John J. Pershing.

Hon. Newton D. Baker, Secretary of War. Throughout the war Secretary Baker stood for a square deal for the Negro soldier and sought to rectify every injustice or case of discrimination that came to his attention.

Theodore Roosevelt

Emmett J. Scott

# SCOTT'S OFFICIAL HISTORY

OF

# THE AMERICAN NEGRO IN THE WORLD WAR

BY

## EMMETT J. SCOTT, A.M., LL.D.

*Special Assistant to Secretary of War*

Author of "Tuskegee and Its People," "Is Liberia Worth Saving?" and
co-Author of "Booker T. Washington, Builder of a Civilization."

Secretary of Tuskegee Normal and Industrial Institute. Eighteen years
PRIVATE SECRETARY TO THE LATE BOOKER T. WASHINGTON

———

A Complete and Authentic Narration, from Official Sources, of the
Participation of

AMERICAN SOLDIERS OF THE NEGRO RACE
*in the*
WORLD WAR FOR DEMOCRACY

———

## *Profusely Illustrated*
*with Official Photographs*

———

A Full Account of the War Work Organizations of Colored Men and Women
and other Civilian Activities including

The Red Cross, the Y. M. C. A., the Y. W. C. A. and the
War Camp Community Service

With Official Summary of Treaty of Peace and
League of Nations Covenant

———

Prefaced with Highest Tributes to the American Negro
*by*
HON. NEWTON D. BAKER, *Secretary of War*
GEN. JOHN J. PERSHING, *Commander-in-Chief, American Exp. Forces.*
*and the late*
COL. THEODORE ROOSEVELT

ADQ 1460

TO

MY WIFE AND CHILDREN

TO WHOSE LOVE AND INSPIRATION

I OWE SO MUCH.

# CONTENTS

4

**6**　　　　　　　CONTENTS (CONTINUED)

## AUTHOR'S PREFACE

The Negro, in the great World War for Freedom and Democracy, has proved to be a notable and inspiring figure. The record and achievements of this racial group, as brave soldiers and loyal citizens, furnish one of the brightest chapters in American history. The ready response of Negro draftees to the Selective Service calls—together with the numerous patriotic activities of Negroes generally, gave ample evidence of their whole-souled support and their 100 per cent Americanism. It is difficult to indicate which rendered the greater service to their Country—the 400,000 or more of them who entered active military service (many of whom fearlessly and victoriously fought upon the battlefields of France) or the millions of other loyal members of this race whose useful industry in fields, factories, forests, mines, together with many other indispensable civilian activities, so vitally helped the Federal authorities in carrying the war to a successful conclusion.

When war against Germany was declared April 6, 1917, Negro Americans quickly recognized the fact that *it was not to be a white man's war, nor a black man's war, but a war of all the people living under the "Stars and Stripes" for the preservation of human liberty throughout the world.* Despite efforts of pro-German propagandists to dampen their ardor or cool their patriotism by pointing out seeming inconsistencies between their treatment as American citizens and their expected loyalty as American soldiers, more' than one million of them (1,078,331), according to the Second Official Report of the Provost Marshal General, promptly responded to, and registered under the three Selective Service calls. More than 400,000 Negro soldiers (367,710 draftees plus voluntary enlistments and those already in the Regular Army) were called to the colors and offered their lives in defense of the American flag during the recent war. Relative to their population, proportionately more Negroes were "drafted" than was true of white men.

The Negro was represented in practically every branch of military service during the Great World War,—including Infantry, Cavalry, Engineer Corps, Field Artillery, Coast Artillery, Signal Corps (radio or wireless telegraphers), Medical Corps, Hospital and Ambulance Corps, Aviation Corps (ground section), Veterinary

Corps, and in Stevedore Regiments, Service or Labor Battalions, Depot Brigades, and so forth.

Nor was this the first instance in the Nation's history that this ever-loyal racial group rightly and cheerfully responded to the tocsin of war and made a military record of which any race might well be proud. In the Revolutionary War, in the War of 1812, in the Mexican War, in the Civil War, and in the War with Spain,— the American Negro soldier has always distinguished himself by bravery, fortitude, and loyalty. His military record has always compared favorably with that of other soldiers.

It is because of the immensely valuable contribution made by Negro soldiers, sailors, and civilians toward the winning of the great World War that this volume has been prepared,—in order that there may be an authentic record, not only of the military exploits of this particular racial group of Americans, but of the diversified and valuable contributions made by them as patriotic civilians.

A notable group of colored Americans, men and women, has joined me in this effort adequately to present a reliable record of the many services and sacrifices that the Negro race has willingly laid upon the altar of Patriotism. It is a matter of profound satisfaction to have had the earnest coöperation of:

CARTER G. WOODSON, A. M., Ph. D., Director of Research, The Association for the Study of Negro Life and History, whose monographs on Negro Life and History appear regularly in the "*Journal of Negro History*," the one publication of its kind in America. Dr. Woodson is a graduate of Harvard University, from which he received the degree of Ph. D., and is an authority on Negro History. His coöperation is, therefore, rightly to be prized as bringing to this work an appreciation of historical values.

RALPH W. TYLER, accredited Negro War Correspondent, who served overseas, representing the Committee on Public Information. Mr. Tyler had full opportunity at the front to know how colored soldiers acquitted themselves in camps and upon the battlefields of France. His letters and official reports sent to America and published through the Committee on Public Information in various white and colored newspapers of the country contained first-hand information concerning Negro troops overseas, and served to keep up the morale of colored Americans at a time when there was much anxiety and complaint among them due to the fact that adequate

news regarding the treatment and activities of Negro soldiers abroad
was not finding its way into the press of the country.

WILLIAM ANTHONY AERY, Publication Secretary of the Hampton
Normal and Agricultural Institute, and MONROE N. WORK, in charge
of the Division of Records and Research at Tuskegee Normal and
Industrial Institute, both of whom, being connected with the largest
industrial schools among colored people in the United States, had
full opportunity to observe the conduct and training of Negro soldiers in the various Vocational Detachments, Students' Army Training Corps, and Reserve Officers' Training Corps units; their counsel
and data furnished have been of material assistance in the preparation of this volume.

MRS. ALICE DUNBAR-NELSON (formerly the wife of Paul Laurence
Dunbar, the "Poet Laureate" of the Negro race), who wrote
Chapter XXVII, entitled: "Negro Women in War Work." Mrs.
Nelson, prominent in educational and literary circles, was actively
engaged during the war in helping to mobilize the colored women of
the country for effective war work, representing the Women's Division of the Council of National Defense; she traveled extensively in
various parts of the country in the effort to promote patriotic activities among the colored women of America, and with eloquent tongue,
trenchant pen, and untiring personal service helped them to make
a record that will stand forever as a monument to the practical value
and absolute dependability of Negro womanhood in a national crisis.

MISS EVA D. BOWLES, Executive Secretary in charge of the
Colored Young Women's Christian Association, who did a notable
piece of work in connection with the War Work Council, not only in
the matter of selecting well-trained women to take charge of Hostess
Houses that were provided at various camps and cantonments, but
in keeping alive the fires of patriotism among the colored women of
the country as she went from place to place lecturing and otherwise
working for the betterment of social conditions in Army camps and
especially in communities adjacent thereto. A full report of the
work done by the organization, which this consecrated young woman
so worthily represents, is contained in Chapter XXVII, entitled:
"Negro Women in War Work."

LIEUTENANT T. T. THOMPSON, Personnel Officer and Historian
of the 92nd Division, to whom I am especially indebted for a large
amount of official data concerning the various activities of this im-

portant Divisional unit of the American Expeditionary Forces. Lieutenant Thompson, by training and experience, was well fitted for the exacting post which was held by him as an officer in the U. S. Army and as a chronicler of the activities and operations of the 92nd Division. The material supplied by him and incorporated in Chapters XI and XII must, therefore, be regarded as official, authentic, and reliable. *It is the one clear record of the activities of the 92nd Division,—that justly famous military unit composed of American Negro officers and soldiers who served their country so gallantly during the recent war.* The data supplied by Lieutenant Thompson has been checked up by various other officers of the 92nd Division, including LIEUTENANT CHARLES S. PARKER, Regimental Adjutant, 366th Infantry, a man of scholarly attainments, judicial poise and clear understanding, and who, also, has supplied definite and important data with reference to the operations of certain Negro units that distinguished themselves by valor when the 92nd Division fearlessly faced the formidable fortress at Metz. It is a matter of great benefit to the Negro Race, and certainly most gratifying to the Author to have had recourse to the official records kept by these colored officers.

I am also especially indebted to CAPTAIN JOHN H. PATTON, Regimental Adjutant of the 370th Infantry Regiment, U. S. A. (better known as the Old Eighth Illinois Regiment) which unit actively participated in many a bloody conflict overseas and won imperishable fame. Captain Patton placed at my disposal the full and complete official record of the "Eighth Illinois" (370th) Regiment and it was largely from that record, of undeniable authenticity, that Chapter XV was compiled.

Grateful reference must also be made to DR. JESSE E. MOORLAND, International Secretary of the Young Men's Christian Association, with Headquarters at Washington, D. C. Dr. Moorland was in charge of all the Y. M. C. A. work conducted among colored soldiers in the various camps and cantonments throughout America as well as overseas, and with a well-selected cabinet of efficient, consecrated young colored men, rendered service of the utmost value in looking after the moral and social welfare of thousands of Negro soldiers who were called to the colors. Each and every Y. M. C. A. Secretary selected for service in camps or cantonments at home or overseas was designated by Dr. Moorland and his large corps of capable helpers coöperated most effectively with the War Work Council. No more notable work was done during the war than that performed by the Young Men's Christian Association among colored soldiers as it received the untutored, untrained and, in many cases unlettered colored men who poured into the various camps, and, largely through the practical help afforded by colored Y. M. C. A. Secretaries, were transformed within a few weeks or months into upstanding, sturdy, forward-looking men. The story of the Y. M. C. A. work among colored soldiers is a story most interesting and worthy of preservation.

CAPTAIN E. L. SNYDER, Y. M. C. A. Secretary, who served for a time at Camp Grant with the 183rd Depot Brigade and later upon three battle fronts overseas, has placed the Author and his Race under many obligations for permitting me to use and in securing for use in this volume a large number of very valuable pictures or illustrations contained herein; they indicate the widespread and varied activities of Negro troops in American camps and cantonments and in service overseas. Many of these illustrations were photographed by him at the front—some being photographed while he was in danger of being wounded or killed by flying pieces of shrapnel, while others were secured from the French Official Photographic Division. They show both American Negro and French Colonial troops in action.

Most or all of the photographs of colored officers have been supplied by these officers themselves at my special request, and I wish in this way to express to them all my grateful acknowledgment, with my sincere regret that the space devoted to illustrations did not permit the publication of all of the photographs so kindly furnished.

Many of these colored officers have furnished me with first-hand information of interest and importance, duly verified by their comrades in arms,—setting forth their individual exploits as well as those of the various units with which they were connected. To all of them, and to all others who have aided me in the preparation of this work, I am profoundly grateful.

In calling attention to these coöperating agencies, I want especially to pay tribute to my loyal and efficient secretary, Mr. William H. Davis, without whose generous support and valued services it would have been difficult for me to have done this work or to have presented a record of the activities of my office during the period of nearly two years I have been serving in the War Department as Special Assistant to the Secretary of War. Since entering upon the duties of that office, Mr. Davis has given a great deal more than time in supporting my various efforts in behalf of Negro soldiers and in the interest of Negro citizens generally; without regard to recompense and without counting time, strength or anything else except a desire to serve to the uttermost,—and I wish in this way and in this place to record my deep indebtedness to him, an indebtedness which must be shared by the Negro people of this country as well, in whose interest and for whose welfare he has served so loyally and unselfishly. I wish also gratefully to acknowledge the help and encouragement I have had from my corps of office assistants, clerks and stenographers, viz: Mr. R. W. Thompson, Mr. Charles Webb, Mr. J. B. Smith, Mrs. Madeline P. Childs, and Miss Ernestine English.

In response to the natural desire and nation-wide demand for an authentic and reliable record of Negro military achievements and other of their patriotic contributions, this volume has been prepared as a lasting tribute to the American Negro's participation in the greatest war in human history. Much of the material, as the reader will note, is based upon first-hand study, official reports and data, and the greatest possible care has been taken in the effort to set forth definitely what has been done—not only by black men in America but by those other brave black soldiers of Africa (Senegalese, Soudanese, and Algerians) who served with the Allies and who rendered such timely and valuable service,—in helping to save to the casket of Freedom the precious jewel of Human Liberty!

*Emmett J. Scott*

Washington, D. C.,
June 15, 1919.

## LOYALTY AND DEMOCRACY OF THE NEGRO PRAISED
## BY THE SECRETARY OF WAR

The following is the testimony of the Honorable Newton D. Baker, Secretary of War, to the loyal and enthusiastic support of colored civilians and the part played by colored soldiers in the war:

In a most encouraging degree, it is being regarded by colored civilians throughout the country, as a privilege and as a duty to give liberally of their substance, of their time, of their talents, of their energy, of their influence, and in every way possible, to contribute toward the comfort and success of our fighting units and those of our allies across the seas.

The colored men, who were subject to draft, are to be commended upon their promptness and eagerness in registering their names for service in the National Army, and likewise mention is made of the relatively low percentage of exemption claims filed by them. Those in the service of their country proved faithful and efficient, and will uphold the traditions of their race.

I want the soldier who did not go over seas to know that he is as much a soldier as though he had taken part in the more spectacular side. I want to insist that the men who were in training in this country are just as much a part of the Army of the United States as if they had gone.

Now, I want to impress this upon you men, that if you feel that things have not been as you would like them—if there have been some things which you think were not as they should have been, you must try to forget them and go back to civil life with the determination to do your part to make the country what it should be.

After all, what is this thing we call "DEMOCRACY" and about which we hear so much nowadays? Surely it no catch-phrase or abstraction. It is demonstrating too much vitality for that. It is no social distinction or privilege of the few, for were it that, it could not win the hearts of peoples and make them willing to die for its establishment. But it is, it seems to me, a hope as wide as the human race, involving men everywhere—a hope that permits

15

each of us to look forward to a time when not only we, but others, will have our respective rights, founded on the generosity of Nature, and protected by a system of justice which will adjust its apparent conflicts. Under such a hope nations will do justice to nations, and men to men. Nor can I believe that this democracy will be attained as a finished and complete thing, but rather with increased education and knowledge its application will enlarge and new meanings be discovered in it. It is not the philosophy of disorder, but of progressive order, not the doctrine of restraint by force, but rather of self-restraint imposed by men who realize that one's own freedom is safest when that of others is equally safe.

NEWTON D. BAKER.

## General Pershing's Tribute to the Negro Soldier

"The stories, probably invented by German agents, that colored soldiers in France are always placed in most dangerous positions and sacrificed to save white soldiers, that when wounded they are left on the ground to die without medical attention, etc., are absolutely false.

"A tour of inspection among American Negro troops by officers of these headquarters shows the comparatively high degree of training and efficiency among these troops. Their training is identical with that of other American troops serving with the French Army, the effort being to lead all American troops gradually to heavy combat duty by a preliminary service in trenches in quiet sectors.

"Colored troops in trenches have been particularly fortunate as one regiment had been there a month before any losses were suffered. This was almost unheard of on the western front.

"The exploits of two colored infantrymen in repelling a much larger German patrol, killing and wounding several Germans and winning the Croix de Guerre by their gallantry, has aroused a fine spirit of emulation throughout the colored troops, all of whom are looking forward to more active service.

"The only regret expressed by colored troops is that they are not given more dangerous work to do. I cannot commend too highly the spirit shown among the colored combat troops, who exhibit fine capacity for quick training and eagerness for the most dangerous work."

JOHN J. PERSHING.

*Above*—Colonel Hayward's "Hell Fighters" in Parade. The famous 369th Infantry of colored fighters marching in New York City in honor of their return to this country after having covered themselves with glory on the blood-stained fields of France.
*Below*—The Buffaloes (367th) Marching up the Avenue in New York on Their Return.

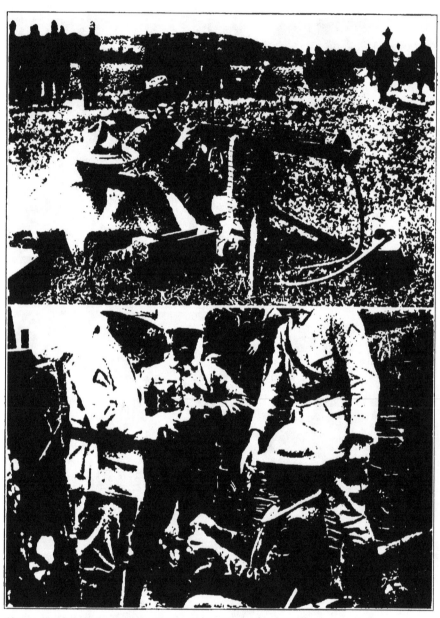

*Above*—American Negro Machine Gunners in the Marne Sector in France.
*Below*—In the trenches; a French Officer explaining operation of the hand grenades to Senegalese and American Negro soldiers.

*Above*—Lt. Rutherford's Minstrels, recruited on board the "Saxonia" on homeward trip, where they amused and entertained over 1700 wounded boys on the way back from France.
*Below*—Transport "Ulua," with her cargo of dusky fighters who are glad to be back home after doing their bit in France. Among them are the 317th Supply Train, 317th Trench Mortar Battery, 325th Field Signal Battery.

MAJOR-GENERAL C. C. BALLOU, COMMANDER OF THE FIGHTING 92nd DIVISION.

*Above*—How the boys enjoyed themselves in France. A group of Negro soldiers off duty around a Y. M. C. A. tent at Villers le Sec (Meuse).
*Below*—A German tank destroyed by allied shell fire in a sector occupied by American Negro Troops.

*Above*—Welcoming a Victorious Hero. Henry Johnson, the American Private who killed four Germans and wounded twenty-two with his bolo knife, and was the First American of any race to receive the Croix de Guerre, being carried in triumph up Fifth Avenue on his return.
*Below*—Negro Stevedores of the National Army Unloading a Transport in the Harbor of Brest.

*Above*—"The Band that Introduced France to Ragtime." Lieut. James Europe's aggregation of
Negro musicians accompanied the 369th Infantry overseas. The music of these dark skinned
players took France by storm. Gen. Pershing borrowed the band for a month to play at
Headquarters of the A. E. F., but sent it back to the regiment when General Gouraud,
the French Commander, begged for its return.
*Below*—Lieut. Maxom and the band of the 814th Infantry on the pier at New York just after
disembarking from the transport Celtic from overseas. Our colored bands were the
wonder of France.

*Above*—"Returning the Colors." Major David Appleton commanding the "Buffaloes," returning the Colors intrusted to this Negro regiment, upon its return from its glorious
service in France.
*Below*—Hon. Charles Evans Hughes Receiving the Colors of the 367th Infantry from Major
Daniel Appleton of the 367th, who is on Justice Hughes' left.

## FORMER PRESIDENT ROOSEVELT ON "THE NEGRO'S PART IN THE WAR"

It is a source of pride and gratification to record the fact that Colonel Theodore Roosevelt, the great former President of the United States, whose sudden and untimely death occurred on January 6, 1919, made his last public appearance and address at a meeting held in Carnegie Hall, New York, on November 2nd, 1918, under the auspices of the Circle for Negro War Relief. It was on this occasion that Colonel Roosevelt paid the following high tribute to the Negro Race in War:

"The Negro has a right to sit at the council board where questions vitally affecting him are considered, and at the same time, as a matter of expediency, it is well to have white men at the board too. And I say that, though I know that there are many men—Dr. Scott is one—whom I would be delighted to have sit at the council board where only the affairs of white men are concerned. As things are now, the wisest course to follow is that followed in the organization of this circle.

"Such an organization as this, though started and maintained with a friendly co-operation from white friends, is intended to prove to the world that the colored people themselves can manage war relief in an efficient, honest and dignified way and so bring honor to their race. Every organization like this Circle for Negro War Relief is doing its part in bringing about the right solution for the great problem which the Chairman has spoken of this evening.

"I do not for one moment want to be understood as excusing the white man from his full responsibility for anything that he has done to keep the black man down; but I do wish to say, with all the emphasis and all the earnestness at my command, that the greatest work the colored man can do to help his race upward is by, in his own person and through co-operation with his fellows, showing the dignity of service by the colored man and colored woman for all our people.

"Let me illustrate just what I mean when I say the advisability of white co-operation and the occasional advisability of doing without white co-operation. Had I been permitted to raise troops to go on the other side, I should have asked permission to raise two colored

17

regiments. It is perfectly possible, of course, that there is more than one colored man in the country fit for the extraordinarily diffi-cult task of commanding one such colored regiment, which would contain nothing but colored officers. But it happens that I only knew of one and that was Colonel Charles Young. I had intended to offer him the colonelship of one regiment, telling him I expected him to choose only colored officers, and that while I was sure he would understand the extreme difficulty and extreme responsibility of his task, I intended to try to impress it upon him still more; to tell him that under those conditions I put a heavier responsibility upon him than upon any other colored man in the country, and that he was to be given an absolutely free hand in choosing his officers, and that on the other hand he would have to treat them absolutely mercilessly, if they didn't come right up to the highest level.

"On the other hand, with the other colored regiment, I should have had a colonel and a Lieutenant-colonel and three majors who would have been white men. One of them, Hamilton Fish, is over there now. One went over and was offered permission to form another regiment. He said no, he would stay with his sunburned Yankees. He stayed accordingly.

"Mr. Cobb has spoken to you as an eyewitness of what has been done by the colored troops across the seas. I am well prepared to believe it. In the very small war in which I served, which was a kind of a pink tea affair, I had a division, small dismounted cavalry division, where in addition to my own regiment we had three white regular regiments and two colored regiments; and when we had gotten through the campaign my own men, who were probably two-thirds Southerners and Southwesterners, used to say, 'The Ninth and Tenth Cavalry are good enough to drink out of our canteens.'

"And terrible though this war has been, I think it has been also fraught with the greatest good for our national soul. We went to war, as Mr. Cobb has said, to maintain our own national self-respect. And, friends, it would have been something awful if we hadn't gone in. Materially, because the fight was so even that I don't think it is boasting, I think it is a plain statement of fact, Mr. Cobb, that our going in turned the scale. Isn't that so? I think the Germans and their vassal allies would have been victorious if we hadn't gone in.

And if they had been victorious and we had stayed out, soft, flabby, wealthy, they would have eaten us without saying grace.

"Well, thank Heaven! we went in, and our men on the other side, our sons and brothers on the other side, white men and black, white soldiers and colored soldiers, have been so active that every American now can walk with his head up and look the citizen of any other country in the world straight in the eyes, and we have the satisfaction of knowing that we have played the decisive part. I am not saying this in any spirit of self-flattery. If any of you have heard me speak during the preceding four years you know that I have not addressed the American people in a vein of undiluted eulogy. But without self-flattery we can say that it was our going in that turned the scale for freedom and against the most dangerous tyranny that the world has ever seen. We acted as genuine friends of liberty in so doing.

"Now after the war, friends, I think all of us in this country, white and black alike, have also got to set an example to the rest of the world in steering a straight course equally distant from Kaiserism and Bolshevism.

"And now, friends, I want as an American to thank you, and as your fellow American to congratulate you, upon the honor won and the service rendered by the colored troops on the other side; by the men such as the soldier Needham Roberts we have with us tonight who won the Cross of War, the greatest War Cross for gallantry in action; for the many others like him who acted with equal gallantry and who for one reason or another never attracted the attention of their superiors and, well though they did, did not receive the outward and visible token to prove what they had done. I want to congratulate you on what all those men have done. I want to congratulate you on what the colored nurses at home have done and have been ready to do, and to express my very sincere regret that some way was not found to put them on the other side at the front. I congratulate you upon it in the name of our country and above all in the name of the colored people of our country. For in the end services of this kind have a cumulative effect in winning the confidence of your fellows of another color.

"And I hope—and I wish to use a stronger expression than 'hope'; I expect—and I am going to do whatever small amount I can do, to bring about the realization of the expectation, I expect that as a result of this great war, intended to secure a greater justice internationally among the people of mankind, we shall apply at home the lessons that we have been learning and helping teach abroad; that we shall work sanely, not foolishly, but resolutely, toward securing a juster and fairer treatment in this country of colored people, basing that treatment upon the only safe rule to be followed in American life, of treating each individual accordingly as his conduct or her conduct requires you to treat them.

"I don't ask for any man that he shall because of his race be given any privilege. All I ask is that in his ordinary civil rights, in his right to work, to enjoy life and liberty and the pursuit of happiness, that as regards those rights he be given the same treatment that we would give him if he was of another color.

"Now, friends, both the white man and the black man in moments of exultation are apt to think that the millennium is pretty near; that the sweet chariot has swung so low that everybody can get upon it. I don't think that my colored fellow-citizens are a bit worse than my white fellow-citizens as regards that particular aspiration. And I am sure you do not envy me the ungrateful task of warning both that they must not expect too much. They must have their eyes on the stars but their feet on the ground. I have to warn my white fellow-citizens about that when they say: 'Well, now, at the end of this war, we are going to have universal peace. Everybody loves everybody else.' I want you to remember that the strongest exponents of international love in public life today are Lenine and Trotsky.

"I will do everything I can to aid, to help to bring about, to bring nearer the day when justice and what in a humble way may be called the square deal will be given. And yet I want to warn you that that is only going to come gradually; that there will be very much injustice, injustice that must not over-much disappoint you and it must not cow you and above all it must not make you feel sullen and hopeless.

"And one thing I want to say, not to you here but the the colored men who live where the bulk of the colored men do, in the South, and that is always to remember the lesson which I learned from Booker Washington: that in the long run, in the long run, the white

man who can give most help to the colored man is the white man who
lives next to him. And in consequence I always felt it my official
duty to work so that I could command the assistance and respect of
the bulk of the white men who are decent and square, in what I tried
to do for the colored man who is decent and square.

"To each side I preach the doctrine of thinking more of his duties
than of his rights. I don't mean that you shan't think of your
rights. I want you to do it. But it is awfully easy, if you begin to
dwell all the time on your rights, to find that you suffer from an
ingrowing sense of your own perfections and wrongs and that you
forget what you owe to anyone else.

"I congratulate all colored men and women and all their white
fellow-Americans upon the gallanty and efficiency with which the
colored men have behaved at the front, and the efficiency and wish to
render service which have been shown by both the colored men
and the colored women behind them in this country."

THEODORE ROOSEVELT.

## TWO FIRST CLASS AMERICANS!

This cartoon, with the above title, was drawn by Mr. W. A. Rogers, the famous cartoonist of the New York Herald, in celebration of the exploit of Henry Johnson and Needham Roberts, the first two American soldiers to win the Croix de Guerre.— Copyright, 1918, by New York Herald Co.

# CHAPTER I

## HOW THE GREAT WAR CAME TO AMERICA

*The Underlying Causes of the War—Racial Hatreds and National Enmities—Germany's Ambition to Rule the World—The Gathering of the War Clouds—Germany's Attempt to Stir Up Trouble Between the United States and Mexico—Events that Led to America's Participation in the War.*

As all the world now realizes, the Great War which came to an end by the surrender of Germany and the signing of an Armistice on November 11, 1918, had its roots in racial hatred and international jealousy between the peoples and rulers of different European countries. What directly brought on the war was the resentment of the Serbians of the effort of the Germanic Austrians to rule them. For centuries the oppression of one race by another had been going on in Europe. All over Europe there were races ruled and exploited by people of another race. The Poles had no government of their own, but were divided among Germany, Russia and Austria. Italians bitterly resented the rule of Austria over large territories, including some great cities, whose population was almost wholly Italian. On the west, the French people of Alsace-Lorraine were held in subjection by Germany. The Czecho-Slovaks of Bohemia were under the control of Austrians; Turkish authority tyrannized over the Armenians, and the Lithuanians were the subjects of Russian masters.

Confident of her ability to overcome all resistance, determined to reduce still more nations and races to subjection and to extend her dominion from the North Sea to the Indian Ocean, Germany entered upon this war to crush friend and foe. The whole civilized world revolted when the German Government declared that its solemn treaty in which it had agreed to the permanent independence of Belgium was only "a scrap of paper," and sent its army into that neutral country. The invasion of Belgium was the act that brought

23

England into the war against Germany; the atrocious treatment of the Belgians and the French by the Germans was the moving force that stirred the American people and prepared them for this country's own entrance into the war even before atrocities committed upon our own citizens forced the issue.

So, in a very literal sense, it may be said that our American soldiers of the Negro Race went over to France to fight for the liberation of the oppressed peoples of Europe. It was a marvelous thing to have occurred, that a race itself so long oppressed should have had the opportunity to help save others from oppression! It is something for every man and woman of the Negro race to be proud of, that our people did eagerly welcome this opportunity and play so glorious a part. The pistol shot which put an end to the life of Archduke Francis Ferdinand, heir presumptive to the Austro-Hungarian throne, at Serajevo, June 28, 1914, turned Europe into a battlefield six weeks later. The Serbians were blamed for the assassination, and on July 23 Vienna sent an ultimatum to Belgrade demanding the punishment of the offenders and Austria's participation in their trial in Serbia. Russia supported Serbia in rejecting the last demand; Germany supported Austria. England, France, and even Italy, then the ally of Austria and Germany, suggested arbitration by the Great Powers. By treaty Germany was obliged to support Austria if attacked by two or more powers, France to support Russia for a similar reason, and Italy to support her allies in case of a defensive war.

Germany deemed Russia's mobilization tantamount to a declaration of war against her and declared war on August 1, 1914. Alleging that France had already begun hostile action against her, Germany declared war on France on the third of August and invaded Belgium in order to attack France. Great Britain declared war on Germany the fourth of August. Italy, deeming Austria the aggressor, proclaimed her neutrality.

But these were merely the culmination of a long-standing conspiracy on the part of Germany and Austria-Hungary soon to be revealed by German propaganda. Germany wished to render France impotent and absorb the Germanic provinces of Russia; she would then be in a position to coerce Great Britain. Austria-Hungary wished to absorb the Balkan Slavs and make her way to the Ægean. For

Germany there was a corollary to the success of the Austro-Hungarian scheme, which, by the bribery of Turkey, would establish German dominion from the North Sea to the Persian Gulf. In November Turkey entered the war on the side of the Central Empires. All this was arranged, even to the minutest detail, at the German Kaiser's Potsdam conference on July 5, 1914. There it was believed that if the corollary did not come into evidence too soon, both Great Britain and Italy would remain neutral. That Japan would enter the war on account of her treaty with Great Britain was thus discounted. Germany attempted to defend her position morally on the ground that she had been attacked by Russia on account of the Pan-Slavonic ambitions of that empire, and by Great Britain on account of the latter's jealousy of her world trade and industry. She was, therefore, "fighting for her existence."

Her enemies in defending themselves entered into treaties for mutual advantages after the war, in case of the defeat of the Central Empires. There was coöperation, but no great unity of action or purpose among them. This gave Germany a great advantage until the spring of 1917, when the United States entered the war. That event, besides bringing the material deciding factor to the Allies' cause, established their war aims upon a world basis of a fight for humanity—of republicanism against absolutism, for the rights of small nations, and "to make the world safe for democracy." All this was to be done by annihilating Prussian militarism and Hohenzollern absolutism. On these humane principles twenty-nine nations arrayed themselves against Germany, of which twenty-four declared war.

The war, which brought to the state of practical application the principles for which the enemies of Germany have been fighting, has been prodigious in geographic and social extent and unprecedented in expenditures of lives and treasure. Through battle, atrocities, and massacres it is estimated that 10,000,000 lives have been sacrificed; that $50,000,000,000 of property, not including the waste of war material, has been destroyed in various ways; that the productive wealth of the belligerents, which in 1914 was estimated at $600,000,000,000, has now been mortgaged for over $200,-000,000,000, much of which now seems unrecoverable.

Germany's initial plan was to place France *hors de combat*

and then obtain a victorious peace over Russia. Austria-Hungary, meanwhile, would attend to the Balkans. The intervention of Great Britain brought this to nought. Germany then directed Turkey to attack Egypt and the Suez Canal, and so strangle Great Britain in the East. The first act of Great Britain was to isolate the German fleet; her second to send an expeditionary force under the command of Sir John French to Belgium and France. The Germans advanced into France to within fifteen miles of Paris, and were then driven back to the Aisne at the battle of the Marne, September 5-12, 1914. Russian armies advanced into East Prussia, were held in the center east of Posen, and overran Austrian Galicia. The Turks were defeated at the Suez Canal on February 2-4, 1915. In the following April the Austro-Germans began a drive in Galicia, which by the following November had carried them eastward to a 450-mile perpendicular extending from near Riga to the Russian frontier.

### Bulgaria and Italy in the War

From March until October the Allies attempted to gain Constantinople from the Peninsula of Gallipoli, and then withdrew to Saloniki in an attempt to defend Serbia, Bulgaria having joined the Central Empires on September 22. Bulgaria overran Serbia and established communication between Berlin and Constantinople via the Orient Railway. Meanwhile Italy had declared war on Austria on May 23, and had invaded Austrian territory, isolating the Trentino and advancing to the River Isonzo. The Russians, advancing through the Caucasus, were defeating the Turks in Armenia.

The sinking of the Lusitania on May 7, 1915, and the atrocities of the Germans in Belgium, the Austrians and Bulgars in Serbia, the Turks in Armenia, and the criminal propaganda in the United States to prevent supplies from going to the Allies, all tended to lower Germany's moral standard in the war. By the naval battle off the Falkland Islands on December 8, 1914, Germany's only fleet on the high seas had been put out of existence; a similar fate soon followed her commerce destroyers. Japan had taken the German-leased territory of Kiao-Chau in China, and soon, out of Germany's oversea possessions of 1,027,820 square miles, none remained. Japan has been fighting down to the end of the war.

The second year of the war, 1915-1916, saw the Germans completing their occupation of the Balkans down to the Saloniki line held by the Allies; there was a British defeat on the Tigris, with the surrender of Kut-el-Amara, on April 28. There were also the battle of Verdun, which began on February 21 and cost the Germans half a million casualties; the sea fight off Jutland on May 31, which left the British Navy in control of the sea; the battle of the Somme in France, July 1-November 13, which regained 170 square miles of territory and secured several strategic positions which five months later forced the great German retreat; General Brusiloff's campaign on the eastern front, which regained 7,300 square miles of territory and captured 358,000 prisoners from June 4 till December, 1916.

On August 27, 1916, Rumania entered the war on the side of Germany's enemies and by the dawn of 1917 had been crushed. In March and April, 1917, took place the German retreat to the Hindenburg line, which surrendered to France nearly 1,500 square miles of territory. There were British victories at the ridges of Vimy and Messines, respectively April 19 and June 7, and the great attack of the French from Soissons to Rheims, which secured 100,000 prisoners. In Mesopotamia the British recovered Kut-el-Amara and on March 11 occupied Bagdad; the Arab kingdom of Hedjaz joined the Allies.

### · Political Events of the Third Year

But the most important events of the third year of the war were political, however—the Russian revolution, March 15, and the entrance of the United States into the war, April 6. The former was brought about without any premeditation by the Cossacks refusing to fire on the Petrograd mob and the Duma taking advantage of the situation and establishing a mild Provisional Government, which opened the country to destructive German propaganda and the rise of the anarchy known as Bolshevism. The moral and material grievances of the United States against Germany culminated in a series of revelations showing the latter's criminality. On January 31 she proclaimed her intensified U-boat campaign, repudiating the promise of May 4, 1916, and on February 28th came the revelation of the Zimmerman note to Mexico and

Japan. Up to the time the United States declared war this country had lost by the illegal operation of U-boats twenty-two ships, amounting to more than 70,000 tons, together with hundreds of lives, most of which, however, had been lost on other neutral ships or on the passenger ships of Germany's enemies.

Early in the fourth year of the war, November 7, 1917, saw the collapse of the Russian Provisional Government and the dominance of the Bolsheviki. They finally drove Russia from the war by the betrayal at Brest-Litovsk, which culminated in the treaty of peace of March 3, 1918. Rumania was forced to make peace on May 6, at Bucharest.

Other events which occupied the closing months of 1917 were equally discouraging for the Allies, whose morale, however, was kept firm through the rapidly augmenting evidences of American aid, which would be decisive. Even here there was fear that this aid could not be brought overseas, due to the intensified action of the U-boats, whose toll of merchant shipping for 1917 had been in the first quarter 1,619,373 tons; in the second, 236,934; in the third, 1,494,473; and in the fourth, 1,272,843. And as yet there were no sure grounds to believe in the great victories which were to come to the Allies a year afterward.

On the western front the battle of Flanders, which had been begun by the British on July 31, ended with the capture of Paschendaele Ridge on the 6th of the following November. There was the abortive battle of Cambrai, November 20-December 5. In October Pétain secured the Chemin des Dames on the Aisne front. Italy advanced over the Bainsizza to within 35 miles of Laibach, between August 20 and October 1, only to be defeated at Caporetto and driven back to the Piave, losing a large part of the Regione of Veneto.

The allied front in Macedonia continued to remain inactive save for the excursions of Greek troops, whose new Government had entered the war on the side of the Allies on the second of July. The war against the Turk, however, showed encouraging signs; in Palestine General Allenby captured Jerusalem on the 22nd of December; in Mesopotamia General Marshall, who had succeeded to the command on the death of Maude on the 18th of November, extended his advance to the Euphrates, and was still ascending the Tigris toward Mosul.

It was known before 1917 closed that Germany, released from war with Russia, was preparing a great offensive. The Austro-German reply to the Pope's peace note of August 1 revealed merely a readiness to talk peace on the basis of the military status quo. President Wilson, in his reply to the Pope on the 27th of September, reaffirmed the great moral issues at stake, but in the chancelleries of the Allies in Europe men like the Marquis of Lansdowne lowered the morale by constantly asking for the war aims of the belligerents, and there was anti-war propaganda abroad. France had her Caillaux and Bolo Pacha, Italy her Giolitti, and England her Irish Sinn Fein.

With these distracting and discouraging influences lightened only by the hope placed in the United States and the faith that the U-boat campaign was being neutralized, the combat was carried for three months into 1918 with forebodings for a long war.

### Germany's Last Great Struggle

Then Germany on March 21, 1918, began her great offensive on the western front with the object of separating the British and French armies by reaching the Channel ports at the mouth of the Somme and then defeating each army in turn and occupying Paris. Between March 21 and July 15 her offensive had passed through four phases, giving her Lys, the Picardy and the Marne salients. She had stretched a 195-mile front to one of 250. However, the Allies held the sectors which bound the salients and also strategic positions on their perimeters. Germany's huge losses prevented her from proceeding further unless at a given point she could break the Allies' line. This in a desperate effort she attempted to do on July 15 by driving across the Marne. She failed and began a highly organized strategic retreat to save her armies.

Meanwhile, the Allies had decided, in April, on unity of command and had placed the conduct of the war in the hands of General Foch. The arrival of nearly 1,000,000 American bayonets in France gave him the opportunity to organize an army of manœuvre.

His attacks begun between Soissons and Chateau-Thierry against the Marne salient on July 18 were unceasing down to the time of the armistice, steadily pushing the German armies east through Belgium and north to the French frontier, a series of battles in which the First American Army played its full part west of the Meuse.

The series of sledge-hammer blows administered by Foch's army began to have their effect not only on the battlefront, but in Berlin and Vienna, in Sofia and Constantinople. The enemy was not reaping the material benefits he had expected to derive from a Bolshevist Russia. There the Czecho-Slovak armies—former prisoners of war released by the Provisional Government—were fighting against the Germans and Bolsheviki and were soon joined by contingents of the Allies and Russians of the educated class. The Allies recognized the belligerency of the Czecho-Slovaks' country—Bohemia—and the national aspirations of the Slavonic subjects of Austria-Hungary.

On the 14th of September the allied armies in Macedonia under General Franchet d'Esperey made an attack which, on the last day of the month, drove Bulgaria to seek unconditional surrender.

On the 15th of September the forces under General Allenby in Palestine annihilated three Turkish armies, which forced the Turks out of the war, on the same terms, October 31.

### Austria Sues for Peace

On the 4th of November, Austria-Hungary, whose note to President Wilson on the 5th of October, asking for a peace parley, had been rejected on the 15th of October, and which was being severely punished by an Italian offensive begun on the 27th of October, accepted an armistice which left her helpless, with revolutionary movements in Vienna, Prague, and elsewhere tending toward the complete dissolution of the dual monarchy of the Hapsburgs. As far back as the 14th of September Austria-Hungary had attempted to have all the belligerents meet in conference, and President Wilson had rejected the proposal on the 17th of September.

On the 6th of October the new German Chancellor, Prince Max of Baden, prepared a peace parley on the basis of the President's

14 Articles of January 8 and subsequent utterances of formulæ for permanent peace. On the 8th of October President Wilson asked for the Chancellor's mandate—did it come from the authorities who had begun and carried on the war or from the people? Germany on the 12th of October pointed out the reforms that were going on in the empire and asked for a mixed commission on the evacuation of the occupied territory in Belgium and France.

To this note President Wilson replied the next day, defining the process by which Germany might receive terms for an armistice, but insisting that the mandate must come from the German people and be preceded by an evacuation of the occupied territories.

Other notes were exchanged, Germany answering on the 21st of October and the President on the 23rd of October; and, respectively, on the 27th and the 5th of November, when the President sent to Germany a memorandum saying that the military advisers of the associated governments were prepared to submit to Germany the terms on which an armistice might be secured.

On the 8th of November the German commissioners received the terms of the armistice at General Foch's headquarters and seventy-two hours were allowed them in which to make answer. The armistice was signed on November 11, 1918.

# CHAPTER II

## THE CALL TO THE COLORS

*Negro Troops That Were Ready When War Was Declared—The Famous 9th and 10th Cavalry, U. S. Army—The 24th and 25th Infantry—National Guard Units of Colored Troops—The 8th Illinois—The 15th New York—National Guard Units of Ohio, Massachusetts, Connecticut, Maryland and Tennessee—First Separate Battalion of the District of Columbia—How All of These Responded to the Call.*

Nearly 400,000 Negro Soldiers served in the United States Army in the Great World War. About 367,710 of these came into the service through the operation of the Selective Draft Law. How this selective draft operated and how the Negro responded to the call to the colors, will be discussed in another chapter. It is a matter of pride, however, to realize that at the instant of the declaration of war, there were nearly 20,000 soldiers of the Negro race in the United States, uniformed, armed, equipped, drilled, trained and ready to take the field against the foe. Proportionately to the total Negro population of America, this was a splendid showing.

Many of these Negro soldiers of the Regular Army and the National Guard had already seen as long and as active service in the field as any of the Regular Army or National Guard regiments of white soldiers. About 10,000 of these Negro troops that were ready when war was declared were in the original four colored regiments of the Regular Army. Of these, the most famous are the 9th and 10th Cavalry. It was the 9th and 10th Cavalry, the Negro troops of the U. S. Regular Army, that saved the day at San Juan Hill for Colonel Roosevelt's Rough Riders, and helped to give him much of his military prestige and fame. The story of the famous charge of these black troops who rushed the Spanish stronghold, singing "There'll Be a Hot Time in the Old Town Tonight," is a familiar story to everyone.

In the war with Spain, in the Philippines, on the Mexican Border, these Negro troops and the two colored infantry regiments of the Regular Army, the 24th and the 25th, won high distinction and merited praise.

Besides these 10,000 Negro soldiers already in the Regular Army, there were nearly 10,000 more in the National Guards of several States, such organizations as the 8th Illinois, the 15th New York, the First Separate Battalion of the District of Columbia, the First Separate Company of Maryland, the 9th Battalion of Ohio, the First Separate Company of Connecticut, Co. L of Massachusetts National Guard and Co. G of the Tennessee National Guard. Some of these, when the United States became a belligerent in the World War, had only recently seen service on the Mexican border.

In the regular army one colored man, Charles Young, of Wilberforce, Ohio, a graduate of West Point, rose to the rank of Colonel, prior to his recent retirement the highest rank attained by any colored man. Benjamin Oliver Davis, of Washington, D. C., rose from the ranks, entering during the Spanish-American War, to Lieutenant-Colonel, and is now stationed with the 9th U. S. Cavalry in the Philippines. Walter H. Loring, retired, another Washingtonian, served with distinction as bandmaster of the Philippines Constabulary Band, and is now a Major. Several colored chaplains of the Regular Army retired with rank of Major, as did one paymaster, Major John R. Lynch, of Chicago. Col. Young was U. S. Military Attaché in the Republic of Haiti, and Lieut.-Col. Davis served in a similar capacity in the Republic of Liberia. Quite a number of colored men were Colonels and Majors in the various National Guard organizations.

### Colored Guard Units Called

The Negro people have always taken particular pride in the records of the four Regular Army units, and they were gratified beyond measure that when war was declared April 6, 1917, there became immediately available not only the Regular Army military units but also the National Guard units, to which reference has been made.

According to the records of the War Department, the Colored National Guard units were called into Federal service as follows:

1st Separate Battauon, District of Columbia National Guard, March 25, 1917; 50 officers, 929 men; Medical Corps attached with 5 officers, 21 men.

1st Separate Company, Maryland, July 25, 1917, 3 officers, 154 men.

1st Separate Company, Connecticut, July 31, 1917, 1 officer, 136 men; 1 officer, 4 men attached.

1st Separate Company, Massachusetts (Co. L), August 5, 1917, 3 officers, 150 men.

9th Separate Battalion, Ohio, August 5, 1917, 14 officers, 600 men; 1 officer, 7 men attached.

8th Illinois Regiment, July 25, 1917, 42 officers, 1,405 men.

15th New York Regiment, July 25, 1917, 54 officers, 2,053 men.

All of those units were afterwards brought up to full strength.

The 15th New York went into final training at Camp Wadsworth, Spartanburg, S. C., where the New York National Guard units were trained; the 8th Illinois went into training at Camp Logan, Houston, Texas, along with the Illinois National Guard; the Separate Battalion of the State of Ohio at Camp Sheridan, Montgomery, Alabama, where the Ohio National Guard units were trained; while the various National Guard Companies of Massachusetts, Maryland, and Tennessee were eventually amalgamated with the troops here mentioned at Camp Stuart, Newport News, Virginia, from which point these units were sent overseas as members of the 93d Division (Provisional), under command of Brigadier General Roy Hoffman.

At the beginning of the war the War Department apparently was uncertain as to just exactly what attitude it should take with reference to having Negroes enlist. Eager youths of the race volunteered their services, but after the four regular military units had been brought up to their proper strength, Negro enlistment was discouraged. A sample of the kind of thing which served to discourage the colored people in the early days of the war was reflected in the following Associated Press telegram, which was sent out from Richmond, Virginia, April 24, 1917:

"NEGRO RECRUITING HALTED

"Richmond, Va., April 24.—No more Negroes will be accepted for enlistment in the United States Army at present. This was the order received by Major Hardeman, officer in charge of the recruiting station here, from the War Department. 'Colored organizations filled,' was the explanation.''

The Negro press and Negro leaders generally became insistent and pressure began to reach the War Department from all parts of the country to make provision for colored troops. The attitude of the Negro people was reflected in the editorial expressions of the colored newspapers. Up to the time of the war there had been among colored people generally a great deal of hostility to the administration at Washington, which was regarded as unfriendly to them, and this attitude of mind is reflected in many of the editorial expressions which then appeared in the colored newspapers.

## Negro Troops in the Post of Honor

Of particular interest to Negro Americans, however, is the fact that on March 25, 1917, the Secretary of War, by order of the President, called the First Separate Battalion, District of Columbia Infantry, National Guard, to the colors to defend the National Capital. This was even before a formal declaration of war. The telegram follows:

*WAR DEPARTMENT TELEGRAM.*
Official Business
Washington, D. C.

2557669 AGO

March 25, 1917.

To Brigadier-General William E. Harvey,
Commanding General District of Columbia National Guard,
Washington, District of Columbia.

Having in view the necessity of affording a more perfect protection against the interference with postal, commercial, and military channels and instrumentalities of the United States in the District of Columbia and being unable with the regular troops available at his command to insure the faithful execution of the laws of the Union in this regard, the President has thought proper to exercise the authority vested in him by the Constitution and laws and to call out the National Guard necessary for the purpose.

I am, in consequence, instructed by the President to call into the service of the United States forthwith, through you, the following units of the

National Guard of the District of Columbia, which the President desires shall be assembled at the places to be designated to you by the Commanding General, Eastern Department, now at Governor's Island, New York, and which said Commanding General has been directed to communicate to you:

First Separate Battalion District of Columbia Infantry, National Guard.

(Signed)  NEWTON D. BAKER,
Secretary of War.

Brigadier-General Harvey at once issued orders for the First Separate Battalion to be mobilized for instruction and muster. Before breakfast following the issuance of this order of March 25, 1917, the entire strength of the battalion was ready for orders and assembled at its armory under command of Major James E. Walker, a colored officer.

The battalion was placed in charge of watching the water supply system, guarding six immense reservoirs, the Potomac River projects, and the various power plants of the District of Columbia, to counter any possible scheme of enemy aliens interfering with these projects and various utilities.

The colored Americans of the District of Columbia and all Washington regarded this assignment of the First Separate Battalion to guard duty within the shadow of the White House as a compliment not exceeded by any since the Negro became a full-fledged citizen of the American Republic. The duty of protecting life and property in the Nation's capital was regarded by them as being comparable to the assignments usually given the guard regiments in England, where men of undoubted loyalty and integrity are given the sacred obligation of protecting St. James's Palace, Westminster Abbey, the Tower of London, and the Houses of Parliament, the places that stand nearest to the welfare and dignity of the British crown.

The men of the First Separate Battalion and the colored citizens of the District of Columbia, and of the whole United States, regarded the call of the First Separate Battalion to the colors as having in it a special compliment from another point of view. It was highly significant that their very *color* which was the *basis of discrimination in time of peace* was considered prima facie *evidence of unquestionable loyalty in time of war.*

In this battalion there were to be found no hyphenates. In fact, the Negro has always proved himself to be 100-per-cent American, without alien sympathies and without hyphenate allegiance. The fact that a colored military unit was placed in this first honor post, to protect the President, the Congress, and the great Executive Departments of the Nation, as well as the vital supply stations that make for the health, happiness, and personal security of the capital of the American Republic, was an honor keenly appreciated.

At about the time that the First Separate Battalion was called out to guard the National Capital the Baltimore Sun, a white newspaper, contained the following expression:

"The Afro-American is the only hyphenate, we believe, who has not been suspected of a divided allegiance."

It was altogether natural that there should be speculation among both white and colored citizens as to why this particular regiment should be the first called to the colors on the eve of the great war declaration. Probably the editorial expression of the Baltimore (Maryland) "Afro-American" may be quoted as to the speculative attitude at least, of colored Americans, which was as follows:

#### "WHY THIS PARTICULAR HONOR?"

"Washington, D. C., has assumed a rather warlike aspect through the calling out of the National Guard to keep an eye on the railway bridges in and around the city, the public buildings, and the water and lighting systems. Strangely enough the First Separate Battalion of colored troopers were mustered in to perform this service, and by this time have perhaps taken the oath, which will incorporate them into the ranks of the regulars.

"In answer to this question of why such honor should be conferred upon the colored troops when the white national guards of the same city are more nearly prepared—the Separate Battalion is still wearing its old blue uniforms—many explanations have been heard in the capital city.

"There are some who have in mind President Wilson's statement that great care should be exercised in calling out the Guardsmen, and every precaution taken that the industrial plants of the country might not suffer by premature loss of workers belonging to the Guards. Should this be the explanation of the Government's move in Washington, then Maryland, New York, Pennsylvania, and Illinois might also expect that their colored troopers will be the first to be called into service.

"However, there is also another whisper going the rounds in the capital of the nation, to the effect that the white regiments of the National Guards have so many foreigners and especially Germans belonging that the Government was afraid to entrust to them the task of watching over Governmental buildings of such immense importance as the Capitol, White House and the houses where the various departments transact their business. It is said that a white trooper on guard at some strategic point might be a German-American and be persuaded to let pass a German confederate armed with dynamite to blow up the Capitol. On the other hand, the colored troopers are known to be *loyal Americans,* and the army officials are certain that no one can pass their lines, not even the Commanding General, unless he has the password.

"For loyalty of this kind our country ought to be willing to pay something. It ought to be willing to pay the price of having its loyal colored men educated for commissioned officers in the very best schools in the nation; it ought to be willing to pay the price of having these citizens enjoy every right and privilege that German-Americans or any others enjoy; it ought even to be willing to have trustworthy colored officers command regiments of white men, which may not be regarded as quite so trustworthy.

"Our Government will do these things, if the Negro will regard his loyalty as an asset, to be sold at the price of citizenship."

Major James E. Walker, the colored officer who was in command of the First Separate Battalion, District of Columbia Infantry National Guard, when it was called to guard the National Capital, was born in Albemarle County, Virginia, September 7, 1874. He attended the public schools and was graduated from the high and normal schools of the District of Columbia. He was connected with the public schools of the District for more than twenty-four years as a teacher and supervisor of the Thirteenth Division and served as such until ordered to the Mexican border with the District of Columbia National Guard in 1916.

His military services began in 1896, when he was appointed first lieutenant in the First Separate Battalion of the National Guard of the District of Columbia. In 1909 he was commissioned captain; in 1912, by and through a competitive examination, he was

commissioned major, after the resignation of Major, now Lieutenant-Colonel, Arthur Brooks.

The First Separate Battalion, under Major Walker, was the
first unit of the District National Guard to be recruited to war
strength in Washington City, and they were among the first troops
to be sent to the Mexican border at the time war threatened between Mexico and the United States in 1916. They immediately
relieved the troops of the regular army and were assigned to the
duty of guarding the water works at Naco, Arizona, which supplied
five or six towns in the vicinity. Aside from his duties there as
battalion commander, Major Walker was selected to act as intelligence officer for the Government.

On March 25, 1917, the battalion was called on to guard the
National Capital, and it was there that the constant vigil of Major
Walker began its inroads on his health. He realized that in selecting his command to safely guard the National Capital, with its
public buildings, water supply, railroads and all other important
facilities, the Government was prompted in its selection by the
high rate of efficiency and undoubted loyalty which his battalion
had established for itself, and in order to continue in this high
regard, he sacrificed health and everything else save that which
makes for the true soldier—duty.

He was ordered to Fort Bayard, New Mexico, to the United
States hospital, for treatment, hoping to regain his health. However the best medical skill was of no avail and he died, April 4,
1918, the first officer of the military forces of the District of
Columbia to give his life for the Nation and world-democracy.
His remains were sent home with military escort, and his body was
interred in Arlington National Cemetery.

His funeral, which was conducted from the Nineteenth Street
Baptist Church, Washington, D. C., of which Rev. W. H. Brooks is
pastor, was attended by a large proportion of the colored citizenship of the District of Columbia, who, despite the cold, bleak day,
followed his remains to Arlington Cemetery.

# CHAPTER III

## OFFICIAL RECOGNITION OF THE NEGRO'S INTEREST

*Appointment of Emmett J. Scott as Special Assistant to the Secretary of War—Difficulties Encountered in Establishing Negro's Status—Opportunities Afforded for Effective Work on Behalf of Colored Soldiers—Better Opportunities for Negro Officers, Soldiers, Nurses, Surgeons and Others Obtained Through This Official Connection.*

On October 5, 1917, the OFFICIAL BULLETIN (published under the direction of the Committee on Public Information), and the Associated Press, carried the following announcement:

### "ADVISOR TO WAR DEPARTMENT

"Secretary Newton D. Baker of the War Department announces that Emmett J. Scott, for eighteen years confidential secretary to the late Booker T. Washington, and at present secretary of the Tuskegee Normal and Industrial Institute for Negroes, has been assigned to duty in the War Department as confidential advisor in matters affecting the interests of the 10,000,000 Negroes of the United States, and the part they are to play in connection with the present war."

This was the first intimation that the Secretary of War had been giving attention to the matter of calling to his side a colored man to advise with him matters concerning colored soldiers and colored Americans generally. There has been very great curiosity on the part of a great many people as to how this appointment came about.

Unfortunately, at the outbreak of the war with Germany there seemed to be in America an epidemic of racial disturbances, such as

40

friction due to the rapid emigration of Negro labor from the South to the North, lynchings of Negro men and women in a number of the states, etc., all of which disturbances were seized upon and magnified through the lens of a well-directed German propaganda, with the manifest purpose of stirring up a feeling of bitterness and unrest among both white and colored Americans. There is ample evidence to support the statement that pro-German influence was for a time diligently at work in the vain effort to dampen the ardor and cool the patriotism of Negro Americans and to thus make them careless or indifferent in support of their country's war program. With a view to stabilizing conditions, as an earnest of the Government's desire to secure the unqualified support of all classes of American citizens, and evidently for the special purpose of reassuring Negroes throughout the country that the Government in general, and the War Department in particular entertained a friendly and just attitude toward them, a representative member of that racial group was appointed by Secretary Baker to serve with him as Special Assistant during the period of the war.

My designation was due primarily to a call during the month of August, 1917, by Dr. Robert R. Moton, Principal of Tuskegee Institute, upon the Secretary of War, in which he pointed out the need and necessity of having in the War Department a colored man in touch with Northern and Southern white people and colored people, who could advise whenever delicate questions arose affecting the interests of the colored people of the United States. Dr. Moton sought to convey the heartening impulse which would come to the colored people of the country if the Government during its period of war should in this direct way recognize the racial group of which he is himself an honored member.

### Correspondence with Julius Rosenwald

Prior to Dr. Moton's call at the War Department to confer with the Secretary of War, the author had been in direct correspondence with Mr. Julius Rosenwald, a member of the Advisory Board of the Council of National Defense, to whom he addressed a letter under date of March 24, 1917, reading as follows:

Tuskegee Institute, Alabama, March 24, 1917.

Mr. Julius Rosenwald,
Member National Defense Board,
Washington, D. C.
Dear Mr. Rosenwald:

I have not been in the slightest degree confused as to what attitude the Negro people should assume in connection with the present threatened war situation, but I have been somewhat concerned at what the attitude of the Administration will be with respect to the Negro people. There are ten millions of us in this country—the only country to which we owe allegiance, etc.

You will note by the attached interview which was sent out by the Associated Press last summer following the Carrizal incident, what I had to say respecting the threatened trouble with Mexico. The Negro people feel just the same way with respect to the German situation.

The point of this letter, then, is to ask you as a member of the National Defense Board as to whether or not you will carefully bear in mind what I have written, and command me and all of us here at Tuskegee most freely in connection with any and all situations in which we can be of service during this crucial hour.

In all former wars in which they have participated, the Negro people have proved by their courage and valor their willingness to fight for American liberty, and I believe they will respond in like measure in the present emergency; and I also believe that the American people will find themselves more and more disposed to accord full appreciation to a people who are willing to lay down their lives in defense of democracy and the well-being of their great country.

My responsibilities here at Tuskegee Institute you know about as fully as any one else, but I wish you to know at the same time my entire willingness to serve the present situation in any way that in your opinion may seem wise and desirable.

Yours very truly,
(Signed)   EMMETT J. SCOTT.

Mr. Rosenwald suggested that the author prepare a resolution expressive of the feelings of the colored people that might be presented to the Council of National Defense. The answer was as follows:

Tuskegee Institute, Alabama, April 7, 1917.

Dear Mr. Rosenwald:

I have your letter of April 4th, and am returning the papers herewith, together with revised resolution which I trust may have your approval.

I am very much gratified to learn that the Council of National Defense is entirely sympathetic and disposed to pass a resolution of this character. It will accomplish very great good. It should be done, however, as you say, in just the right way.

Throughout the South there is considerable apprehension at this time as to whether or not the Negro people are going to remain loyal to the country in this crisis. There need be no fears on this score. As I sought to express in my letter of March 24, the American people, I believe, will be disposed more and more to remove such handicaps and to right such injustices as we now struggle against after the settlement of this great emergency which now faces our common country. I have referred to the patriotism of the Negro rising above wrongs and injustices so as to disarm that element of our people who are urging that the Negro emphasize his wrongs and injustices so as to force from the Government his recognition of his guaranteed rights under the Constitution, etc. My thought and idea is that a sentence of this character will take note of the fact that the Negro does labor under certain handicaps and injustices and yet rises above it in the face of national emergency and need. I hope that the resolution as drafted may have your approval.

With best wishes, I am,

Yours very truly,<br>(Signed)  Emmett J. Scott.

The Resolution as finally drafted and submitted to Mr. Rosenwald follows:

"1.   There are in the United States ten million Negro people. These people have shown allegiance to no country other than the United States. They are in a peculiar and noble sense the children of a united republic. They possess a patriotism which has always risen above wrongs and injustices. There are no hyphenates among them. These people take pride in the fact that it was the charge of Negro troops at San Juan Hill in the Spanish-American War that turned the tide there, and that Negroes have fought bravely in every war in which this country has engaged. The Negro was with Jackson at New Orleans, with Perry on Lake Erie, and 180,000 Negro soldiers served in the Civil War.

"2.   The Government and the people of the United States are deeply sensible of the loyal support rendered by the Negroes of America to their country in past days of national emergency and need.

"3.   Therefore, Be It Resolved, That the Council of National Defense and the Advisory Commission thereto, in joint conference assembled, urge that this Government shall, without regard to racial, political or geographical divisions, give due heed to, and exercise appreciation of the past loyalty of its Negro citizens and of their eager desire to bear anew a generous and helpful part in the common cause of the national defense.''

There were still some doubts and misgivings, however, as to whether the Council of National Defense should pass the resolution, which led to further correspondence:

Tuskegee Intitute, Alabama, April 17, 1917.

My Dear Mr. Rosenwald:

I do most earnestly urge that the resolutions, preamble and all, be published. My reasons rest on the concrete fact that the opinion prevails in many quarters that colored men are not desired by the Administration to have any part in the prosecution of this war. For instance, as I write, I have before me now a letter just received from a man who is probably the most prominent colored physician of Philadelphia, with this paragraph:

> The war. There is not much to be said about it. Mr. Wilson has plainly shown that he would like to get along as much as possible without the Negro. I see in tonight's ''Bulletin'' that it has been decided for the first time in two years to enlist colored men for the regular infantry and cavalry. Active enlistment campaigns are going on here for crews for various warships, but Negroes are not wanted save as waiters and lackeys. It is hard to be loyal and patriotic under these circumstances, though it will not do any good to be otherwise.

This same thing is being said over and over again by other colored men, and by many of the colored newspapers of the country. I enclose two statements I have just clipped from one of our most prominent colored newspapers. I have kept watch on this phase from the beginning, and fundamentally this was back of my original communication to you.

I appreciate the point of view suggested by members of the Council, and am of the opinion that what I have here suggested and mentioned bears out the fact that there is an existing feeling that there is ''some evidence (or feeling) of discrimination sentiment,'' if not in action. The compelling reasons, in my opinion, overbear the suggested objections. I have taken occasion to mention the matter to Dr. Moton and he concurs with me in my conclusion.

With thanks always for your interest and generous support of all that concerns us as a race, I am

Yours very sincerely,

(Signed)  EMMETT J. SCOTT.

## After the Race Was Recognized

Shortly after the author's appointment as Special Assistant to the Secretary of War, hundreds of letters poured into the War Department from colored citizens residing in all parts of the country, commending Secretary Newton D. Baker for his action in selecting a colored man to represent the interests of that racial group during the period of the War, and expressing their satisfaction with the particular choice which had been made. The sentiment of the white South with reference to this appointment is best conveyed by the following typical editorial expression which appeared in the Mobile News Item, a white newspaper published in the heart of the South: "The appointment is a wise move and a wise selection. While the Government is coordinating all the interests of the country in the movement to win the war with Germany, it should not overlook the colored people. Thousands of them have been drafted and are being trained for duty in the trenches. They are to wear their country's uniform and represent their country in the greatest conflict of all times. Millions will stay at home tilling the fields and working in the country's industries. They have their problems no less than others, and it is well that one who knows them so intimately is to advise the Government how to meet these problems."

The colored newspapers were equally responsive in their endorsement of the new policy adopted by Secretary Baker as indicated by his appointment of a representative of the Negro race to advise him on all matters affecting the interests of that particular group during the period of the war, and in numerous editorial comments and special articles warmly commended the selection.

## Endorsed by Leading Citizens

Important white Americans, including such representative citizens as Mr. George Foster Peabody, the New York philanthropist, and Mr. Julius Rosenwald, a member of the Advisory Commission of the Council of National Defense, approved the appointment at various times and have given the author the warmest encouragement and support; without such encouragement and support from colored Americans and white Americans alike, it would have been most difficult to handle even a small proportion of the many problems which came to the office.

Mr. Rosenwald, in an address at the Tuskegee Normal and Industrial Institute, of which he is a trustee, speaking to the officers and teachers and students of the school, March 12, 1918, said:

"In noticing this flag, this Service Flag, hung here in the Chapel, I could not help but feel that there ought to be one very large star there, because the Secretary of War said to me—although I was not directly responsible, and I wanted to deny the responsibility, while I would have been proud to claim it, for Mr. Scott's coming into the War Department—but, notwithstanding that, the Secretary of War has thanked me over and over again, as a Trustee of Tuskegee Institute, for the service he is rendering the War Department and the Nation. When the question came up, I said that nothing would please me better than to see Mr. Scott in Washington, in the War Department, and, of course, none of us would question but what we would all be proud of him in that work as we always have been in everything he has undertaken. There was no question about his making good. That was a foregone conclusion, and as a Trustee I know you, teachers and students of Tuskegee, share that pride with me and the other Trustees in having Mr. Scott in that conspicuous position. Certainly no prouder honor could come to anyone!"

Professor Kelly Miller, Dean of the College of Arts and Sciences, Howard University, a colored college professor of high standing, at a mass meeting of the colored citizens of the District of Columbia at the Dunbar High School, October 22, 1917, also in referring to the appointment said:

"The thanks of the race, amounting almost to gratitude, are due the Secretary of War for his statesmanlike grasp of the situation in designating one of our number to help in bringing the race into sympathetic understanding and cheerful coöperation with the plans and purpose of the Government as they relate to the great struggle in which the world is now involved. Secretary Baker in meeting the impending military emergency has laid the basis of a broad and far-reaching statesmanship. I have always contended, and shall always contend, that the fundamental grievance of the Negro against the American people consists in the fact that he is shut out from participation in the making and administering of the laws by which he is governed and controlled. The nation cannot expect that the Negro will always remain an ardent, enthusiastic citizen, eager to play his part, if he is to be forever shut out from equal participation in and protection under the law. It is imposing too great a tax upon the docility even of the Negro, to make him the victim of harshly enforced discriminatory laws and expect that he will forever exhibit this patriotism and loyalty with ecstatic enthusiasm and paeans of joy. The race may rest assured that its interest will be looked after and safeguarded so far as the military situation is concerned as long as Emmett J. Scott sits at the council table.

"I regard the appointment of Mr. Scott, as Special Assistant to the Secretary of War, as the most significant appointment that has yet come to the colored race. Other colored men have been appointed to high office under different administrations, but the appointments have been mainly a reward for political service, or representation of a contributing element to party success. Such appointments are altogether worthy and desirable, but they are not supposed to carry with them any particular function affecting the welfare of the colored race. The appointment of Mr. Scott, on the other hand, is for the express purpose of securing the cheerful coöperation of the Negro race in the accomplishment of the greatest task to which our Government has committed itself. This is not merely representation for the sake of political reward, but representation carrying with it the vital governmental function."

Shortly after the appointment of the Special Assistant, letters written by a number of representative colored Americans in all sections of the country, and representing many of the leading Negro organizations, denominations, etc., were received by the Secretary of War, to which he made reply similar in tenor to that indicated in the correspondence printed below:

Financial Department of the A. M. E. Church,
Washington, D. C.

October 8, 1917.

Hon. Newton D. Baker,
Secretary of War,
Washington, D. C.

Dear Sir:

Please allow me to express to you my very great delight and appreciation of your appointment of Mr. Emmett J. Scott as a special assistant or aid of the War Department to represent the Colored race during this war period.

The selection and appointment of capable colored men to such positions of trust and responsibility will prove of very great value in the work of a proper adjustment of matters so vital to the best interest of our common cause.

This act of yours is a fitting recognition of the Negro's high sense of patriotism and faithfulness to duty as well as his fitness and willingness to contribute his best in mind and spirit to the cause of right.

Very sincerely yours,

(Signed)  JOHN R. HAWKINS,
Secretary, Financial Department, A. M. E. Church.

### The Reply

War Department
Washington
Office of the Secretary of War

October 9, 1917.

My Dear Mr. Hawkins:

I have received your letter of October 8th and am delighted to know that the appointment of Mr. Scott is meeting with such general approval among his people.

I have long known of his splendid character and of his attainments, and it is source of comfort to me to know that I can have the benefit of his advice more constantly, now that he has accepted a permanent relation to my office.     Cordially yours,

(Signed)  NEWTON D. BAKER,
Secretary of War.

Mr. John R. Hawkins,
1541 Fourteenth Street N. W.
Washington, D. C.

*Above*—Official Photograph of American Negro Troops at drill. Bringing up the machine guns.
*Center*—American Negro Troops brigaded with the French Army, drilling under French Officers
with French machine guns.
*Below*—A Company of Negro Infantry wearing French helmets, as they were brigaded with French
Troops. Photo taken at Herpunt, in the Meuse Sector.

Colored soldiers who served overseas under General Pershing returning to their homes in St. Louis amid the cheers of the people.

*Above*—Two Officers Who Won the Croix de Guerre. Capt. Stewart Alexander on the left, and Lieut. Frank Robinson, both decorated by the French for conspicuous bravery on the field of battle.
*Below*—Three Negro Officers Who Won Distinction Overseas. Left to right: Lieut. Wm. Andrews, Commanding Negro Casuals, of Chicago; Lieut. H. A. Rogers of Richmond, Va., and Lieut. J. A. Rucker of Natchez, Miss.

The return of the 369th (Old 15th New York National Guards)    Passing the Plaza on parade.

*Above*—Colored Troops on Sentry Duty Near the Front Lines.
*Below*—American Camp for Colored Troops in France.

*Left*—First Negro Officer to be Decorated. Lieut. Robert C. Allen of the 372nd Infantry was mentioned in Army orders and awarded Distinguished Service Cross for gallantry in action. His home is in Springfield, Ohio.
*Right*—Lieut. Robert L. Campbell. Company L, 368th U. S. Infantry, awarded the Distinguished Service Cross by order of General Pershing for bravery in fighting in the Argonne Forest.

## Letter of Credentials

To make my work effective as I went from camp to camp, Secretary Baker addressed a letter to Division and Brigade Commanders which was inclusive enough to give me authority to make any inquiries I deemed necessary to be made in camps or cantonments regarding conditions affecting Colored Troops.

The Secretary of War's letter read as follows:

War Department
Washington
Office of the Secretary of War
November 1, 1917.

*TO DIVISION AND BRIGADE COMMANDERS:*

I have appointed Mr. Emmett J. Scott, of Tuskegee Institute, Alabama, as a Special Assistant to the Secretary of War, to advise with respect to the colored people of the United States, colored drafted men, and the colored men who constitute units of National Guard Divisions.

He will be visiting National Army cantonments and National Guard camps, and it is my desire that he be given every opportunity to follow up the work I have entrusted to his care.

He will personally present this letter.

(Signed)     NEWTON D. BAKER,
Secretary of War.

## How the Office Has Functioned

There was considerable misunderstanding and false impression at the beginning as to the real function of the office of "Special Assistant to the Secretary of War," as to the real scope and limitations of the appointment, and as to the real purpose that called the author to Washington. Judging from thousands of letters he received, covering every subject imaginable, and from various public comments and utterances during a period of twenty-one months, it would seem that he had been appointed a "Special Committee of One" to adjust and settle at once any and all matters and difficulties of whatsoever kind and nature which had any bearing upon the race problem in America.

Some of the correspondents, and a few critics, seemed to forget that this appointment was never intended to be an immediate cure for all of our racial ills in America. My call to the Nation's Capital was to advise in matters affecting primarily the interests of colored draftees and colored soldiers, as well as to render counsel and assistance in those matters, including the interests of soldiers' families and dependents, and, in a sense, the morale of Colored Americans generally during the war. Some seemingly failed to remember that the race problem in America has been pending ever since the Civil War; that certain phases of that problem have remained troublesome and unsolved even in the ordinary times of peace in spite of the vigorous and consecrated efforts of prominent race leaders who have ably pleaded our race's cause before the bar of public opinion for the past fifty years. It was therefore manifestly unfair to expect that the mere appointment of a "Special Assistant to the Secretary of War" would effectually abolish overnight all racial discriminations and injustices, some of which were sanctioned by law; or that the Special Assistant would be able to solve, during twenty-one months of the critical and abnormal period of war, all those intricate problems affecting the Negro race in America that others were unable to solve in fifty years of peace. While the author has never minimized any wrong, nor acted in the role of an apologist, nor condoned any injustice visited upon a single member of the Negro race, either before or during the recent world war, yet he has diligently directed his efforts towards securing the best possible results obtainable out of every situation that has arisen.

# CHAPTER IV

## THE WORK OF THE SPECIAL ASSISTANT

*Guarding the Interests of Negro Soldiers and Civilians—Promoting a Healthy Morale—Cases of Alleged Discrimination Against Negro Draftees—The Edward Merchant Case—The John D. Wray Case—How Justice Was Secured—A War Department Inquiry—Training for Colored Officers.*

At the time that the Special Assistant to the Secretary of War was called to Washington, in October, 1917, the war was in progress and the first draft law was being enforced. His first duties consisted principally in urging the equal and impartial application of the Selective Service Regulations to black men and white men alike, and formulating plans calculated to promote a healthy morale among Negro soldiers and civilians. In his effort to properly represent the interests of Negro draftees throughout his tenure of office, he received and keenly appreciated the prompt and cordial coöperation and support of the Secretary of War and of the Provost Marshal General's office. While it is true, and only fair to state, that Negro men, in many cases, were not treated as equitably and justly as white men in the application of the draft law, and that in certain sections they were made victims of many errors, irregularities, and injustices in the matter of classifications, inductions, etc., yet it is a fact that three Local Draft or Exemption Boards were removed from office by the Secretary of War, because it was proven that these Exemption Boards had flagrantly violated the Selective Service Regulations by discriminating against Negro draftees; furthermore, it was ordered that all wrongful classifications, etc., made by them should be corrected forthwith. The office was also instrumental in obtaining justice for a large number of Negro draftees who sent in countless letters, affidavits, and the like, registering their complaints against the unfair treatment of various Draft Boards; and the victories won in their cases, together

51

with the wide newspaper publicity connected with the removal of three local Draft Boards mentioned above, because of their unfairness and injustice to Negro men, served as helpful and warning precedents and had a most salutary effect in the application of the second and third draft laws.

In handling these numerous cases of alleged discrimination and injustice, much correspondence passed between the office of the Special Assistant and the office of Provost Marshal General E. H. Crowder and numerous telephone messages and personal conferences were required.

### Some Typical Correspondence

A small portion of the correspondence in typical cases is hereto appended that indicate the efforts made on behalf of Negro draftees as well as the sympathetic attitude of the Provost Marshal General's office in its partially successful effort to correct abuses and injustices that arose in the application of the Draft Law by various Local Boards:

Provost Marshal General—Army.

February 21, 1918.

Adjutant General,

Jackson, Mississippi.

Number 4496.—Case of Edward Merchant of Local Board of Leake County, serial number 792, has again been brought to this office. Please direct the board to wire at once if they did or did not grant discharge to this registrant prior to November 13, and transmit original reply from local board by mail after wiring contents.

(Signed) CROWDER.

———

State of Mississippi
The Adjutant General's Office
Jackson, Miss.

February 22nd, 1918.

FROM: Adjutant General Mississippi.
TO: F. E. Leach, Govt. Appeal Agent, Carthage, Mississippi.
SUBJECT: Status Edw. Merchant.

I am directed by the Governor to inform you that the Provost Marshal General desires the Local Board of Leake County to advise the status of Edward Merchant, therefore, please answer the following questions on the bottom of this letter.

Did the local board grant Merchant a discharge from the draft?
If a discharge was granted, was it issued prior to November 13th?

(Signed) EDW. C. SCALES,
Brigadier General.

---

Carthage, Miss., Feb. 23, 1918.

1st. Records of Local Board show that Edward W. Merchant was discharged by them on reconsideration of his claim.

2nd. Date of discharge is November 7, 1917.

F. E. LEACH,
Govt. Appeal Agt., Leake County, Miss.

---

War Department, Washington.

February 26, 1918.

Memorandum for the Provost Marshal-General's Office:

Attention of

Major Roscoe S. Conkling, Judge Advocate.

With further reference to the case of Edward Merchant, of Leake County, Mississippi, who was transferred from Camp Pike, Little Rock, Arkansas, to Camp Upton, New York, and to your memorandum bearing on his case which you forwarded me under date of February 14th.

I am venturing to raise the question as to whether or not this man is not entitled to discharge under the Selective Service Regulations in view of the fact that the Local Exemption Board of Leake County, Mississippi,—on the 7th day of November, 1917, actually discharged Edward Merchant, as stated in affidavit filed by H. N. McMillan, Circuit Clerk, of said County—notwithstanding the disinclination of the State authorities of Mississippi to recommend such discharge.

The said Edward Merchant, whose letter I brought to your attention under date of January 25th, states that he has "a mother 50 years old and feeble, a wife and baby," and that his wife is pregnant and not able to perform any work whatsoever, that he is their only support and in the shape they are in it will be impossible for the Government allowance to keep them from suffering. This man is also a productive farmer, and it appears from all the evidence at hand that the decision of the Local Board discharging him was wise and just, and should be affirmed.

This man's case was up twice before the Local Board of Leake County, Miss., after which he was discharged, and in your memorandum to me, of February 9th, you stated: "This was apparently in accordance with Compiled Rulings No. 12 (m) of this office, and it appears that the man (referring to Edward Merchant) should have been discharged from service.''

In telegram of February 12th, the Provost Marshal General (see last clause of telegram) asks the Adjutant General at Jackson, Mississippi, to ''Please advise why Adjutant General's office recommended that registrant be held to service.'' I fail to find, in the documents you kindly transmitted (and which are hereby returned as requested) any satisfactory reply to the inquiry above quoted, and in view of the discharge granted Edward Merchant by his Local Board (verified by the affidavit of the Circuit Court Clerk of Leake County) it does seem that a serious injustice has, in some way, been done this registrant, inasmuch as the telegram from ''Scales'' (presumably the Adjutant General of Mississippi) states ''that the records submitted to State headquarters did not grant an exemption from the draft.'' Will you, therefore, kindly have a full investigation of this case made, and ascertain if the action of the Local Board was properly made known to the State authorities. I would very much appreciate a further report on the findings in this case, as soon as the reasons for ignoring or over-ruling the action of the Local Board by the State authorities can be ascertained.

(Signed)  EMMETT J. SCOTT,
Special Assistant to Secretary of War.

———

March 4, 1918.

FROM:  Office of the Provost Marshal General.
TO:  The Adjutant-General of the Army.
SUBJECT:  Case of Edward Merchant, Serial No. 792, Order No. 109, Ofahoma, Leake County, Mississippi.

1. Your attention is respectfully invited to the case of Edward Merchant, Serial No. 792, Order No. 109, Ofahoma, Leake County, Mississippi, inducted into military service by operation of the Selective Service Law and forwarded to Camp Pike, thence transferred to Camp Upton, where he now is. As a matter of identification, it is stated that Merchant was at Base Hospital, Ward G-6, Camp Upton, on February 12th.

2. This case has been under investigation by this office for more than two months, and it appears that on November 7, 1917, after due and proper reconsideration of the facts, the local board of the proper jurisdiction granted a discharge on dependency grounds; that through an error or negligence the man was not discharged from service.

3. It appears that the regular procedure prescribed by the regulations has been followed up to the point of transmittal of the final recommendation to the Camp Commander, and that through an error of the

State headquarters, the man has been held to service. It therefore appears that the discharge should have been issued, in due course, more than three months ago.

4. A special request is made that prompt action be taken in this matter, as severe hardship and distress is reported to this office from various sources, due to this failure of the proper functioning of local officials, and that this office be advised of the final disposition of the case in order that it may speedily inform the parties interested.

E. H. CROWDER,
Provost Marshal General.
By Roscoe S. Conkling,
Major, Judge Advocate.

———

201 (Merchant, Edward) E. M. 1st Ind.
War Dept., A. G. O., March 7, 1918.—To the Commanding General 77th Division, Camp Upton, Yaphank, N. Y., for investigation, necessary action and report.

By order of Secretary of War:

J. W. RILEY,
Adjutant General.

———

201 (Merchant, Edward) 2nd Ind.
Hdq., 77th Division, Camp Upton, New York, March 15, 1918.—To Commanding Officer, 367th Infantry, for compliance with the first indorsement hereon.

By Command of Brigadier-General Johnson:

LOUIS B. GEROM,
Capt., Field Artillery, N. A., Asst. to the Adjutant.

———

111 K            3rd Ind.
Hq. 367th Inf., Camp Upton, N. Y., 19th March 1918.—To Comdg. Gen'l, Camp Upton.

Private Edward Merchant states that on being inducted into the service at Camp Pike, he was informed that his certificate of discharge on account of dependent relatives was unnecessary, as he was to be discharged for physical disability. This not being done, he wrote to his mother who appeared before the Board and obtained the certificate which is inclosed herewith.

W. G. DRANE,
Lieutenant-Colonel, 367th Infantry, Administrative Officer.

March 28, 1918.

Memorandum for Colonel Easby-Smith:
In re Edward Merchant, Leake County, Miss.

The discharge of this registrant was recommended by this office in our letter of March 4th to the Adjutant General of the Army. We have received no advice that such discharge has been granted.

### History of the Case

December 26, 1917, registrant wrote Special Assistant Emmett J. Scott of the War Department, stating that his Local Board had, by order of the Adjutant General of Mississippi, reopened his case and granted his exemption. November 7, 1917, his discharge was refused by the Camp Commander.

January 25th, Mr. Scott referred the matter to this office.

February 11th, the Adjutant General of Mississippi advised that the Local Board for Leake County had refused to grant exemption to the registrant. The certificate of the Secretary of the Local Board showed that the discharge of the registrant was recommended by his Local Board on November 7, 1917.

On February 18th, the matter was presented by Senator Williams.

On February 27th the Adjutant General advised that their records show that the discharge of the registrant was actually recommended on November 7, 1917. The error in the case was obviously in the office of the Adjutant General of Mississippi.

March 4th, discharge recommended by this office in letter to The Adjutant General of the Army.

March 22nd, memorandum from Mr. Scott, "Is this in accordance with the decision reached?"

JAMES H. HUGHES, JR.,
1st Lieut., Infantry, R. C.

---

## The John D. Wray Case

September 3, 1918.

Memorandum for Colonel Roscoe S. Conkling,
Office of the Provost Marshal-General:
Dear Colonel Conkling:

Mr. John D. Wray, who is a substantial Negro farmer engaged in Coöperative Extension Work, headquarters A. & T. College, Greensboro, North Carolina, has written me the enclosed letter concerning certain definite cases of alleged injustice to colored draftees in said State, and I wish to bring the same to your attention for such investigation as they may merit. Sincerely yours,

(Signed) EMMETT J. SCOTT,
Special Assistant to Secretary of War.

Enclosures.
WHD

---

September 9, 1918.

Honorable Emmett J. Scott,
Special Assistant, Office of The Secretary of War.
Washington, D. C.

Dear Sir:—Your letter of September 3, with enclosure from Mr. John D. Wray attached, has been referred to The Adjutant General of North Carolina with instructions to have an immediate investigation made of the matters complained of in Mr. Wray's letter and to make a report of the results of said investigation.

Upon receipt of this report you will be further advised.

(Signed) E. H. CROWDER,
Provost Marshal General.
By Roscoe S. Conkling,
Lieut. Colonel, J. A., Chief, Classification Division.

JDL

---

October 11, 1918.

Mr. Emmett J. Scott,
Special Assistant,
Office of the Secretary of War,
Washington, D. C.

Dear Sir:
There is returned herewith a letter from John D. Wray of Greensboro, North Carolina, which accompanied your memorandum of the 3rd ult., together with photostat copies of reports from the Adjutant General of North Carolina and from various Local Boards, relating to the cases of the several registrants named in the complaint filed with you by John D. Wray.

(Signed) E. H. CROWDER,
Provost Marshal General.
By Roscoe S. Conkling,
Lieut. Colonel, J. A., Chief, Classification Division.

WGdeR—gm
Encls.

War Dept., P. M. G. C., September 9, 1918.—To The Adjutant General, Raleigh, N. C.

1. Referred.

2. Nothing could be more harmful to the Administration of the Draft than to have an impression prevail that race discrimination exists in any section of the country.

3. You are requested, therefore, to cause an immediate investigation to be made of the matters complained of in the attached letter, and upon completion of the investigation, to make a full report to this office.

4. It is suggested that, in making such investigation, the attached letter from Mr. John D. Wray be treated as confidential.

(Signed)   E. H. CROWDER,
Provost Marshal General.
By Roscoe S. Conkling,
Lieut. Colonel, J. A., Chief, Classification Division.

The following communication is typical of the manner in which the author took up a number of matters involving injustice to colored workers in the departmental service at Washington and elsewhere:

March 21, 1918.

Memorandum for Dean F. P. Keppel, 3rd Assistant Secretary of War:
Dear Dean Keppel:

I very much hope it will be possible to hold up the suggestion which has been made—to eliminate all of the colored messengers who have successfully passed the Civil Service examination for that grade, and have thereby secured their positions through Civil Service regulations in the Procurement Division, Office of Chief of Ordnance, War Department, Washington, D. C. Such a recommendation has been made, and, I understand, is being seriously considered.

It is highly desirable, in my judgment, to ameliorate rather than inflame Negro public opinion here at the National Capital by these movements and suggestions of one kind or another which seem to indicate a willingness to altogether disregard this group of people who are striving in every way possible to support our Government.

(Signed)   EMMETT J. SCOTT,
Special Assistant to Secretary of War.

### Nation's Call to All Alike

Likewise, in the Camp Lee (Virginia) case, the Special Assistant found hundreds of educated young colored draftees, many of them college graduates, hailing from some twenty or more of the leading educational institutions of our country, all assigned to stevedore regiments and labor battalions, without any regard for their educational or technical qualifications, limited to the use of the spade, pickaxe, and shovel and to the digging of ditches, trenches, and the like, instead of being permitted to be trained as infantrymen with gun and bayonet. In direct response to repeated representations made by the author, hundreds of these men were transferred to infantry, artillery, and other units where they could more effectively and more agreeably serve their country, and the Secretary of War issued the following public statement, which was published in The Official Bulletin, of December 4, 1917, indicating his attitude with reference to such discriminations:

"War Department,
"Washington, November, 30, 1917.

"Mr. Emmett J. Scott,
"Special Assistant, War Department:

"Referring to various telegrams and letters of protest received at the Department, to which you have called my attention, concerning certain alleged discriminations against colored draftees, I wish to say that a full investigation of the matters complained of has been ordered.

"As you know, it has been my policy to discourage discrimination against any persons by reason of their race. This policy has been adopted not merely as an act of justice to all races that go to make up the American people, but also to safeguard the very institutions which we are now at the greatest sacrifice engaged in defending and which any racial disorders must endanger.

"At the same time, there is no intention on the part of the War Department to undertake at this time to settle the so-called race question. In this hour of National emergency and need white and colored men alike are being called to defend our country's honor. In the very nature of the case some must fight in the trenches, while others must serve in other capacities behind the firing line.

"I very much regret what seems to be a certain amount of over-worked hysteria on the part of some of the complainants who seem to think that only colored draftees are being assigned to duty in Service Battalions, whereas thousands of white draftees already have been, and more of them necessarily will be, assigned to duty in such Service Battalions.

"Some of the complaints or charges of discrimination seem all the more unwarranted in view of the fact that there is far less hazard to the life of the soldier connected with the Service Battalion than is true in the case of the soldier who faces shot and shell on the firing line. Furthermore, the attitude of the War Department toward colored soldiers is clearly shown by the following facts: More than 626 of the 1,250 colored men who completed the course at the Reserve Officers' Training Camp, at Fort Des Moines, Iowa, have been commissioned as officers in the United States Army, nearly 100 colored physicians and surgeons have received commissions as officers in the Medical Reserve Corps, and a full fighting force of 30,000 colored soldiers, including representatives in practically every branch of military service, will constitute the Ninety-second Division, to be detailed for duty in France under General Pershing.

"The relations between the colored and white men in the camps containing both have been worked out on a very satisfactory basis, and little or no trouble seems likely to arise. All of my reports indicate that the colored men are accepting this as an opportunity to serve and not an occasion for creating discord or trouble, and white men and officers are passing over the question of race difference in a helpful spirit. What we need in this emergency is the help of right-thinking people in the cities and towns around the camps, and we are getting that coöperation so generally that our course seems free from embarrassment if German propagandists, who want to make discord by stirring up sensitive feelings, are simply not allowed to do their work.

"As a matter of fact, the colored people and the white people in this country have lived together now for a good many years and have established relationships in the several parts of the country which are more or less well organized and acquiesced in. Gradually the colored people are acquiring education in the industrial arts, and are rendering themselves more and more useful in our civilization and more and more entitled to our respect. On the other hand, the white people are coming more generally to realize the value of the good citizens among the colored people through their industrial importance and their eager desire to learn and qualify themselves for usefulness in the country, and this has brought about a growth of good feeling, marred, it is true, here and there by such incidents as that at Houston and that at East St. Louis, which grew out of sad misunderstandings and were perhaps contributed to, in at least one of these instances, by the malicious activities of people who would rejoice to see any embarrassment come to us as a sign of weakness against our enemy. Therefore, unrest among the colored people and suspicion of the Government on their part are, by all means, to be discouraged at a time like this.

"We are bending all our energies to the building up of an Army to defeat the enemy of democracy and freedom, and the Army we are building contains both white and colored men. We are expecting that they will all do their duty, and when they have done it they will be alike entitled to the gratitude of their country.

(Signed)  "Newton D. Baker,

"Secretary of War."

### Cases of Unfair Treatment

Every case of racial discrimination or injustice that was brought to official attention, involving either Negro draftees and soldiers or Negro war workers and civilians, was taken up and brought to the attention of the proper officials of the Government, including the War and other Departments, the Military Intelligence Bureau, and in some cases the Department of Justice. The Special Assistant to the Secretary of War regarded all such cases of unfair treatment as calculated inevitably to affect the morale of the Negro people, the maintenance of which was such an essential factor in the winning of the war.

The official files of the Adjutant-General of the Army, which is the administrative branch of the War Department, as well as the files of the Office of the Secretary of War, contain scores and scores of memoranda which the Special Assistant has submitted in the interest of Negro soldiers, Negro chaplains and Negro officers in the National Army, now known as "The Army of the United States." They reveal a strenuous effort to have the worth of the Negro as a soldier fitly recognized by the formation of combatant Negro units in addition to the noncombatant units, known as Stevedore and Labor battalions and the like, to which latter class of military service Negro soldiers, at the beginning of the war and regardless of their educational and special qualifications, seemed to be disproportionately assigned, if not completely doomed. An effort in behalf of the proper training and increased utilization of Negro men as infantry and artillery officers, as medical officers, as chaplains, and of colored women as army nurses and the like, likewise, in part, succeeded because it was worthy in itself and received the hearty, intelligent, and continuous support of practically the entire Negro press of America, to whom the Special Assistant to the Secretary of War owes so much personally as well as officially for the most loyal and valuable help rendered during his tenure of office in the War Department.

To any one who is acquainted with the military status of the American Negro before the war with Germany, and who is familiar with the organized and determined efforts that had to be put forth to have the merits and rights of Negro soldiers suitably recognized, there must come the conviction that the privileges, opportunities, and honors accorded him during the war were, in spite of some discouragement, not merely incidental or accidental; but were due, in some measure at least, to the fact that the Negro soldiers were permitted to have a "friend at court" who was backed up by the best thought and sentiment of the Negro race and by influential white friends of that race in formulating and carrying forward a constructive program that has given to them quite a number of military and other advantages never before enjoyed in the history of our country. While the Special Assistant to the Secretary of War would not by any means exaggerate the importance of the office which he has been holding in the War Department, nor assume any credit which does not rightfully belong to it, yet it is highly significant and proper to note the contrast between the condition of the Negro in the United States at the beginning of the war and the military opportunities and advantages which our race acquired during the progress of the recent world-wide conflict.

Before the European war the Negro was represented in only two branches of the United States Army, namely, the Ninth and Tenth Cavalry, and the Twenty-fourth and Twenty-fifth Infantry units, comprising all told less than 10,000 men, and less than a dozen Negro officers; while during the war, approximately twelve hundred (1200) Negro officers were admitted into practically every branch of military service, including Field Artillery, Coast Artillery, Cavalry, Infantry, Engineer Corps, Signal Corps (radio or wireless telegraphy, etc.), Medical Corps (physicians, surgeons. dentists, etc.), Hospital and Ambulance Corps, Veterinary Corps, Sanitary and Ammunition Trains, Stevedore Regiments, Labor Battalions, Depot Brigades, and quite a number of them served as Regimental Clerks, Surveyors, Draftsmen, Auto Repairers, Motor Truck Operators, several Regimental Adjutants, one or more Judge

Advocates and a number of Negro Military Intelligence Officers, Negro chemists, Negro mechanics;—indeed, the Negro served in nearly every branch of the Army with the exception of the Air Section of the Aviation Corps (operating airplanes, etc.).

These increased opportunities for Negro men and officers were not a matter of *chance*, for they would not have been possible if the "*fight for a chance to fight as Negro combat units*" had not been successful. The Special Assistant to the Secretary of War made a systematic effort to mobilize college-trained Negro men for Artillery and other technical branches of military service, including the 317th Engineer Regiment, the 325th Field Signal Battalion, and as Negro officers for the 92nd Division, etc., realizing, as he did, the imperative necessity of obtaining the very best material his race could afford in trying out this most important, this historic, and now successful military experiment. Scores of technically qualified young men were enabled to consummate their desire to render that particular service in the Army for which they were best fitted by talent and special training.

Perhaps one of the most important and far-reaching projects developed by the War Department was the provision for the training of nearly 20,000 young colored men in military science and tactics, at Government expense, in conjunction with their general education, through Students' Army Training Corps and Vocational Detachments, established in some twenty or more of the leading colored schools, institutes, colleges, and universities of the United States. Similar provision has also since been made for the formation of Reserve Officers' Training Corps for colored men in a number of colored educational institutions, North and South.

Another useful function performed by the Special Assistant to the Secretary of War, and one which has afforded him as much genuine satisfaction as any other service he has rendered in the War Department, is the matter of looking after hundreds, if not thousands of cases relating to voluntary and compulsory allotments, extra Government allowances and compensations, war risk insurance, and the like, due to the families and dependents of enlisted men and of deceased Negro soldiers. The Special Assistant to the Secretary of War has personally looked after or handled through his office many of these cases pending before the Bureau of War

Risk Insurance at Washington, believing that one of the best services he could render the Negro soldier was to protect the financial interests of his wife, his little ones, or other dependents.

## Training of Colored Officers

Along with many others the Special Assistant to the Secretary of War fought for the establishment of the Fort Des Moines Reserve Officers' Training Camp for Negro officers; likewise, after his appointment in the War Department, he used every argument and resource at his command to induce the War Department to make adequate and equal provision for the training of Negro officers in connection with the various camps and cantonments where the National Army was being developed. Never before in the history of our country did we have a Special Officers' Training Camp for the training of Negro officers, to serve in the United States Army, like the one which was conducted by Army officers at Fort Des Moines, Iowa, from June 15 to October 15, 1917, where nearly 700 Negro officers were commissioned; or like the Third, Fourth and Fifth Series of Reserve Officers' Training Camps that were later conducted for the benefit of enlisted men, Negroes and whites alike, in conjunction with the National Army camps and cantonments throughout the country.

The admission of Negro officers into Field Artillery units was only secured after a struggle. It seemed difficult to convince certain subordinate members of Secretary Baker's staff that Negro men possessed the mentality and college training considered as a necessary prerequisite to being trained as Field Artillery officers, but with the creation of the 349th, 350th and 351st Field Artillery regiments (all Negro organizations) the "ice was broken" and quite a number of Negro soldiers, hailing from some of the leading colleges and universities of America, were trained as artillery officers.

The retirement of Colonel Charles Young from active service occasioned much feeling among the colored people. This is referred to elsewhere in this volume. Nothing gave the Special Assistant to the Secretary of War greater pleasure than to coöperate with the friends of Colonel Young to bring about his call to active duty again through the following order:

*Above*—"The Raw Material of Soldiers." Negroes drawn in the selective draft arriving at the cantonment. Compare this photograph with the one below.
*Below*—"Six Months Later." American Negro troops marching along a French road toward the front. Six months before this picture was taken they were undrilled civilians.

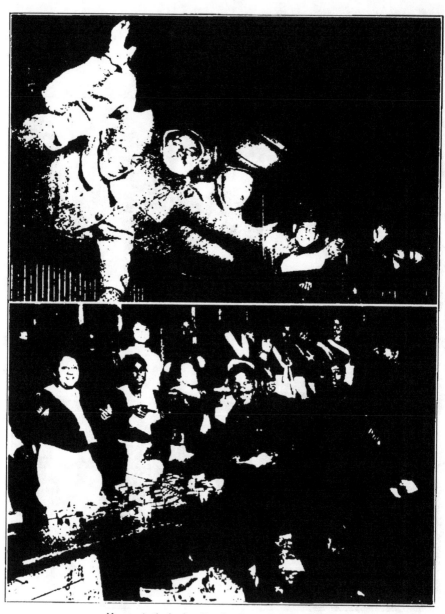

*Above*—Arrival of a Bunch of the Chicago Boys.

*Below*—Happy return of (the old 15th Inf.) New York's famous colored regiment; receiving their shares of cigarettes and chocolate handed out to the boys at the chicken dinner given them at 71st Regiment Armory

*Above*—How Our Soldiers Came Home. American Negro troops boarding the boat in New York Harbor for Camp Merritt, N. J., demobilization camp.

*Below*—It is said that the Negro, because of his constant cheerfulness makes the best soldier. However that may be, it is certain that these three specimens have acquired a reputation for being the most zealous workers in their company and are shown as the three prize men of the company.

These four officers of the 366th Infantry were in some of the heaviest fighting of the war. Left to right they are: Lieut. C. L. Abbott of South Dakota, Capt. Jos. L. Lowe, Pacific Grove, Calif.; Lieut. A. R. Fisher, Lyles. Ind., who won the Distinguished Service Cross, and Captain E. White of the 92nd Division (Buffaloes) of Pine Bluff, Ark.

*Above*—One of the big Y. M. C. A. tents near the front in France. The "Y" gave the same service to the Negro Troops as to the white soldiers.
*Below*—French Colonial Troops (Senegalese) being drilled in use of rifle grenades on the Marne.

*Above*—Baptism for Army Men. Colored troops of the U. S. Army receiving Holy Baptism at the Norcross Rifle Range, Camp Gordon, Ga.
*Below*—Part of Squadron "A," 351st Field Artillery, colored troops on the Transport Louisville. These men are mostly from Pennsylvania.

WAR DEPARTMENT.

The Adjutant General's Office.

Washington, Nov. 6, 1918.

*FROM:*     The Adjutant General of the Army.

*TO:*       Col. Charles Young, U. S. Army (retired),

              1912½ Fourteenth St., N. W.,

              Washington, D. C.

*SUBJECT:* Assignment.

The Secretary directs as necessary in the military service that you proceed to Camp Grant, Rockford, Illinois, and report in person to the Commanding General of that camp for assignment to duty in connection with the Colored Development Battalions at Camp Grant.

WILLIAM KELLY, JR.,

Adjutant General.

One of the most important functions of the office of the Special Assistant to the Secretary of War was to help maintain a healthy morale among Negro soldiers and the twelve million colored Americans, whose continued loyalty was so severely tried during the war. In coöperation with the Committee on Public Information, he conducted a systematic campaign of publicity through the Negro press, the Official Bulletin, leading white newspapers and magazines, etc., which kept the colored people and the country at large fully informed as to the aims and policies of the Government and especially as to the attitude of the War Department with reference to opportunities offered and treatment accorded colored draftees and soldiers. This campaign did much to reassure the colored soldiers, to maintain the morale of colored Americans generally, and to vitalize their efforts toward winning the war.

While it was not possible to accomplish even a small proportion of favorable results in all of the matters which arose; and while in many instances the full measure of justice was not accorded Negro soldiers, sailors, and civilians, it yet remains a fact that during the whole period of the war the office of Special Assistant continued to urge a program of One Hundred Per Cent Americanism, it sought to obtain for them the fullest measure of opportunity possible and to promote friendly feelings between white and colored citizens of the country, based upon the highest ideals of justice and fair play.

# CHAPTER V

## THE NEGRO IN THE NATIONAL ARMY

*Selective Service Law the Most Complete Recognition of the Citizenship of the Negro, North and South—All the Duties and Responsibilities of Patriots Imposed Upon the Negro by the Draft Act—Tribute by the Provost Marshal General to the Colored Soldier—Assignment of Negro Draftees to Cantonments.*

On May 18, 1917, Congress enacted what came to be known as the Selective Service law. As stated in the First Report of the Provost Marshal General, "It was unequivocal in its terms. It boldly recited the military obligations of citizenship. It vested the President with the plenary power of prescribing regulations which should strike a balance between industrial and economical need on the one hand and the military need on the other. It provided that men could be summoned for service in the place in which it would best suit the common good to call them. It was a measure of undoubted significance and power and flung a fair challenge at the feet of those doubters who did not believe that the country would respond to a draft upon the man-power of the republic."

It is of moment to state that on June 5, Registration Day, a number of representative colored citizens served as Selective Service registrars to the entire satisfaction of the Provost Marshal General. There was complaint, however, that so small a number of colored men were permitted to serve as Selective Service registrars, considering the large number of colored men who were called upon to register under the draft.

Under the first selective draft 9,586,508 men between the ages of 21 and 31 were registered; of this number 8,848,882 were whites and 737,626 were colored. Thus it appears that the total registration of citizens of African descent was nearly eight per cent of the entire (racially composite) registration. Of the number of white and colored draftees who were *certified* for service, official figures show that, in the first draft, 75,697 colored men, or 36.23 per cent of the total number were called to the colors and served as soldiers; while 711,213, or 24.75 per cent of the total number of white men certified were called to the colors and served as soldiers. On this particular point I quote directly from Provost Marshal General Crowder's First Report: ·

"Thus it appears that out of every 100 colored citizens called 36 were certified for service and 64 were rejected, exempted or discharged; whereas out of every 100 whites called 25 were certified for service and 75 were rejected, exempted, or discharged."

Further drafts during the course of the war led to increasingly large numbers of whites being called to the colors, and of course increasingly large numbers of colored selectmen as well. Nineteen months brought the total enrollment for service up to twenty-four million (24,000,000), including those who were enrolled under subsequent calls, which were put into operation as the result of Congressional legislation, which afterwards enrolled even those men who reached the age of 45 years.

Under the law, as has been stated, no difference was made as between white and colored citizens. The citizenship of the Negro as provided in the Thirteenth Amendment to the Constitution was fully recognized; color and race were not material, and the regulations for the purpose of classification did not exempt the Negro. A comparison of white and colored registration at the end of the war discloses the following facts: That between June 5, 1917, and September 12, 1918, there were registered 21,489,470 whites and 2,290,527 Negroes, the proportion of colored registrants to the whole being 9.63 per cent. The figures above, however, do not include some 300,000 additional registrants during September and October.

The Mobilization Division of the Provost Marshal General's Office furnished the following table (December 16, 1918), showing the total number of white and colored men called under the Selective Service Draft Regulations during the entire war as shown by States:

| State | White | Colored |
|-------|-------|---------|
| Alabama | 36,172 | 25,674 |
| Arizona | 8,308 | 77 |
| Arkansas | 33,217 | 17,544 |
| California | 71,026 | 919 |

| | | |
|---|---:|---:|
| Colorado | 24,178 | 371 |
| Connecticut | 33,802 | 941 |
| Delaware | 3,879 | 1,365 |
| District of Columbia | 6,576 | 4,000 |
| Florida | 12,769 | 12,904 |
| Georgia | 34,748 | 34,303 |
| Idaho | 13,222 | 95 |
| Illinois | 178,036 | 6,754 |
| Indiana | 70,701 | 4,579 |
| Iowa | 70,899 | 929 |
| Kansas | 43,761 | 2,127 |
| Kentucky | 48,977 | 11,320 |
| Louisiana | 29,230 | 28,711 |
| Maine | 16,415 | 50 |
| Maryland | 26,211 | 9,212 |
| Massachusetts | 82,765 | 1,200 |
| Michigan | 99,027 | 2,395 |
| Minnesota | 76,406 | 511 |
| Mississippi | 21,182 | 24,066 |
| Missouri | 67,920 | 9,219 |
| Montana | 27,965 | 198 |
| Nebraska | 31,520 | 642 |
| Nevada | 3,227 | 26 |
| New Hampshire | 9,174 | 27 |
| New Jersey | 69,974 | 4,863 |
| New Mexico | 9,082 | 51 |
| New York | 260,759 | 6,193 |
| North Carolina | 40,740 | 20,082 |
| North Dakota | 19,087 | 87 |
| Ohio | 139,695 | 7,861 |
| Oklahoma | 61,287 | 5,694 |
| Oregon | 18,182 | 68 |
| Pennsylvania | 197,336 | 15,392 |
| Rhode Island | 11,785 | 291 |
| South Carolina | 19,909 | 25,798 |
| South Dakota | 22,132 | 62 |
| Tennessee | 44,405 | 17,774 |
| Texas | 91,583 | 31,506 |
| Utah | 11,631 | 77 |
| Vermont | 7,294 | 22 |
| Virginia | 37,295 | 23,541 |

| | | |
|---|---:|---:|
| Washington ................................ | 30,912 | 173 |
| West Virginia ............................. | 41,362 | 5,492 |
| Wisconsin ................................. | 75,261 | 224 |
| Wyoming ................................... | 8,095 | 95 |
| Alaska .................................... | 1,957 | 5 |
| Hawaii .................................... | 5,523 | .... |
| Porto Rico ................................ | 15,787 | .... |
| Totals .................................... | 2,442,586 | 367,710 |

Of the colored men who were classified, 51.65 per cent were put in Class I, while of the whites between the same dates who were registered 32.53 per cent were put in Class I.

The Provost Marshal General at some length offers an explanation of the high figures for colored registrants in Class I, but the essential fact stands that under the Selective Service Regulations 51.65 per cent of the colored registration was placed in Class I, while only 32.53 per cent of the whites were so classified. The Provost Marshal General in his Second Annual Report to the Secretary of War discusses ''The Negro in Relation to the Draft.'' Officially he states:

''The part that has been played by the Negro in the great world drama upon which the curtain is now about to fall is but another proof of the complete unity of the various elements that go to make up this great Nation. Passing through the sad and rigorous experience of slavery; ushered into a sphere of civil and political activity where he was to match his endeavors with those of his former masters still embittered by defeat, gradually working his way toward the achievement of success that would enable both him and the world to justify his new life of freedom; surrounded for over half a century of his new life by the spectre of that slavedom through which he had for centuries past laboriously toiled; met continuously by the prejudice born of tradition; still the slave, to a large extent, of superstition fed by ignorance—in the light of this history, some doubt was felt and expressed, by the best friends of the Negro, when the call came for a draft upon the man-power of the Nation, whether he would possess sufficient stamina to measure up to the full duty of citizenship, and would give to the Stars and Stripes, that had guaranteed for him the same liberty now sought for all nations and all

races, the response that was its due. And, on the part of many of
the leaders of the Negro race, there was apprehension that the sense
of fair play and fair dealing, which is so essentially an American
characteristic, would not, nay could not, in a country of such diversified views, with sectional feeling still slumbering but not dead, be
meted out to the members of the colored race.

"How groundless such fears, how ill considered such doubts,
may be seen from the statistical record of the draft with relation to
the Negro. His race furnished its quota, and uncomplainingly, yes,
cheerfully. History, indeed, will be unable to record the fullness
of his spirit in the war, for the reason that opportunities for enlistment were not opened to him to the same extent as to the whites.
But enough can be gathered from the records to show that he was
filled with the same feeling of patriotism, the same martial spirit,
that fired his white fellow citizen in the cause for world freedom.

### No Discrimination Shown

"As a general rule, he was fair in his dealings with draft
officials; and in the majority of cases, having the assistance of his
white employers, he was able to present fairly such claims for defer-
ment or discharge as he may have had, for the consideration of the
various draft boards. In consequence, there appears to have been
no racial discrimination made in the determination of his claims.
Indeed, the proportion of claims granted to claims filed by members of the Negro race compares favorably with the proportion of
claims granted to members of the white race.

"That the men of the colored race were as ready to serve as their
white neighbors is amply proved by the reports from the local
boards. A Pennsylvania board, remarking upon the eagerness of
its colored registrants to be inducted, illustrated this by the action
of one registrant, who, upon learning that his employer had had
him placed upon the Emergency fleet list, quit his job. Another
registrant, who was believed by the board to be above draft age,
insisted that he was not, and, in stating that he was not married,
explained that he 'wanted only one war at a time.'

General Crowder requested a statement as to the coöperation
shown the office of the Special Assistant to the Secretary of War
by the Provost Marshal General's office in the matter of selective

service administration as it affected the Negro people, especially in reference to complaints which were from time to time received from his office. He quotes in his Report the following extract from a memorandum written to him by the Special Assistant under date of December 12, 1918:

" 'Throughout my tenure here I have keenly appreciated the prompt and cordial co-operation of the Provost Marshal General's office with that particular section of the office of the Secretary of War especially referred to herein. The Provost Marshal General's office has carefully investigated and has furnished full and complete reports in each and every complaint or case referred to it for attention, involving discrimination, race prejudice, erroneous classification of draftees, etc., and has rectified these complaints whenever it was found, upon investigation, that there was just ground for the same. Especially in the matter of applying and carrying out the Selective Service Regulations, the Provost Marshal General's Office has kept a watchful eye upon certain local exemption boards which seemed disinclined to treat Negro draftees on the same basis as other Americans subject to the draft law. It is an actual fact that in a number of instances, where flagrant violations have occurred in the application of the draft law to Negro men in certain sections of the country, local exemption boards have been removed bodily and new boards have been appointed to supplant them. In several instances these boards so appointed have been ordered by the Provost Marshal General to reclassify colored men who had been unlawfully conscripted into the Army or who had been wrongfully classified; as a result of this action hundreds of colored men have had their complaints remedied and have been properly reclassified.'

The Special Assistant also ventured in the same memorandum which Gen. Crowder quotes, to say:

" 'In a word, I believe that the Negro's participation in the war, his eagerness to serve, and his great courage and demonstrated valor across the seas, have given him a new idea of Americanism and likewise have given to the white people of our country a new idea of his citizenship, his real character and capabilities, and his 100 per cent Americanism. Incidentally, the Negro has been helped in many ways, physically and mentally and has been made into an even more satisfactory asset to the Nation.' "

## A Problem for the War Department

In view of the restiveness which obtained in the South with reference to sending colored soldiers into the training camps an acute problem was presented to the War Department. Toward the latter part of August, 1917, a conference was held to discuss this question. It was attended by a number of educators who were in Washington for the purpose of being present at an Educational Conference which had been called by Hon. P. P. Claxton, United States Commissioner of Education, an appointment having been made with the Secretary of War, at which conference the whole question was discussed at some length. Present were Mr. George Foster Peabody, New York, philanthropist and unfaltering friend of the Negro; Mr. Oswald Garrison Villard, then editor and owner of the New York Evening Post; Dr. T. H. Harris, State Superintendent of Education for Louisiana; Dr. Thomas Jesse Jones of the Phelps-Stokes Fund Foundation; and such prominent colored men as Dr. Robert R. Moton, Principal of the Tuskegee Normal and Industrial Institute; Dr. John Hope, President of Morehouse College; Bishop George W. Clinton of the A. M. E. Z. Church, and a number of others, including the author. This conference was followed by another which was held by Mr. Peabody, Dr. Moton, and the author, with Messrs. Walter Lippman and Felix Frankfurter, who were advising the Secretary of War at that time in matters relating to the colored people. At this latter conference it was substantially agreed that while the South might object to having colored men from Northern states sent into the various camps and cantonments of the South, it could not well refuse an acceptance of the principle of having such colored selectmen as might be called in such states trained in the cantonments of the states in which they lived.

Considerable hardship followed, however, as the result of this principle; as, for instance, while Alabama has a large colored population, colored soldiers were not sent to Camp Sheridan, Alabama, where a camp was located, but instead were sent to Iowa, because Camp Sheridan was not a cantonment but a camp at which the Ohio National Guardsmen were trained,—the colored battalion from Ohio for a while, along with the whites; but the colored selectmen from

Alabama could not be trained at this camp under the program agreed upon. Camp Gordon, Atlanta, Ga., however, was called upon to accept colored registrants from Georgia because it was a cantonment rather than a camp, and the same thing was true of Camp Jackson, South Carolina, to which colored selectmen of South Carolina were assigned.

The first call for colored selectmen was under date of September 22, 1917, the men being distributed as follows:

*Approximately*

| | |
|---|---:|
| To Camp Devens, Ayer, Mass., its own colored quota............ | 600 |
| To Camp Upton, Yaphank, L. I., New York, its own colored quota | 5,800 |
| To Camp Dix, Wrightstown, N. J., its own colored quota and Florida colored quota.................................... | 4,500 |
| To Camp Meade, Annapolis Junction, Md., its own colored quota and Tennessee colored quota............................. | 6,100 |
| To Camp Lee, Petersburg, Va., its own colored quota............ | 6,300 |
| To Camp Sherman, Chillicothe, Ohio, its own colored quota, and Oklahoma colored quota.................................... | 3,000 |
| To Camp Jackson, Columbia, S. C., its own colored quota........ | 5,900 |
| To Camp Gordon, Atlanta, Ga., its own colored quota........... | 9,000 |
| To Camp Pike, Little Rock, Ark., its own colored quota, and Louisiana colored quota.................................... | 9,600 |
| To Camp Custer, Battle Creek, Mich., its own colored quota...... | 600 |
| To Camp Grant, Rockford, Ill., its own colored quota and North Carolina colored quota.................................... | 7,200 |
| To Camp Taylor, Louisville, Ky., its own colored quota.......... | 3,000 |
| To Camp Dodge, Des Moines, Ia., its own colored quota and Alabama colored quota..................................... | 6,600 |
| To Camp Funston, Ft. Riley, Kas., its own colored quota and Mississippi colored quota.................................. | 8,300 |
| To Camp Travis, Ft. Sam Houston, Texas, its own colored quota.. | 6,500 |
| To Camp Lewis, Washington, D. C., its own colored quota....... | 400 |
| Total.............................................. | 83,400 |

The effect of the above distribution was in many cases to throw, in the beginning, the colored selectmen of Georgia, for instance, with some 30,000 selectmen from the North and East; the same thing was true at Camp Pike, Arkansas, to which some 30,000 Western selectmen were first sent. Under this program it was proved that colored and white men could be trained together in Southern camps without friction. Long before the nineteen months of the war had ended, colored selectmen were being sent into practically every camp in the South, and it is a matter of congratulation to both races that no such friction and trouble followed as had been feared beforehand.

The draft revealed the fact that the Negro could stand the high physical tests of the Selective Service Regulations, a smaller proportion of his number proportionately being rejected than was true of the rest of the composite American population. Americans generally were more or less amazed to find that the Negro not only stood up physically, but that in many important respects where he was supposed to be "off color" his record stood the test.

# CHAPTER VI

## A CRITICAL SITUATION IN THE CAMPS

*Race Problems that Had to be Solved—Fear of the Southern Whites that Trouble would Follow the Training of Negro Troops in the South—Situation Complicated by the Houston Riot—Protest of the Governor of South Carolina—Dr. Scott Called to Spartanburg, S. C., to Allay Trouble There—How the Negro Soldier Finally Won the Respect and Confidence of the South.*

Secretary Baker would not brook discrimination against colored soldiers. It is of official record that at no time during the war period did the Secretary of War give countenance to the practice of discrimination against colored soldiers because of their race. On the contrary, there are many instances which may be cited to prove that he was sincerely and vigorously opposed to any exhibition of race prejudice, and that officers and men have met with severe and condign punishment for acts in contravention of justice to the colored defenders of the flag.

It will be remembered that just after the Houston riot in Texas, during the month of August, 1917, there was a common feeling throughout the South that no more colored troops should be stationed on Southern soil. Many problems, therefore, had to be solved in connection with sending the Negro soldiers into the various camps. There was the fear, ill concealed in the North as well as in the South, that if Negro soldiers, in large numbers, were sent into any particular camp they would be a menace to the surrounding population and to peace and order.

When the time came to call colored troops under the draft, so strongly did some of the Southern States feel on this subject that officials and citizens visited Washington to protest against such troops being sent into their States for training. This was notably true of South Carolina, a visit to Washington being made by Governor Manning, who most strongly conveyed to the War Depart-

75

ment the feeling of the citizens of that commonwealth. The War Department, however, adhered to its policy of sending colored units of National Guard organizations to the camps where such National Guard Divisions were to be trained, whether it happened to be in the North or the South.

Under this program it so happened that the 8th Illinois Regiment, colored, was sent with the remainder of the Illinois National Guard to Camp Logan, Houston, Texas, where the riot, just referred to, had occurred in August of the same year. The 8th Illinois was commanded from Colonel to corporal by colored officers, Col. Franklin A. Denison being in command. The old fires of resentment were rekindled and it was difficult to predict what would follow. Col. Denison, himself a native of Texas and an attorney who had won wide prestige as Assistant City Prosecuting Attorney, and afterwards Assistant Corporation Counsel of Chicago, handled his men wisely and well, and no outbreaks occurred between the white citizens of the town and these colored soldiers who were being trained for service overseas. Week by week during the course of the training Col. Denison and his men won the confidence of the best white and colored citizenship of the town. He asked for a "square deal" for his men, and he resolved that they should not suffer because of the former riot, with which they had nothing to do, although at several places en route to Houston from Illinois they were jeered at along the way, stoned in one or two places, and a riot was barely averted at a way station in Texas.

The Ninth Ohio was sent to Camp Sheridan, Montgomery, Alabama, the capital of the Confederacy, along with the Ohio National Guard Division. Organizations of colored citizens under the leadership of Mr. Victor H. Tulane, a trustee of Tuskegee Institute and friend and counselor of the late Booker T. Washington, took charge of the matter of bringing the colored and white people of the city into agreement so that there should be no untoward incident while the Ohio battalion was at Montgomery. A change as to sentiment soon followed among the citizens of various cities throughout the South where National Guard Camps, or National Army Cantonments were located, when the colored soldiers began to show by their demeanor that they were bent upon serious business and that they were disposed to go about their business without molesting the common citizenship, asking only that they in turn be not unfairly treated.

It is to the credit of the South that outside of the common friction which always occurs where any group of soldiers are gathered, whether they be white or black, no clash of the kind feared took place during the whole period of the training. City officials, judges, and chiefs of police began to speak in the highest terms of the men, expressing in nearly every instance great surprise that none of the anticipated troubles had occurred. The relations between the colored and white soldiers in the camps, with rare exceptions, were pleasant and friendly; and where those exceptions occurred it was due more or less to the policies pursued by such authorities as were fearful of untoward results rather than to any other reason.

Shortly after the Special Assistant was called to service, the Secretary of War held a conference with Mr. Raymond B. Fosdick, Chairman of the Commission on Training Camp Activities, and the author, making a survey of the whole situation with reference to the presence of these colored men in the various camps and cantonments and expressing the hope and idea that the Commission on Training Camp Activities would make full provision for the entertainment, recreation, and amusement of colored soldiers, such as was being provided for white soldiers. Mr. Fosdick, as the responsible executive officer of this important work, most enthusiastically developed and carried out this program. His representatives in the various States coöperated, more or less slowly to begin with, but in the end most enthusiastically, to provide proper recreation and amusement for colored as well as for white. It is a fact to be noted, however, that the War Camp Community Service organization made provision for colored soldiers in only one city during the first seven months after they were drafted, but between May, 1918, and August 5 of the same year, six or eight clubs were opened in various cities.

### Military Training An Educational Uplift

While the Field Signal Battalion and some of the Headquarters companies of the 92nd Division were composed of specially trained enlisted men, and well educated men selected from the draft, there was an amazing amount of illiteracy when the Division was first organized. As the trains from the South brought the men into the camps during the bleak days of November, 1917, they were a spectacle to behold. Hundreds coming directly from the cotton and corn fields or the lumber and mining districts—frightened, slow-footed, slack-shouldered, many underfed, apprehensive, knowing little of the purpose for which they were being assembled and possibly caring less—the officers but recently from the training camp received them.

. The task of making soldiers of such raw material presented a most discouraging problem. Night school with the veriest rudiments of elementary training and talks on the simple rules of better living and army sanitation were conducted by the officers of every organization in connection with the daily drill schedules. The officers of the 92nd Division determined to make men of this material, men capable of occupying a larger place in the community life at the same time that they were making soldiers of them, fitted to fill the place in a modern fighting machine such as was being built by the United States Army. Without exception the men showed that they were eager to learn; and as the stoop came out of their spines, the shamble from their gait, they learned to read and write their names. On the first pay-roll of one regiment of the 92nd Division 90 per cent of the men being unable to write, made their marks. Five months of night school eliminated this condition and in its place came smartness in drill, cleanliness in billets, discipline, a pride in the uniform, respect for the flag, and the ability to sign their names to the pay-rolls. When that same regiment which had had 90 per cent of its members unable to write their names was on its return trip South to be mustered out of the service, Red Cross workers in two cities marveled at the improvement in the men's appearance, some doubting that they were the same men who had passed these points going into the draft. The difference was not one of appearance alone, for every one of those same men gave Uncle Sam a receipt in his own handwriting for his final pay and was capable of correcting any error that might have been made by the clerk.

All of the new influences which the colored soldier met in the camp conspired to give him a new vision, and the testimony from such widely separated points as Camp Dodge, Ft. Des Moines, Iowa, and several of the camps in the South will illustrate the change which soon came to be noted as to the conduct and demeanor of the colored soldier.

*Collier's Weekly* dispatched one of its staff contributors, William Slavens McNutt, to make a round of all the camps and cantonments and to report conditions as he found them. In one of these articles entitled, "Making Soldiers in Dixie," Mr. McNutt devoted considerable space to the description of the change which was taking place in the Southern cities and towns, and even in some of the Southern camps where colored soldiers and Southern white men were being trained for overseas service. In this article Mr. McNutt reported 'visits made by him to two Southern camps and paid many compliments to the Negro soldiers because of their solemn attitude toward the war and the earnestness with which they undertook and passed through the ordeal of training.

## A Situation at Spartanburg, S. C.

But it was not all easy sailing in all the camps and there was considerable jarring from time to time and enlightening wisdom and firmness were required to overcome certain threatening situations. One of these stands out in my memory particularly just now, and is probably being related for the first time. At Spartanburg, South Carolina, where the New York National Guard units were being trained, there developed a little trouble. The 15th New York Regiment (colored) under command of Col. William Hayward, which regiment afterwards came to be known as the 369th, won enduring fame in France, being the first colored combat regiment to go overseas. On October 22, 1917, Col. Hayward came personally to the War Department to place before it the highly inflammable situation existing at Spartanburg, South Carolina, near which city Camp Wadsworth was located. Spartanburg is a small Southern city which closely follows what are usually regarded as Southern traditions and prejudices in the treatment of the Negro. Some of its citizens rather felt that something was needed to let the jaunty Negro soldiers from New York "know their place," and so one Sunday evening when a colored soldier, Noble Sissle by name, stepped into a white hotel to buy a New York newspaper, the proprietor walked up to him, it is stated, and with an oath demanded to know why he did not remove his hat.  Sissle, holding the newspaper in one hand and his change in the other, did not quickly enough respond to the demand and his hat was knocked from his head.  When he reached down to pick it up and arose he was all but felled by a blow, and as he retreated toward the door was kicked by the irate proprietor.  On the sidewalk, awaiting Sissle's return, was Lieut. James R. Europe, a colored officer, bandmaster of the 15th New York Regiment.  A group of colored and white militiamen "rushed" the hotel, but were "called to attention" by Lieut. Europe, who demanded that the crowd disperse.

The New York militiamen expressed themselves as being violently opposed to the treatment which had been visited upon Sissle; and so the next night a group of these soldiers banded together and began marching to Spartanburg, several miles away, to "shoot it up" as the soldiers at Houston had "shot up" that town after the clash with the Houston police in the August preceding.

It was only because of Col. Hayward's courage and firmness in overtaking these men, and in safely bringing them back to camp that another Houston riot was for the moment averted.

The feeling grew more and more intense, however, and Col. Hayward, to ward off another "situation," came to the War Department.  The Special Assistant to the Secretary of War was hastily summoned by the Secretary of War and ordered to proceed to Spartanburg.  The atmosphere, it was easily observed, was surcharged.  Col. Hayward called his officers together, advised them of the object of the mission of the Special Assistant to the Secretary of War and had all non-commissioned officers of the regiment assemble.  Col. Hayward then withdrew and carried with him every commissioned officer of the regiment.  Non-commissioned officers usually prove themselves to be the backbone of a regiment, and it was these men that Col. Hayward desired I should address.  These men and the Special Assistant to the Secretary of War were thus left alone to discuss the delicate situation face to face and in the frankest way possible.  My address to these men was an appeal and admonition to do nothing that would bring dishonor or stain to the regiment or to the race which they represented; that whatever of violence they should do in the present difficulty would only react upon their race throughout the country, and that the situation was potentially dangerous, in that it was hardly to be expected that the country would stand for another riot of the Houston character, despite the fact that the men, when visiting the town, had suffered rebuffs and mistreatment which had tried their patience and caused them to wish to visit violence upon the community.

As the Special Assistant now recalls that dramatic setting in the late afternoon of that Fall day, there is nothing in the service rendered by him in the War Department which he remembers more vividly, or as being more serviceable than that appeal addressed to these men, that they should listen to the counsel of patience for the Great Cause, even in the face of studied insult and maltreatment. Afterward many of the men, with tears streaming down their faces, approached him and voiced how bitterly they felt in the face of the insults which had been heaped upon them from time to time as they passed through the town, but at the same time they told him of their willingness to listen to the counsel which had been addressed to them for the sake of the Negro race, and for all that was at stake for it and the country during the war.

The War Department faced three situations: It could keep the regiment at Camp Wadsworth and face an eruption, and possibly further anger the white citizens who were opposing the retention of the regiment there, while at the same time inflaming the men of the regiment and many of the white New York guardsmen who were restive under the treatment accorded the colored soldiers, or the regiment could be removed to another camp and thereby convey the intimation that whenever any community put forward sufficient pressure, the War Department would respond thereto and remove soldiers from such location, whether they had given provocation for such demand or not. As a third alternative the Department could order the regiment overseas. The latter alternative was decided upon, and soon after reaching New York the 15th New York was on its way overseas.

The story of its wanderings from camp to camp in America, of its ship breaking down after being two days at sea, and of its return to New York harbor, of its finally reaching France, and of the glorious record it achieved as the 369th Infantry will be recounted again and again by the heroic survivors for years to come.

# CHAPTER VII

## COLORED OFFICERS AND HOW THEY WERE TRAINED

*First Officers' Training Camp for Colored Men at Fort Des Moines, Iowa—Major J. E. Spingarn's Fight for the Establishment of This Camp—Methods of Training Reserve Officers—Negro Educational Institutions Furnish Personnel—Seven Hundred Colored Officers Commissioned at Fort Des Moines.*

While the great nations in Europe were flooding the continent with human blood, leaders in American political thought saw that the United States would sooner or later become a partner in the great cataclysm. The weakness of our Army and Navy crystallized into a national slogan, "Preparedness." Accordingly, several leading citizens in New York and vicinity organized a civilian camp at Plattsburg, N. Y. The purpose of this camp was to fit men to take examinations for commissioned officers for the new National Army which was inevitable. The Government endorsed the proposition and furnished aid to the extent of upkeep and living expenses during the period of training.

But "Plattsburg" was a voluntary—almost a social camp, and true to American tradition no colored men could be admitted to such a camp with white men. When the United States entered the great European war, Congress authorized the establishment of a number of training camps for white officers, the number to be left to the discretion of the Secretary of War. No provision was made for the training of colored officers. After repeated efforts of various kinds, a committee composed of representative citizens, headed by Dr. Joel E. Spingarn of New York City, held a conference with the military authorities. The efforts of the committee were fruitless for the time being, at least, and the committee was dissolved. The project was later taken up by the students of Howard University together with a few members of the faculty

82

and students from other colleges, from Lincoln University, Fisk University, Atlanta University, Morehouse College, Tuskegee Normal and Industrial Institute, Hampton Agricultural and Industrial Institute, Virginia Union Seminary, and Morgan College.

### Efforts of Dr. Spingarn

Dr. Joel E. Spingarn consulted Gen. Leonard Wood, who was at this time in charge of the Eastern Department, Governor's Island, New York, about the establishment of a "Plattsburg" for colored men. General Wood gave assurance that the same aid and assistance could be given a camp for colored men that were given the camp for white men, provided 200 men of college grade could be secured. Dr. Spingarn set out upon a vigorous campaign, sending letters and circulars in every direction and personally visiting Howard University and kindred institutions. Success crowned his indefatigable industry, but not without great opposition.

Dr. Spingarn's efforts, by many of the important newspapers and leaders of the race, were referred to as being designed to bring about the establishment of a "Jim Crow Camp" for training colored officers. The agitation grew quite violent at times, particularly because of the fact that Dr. Spingarn was Chairman of the Executive Committee of the National Association for the Advancement of Colored People, an organization generally regarded as standing uncompromisingly for the rights of the Negro people. In his efforts to secure the establishment of this camp Dr. Spingarn had the coöperation of his aide, Dr. W. E. B. DuBois, Editor of *The Crisis,* also regarded as an uncompromising champion of the Negro, and of Col. Charles Young, United States Army, and such virile speakers and leaders as William Pickens and others. The agitation among the Negro group and the recognized friends of the Negro grew so warm that for a while divided counsels threatened the establishment of a camp. Whether through a fortunate or unfortunate turn of circumstances, while this agitation was at its height, Congress declared that a state of war existed between the United States and the Imperial German Government. Immediately, civilian training camps were abolished and fourteen Government camps were established for the training of officers.

Strange and paradoxical as it may seem, America, while

fighting for the democratization of the peoples bf far-off Europe, was denying democracy to a part—an honest, loyal and patriotic part—of her citizens at home. Fourteen camps were instituted for the training of *WHITE* officers—none for colored officers, nor were colored men admitted to any of the fourteen camps.

The next best thing seemed to be a separate camp. The students were joined by faculty members and an executive committee was organized with Prof. T. Montgomery Gregory as Chairman. *Colored men were fighting the Government in order to wring from it permission to fight for it.* The President and Deans of the University gave full coöperation. A convention of the student body was called on Tuesday, May 1, 1917, when money was raised by students and faculty for the dispatch of delegates to take up this matter with the student bodies of various schools.

At the suggestion of Prof. Gregory, the Executive Committee was transformed into the Central Committee of Negro College Men with Mr. C. Benjamin Curley as Secretary, and an office was opened in the basement of Howard University Chapel. The work was so organized that the secretary was in control of the situation at all times and his office became the radiating center from which the latest information was flashed throughout the country. Letters and telegrams flooded the office in quest of details and instructions. The delegates announced success in obtaining in ten days, 1,500 names to be presented according to agreement, to the War Department as a justification for the appeal for an ''Officers' Reserve Training Camp for Colored Men.''

Meanwhile the committee interviewed Congressmen, leaving a copy of the following card on each Congressman's desk:

### TRAINING CAMP FOR NEGRO OFFICERS

Our country faces the greatest crisis in its history; the Negro, as ever, loyal and patriotic, is anxious to do his full share in the defense and support of his country in its fight for democracy. The Negro welcomes the opportunity of contributing his full quota to the Federal army now being organized. He feels very strongly that these Negro troops should be officered by their own men. The following statement presents the facts upon which we base our request for an officers' reserve training camp for Negroes.

1 (a)   Fourteen officers' training camps are to be opened on May 14, 1917, to provide officers for the new Federal Army.

(b)   No officers are to be commissioned unless they receive training in one of these fourteen training camps:

(c)   The War Department has stated that it is impracticable to admit Negroes to the fourteen established camps;

2 (a)   The Negro is to furnish his proportionate quota in this army;

(b)   It seems just that the competent and intelligent Negroes should have the opportunity to lead these troops;

(c)   One thousand Negro college students and graduates have already pledged themselves to enter such a training camp immediately;

(d)   In addition men in the medical profession desire to qualify for service in the Medical Corps, and there are other competent men ready to qualify for other specialized corps provided for;

(e)   Records of Negro officers and troops warrant the provision for Negro officers to lead Negro troops.

Lieut. Col. Young,            Major Loving
Capt. Davis                   Major Walker

3.   Therefore, the Negro race requests the establishment of an officers' reserve training camp for Negroes.

CENTRAL COMMITTEE OF NEGRO COLLEGE MEN.
Signed:

FRANK COLEMAN, Chicago,        T. M. GREGORY, Harvard,
W. DOUGLAS, Lincoln,           C. H. HOUSTON, Amherst,
W. A. HALL, Union,             L. H. RUSSELL, Cornell,
M. H. CURTIS, Howard,          C. B. CURLEY, General Secretary,
                  Howard  University, Washington, D. C.

Over 300 Senators and Representatives signified approval, and the War Department was soon the center of a storm of telephone calls and personal interviews.

The colored churches in the District of Columbia were interested. Dr. J. E. Moorland advised that the Y. M. C. A. branches throughout the country be used as recruiting stations, a valuable suggestion which was readily accepted. Frequent mass meetings were held by the Howard students; and when additional funds were needed a concert was given in the chapel. A little later the University Dramatic Club repeated its performance of "Disraeli" through the courtesy of the management of the Howard Theater, at which time over $125 was raised.

With 1,500 names in the hands of the War Department on May 7, the campaign became more heated. Press articles were sent out by the committee. The following is one of a large variety:

"THE COLORED PEOPLE OF THE COUNTRY MAKING STRENUOUS EFFORTS TO SECURE TRAINING CAMP FOR COLORED OFFICERS.

Headquarters and Recruiting Station at Howard University.
"According to the best authorities about 83,000 Negroes will be drafted for the New Federal Army. The Negroes welcome this opportunity of serving their country, and sharing their full responsibilities in this time of national peril. They feel, however, that Negro troops thus raised should be officered by men of their own race and are making strenuous efforts to secure a training camp in which such officers can be prepared. The War Department has stated that it is impracticable to admit Negroes to the fourteen camps for officers to be opened on May 14, 1917. And it has also stated that no officers are to be commissioned unless they receive training in one of these camps. This means that unless some provision is made whereby colored men may be trained for officers these 83,000 Negro troops will be officered exclusively by white officers; and that Negroes qualified both mentally and physically to serve as officers will be forced under the conscription law to serve as privates. The colored man is willing and ready to carry out the duties imposed upon him as an American citizen, and feels that he should be given the same opportunities in the performance of these duties as are given to other American citizens. The Negroes from every section are requesting that the Government provide means whereby colored officers may be trained. The appeal is just, reasonable, and practicable. The proposition is squarely up to the Government. This is no time for sectional differences and race prejudice and the highest patriotism demands that every American citizen be given the opportunity to serve his country in the capacity for which he is best fitted.

"Over one thousand colored men have sent their names to their headquarters at Howard University, and hundreds of others are arriving by mail and telegrams.

"Why should not colored troops be officered by colored men? Their records show them to be competent and efficient, and to deny any class of citizens the opportunity of rendering its best service belies the very theory of our democracy, and the basic principle for which the present war is waged. Our American statesmen should frown upon any procedure that does not offer an equal opportunity for all at all times, but more especially at a time when our country is faced by a foreign foe."

An important conference was held in Washington with Dr. Robert R. Moton, Principal, and Mr. Emmett J. Scott, Secretary of the Tuskegee Normal and Industrial Institute, by Dean George W. Cook and Professor T. Montgomery Gregory of Howard University and the valued support of Tuskegee Institute enlisted in behalf of the Officers' Reserve Training Camp. The work in Congress was kept up. Communications were sent to President Wilson, Secretary Lansing, Secretary Baker, and other Cabinet officers. Finally there were two important conferences: the one at the War College where President Newman of Howard University, Deans Miller, Cook and Moore, Professors Tunnell and Gregory, Mr. H. E. Moore, Doctors Marshall and Cabannis met and discussed the matter with Major Kingman, then head of the War College; the other with Secretary Baker the following day, when he practically assured the same committee of the establishment of the camp.

"The question of location, it was said, was the only remaining obstacle; to offset this the grounds and buildings of Howard University were offered by the authorities, but were not accepted for various reasons. The tension was then at its height and just as a more extensive campaign was about to be launched President Newman was notified that the camp would be established. This happened about 7 P. M., May 12, 1917.

"The authorization of the camp brought joy unspeakable to the hearts of the committee and students. Smiles and handshakes soon made the campus seem like an old-fashioned Methodist prayer meeting and the news was heralded far and wide. The following was sent to all those who had submitted their names:

"'Dear Sir:
"'The War Department has announced that a camp to which colored men can be admitted to be trained as officers will be established at Fort Des Moines, Iowa, June 15th. Twelve hundred fifty men will be admitted. Two hundred fifty will be selected from the regular army and one thousand from the various states and the District of Columbia on a pro rata basis. The camp will be organized and maintained on the same regulations as all the other camps now in operation.

"'There will be recruiting stations throughout the country to which applicants must report for physical and mental examinations. The mental training will be rigid and none but thoroughly qualified men ought to apply.

" 'Successful applicants must pay their transportation to the camp. They will be reimbursed at the rate of 3½ cents per mile from their homes to Des Moines by the shortest route. The men will be paid while in camp but the exact amount has not yet been determined. Additional information will be given to the Press as soon as the War Department issues it. Watch the papers from this date. The race is on trial. Come to camp determined to make good.

" 'Yours truly,

C. BENJ. CURLEY,

General Secretary,

Central Committee of Negro College Men.'

Howard University,
    Washington, D. C.
        May 23, 1917.

"Of the 1500 names submitted, these were almost without exception men from colleges and averaged between 18 and 25. The War Department in the interim suggested that in as far as possible only men between 25 and 40 be included. This meant additional work, but the committee met it cheerfully and augmented its already widely advertised propaganda by numerous press articles. The following is one of the many:

" 'Howard University,
" 'Washington, D. C.,
" 'May 24, 1917

" 'Dear Brother:

" 'A Reserve Officers' Training Camp, accommodating 1250, at Des Moines, Iowa, for Colored men, to start June 15th. Such was the official announcement of the War Department last Saturday, May 19th.

" 'Stop but a moment, brother, and realize what this means. At present, we have only three officers of the line in the army; in less than four months we shall have 1250 officers. Our due recognition at last. But no one who was not in the fight knows what a struggle we had to obtain the camp. Only a few of those in authority would support the project; most of them did not want to consider it; and the remainder were bitterly against it. "Why waste time trying to train Negroes to be officers," they said, "when the Negro can't fight unless he is led by white officers?" The truth is, the Negro has had no chance to fight under his own leadership. Now the chance has come; the greatest opportunity since the Civil War. But what if we fail? Eternal disgrace! Our enemies will say forever: "Oh, yes, the Ninth and Tenth were uneducated men; but just as soon as the Negro gets a little education he becomes a coward." There is a terrible responsibility resting upon us. The Government has challenged the Negro race to prove its worth, particularly the worth of its educated leaders. We must succeed and pour into the camp in overwhelming numbers. Let no man, slack.

"'Some few people 'have opposed the camp as a "Jim Crow" camp; they say we are sacrificing principle for policy. Let them talk. This camp is no more "Jim Crow" than our newspapers, our churches, our schools. In fact, it is less "Jim Crow" than our other institutions, for here the Government has assured us of exactly the same recognition, treatment, instruction and pay as men in any other camp get. The Government bears all expenses, including transportation, uniform, and keep; and, in addition, pays a salary of not less than $75 a month while in training. When commissioned, the lowest salary is $145 a month. But the salary, though not to be despised, is not the fundamental element. Our great task is to meet the challenge hurled at our race. Can we furnish officers to lead our own troops into battle; or will they have to go again (and if they have to go now, they will go forever) under white officers?

"'Let us not mince matters; the race is on trial. It needs every one of its red-blooded, sober minded men. Doctors, lawyers, teachers, business men, and all men who have graduated from high school. Let the college student and graduate come and demonstrate by their presence the principles of virtue and courage learned in the academic halls. Up, brother, our race is calling.

"'We cannot tell you how to register just now; but in a few days we shall know everything. What you are to do NOW is to send this letter to another brother and tell him to do the same, to pass the word along, and to stir up all the enthusiasm in your district. Watch all the papers and when you see news distribute it. Look for all bulletins; and, above all, be ready!

"'Just think a moment how serious the situation is. Peal the war tocsin; stand by the race. If we fail, our enemies will dub us COWARDS for all time; and we can never win our rightful place. But if we succeed— then eternal success; a mighty and far-reaching step forward; 1250 Colored Army officers leading Negro troops. Look to the future, brother, the vision is glorious!

"'Ever your brothers,

"'CENTRAL COMMITTEE OF NEGRO COLLEGE MEN.'"

As a result of these persistent efforts a training camp for colored officers was authorized by the Secretary of War on the 19th of May and soon thereafter the candidates for commissions set out for Fort Des Moines, Iowa, where they were to undergo training. The Honorable Champ Clark, Speaker of the House of Representatives, said that this marked "an epoch in American history and a new day for the Negro."

The student officers were put through weeks of intensive training under Col. C. C. Ballou, his staff, and a group of colored non-commissioned officers from the four colored regiments of the Regular Army. The Presidents and other officers of the various colored institutions of learning whose officers, teachers and students were in training visited the camp and spoke to the officer-candidates. Dr. George W. Cabannis, a colored physician of Washington, D. C., voluntarily gave up his practice and enlisted in the Y. M. C. A. work as a Secretary, and took charge of the Y. M. C. A. tent at Ft. Des Moines, working in closest coöperation with Col. Ballou and his military aides.

It was expected that the training would last three months. At the end of that period, however, the War Department decided to continue training for another month. Suspicion became rife among the men; many of them dropped out, giving as a reason that "the War Department never intended to commission colored men as officers in the army."

There were only a few of those faint-hearted fellows, however; the great majority remained, and on October 14, 1917, Col. W. T. Johnson of the Adjutant General's Office arrived at Ft. Des Moines with commissions for 639 officers,—106 captains; 329 first lieutenants, and 204 second lieutenants.

On that day, October 14, 1917, amidst impressive ceremonies, the 17th Provisional Training Regiment, as the Fort Des Moines Training Camp was called, was formed on the drill-ground facing the Administration building; here with bared heads and uplifted hands these 639 members of the regiment (the unsuccessful members having been dismissed) took the solemn oath which was administered by Col. Johnson, Chief of the Division of Training Camps, War Department.

On the next day, October 15, the successful candidates received commissions and were ordered to report after fifteen days' leave of absence to their respective camps. In equally divided groups the 639 officers were sent to the following camps, reporting for duty on the 1st of November, 1917: Camp Funston, Kansas; Camp Dodge, Iowa; Camp Grant, Illinois; Camp Sherman, Ohio; Camp Meade, Maryland; Camp Dix, New Jersey; Camp Upton, New York.

It was at these widely distributed camps that the various units of the 92d Division (the authorized colored Division) were trained.

Some of the difficulties which befell the 92d Division are to be ascribed to the fact that the units of the Division were never united until they reached France, being trained in the seven camps here mentioned; this was true of no other division of the army sent overseas.

On October 15, 1917, impressive exercises were held in the Y. M. C. A. tent, Dr. George W. Cabannis of Washington, D. C., presiding, following the bestowal of the commissions. A program had been hastily arranged. Addresses were made by Brigadier General C. C. Ballou, who had started the training at Fort Des Moines and who had been made a Brigadier General and assigned to Fort Dodge; by Col. Hunt, who had succeeded Col. Ballou in charge of the 17th Provisional Training Regiment training camp; by Dr. Daniel Hale Williams of Chicago, Illinois, who was present as a visitor, and by one or two officers of the 17th Regiment Training Camp. The Special Assistant to the Secretary of War also spoke upon this occasion, having been detailed by the Secretary of War to represent him at the exercises in connection with the bestowal of the commissions.

# CHAPTER VIII

## TREATMENT OF NEGRO SOLDIERS IN CAMP

*Men from the South Sent to Northern Camps to Face a Hard Winter—Attempts at Discrimination Against Negro Soldiers and Officers—Firm Stand of the Secretary of War Against Race Discrimination—General Ballou's "Bulletin No. 35"— Members of Draft Boards Dismissed for Discrimination Against the Race.*

The treatment of Negro soldiers in the various camps and cantonments of the country was a subject much discussed during the war. Reports of discrimination against colored soldiers because of race and color were heard upon all sides and at times the colored people were greatly exercised when alleged situations of a particularly outrageous character came to their ears. The morale of the race was at times lowered to a degree that was little short of dangerous. Prompt and vigorous action, however, on the part of officers high in command led to a correction of many of the evils complained of, and in this way countless episodes pregnant with the possibility of serious clashes and violent conflicts were happily adjusted and no end of trouble thus averted.

Before going into the analysis of a number of exceptionally trying instances of color discrimination—incidents that more than once attracted nation-wide attention—it might be well to make note of the manner in which the colored troops were apportioned throughout the country. As was perfectly natural, by virtue of the immense Negro population, the South furnished the bulk of the colored men called through the selective draft law. If the unwritten custom of assigning men to the camps nearest the place from which they were drawn had been carried out to the letter, the camps in Mississippi, Alabama, Georgia, Louisiana, and South Carolina would have been made up in many cases almost exclusively of Negro soldiers. For this reason, and to prevent concentration of over-large contingents of colored soldiers at any one camp,—a policy frankly decided upon long before the Special

Assistant came to the War Department—thousands of colored draftees found their way to the North in the fall of 1917, being stationed at Camps Grant, Illinois; Funston, Kansas; Dodge, Iowa; Zachary Taylor, Kentucky; Sherman, Ohio; Meade, Maryland; Custer, Michigan; Dix, New Jersey; Upton, New York, and Devens, Massachusetts—all of these classed as Northern States from the Southern soldiers' climatic standpoint. The climate of the North—with its long winter, unusually severe in 1917-18—proved to be the source of much suffering, on account of its deadly effect upon colored soldiers bred and born amid the magnolia blossoms and in the balmy atmosphere of the "sunny South." These colored soldiers faced the hard winter of 1917 with sinking hearts and grave apprehensions, and with an equipment in many instances far from adequate, owing to the haste with which the preparations for war were made. There was great suffering among colored and white soldiers, and the mortality from pneumonia and like troubles was alarmingly heavy among the unacclimatized colored men from the South. Nevertheless, they bore their sufferings with a fortitude that approached the heroic.

It was unjust, but not strange, that there should be many attempts at discrimination against Negro officers and soldiers in many of the camps, particularly those in the South, and in other sections where white soldiers from the South were brought into contact with colored troops. Prejudice, based on race, was something too deeply implanted in the mental fabric of an element of the American people, it seemed, to be overcome over night through any pressure the war might bring to bear. Clashes between white and colored soldiers happened North and South, after a sporadic fashion, but at no time were their clashes so general or persistent as to endanger the well-being of the Army as a whole.

In many sections of the South violent protests against the quartering of colored troops were registered with the War Department, and the Governors, Senators, and Representatives of more than one State filed formal objections with the President of the United States and the War Department, insisting that Negro troops be not stationed at the camps within their borders. The War Department steadily declined to be moved by these protests and pursued unhesitatingly its practice of stationing units of troops, colored and white, at whatever posts the exigencies of the service seemed to make their presence expedient or necessary. The dignified bearing of the Negro soldiers and their studious avoidance of any excesses, however, tended to mollify the feelings of the Southern people and they finally began to accept them, not as an inescapable burden "wished upon them," but with genuine pride in their progress, declaring that they were a part and parcel of the South and should be accorded full credit for their unquestioned valor, patriotism and loyalty.

### The Houston Episode

The unfortunate episode at Houston, Texas, in 1917, which precipitated a so-called "race riot," in which were involved a number of the soldiers of the 24th Infantry, Regular Army, had its origin in the prejudice of a portion of the citizens of Houston against Negro soldiers, and the reciprocation of this dislike by the colored soldiers themselves. The clash that took place in that city in August, 1917, marked the beginning of the end of the disorder that had obtained throughout the earlier months of the stay of the colored troops at Houston, for afterwards, when the Eighth Illinois Regiment came to Camp Logan from Chicago and the West, there were but few ebullitions of race feeling between the whites and the men of the Eighth. The execution of thirteen of the colored soldiers implicated in the Houston riot was one of the dark spots on the escutcheon of the Army, but it did not dampen the ardor of the colored men who went to the front for the Stars and Stripes. They realized that neither the meanness of those who fomented the riot, nor the undue haste that led to the summary execution of the soldiers convicted of being guilty of murder and mutiny, was typical of the feeling of the great body of the American people, nor of even the large majority of Southern white people of real influence and standing.

Incipient race riots were reported at frequent intervals at various stations, North and South. Of these, mention might be made of the magnified reports of a fracas said to have occurred between Negro soldiers and the police at Newport News, Virginia, in September, 1918, and of other affairs of no great seriousness that were reported at Camp Upton, Camp Merritt, Camp Grant, and one or two others. Many minor encounters grew out of the refusal of white soldiers to salute colored officers, and of efforts to draw the color line in places of recreation and amusement. Most of these cases were adjusted by the commanding officers of the army camps.

At Camp Grant, Illinois, General Thomas H. Barry, Commanding General, faced this question as soon as it was presented. A newspaper reporter started a campaign of inquiry among certain of the white soldiers to ascertain whether or not they meant to salute colored officers. The question began to run through the camp, but this reporter was challenged by General Barry in the presence of others to cease his activity. The General plainly stated that in that particular camp the Commanding Officer designated by the War Department alone was in command, without the aid of journalistic helpers, and that the only color recognized in Camp Grant was to be the "O. D."—the olive drab of the Army uniform.

### How General Bell Acted

At Camp Upton, New York, General F. Franklin Bell met a similar situation without hesitation:

"Now, gentlemen," said he, "I am not what you would call 'a Negro lover.' I have seen service in Texas, and elsewhere in the South. Your men have started this trouble. I don't want any explanations. These colored men did not start it. It doesn't matter how your men feel about these colored men. They are United States soldiers. They must and shall be treated as such. If you can't take care of your men, I can take care of you; and," said he in conclusion, "if there is any more trouble from your men you will be tried, not by a Texas jury but by General Bell, and not one of you will leave this camp for overseas." And he thus dismissed them.

General Bell was talking to white officers of a Southern regiment that came to Camp Upton. The remarks quoted above followed a fracas between white soldiers of this Southern regiment and colored soldiers whom the white soldiers attempted to throw out of the Hostess House, while he was Commanding General there.

At Camp Lee, Virginia, General Adelbert Cronkhite was reported in the Richmond, Virginia, daily newspapers and in the camp newspaper as saying:

"I met some junior officers who said they were not keen on saluting Negro officers. They would not feel that way if they understood the spirit of the salute. If one of them came from a town where there was an old Negro character, one of those old fellows who do odd jobs around and is known to everybody, he'd at least nod his head and say, 'Howdy, uncle.' Now, suppose through some freak of nature this old Negro should be transplanted into an officer's uniform; the salute would be merely saying to him 'Howdy, uncle,' in a military way."

It is fair to say that General Cronkhite disavowed responsibility for the appearance of a certain article in the *Richmond Times Dispatch* and said that he had never made a statement in the way it was quoted in the article. He explained, however, that "the idea involved in this statement expressed in becoming language is the expression of my idea and was not based on any special case," whatever that may mean! General Cronkhite also said that his statement was not an official one and had not therefore been published by him in the official bulletin of the command.

Attempts at segregation were charged against the Quartermaster's Depots at Chicago and at St. Louis, where color discrimination was alleged in the matter of appointments, promotions, and working conditions, and where unfairness was said to exist in the withholding from the colored employees of the use of toilet facilities, as well as restrictions in the service of the depot restaurants, cafeterias and the like. Whenever these cases were called to the attention of the War Department they were carefully inquired into, to develop the facts. In more instances than the Special Assistant can now recall, remedial action was taken by the officials in charge of the stations under criticism. Discriminating orders were rescinded, restrictions modified, and favorable interpretation of ambiguous regulations was secured in many of the cases that came to the War Department.

### Gen. Ballou's Bulletin No. 35 at Camp Funston

Perhaps no single incident in the camp life of the Army attracted so large a measure of attention at the hands of the

*Above*—This is how the Western Front in France looked most of the time. The Germans kept down in their trenches and the Allies in theirs, with barbed wire entanglements of No Man's Land between them. Negro soldiers with machine guns.

*Below*—Another corner of the Fighting Front. American Negro Soldiers and French Colonials firing rifle grenades.

*Above*—Dancing; a Favorite Diversion of Colored Soldiers When Off Duty.
*Below*—Young Women's Christian Association Camp, Louisville, Ky.

*Above*—After the capture of Cantigny. Colored troops won glory in taking this city from the Germans. Photograph shows American Negro soldiers cleaning up the ruins with flame throwers and grenades.
*Below*—American Negro soldiers throwing hand grenades from a French trench into No Man's Land.

Some of Philadelphia's Negro Soldiers. Photo of colored troops who were wounded or gassed in the fighting in France. They are all from Philadelphia.

*Above*—One of the most important parts of war is keeping up communication with the front. Telephone lines must be maintained no matter how heavy the enemy's fire. This French Official Photograph shows Senegalese troops carrying telephone lines forward to observation posts.
*Below*—American Negro Soldiers and French tanks. This is the way the colored infantrymen advanced on the Somme.

*Left.*—One of General Pershing's colored veterans enjoying a bit of cake baked at the American Red Cross Canteen at Is-Surtile. *Right.*—He Captured the Kaiser. Corporal Fred McIntyre of the 369th Infantry with the photograph of the Kaiser which he captured from a German officer in his dugout.

*Above*—Some of the Chicago Girls Welcoming Home One of the Boys of the 370th (Old 8th Illinois National Guard).
*Below*—The Salvation Army Draws No Color Line. Soldiers of the 351st Field Artillery are receiving candy from Salvation Army lassies. on their return to New York.

*Above*—Negro Troops in Camp in France. This temporary shelter was not far from the front line. The men are wearing their trench boots and the top of shelter is covered with branches of trees, a form of camouflage intended to prevent detection by enemy aeroplanes
*Below*—Routing the enemy with cold steel.—From Photo and Painting

colored people as "Bulletin No. 35," issued to the officers and soldiers of the 92d Division by General C. C. Ballou, commanding officer of the Division, with headquarters at Camp Funston, Kansas.

The issuance of the Bulletin came about because of the refusal of the manager of a theater at Manhattan, Kansas, to admit a sergeant of the 92d Division, because of the possible objection of his white patrons.

The interpretation placed upon the order by most people was that General Ballou requested and indirectly "ordered" that Negro officers and soldiers refrain from exercising their prerogatives as citizens in the matter of attending places of public amusement or recreation, if their presence seemed offensive to the white patrons of such resorts and likely to provoke racial friction. The colored press was particularly bitter and many newspapers pronounced the "order" an "insult" to the Negro race. At various public gatherings of colored people General Ballou's resignation as commander of the 92d Division was demanded, and at no time during his incumbency as the head of the Division was General Ballou able to regain the confidence of the colored masses, with whom he had been immensely popular prior to this episode, in recognition of his valued and sympathetic services as supervisor of the Officers' Training Camp at Fort Des Moines, Iowa, from which came 639 colored men, graduating with commissions as captains and first and second lieutenants.

The full text of "Bulletin No. 35," as issued by General Ballou was as follows:

Headquarters 92d Division,
Camp Funston, Kans., March 28, 1918.

"1. It should be well known to all colored officers and men that no useful purpose is served by such acts as will cause the 'color question' to be raised. It is not a question of legal rights, but a question of policy, and any policy that tends to bring about a conflict of races, with its resulting animosities, is prejudicial to the military interest of the 92d Division, and therefore prejudicial to an important interest of the colored race.

"2. To avoid such conflicts the Division Commander has repeatedly urged that all colored members of his command, and especially the officers and non-commissioned officers, should refrain from going where their

~resence will be resented. In spite of this injunction, one of the sergeants of the Medical Department has recently precipitated the precise trouble that should be avoided, and then called on the Division Commander to take sides in a row that should never have occurred had the sergeant placed the general good above his personal pleasure and convenience. This sergeant entered a theater, as he undoubtedly had a legal right to do, and precipitated trouble by making it possible to allege race discrimination in the seat he was given. He is strictly within his legal rights in this matter, and the theater manager is legally wrong. Nevertheless the sergeant is guilty of the GREATER wrong in doing ANYTHING, NO MATTER HOW LEGALLY CORRECT, that will provoke race animosity.

"3. The Division Commander repeats that the success of the Division with all that success implies, is dependent upon the good will of the public. That public is nine-tenths white. White men made the Division, and they can break it just as easily if it becomes a trouble maker.

"4. All concerned are again enjoined to place the general interest of the Division above personal pride and gratification. Avoid every situation that can give rise to racial ill-will. Attend quietly and faithfully to your duties, and don't go where your presence is not desired.

"5. This will be read to all organizations of the 92d Division.

"By command of Major-General Ballou:

(Signed) "ALLEN J. GREER,

"Lieutenant Colonel, General Staff,

"Chief of Staff."

Commenting in an editorial of the issue of April 13, 1918, upon the order as issued by General Ballou, *The Advocate,* a colored newspaper of Cleveland, Ohio, printed the following:

### GENERAL BALLOU'S ORDER.

Major General Ballou has just issued an order to the Colored men of his division which is, to say the least, "extry."

In part, the order calls for the exercise of care on the part of the commissioned and non-commissioned officers and men of the division in shunning places where they have reason to believe that their presence will be resented. It is an apparent appeal for lessening the "racial issue" controversies.

The order might possibly be considered "perfectly harmless" and of the "vaudeville type" of monologues if it were not for the paragraph, "White men made possible the division, and white men can break it up."

We expected better than this of Major General Ballou in this day of bitter warfare when the President is calling upon all America—white and black, we presume—to rally to the Flag and help to crush "the foe of humanity."

We can only urge our race to forgive General Ballou, "he knows not what he says."

*WE ARE NOT IN FAVOR OF THE MEN OF ANY DIVISION SEEKING TO STIR UP "RACIAL STRIFE."* We feel that *NOW IS NOT THE TIME* for injecting any such issue into the already over-crowded portfolio of Uncle Sam.

Let us help "lick the Kaiser" FIRST and then thrash out our local difficulties.

We do not want to be classed in the President's list of "creatures of passion, disloyalty and anarchy," therefore let us say "shoo fly" to General Ballou's "undiplomatic paragraph."

Now, all together—let's get the Kaiser!

Many similar expressions of resentment appeared in the Negro press.

A news report, sent out shortly after the issuance of the Ballou Bulletin No. 35, preliminary to the publication of a letter sent by General Ballou to me, in response to my request for a statement that might give the purpose that prompted the Commander of the 92d Division to issue the bulletin, said:

"It transpires that while Major General C. C. Ballou, of the 92d Division, was addressing the men under him through Bulletin No. 35, he was at the same time pressing the prosecution of the theatrical manager who had discriminated against a sergeant of the Division.

"The prosecution of the manager of the Wareham Theatre for discrimination on account of color, instigated at General Ballou's request, was, after being twice continued, tried in Police Court at Manhattan, Kansas, a few days ago, and resulted in the conviction of the defendant and the imposition of $10 and costs. It is generally assumed that the conviction of the theatrical manager will serve to prevent a repetition of the offense, and will deter other theater owners and managers from making discrimination on account of color. General Ballou followed the same course here as he did at the Officers Training School at Des Moines, Iowa, last summer, namely: while admonishing his men to refrain from precipitating racial disturbances, to prosecute those who should discriminate against his men."

General Ballou's letter to the author said:

Headquarters 92d Division,
Camp Funston, Kansas, April 22, 1918.

My Dear Mr. Scott:

I have your request that I make a brief statement relative to Bulletin No. 35, these Headquarters. There seems to be no good reason why I should not do so.

Here are the preliminary facts:

A soldier of this Division got into trouble with a theater manager at Manhattan and reported it to me. I at once ordered an investigation, placed the facts before the Division Judge Advocate and was informed by him that the theater manager had violated the law. I then put the case in the hands of the United States Attorney and requested the prosecution of the theater manager. The case was set for April 22d. I then issued Bulletin No. 35, which, in brief, is counsel to my soldiers to avoid race troubles. This Bulletin was given out to the colored press of the country, accompanied by an entirely misleading letter that not only completely suppressed all mention of any prosecution of the theater manager, but directly and falsely conveyed the impression to editors and readers that I had not done so. The most prejudiced person will, I think, at once see that this was a malicious attempt to stir up race feeling by misrepresentation.

#### GOOD ORDER AND MILITARY DISCIPLINE FOUNDATION STONES.

The character of Bulletin No. 35 was that of advice, as already stated. This advice was ordered published to the Division. It had nothing to do with any policy of segregation, or with any policy outside of the military establishments. Its purpose was to prevent race friction, with the attendant prejudice to good order and military discipline. Good order and military discipline are the foundation stones of the military service. They are indispensable. Nothing connected with the service of the colored troops has ever been so threatening to good order and discipline as race troubles have been, and it is well-known that our enemies have sought to profit by this fact ever since there was a prospect of war. No stone has been left unturned. There have always been foes of our country ready to aggravate the grievances of the colored people on the one hand and to stir up the whites on the other. It was no mere coincidence that the East St. Louis atrocities occurred in a city filled largely with German sympathizers.

There is little doubt that the same influence egged on both whites and blacks at Houston. Most troubles have small beginnings. At Houston they grew from the fact of colored soldiers entering cars reserved for whites, and other similar matters. Great wrongs were eventually committed on both sides, culminating in the killing of a score or more of white people and the hanging of thirteen Negroes. In the midst of all the feeling and excitement caused by the East St. Louis and Houston troubles, the colored officers' training camp at Fort Des Moines won golden approbation all over the United States, made thousands of friends for the colored race and achieved a glorious success. It did all of this by following precisely the advice that was repeated to the 92d Division in Bulletin No. 35.

"BY THEIR FRUITS YE SHALL KNOW THEM."

Our enemies do not wish the United States to have its military power increased by colored soldiers, and they stand ready to add fuel to every race discord in order to embarrass our country as much as possible in this war. Is it any wonder then, in view of what the enemy has accomplished in the past and is seeking to accomplish again, that the Commander of the colored Division seeks to nip troubles in the bud, and while prosecuting white men for their offences against his soldiers, urges the soldiers to do their part to keep the peace and promote harmony.

I have shown that my position and action were deliberately and maliciously misrepresented to the colored people by the suppression of the news of my prompt prosecution of the theater manager, and by falsely conveying the impression that I had taken no such action. The entire letter that accompanied Bulletin No. 35 to the press of the colored people was a misrepresentation of my attitude and of the facts in the case, and no fair-minded person, when the facts are known, as stated above, can fail to see the work of an enemy—an enemy of our country and an even greater enemy to the colored race. Is the colored race going to "fall" for such schemes? I think not. I think they will contrast the work of the trouble-maker with the solid achievements of the colored officers' training camp at Fort Des Moines and of the 92nd Devision, and consider thoughtfully the words—"By their fruits ye shall know them."

Sincerely,

C. C. BALLOU,

Major-General, Commanding 92d Division.

## Baker Against Discrimination

Early in the summer of 1918, a flood of complaints reached the War Department from many of the camps, the burden of which was that the Negro soldiers were being grossly mistreated by their white officers, ofttimes physically assaulted, called by names that were highly insulting—such as "nigger," "coon," "darkey," and worse, and that the colored men were forced to work under the most unhealthy and laborious conditions, with a certain penalty of long periods of imprisonment in guard-houses and stockade and other cruel and unusual punishments if they dared to resent any indignity or failed to perform "impossible" tasks. In many cases, it was alleged, opportunity for advancement was refused to colored men of ability, and all the assignments worth while were given to white men, some of whom had doubtful qualifications.

Besides the complaints growing out of unfair treatment of colored men in the camps numerous instances of unequal standards and straightout discrimination in the operation of the selective draft law were reported as being practiced by the draft officials in several States, particularly in the South. The claim was made, and almost invariably substantiated by reliable testimony, that colored men, palpably unfit for military service, and others who were entitled to exemption under the law, were "railroaded" into the army while other men with no legitimate excuse for exemption were allowed to escape the requirements of the draft system. The situation reached such a stage, by reason of the growing disregard for fair play and the honest interpretation of the law, that Secretary Baker felt called upon to check the infractions by Exemption Boards and the unfair treatment of Negro soldiers in the camps by issuing a clean-cut statement to the effect that "the War Department will brook no discrimination, based upon race or color," and that all instances of unfairness in the Army on this score would meet with speedy correction, with adequate punishment for all violators of the military regulations bearing on the rights and privileges of soldiers.

As indicating the general attitude of some Army officers in carrying out the instructions of the War Department, there may be mentioned the particular attitude of certain officers in charge of units of the so-called Labor Battalions. The pressure from colored people throughout the country and from other sources as well became so strong that the War Department found it necessary to issue a certain memorandum changing the former decision (which called for white sergeants) to a decision which required that the non-commissioned officers in the Reserve Labor Battalions should be "all white or all colored" instead of "white." The effect of this immediately was to eliminate in many camps the colored men who were serving as non-commissioned officers and to substitute white men, no matter how unfitted such white non-commissioned officers were for the duties required of them. No element contributed to more unrest among the colored men who were drafted than this organization of Reserve Labor Battalions.

It was a situation of this character which inspired the uncompromising memorandum of the Secretary of War to the Special Assistant under date of November 30, 1917, of which this paragraph stands as the "keynote":

"As you know, it has been my policy to discourage discrimination against any persons by reason of their race. This policy has been adopted not merely as an act of justice to all races that go to make up the American people, but also to safeguard the very institutions which we are now, at the greatest sacrifice, engaged in defending, and which any racial disorders must endanger."

It will be noted that the same fundamental principle of simple justice to all defenders of the flag was reiterated in the interview made public July 1, 1918, when it seemed that the earlier proclamation failed to prove as effective as the Secretary of War had hoped it would be in wiping out color proscription in the army. In consequence of the firm stand of Secretary Baker against discrimination against colored men on the part of draft boards, several offending members of these boards were separated from their positions, and in one notable instance, in Fulton County (Atlanta), Georgia, an entire Exemption Board was summarily removed, upon proof of improper manipulation of the Selective Draft Law in its application to colored registrants.

In keeping with the insistence upon a "square deal" for all, there came a marked improvement in the morale of the camps where much trouble had been made for colored soldiers through the petty meanness practiced by the so-called "Military Police." Reports had come into the War Department in immense volume to the effect that there was increasing friction between colored soldiers and the Military Police, in charge of order and general discipline in the camps. Colored soldiers complained that they were kept more closely confined to the camps than were white soldiers; that they had the greatest difficulty in obtaining passes to go to town or to visit relatives, and that they were punished more severely than were white soldiers for trivial offenses. The "bad blood" between the "M. P." and the colored soldiers frequently led to free fights, near "race riots," and the "rushing" of the guards in an attempt to leave the camp, regardless of the possession of passes. Wherever the blame may be placed for these outbreaks, a systematic effort was made to remedy the evils complained of, and a memorandum from the Morale Branch of the War Department, commenting upon the matter, carried the observation that: "The action that has been taken at these camps, as reported to this office, indicates that a genuine effort has been made to correct any abuses that may have existed."

A further evidence of the potency of the rigid policy of the War Department to stamp out as far as was possible the evil of race prejudice on the part of officers in their relation to colored soldiers, is found in the case of Captain Eugene C. Rowan, of the 162d Depot Brigade, with headquarters at Camp Pike, Little Rock, Arkansas. Upon positive proof, adduced by evidence given before a court-martial, Captain Rowan was found guilty of wilful disobedience of the orders of a superior officer and was ordered by the War Department to be dismissed from the service. The case attracted more than ordinary attention because of the fact that it was the first instance wherein the color question had figured in an action against a white officer of the Army, in a National Army court of inquiry. Captain Rowan was charged with having refused to obey an order issued by the Brigade Commander, Colonel Frederick B. Shaw, calling for a troop formation, because, it was asserted, both colored and white soldiers were included in the formation. The defense attempted to justify Captain Rowan in his disobedience of explicit military orders on the ground that he was a native of Georgia, had long resided in Mississippi, and that in keeping with his own personal feelings and a definite promise made to his men, he did not desire to give any order that would compel white men to "lower their self-respect." The dismissal of Captain Rowan followed his conviction by the court-martial, and the judgment of the Army tribunal was promptly sustained by the War Department at Washington.

A number of other cases are on record where white officers were separated from the service for discrimination against colored soldiers and for unwarranted acts of cruelty in dealing with them.

## CHAPTER IX

## EFFORTS TO IMPROVE CONDITIONS

*Secretary Baker and the Trying Situation at Camp Lee, Virginia—
Reports on Investigations at Numerous Camps—Improved Con-
ditions Brought About Gradually—Help for Colored Draftees—
The Case of Lieutenant Tribbett and Similar Cases of Race
Prejudice.*

---

*From Secretary of War—Memorandum for Mr. Scott.*

Should you not go personally to
Camp Lee and investigate? Then I
can go and finish the job.

BAKER.

---

The attitude of Secretary Baker toward a trying situation at
Camp Lee, Petersburg, Virginia, and his vigorous handling of the
charges of racial discrimination that were rife at that military
station, was significant of his consistent policy with respect to the
colored soldiers throughout the entire war period. The above memorandum was sent to the Special Assistant by the Secretary about
the last of November, 1917, in response to a report which the
former had made to him touching the conditions complained of at
Camp Lee, and which had formed the basis of the longer memorandum, making known, in language unequivocal and of extraordinary
force, the Secretary's antagonism to all practices of discrimination
in the Army based on race or color.

At Camp Lee there was much dissatisfaction among the colored
soldiers. The reports which came to hand embodied the universal
complaint that "the whole atmosphere in regard to the colored
soldier at Camp Lee is one which does not inspire him to greater
patriotism, but rather makes him question the sincerity of the great
war principles of America." The efficiency of the War Department
was interfered with, it was stated, because of this unwholesome
atmosphere. The colored soldiers were compelled to work at menial

tasks, regardless of their educational equipment or aspirations for higher duties, and discontent reigned because it was said the white soldiers were given genuine, intensive military training, while Negroes were not given enough drilling to give them the simplest rudiments of real soldier life and were not permitted to fire a gun. The statement was made that if the Negroes were allowed to be trained for combatant service, as white soldiers were, thousands would be inspired to enter the work more whole-heartedly, and the Labor Battalions would also show a larger measure of efficiency by the inculcation of a feeling that colored men were getting a "square deal." Not a few of the men asserted plainly that it was useless for colored men to try to improve themselves at Camp Lee, as white officers openly admitted to them that sergeants and an occasional sergeant-major was as high as the Negro might hope to reach, no matter what might be his intellectual attainments or executive ability.

Mr. C. H. Williams, of the Hampton Institute, Virginia, a young colored man of superior training, was designated by the Committee on Welfare of Negro Troops of the War Time Commission of the Federal Council of Churches to visit all the cities where military camps were located, to make a survey of conditions as they affect colored troops. Under an arrangement he filed with the Special Assistant a copy of each of his reports, so that they might be followed up from time to time inside of the War Department so as to change conditions where necessary. Mr. Williams sought to get the exact facts as to the feeling of the colored soldiers as well as of the colored population in the camp cities, and as he went from one part of the country to the other he also got a line on Negro public opinion generally. Practically all the camps and cantonments where colored troops were located were visited by him as well as by the Special Assistant.

Mr. Williams submitted a survey of conditions as they existed. His survey included inquiry into the social and religious conditions and the state of mind of the colored troops generally and made recommendations as to the steps that should be taken to bring about a correction of the ills complained of. At some points he found the situation fair, in others not good, and in many it was inexcusably bad. All of this had to do in the most direct fashion with the morale of the colored soldiers, and hence the remedy to be sought for the unfavorable circumstances indicated in Mr. Williams's reports was regarded by the Special Assistant as a mission of the highest and most pressing importance.

### COMPLAINTS LODGED BY COLORED SOLDIERS IN CAMP

"Discrimination as to the issuance of passes to leave the camps—that white soldiers were allowed to go at will, while Negroes were refused permission to leave.

"Unfair treatment, oftimes brutality, on the part of Military Police.

"Inadequate provision for recreation.

"Unfair treatment, ofttimes brutality, on the part of Military Police. and denial of the enjoyment of privileges in the huts, where colored huts had not been provided.

"White non-commissioned officers over colored units, when the colored men were of a higher intellectual plane than the whites who commanded them.

"Lack of opportunity for educated Negroes to rise above non-commissioned officers in the Reserve Labor Battalions.

"Confinement to the guard house for long periods and compelled to pay heavy penalties for minor infractions of the rules of camp, or for disobedience of unreasonable commands.

"Frequently, lack of proper medical attention and treatment.

"Negro soldiers compelled to work at menial tasks, and denied sufficient drill work and not allowed training in manual of arms and denied an opportunity to fire a gun, in many instances.

"Insufficient number of Hostess Houses—especially in the earlier stages of the war. Insufficient number of chaplains in most camps, in earlier stages of the war. Never enough of either of these helpful agencies at any stage of the war.

"Slow discharge of colored men in labor battalions after the armistice.

"At more than one camp—Humphreys notably—colored men had practically no sanitary conveniences, bathing facilities, barracks, mess halls, Y. M. C. A. service, during the war period, until after white soldiers had left the station.

"Use of abusive language to the colored soldiers by white officers and calling them by opprobrious names.

"Working with civilians, soldiers getting $30 per month, and the civilian, doing identical work, getting from $3.50 to $5.00 per diem.

"Too many tent camps for Negroes, while whites are given barracks.

"Reluctance of white officers to recommend colored men for induction into the Officers' Training Camps.

"Men with venereal diseases not segregated in the matter of washing mess kits and general use of camp facilities from those not so infected.

"During winter of 1917-18, general complaint was made of insufficient clothing, shortage in supply of overcoats, inadequate bedding, and tents without flooring and ofttimes situated in wet places, where ice formed in winter and where mud and malaria flourished at other times. A statement came from Camp Alexander, Va., that during the winter of 1917-18 men died like sheep in their tents, it being a common occurrence to go around in the morning and drag men out frozen to death. It took a long time for this situation to get to the authorities, but when it did get to the proper officials, steps were taken to correct the trouble.

"Men pronounced unfit for overseas service, and often in cases where they were unfit for any kind of military duty, were kept at the camps and forced to work.

"Alleged essential labor required at many stations on Sundays.

"Made to work in rain and cursed when any dissatisfaction was shown. 'Gotten even with' by commanders if report was made of conditions to higher officers or to outsiders.

"Promise of officials to muster out first the men in tent camps not promptly kept.

"Passes refused colored men, even when messages of critical illness of parents or near relatives had been received."

The Camp Lee situation being of a piece with the conditions obtaining at most of the army stations where colored men were located, it may be dwelt upon at length to illustrate the plan of research and operation which was adopted to ameliorate the ills that were brought to the attention of the Special Assistant and laid before the Secretary of War, with suggestions and recommendations looking toward a speedy betterment.

Letters were sent to the War Department by the men and communications of the same tenor doubtless went outside to their friends. Telegrams and protests were received from representatives of several colored protective organizations, prominent ministers, leading editors, college heads, and men of affairs generally, and other communications sent to them were forwarded to me in Washington, asking that vigorous action be taken to assist in the unraveling of the problem confronting the men at Camp Lee. One very urgent letter was sent by the Governor of a State, intimating that he was confident that discriminations against colored soldiers were practiced at Camp Lee, but declared it to be his belief that this was without the knowledge of the War Department. "I respectfully request that you make an investigation of the situation there at the earliest possible moment," concluded the Governor. These very timely requests were most cheerfully complied with.

That an improved state of affairs was brought about at Camp Lee is evidenced by a report submitted to the Special Assistant under date of February 20, 1919, by Louis L. Watson, Jr., of 603 L Street, Southeast, Washington, D. C., formerly Captain of Infantry, United States Army, after an exhaustive inquiry, covering every phase of Army life at that point, in its relation to the treatment of the Negro and the opportunities afforded him.

Captain Watson, at the outset of his communication, refers to "the evolution of a somewhat equitable military régime, as far as the races are concerned," which has a decidedly hopeful ring, and which hope is given quite a considerable realization before his final paragraph is reached. Noting his observations as "a race man on the scene, seeking to correct the most flagrant violations of military law," and his purpose to "get things done," rather than to pile up dry statistics, Captain Watson concluded his introduction by saying: "The following recapitulation, however, is quite true in the large, and inclusive of *camp improvements worked out in the last five months.* I hope you may find it of value."

### Captain Watson's "Recapitulation"

Said Captain Watson, in recapitulating the results that had been secured at Camp Lee in the five months of intensive inquiry and practical reformatory effort:

"Until about the middle of July, 1918, there had been several colored officers at Camp Lee, but none had remained for more than twenty-four hours. Then came Lieut. Myron McAdoo, commissioned second lieutenant from the ranks of the 9th Ohio. He was assigned to the 13th Battalion Replacements Training Center to serve with white officers until the 15th of August, when five first lieutenants and three second lieutenants, colored, were assigned to the outfit—1st Lieuts. Allan Turner, Frank M. Goodner, Chas E. Roberts, G. Cleveland Morrow and Louis L. Watson, Jr., and 2nd Lieuts. Leonidas H. Hall, Joseph L. Johnson, Gloucester A. Price. Moreover, until this time there had been relatively few non-commissioned officers, colored, in the camp and a large percentage of these were corporals of little ability or promise. It was characteristic of white officers to ignore men of ability and to make non-commissioned officers of the illiterate funny fellows who could furnish entertainment for them in the orderly room with their antics and shameful ignorance. But what was even worse than this came the report that in other sections of the camp, where there were not even non-commissioned officers of this caliber, white officers were inflicting bodily punishment upon ignorant enlisted men of color. This of course is contrary to all military law and custom. As far as I know, however, none of this happened after the colored officers came to camp.

"The colored officers immediately launched a discreet educational campaign to combat this condition. Their presence alone did much to put a stop to this practice, but the fact that they used considerable tact in spreading knowledge of the law in such cases, did even more. It became apparent almost immediately that colored enlisted men were growing cognizant of their right to redress and the way to get it, and ill-treatment reduced itself to the personal factor entirely, which is not illegality so much as it is inefficiency in handling men, and not politic.

"At the same time the colored officers set out to get more non-commissioned officers worthy of their rank, by a careful selection and promotion of the men in the four companies of the battalion. This being the only combatant organization of colored men in the camp it took the lead in efficient colored non-commissioned officers. The efficiency of these men was highly commendable.

"In view of the prevalent antagonistic public sentiment against the rise of colored men in these parts the promotion of four colored First Lieutenants to Captaincy on the 10th of September, 1918, and their subsequent assignment to the command of the companies of the Battalion with a commissioned personnel of an average of ten white first and second lieutenants, including the former company commanders, is nothing short of marvelous. *I shall not recount in detail your work in bringing this condition about except to say that your investigation in this matter alone proved to officials in the camp that colored men could get a hearing in the War Department,* and it would not be good policy to violate the integrity of their office with prejudicial treatment of colored officers and enlisted men under their command. The Battalion had on an average of forty white first and second lieutenants serving in companies under colored captains. These officers were from almost all walks of life. Among them were a lawyer and school teacher from Alabama, a light-weight pugilist from Louisiana, an owner of orange groves from Florida, a ranchman from

Texas, a coalmine owner formerly from Virginia, and several stockbrokers, contractors, electrical engineers, merchants, graduate and undergraduate students of the large Eastern and Western Universities, as well as two "movie" actors, one principal of a Pennsylvania high school, and the son of a classmate of the great Gen. Joffre. Most of these officers were originally from the South.

"Of the company commanders, one had done twenty-four years and another eleven years in the Regular Army, while the other two were from civil life, one a graduate from Massachusetts State College and the other a graduate of Howard University. The Battalion Commander was a criminal lawyer with a large practice in Shreveport, Louisiana. All worked together and made the Battalion the most efficient and the most praised organization in all the Replacements Camp. There was no hesitancy on the part of the commanding officer to point to the 13th Battalion as an example in drill, parade, and administration.

"When the 13th Battalion was completely demobilized and I was attached to the 1st Development Battalion I had the opportunity to observe the working of organizations of colored enlisted personnel under the command of white officers. I found this organization, in contrast to the 13th Battalion which I had just left, to be poorly disciplined and overburdened with complaints concerning mess. Regulations were wholly ignored where punishments were concerned and general dissatisfaction was spread over the entire outfit. The morale was very low among the enlisted men and the officers unconcerned. From my observations this condition appeared inexcusable.

"I will conclude this resumé with a statement of several definite and unbiased convictions growing out of my experience and observations:

"(1)   Colored officers show marked superiority over white officers of the same grade.

"(2)   A mixed organization of both white and colored officers is a very efficient machine and works out to perfection from a purely military point of view because a man's race pride will not allow him to neglect his duty and thus bring down criticism from officers of the other race. Each tries to excel.

"(3)   Wherever it is possible colored troops should have colored officers. There is no doubt that the interests of our troops are better conserved by colored officers.

"(4)   *Your eagerness to correct evils in the camp and your effective work in this regard have done more than any other single factor to make life tolerable for colored officers and enlisted men here.* Assuming conditions at this camp to be the average in Southern cantonments such an office as yours held by a man of the race is indispensable to the welfare of the colored soldier. Very respectfully,

(Signed) Louis L. Watson, Jr.,
Formerly Capt. Inf. U. S. A.

### Help for Colored Draftees

The National Medical Association, under the active leadership of Dr. George E. Cannon, of Jersey City; Dr. A. M. Curtis, of Washington, D. C.; Dr. A. M. Brown, of Birmingham, Alabama; Dr. E. T. Belsaw, of Mobile, Alabama; Dr. M. O. Dumas, of Washington, D. C., and Dr. W. G. Alexander, of Orange, New Jersey, exerted a helpful interest in the welfare of the medical men drawn in the draft. The Special Assistant took up the cases of many colored doctors who had been drafted and assigned to service battalions or as mere privates in the infantry organizations, with a view of having them transferred to the Medical Corps, where they might render a more effective service to their country along the line of their professional equipment.

Another investigation, which may properly find a place in this chapter on the treatment of colored soldiers in the camps, is that which resulted in the admission of colored draftees, regardless of the time of their call, into the training schools for officers. The number permitted to enter at the outset was unusually small, and these were restricted to draftees who had been conscripted prior to January 5, 1918. The number recommended by their camp commanders was not at all commensurate with the abilities of the men who desired to take advantage of the Government's plan of developing officer material, and was reported to be so niggardly as to amount almost to an ignoring of the explicit order of the Secretary of War that no form of injustice or discrimination be practiced against any soldier because of race or color. There were also persistent rumors that an attempt was being made to promote white non-commissioned officers in Negro units to commissioned officers, which could have no other result than to fill all of the line-officer places with white men and make it impossible for a Negro non-commissioned officer, no matter how efficient or how intelligent he might be, to rise above that rank. Another flood of protests came into the War Department from colored men in the army and from colored people everywhere. Those in authority were apprised of

*Above*—A detachment of American Negro Infantrymen Operating in the Front Line Trenches
*Below*—Here is a photograph right from the front, an unusual picture showing how the trenches really looked. These are American and French Colonial colored soldiers in a French trench.

*Above*—One of the Docks at Bordeaux Where Negro Stevedore Regiments Played a Vital Part in the War in Unloading Supplies for Our Troops. Transportation of supplies is just as important a part of war as firing guns at the enemy. All the armies in the world could not have defeated Germany if it had not been for the Service of Supply, getting the guns, ammunition, equipment and food to them.
*Below*—To give an idea of the enormous quantities of supplies handled by Negro stevedore regiments, here is a photo of a few cook stoves that came in one shipment.

*Above*—On the Docks at Brest, another French port where colored stevedore regiments were the chief reliance in getting supplies through to the boys at the front.
*Below*—It took tens of thousands of motor trucks to get supplies from docks to the front in France. These had to be shipped from America and here are a few in Assembling Yard at St. Nazaire, France, with cases and barrels of gasoline and oil in the foreground. If it had not been for Negro stevedore regiments, these trucks could not have been taken off the ships.

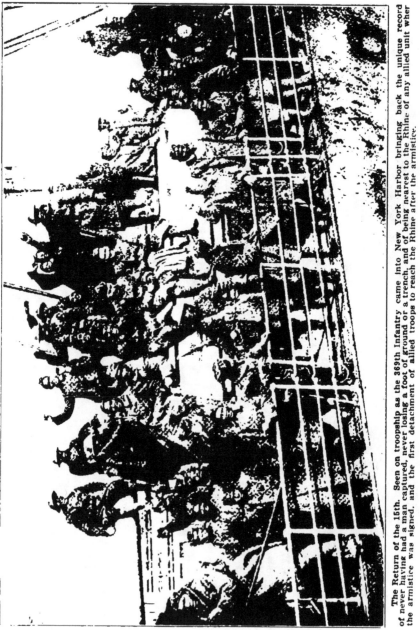

The Return of the 15th. Seen on troopship as the 369th Infantry came into New York Harbor bringing back the unique record of never having had a man captured, never losing a foot of ground or a trench, and of being nearest to the Rhine of any allied unit when the armistice was signed, and the first detachment of allied troops to reach the Rhine after the armistice.

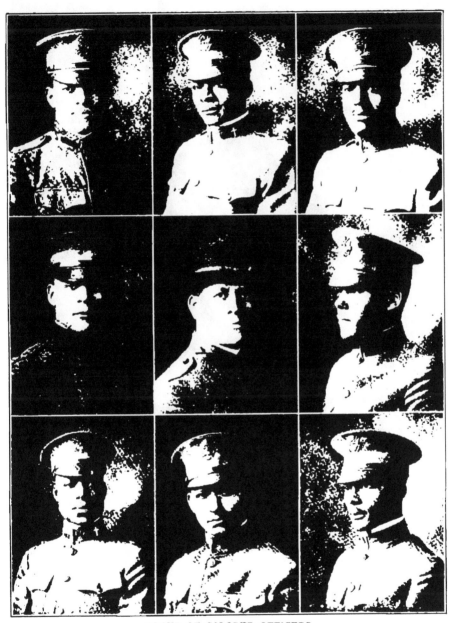

### GROUP OF COLORED OFFICERS

Reading left to right—*Top*—1st Lt. Chas. Lane, 367th Inf.; Chaplain E. H. Hamilton, Camp
  Mead; 2nd Lt. E. P. Sawyer, 367th Inf.
*Center*—1st Lt. J. H. N. Waring, 367th Inf.; 2nd Lt. R. W. Fearing, 367th Inf.; 1st Lt. J. W.
  Clifford, 367th Inf
*Bottom*—Chaplain F. C. Shirley, Camp Mead; Capt. Chas. Garvin, Med. Corps, 367th Inf.;
  2nd Lt. H. D. Smith, Depot Brig. Camp Mead.

*Above*—The Only Negro General Court Martial Board Which Ever Existed. Photograph shows the General Court Martial of the 370th Infantry (8th Illinois National Guard) convened at Camp Logan, Houston, Texas. Officers in picture indicated by numbers following: 1—Lieut. F. P. Boss, 2—Capt. L. Jackson, 3—Capt. James C. Hall, 4—Capt. George M. Allen, 5—Major (Now Lieut. Col.) Otis B. Duncan, President; 6—Capt. Wm. B. Crawford, 7—Lieut. C. N. Hinton, 8—Lieut. Louis C. Washington, 9—Capt. L. E. Johnson, Counsel for Defense; 10—Lieut. R. A. J. Shaw, Judge Advocate, 11—Court Reporter McCarty.
*Below*—War Camp Community Service Club for Colored Soldiers, Louisville, Ky.

*Above*—What real war looks like. Photograph of American Negro soldiers going into action in the attack on Cantigny. American Infantry is co-operating with French tanks.
*Below*—In the Trenches. The smoke is from explosion of a hand grenade just thrown by the American Negro Soldier at the right.

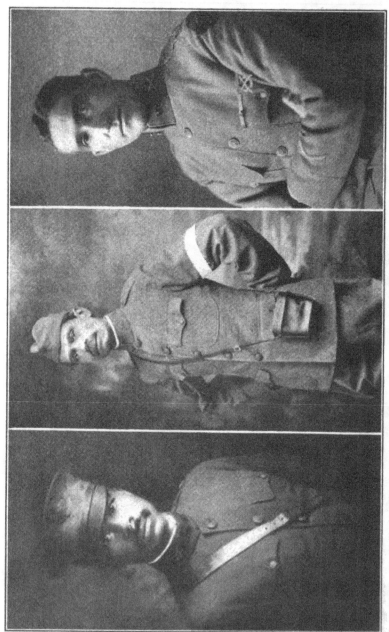

*Left*—Major Adam E. Patterson. Judge Advocate 92nd Division in France.
*Center*—Ralph W. Tyler. War Correspondent who accompanied U. S. Negro troops to France. Accredited representative of the
Committee on Public Information.
*Right*—Major Dean. one of the three Negro Officers of this rank in the U. S. Army.

the unrest that existed. The Secretary of War gave orders that ample provision be made for the induction of properly qualified colored men into the Officers' Training Schools. In the end, training camps for colored candidates for officers' commissions were made available at Camp Taylor for field artillery; at Camp Pike for infantry, and at Camp Hancock for machine gun training.

### The Case of Lieutenant Tribbett

An instance of the workings of race prejudice, in its relation to colored officers, was found in the case of Lieutenant Charles A. Tribbett.

Lieutenant Tribbett was from New Haven, Conn., and was graduated from the Officers' Training Camp at Des Moines, Iowa, and assigned to duty with colored troops at Camp Upton, Yaphank, Long Island. While on that duty, the records of the War Department show that he was ordered to proceed by the usual means of transportation to the army post at Fort Sill, Okla., for instruction in aviation. When the train on which he was traveling stopped at a station near Chickasha, Okla., it was boarded by a sheriff and party, who arrested Tribbett, who was in regulation military uniform, for riding in a car with white people. In spite of his protest that he was an officer of the United States Army, traveling under orders, on Government business, he was forcibly removed from the car and imprisoned in the county jail, and subsequently fined. Following an appeal to the War Department, Tribbett was released and permitted to resume his journey to Fort Sill, where he resumed his military duties.

The matter was brought to the attention of the War Department by Mr. George W. Crawford, of New Haven, Conn., and Mr. Robert L. Fortune, of Chickasha, Okla., who protested against the mistreatment to which Lieutenant Tribbett had been subjected. These well-posted attorneys set up the contention that as an interstate passenger, traveling under orders on Government business, he was not subject to the jurisdiction of the State authorities, and gave notice that they would exhaust every resource to gain adequate redress for their client.

The case was cited for investigation by the Department of Justice, and is still pending. Here was a flagrant instance of injustice to an officer of the United States Army, in the full uniform of the military service, on Government business and traveling on a road under Government supervision. From every viewpoint it was a case for Federal intervention. All the available evidence seemed to indicate that the arrest of Lieutenant Tribbett was an inexcusable usurpation of authority on the part of the civil officials of the State of Oklahoma, and for this reason the Special Assistant to the Secretary of War felt warranted in urging that the whole matter go to the Department of Justice for adjudication by the Federal Government. General Ansell, Acting Judge Advocate General, who has conducted a campaign against the army system of court-martial as being "unfair," did not move to have the case of Lieutenant Tribbett pressed on its merits, and therefore nothing officially has been done,

### Treatment of Colored Soldiers Overseas

An important matter, in connection with the treatment of colored soldiers in the camps, which ought not to pass without mention, was the suggestion made by the Special Assistant to Mr. George Creel, Director of the Committee on Public Information, looking to an investigation of conditions among colored soldiers in France. The morale of the colored people in America was noticeably lowered by ugly rumors that came by devious and winding ways from abroad, and the Special Assistant thought it worth while to have a commission named, made up of representative men, in whom the masses had implicit confidence, to give this situation a searching investigation and make a full report thereon, to set at rest the uneasiness and anxiety that was alarmingly prevalent toward the end of the summer of 1918. The mails and cables were congested, and for weeks and weeks not a word could be had by relatives at home from their loved ones battling for freedom and democracy across the seas. The following letter addressed to Mr. Creel more fully explains the motive which prompted the Special Assistant to offer the suggestion that a special inquiry be made and the remedy be applied:

Washington, D. C., August 10, 1918.

Dear Mr. Creel:

Recently in a conference with the head of the Military Intelligence Bureau, the matter was discussed of having two or three representative colored men go to France for the purpose of making an investigation of the facts with respect to several matters indicated herein.

1. A military man who is qualified to make a free and full investigation of the general treatment being accorded colored troops on the French and other fronts. There has been, and still continues, considerable propaganda and rumor to the effect that colored soldiers are being mistreated and discriminated against. Letters have come to the Office of the Secretary of War and to me, the same being forwarded by United States Senators in some instances, etc., to the War Department conveying these complaints. The information which would be secured first-hand by the military man suggested would be (under such direction as you might approve) conveyed to the Negro people of the United States through the Negro newspapers, public meetings, public speakers, the *Committee of One Hundred* of the Public Speaking Division, etc.

(2) Two other representatives, not necessarily military men, but of sound judgment, capable of studying the facts and coöperating with the military representative, above referred to, in making a full report of existing conditions abroad with respect to colored men at the front as well as those behind the lines (referring to service battalions, stevedore regiments, etc.).

The joint testimony of these men would satisfactorily establish the facts and enable us to do a good piece of work in disposing of these damaging rumors which are being continually circulated.

In this connection, I wish to state that, at a meeting held in New York City, Monday, August 5th, attended by officials of the Federated Council of Churches, by a representative of the Surgeon General's Office, a representative of the Military Intelligence Bureau, Mr. George Foster Peabody (the well-known New York philanthropist) and others, including the undersigned—the same suggestion was made that a commission of colored men in whom they have confidence be sent abroad for the purpose of studying the situation above indicated, and the matter was broached by Mr. Henry A. Atkinson, of the National Committee on Churches and Moral Aims of the War, of New York City, who expressed the opinion that it would be highly desirable for the Government to take the initiative in this matter.

There is more depressed morale among the colored people than is generally supposed, due to stories of unfair treatment of colored men in various camps in America as well as abroad. Under the circumstances, I am quite seriously of the opinion that such a commission as herein suggested would accomplish very great good.

An interview with you, at your convenience, would be very much appreciated. Will you kindly let me hear from you directly or through Mr. Byoir, Associate Chairman.            Sincerely yours,

(Signed)  EMMETT J. SCOTT,
Office of the Secretary of War.

The proposal outlined in the above letter was given serious consideration by Mr. Creel, by the Morale Branch of the War Department, and by a number of officials of the War Department, who readily recognized the gravity of the situation which confronted them, with reference to the attitude of the Negro mind of the nation on this matter of the treatment of colored soldiers overseas. There is strong ground for the belief that some steps of the nature suggested would have been taken by the authorities in charge of war operations had not the conflict come to an abrupt end in November, 1918, many months earlier than even the initiated dared to hope for.

It is not without the range of probability that the movement, already set in motion by the Conference of Negro Editors and Leaders in the preceding summer, to send to France a competent representative of the Negro press, to report accurately and fully the activities and conditions of the colored troops, received a positive impetus by the letter to Mr. Creel. Action to relieve the tension referred to, was apparently "speeded up." Within a month after this suggestion that a commission be appointed to inquire into what the colored troops were actually doing on the battlefields across the water, Mr. Ralph W. Tyler, an experienced newspaper man of the race, was on his way to France as the accredited representative of the Committee on Public Information, commissioned as a war correspondent on the staff of General Pershing, and directed to chronicle the labors and achievements of the colored soldiers. Later Dr. Robert Russa Moton, Principal of Tuskegee Institute, as told elsewhere, was delegated by the President of the United States and the Secretary of War to go to France on a special mission, which had in mind the promotion of the welfare of the colored troops, and the maintenance of the morale of the Negro people in this country, by taking them fully into the confidence of the Government on all matters relating to their sons who had gone abroad to risk their lives in defense of the Stars and Stripes.

# CHAPTER X

## THE NEGRO SOLDIERS OF FRANCE AND ENGLAND

*French Colored Colonials the First Black Soldiers to Take Part in the War—The Story of These Senegalese Fighters—Their Important Part from the Beginning of the War—The Fight for the African Colonies—German Employment of Negro Troops in the Early Part of the War.*

From the very beginning of the European war, in 1914, soldiers of the Negro race had a great and growing share in the fighting. For nearly three years before America's entry into the conflict these colored "Colonials" from the French and British Colonies in Africa and Asia, had been taking part in the warfare on European soil, while in the fierce but little heard of campaign that resulted in the crushing of German authority in East Africa, it was the Negro troops who bore the chief burden and brunt of the fighting.

At my request, Colonel Edouard Réquin of the French Military Commission to the United States, has prepared the following state-ment of the participation of French Negro troops in the Great War:

"France has had colored troops ever since it has had colonies. These troops have participated in all our expeditions overseas; they have been the best instrument of our colonial expansion. Algerian troops (Arabs and Kabyles) fought in France in 1870-71 against Germany.

"But it was for the first time, in 1914, that *black troops* (Sene-galese and Soudanese) took part in the European war against an enemy as redoubtable as Germany. If it is asked what have been the results of this experience there is only one answer: they have been excellent.

"The black troops of Africa are grouped either by battalions or by regiments with our colonial French troops. The reason is that the colonial officers understand them thoroughly, and that the men themselves, in fighting together in the colonies, have acquired a mutual confidence in each other.

117

Recruited among the warrior tribes of Senegales and the Soudan these troops have great combatant qualities. They are particularly apt for attack and counter-attack, but they are primitive men without civilization—*men who cannot be compared from this point of view with colored Americans.* The black French soldiers are excellent grenadiers, but they are less prepared in the use of the machine gun and the automatic rifle, which demand a certain mechanical aptitude. They receive the same instructions as the French soldiers; these instructions are given to them by white officers and non-commissioned officers who understand them well, and who for this reason ought to be changed as little as possible.

"The characteristic of the black soldier is an entire devotion to these officers who have merited it and whom they will never abandon. In other words, the valor of the colored unit depends essentially on grouping and leadership.

"Colored troops won' distinction for themselves at Dixmude in 1914; at Verdun; on the Somme in 1917; on the Aisne, and more recently still in the counter-attack which forced back the Germans north of Compiegne.

### Salute Their Flag and Die

"These troops are not only devoted to their officers, they are equally devoted to France, whom they serve most loyally, and to the flag which represents France. The following example may be cited as an illustration: One day in 1916, on the Mediterranean, a transport carrying a battalion of Senegalese was torpedoed by a Boche submarine. It was impossible to save everybody. The last who remained on board lined the deck, saluted the flag, and went to the bottom with a discipline and a self-abnegation which must remain an example to all the world.

"It is because these soldiers are just as brave and just as devoted as white soldiers that they receive exactly the same treatment, every man being equal before the death which all soldiers face. In the French Army white and black wounded soldiers are cared for in the same hospital by the same personnel, so that just as we have delivered these black men from African barbarism so we have given them civilization and justice; it is their duty in turn to defend among us that justice and that civilization against Prussian barbarism.

"I recall a design in the Parisian magazine '*L'Illustration*' which represents a Senegalese guarding some German prisoners. This black soldier said with a smile to a visitor who approached to see the Boche: 'I suppose you have come to see the savages, is it not so?' There was in this irony which the artist placed in the black man's mouth an infinitude of truth.

"There is one difficulty which presents itself in connection with colored French troops—a difficulty which results from the climate. The blacks of Sengal are accustomed to a very hot climate and stand our winters very badly, so the French Command, anxious to conserve their health, sends them during the winter to the camps in the south of France, or to Algeria. This inconvenience, however, is only relative; for the black soldiers perfect their instructions in the southern camp and in spring once more take their place in combat beside the white soldiers.

"To sum up, it may be said that, contrary to the opinion so often stated in times of peace by the adversaries of the colonial French expansion necessary to every modern state, the French colonies, far from enfeebling the military effort of the metropolis in face of the common enemy, have on the contrary augmented that power. Not a single territory which we occupied in Africa or in Asia has been abandoned. No serious revolt has been produced outside of a few local agitations provoked by German agents. All those colonies have given us volunteers—Arab, Kabyles, Moroccans, Tunisians, by hundreds of thousands, Senegalese, Madagascans, Somalis, and even Indo-Chinese, have come to fight on French soil in order to defend the liberty of which they have learned under our aegis to appreciate all the benefits.

"The fact that certain countries like Morocco, not yet pacified, furnish us with soldiers taken from the faithful tribes—and tribes that we ourselves fought only yesterday—is one of the most extraordinary illustrations that could be cited.

"All this honors those men who are in charge of the organization of these colonies and the methods which they apply there. It shows equally what prodigious faculty of assimilation the French possess. If one considers that in North Africa the Mohammedan group has been essentially refractory to all foreign intervention, the voluntary participation of colored men in the defense of French soil consecrates definitely the motivating principles of our colonial expansion.

"It is wholly apart from every question of national interest, and solely from the point of view of humanity and morals that the role played by France outside of France itself received its noblest justification."

### The Negro Forces of Britain

Less has been heard of the part played in the war by British Colonials of the Negro race. Before going into further detail about the French Colonials, let me quote here an article from the London *Spectator*, one of the most influential British journals, which gives an excellent summary of the way in which the Negro served under "the meteor flag of England."

"Sir Auckland Geddes said the other day that, for every man in the Army who was actively engaged in fighting at a given moment, twenty-four men were hard at work in connection with the war. The statement illustrated the complexity of modern warfare and the importance of the unarmed laborer as an assistant to the fighting man. In the present war this is generally understood, but it was not always so. When we invaded Crimea we had no labor corps. The troops on the plateau above Balaclava through the winter of 1854-55 starved within a few miles of abundant supplies because there was no proper means of transport and no road along which vehicles could move rapidly. The General declared that he could not spare soldiers from the trenches for roadmaking; the trenches were indeed very thinly held. No one at the War Office had foreseen the necessity of enlisting large gangs of laborers to keep the troops properly fed and equipped, and it was not till after months of hardship that a corps of navvies was sent out to the Crimea. Nowadays this would be done as a matter of course.

"It is a common knowledge that there are in France many thousands of British workers who never hear a shot fired, but are nevertheless indispensable to the comfort and efficiency of the army. The problem of finding labor for the manifold tasks that have to be performed—not merely in constructing fortifications, but in making new roads and railways, in unloading ships, and in transporting the stupendous quantities of food, munitions and stores of every kind that a modern army requires—is as important and difficult as any problem of the war. The Germans have tried to solve it by compelling the people of the occupied territories to work for them, but this forced labor is probably inefficient as a rule because the poor slaves are ill fed and harshly treated. We have done better because we have called on the immense reserves of colored labor in the empire to supply voluntary workers, who are well fed and well paid, and cheerfully assist us in the struggle for liberty.

"Sir Harry Johnston's little book on the part that the colored races are playing in the war is interesting and informing, especially from this point of view. He begins by reminding us that:

"'The United Kingdom of Great Britain and Ireland rules more or less directly some 44,700,000 Africans, about 1,700,000 Aframericans in the West Indies, Honduras and Guiana, and about 338,000 Oceanic Negroes, Melanesians and Polynesians in the Pacific archipelagoes. And in addition the Daughter Nation of the South African Union governs another 4,000,000 of Bantu Negroes, Hottentots and half breeds; lastly, the Commonwealth of Australia and the Dominion of New Zealand are responsible for the safe keeping and welfare of about 400,000 Papuans, 150,000 Australoids and 100,000 Polynesians, Melanesians and Micronesians.'

"Our Asiatic subjects are more than six times as numerous, but our fifty-one million Negroes are not greatly inferior in numbers to the sixty-one million white people within the Empire, and their help, freely and loyally tendered, has been most valuable. The author proves his case by taking each Negro country in turn, describing its races and showing what they have done in the war. British West Africa naturally comes first. Nigeria alone contains over sixteen million Negroes, some of whom are among the best native troops that we have. The French Senegalese battalions have done magnificent service on the Western front, and their southern neighbors under our rule have an equally fine record in the African campaigns. The Hausa of Nigeria and the Mandingoes of Gambia and Sierra Leone make first-rate soldiers, and have faced German troops and their machine-gun fire without flinching.

"Ebrima Jalu, a Mandingo sergeant-major in the West African Frontier Force, received the D. C. M. in 1916 for his gallantry in a severe action in the Cameroons. When his white officer had been killed, he took command of his sector and directed the guns for several hours until another officer could reach him. Sergt.-Maj. Ebrima Jalu is not the only hero of his race. It is good to know that all these West African troops, perhaps thirty thousand in number, are volunteers, and that they enlist with the warm approval of their people. We could hardly have better testimony to the popularity of British rule in West Africa than the anecdote which Sir Henry Johnston cites from Southern Nigeria early in the war:

" 'The people of New Calabar and their hereditary enemies, the people of Okrika, had now sworn blood brotherhood (lest their intertribal quarrels should embarrass us), and had brought in £1,000—each tribe contributing £500—which they begged the local Political Officer to forward as a token of personal loyalty to the King. They wrote letters in broken English saying that they wanted to help in the Great War because they were grateful for having such good and kind rulers. This means a great deal when one realizes what keen, hard-headed traders are the few headmen with money, and how comparatively poor (except in foodstuffs) are the masses of the people.'

"Attempts were made by Turkish agents to rouse the Mohammedans of Nigeria against us, but not even the ruling Fula caste, whom we had to fight when we took over Nigeria, would pay any attention to these sedition-mongers.

"Incidentally the author tells us that the Negroes of German East Africa are akin to those of British East Africa and Nyasaland, and like them use Swahili as a *lingua franca*. They were well treated by Major von Wissmann and other early administrators, but in recent years their interests have been completely subordinated to German greed:

" 'The general cry of the natives in German East Africa since victories of the Allied troops has been, "Watu wa kumina-tano wametoka; wasirudi." ("The people of '15' have departed; may they never return.") The "15" refers to the lowest number of lashes with hippopotamus hide which were administered by the Germans for minor offenses. The natives would regard with terror any possibility of the return of the Germans. In one district where a small British column temporarily occupied the country and were welcomed by the natives, the latter were massacred when the Germans returned.' "

The loyalty and devotion of the British and French Negro colonials to the flags and governments of the British Empire and the French Republic, respectively, is in sharp contrast to the feeling toward the German government and the German flag among the Negro population of those sections of Africa which were held as German colonies, but which under the terms of the Treaty of Versailles have been taken away from that country. While other considerations than the rights of the Negroes themselves may have and doubtless did enter into the considerations that led to the decision of the Peace Conference to take her colonies away from Germany forever, this decision can nevertheless be properly regarded as a fulfillment of the wish and desire of every American citizen of the Negro race.

### German Atrocities in Africa

The record of German duplicity and cruelty in Southwest Africa as disclosed in the official reports of the British administrator embodies many of the stories of these atrocities. Between 1904 and 1911 the numbers of three native races were reduced from 130,000 to 37,742. The decrease was brought about by a war of extermination undertaken by the Germans against tribes with whom they had made agreements—the "scrap of paper" over again. The Kaiser undertook by the treaties "to give his All-Highest protection to the chief and his people." As soon as the Germans had sufficient force on the spot they tore up the treaties, goaded the natives into rebellion, and then massacred them. The German Governor Leutwein avows the crime as cynically as Bethmann-Hollweg admitted the crime against Belgium. He simply says:

"The specific provisions of the agreement did not matter; the fact of their conclusion was sufficient. The manner of the carrying out of those agreements thus depended entirely on the power which stood behind the German makers of the agreements. So long as the German Government in the protectorate had no means of enforcing its power the agreements were of small significance. After this state of affairs had been changed the agreements were, in practice, dealt with uniformly without regard to their stipulated details. So the native tribes were all in the same way, as a whole, whether it was arranged or not, made subject to German laws and

German jurisdiction and received German garrisons.'' That was
how the Kaiser's ''protection'' was given. Then came the slaughter.

All the records in the report are from the archives at Windhoek, from sworn statements made by Europeans familiar with the
country, by native chiefs, and from the writings of Leutwein, who
was governor from 1894 to 1905, and other German authorities.
Every injustice and atrocity dealt with is a substantial fact.

The death of a native from a thrashing was not regarded by
the German courts as murder. Leutwein says: ''The natives could
not understand such subtle distinctions. To them murder and
beating to death were one and the same thing.''

Government of this kind impelled the Herrero rebellion.
Samuel Kariko, son of Under-Chief Daniel Kariko, stated on oath:
''Our people were shot and murdered; our women were ill-treated;
and those who did this were not punished. Our chiefs consulted and
we decided that war could not be worse than what we were under-
going. We all knew what risks we ran, yet we decided on war, as
the chiefs said we would be better off even if we were all dead.''

Johannes Kruger, appointed by Leutwein as chief of the
Bushmen and Berg-Damaras of the Grootfontein area, stated on
oath with regard to the campaign of Gen. von Trotha: ''I went
with the German troops right through the Herrero rebellion. The
Afrikander Hottentots of my werft were with me. We refused to
kill Herrero women and children, but the Germans spared none.
Two of my Hottentots, Jan Wint and David Swartbooi, were
invited by the German soldiers to join them in violating Herrero
girls. The two Hottentots refused to do so.''

Hendrik Fraser of Keetmanshoop stated on oath: ''On one
occasion I saw about 25 prisoners placed in a small inclosure of
thorn bushes. They were confined in a very small space, and
the soldiers cut dry branches and piled dry logs all around them—
men, women, and children and little girls were there. The prisoners were all alive and unwounded, but half starved. Having piled
up the branches, lamp oil was sprinkled on the heap and it was
set on fire. The prisoners were burnt to a cinder. I saw this
personally.''

The official photographs of natives hanged by Germans, are
pitiful. Capt. L. Fourie, S. A. M. C., district surgeon at Windhoek,

states: "Executions were carried out in a very crude and cruel manner. The prisoner was conducted to the nearest tree and placed on an ammunition, biscuit, soap, or other box or convenient object, and the rope, after being run around his neck and through a fork of the tree, was fixed to the trunk. The box was removed and death resulted from asphyxiation. In other instances the condemned prisoner was strangled by merely hoisting him off his feet by utilizing the fork or branch of a tree. When the rope was not available, telegraph or telephone wire or other convenient material was used. Very rarely could death have resulted instantaneously."

Such had been the history of German East Africa which was completely captured and taken over by the British early in the World War. Here the Germans sought to resist the British forces, consisting of native and Boer regiments from the British South African colonies, under the command of Boer officers, by compelling Negroes to fight them against the invaders. Their resistance was half-hearted; even the least intelligent African native could feel neither loyalty nor respect for the brutal and tyrannical German officers and Colonial officials, and the Germans were left practically to conduct their resistance unaided. The extension of the British protectorate over German East Africa was hailed with joy by all the natives.

If the author has digressed from his theme of the Negro Soldiers of France, it is because he has wished to draw a picture of the contrast between the loyalty of the French and British Colonials on the one hand and the hatred and terror inspired by Germany wherever that nation has attempted to establish colonies and rule the natives. To the French, who draw no color line, there is nothing startling or worthy of special comment in the fact that in the armies of France in the Great War, two colored soldiers reached the rank of General, and four the rank of Colonel. And the French as a race are proud of the exploits of "Les Joyeux" (the happy ones), the Negro soldiers of the special corps called officially "Bataillons d'Afrique."

It was "Les Joyeux" who electrified the entire sector when on May 27, 1918, the Germans attempted to storm their defenses. Although the enemy attacked in superior numbers, the "Joyeux," fight-

ing desperately, with entire disregard to numbers, held their ground
and every yard of the line of barbed-wire entanglement fronting
the French trenches was ornamented with dead Germans. Some
of the enemy elements which succeeded in penetrating the trenches
were slaughtered with bayonets and grenades. Supreme abnegation
was shown by the war-hardened "Joyeux," who checked the powerful German assaults. The line of trenches was firmly held and
communication was kept open between the various defending
elements.

On the night of May 28 the First Battalion of the Chasseurs
d'Afrique fell back in an orderly manner, having fulfilled the mission intrusted to it and picking up the equally weary elements of
the Third Battalion, which had struggled no less gloriously. After
an all-night march of twenty kilometers (twelve miles) they arrived
at their destination without abandoning any material, the machine
gunners carrying their pieces on their backs. Several of the
"Joyeux" spoke of this moving night march with heroic simplicity.

"We were counted and reconstituted," said one of, them.
"About midnight of May 29, 1918, without taking a rest, we
again went to the front. On June 1 we launched an attack, making
a formidable charge, which caused the boches to renounce their
attempt to advance."

### Many Deeds of Heroism

Many deeds of heroism were performed by these men. One of
the battalions taking part in the action was composed of very
young men and had arrived on the French battlefields as late as
January 3, 1918, after distinguishing itself in Morocco by its ardor
and endurance. The esprit de corps animating this battalion was
most chivalrous.

Four "Joyeux" in the night of May 28th, saw their company
commander, Lieutant Marechal, fall in a boyau pierced by enemy
bullets. Not wishing to lose the body of their chief, the valiant
four resisted the Germans with grenades, holding them at bay.
After they had recovered the body the same four "Joyeux" carried
it all the way during the terrible back-breaking twenty kilometer
retreat. On the morning of May 29, although harassed by fatigue
and lack of sleep, they organized a short funeral service, glorifying
the officer who had fallen at their head. On June 1 the same

battalion, supported by two companies of other battalions, after being almost submerged by the German waves, threw itself, the officers leading with drawn revolvers, into a hand-to-hand encounter with the Germans, who fell back in disorder, abandoning their field and machine guns.

The Germans applied the common name of "Frenchmen from Africa" to the soldiers of all the French regiments which in time of peace served in Africa, including legionnaires, zouaves, "Joyeux," colonials, mitrailleurs—Arab and black sharpshooters recruited in northern Africa—Spahis and African chasseurs. These corps were especially feared by the enemy and formed one of the firmest bulwarks of the allied defense.

The annals of the French Army in the Great War are filled with records of individual heroism on the part of the French Colonial troops. Here is the official record of Fako Doumbia of the Fifty-first Senegalese Battalion, serving at the observation post of the trench. He was three times buried by projectiles, three times released himself, resumed his post with the greatest calmness, and continued on duty until relieved by the commandant of his company.

Fort Douaumont, which had gained renown for its obstinate and prolonged defense by the French during the German rush at Verdun in 1916, was defended by the Huns with equal obstinacy when the French began their counter-attack in 1918, but was recaptured at last. In the course of the attack a battalion of the "Tirailleurs," together with one of the "poilus," was held up by an artillery barrage in front and machine-gun fire on the flanks. A veteran lieutenant of the Tirailleurs cautiously raising his head shouted to his men: "How now, Tirailleurs, are we going to stick here? Forward!" The Tirailleurs immediately bounded forward, carrying the "poilus" with them in their rush. They passed the barrage and captured the fort and raised the tricolor once more upon its walls.

On March 1, 1916, a battalion was organized at St. Raphael from the veterans of the previous campaign and recruits recently arrived from Africa. After three months' training, to give the necessary cohesion, the battalion was sent to the front on June 1, and went into the trenches on the Oise, and then on the Somme, taking its part in all the battles. At the end of October the battalion went into winter quarters near Arachon, where it was put under "intense" training, and on March 19, 1917, joined the armies of the North and Northeast on the line of the Aisne, where it was attached to a regiment of Colonial infantry with which it took part in the spring offensive. On April 16 and 17 it distinguished itself greatly at the farm of Noisy, the men dying at their posts rather than abandon the position which they had taken. In May it served at the Mill of Lafaux, and in June and July was in the trenches in the reconquered part of Alsace. During July-August it took part in the defense of the plateaux of Craonne and California and fought on the Chemin des Dames.

These places are mentioned to show that the battalion was always at the seat of the hottest fighting, and wherever it was called upon to serve, whether in attack or in defense, it attracted attention by its courage, devotion and self-sacrifice. The quality of these gallant soldiers will be shown by a few quotations from the "citations á l'ordre" for a single day:

"Kofi Alla, private: Cool and collected; courageously led his comrades on April 16, 1917, to an assault of the enemy positions. Although wounded, continued to throw his bombs on a hostile machine gun and only left his post when his strength gave out."

"Moderi Comba, private: Very devoted and courageous; on April 16, 1917, dressed, under fire, the wounds of his lieutenant and returned to his post in the line."

"Demba N'Daigne, private: Very courageous. On April 16, 1917, taking the quick firing gun of one of his wounded comrades, stopped by his fire an attempted bombing attack by the enemy."

"Namadon N'Daigne, sergeant: On April 1, 1917, distinguished himself among the bravest of those who advanced against a German counter-attack and formed a first line of defense behind the barbed wire."

"Donga Thiam, private: On April 16, 1917, being with a group of bombers and all his comrades having become casualties continued alone to cast his bombs into the enemy's trench."

"Eli Diot, corporal: Showed remarkable courage in the attack on the enemy's lines on April 16, remained at his post, although seriously wounded and never ceased to encourage his comrades."

It was with records like these, made by men of their own race though under different flags, that the Negro soldiers of America had to compete. That they did compete, and nobly upheld the tradition of valor established by these French soldiers of their own color, is a source of much satisfaction.

A STUDY IN BLACK AND YELLOW

# CHAPTER XI

## THE NEGRO COMBAT DIVISION

*Full Detailed Account of the Organization and Fighting Campaigns of the Famous Ninety-Second, as Recorded by the Division's Official Historian—Complete Official Reports of Every Battle in Which the Ninety-Second Took Part—Commendation by Commanding Officers.*

*Pursuant to War Department Orders, the 92nd Division was organized November 29, 1917, from the first contingent of Negro draftees arriving at the various camps and cantonments throughout the United States during the latter part of the month of October, 1917. The entire enlisted personnel was made up of Negroes and represented practically all the States in the Union. The Staff and Field Officers, officers of the Supply Units, Quartermaster Corps, Engineers' Corps, and of the Artillery Units, with few exceptions, were white. The remainder of the commissioned personnel, comprising about four-fifths of the whole, were colored.

The plans of the War Department did not provide a separate cantonment for this division. It was therefore necessary to distribute its various units among seven widely-separated camps. This distribution was effected as follows:

| Name of Camp | Location | 92nd Division Units |
|---|---|---|
| Funston | Ft. Riley, Kansas | Division Headquarters |
| | | Headquarters Troop |
| | | 349th Machine-gun Battalion |
| | | Divisional Trains |
| Dodge | Des Moines, Iowa | 366th Regiment of Infantry |
| Grant | Rockford, Ill. | 365th Regiment of Infantry |
| | | 350th Machine-gun Battalion |

---

*The information contained in this chapter with reference to the organization, operations and other data of the 92nd Division has been supplied for this work by First Lieut. T. T. Thompson of the 92nd Division, who accompanied it to France and served during the whole period at Headquarters at Camp Funston and in France as acting Personnel Officer. He was specially detailed as Historian of the 92nd Division.

| | | |
|---|---|---|
| Sherman | Chillicothe, Ohio | 317th Engineers Regiment |
| | | 317th Engineers Train |
| | | 325th Field Signal Battalion |
| Meade | Annapolis Jct., Md. | 368th Regiment of Infantry |
| | | 351st Field Artillery |
| Dix | Wrightstown, N. J. | 349th Field Artillery |
| | | 350th Field Artillery |
| | | 317th Trench Mortar Battery |
| Upton | Yaphank, New York | 367th Regiment of Infantry |
| | | 351st Machine-gun Battalion |

At the time of organization the Staff Officers of the Division were as follows:

| | | |
|---|---|---|
| CHARLES C. BALLOU | MAJOR GENERAL | COMMANDING DIVISION |
| Chauncey Dewey | Captain F. A. | Aide-de-Camp |
| Allen J. Greer | Lt. Colonel G. S. | Chief of Staff |
| *Harry L. Hodges | Major Inf. | Assistant Chief of Staff |
| Sherburne Whipple | Major Inf. | Division Adjutant |
| Robert P. Harbold | Major Inf. | Division Inspector |
| Edward L. Glasgow | Colonel Q. M. C. | Division Quartermaster |
| Perry L. Boyer | Lt. Colonel M. C. | Division Surgeon |
| Philip S. Gage | Major Ord. C. | Division Ordnance Officer |
| Alfred M. Craven | Major J. A. G. D. | Division Judge Advocate |
| Thomas C. Spencer | Major Inf. | Division Signal Officer |

*Never reported.

The 183rd Infantry Brigade comprised the 365th and 366th Regiments of Infantry and the 350th Machine-gun Battalion, and was organized as follows:

| | | |
|---|---|---|
| MALVERN H. BARNUM | BRIGADIER GENERAL | BRIGADE COMMANDER |
| Edmund A. Buchanan | Major | Brigade Adjutant |

365th Regiment of Infantry

| | | |
|---|---|---|
| VERNON A. CALDWELL | COLONEL | REG'L COMD'R |
| John J. Ryan | Lt. Colonel | Regiment |
| Frederick E. Sweitzer | Captain | Regimental Adjutant |
| James E. Abbott | Major | Comd'g 1st B'n |
| Charles W. Mason | Major | Comd'g 2nd B'n |
| William F. Robinson | Major | Comd'g 3rd B'n |

366th Regiment of Infantry

| | | |
|---|---|---|
| RALPH W. PARROTT | COLONEL | REG'L COMD'R |
| Adelbert G. Aldrich | Captain | Reg'l Adjutant |
| James E. McDonald | Major | Comd'g 1st B'n |

| Ralph Leavitt | Major | Comd'g 2nd B'n |
| Horace F. Sykes | Major | Comd'g 3rd B'n |

### 350th Machine-gun Battalion

| GEORGE M. LEE | MAJOR | B'N COMD'R |
| Dennis M. Matthews | 1st Lt. | Actg. B'n Adjutant |

The 184th Brigade was organized as follows:

| WILLIAM H. HAY | BRIGADIER GENERAL | BRIGADE COMMANDER |
| Herman S. Dilworth | Major | Brigade Adjutant |

### 367th Regiment of Infantry

| JAMES A. MOSS | COLONEL | REG'L COMD'R |
| William C. Doane | Lt. Colonel | Regiment |
| Fred W. Bugbee | Lt. Colonel | Unassigned |
| Frederic Bull | Captain | Regimental Adjutant |
| Charles L. Mitchell | Major | Comd'g 1st B'n |
| Wilford Twyman | Major | Comd'g 2nd B'n |
| Fitzhugh L. Minnegerode | Major | Comd'g 3rd B'n |

### 368th Regiment of Infantry

| WILLIAM P. JACKSON | COLONEL | REG'L COMD'R |
| William S. Mapes | Lt. Colonel | Regiment |
| Harry Armstrong | Captain | Regimental Adjutant |
| Henry S. Terrell | Major | Comd'g 1st B'n |
| Max A. Elser | Major | Comd'g 2nd B'n |
| William R. Pope | Major | Comd'g 3rd B'n |

### 351st Machine-gun Battalion

| ROBERT M. BARTON | MAJOR | B'N COMD'R |
| Oscar C. Brown | 1st Lt. | B'n Adjutant |

The 167th Field Artillery Brigade was organized as follows:

| JOHN H. SHERBURNE | BRIGADIER GEN. | BRIGADE COMMANDER |

### 349th Field Artillery Regiment

| DAN T. MOORE | COLONEL | REG'L COMD'R |
| Charles S. Blakely | Lt. Colonel | Regiment |
| Royal F. Nash | Captain | Reg'l Adjutant |
| William F. McCleave | Major | B'n Commander |

### 350th Field Art. Regiment

| FRED T. AUSTIN | COLONEL | REG'L COMD'R |
| Walter E. Prosser | Lt. Colonel | Regiment |
| William Heffner | Captain | Regimental Adjutant |
| Allen McBride | Major | B'n Commander |

### 351st Field Art. Regiment

| | | |
|---|---|---|
| WILLIAM E. COLE | COLONEL | REG'L COMD'R |
| Edward L. Carpenter | Lt. Colonel | Regiment |
| Earl Briscoe | Major | Comd'g 1st B'n |
| Wade H. Carpenter | Major | Comd'g 2nd B'n |

The 317th Engineers' Regiment was organized as follows:

| | | |
|---|---|---|
| EARL I. BROWN | COLONEL | COMD'G REGIMENT |
| Henry A. Finch | Lt. Colonel | Regiment |
| Charles Ecton | Captain | Reg'l Adjutant |
| William H. Ferguson | Major | Comd'g 1st B'n |
| Arthur E. Wenige | Major | Comd'g 2nd B'n |

### 317th Engineers' Train

| | | |
|---|---|---|
| PITTMAN E. SMITH | 1st Lt. | Train Comd'r |
| Ether Beattie | 2nd Lt. | Tr. Adjutant |

The 325th Field Signal Battalion was organized as follows:

| | | |
|---|---|---|
| IRVING DEEMS | MAJOR | B'N COMMD'R |
| Luther N. Hull | Captain | B'n Adjutant |

The 317th Supply Train was organized as follows:

| | | |
|---|---|---|
| OTTO W. RETHORST | MAJOR | TR. COMD'R |
| John N. Douglass | Captain | Tr. Adjutant |

The 317th Ammunition Train was organized as follows:

| | | |
|---|---|---|
| HENRY B. CLARK | COLONEL | TR. COMD'R |
| Allan R. Williams | Major | Comd'g Horse Sec. |
| Charles C. McClure | Major | Comd'g Motor Sec. |
| Charles C. Hoag | Captain | Adjutant Mot. Sec. |
| Edward F. Springer | Captain | Adjutant Horse Sec. |

The 317th Sanitary Train:

| | | |
|---|---|---|
| DAVID B. DOWNING | MAJOR, M. C. | TR. COMD'R |
| Edward B. Simmons | Captain, M. C. | Comd'g Ambu. Sec |

The 317th Trains Headquarters and Military Police:

| | | |
|---|---|---|
| ISAAC S. JENKS | COLONEL | TR. COMD'R |
| Joseph C. Wilson | Captain | Tr. Adjutant |

The 349th Machine-gun Battalion:

| | | |
|---|---|---|
| ROBERT S. STERRETT | MAJOR | B'N COMD'R |
| Arthur Hubbard | 1st Lt. | B'n Adjutant |

The Division Headquarters Troop:

| | | |
|---|---|---|
| EDWARD J. TURGEON | CAPTAIN | TROOP COMD'R |
| Marion C. Rhoten | 1st Lt. | Troop |
| Sidney D. Frissell | 1st Lt. | Troop |
| Arthur R. Williams | 2nd Lt. | Troop |

## The Training in France

The organization and training of the Division extended over a period of five months. In May, 1918, the Division was ordered overseas to join the American Expeditionary Forces in France. The first contingent embarked at Hoboken, N. J., on June 10, 1918, and reached Brest (Finisterre) on the 19th day of June, 1918. During the same month the Infantry Units, the Divisional Trains and the Field Artillery Brigade, elements of the division which had not embarked with the first contingents, reached France and went immediately into a secondary period of intensive training.

Bourbonne-les-Bains (the baths of the Bourbons), in Haute Marne, was the first training area of the 92nd Division in France. Bourbonne is a historic little town of five or six thousand inhabitants, situated almost midway between the lower reaches of the Marne on the west and the Moselle on the east, in the northeastern part of the country. To the east about one hundred miles flows the Rhine, while to the southeast at a less distance lies the border of Switzerland. Sixty miles north of the town, the battle line ran angling to the southeast and thirty miles northwest was Chaumont, the headquarters of the American Expeditionary Forces. Like most of the towns of France, Bourbonne-les-Bains counted its age in centuries. In peace times its natural hot-water baths attracted health-seekers from all parts of the country. Tradition relates that the hot mineral waters of the surrounding springs had not only been a favorite gathering place for the Bourbon kings in the Middle Ages, but of the Romans as well, many centuries before. In the old city park, at the foot of the hill, near where a moving-picture theater now stands, may be seen the ruins of ancient Roman colonnades, standing near an excavation in the solid rock. This excavation until recently was still used as a swimming pool, into which the same hot springs continue to flow.

The various units of the Division, except the Artillery Brigade and the Ammunition Train, were quartered in the numerous villages extending in a semicircle to the north and east of Bourbonne, ranging from six to sixteen kilometers from Division headquarters, which was established in the city. Following the plan of quartering the American army as it entered France, the soldiers were billetted in buildings vacated by the French people. These buildings consisted of public halls, hotel buildings, barns and in many instances the homes of families where available space could be found.

The training period continued through eight weeks, embracing all phases of offensive and defensive tactics found necessary to meet the actual methods in use in the allied armies. In the meantime, the complete Artillery Brigade and the Ammunition Train reached France and went into training July 18 at Montmorrillon, in the department of Vienne, the training area for artillery units.

### Takes Over the St. Die Sector

Leaving this training area about the 7th of August, 1918, the Division moved up by stages to take over its first sector. Leaving Bourbonne-les-Bains, the Division established temporary headquarters at Bruyères, Vosges, remaining twelve days, during which time the Division was equipped for front line duty. From Bruyères the Division moved up by marches to St. Die on the 21st of August, and took over its first sector on the 25th of August, 1918.

From St. Die to the Rhine is not more than a day's march. From the towers and other elevations of the city, the dim outlines of the distant mountains—the foothills of the Alps—covered with impenetrable forests, are plainly visible. The clear and shallow waters of the river Meurthe flow through the heart of the city. A quaint bit of history connected with St. Die is that it gave the name to the continent of America. This is explained by large placards posted in different parts of the city to welcome incoming American troops, by the announcement in French that the city of St. Die is the "Marraine" of America, because it was for Americus Vespucius, a St. Diean monk, that the continent was named. One of the leading streets terminating at the square known as the "Place de Jules Ferry" is called "Rue de President Wilson." The headquarters of the Division in this city of 10,000 inhabitants, was located in the historic old building formerly used by the Bishop of Eastern France as office and prefecture.

This rambling old building crowns the single eminence of the city and part of it is still used for church services by the native population.

The St. Die sector formed the southeastern tip of the great battle line which extended from the North Sea to the borders of Switzerland. Across the line opposite the sector lay Alsace. Beyond the Alsatian strip of country lay impenetrable mountains and forests. Physical barriers made extensive military movements impracticable, and for this reason the sector was comparatively a quiet one and usually assigned to inexperienced divisions coming into the front line for the first time. The city of St. Die, on the French side, was easily within range of enemy guns, and Saales, the Alsatian city opposite St. Die, was as easily within the range of our own artillery, but through a tacit understanding, neither of these cities suffered from artillery bombardment from opposing forces, although the villages and roads beyond were frequently bombarded.

### The Baptism of Fire and Gas

With the coming of American troops, the sector became more active. The 92nd Division in this sector relieved the 6th Infantry, American Expeditionary Forces, and French units of the 33rd Army Corps, with which the 6th Infantry had been brigaded, less the French artillery which supported the 92nd Division. The Artillery Brigade of the 92nd Division was still in training at Montmorrillon. In a raid on the 16th of August, nine days before the 92nd took over the sector, the 6th Infantry had captured the village of Frapelle and extended its front line trenches. As a result of this loss, the 92nd found the enemy on the offensive and received its baptism of fire and gas on August 25, 1918. Amid intermittent shelling with shrapnel and gas, the front line trenches were taken over by three companies respectively from the 368th and 365th Regiments, two companies of the 367th Infantry, and five companies of the 366th Infantry, with other combat units in reserve and support.

From the 25th of August until the Division was relieved on the 20th of September, the principal activities consisted of patrolling and raiding parties, with artillery and aerial bombardment of enemy positions. Skirmishes between raiding parties were frequent. One of the most intense engagements during this period was on the night of the 31st of August, 1918, when the enemy made an attempt in force to retake Frapelle. In this attack the enemy was supported by intense artillery bombardment, employing mustard gas and flame projectors, but was repulsed with heavy losses. Our casualties were 34 wounded and gassed and four killed, including First Lieutenant Thomas Bullock, 367th Infantry, the first officer of the Division to meet death at hands of the enemy.

On the following day, the enemy attacked our forces at Ormont, after heavy artillery barrage, but were driven back by the 366th Infantry. In this attack more than 12,000 shells were fired into our front line trenches between the hours of 12:30 and 3:00 in the afternoon. After this intense barrage the enemy charged our gun fire. In this action, the 365th were commended for repelling the enemy's attack.

Following the enemy's defeat at Hermanpère, the enemy attempted a raid at Frapelle but was repulsed by our infantry, assisted by artillery barrage. Among the casualties on this date, Lieutenant Aaron Fisher of the 366th Infantry, later awarded a Distinguished Service Cross, was seriously wounded.

### Negro Soldiers Eager to Attack

No immediate offensive operations were attempted by our forces at this time. Our officers and soldiers pleaded for an opportunity to attack the enemy, to assume the offensive; especially was this true at Senones, where our patrolling parties entered the town and mingled with its occupants, and brought back valuable information, but it was deemed inadvisable at that time. Troops not actively engaged in holding positions and repelling the enemy attacks were extending and repairing trenches and dugouts. The entrenchment system was inadequate for the protection of the troops and out of repair from long non-use. In the meantime it developed that notwithstanding the incessant activities of the enemy, he was nevertheless falling back and taking up new positions to the rear. Numerous patrolling parties sent out from our lines returned after long patrols and reported failure to come in contact with the enemy. In many cases enemy trenches were found abandoned. This was regarded as indicating that the enemy was not anxious to meet our troops in a general engagement.

At Hermanpère, La Fontenelle, La Raniese, Vanifosse, Ban de

Sapt, Denipaire, Robedeau, Coichots, Ravines, Germanfaing, Moyen-moutier—villages occupied by the 92d in this zone of operations—the enemy kept up incessant bombardment, including a variety of gas shells. During the latter days of September aerial activity, both bombing and reconnaissance, increased daily.

## A Duel in the Air

Near Raon L'Etape, on the 15th of September, our troops witnessed their first airplane duel. A German aviator, steering a combat plane of the larger Fokker type, entered our lines at an altitude of 8,000 feet. The enemy plane was reported by observers at 14 hrs. At 14:40 hrs. a combat plane from the French aero squadron which was coöperating with our forces in this area, had sighted the enemy plane and was climbing rapidly to give battle. Taken by surprise, the Boche aviator circled and attempted to rise to the level of his antagonist, but the French lieutenant was now opening his batteries on the port side of the Boche plane at a superior height of 800 feet. The accurate aim and superior maneuvering by Lieut. Fagon enabled him to reach the vitals of the Boche plane before the latter could bring his machine into position to defend himself effectively. After twenty minutes of circling, swooping, diving and sparring for advantage, the German plane with its propeller shot away, crashed headlong to earth, its occupant pierced many times with machine-gun bullets.

During the week of September 14, 1918, one of the raiding parties of the 366th Infantry surprised and captured a group of five German soldiers, the first prisoners taken by the 92nd Division. Other raiding parties captured enemy rifles, machine-guns and message dogs. In the meantime two members of one of our own patrolling parties fell into the hands of the enemy. In this way the Germans learned for the first time that the 92nd Division, the opposing force which faced them, was made up of American Negroes. With this information, the Germans changed their tactics for the moment and launched into our trenches the first propaganda which reached us. On the morning of the 12th of September, a section of the 367th Infantry was bombarded with what at first was thought to have been gas shells. On closer inspection it was found to be

circular printed matter.  Printed in good English, a copy of this
circular read as follows:

"To the Colored Soldiers of the American Army"

"Hello, boys, what are you doing over here?  Fighting the Germans?
Why?  Have they ever done you any harm?  Of course some white folks
and the lying English-American papers told you that the Germans ought to
be wiped out for the sake of Humanity and Democracy.

"What is Democracy?  Personal freedom, all citizens enjoying the same
rights socially and before the law.  Do you enjoy the same rights as the
white people do in America, the land of Freedom and Democracy, or are
you rather not treated over there as second-class citizens?  Can you go into
a restaurant where white people dine?  Can you get a seat in the theater
where white people sit?  Can you get a seat or a berth in the railroad car,
or can you even ride, in the South, in the same street car with white people?
And how about the law?  Is lynching and the most horrible crimes connected
therewith a lawful proceeding in a democratic country?

"Now, this is all different in Germany, where they do like colored people,
where they treat them as gentlemen and as white people, and quite a number
of colored people have fine positions in business in Berlin and other German
cities.

"Why, then, fight the Germans only for the benefit of the Wall street
robbers and to protect the millions they have loaned to the British, French,
and Italians?  You have been made the tool of the egotistic and rapacious
rich in England and in America, and there is nothing in the whole game for
you but broken bones, horrible wounds, spoiled health, or death.  No satisfaction whatever will you get out of this unjust war.

"You have never seen Germany.  So you are fools if you allow people
to make you hate us.  Come over and see for yourself.  Let those do the
fighting who make the profit out of this war.  Don't allow them to use you
as cannon fodder.  To carry a gun in this war is not an honor, but a shame.
Throw it away and come over into the German lines.  You will find friends
who will help you along."

Be it said to the honor and credit of the many thousands of
Negro officers and soldiers to whom this propaganda was addressed,
the invitation had no effect other than to present an intimate view
of German methods and to confirm in our men a loftier conception
of duty.

On the 20th of September, 1918, the 92nd Division was relieved
in the St. Die sector by the 81st (the Wildcat Division).  During the

four weeks the Division held this sector, all enemy attacks were repulsed, a number of prisoners and quantities of material were captured, trenches and roads were constructed and repaired, and most important of all, the Division demonstrated its ability to fight in or out of the trenches as it had been trained in the back areas.

### Second Sector Held by the 92nd Division

Beginning on the 21st of September, 1918, the Division left the St. Die sector, dropping down into the Corcieux zone for entrainment. Orders from the Commander-in-Chief of the American Expeditionary Forces directed the Division to proceed to the Department of the Meuse and take up position as a Corps Reserve unit. From Corcieux and other nearby entraining points, the various units of the Division, less the artillery and Ammunition Train, were entrained and en route to the Argonne region within twenty-four hours after orders were received.

Preparations for the great drive of the Allies which had been scheduled to begin on the 25th of September, 1918, were almost complete. More than 650,000 American troops were hurrying day and night to take up their places in the line. The whole Hindenburg line contained no section more difficult than that assigned to the American Army. This great offensive operation was a part of the general program to break the German line. The objective for the American Army was a point opposite Sedan on the Meuse, to reach which it was necessary to drive the enemy entirely out of the Argonne, a section he had held tenaciously for four years.

The distance of more than three hundred miles was covered by the 92nd Division in troop trains by the afternoon of the 23rd. With all equipment and supplies each unit was in place by the morning of the 24th of September. Division headquarters was established in echelons at Triacourt and Beauchamp, sixteen kilometers apart.

The Argonne is a narrow oblong strip of territory extending almost north and south between the Aisne and the Aire, with a ridge of hills through almost its entire length, skirted by the river valleys on either side. Several villages are located in the region, but the greater part is densely wooded, with gorges and ravines. In length it is nearly thirty miles from Grand Pré at one end to Triacourt at the other, and varies in width from eight to fifteen miles. The entire section is crossed by only two main wagon roads and one railroad. On the western side is St. Menehould, on the eastern side is Clermont. To the east a few kilometers lies battered Verdun, while westward of St. Menehould 90 kilometers lies naked Rheims. The line of railroad running from Metz to Paris and passing through Verdun, Clermont, St. Menehould, and Rheims, bisects the Argonne forest at Les Islets. The entire area of the strip is less than 500 square miles and yet because of the rugged terrain and impassable forests, the Allies found this section the most difficult of the whole line from which to dislodge the enemy. Throughout the whole period of the war this forest remained the scene of the fiercest struggles. It was overrun in 1914 when the German army advanced to the Marne after driving its wedge between Verdun and Rheims. After four years of fighting in which the German army had been pushed back gradually, that portion of the Argonne between the line of railroad and Grand Pré still remained in the hands of the enemy. On the date of the beginning of the Argonne-Meuse offensive, more than 21 divisions of the American Army held this portion of the line, while the enemy had more than 40 divisions opposite.

A change in the disposition of allied troops made it necessary for the 368th Infantry to take over the sector opposite Binarville on the 25th of September. At this time the 368th Infantry was commanded by Colonel Fred R. Brown with the following battalion commanders: First battalion, Major John H. Merrill; second battalion, Major Max Elser; third battalion, Major Benjamin F. Norris. For this engagement, the regiment coöperated with the French forces, the 4th French Army, commanded by General Gourard. Moving over from Vienne-le-Chateau it took up a position on the left of the American forces and on the right flank of the French.

The sector held by the 368th Regiment formed an irregular triangle projecting forward beyond the general line. In front of this position vast stretches of enemy wire entanglement extended at intervals in all the intervening "no-man's-land." Beyond this wire entanglement were numerous concealed machine-gun emplacements. At this point the fighting was harder than anything the Division had experienced up to that time. At least two unsuccessful attempts were made to advance before the first objectives were reached. The total casualties exceeded 450 men killed, wounded and gassed. Among the casualties in this action, the following officers were killed: Lieut. Norwood C. Fairfax and Captain Walter Green of the 368th Infantry. During the five days in which the 368th held this position a total advance of five kilometers was made and the village of Binarville was taken.

### Infantry Activities of the Division

The following statement indicates somewhat in detail the Infantry activities of the 92nd Division: On August 23, 1918, the entire 92nd Division except the artillery moved from the training area into the St. Die (Vosges) sector, to relieve the 5th Regular U. S. Army Division. The front line trenches of this sector were established 60 days after the opening of the war and had not changed until the taking of the village of Frapelle. More than three years of attack and counterattack had caused both the French and Germans to conclude that the Vosges Mountains offered too many difficulties for either to advance and hold. This bit of rugged terrain had been used by both sides as a "rest sector." About the middle of August, 1918, the 6th Infantry of the 5th Regular U. S. A. Division in an early morning surprise attack captured the village of Frapelle. This is said to have been the first town taken by an American unit independent of any assistance from the French. Frapelle controlled a very important highway and its loss by the Germans threatened a railroad which was much used to convey troops and military supplies into Southeast Alsace.

Before the 6th Infantry had time to reorganize to hold the newly captured territory, the 366th Infantry (colored troops) was ordered to relieve them. The Germans were very angry at this loss and hurriedly moved Prussian troops in to replace Alsatian Guards (second class troops) and supplemented the sector artillery with many heavy guns. Counterattacks began immediately upon the arrival of the new troops and many efforts were made to retake the village. The casualties of the 6th Infantry were probably larger than the accomplishment would seem to merit. While the relief of the 6th Infantry by the 366th was in progress a bombardment of Frapelle took place which lasted four hours, and not a wall in the entire town was left standing. The Catholic church steeple was the last to topple over. That this had ceased to be a "quiet sector" was learned by the first company of the 366th Infantry the very night they entered the trenches, for two men were killed and six severely wounded before the relief was completed. In this sector the "dough-boys" of the 366th were first introduced to a flame-projector attack. There the Germans also had air-superiority, and when the weather was clear, the front line trenches were bombed from above.

In addition to their systematic daily program of artillery fire, one and at times two barrages were placed over the front line positions. Aeroplanes flying above often directed the fire for more than thirty minutes at a time before being driven away by the French anti-aircraft guns. The roads traveled by the supply trains were bombed, shelled with shrapnel, high-explosive and gas shells every night.

### Enemy Defeated with the Bayonet

After the first week in this sector the men of this (366th) regiment, not only took complete possession of "no-man's-land," but made nightly patrols over the first and second line trenches of the enemy. One bright Sunday morning after being in the trenches two weeks, the Germans following closely behind a most terrific bombardment, which battered down two front line dugouts, entered the front line trenches and after a hand-to-hand bayonet encounter were forced to retire in complete disorder. After this first and only time that the Germans actually entered the trenches, they seemed to conclude that the Negro infantryman knew how to use "cold steel" and that he was not to be driven from his post. Snipers, machine guns and artillery alone were used against him after that one attack. At night motor trucks armed with light artillery and machine guns were sent forward to commanding positions on the enemy side and the strong points shelled. With the aid of bright rockets on moonlight nights during the early part of September, 1918, these same trucks were used, and often very effectively, against the patrols in "no-man's-land."

During the 28 days in the St. Die sector the men of the 366th Regiment gained a confidence in themselves and their weapons, such as could never have come in a camp or training area. They learned coördination and a real love for the war game. It became difficult to send out small patrols, for every officer and man desired to participate. Company commanders in order to settle disputes as to priority among the volunteers for night patrols and raiding parties were compelled to promise places days in advance of orders.

Many officers of the 366th Infantry think the regiment lost its best opportunity in this sector because orders were never received allowing them to advance. The mission of the regiment was to reorganize the captured territory and hold at any cost. They did this and more. Raiding parties succeeded in driving the German patrols from "no-man's-land" and out of their own front line trenches at night, without assistance from the French sector artillery, which was inactive most of the time, and being situated beyond range was ineffective in silencing enemy batteries when it did fire. Ten days before leaving the sector it was generally recognized that the regiment had superiority in all arms and could, it is believed by its officers, have gone over and captured the villages of Beaulay and Provenchires, thereby bettering their position, with fewer casualties than were sustained by remaining in the valley of the Fave.

### The March to the Argonne

Relieved by the "Wildcat" Division and a battalion of French troops the 366th Infantry, weary and badly rest-broken, moved back for what was rumored to be a rest. After a 20-kilometer march with heavy packs over the flinty roads of the Vosges Mountains to the railroad, they were entrained with other units of the 92nd Division and rushed to the village of Le Chemin, arriving there on the morning of the 23rd of September, 1918. The 92nd Division Headquarters was established at St. Menehould. At seven o'clock in the evening of September 23rd, in a very heavy rain, a start was made for the Forêt d'Argonne. The march from St. Die to Granges, which was very hard on the men, proved disastrous to the horses and mules. The road from Le Chemin to Camp D'Italien was strewn with dead animals and equipment which had to be abandoned for want of transportation. Most of the men of the 1st and 3rd Battalions of this regiment removed their shoes, while on the train, for the first time in ten days; this condition was but a trifle worse with the officers and men of the 2nd Battalion, who had been in the front line trenches twenty days under the most terrifying artillery fire. In recognition of the splendid services rendered during this period eighteen Distinguished Service Crosses were awarded the men of this battalion.

Resting in the woods of Camp d'Italien without shelter except from pup tents during the day of the 24th, another start was made that night and after marching nine kilometers, a part of which was over the famous Verdun highway, Camp Cabaud was reached early in the morning and rest once more established. The march over the Verdun highway that night will never be forgotten by the thousands of soldiers racing for a place in the great offensive of the First American Army. Several miles of trucks were stranded along this highway; congestion was never worse on any ·oad. After several days' rain the shell-torn roads caused some of the trucks to turn end for end; some were on one side, while others were completely upside down. Every effort on the part of the Military Police failed to keep trucks and troops moving. Ammunition having the right of way over everything, forced infantry and even ambulances to halt.

### Roads Blocked with Trucks

Determined to keep transportation moving, trucks were ordered forward over the left side of the road, when the right had become solidly· blocked. Despite the skill and ingenuity of higher commanders, for both Major Generals and Brigadier Generals left their automobiles and vied with Colonels in spending every human energy in an effort to open the roads, the left side of the road became blocked about midnight and for seven kilometers trucks and troops were banked together in mud and mire. The infantry, moving forward by file in small detachments, finally reached the woods above Passavant-en-Argonne about 5 o'clock in the morning. The sky, though cloudy that night after the rain, was well lighted by the continuous flash from the big guns. The roar was deafening. Hearing one speak in ordinary tones beyond a few feet was impossible, though we were ten to twelve kilometers from the battery positions. It was not the ordinary noise of the battle front that night; every soldier knew that a something different was "coming off." Single guns could not be heard; no, not even single batteries; it was just one continuous roar. So numerous were the guns and so regular the fire that the discharge could not be distinguished from the burst of the shells.

Secret Field Order No. 13, Headquarters 92nd Division, made this division, less the 368th Infantry, a Corps Reserve and designated its station as "the woods north of Clermont." Hardly had these woods (Camp Cabaud) been reached when, by verbal order of the Brigade Commander, the 1st Battalion of the 366th Infantry was ordered to go forward and build a road across "no-man's-land." The artillery of the First Army had done its work well, the infantry attacking waves of the assaulting divisions were moving forward. In order that the heavy guns, ammunition, and supplies might follow in close touch with the rapidly advancing troops, roads had to be built in great haste.

Amid gas, shrapnel, and high explosive shells, with but few casualties, this battalion did its work. So rapid was the advance the first few days that the entire 183rd Brigade, which included both the 366th and 365th Infantry, were ordered, in conjunction with the 317th Engineers (also of the 92nd Division), to move forward and engage in the work of making roads. In speaking of this work, General Pershing says in his report to the Secretary of War, dated November 20, 1918: "We had gained our point of forcing the battle into the open and were prepared for the enemy's reaction, which was bound to come as he had good roads and ample railroad facilities for bringing up his artillery and reserves. *In the chill rain of dark nights our engineers had to build new roads across spongy, shell torn areas, repair broken roads beyond no-man's-land, and build bridges.* Our gunners, with no thought of sleep, put their shoulders to the wheels and drag-ropes to bring their guns through the mire in support of the infantry, now under the increasing fire of the enemy's artillery. Our attack had taken the enemy by surprise, but, quickly recovering himself, *he began to fire counterattacks in strong force, supported by heavy bombardments, with large quantities of gas.*"

### Third Sector Held by the Division

About the 5th of October the 92nd Division was withdrawn from this sector and ordered to the Marbache sector. This sector extended along the Moselle river from Marbache to Pont-a-Mousson, a distance of 16 kilometers. The troops of the Division took up a position on a line crossing the river at right angles and resting on both sides of the picturesque stream. Division headquarters was established at Marbache. The elements of the Division were distributed in Belleville, Millery, Saizerais, Dieulouard, Pont-à-Mousson, Jezainville, Loisy, Ste. Genevieve, Ville-au-val, Norroy, Montauville, Port-sur-Seille, and Lesmesnils.

This section lies directly south of Metz in distances varying from 10 to 14 kilometers. According to the plans of the Commander-in-Chief, Metz was selected as one of the next important objectives in the forward movement of the American Army. With several lines of railroads centering at Metz and passing into Germany, its use as a base of the German army, and its location, it was considered an important strategic point. At the same time it was strongly protected by many outlying forts manned with powerful guns.

In the chosen plan of isolating Metz, the 92nd Division would have occupied a prominent place between the Moselle and the Seille and nearer than any other unit to German soil (Lorraine). These plans were interrupted by the signing of the armistice on November 11, 1918.

The position of the enemy opposite the 92nd Division in the Marbache sector was strengthened by the fortifications of Metz. For this reason, the enemy was not falling back in this region as he was doing in other parts of the now shattered Hindenburg line farther to the north, but was stubbornly holding his ground until forced to fall back.

Active operations commenced in this sector about the 8th of October. The 69th French Artillery was relieved from the Division on the 10th of October by the 62nd Field Artillery Brigade, American Expeditionary Forces. By the middle of October the greater part of the Division's forces had crossed to the east bank of the Moselle and was pressing the enemy steadily back to second line positions. Patrols and raiding parties kept in constant touch with the enemy all along the front, with ever-increasing artillery bombardments. During the early days of November the enemy was driven from numerous positions which he held for many months and which were strongly fortified. Reference to this series of rapid offenses launched by the 92nd Division, in which the enemy was routed, is made in the following memorandum from the Commanding General:

A. P. O. 766

7 November 1918.

OPERATING MEMORANDUM NO. 41.

1. When the Marbache sector was taken over by the 92nd Division, the Germans owned "No-man's-land" and were aggressive. They held Belle Air Farm, Bois de Tete d'Or, Bois Frehaut, Voivrotte Farm, Voivrotte Wood, Bois de Cheminot, Moulon Brook.

2. The consistent, aggressive action of our patrols, night and day, has resulted in many casualties to the enemy, and the capture of many prisoners.

3. Each of the places named above has been raided, as has Eply also, and patrols have penetrated north nearly to the east and west line through Pagny. The enemy has been driven northward beyond Frehaut and Voivrotte Woods, and eastward from Cheminot Woods across the Seille, destroying the Cheminot Bridge, flooding the Seille and attempting to destroy the Seille bridge—evidence of the fact that he regards the 92nd Division as an uncomfortable neighbor, with whom *he intends to avoid close relations in the future.*

4. West of the river excellent results have also followed energetic offensive action. The enemy has suffered losses in killed, wounded, and prisoners during the brief occupancy of this part of the sector.

5. The results should greatly stimulate and encourage every man of the Division. With the prospect of efficient artillery support in the future, there will be no let-up in the hammering of the enemy wherever found.

6. Unit commanders will promptly submit reports of all specially meritorious action of officers and enlisted men, in order that the same may be appropriately recognized.

7. This will be read to all troops of the 92nd Division.

By Command of Major-General Ballou:

(Signed) ALLEN J. GREER,

Colonel, General Staff, Chief of Staff.

Our own artillery brigade and ammunition train complete, joined the Division about the 18th of October, 1918. The splendid work of the artillery units soon showed itself in the effective support given in the capture of objectives taken from well-trained and seasoned soldiers—positions that had been organized and strengthened for more than four years.

An attack on Pagny and other positions of the enemy was ordered by the Commanding General of the 183rd Brigade, 92nd Division, to start at 5 A. M., November 10, 1918. This attack was under way and progressing when orders to cease hostilities were received on the morning of the 11th of November. A report of that operation is appended. Another report by the Division Commander is also appended.

HEADQUARTERS 183RD BRIGADE

A. P. O. No. 766, France,

November 19, 1918.

FROM:      Commanding General, 183rd Brigade.
TO:         Commanding General, 92nd Division.
SUBJECT:  Report on Offensive Operations.

1. On November 8, 1918, the 183rd Infantry Brigade was garrisoning a portion of the Allied line immediately east of the Moselle river and extending from Pont-à-Mousson (east bank of Moselle river inclusive to Clemery, exclusive). This portion of the general front was known as Marbache Sector. Marbache Sector was normally divided into sub-sectors, namely, the sub-sector Seille, and the sub-sector Mousson. The sub-sector Seille comprised one center of resistance, the sub-sector Seille two, namely from East to West Les Menils and Mousson.

2. On November 8, 1918, plans were made at Brigade Headquarters for an attack to be executed on the morning of November 10, on the Bois Frehaut and the Bois Voivrotte by two battalions of infantry, each battalion supported by its machine-gun company. The co-operation of the divisional artillery was procured for this attack. Trench mortars and 37-mm. guns were to support the attack. The object of this attack was to capture and hold the Bois Frehaut and the Bois Voivrotte with the object of advancing the line of observation of the Marbache Sector to the northern boundary of these woods.

Operation Order No. 7, Hq. 183rd Brigade, Nov. 8, was issued describing the details of this attack.

3. The attack was to be made on the Bois Frehaut by the 2nd Bn., 365th Inf., Major Warner A. Ross, commanding. The attack on the Bois Voivrotte was to be made by two platoons, 2nd Bn., 366th Inf. At the zero hour, one platoon, 366th Inf., was to occupy the Bois Cheminot in order to cover Cheminot bridge.

4. On Nov. 8 Marbache Sector was garrisoned as follows: C. R. Seille, by the 3d Bn., 366th Inf. and Co. A, 350th M. G. Bn.; C. R. Les Menils, by the 3rd Bn., 365th Inf. and Co. B 350th M. G. Bn.; C. R. Mousson, by the 1st Bn., 365th Inf. and Machine Gun Co., 365th Inf.

The 2nd Bn., 366th Inf., and Co. C, 350th M. G. Bn., were in support position southern part Forêt de Facq. The 2nd Bn. 365th Inf., and Co. D, 350th M. G. Bn., were in support position western part Forêt de Facq. The

1st Bn., 366th Inf., and the M. G. Co., 366th Inf., were held as Brigade Reserve at Bezaumont.

5.  On the afternoon of Nov. 9, the 2nd Bn., 365th Inf., was in Pont-à-Mousson, the 2nd Bn., 366th Inf., in the northern part of Forêt de Facq, where they had been placed in preparation for the attack as specified above. The zero hour for the attack had been given for 5 A. M., November 10.

6.  The plans for the attack were changed by telephone instructions from the Commanding General, 92nd Division, to the Commanding General, 183rd' Brigade, received 12:45 A. M., Nov. 10. These instructions were to the effect that the second American Army would attack on the morning of Nov. 10 at 7:00 A. M.; that the 92nd Division would attack at that hour, pushing the advance as expeditiously as possible, and holding all captured ground.

Telephone messages were immediately sent the attacking troops, changing the hour for the attack from 5:00 to 7:00 A. M. The Commanding General, 183rd Brigade, with the Brigade Adjutant, started out at 2:00 A. M. by automobile to consult the Commanding Officer, 365th Inf. and 366th Inf., with reference to the change in plans. Both of these officers were notified as to the new plans, and given preliminary instructions as to their execution. The Brigade Reserve Bn. was ordered alerted and moved to Camp Schnable, Forêt de Facq. The supporting artillery was notified as to the change of plans.

7.  At 6:15 A. M., Nov. 10, F. O. No. 24, C. S. 92nd Div. was received.

At 7:00 A. M., Nov. 10, attack as specified in Operation Orders No. 7 above was launched.

At 7:25 A. M., F. O. No. 19, 183rd Brigade, was issued. This order was based on F. O. No. 24, 92nd Division, as above, and required the advance to be pushed beyond the objective as ordered in Operation Order No. 7. It was in accord with verbal instructions given Regimental Commanders the early morning of Nov. 10.

8.  At 8:00 A. M., information was received that the French Division on our right was not attacking. Telephone instructions were then sent to the Commanding Officer 366th Inf. to hold his 3rd Bn. in C. R. Seille, and to have his 3rd Bn. maintain liaison between the French Division on our right and the attacking troops.

At 8:12 A. M., a pigeon message was received from the C. O. 2nd Bn., 366th Inf., by runner, and relayed by telephone, to the effect that the Bois Voivrotte had been completely occupied and that three prisoners had been taken.

At 9:00 A. M. a message was received that sharp fighting by machine guns was going on in the Bois Voivrotte and the Bois Frehaut.

At 10:00 A. M., a runner message was received from the Commanding Officer, 2nd Bn., 365th Inf., to the effect that they were being heavily shelled in the Bois Frehaut by enemy artillery, and requesting counter battery fire; it was also stated that their advance had almost reached the northern edge of Bois Frehaut. Heavy artillery was asked to counter-fire on enemy artillery, which they promptly did.

At 10:30 A. M. a message from the Division was received that the attack of the 367th Inf., 184th Brigade, had been repulsed (on our left), but that two companies were being sent forward to reinforce their attack.

At 11:15 A. M., a message from the C. O. 2nd Bn., 365th Inf., to the effect that Bois Frehaut was completely occupied, that Boches were shelling woods with gas and high explosives, and requesting counter battery fire.

At 11:16, Heavy Artillery asked to counter fire on German battery, which they promptly did.

At 11:30, the Commanding General, 167th F. A. Brigade, called in consultation in reference to artillery preparation for a further advance. After consultation, it was decided to bring forward reinforcements, and to launch a new attack on the strong enemy positions of Champey, Bouxières, and La Cote at 5:00 P. M.

11:50—Telephonic orders to Commanding Officer, 365th Inf., to move his 1st Bn. to the northern edge of Forêt de Facq as Brigade reserve, and to move his P. C. to C. R. Les Menils, and take command of the advancing troops of his regiment.

12:00 M.—Information from Commanding General, 92nd Div., that one Bn., 368 Inf., was moving to Pont-à-Mousson, east bank of river, as reserve of 183rd Brigade; that 368th Inf., less one Bn., would be concentrated at Camp Schnable as Division Reserve.

1:05 P. M.—F. O. No. 20, 183rd Brigade, issued; 2:00 P. M., 365th Inf. reports capture one Boche, Bois Frehaut.

3:05 P. M.—Telephonic message from C. O. 2nd Bn., 366th Inf., that he had withdrawn his lines to southern edge of Bois Voivrotte because of heavy enemy shelling, high explosives and gas in woods.

3:55 P. M.—Orders received from Commanding General, 92nd Division, not to launch attack as planned for 5:00 P. M., but to consolidate positions gained, holding them at all costs against possible counter-attacks.

4:00 P. M.—Telephonic message sent Commanding Officer 365th-366th Inf., C. G. 167th F. A. Brigade to this effect.

4:10 P. M.—Operation Memo. Hq. 183rd Brigade issued.

5:50 P. M.—Telephonic instructions to C. O. 365th Inf., 366th Inf., and C. G. 167th F. A. that attack specified in F. O. No. 20 would be made at 5:00 A. M. on Nov. 11.

6:00 P. M.—F. O. No. 21 issued.

6:30 P. M.—F. O. No. 25cs 92nd Division received.

7:30 P. M.—Message from C. O. 365th Inf. that 1st Bn. was moving into Bois Frehaut to support of 2nd Bn.

*November 11.*—5:00 A. M., attack launched as ordered in F. O. No. 21.

Attacking troops met by strong enemy artillery, machine gun and infantry fire. Troops on right had reached the outskirts of Bouxières by 7:30 A. M. Troops on left had advanced a short, distance, but had been forced to retire to woods.

7:18 A. M.—Telephonic message from Division to the effect that Armistice signed, effective at 11 hours, 11th Nov.; that all hostilities must cease at that hour. All firing ordered stopped by our troops by 10:45 A. M. Firing stopped promptly at that hour.

The line held by our troops at the cessation of hostilities was as follows: Line shown by co-ordinates, Map, Pont-à-Mousson, 1/20,000.

65-97; 76; 98 (Ferme de Ponce); 81:02 (N. W. corner) Bois Frehaut; 92-02, N. W. corner Bois Frehaut, 93-01; 95-01; 95-95; 01-96, N. W. corner Bois Voivrotte; 07-97, N. E. corner Bois Voivrotte; 06-92, La Voivrotte Ferme; 02-87; Norroy, thence East and S. E. as formerly held; 19-86; Bois Cheminot, held as an advance post.

9.  The enemy units engaged between the Moselle and the Seille were, from west to east, the 86th and 30th Regiments of Infantry, 31st Landwehr Brigade, and the 47th Infantry Regiment. These regiments were supported by one Bn. of Sharpshooters. East of the Seille river were the 70th Infantry Regiment and the 6th Grenadiers, formerly 10th Division.

10.  SUMMARY:  (a) Our advance was for about a depth of 3½ kilometers. When this Brigade took over the sector just east of the Moselle river there was a deep re-entrant next to the river, due to the St. Mihiel drive which advanced the line several kilometers on west bank of the Moselle river. while the line on the east bank remained in place.

The attack on the morning of Nov. 10, by the units of this Brigade, wiped out this re-entrant, by advancing our lines on the east bank of the Moselle river a distance of 2¼ km.

The advance thus made was held against heavy artillery and machine gun fire and high concentration of gas. The attack was renewed on the morning of Nov. 11, lines being advanced a distance of 3¼ km., an original line. Our liaison with the troops west of the river was thereby greatly improved.

(b) A total of six prisoners was captured; three in the Bois Frehaut and three in the Bois Voivrotte.

(c) The following material was captured: 1,000 (approximately) grenades, all types; 5,000 (approximately) rounds ammunition; 25 (approximately) boxes M. G. ammunition, in belts; 50 (approximately) rifles and bayonets, 10 (approximately) pairs field glasses, 4 (approximately) machine guns, 6 carrier pigeons, 1 signal lamp and battery, 2 **Verey pistols, 3 carbide lamps,** 100 helmets. Many overcoats, boots, canteens, belts, and other articles of equipment were left by the fleeing enemy.

(d) The following were our casualties:

|  | Killed | Wounded | Gassed | Missing | Total |
|---|---|---|---|---|---|
| 365th Infantry ........... | 14 | 67 | 211 | 8 | 300 |
| 366th Infantry ........... | 17 | 52 | 63 | 0 | 132 |
| 350th M. G. Battalion..... | 1 | 0 | 11 | 0 | 12 |
| Total .................. | 32 | 119 | 285 | 8 | 444 |

(e) Full use was made of auxiliary arms, machine guns, 37 mm. guns, Stokes mortars, and rifle grenades. All of these weapons, except Stokes mortars, were brought into play in the heavy fighting in the Bois Frehaut to combat enemy machine-gun nests. 37 mm. guns were pushed well to the front when direct fire at machine-gun positions could be obtained. It was to the extensive use of these weapons that the rapid advance through the Bois Frehaut was due. Machine guns were used frequently to cover the flanks of the attacking infantry. They aided materially in protecting the N. E. corner of the Bois Frehaut from an enemy counter-attack from Bouxières. Trench mortars were placed in position after the Frehaut woods were taken, to cover the new front.

(f) No tank or gas troops were available for this attack. Regtl. and Bn. gas officers and N. C. O.'s rendered valuable assistance in disinfecting infected areas, posting gas alarm sentinels, and upholding gas discipline.

(g) The divisional artillery supported both attacks with a rolling barrage, preceding the troops. These barrages were very well laid and proved effective. It also rendered valuable work in placing heavy concentration fire on enemy strong points and machine-gun nests. Its counter-battery work was excellent.

(h) The attack was executed over a very difficult terrain. For a distance of about 1½ km. in front of our lines, the terrain was open, heavily wired with a downward slope. It was well registered by the enemy artillery, as the numerous shell holes over its surface indicated. The Bois Frehaut is a wood of about 1,500 meters square and breaks the western half of the sector attacked, about 700 meters to the east of the Bois Voivrotte, a small wood about 600 meters square. Both of these woods were a mass of heavy German wire, much of it new. Their edges were protected by bands of heavy wire and chevaux-de-frise. Both of these woods were at the foot of and north of the ridge of which Eon hill, a hill 358 meters high, is the summit. From their southern slopes the ground rises slightly for a distance of about 700 meters, then falls again to a deep ravine traversing the Bois Frehaut from east to west. It then rises again, culminating in La Cote hill, a hill 1,500 meters north of the Bois Frehaut, and 87 meters higher than the highest point of the Bois Frehaut, namely, Hill 260.8. This hill is heavily wooded on its summit, and was strongly held by infantry, machine guns, trench mortars, and light artillery. The southern slopes of this hill were protected by a small wood about 500 meters square about 200 meters north of the Bois Frehaut and by the strongly fortified towns of Bouxières and Champey. These towns, together with the small wood in question, were heavily garrisoned by enemy infantry and machine guns. They formed together a dominating and strongly organized position, protected by heavy bands of wire. Numerous tank traps had been prepared south of this position. These positions dominated the Bois Voivrotte, the Bois Frehaut and the ground to the north.

*Conclusion.*—The lines held by the Germans were unusually strong, being the result of four years of stabilization in that sector. Their artillery was most active, as unquestionably during these years they had registered on every point of importance in the sector. Furthermore, their positions were the first line of defense of Metz. The troops occupying them were young efficient men and not old soldiers from a rest sector.

From the time we entered the sector, our patrols were very active, so much so that we took complete possession of "no-man's-land." After the first few days we were unable to find any German patrols outside their lines.

Previous to November 10, we made several reconnaissances in force (that is, employing a company in each instance) to ascertain if the Germans were still holding their lines. The abundance of machine-gun fire developed in each case, showed that they were.

Our attack on the morning of November 10 was the first offensive move made by the Brigade which required artillery preparation. The Commanding Officers of units making the attack, and also of the artillery, were constantly stating that they were hurried into these movements without proper preparation. Had they been familiar with such operations, the time allowed would have been sufficient. Our artillery was having its first experience in the line and was meeting with the usual difficulties: Lack of transportation, unfamiliarity with sector, little opportunity to register on probable targets, etc.

There is no doubt that some details of the operation were not carried out as well as might have been done by more experienced troops. These were the results of mistaken judgment due to lack of experience, rather than to lack of the offensive spirit. These minor features have no effect on the general outcome.

From my intimate contact with the troops making these attacks, I can state definitely that these men were just finding themselves. The improvement in the aggressive spirit from day to day was manifest.

As a summary, I desire to again call attention to the following: 1st, that we were operating in a sector that had been organized for defense against us for over four years, and was made unusually strong on account of being in front of the great fortress Metz; 2nd, that our inexperienced troops were operating against trained soldiers of the greatest military power of the world; 3rd, that from the time we entered the sector our troops were constantly on the offensive; 4th, to the success that was obtained, viz., removing the reentrant and advancing our lines 3½ kilometers.

(Signed) MALVERN HILL BARNUM,
Brigadier General, U. S. A.

Major A. E. Sawkins, commanding the Second Battalion of the 366th Infantry, in referring to the same offensive operations of November 10th and 11th, 1918, said:

2nd Battalion, 366th Infantry,
17th November, 1918.

FROM:     Battalion Commander.
TO:         Commanding General, 92nd Division.
SUBJECT:  Conduct of troops in action.

1. Reference to action in which this battalion was engaged in Bois de la Voivrotte on 10th and 11th November, 1918, the following report is made on conduct of officers and men while in action.

Troops: 2nd Bn. 366th Infantry, Company C, 350th M. G. Bn. attached. Company A, 366th Infantry.

Officers and men deserving special mention have been recommended in other communications. An observation of the general conduct of officers and men is the reason for this report. *I desire especially to call to the attention of the Division Commander the fact that the handling of their units by the company and platoon commanders was all that could be expected from the most experienced officers.* There was an absolute lack of any disorder, and I cannot say too much in praise of the manner in which these officers handled their men. The men responded as though at a maneuver, and although without food or sleep for 48 hours at time of the attack on morning of the 11th November, the men went into action in such a manner that I feel proud to command such fine, soldierly troops.

(Signed) A. E. SAWKINS,
Major 366th Infantry.

The Commanding General of the 92nd Division reported as to these operations of November 10-11, 1918, as follows:

HEADQUARTERS NINETY-SECOND DIVISION
American Expeditionary Forces
A. P. O. 766

30 November, 1918.

FROM:        The Commanding General, 92nd Division.
TO:          The A. C. of S., G-3, G. H. Q.
SUBJECT:     Report on Operations 10-11 November, 1918.

1. This report made pursuant to paragraph 3, G. O. 196, G. H. Q., American Expeditionary Forces, 1918, embodies the operations of this Division during the period 10-11th November, 1918.

### (1) *Situation at Beginning of Operations*

On November 9, 1918, it having been reported that the enemy, disorganized, was retreating along the entire front, the Commanding General of the 2nd Army, of which this division is an element, gave the order for an attack at 7 hours, 10th November, 1918, along its entire front, following the enemy in his withdrawal, pushing with all energy to secure decisive results, and holding all ground taken. The mission assigned to the Division was to push forward west of the Seille river, along the heights on both banks of the Moselle river in the direction of Corny, maintaining liaison with the 32nd Army Corps (French) and the 7th Division on the left. The western boundary of its zone of action being the same but extending north—Preny (Excl.) —Gorze (excl.). At the beginning of operations 10th November, 1918, the 92nd Division of the 6th Corps, 2nd Army, with three regiments in line and one in reserve, P. C. Marbache, held the Marbache sector, constituting the existing front of the 6th Corps and extending from Clemery (Excl.) to Preny (Excl.). The 165th D. I. (Fr.), P. C. Custines, occupied the sector on the right. The 7th Division, P. C. Euvezin, occupied the sector on the left. The Divisional limits were as follows:

Eastern Boundary.—Port-sur-Seille (incl.)—Ste. Genevieve (incl.)— Bezamont (incl.)—Ville-au-Val (incl.)—Autreville (incl.)—Belleville (incl.) —Marbache (incl.)—Sazerais (incl.).

Western Boundary.—Preny (excl.)—Eastern edges of B. des Rappes— Villers-sous-Preny (excl.)—about one kilom. west of Montauville—Gezoncourt (incl.)—Rogeville (incl.).

Southern Boundary.—Roiseres-en-Haye (excl.)—St. Georges (excl.).

The portion of the sector east of the Moselle was divided into two subsectors. The dividing line being—Ste. Genevieve (inclusive) north through southern portion of Forêt de Facq to a point on the Atton-Morville road about two km. N. E. of Atton (381.2—234.6) then N. E. along road for 1 km. to road cross, then north by west along Ste-Genevieve-Les Mennils road to road cross at (381.5—236.5) (1:50,000) Cheminot map, thence east by north along road to front at point 383.0—237.2. This portion of the sector was organized in successive positions, viz.:

(a) A covering position consisting of a line of observation and a zone of resistance and including the special defense position of the region of Aon.

(b) A position of resistance consisting of a high line and a low line.

The garrison east of the Moselle consisted of the 183rd Brigade and elements of Divisional Machine-Gun Battalions (349th) with Division and corps artillery support. The 366th Infantry with one battalion in line, one battalion in support, one battalion in reserve, garrisoned the sub-sector east of the Division line. This will be referred to as C. R. Seille. The other sub-sector east of the Moselle was garrisoned by the 365th Infantry with two battalions in line and one in support. The areas occupied by these two battalions were referred to as C. R. Les Mesnils and C. R. Mouson respectively. The region included between the Moselle and the western boundary of the division area was known as the C. R. Vandières, it was garrisoned by the 367th Infantry with one battalion in line, one battalion in support, and one battalion in reserve.

At the commencement of operations units of the Division were disposed in conformity with its defensive mission announced in F. O. No. 19, Hqs. 92nd Division, 11 October, 18 (See Appendix "A"), and amplified by F. O. No. 20, Hqs. 92nd Division, 24 October 18, Appendix "B," F. O. No. 23, Hqs. 92nd Division, 8 November, 1918 (See Appendix "C").

In the event of forward movement, advance P. C.'s had been selected after reconnaissance and had been announced. The Division advance P. C. was at Ville-au-Val.

On 10 November, 1918, at 3:30 hours, F. O. No. 4, Hqs. 6th Army Corps issued prescribing interalia as follows:

"1. It is reported that the enemy, disorganized, is withdrawing along the entire front.

"The second army will attack at 7 hours, 10th November, and follow closely the enemy in his withdrawal, pushing him with all energy to secure decisive results, and holding all grounds taken.

"2. The 6th Army Corps will attack in conjunction with the 4th Army Corps on the left.

"3. (a) *The 92nd Division* will push forward west of the Seille River along the heights on both sides of the Moselle River in direction of Corny. It will maintain liaison with the 32nd Army Corps (Fr.) on its right and the

7th Division on its left; Western boundary of its zone of action being as at present, extended North as follows: Preny (excl.)—Gorze (excl.).

"Artillery taken forward will be limited to that which can be fully horsed and adequately supplied with ammunition.

"(b) *Corps Artillery.* Counter battery work on such targets as may be designated by the Chief of Artillery.

"(c) *The 115th Engineers.* Company D at disposal of Commanding General, 92nd Division. Regiment (less Company D) will await orders in Forêt de Puvenelle. It will be in readiness to promptly repair the bridge across the Moselle River at Pont-à-Mouson and to open and maintain road communications North therefrom.

"(d) *The Chief of Air Service* will make the necessary assignments of Artillery, infantry and command planes, and will prescribe the observation to be executed by the 10th Balloon Company.

"(e) *Corps Signal Troops* will maintain communication between 92nd Division, Corps Artillery, 115th Engineers, Corps Air service and these headquarters."

　•　　•　　•　　•　　•　　•　　•　　•　　•　　•　　•

In conformity with the foregoing, the Division Commander having received advance information, issued F. O. No. 24, Hqs. 92nd Division, 3 hours, 10 November, 1918, as follows:

HEADQUARTERS 92ND DIVISION<br>AMERICAN EXPEDITIONARY FORCES, A. P. O. 766,

10 November, 1918, 3 hours.

*Field Order No. 24.*

1. 2nd Army attacks at 7 hours, 10 November, 1918. 6th Corps attacks with Western boundary same as at present, extending north—Preny (excl.) Gorze (excl.). Eastern limit of action—Seille River.

2. 92nd Division will attack in direction of Corny, advancing from present front at 7 hours, 10 November, 1918. Decisive results will be obtained and all ground taken will be held.

3. (a) Division Artillery will support advance with standing and rolling barrage east of the Moselle in initial phase of advance, thereafter following advancing infantry with all mobile elements and supporting further advance as occasion presents.

(b) 183d Infantry Brigade will attack east of the Moselle River with elements of two battalions in line maintaining liaison with the 165th Division (Fr.) on the right.

(c) 367th Infantry will attack west of the Moselle with two companies in line maintaining close contact with elements of the 7th Division on its left.

(X) Liaison between advancing elements east and west of the Moselle will be maintained by all means possible. Strong combat liaison between all advancing elements will be maintained and liaison from front to rear will be given particular attention.

(Y) Division reserve will await orders in alert positions.

4. Administrative instructions follow.

5. P. C.'s later.

By command of Major General Ballou.

(Signed) ALLEN J. GREER,
Colonel, General Staff.
Chief of Staff.

The detailed dispositions of the infantry and artillery units in each of these C. R.'s (Centers of Resistance) are shown in the annexed reports of the Commanding General, 183rd Brigade, Commanding General 167th Field Artillery Brigade, and the C. O. 367th Infantry, which are hereto appended, and marked appendices "D," "E," and "F" respectively.

(2) *The Attack—A Chronological Statement of Enemy Units Engaged—Time and Place.*

**1918**

9 November, 23 hour. Instructions received from 6th Army Corps in advance of F. O. No. 4, 6th Army Corps, 10 November, 1918, relative to projected offensive along front of 2nd Army.

9 Nov. 23 hr.—Instructions given to C. G. 183rd Brig., C. G. 167th F. A. Brig., C. O. 337th Inf., relative to projected attack and in advance of F. O. No. 24, Hqs. 92nd Div., issued.

10 Nov. 3 hr.—10 November, 1918, at 3 hours. The exact time when these instructions were received and detailed action taken shown on appended reports.

10 Nov. 4 hr.—Received F. O. No. 4, Hqs. 6th Army Corps, dated 10 November, 3:30 hrs., prescribing attack and confirming telephone instructions.

10 Nov. 7 hr.—Attack initiated along front east of Moselle between Moselle and Seille Rivers. Division reserve in alert position at the time of the attack.

10 Nov. 8 hr.—Information received that the French Division on right was not attacking, whereupon C. O. 365th Infantry was directed to hold 3rd Battalion in C. R. Seille maintaining liaison with the French on right.

10 Nov. 9:30 hr.—Attack by 367th Infantry west of Moselle not prosecuted because of failure of the 56th Infantry, 7th Division, to capture Preny. The report of the C. O. 367th Infantry at pages 2 and 3 shows the facts and reasons.

10 Nov. 11 hr.—All first objectives east of Moselle were attained. The exact progress of the attack and orders and messages sent and received are

shown clearly in the appendices. They are not reproduced in great detail here.

11 Nov. 1:40 hr.—C. G. 184th Brig. directed to proceed with two remaining battalions and other remaining combat elements of the 184th Brigade to Forêt de Facq, locating P. C. at crossroads at 382.5—233.3. Field and combat trains to same position after dark. Command to be placed off road awaiting employment.

11 Nov. 3:59—Artillery directed to put down barrage on northern edge of Bois de la Voivrotte, this point not being occupied by our troops.

11 Nov. 4:13—Five o'clock advance called off. Divisional Artillery and 6th Corps notified. Advance troops directed to organize first position.

11 Nov. 16:30—Received F. O. No. 5, 6th Army Corps, 10 November, 1918, 18 hr., directing continuation attk.

10 Nov. 18 hr.—Issued F. O. 25, Hqs. 92nd Division, 10 November, 1918, 18 hr. (Annxd. as appendix "G"), continuation of attack directed.

11 Nov. 5 hr.—Attack launched on front of 183rd Brigade between Seille and Moselle Rivers, direction as before.

7:10 hr.—Information from 6th A. C. received that armistice had been signed, effective 11 hr., 11 November, 1918. Attacking troops met by strong enemy artillery, machine-gun and infantry fire.

11 Nov. 10:45 A. M.—All firing by our troops ceased in accordance with armistice.

### (3) *Statement of Enemy Units Engaged, Time and Place.*

Inasmuch as the 367th Infantry operating west of the Moselle made no advance due to the fact that it was necessary that the 7th Division should first capture Preny before an advance was practicable. No report is made here of enemy units engaged west of Moselle. The same condition applies under subheads (4) and (5) of this report. The report of the Commanding General of the 183rd Brigade under these heads is adopted with some modifications as the report of the Division and to that extent is embodied herein.

The enemy units engaged by elements of the 183rd Brigade between the Moselle and the Seille were, from west to east, the 96th and 30th regiments of infantry, 31st Landwehr Brigade, and the 47th Infantry regiment. These regiments were supported by one battalion of sharpshooters. East of the Seille River the 70th Infantry regiment and the 6th Grenadiers, formerly 10th Division, were encountered. See report of the Commanding General 183rd Brigade, appended.

### (4) *Summary.*

Our advance was for a depth of 3½ km. When this Brigade took over the sector just east of the Moselle River there was a deep re-entrant next to the river, due to the St. Mihiel drive, which advanced the line several kms.

on the west bank of the Moselle, while the line on the east bank remained in place.

The attack on the morning of the 10th of November, by one battalion, 365th Infantry, and the Machine Gun company of that regiment, and one battalion 366th Infantry supported by Company C, 350th Machine Gun Battalion, wiped out this re-entrant, by advancing our lines on the east bank of the Moselle River a distance of 2½ km.

The advance thus made was held against heavy artillery and machine-gun fire and high concentration of gas. The attack was renewed on the morning of the 11th, the lines being advanced to the northern edge of the Bois Frehaut, a distance of 3½ km. from an original line. Our liaison with the troops west of the line was thereby greatly improved.

The line held by our troops at the cessation of hostilities was as follows: (Details already given).

A total of six prisoners were captured, three in the Bois Frehaut and three in the Bois Voivrotte.

The following material was captured: 1,000 grenades, 5,000 rounds of ammunition, 25 boxes of M-G ammunition in belts, 50 rifles and belts, 10 pair of field glasses, 4 machine-guns, 6 carrier pigeons, 1 signal lamp and battery, 2 Verey pistols, 3 carbide lamps, 100 helmets, many overcoats, boots, canteens, belts, and other equipment left by the fleeing Germans.

The following were our casualties:

|  | Killed | Wounded | Gassed | Missing | Total |
|---|---|---|---|---|---|
| 365th Infantry ........... | 14 | 67 | 211 | 8 | 300 |
| 366th Infantry .......... | 17 | 52 | 63 | 0 | 132 |
| 350th M-G Battalion...... | 1 | 0 | 11 | 0 | 12 |
| Total for Brigade..... | 32 | 119 | 285 | 8 | 444 |

Full use was made of auxiliary arms for this attack—Machine-guns, 37-mm. guns, Stokes mortars, and rifle grenades.

No tank or gas troops were available for the action.

The Divisional Artillery supported both attacks, with a rolling barrage preceding the troops in placing heavy concentration fire on enemy strong points and machine-gun nests.

The attack was executed over a very difficult terrain. For a distance of about 1½ km. in front of our lines the terrain was open, heavily wired, with a downward slope. It was well registered by the enemy artillery as the numerous shell-holes over its surface indicated. The Bois Frehaut is a wood of about 1,500 meters square and breaks the western half of the sector attacked, about 700 meters to the east of the Bois Frehaut, and about on a line with the southern edge of the Bois Voivrotte, a small wood of about 600 square meters. Both of these woods were a mass of heavy German wire, much of it new. Their edges were protected by heavy bands of wire and chevaux-de-frise. Both of these woods were at the foot of and north of the ridge of which Eon hill, a hill 358 meters high, is the summit. From their southern slopes, the ground rises slightly for a distance of about 700 meters, then falls again to a deep ravine traversing the Bois Frehaut from east to west. It then rises again, culminating in La Cote hill, a hill 1,500 meters north of Bois Frehaut and 87 meters higher than the highest point of the Bois Frehaut, namely Hill 260.8. This hill is heavily wooded on its summit and strongly held by infantry, machine guns, trench mortars and light artillery. The southern slopes of this hill were protected by a small wood about 500 meters square, about 200 meters north of the Bois Frehaut and by the strongly fortified towns of Bouxières and Champey. These towns together with the small wood in question were heavily garrisoned by infantry and machine guns. They formed together a dominating and strongly organized position protected by heavy bands of wire. Numerous tank traps had been prepared south of this position. These positions dominated the Bois Voivrotte, the Bois Frehaut and the ground to their north. In the area west of the Moselle, the ground in front of the position slopes to the north into a basin with little or no cover. On the west Preny heights rise precipitously out of the plain and the town and citadel dominate the entire basin up to Preny and beyond.

This basin is enfiladed from the right by enemy artillery N. E. to S. E. over an arc of 140 degrees in part by direct fire. Moulon creek crosses the basin from west to east about 1 km. in front of position.

Creek line formerly held by enemy as advanced night outpost, taken by us and held for same purpose. This line in daylight can be reached by infiltration or by patrols but owing to flanking fire from Preny has been found untenable except at night, any small body of troops attracting both machine-gun and artillery fire under conditions of fair visibility.

At the time of our attack east of the Moselle, there was no general retirement immediately on our front. A vigorous resistance was interposed by the enemy. The attack was made on very brief preparation, too brief in view of the strength of the enemy positions, which were very strongly held. The wire entanglements about Bouxières rendered a very considerable artillery preparation necessary to make a further advance possible. The attack was to have been continued with this preparation had not the armistice occurred. A decided improvement in offensive spirit and aggressive action was shown by all troops engaged.

(Signed) CHARLES H. MARTIN,
Major General Commanding.

## After the Armistice Was Signed

Immediately following the signing of the armistice, the 92nd Division was named among those divisions scheduled to embark for the United States in the first available transportation. The various units of the division were withdrawn gradually from front line positions to back areas for rest and renovation.

At this time the rail facilities of France were taxed to the utmost in transporting supplies into the area to be occupied by the allied armies according to the terms of the armistice. In addition to the hundreds of troop trains going forward daily, all wagon roads leading toward the region of the upper Rhine were crowded with troops forming the army of occupation. After waiting five weeks at Marbache, transportation was finally supplied and the Division moved down to Maronne for entrainment on the 19th of December, 1918. Leaving Maronne between the 19th and 22nd of December the elements of the Division arrived at Mayenne, in the zone of the embarkation center, on the morning of the 24th of December. Pending orders to move forward to Brest, the units of the Division were billeted in the following towns and villages: Mayenne, Ambrières, Domfront, La Chapelle, Couterne, Lassay, Villaines, Javron. In this section, formerly a part of old Brittany, many evidences remain of the earliest days of the country's settlement. One of the principal roads leading through the section was laid out by Julius Caesar, more than fifty years before the birth of Christ; at Domfront the old fort built by the Roman legions remains in a remarkable state of preservation. The language of the ancient Bretons is often spoken by the people at this time.

Five weeks were spent in this area completing preliminaries incident to embarkation and waiting for transportation to the seaboard. The last units left Mayenne on the 29th of January, passing through the forwarding camp at Le Mans and arriving at Brest the first week in February. The first transports left Brest bearing our troops homeward on the 5th of February and were followed by others throughout the month and until the 12th of March, when the last unit of the 92nd Division landed at Hoboken, completing nine months of foreign service.

## Casualties of the Division

The total number of casualties in the 92nd Division was as follows:

| | Officers | Enlisted Men |
|---|---|---|
| Killed in action | 6 | 208 |
| Died of wounds | 1 | 40 |
| Died of Disease | 1 | 43 |
| Died of other causes | 0 | 9 |
| Severely wounded | 6 | 203 |
| Slightly wounded | 46 | 348 |
| Gassed | 43 | 672 |
| Missing | 0 | 20 |
| | 103 | 1,543 |

Total—1,646

## Personal Conduct of Troops

The statistics of the Judge Advocate's Department show that the individual conduct of the soldiers of the 92nd Division was highly creditable. Both in number of offenses committed against military law and the nature of the offenses, the record of the 92nd·Division compares most favorably with that of any other Division in the American Expeditionary Forces. The only case of a conviction with death penalty assessed applied to a soldier who was not a member of the 92nd Division, but whose trial was held in the Division's courts for convenience.

During the month of October, twelve hundred enlisted men were granted furloughs with privilege of visiting Aix-les-Bains, the leave center for soldiers of the American Expeditionary Forces. The report of the Commanding Officer of Aix-les-Bains leave area is referred to in the copy of General Order 31 given below:

HEADQUARTERS 92ND DIVISION
AMERICAN EXPEDITIONARY FORCES
A. P. O. 766

7·November, 1918.

General Orders No. 31.

1. The Division Commander desires to make known to the members of this command the fact of his appreciation of the exemplary conduct of the

men composing the first and second leave quotas at Aix-les-Bains during October, 1918.

The Commanding Officer of Aix-les-Bains reports that the neatness, general appearance, and military courtesy of the men of the 92nd Division while on leave, was highly commendable.

By Command of Major General Ballou.

(Signed) ALLEN J. GREER,

Colonel, General Staff,

Chief of Staff.

OFFICIAL:

EDW. J. TURGEON,

Major, Infantry.

Adjutant.

### The Artillery Brigade

From the outset of the 92nd's organization, it was a problem to get together and build up an artillery brigade that would in all essentials be thoroughly efficient and dependable. In such warfare as the European war entailed, the artillery arm was of the greatest importance. It was doubted whether or not an artillery brigade made up of Negro soldiers could be developed and sufficiently trained in the technique of artillery to make an effective fighting artillery unit. Men were needed for this branch of the service who were educated and who could be depended upon to know fractions and be able to read scales, deflections, and other technical details. In the ordinary run of the enlistment, the draft did not furnish enough men qualified along these lines to build up the artillery regiments, and it therefore became necessary for the officers of the artillery brigade to make special canvasses to secure a sufficient number of qualified men. In this work, voluntary enlistments were called for. In the course of time enough men were enlisted to make up the Artillery Brigade. Tuskegee Institute furnished a group of students. Baltimore, Pittsburg and other cities furnished men from the high schools and other institutions. Through this special canvass the great bulk of the artillery troops was secured.

In recruiting these men, specially qualified for the artillery regiments, through the process of voluntary enlistments, much credit is due the following officers of the Brigade: General John H. Sherburne, Colonels Fred T. Austin, William E. Cole, Dan T. Moore; Lieutenant-Colonels Walter E. Prosser, Edward L. Carpenter,

Charles L. Blakely; Captains Royal F. Nash, William Heffner, and Lieut. Harry K. Tootle. The last named officer made personal canvasses in the churches and schools of Pittsburg and other cities.

As a result of this plan of building up the Artillery Brigade, the three regiments were made up of picked men, forming the first artillery brigade of Negroes ever organized in the world. During the training period and afterward on the battlefield, General Sherburne frequently expressed the opinion that his artillerymen were the equals of any artillerymen in the American Expeditionary Forces. Even during the short time in which the artillery was engaged, the high degree of efficiency was evidenced by the accuracy and effectiveness of their barrages and bombardments as laid down by these Negro gunners.

The following is a copy of the last General Order issued to the Brigade by General Sherburne just before his transfer from the Division to take up other duties:

HEADQUARTERS 167TH FIELD ARTILLERY BRIGADE
92ND DIVISION, A. E. F.

3 February, 1919.

General Orders No. 1.

1. In leaving the 167th Field Artillery Brigade, to take up other duties, the Brigade Commander wishes to record in General Orders the entire satisfaction it has given him to have commanded the Brigade, the first Brigade of Negro artillerymen ever organized. The satisfaction is due to the excellent record the men have made. Undertaking a work that was new to them, they brought to it faithfulness, zeal, and patriotic fervor. They went into the line and conducted themselves in a manner to win the praise of all. They had been picked for important work in an offensive which had been planned to start after November 11.

2. The Brigade Commander will ever cherish the words of the Commander-in-Chief, the compliments he paid in all sincerity to this Brigade, while he watched it pass in review last Wednesday. He wishes the Brigade to understand that these words of appreciation were invoked because each man has worked conscientiously and unflaggingly to make the organization a success.

3. The Brigade Commander feels that he should also make an acknowledgment in General Orders of the remarkable esprit-de-corps displayed by the officers of the brigade. They were pioneers in a field where, at the start, success was problematical. This being the first brigade of its kind ever organized, it has been only natural that the work of the men should have

featured prominently, yet the same prominence and the same praise should be accorded the officers. While the Brigade Commander takes this occasion to praise splendid work, he believes the greatest praise will come from the men themselves, not only now, but ever in greater measure when they have returned to civilian life and have secured the perspective of time and experience that will teach them how fortunate they were in making the race's initial effort as artillerymen under officers who were both skillful artillerymen and sympathetic leaders.

By Command of Brigadier General Sherburne.

(Signed) HARRY KING TOOTLE,
First Lt. F. A., U. S. A.
Acting Adjutant.

### Praised by General Pershing

The passage in the foregoing General Order from General Sherburne, in which allusion is made to the compliments from the Commander-in-Chief, refers to the address delivered to the assembled units of the 92nd Division at Le Mans on the 28th of January, 1919. On this occasion General Pershing reviewed the troops of the Division for the last time before its embarkation for the United States. In the course of his address to the officers and soldiers of the Division, the Commander-in-Chief, General Pershing, said:

"I want you officers and soldiers of the 92nd Division to know that the 92nd Division stands second to none in the record you have made since your arrival in France. I am proud of the part you have played in the great conflict which ended on the 11th of November, yet you have only done what the American people expected you to do and you have measured up to every expectation of the Commander-in-Chief. I realize that you did not get into the game as early as some of the other units, but since you took over your first sector you have acquitted yourselves with credit, and I believe that if the armistice had not become effective on the 11th day of November, the 92nd would have still further distinguished itself. I commend the 92nd Division for its achievements not only in the field, but on the record its men have made in their individual conduct. The American public has every reason to be proud of the record made by the 92nd Division."

The following memorandum, issued on the date on which Major General Ballou left the Division as Commander to take up other duties to which he had been transferred, marks the last official order from the officer to whom, more than to any other individual, is due the credit for organizing and training the first Division of American Negro soldiers ever placed in the field:

HEADQUARTERS 92ND DIVISION
American Expeditionary Forces
A. P. O. 766

18 November, 1918.

*Memorandum:*

Five months ago today the 92nd Division landed in France.

After seven weeks of training, it took over a sector in the front line, and since that time some portion of the Division has been practically continuously under fire.

It participated in the last battle of the war with creditable success, continuously pressing the attack against highly organized defensive works. It advanced successfully on the first day of the battle, attaining its objectives and capturing prisoners. This in the face of determined opposition by an alert enemy, and against rifle, machine-gun and artillery fire. The issue of the second day's battle was rendered indecisive by the order to cease firing at eleven A. M.—when the armistice became effective.

The Division Commander, in taking leave of what he considers himself justly entitled to regard as *his* Division, feels that he has accomplished his mission. His work is done and will endure. The results have not always been brilliant, and many times were discouraging, yet a well organized, well disciplined and well trained colored Division has been created and commanded by him to include the last shot of the war.

May the future conduct of every officer and man be such as to reflect credit upon the Division and upon the Colored race.

By Command of Major General Ballou:

(Signed)   ALLEN J. GREER,
Colonel. General Staff,
Chief of Staff.

OFFICIAL:
EDW. J. TURGEON,
Major, Infantry,
Adjutant.

## Changes in Official Personnel

Through the process of transfers and promotions, many changes occurred in the official personnel of the numerous elements of the 92nd Division. The same was true on a larger scale of the entire

American Expeditionary Forces. In keeping with military methods of promotions, transfers, etc., every promotion, transfer, or discharge resulted in a chain of promotions or transfers or vacancies in all units affected. Through this method, every unit of the A. E. F. experienced a continual changing and shifting of its official personnel. This was true of Field officers as well as Staff officers. Among the names of officers who made up the Staff of the 92nd Division when it sailed for France in 1918, not one was on the roster when the Division returned.

The following synopsis, with military record, of the Division Commanders gives an idea of the changes in the General Staff:

*Commanding General:—*

1. Major General CHARLES C. BALLOU: Born in Orange, Schuyler County, New York, June 13, 1862. Entered West Point June 6, 1882, by appointment from Fourth District, Illinois. Graduated June 12, 1886. Commissioned 2d Lt., 16th Infantry, July 1, 1886, and served in that regiment in Texas, Utah, and Sioux campaign of 1890-91 in South Dakota. Promoted 1st Lt., 12th Infantry, April 23, 1893. Served in Florida, Alabama, Oklahoma, Nebraska, Kansas, Georgia, Illinois, Virginia, Pennsylvania and Missouri. Mustered in 8th and 9th Illinois Volunteers at Camp Tanner, 1898. Promoted Captain, 12th Infantry, March 2, 1902. Served in that regiment as captain in the Philippine Insurrection, during which time he' participated in several battles and small actions. Name sent to Senate by President Roosevelt for confirmation for brevet of Major for "distinguished gallantry in action near Anzeles, Luzon, P. I.," August 16, 1899. Quartermaster 12th Infantry. Transferred to 15th Infantry February, 1904. Quartermaster 15th Infantry. Commissary 15th Infantry. Transferred to 12th Infantry, February, 1906. Detailed in Quartermaster Department October, 1908. Promoted Major 7th Infantry, June 26, 1909. Duty in Quartermaster General's office 1909-10. Transferred to 24th Infantry in 1912. Lt. Colonel 24th Infantry February 7, 1915. Commanded 24th Infantry during portion of campaign in Mexico. Colonel of Infantry July 19, 1916. Conducted Training Camp for Colored Officers, Ft. Des Moines, Iowa, 1917. Brigadier General, August, 1917. Commanded Depot Brigade, Camp Dodge, Iowa, September and October, 1917. Major General, November 28, 1917. Organized, trained and commanded 92nd Divi-

sion, October 26, 1917, to November 19, 1918. Attended Infantry and Cavalry School at Ft. Leavenworth Field Officers' School, and War College. Five times in Philippine Islands. Sailed for France June 10, 1918. On front line August 24 to November 19, 1918.

2. Major General CHARLES H. MARTIN: Commanded 86th Division prior to transfer to 92nd Division. Organized 86th Division at Camp Grant, Ill. Camp Commander Camp Grant, Ill., 1917-18. Commanded 92nd Division from November 19, 1918, to December 15, 1918.

3. Brigadier General JAMES B. ERWIN: Cadet U. S. Military Academy June 12, 1875. Second Lieutenant, Cavalry, June 12, 1880. First Lieutenant, 4th Cavalry, March 18, 1886. Captain, 4th Cavalry, March 18, 1896. Major, 9th Cavalry, April, 1903. Lieutenant Colonel, Inspector General's Department, May, 1911. Colonel, January, 1914. Brigadier General, August, 1917. With 82nd Division to December 27, 1917. Organized and served with 6th Division to December 14, 1918. Commanding 92nd Division since December 15, 1918. Honor Graduate Infantry and Cavalry schools, class 1883. Inspector General 1906-10 and 1911-15. Adjutant General September, 1914-August, 1915. Served in Indian wars, Philippine Insurrection, Punitive Expedition in Mexico, and European War, 1914-18.

*Aides-de-Camp:*—

Staff of General Ballou—Captain Chauncey Dewey.

Staff of General Martin—Captain J. E. Eddy, Captain E. H. Spencer, Captain Gordon McCormick.

Staff of General Erwin—Lieutenant Charles H. Cox, Lieutenant Henry B. Tompkins.

*Chiefs of Staff:*—

1. Colonel ALLEN J. GREER: Appointed Second Lieutenant, 4th Tennessee Volunteers, July 5, 1898. Second Lieutenant 4th Infantry, October 5, 1899. Appointed First Lieutenant, July 1, 1901. Transferred to 26th Infantry, September 29, 1904. Twenty years continuous service in grades of second and first lieutenants, captain and major in regular army. Appointed Lieutenant Colonel and assigned to duty as Chief of Staff, 92nd Division, November 2, 1917. Promoted to rank of Colonel, August, 1918. Continuous service as Chief of Staff with 92nd Division until December 4, 1918.

2. Colonel GEORGE K. WILSON: Regular Army, May 1, 1898.

Second Lieutenant, Infantry, June, 1900. First Lieutenant, May, 1904. Captain, April, 1915. Major, August, 1917. Lieutenant Colonel, June, 1918. Colonel, October, 1918. Transferred to 92nd Division as Chief of Staff, December 4, 1918.

*Assistant Chiefs of Staff:—*
Lieutenant Colonel James P. Barney, Major Frederick P. Schoonmaker, Lieutenant Colonel Van L. Willis, Major Charles S. Buck, Major Donald J. McLachlan, Lieutenant Colonel John D. Sayles, Major Harding Polk, Major H. L. Taylor, Lieutenant Colonel James L. Cochran.

*Division Adjutants:—*
Major Sherburne Whipple, Captain Edward J. Turgeon (Acting), Major Alfred E. Sawkins, Major Ralph H. Leavitt, Major Edward J. Turgeon.

*Division Inspectors:—*
Major Robert P. Harbold, Major Clifford D. Davidson, Major Clifford B. King, Major Clifford D. Davidson.

*Division Quartermasters:—*
Colonel Edward L. Glasgow, Major Odiorne H. Sampson, Major Joseph T. Byrne.

*Division Surgeon:—*
Lieutenant Colonel Perry L. Boyer, Lieutenant Colonel Jonas T. White.

*Division Ordnance Officer:—*
Major Philip S. Gage, Captain Warner F. Russell.

*Division Judge Advocate:—*
Major Alfred M. Craven, Major Adam E. Patterson.

### Visitors to the Division

During the sojourn of the 92nd Division in France, several distinguished visitors, all of whom were interested in war work of one phase or another, called at headquarters, or visited camps where our troops were quartered.

In July, Miss Elsie Janis, famous actress and movie star, in company with her mother, visited the Division at Bourbonne-les-Bains. The coming of Miss Janis had not been generally announced.

It was therefore only a small group of soldiers whom she entertained in an impromptu program in the city park on the afternoon of her visit.

Mr. Ralph W. Tyler, of Columbus, Ohio, editor and writer, and formerly Auditor of the Navy under President Roosevelt, visited the Division during the month of October and remained throughout several weeks in the Marbache sector. Mr. Tyler visited a number of organizations of Negro troops not included in the 92nd Division. During his tour he represented the Committee on Public Information.

Dr. R. R. Moton, principal of Tuskegee Institute, in company with Mr. Thomas Jesse Jones, national educator, Mr. Nathan Hunt of Tuskegee Institute, and Mr. Lester A. Walton, of the New York Age, visited the Division in December at Marbache. Dr. Moton came as the representative of the administration at Washington and directly from the War Department to bring official greetings to Negro troops in France. Dr. Moton discharged this mission in a manner creditable to himself and to the race.

Dr. John Hope, President of Moorehouse College, Atlanta, Georgia, energetic Y. M. C. A. worker, visited the Division from time to time in connection with Y. M. C. A. work.

Dr. W. E. B. DuBois, editor and writer, visited the Division during the months of December and January.

# CHAPTER XII

## CITATIONS AND AWARDS, 92ND DIVISION

*Officers and Men of the Famous Negro Division Whose Heroic
Conduct Gained for Them the Distinguished Service Cross—
Details of Their Deeds of Heroism in Action—Special Mention
of Officers and Men by Various Commanding Officers.*

The gallant Ninety-second Division, composed entirely of colored
American troops, received a great number of citations and awards
for meritorious and distinguished conduct on the battlefields of
France, and besides those who earned the coveted medals there were
many more members of the Division who were specially mentioned
in communications from Headquarters and by the commanding
officers of the various units, as appears hereafter. The lists given
below, however, are necessarily incomplete, as many recommendations for awards were still under consideration when this volume
went to press.

The following is reproduced from a January (1919) issue of the
Army and Navy Journal:

"COLORED TROOPS OF THE A. E. F. VARIOUSLY HONORED."

"Colored troops forming the 92nd Division of the A. E. F. have
recently been awarded many honors. The entire 1st battalion of the
367th Infantry have been cited for bravery and awarded the Croix
de Guerre by the French military authorities.

"The citation was made because of the bravery and fine service
of the battalion in the last engagement of the war, the drive toward
Metz on November 10 and 11.

"Major-General Martin, U. S. A., commanding the 92nd Division, has cited a number of colored officers, noncommissioned officers
and privates of the 365th Infantry for meritorious conduct in action
at *Bois Frehaut* on November 10 and 11. The officers cited are
Captain John L. Allen, Lieuts. Leon F. Stewart, Frank L. Drye,

Walter Lyons, David W. Harris, Benjamin F. Ford, George L. Gains, and Russell C. Atkins, all U. S. A. In another order, Lieut. Nathan O. Goodloe, of the machine-gun company of the 368th Infantry, was commended for meritorious conduct in the Argonne Forest. In the entire Division, fourteen colored officers and forty-three enlisted men have been cited for bravery in action and awarded the Distinguished Service Cross. The total casualties suffered by the Division since its arrival in France number 1,748. Of officers, six were killed in action and one died of wounds; 46 officers were wounded and 39 gassed. Of enlisted men, 31 died of wounds, 203 were killed in action, 543 were wounded, 661 were gassed, 40 died of disease, and 28 were reported missing."

The following letter of commendation is self-explanatory:

HEADQUARTERS FIRST BATTALION, 367TH INFANTRY

FROM: Commanding Officer, 1st Battalion, 367th Infantry.

TO: Commanding Officer, 367th Infantry.

SUBJECT: Conduct of Company A.

1. I wish to call attention of the regimental commander to the meritorious conduct of Company A on the night of November 2 and 3.

2. Under intense shell fire of gas and H. S. lasting two hours, the company maintained its advanced positions, staying there without any shelter and finally repelling the enemy raid and capturing one prisoner.

3. The conduct of Captain Peter McCall, his officers and men was such as deserves the highest commendation, and in my opinion merits mention.

(Signed) CHARLES L. APPLETON,

Major, 367th Infantry.

Extended space would be required to detail the meritorious work of the individual units of the Division throughout the several operations in which it participated. In the Argonne-Meuse offensive, after overcoming its first extreme difficulties, the 368th Infantry performed gallant service. Among the officers whose conduct was mentioned for gallantry in the Argonne were Captain T. M. Dent, promoted after commendation for special bravery and heroism; Captain R. A. Williams, who also won commendation of his regimental commander for skillful handling of his troops in the crucial advance through the Argonne; Lieut. Charles G. Young and Captain Thomas E. Jones, of the 368th, who each won the D. S. C. for extraordinary heroic service and gallant conduct in the Argonne Forest.

Of the 367th Regiment, the unit organized and trained by Colonel James A. Moss, much could be said of its excellent record, both in the St. Die sector and in the Argonne and on the Moselle in front of Metz. In this last-named position it rendered its most distinguished service during the closing days of the war. On the 10th of November, an attack was made on Pagny, a stronghold of the German line opposite the Metz forts. In the general advance, two battalions of the 56th Infantry, a white unit on the left of the 367th, after advancing a half mile abreast of the 367th, became hopelessly entangled in the enemy's wire entanglements and were being slaughtered by German machine-gun batteries. Our own advance was stopped, and a part of the 367th was sent to the rescue of the 56th in order to cover their withdrawal from the perilous position. The 367th dispatched two machine-gun companies, one of their own and the other from the 350th machine-gun battalion. A counter fire was turned on the German positions, which silenced their batteries, while the 56th retired leaving a third of their men dead or wounded. In the meantime the 367th held the position until relieved by reinforcements from the 56th and then resumed their advance toward Pagny. Doubtless the entire forces of the 56th would have been wiped out but for the timely rescue of the 367th. For this action the entire battalion was cited by the French commanding officer under whom the 56th was brigaded.

### Awarded the Distinguished Service Cross

The Distinguished Service Cross of the United States was awarded to the following officers and men of the 92nd Division, for the heroic deeds and exploits stated after their respective names:

HORTON, VAN, Corporal, Company E, 366th Inf. (A. S. No. 2168859). Medal Number 431. For extraordinary heroism in action near Lesseau, France, 4 September 1918.

During a hostile attack, preceded by a heavy minenwerfer barrage, involving the entire front of the battalion, the combat group to which this courageous soldier belonged was attacked by about twenty of the enemy, using liquid fire. The sergeant in charge of the group and four other men having been killed, Corporal Horton fearlessly rushed to receive the attack and the persistency with which he fought resulted in stopping the attack and driving back the enemy.

Home address: Mrs. Minnie Horton, mother, Route 5, Box 93, Athens, Ala.

Medal presented to above named soldier Dec. 2, 1918, near Pont-à-Mousson.

FISHER, AARON R., 2nd Lieut., 366th Infantry, Medal No. 432. For extraordinary heroism in action near Lesseau, France, 3 September 1918.

Lieut. Fisher showed exceptional bravery in action when his position was raided by a superior force of the enemy by directing his men and refusing to leave his position although he was severely wounded. He and his men continued to fight the enemy until the latter were beaten off by counter attack.

Home address: Benjamin Fisher, father, General Delivery, Lyles, Indiana.

Lieut. Fisher was evacuated to Base Hospital No. 45, Sept. 18, 1918, consequently his medal was not presented to him while in the Division.

WILLIAMS, JOE, Pvt., Company E, 366th Inf. (A. S. 2169035). Medal No. 433. For extraordinary heroism in action near Lesseau, France, 4 September 1918.

Private Williams was a member of a combat group which was attacked by twenty of an enemy raiding party, advancing under heavy barrage and using liquid fire. The sergeant in charge of the group was killed and several others, including Private Williams, were wounded. Nevertheless, this soldier with three others fearlessly resisted the enemy until they were driven off.

Home address: Mrs. Carrie Gordon, friend, Octon, Ala.

Medal presented to above named soldier Dec. 2, 1918, near Pont-à-Mousson.

BROWN, ROY A., Pvt., Co. E, 366th Inf. (A. S. 2168841). Medal No. 434. For extraordinary heroism in action near Lesseau, France, 4 September 1918.

Private Brown was a member of a combat group which was attacked by twenty of an enemy raiding party, advancing under a heavy barrage and using liquid fire. The sergeant in charge of the group was killed and several others, including Private Brown, were wounded. Nevertheless, this soldier with three

**SECRETARY BAKER'S WAR CABINET.**

*Top Left to Right*—Hon. Benedict Crowell, Assistant Secretary of War; Hon. E. R. Stettinius, Second Assistant Secretary of War; Dr. Ernest Martin Hopkins, President Dartmouth College, Special Assistant.

*Center*—Hon. Newton D. Baker, Secretary of War.

*Below*—Dr. F. B. Keppel, Third Assistant Secretary of War; General P. C. March, Chief of Staff U. S. Army, and Dr. Emmett J. Scott, Special Assistant to the Secretary of War, representing the interests of the Negro Race of the United States

GROUP OF COLORED OFFICERS.

*Top, Left to Right*—1st Lt. B. A. Jackson, 350th Mchn. Gun Bn.; 1st Lt. Abraham Morse, 367th Infantry; 1st Lt. Herman L. Butler, 366th Infantry.
*Center*—Capt. Wm. B. Campbell, Personnel Adj. 317th A. T.; 1st Lt. Chas. H. Fearing, 365th Infantry; Capt. Alonzo Campbell, 367th Infantry.
*Below*—1st Lt. Geo. B. Cooper, 367th Infantry, Supply Officer; 1st Lt. Benjamin F. Ford, 365th Inf.; 1st Lt. Anderson Trapp, 366th Inf.

*Above*—Negro troops returning to camp behind the lines after a strenuous day on the Western Front during operations on the Marne.
*Center*—Officers of Dental Corps attached to various units of the 92nd Division. With the exception of Capt. Jacob Brause, Division Dentist, all were Negroes.
*Below*—The American Red Cross knew no color line and sought to render the same service to Colored as to White troops.

CONFERENCE GROUP COLORED EDITORS in Washington during the war.
Reading left to right. *Front Row.*—Former Gov. P. B. S. Pinchback, Charles W. Anderson, Maj. L. P. DeMonial, Dr. Emmett
J. Scott, Chairman, Col. Edouard Requin, Dr. Robert R. Moton, Judge R. H. Terrell, Dr. W. E. B. DuBois, Major J. E.
Spingarn, Chris J. Perry, Rev. Ernest Lyon.
*Second Row.*—W. H. Steward, Dr. A. M. Curtis, W. T. Andrews, Dr. W. H. Davis, Benj. J. Davis, Henry A. Boyd, R. S. Abbott,
John Mitchell, Jr., J. H. Murphy, G. W. Knox, J. A. E. Manning.
*Third Row.*—Dr. Maurice Curtis, Dr. H. M. Minton, J. C. Dancy, H. C. Smith, E. A. Warren, C. K. Robinson, J. E. Mitchell,
Ralph W. Tyler, R. W. Thompson, N. C. Crews.
*Fourth Row.*—Dr. S. A. Furniss, R. C. Bruce, P. B. Young, Geo. W. Harris, Dr. W. H. Brooks, Jas. A. Cobb, Dr. J. R.
Hawkins, C. N. Love, W. J. Singleton, W. L. Houston, Wm. E. King.
*Fifth Row.*—Dr. R. E. Jones, Maj. A. W. Washington, Robt. L. Vann, A. H. Grimke, Prof. Geo. W. Cook, Capt. Arthur S
Spingarn, F. H. Moore.

*Left*—Colonel Charles Young, Veteran Ranking Negro Officer of the Regular U. S. Army. Commissioned from West Point. Detailed to active service at Camp Grant during the war. *Right*—Major General Enoch H. Crowder, Provost Marshal General of the United States Army.

Top, Left—Capt. Moody Staten, 317th Military Police. *Center* 2nd Lt. Charles Udell
   Turpin, 365th Infantry. *Below*—1st Lt. E. C. Morris, 366th Infantry.
*Center Panel*—Major James E. Walker, 1st Separate Battalion, District of Columbia N. G.
*Top, Right*—Capt. Thos. E. Jones, 368th Infantry, 92nd Div., Awarded Distinguished Service
   Cross for bravery at Argonne Forest.
*Right Center*—Capt. Samuel Reid, 317 A. T., Veteran of Spanish War and Philippine In-
   surrection; served over thirty years in United States Army, retired since close of the
   war.
*Below*—Sergt. Rufus Pinckney, Baltimore, Md., 1st Separate Company, 372nd Inf., wears
   highest honors from French Government; captured 15 Germans, saved French
   Officer's life, fought in Champagne, Argonne and at Verdun

## GROUP OF LEADING WOMEN WAR WORKERS.

**Center**—Miss Eva D. Bowles, Secretary of Colored Women's War Work in cities, National Board of the Young Women's Christian Association.

**Above, Left**—Miss May B. Belcher, Field Worker among colored women of War Work Council; a graduate of Sargent School, studied at Moody Institute and later Secretary of Phyllis Wheatley Branch, Y. W. C. A. in St. Louis.

**Right**—Alice Dunbar Nelson (formerly Mrs. Paul Laurence Dunbar), recognized leader in mobilization of colored women of the United States for War Work under auspices Council of National Defense.

**Below, Left**—Miss Mary E. Jackson, Special Industrial Worker among colored women for War Work Council.

**Right**—Mrs. Louise J. Ross, Chairman New Orleans Chapter American Red Cross, recognized leader of the race in the South

*Above*—American Negro Soldiers in hospital, Glasgow, Scotland, receiving cigarettes and chocolates from Red Cross Chaplain Thos. E. Swan and a visit from Mrs. Jas. Gardiner, one of the Red Cross Workers.

*Below*—Sergeants of Headquarters Company 372nd Infantry "somewhere in France" just before the big drive.

others fearlessly resisted the enemy until they were driven off.

Home address: Mrs. Ellen Brown, mother, 620 Madison St., Decatur, Ala.

Medal presented to above named soldier Dec. 2, 1918, near Pont-à-Mousson.

MERRIFIELD, ED., Private, Co. E, 366th Inf. (A. S. No. 2817823). Medal No. 435. For extraordinary heroism in action near Lesseau, France, 4 September 1918.

Although he was severely wounded, Private Merrifield remained at his post and continued to fight a superior enemy force which had attempted to enter our lines, thereby preventing the success of an enemy raid in force.

Home address: Mrs. Lucinda Merrifield, mother, Greenville, Illinois.

Private Merrifield was evacuated to Base Hospital No. 17, Sept. 30, 1918, consequently his medal was not presented to him while in the Division.

HAMMOND, ALEX., Private, Co. E, 366th Inf. (A S. No. 2169003). Medal No. 436. For extraordinary heroism in action near Lesseau, France, 4 September 1918.

Although he was severely wounded, Private Hammond remained at his post and continued to fight a superior enemy force which had attempted to enter our lines, thereby preventing the success of an enemy raid in force.

Home address: Will Hammond, father, Rt. 1, Harvest, Ala.

Private Hammond was evacuated to Base Hospital No. 17, Sept. 30, 1918, consequently his medal was not presented to him while in the Division.

BELL, GEORGE, Private, Co. E, 366th Inf. (A. S. No. 2168986). Medal No. 437. For extraordinary heroism in action near Lesseau, France, 4 September 1918.

Although he was severely wounded, Private Bell remained at his post and continued to fight a superior enemy force which had attempted to enter our lines, thereby preventing the success of an enemy raid in force.

Home address: Mrs. Clara Bell, mother, Rt. 2, Athens, Ala.

Private George Bell, Co. E, 366th Inf., deceased, Sept. 16, 1918.

CLINCY, WILL, Private 1st Cl., Company F, 366th Inf. (A. S. No. 2169151). Medal No. 438. For extraordinary heroism in action near Frapelle, France, 4 September 1918.

Private Clincy showed exceptional bravery during an enemy raid. His teammate on an automatic rifle having been mortally wounded and although he was himself severely wounded, he continued to serve his weapon alone until the raid was driven back.

Home address: John Clincy, father, 2616-6th Alley, N. Birmingham, Ala.

Private 1st Class Will Clincy, Co. F, 366th Inf., was evacuated to Base Hospital (no record of number), Sept. 4, 1918, consequently his medal was not presented to him while in the Division.

YOUNG, CHARLES G., First Lieut., 366th Infantry. Medal No. 931. For extraordinary heroism in action near Binarville, France, 27-28 September 1918.

Lieutenant Young, while in command of a scout platoon, was twice severely wounded from shell fire, but refused medical attention and remained with his men, helping to dress their wounds and to evacuate his own wounded during the entire night, and holding firmly his exposed position covering the right flank of his battalion.

Home address: Mrs. Millie G. Young, wife, 1802 Greenlaw St., Austin, Texas.

WATKINS, LEWIS, Private 1st Class, Co. A, 350th Machine Gun Battalion (A. S. No. 2816183). Medal No. 1139. For extraordinary heroism in action near Eply, France, 4 November 1918.

Private 1st Class Watkins accompanied an infantry patrol, acting as gunner with a heavy machine gun. When a large party of the enemy had worked around the flank of the patrol and was advancing across a road along which the patrol was withdrawing, Private Watkins went into action with his gun at a range of less than 100 yards, although the order to withdraw had been given. Displaying exceptional coolness and bravery under heavy rifle and machine-gun fire, he succeeded in dispersing the enemy. He was the last of the patrol to retire.

Medal presented to above named soldier December 2, 1918, near Pont-à-Mousson.

LAWRENCE, JACKSON S., Major Medical Corps, 368th Infantry. Medal No. 1052. For extraordinary heroism in action at Binarville, France, 30 September 1918.

Major Lawrence with two soldiers voluntarily left shelter and crossed an open space fifty yards wide, swept by shell and machine-gun fire, to rescue a wounded soldier, whom they carried to a place of safety.

Home address: Mrs. Florence McC. Lawrence, wife, 405 S. 42nd St., Philadelphia, Pa.

Medal presented to above Officer November 26, 1918, at Villers-en-Haye.

DAVIS, THOMAS H., Private 1st Class, Sanitary Detachment, 368th Infantry (179930). Medal No. 1053. For extraordinary heroism in action at Binarville, France, 30 September 1918.

Private Davis with an officer and another soldier voluntarily left shelter and crossed an open space fifty yards wide, swept by shell and machine-gun fire, to rescue a wounded soldier, whom they carried to a place of safety. ·

Home address: Mrs. Francis Davis, mother, 49 West Lincoln St., Hampton, Va.

Medal presented to above named soldier November 26, 1918, at Villers-en-Haye.

HANDY, EDWARD H., Private 1st Class, Company B, 368th Infantry (1799754). Medal No. 1054. For extraordinary heroism in action at Binarville, France, 30 September 1918.

Private Handy with an officer and another soldier voluntarily left shelter and crossed an open space fifty yards wide, swept by shell and machine-gun fire, to rescue a wounded soldier, whom they carried to a place of safety.

Home address: Mrs. Rosena Gibson, sister, 2627½ Virginia Ave., Washington, D. C.

Medal presented to above named soldier November 26, 1918, at Villers-en-Haye.

RIVERS, TOM, Private, Co. G, 366th Inf. (No. 2169507). Medal No. 1633. For extraordinary heroism in action near the Bois de la Voivrotte, France, 11 November 1918.

Private Rivers, although gassed, volunteered and carried important messages through heavy barrages to the support companies. He refused first aid until his company was relieved

Home address: Mrs. Cornelia Rivers, wife, R. F. D. 2, Box 7, Opelika, Ala.

Medal presented to above named soldier December 11, 1918, at Maron.

Lewis, Bernard, Private, Co. A, 368th Infantry. Medal No. 858. For extraordinary heroism in action near Binarville, France, 30 September 1918.

Private Lewis, during an attack on Binarville, volunteered to go down the road that leads into the village, to rescue a wounded soldier of his company. To accomplish his mission, he was compelled to go under heavy machine gun and shell fire. In total disregard of personal danger he brought the wounded man safely to our lines.

Home address: Mrs. Martha Lewis, mother, 135 E. St., N. W., Washington, D. C.

Medal presented to above named soldier November 8, 1918, at Villers-en-Haye.

James, Joseph, Hqrs. Co., 368th Infantry (1798927). Medal No. 1731. For extraordinary heroism in action near Binarville, France, 30 September 1918.

Private James went to the aid of a wounded companion under very severe machine-gun and artillery fire and brought him to cover. He stayed with the wounded man, giving him all possible aid until assistance came, when he returned to his place with the platoon.

Home address: Mrs. Martha James, mother, 1622 N. Alder St., Philadelphia, Pa.

Medal presented to above named soldier January 2, 1919.

Jones, Thomas Edward, 1st Lieut., Med. Corps, 368th Inf. Medal No. 1844. For extraordinary heroism in action near Binarville, France, 27 September 1918.

Lieutenant Jones went into an open area subjected to direct machine-gun fire to care for a wounded soldier who was being carried by another officer. While dressing the wounded runner a machine-gun bullet passed between his arms and his chest and a man was killed within a few yards of him.

Home address: Mrs. Leonie Jones, wife, 509 O St., N. W., Washington, D. C.

Medal presented to above Officer January 2, 1919.

BRECKENRIDGE, ROBERT M., Private 1st Class (Deceased), Company H, 365th Infantry (1967624). For extraordinary heroism in action at Ferme de Bel Air, France, 29 October 1918.

Although severely wounded in the leg from shell fire, Private Breckenridge, an automatic rifleman, continued in action, crawled forward for a distance of 100 yards to a position where he obtained a better field of fire, and assisted preventing an enemy party from taking a position on the company's flank. In spite of his wound, Private Breckenridge continued to use his weapon with great courage and skill until he was killed by enemy machine gun fire.

Next of kin: Amelia Wilson, mother, Route 5, Box 95, Hennessey, Oklahoma.

POLLARD, RUSSELL, Corporal, Co. H, 365th Infantry (1967745). Medal No. 1899. For extraordinary heroism in action at Bois Frehaut, France, 10 November 1918.

During the assault at Bois Frehaut, Corporal Pollard, a rifle grenadier, conducted his squad skillfully in firing on hostile machine guns, until his rifle was broken. He then used his wire-cutters with speed and skill under heavy shell and machine-gun fire. Although wounded in his right arm, he continued to cut the wire with his left hand, and assisted his men in getting through it, until ordered to the dressing station a second time by his company commander.

Home address: Caroline Pollard, mother, Weatherford, Texas.

PURSLEY, EARL, Private 1st Class, Medical Detachment, 366th Infantry (2170837). Medal No. 1900. For extraordinary heroism in action near Lesseux, France, 4 September 1918.

Private Pursley voluntarily carried a wounded soldier from an exposed position under intense enemy shell fire for a distance of 400 yards to dressing station. He then immediately returned to the position and helped to dig out men who had been buried by the explosion of a shell.

Home address: Earl Pursley, father, General Delivery, Hickman, Ky.

Medal presented to above named soldier 2 January 1919.

## Special Mention of Officers and Men

There were issued from Headquarters of the 92nd Division and also by the Commanding Officers of the various units of the 92nd Division through successive periods expressions of special commendation of various officers and soldiers. Among those which may be quoted are the following:

Company M, 368th Infantry,
Trench Brealau, 94.1-71.75,
3 October, 1918.

*FROM:*      The Commanding Officer, Co. M. 368th Inf.
*TO:*          The Commanding Officer, 3rd Battalion.
*SUBJECT:*   Lt. T. M. Dent, 368th Inf.

1. I desire to call the attention of the Battalion Commander to the work of First Lieutenant T. M. Dent, 368th Infantry, during the days covering the advance from Vienne-le-Chateau.

2. Lieut. Dent was the only officer present with me during the greater part of that time and his conduct was at all times characterized by fearlessness and initiative. His platoon captured a German automatic rifle which covered the bridge crossing the Vallee Moreau and he later on the same day, 28th September, led his platoon to the wire in front of Trench Clotilde at 92.5-73.5, but owing to heavy machine-gun fire from his right was unable to remain there or to penetrate the unbroken wire.

3. In the event of another detail from this Company to the First Corps Schools, I request that this officer be given the opportunity to further increase his value to the service by attending said schools.

R. H. WILLIAMS,
Captain, 368th Infantry,

—

Headquarters 92nd Division,
Army Post Office No. 766.
American Expeditionary Forces.
October 11, 1918.

General Orders No. 27.

1. The Commanding General desires to call the attention of the entire command to the excellent work and meritorious conduct of Captain R. A. Williams and First Lieutenant T. M. Dent, both of the 368th Infantry. During the days of the fight around Vienne-le-Chateau both of these officers

displayed courage and leadership, and their conduct should be an example to the other officers of the Division.

2. The Division Commander desires to commend the conduct of Private Philip Estrada (1766914), Battery A, 350th Field Artillery, who at the risk of his own life saved Corporal Alfred Tinson (1767196), Battery B, 350th Field Artillery, from drowning on or about the 8th day of August, 1918.

By Command of Major General Ballou.

(Signed)  ALLEN J. GREER,
Lieut.-Colonel, General Staff,
Chief of Staff.

—

HEADQUARTERS 92ND DIVISION
A. P. O. 766

28 November, 1918.

General Orders No. 35.

* * *

II. PVT. BERT WALKER, 367th Infantry.

The Division Commander desires to commend in orders the meritorious conduct of Pvt. Bert Walker, 367th Inf. Pvt. Walker, on November 9, 1918, in the vicinity of Villers-sous-Preny—after it was learned that the road leading to Villers-sous-Preny had been so heavily shelled by gas shells as to make it almost impassable—volunteered to assist in carrying gas masks down this road to organizations in position, and made several trips through this gassed area, helping to equip and protect against a heavy gas attack which troops were later subjected to.

III. LIEUT. E. B. WILLIAMS, 367th Infantry.

The Division Commander desires to call the attention of the entire command to the excellent work and meritorious conduct of Lieut. E. B. Williams, 1st Battalion Gas Officer, 367th Infantry. During the action around Villers-sous-Preny this officer was gassed, but maintained his post until all shellholes were properly covered and his entire area free from gas. Lieut. Williams refused to rest until ordered to do so by his superior officer.

By Command of Major General Martin.

(Signed)  ALLEN J. GREER,
Colonel, General Staff,
Chief of Staff.

Official:
EDW. J. TURGEON,
Major, Infantry, U. S. A.,
Adjutant.

29th November, 1918.

General Orders No. 36.

I.  2ND LIEUT. NATHAN O. GOODLOE, 368th Infantry.

The Division Commander desires to call the attention of the entire command to the excellent work and meritorious conduct of 2nd Lieutenant Nathan O. Goodloe, Machine Gun Company, 368th Infantry.  During the operations in the Forêt D'Argonne, September 26 to 29, 1918, this officer was attached to the 3rd Battalion of his regiment, and on September 28, during the course of action, it became necessary to reorganize the Battalion and withdraw a part of it to a secondary position, and he rendered valuable assistance.  The movement was carried out under a continual machine-gun fire from the enemy, and Lieut. Goodloe's calm courage set an example. that inspired confidence in his men.

II.  WAGONER TOM BROWN (1725697), Hq. Det., 351st M. G. Bn.

The Division Commander desires to commend in orders the meritorious conduct of Wagoner Tom Brown, 1725697, Headquarters Detachment, 351st . Machine Gun Battalion, who, as driver with a combat wagon carrying ammunition to organizations going into action near Vienne-le-Chateau, in the Argonne Forest, on September 27, 1918, displayed marked devotion to duty, exceptional coolness, and great courage under fire.  The ammunition was hauled over a shell-swept road and Wagoner Brown insisted on completing his work, even after his wagon and horses had been hurled into a ditch; he, despite a painful injury, worked faithfully until he had extricated his horses, and his conduct was such as to merit having it called to the attention of members of the Division as worthy of emulation.

By Command of Major General Martin.

(Signed)  ALLEN J. GREER,
Colonel, General Staff,
Chief of Staff.

Official:
EDW. J. TURGEON,
Major, Infantry,
Adjutant.

1st December, 1918.

General Orders No. 37.

1.  The Division Commander desires to commend in orders for meritorious conduct in action at Bois Frehaut near Pont-à-Mousson, France, November 10-11, 1918, the following named officers and enlisted men:

Major E. B. Simmons, Regimental Surgeon, 365th Infantry;
Captain John H. Allen, Machine Gun Company, 365th Infantry;
1st Lieut. Leon F. Stewart, 2nd Bn. Scout Officer, 365th Infantry;
1st Lieut. Frank L. Drye, Company "E", 365th Infantry;
1st Lieut. Walter Lyons, Company "G", 365th Infantry;
1st Lieut. Bravid W. Harriss, Company "H", 365th Infantry;
1st Lieut. Benjamin F. Ford, Company "H", 365th Infantry;
2nd Lieut. George L. Gaines, Company "G", 365th Infantry;
2nd Lieut. Russell C. Atkins, Company "H", 365th Infantry;
Sergeant Richard W. White, 2073368, 2nd Bn. Scouts, 365th Infantry;
Sergeant John Simpson, 2074325, M. G. Co., 365th Infantry;
Sergeant Robert Townsend, 1967208, Company "E", 365th Infantry;
Sergeant Solomon D. Colston, 2073518, Company "E", 365th Infantry;
Sergeant Ransom Elliot, 1967307, Company "G", 365th Infantry;
Supply Sergeant Charles Jackson, 2073816, Company "H", 365th Inf.;
Corporal Thomas B. Coleman, 1967082, Company "E", 365th Infantry;
Corporal Albert Taylor, 2091596, Company "E", 365th Infantry;
Corporal Charles Reed, 2073745, Company "G," 365th Infantry;
Corporal James Conley, 2073730, Company "G", 365th Infantry;
Private 1st Class Jesse Cole, 2817706, Company "G", 365th Infantry;
Private 1st Class Earl Swanson, 1967391, Company "G", 365th Inf.;
Private 1st Class James Hill, 2091205 (deceased), Co. "H", 365th Inf.;
Private 1st Class Charles White, 2089235, Company "H", 365th Inf.;
Private George Chaney, 2655690, Company "H", 365th Infantry.

II. The Division Commander desires to commend in orders for meritorious conduct in action as specified below, the following named officers and enlisted men:

During action near Frapelle, France, September 3, 1918:
Sergeant Isaac Hill, 2169092, Company "F", 366th Infantry.
During action near Lesseux, France, September 7, 1918:
1st Lieut. John Q. Lindsey, Company "E", 366th Infantry.
During action near Heminville, France, November 10-11, 1918:
1st Lieut. Edward W. Bates, Medical Corps, Ambulance Co. No. 368;
Sergeant Werter L. Gross, 2167835, Company "A", 366th Infantry.

By command of Major General Martin:

        (Signed) ALLEN J. GREER,
           Colonel, General Staff,
             Chief of Staff.

Official:
EDW. J. TURGEON,
Major, Infantry, U. S. A.,
Adjutant.

HEADQUARTERS NINETY-SECOND DIVISION
Army Post Office No. 766
American Expeditionary Forces

6th December, 1918.

General Orders No. 38.

I. SERGEANT RUFUS B. ATWOOD, 1974547, 325th Field Signal Battalion.

The Division Commander desires to call the attention of the entire command to the excellent work and meritorious conduct of Sergeant Rufus B. Atwood, 1974547, 325th Field Signal Battalion. On the morning of November 10, 1918, while returning to the switchboard in Pont-à-Mousson, a shell struck the house in which the switchboard was being operated, breaking all the lines. Sergeant Atwood rendered valuable assistance to the officer in charge in reconstructing the switchboard and connecting new lines under heavy shell fire. When the ammunition dump began to explode in the same neighborhood, he remained on the job, tapping new connections. After repairs were made from the first explosion, there were two to follow which completely wrecked the switchboard room and tore out all the lines which were newly fixed. Sergeant Atwood was left alone, and he established a new switchboard and the same connections they had at first. The coolness with which he went about his work and the initiative he took in handling the situation justifies his being mentioned in orders.

II. PRIVATE CHARLES E. BOYKIN (Deceased), Co. "C", 325th Field Signal Bn.

The Division Commander desires to commend in orders the meritorious conduct of Private Charles E. Boykin, Company C, 325th Field Signal Battalion. On the afternoon of September 26, 1918, while the 368th Infantry was in action in the Argonne Forest, the Regimental Commander moved forward to establish a P. C. and came upon a number of Germans, who fled to the woods, which were found to be alive with machine guns. The Commanding Officer ordered the woods searched to the top of the hill, the officer in charge of the scouting called for volunteers, and Private Boykin, a telephone lineman, offered his services and set out with the rest of the detail. While trying to flank an enemy machine gun another opened fire, killing him instantly.

By command of Major General Martin:

(Signed)   ALLEN J. GREER,
Colonel, General Staff,
Chief of Staff.

Official:
EDW. J. TURGEON,
Major, Infantry, U. S. A.,
Adjutant.

HEADQUARTERS 92ND DIVISION

A. P. O. 766

16 November, 1918.

General Orders No. 32.

I. The Commanding General wishes to call the attention of the command to the excellent and meritorious conduct of the following officers and enlisted men:

Major Warner A. Ross, 365th Infantry.

Captain William W. Green, 365th Infantry.

Sergeant Rufus Bradley, 2073505, Company E, 365th Infantry.

Bugler Junius Jules, 2075822, Company H, 365th Infantry.

During the advance of November 10, 1918, in the action of Bois Frehaut, these officers and men displayed such exceptional bravery and coolness under fire as to merit commendation in orders.

This order will be read to the command at first assembly after its receipt.

II. The Commanding General wishes to call the attention of the command to the excellent and meritorious conduct of the following officers and enlisted men of Company A, 366th Infantry:

1st Lieutenant William H. Clark, 1st Lieutenant William Jones, 1st Sergeant Eugene Love, Sergeant Gus Hicks, Sergeant Richard Parker, Sergeant James E. Green, Corporal John H. James, Corporal Fred Lewis, Corporal Ben L. Moore, Bugler Irvin Turpin, Pvt. 1st Cl. Fred Littlejohn, Pvt. 1st Cl. Ed Martin, Pvt. 1st Cl. Riley Porter, Pvt. 1st Cl. Ames Robertson, Pvt. 1st Cl. Mathew Rose, Pvt. 1st Cl. Lonnie Rice, Pvt. 1st Cl. Richard Wells, Pvt. 1st Cl. Henry Williams, Private Conce Cooks, Private Willis Coles, Private Charles Dozier, Private Frank W. Franklin, Private Harvey Hite, Private Leonard Morton, Private Clarence Leake.

In the action near Bois de Voivrotte, France, on November 11, 1918, these officers displayed such excellent qualities of leadership and courage, and the men such heroic conduct and attention to duty under fire, as to merit commendation in orders.

This order will be read to the command at first assembly after its receipt.

By command of Major General Ballou.

(Signed)   ALLEN J. GREER,
Colonel, General Staff,
Chief of Staff.

Official:

EDW. J. TURGEON,
Major, Infantry, U. S. A.,
Adjutant.

HEADQUARTERS 372ND INFANTRY
S. P. 179, France
Granges, Vosges.

December 23, 1918.

(1383)

FROM:        The Acting Adjutant.
TO:          Captain Clarence S. Janifer, 92nd Division, American E. F.,
             France.
SUBJECT:     Decoration.

1. It is with pleasure that I inform you that you have been awarded a Croix de Guerre with citation in the orders of the 157th Division. The approval of the award was received from the Personnel Section, G. H. Q., American E. F., on December 14th.

2. The citation is as follows:

*1st Lieut. Clarence S. Janifer, M. C. Surgeon 3rd Battalion 372nd Infantry.*

"Fearless to danger, established his First Aid Post on the battlefield in front of Bussy Farm September 28, 1918, following the Battalion in the open fields, giving help and relief to the wounded and dying at first hand."

Pending the receipt of the official citation from the 157th Division, this letter will serve as authority for the wearing of the Croix de Guerre with a silver star.

(Signed)   PRESTON F. WALSH,
             Captain Infantry, U. S. A.

I certify that the above letter is a true copy.

. T. T. THOMPSON,
             1st Lt., Inf., U. S. A.

——

There were many such commendations of individual soldiers issued during the period of the stay of the 92nd Division in France.

No officer in the 92nd Division won the respect and devotion of his men more completely than did Brigadier-General Malvern-Hill Barnum, commanding the 183rd Brigade. That General Barnum felt a deep attachment to his command is shown by the following letter addressed to the entire brigade:

A. P. O. 714, France.
22 December, 1918.

From:      Malvern-Hill Barnum, Brigadier-General, U. S. A.
To:        The Officers and men of the 183rd Brigade.
Subject:   Relief from command.

The order detaching me from command of the 183rd Brigade was unexpected and coming, as it did, just as the Brigade was moving, made it impossible for me to give expression to my regret at having to sever an association of over a year and one that will be one of the pleasantest recollections of my Army career.

Having organized and trained the 183rd Brigade and commanded it through its active service in the present war, I can speak for the willing compliance to all requirements that made the work very enjoyable. When men work with their hearts as well as their heads and hands, the best results are certain to follow.

I feel that the officers and enlisted men of the Brigade may justly be proud of the record made and I believe that history will accord them no little credit.

I trust that each one will do his utmost to insure to the Brigade the finest record possible during the remainder of its period of service.

Finally in returning to their homes I trust that each one will take with him a high sense of responsibility as an American citizen and a keen desire to perform faithfully whatever duties fall to him in the future.

With such a heritage from his Army service each one will not only have helped win the war and thus rendered a great service to humanity, but will himself have become the gainer through the remaining years of his life.

(Signed)  MALVERN-HILL BARNUM.

This letter will be published to all members of the command at the earliest opportunity.

By order of Colonel Parrott.

Hq. 366th Infantry.                                    (Signed)  R. D. McCORD,
December 24, 1918.                                        Capt. and Adjt., 366th Inf.

# CHAPTER XIII

## THE STORY OF "THE BUFFALOES"

*Glorious Record of the 367th Infantry Regiment—Colonel James A. Moss—Presentation of Colors at the Union League Club— The "Buffaloes" in France—How They "Saw It Through" at Metz—Their Heroic Conduct Under Fire—Regimental Colors Decorated by Order of the French High Command—A Tribute From France to "These Sunburned Americans."*

Quite naturally, and with pardonable pride, all the officers and men of each unit of the 92nd Division regard their particular unit as having contributed most to the glory of that Division and to the record of the achievements of Negro troops upon battlefields overseas. However, it will probably not be disputed that the 367th U. S. Infantry was, in some respects, the most notable unit of the 92nd Division.

The 367th Regiment was organized at Camp Upton, N. Y., on November 3, 1917, pursuant to Order No. 105, War Department, 1917, and Special Order No. 72, Headquarters 77th Division, 1917. Colonel James A. Moss, Lieutenant Colonel William G. Doane, Majors Charles L. Mitchell, Fred W. Bugbee and William H. Edwards were assigned to and joined the regiment, 3rd November, 1917, per Order No. 105, War Department, 1917.

Pursuant to telegraphic instructions from the War Department, 2nd November, 1917, Major Henry N. Arnold, Inf. R. C., was transferred to the regiment *vice* Major William H. Edwards, transferred to the 306th Machine Gun Battalion.

The Captains of the regiment (with the exception of the Regimental Adjutant, Commanding Officers' Headquarters and Supply Companies), also the 1st and 2nd Lieutenants, graduated from the Officers' Training Camp, Fort Des Moines, Iowa, were assigned to and joined the regiment 3rd November, 1917, per Special Order 72, Headquarters 77th Division, 1917.

190

The Regimental Adjutant, Captain Frederic Bull; Commanding Officer, Headquarters Company, Captain Benjamin F. Norris, and Supply Officer, Captain Charles L. Appleton, were transferred to the regiment 3rd November, 1917, from the 152nd Depot Brigade, 77th Division, per Special Order No. 72, Headquarters 77th Division, 1917.

The enlisted personnel of the regiment was assigned from selective draft men, who joined as follows:

In November, 1917: New York, N. Y., 1,198; Camp Devens, Mass., 22; Camp Custer, Mich., 301; Camp Lewis, Wash., 100.

In December, 1917: Camp Travis, Tex., 300; Camp Pike, Ark., 600; Camp Lee, Va., 300.

Six enlisted men from the Regular Army were transferred to the regiment.

During the period, 3rd November, 1917, to 31st December, 1917, the troops of the regiment were given training and instruction daily, Saturdays, Sundays, and holidays excepted, in the prescribed course of instruction for officers and men.

The field officers, regimental adjutant, regimental supply officer, regimental surgeon, and the commanding officers of the Headquarters Company, nine in all, were white, while all the company officers (87), except the commander of the Headquarters Company; the medical officers, except the regimental surgeon; the dental surgeons, and the chaplain, 97 in all, were colored officers. The colored officers, with the exception of the chaplain, were all graduates of the Fort Des Moines (Iowa) Officers' Training Camp.

The enlisted men (3,699) were drafted from various parts of the country, quotas having come from Camp Devens, Camp Custer, Camp Lewis, Camp Lee, Camp Pike, Camp Travis, and about 1,500 from New York and Brooklyn. An enlisted training cadre of 19 men was assigned to the regiment from the 25th U. S. Infantry.

Being trained at Camp Upton, near New York City, the attention of the metropolitan press was focused upon this particular regiment, which was commanded by a Southern officer, Colonel James A. Moss, a West Point graduate, who was born in Louisiana. Colonel Moss early began to put the 367th Infantry "on the map" after the regiment was organized; first by speaking before the Union League Club and other important organizations in the City of New York, and by the formation of the 367th Infantry Welfare League, the object of which was to keep open the line of communication with the home ties that the colored soldiers had left behind. Colonel Theodore Roosevelt became its Honorary President, following an address he made to the men of the regiment at Camp Upton, October 18, 1917. Colonel Roosevelt was delighted with the regimental singing and was fervent in his praise of the men. The officers of the League were: Colonel Theodore Roosevelt, Honorary President; Hon. Charles W. Anderson, First Vice-President; Dr. W. M. Moss, Second Vice-President; Dr. William Jay Schieffelin, Treasurer; Captain Walter B. Williams, Secretary; George W. Lattimore, Field Secretary, and Colonel James A. Moss, Commandant, 367th Infantry.

This regiment paraded with the 77th Division through the streets of New York City on the occasion of the celebration of George Washington's birthday, February 22, 1918, and was acclaimed by the metropolitan press as presenting a fine soldiery appearance; this was especially noteworthy in view of the fact that nearly one-half of the men had been drafted from the far South and had come up from cotton plantations and fields without previous military experience.

### Union League Club Presents Colors

A particularly notable incident in connection with the stay of the 367th Infantry at Camp Upton was the "presentation of colors" by the Union League Club on Saturday, March 23, 1918. The Union League Club during the Civil War always stood firmly and boldly for equal rights of American citizens, regardless of color. It decided, in 1863, to enlist Negroes of New York State in the Union Army and within one month raised $18,000 for that purpose and in November, 1863, one thousand and twenty Negroes—a regiment—were in training on Riker's Island. There remained in addition six hundred men, who formed the skeleton of a second regiment which the club subsequently raised. These regiments were known during the Civil War as the Twentieth and Twenty-sixth U. S. Colored Troops. Later the club assisted in the recruiting of two more colored regiments. The recruiting of Negro soldiers, however, was not regarded with general favor. The then Governor

Above—A group of colored clerks employed in the Bureau of War Risk Insurance.
*Front Row*, Left to Right—Miss V. L. Comer, Atlanta, Ga.; Mrs. F. Alston, Mobile, Ala.; Mr. W. Bernard Gardner, Philadelphia, Pa.; Miss V. B. Adams, Washington, D. C.; Miss F. M. Botteese, Washington, D. C.; Miss B. Kebble, Waco, Tex.
*Second Row*, Left to Right—Miss C. J. Tarby, Boston, Mass.; Miss E. M. Cameron, Birmingham, Ala.; Mrs. H. L. Johnson, Washington, D. C.; Miss E. R. Nelson, Laurel, Miss.; Mrs. E. T. Albert, Washington, D. C.
*Below*—Officials of Young Men's Christian Association Department for Colored Troops.
*Front Row*, Left to Right—Wm. J. Faulkner, Placement; Jesse E. Moorland, Executive Secretary; Robert B. DeFrants, Personnel.
*Back Row*, Left to Right—Geo. L. Johnson, Religious Work; Max Yergan, Overseas; J. Francis Gregory, Religious Work.

*Above*—Group of Depot Company Sergeants of the 372nd Infantry behind the lines
waiting for orders to advance.
*Below*—Truck Train of 365th Infantry unloading troops at Bruyères. It required the
services of 500 big army trucks for three days and nights to transport the 92nd
Division from Bourbonne-les-Bains to this point in the Vosges zone.

*Above*—Group of typical French Colonials. These Senegalese Troops were brought directly from the Colonies in Africa for the war, as fully related in Chapter X of this volume.

*Below*—German prisoners of war being brought into camp by the Negro soldiers who surprised a large detachment and took them prisoners.

This group of Colored physicians served during the war as lecturers under Captain Arthur B. Spingarn, Surgeon General's Office, U. S. Army, visiting camps and cantonments and instructing Negro soldiers upon the subject of Sex Hygiene. Center—Captain Arthur B. Spingarn. Left, top—Dr. Ralph Burnette Stewart of Washington, D. C. Below—Dr. C. V. Roman, Nashville, Tenn. Right, top—Dr. A. B. Jackson, Philadelphia, Pa. Below—Dr. Roscoe C. Brown of Richmond, Va.

*Left*—Motor Corps Women did much for the comfort of sick and wounded during the war and after. Two are here shown doing their bit in helping a wounded hero from ambulance into a theatre where a show was given for wounded Colored soldiers.

*Right*—One of the thousands of Young Negro American Boy and Girl Red Cross Workers who took part in the Nation-wide drive for war funds.

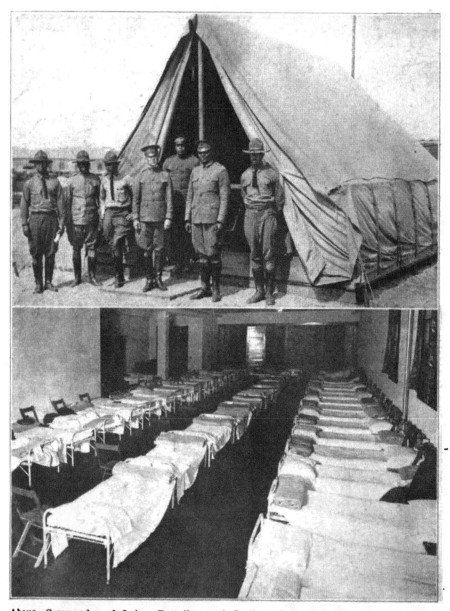

*Above*—Commander of Labor Battalion and Staff at Governor's Island. Capt. E. S. Jones was Commander of the U. S. Labor Battalion stationed at this point.
*Below*—Baltimore War Camp Community Circle. Some of the beds at the War Camp Community Service Colored Club which is typical of many such clubs organized throughout the entire United States.

*Above*—Group of colored woman war workers of the New Orleans Chapter of American Red Cross.

*Below*—Negro Sailors enjoying a few hours' "liberty" in the restrooms, American Red Cross Headquarters, New Orleans.

No. 2461-5-5

### AMERICAN EXPEDITIONARY FORCES

*Corps Expéditionnaires Américains*

IDENTITY CARD
*CARTE D'IDENTITÉ*

Name *Dee Jones*
Nom

Rank *Captain 366th Inf.*
Grade

Duty *Supply 366th Inf.*
Fonction

Signature
of Holder

Signature
du Titulaire *Dee Jones*

*Above, Left*—Ernest P. Attwell, who did organization work among the colored people for Food Administration. *Center*—1st Lt. Denton J. Brooks, Regimental Insurance Officer, 365th Infantry, who covered members of his regiment with over $29,000,000 War Risk Insurance. *Right*—Chas. H. Williams, Special Investigator for Committee on Welfare of Negro troops and conditions existing among Negro soldiers in camps and war camp community centers.

*Below*—Capt. Dee Jones, and sample Identification Card printed in English and French carried by all American soldiers of Expeditionary Forces in Europe. On each identity card was shown photo of its owner and a number corresponding with metal tag worn by each soldier of New York State not only refused his authority, but withheld his sanction of the movement, and it became necessary for the Union League Club to obtain the proper authority from the War Department at Washington. It was not a matter of surprise, then, that the Union League Club decided to present a "stand of colors" to the 367th Infantry that comprised so large a number of colored draftees from New York City and State for service in the World War.

The 367th Infantry regiment was a part of the first contingent of the 92nd Division that sailed for overseas, leaving the port of embarkation at Hoboken, N. J., on June 19, 1918, and arriving at Brest, France, on June 29, 1918. The regiment made a notable record in France—the entire First Battalion of the 367th (Buffalo) Infantry being cited for bravery and awarded the Croix de Guerre, thus entitling every officer and man in the battalion to wear this distinguished French decoration. This citation was made by the French Commission because of the splendid service and bravery shown by this battalion in the last engagement of the war, Sunday and Monday, November 10 and 11, in the drive to Metz. *This battalion went into action through a valley commanded by the heavy German guns of Metz, and held the Germans at bay while the 56th Regiment retreated, but not until it had suffered a heavy loss.* In the record of operations of the 92nd Division as a whole, the detailed statement of the glorious part played by the 367th Infantry (see Chapters XI and XII) will be noted. It may be said that this unit lived up to its regimental motto—*"SEE IT THROUGH."*

Particular reference is made to this regiment (the 367th U. S. A.), not only because its splendid record at home and achievements overseas merits special mention, but also for the purpose of bringing out in bold relief the fact that it is possible for a white man born and bred in the South to learn to appreciate the real worth of the Negro soldier and, whenever placed in command of them, to treat them as all American soldiers should be treated and to accord to them a full measure of respect, opportunity, and credit. This has been notably true in the case of Colonel James A. Moss, Commanding Officer of the regiment, who enjoyed the confidence and even the affection of the men of his command. It will be interesting, in this connection, to read the tribute which he paid to the Negro as a soldier and military officer, and which was issued as an "*Introduction*" to a booklet concerning his regiment of colored soldiers:

STATEMENT BY

COLONEL JAMES A. MOSS, COMMANDING 367TH INFANTRY, U. S. A.

"Having been born and reared in the State of Louisiana, whose confines I did not leave until I went to West Point at the age of eighteen, and having served eighteen years with colored troops, including two campaigns, what I say about the colored man as a soldier is therefore based on many years' experience with him in civil life and in the Army—in peace and in war, in garrison and in the field.

"If properly trained and instructed, the colored man makes as good a soldier as the world has ever seen. The history of the Negro in all of our wars, including our Indian campaigns, shows this. He is by nature of a happy disposition; he is responsive and tractable; he is very amenable to discipline; he takes pride in his uniform; he has faith and confidence in his leader; he possesses physical courage—all of which are valuable military assets.

"The secret of making an efficient soldier out of the colored man lies in knowing the qualities he possesses that are military assets, and which I have named, and then appealing to and developing them—that is, utilizing them to the greatest extent possible.

"Make the colored man feel that you have faith in him, and then, by sympathetic and conscientious training and instruction, help him to fit himself in a military way to vindicate that faith, to 'make good.' Be strict with him, but treat him fairly and justly, making him realize that in your dealings with him he will always be given a square deal. Commend him when he does well and punish him when he is refractory—that is to say, let him know that he will always get what is coming to him, whether it be reward or whether it be punishment. In other words, treat and handle the colored man as you would any other human being out of whom you would make a good soldier, out of whom you would get the best there is in him, and you will have as good a soldier as history has ever known—a man who will drill well, shoot well, march well,

obey well, fight well—in short, a man who will give a good account
of himself in battle, and who will conduct and behave himself
properly in camp, in garrison and in other places.

"I commanded colored troops in the Cuban campaign and in
the Philippine campaign, and I have had some of them killed and
wounded by my very side. At no time did they ever falter at the
command to advance nor hesitate at the order to charge.

"I am glad that I am to command colored soldiers in this, my
third campaign—in the greatest war the world has ever known.

(Signed)   "JAS. A. Moss,<br>"Colonel 367th Infantry."

Colonel Moss has the reputation of being one of the best-
known military authors in the world. He has written twenty-six
military books, of which several have been for years regarded as
standard. His "Manual of Military Training" has been called
the "Encyclopædia Britannica of the Army." His "Officers'
Manual," a guide in official and social matters, is used by prac-
tically every young officer entering the Army. His "Privates'
Manual" was adopted several years ago by the United States
Marine Corps, and a copy is placed in the hands of every recruit.
Other books of his, such as "Non-Commissioned Officers' Manual,"
"Army Paperwork," "Infantry Drill Regulations Simplified,"
"Field Service," "Riot Duty," "Company Training," and
"Applied Minor Tactics," are also regarded as standards among
all military men. Since his graduation from West Point in 1894
Colonel Moss's service has been distinguished. It includes a record
of three campaigns. In addition, he was aide-de-camp for three
years to Lieutenant-General Henry C. Corbin, during which time,
although only a captain in the Regular Army, he had the rank, pay,
and allowances of lieutenant-colonel. For three years he was
instructor at the Army Service Schools, Fort Leavenworth,
Kansas. In 1911 and 1912 he was on special duty in the office of
the Chief of Staff of the Army, General Leonard Wood, by whom
he had been specially selected to reduce and simplify the administrative work of the Army. Not only is he the father of the present
system of Army correspondence, but he also gave to the service
the new, simplified pay and muster rolls, and several other labor-

saving blank forms that have done much to reduce military administrative work.

Perhaps the secret underlying the splendid relations that continually existed between this Southern white Army officer and the colored soldiers and officers of his command, is partly disclosed in the brief biographical sketch of his military career given above, for, whenever a *THOROUGHLY EDUCATED WHITE MAN* meets the *EDUCATED TYPE AND BETTER CLASS OF NEGRO MEN*, like most if not all of those comprising the officer-group of the 367th Regiment, the difficulties connected with the so-called Race Problem are simplified and reduced to the minimum.

The success of the 367th U. S. Infantry therefore strongly suggests (1) that whenever white men are put in command of Negro troops they should be of that high intellectual and moral caliber that will enable them to appreciate, bring forth, and develop the best that is in the colored men of their command; and (2) that Negro officers are more and more demonstrating their fitness and capacity to command men of their own race.

# CHAPTER XIV

## RECORD OF "THE OLD FIFTEENTH"

*The Glorious Story of the 369th United States Infantry, Formerly of the New York National Guard—The Regiment That Never Lost a Man Captured, a Trench, or a Foot of Ground—First Negro Troops to Go into Action in France.*

The first effort to organize a colored National Guard regiment in New York City was sponsored by Charles W. Fillmore, a colored citizen, who afterwards was commissioned a Captain in the "15th" by Col. Hayward. The effort to secure proper approval of such a regiment was more or less abortive until Gov. Charles S. Whitman, following the gallant fight of Negro troops of the Tenth Cavalry against Mexican bandits at Carrizal, authorized the project and named Col. William Hayward, then Public Service Commissioner, to supervise the task of recruiting an organization. It was found that there were more than two hundred Negro residents of the city who had seen service in the regular army, or in the militia of other states. With these as a nucleus the work of recruiting began on June 29, 1916.

By the first of October, ten companies of sixty-five men each had been formed, and the regiment was then recognized by the State and given its colors. By April 8, 1917, the regiment had reached peace strength, with 1,378 men, and was recognized by the Federal Government. Two weeks later the organization was authorized to recruit to war strength. The 600 men needed were recruited in five days after the applicants had been subjected to a physical examination more stringent than that given in the regular army. The first battalion of four companies was recruited in Manhattan; the second battalion was composed of Brooklyn men, and the third of men from Manhattan and the Bronx. "There is no better soldier material in the world," said Col. Hayward, following the organization of the regiment. "Given the proper training, these men will be the equal of any soldiers in the world."

Col. Hayward in a personal memorandum to the author submitted the following diary of dates in the history of the 15th New York, which afterwards became the 369th Infantry prior to its going overseas:

"July 15, 1918, mobilized at various halls and meeting places where regiment was recruited and went to Camp Whitman, near Poughkeepsie, N. Y., for muster-in to United States service;

"August 2, Machine Gun Company sent to Ellis Island to guard German spies and internes;

"Two companies—1st Battalion, Harrison, N. J., for guard duty on Jersey railroads and certain essential factories.

"One company—1st Battalion, guarded tunnels and bridges New York Central and other railroads from New York City to the Adirondack Mountains in small detachments;

"One company, in and around New York City, including guard duty on seized German ships;

"Second Battalion, less one company, pioneered Camp Upton.

"Fourth company, on guard over Iona Island near West Point and Bear Mountain;

"Third Battalion, pioneered Camp Dix.

"First week in October, Regimental Headquarters, 2nd and 3rd Battalions, Headquarters and Supply Companies to Camp Wadsworth, Spartanburg.

"October 12, assembled and secretly transported at 9 to 10 A. M. via Fifth avenue busses and elevated railroads and on foot in various parts of New York City to dock at 95th street and East River, and transported to Hoboken. Embarked on transport "Hoboken." Second day at sea ship broke down and limped back to Hoboken. Regiment moved to Camp Merritt.

"October 23, back to Hoboken to sail October 27. Owing to incomplete equipment, unable to sail and battalions stationed at Camp Mills, Park Avenue Armory, Van Cortlandt Park, 2nd Field Armory and other armories in New York City.

"November 12, moved secretly with colors cased and drums forbidden to play, at 10 A. M. by train to Hoboken and marched through the principal street to transport "Pocahontas" at Pier 3. Ship on fire and regiment remained on board, sailing again December 3.

"December 4, collision at sea;

"December 5, regiment repaired ship;

"December 27, landed at Brest. Right side up."

In sending the diary, Col. Hayward adds the following significant statement:

"We had no wrecks, no fires, no explosions, no escaped prisoners during our tour, prior to sailing. Gen. Hoyle, Commanding General Eastern Department, said ours was the only regiment, regular or national guard, on this duty against which no complaint had been filed by civilians or others."

### Training the Regiment

Training the men presented some difficulty. At first they were drilled in Lafayette Hall, 132nd street and Seventh avenue, New York City. But the place was altogether too small and many of the fifty squads which drilled nightly had to take to the streets to carry out the maneuvers of their drill sergeants. Later they went for three weeks to Camp Whitman. An announced plan to send the regiment to train at Camp Wadsworth, Spartanburg, S. C., caused a storm of protest from the citizens of the South Carolina town.

"The most tragic consequences," they insisted, "would follow the introduction of the New York Negro with his Northern ideas into the community life of Spartanburg." The Spartanburg Chamber of Commerce drafted resolutions protesting against the training of Negro troops at Camp Wadsworth, which were sent to New York State officials. The resolutions, however, had less weight than the exigencies of war and, early in October, the 15th Negro Infantry detrained at Camp Wadsworth. The "tragic consequences" did not materialize. Certain stores refused to serve Negro customers and were, in turn, boycotted by the white soldiers, but the chief result of the Fifteenth's visit to Spartanburg was an increased respect in some measure, at least, for the black soldier.

While at Spartanburg the regiment was supplied with the latest things in trench shoes, heavy underwear, and other overseas supplies. This led the men to expect immediate transfer overseas. They were, indeed, ordered overseas, but as Colonel Hayward's memorandum quoted above indicates, the regiment

made three distinct starts for France before it finally got away
from America. The accident that caused the first turning back
occurred when still in sight of the Narrows. The vessel was disabled by a bent piston rod and had to put back to the Brooklyn
Navy Yard for repairs. Four days later the ship put out again,
only to halt when fire was found in the reserve coal bunker.
Putting back to Hoboken, the sorely tried Fifteenth counted the
hours until a new transport could be obtained. Hours became
days, and days weeks, but still no other ship offered.

### Delayed by Storm and Collision

Finally, on December 3, 1917, the Navy Department notified
the transport's commander to put to sea. But while the pier
lines were being cast off a storm started to blow up, and by the
time the "Pocahontas"—nameless at the time—reached the outer
bay, the greatest blizzard of the year was raging. Clouds of snow,
through which nothing could be seen, forced the "Pocahontas" to
drop anchor. She had hardly done so when a huge hulk, appearing
suddenly through the murk, bore down upon the transport's bow
and cut a ten-foot hole in her side. Then the storm abated in the
bay, but a new one arose below decks, where 3,000-odd exasperated
soldiers were maintaining their belief that no such place as France
existed. The captain of the transport was for turning back again
to the Navy Yard. The hole was above the water-line, he admitted,
and there was no great danger impending as a result of the
collision, he said. Nevertheless there would be an inquiry, and it
was necessary that he be present to state his case.

"I can see no reason for turning back except that of fear,"
said Col. Hayward to the captain. The captain did not turn back.
There was an ambulance assembly unit on board with electric
drills. Ten hours, it was said, would suffice to make sufficient
repairs to enable the vessel to proceed. The bent plates were
drilled out and double planking erected in their place. Concrete
was then poured between the planks. The result was not elegant,
but the ship was water-tight and best of all, still bound for France.

Brest was reached on December 27 without incident except for
an epidemic of German measles which attacked the crew of the

transport, but which was escaped by nearly all officers and men of the Fifteenth.

From Brest the regiment was transferred to St. Nazaire, where the troops were put to work constructing a huge railroad yard, building roads, and unloading ships. The fact of being in the country "where the war is" helped the impatient soldiers to endure their lot for awhile, but before long there was a general feeling that "while stevedoring may be all right, it is not war," and the officers were besieged with apologetic and respectful queries, "When do we fight?"

### Guarding German Prisoners

The answer was assumed to have been supplied when, early in January, the Third Battalion was ordered to Colquidan, in Brittany, where there was a big American artillery camp. It turned out, however, that peace was still longer to bear down upon the spirits of the Fifteenth. At Colquidan, they found, as well as an American artillery camp, there was also a large German prison camp, and it was for the purpose of guarding this camp that their services were required.

Three weeks passed, and then the Third Battalion received orders to join the rest of the regiment at Givry-en-Argonne, there to be formally transferred to the French high command and to be known as the 369th Regiment d'Infanterie Etats Unis (United States Infantry). Actual fighting was still afar off, it seemed to the soldiers, for they were put to training under French officers. One hundred and twenty picked men and a number of officers were sent to the French Divisional Training School, where they were taught to use the French arms, including grenades, French bayonets, rifles and machine guns. Upon the completion of the course others of the former Fifteenth were sent to take this training.

They proved apt pupils. In grenade-throwing they easily out-did their instructors, and in bayonet work they demonstrated great skill. They surprised the French, also, with the manner in which they acquired the French language. Many of them were talking quite fluently after a week with their French comrades. It turned out, however, that many of the soldiers hailed from Louis-

iana, and that their new environment merely had revived forgotten memories of the French language.

In May the regiment went to the Main de Massiges, a part of
the French line which offered the greatest danger as well as the
greatest opportunity for training in trench warfare and raiding.
A small number of the Fifteenth's men were sent with each French
company, with instructions to observe all regulations and
familiarize themselves with the tactics of the French. The French
"poilus" were delighted with their colored comrades and soon
sought to teach them all they knew.

After two weeks' experience obtained in the manner described,
the 369th was sent into action in the Bois d'Hauze, Champagne,
where the regiment, unassisted by the French, held a complete
sector, which in length constituted 20 per cent of all territory held
by American troops at the time. In this action, which lasted until
July 4, 1918, when the colored soldiers, their ranks thinned by the
deadly German fire and completely worn out, were relieved by the
4th French Chasseurs-à-pied.

### Fighting Ability Recognized

By this time the fighting effectiveness of the Negro troops
from New York was recognized by the high command, and after
resting behind the lines for a few weeks they were transferred and
placed in the path of the expected German offensive at Minancourt,
near Butte de Mesnil, where they bore the brunt of the German
attacks of July 15 and thereafter. Against the enemy in this
action the old Fifteenth was completely successful, holding against
the German fire, repelling German attacks and by counter-attacks
becoming possessed of the front line German trenches.

At the end of July the regiment, after a three days' march to
the rear, went into training for open warfare, but had hardly
started work when a hurry call was sent to them to take over the
same place in the line which they had left a few days before.
Motor lorries were impressed and the New York soldiers hastened
back to the front, arriving in time to assist in repelling the most
violent German attacks.

During the action which followed it was the policy of the
French strategists to retreat from the lines then held, after having

"gassed" all the dug-outs. The advancing Germans thereupon were met with such heavy shell fire that they were forced into the underground shelters and so fell by the hundreds, victims of the noxious fumes released by the French.

The men of the 369th, advancing again after this defeat of the enemy, found enough Mauser rifles lying beside the dead Germans to equip an entire brigade. Finding the German Mauser to resemble the Springfield formerly used by the American troops and preferring it to the French weapon furnished them, the men of the Fifteenth promptly adopted the captured rifle, and it was with considerable difficulty that the French equipment was finally restored to them.

### Wins the Croix de Guerre

Early in September the men of the 369th were transferred from the 16th French Division, in which they had been serving, and made an integral part of the 161st French Division. And then, on the morning of September 26th, they joined with the Moroccans on the left and native French on the right in the offensive which won for the entire regiment the French Croix de Guerre and the citation of 171 individual officers and enlisted men for the Croix de Guerre and the Legion of Honor, for exceptional gallantry in action. The action began at Maison-en-Champagne; it finished seven kilometers northward and eastward and over the intervening territory the Germans had retreated before the ferocious attacks of the Fifteenth and its French comrades.

A month later a new honor came to the regiment—the honor of being the first unit of all the Allied armies to reach the River Rhine. The regiment had left its trenches at Thann, Sunday, November 17, and, marching as the advance guard of the 161st Division, Second French Army, reached Blodelsheim, on the left bank of the Rhine, Monday, November 18. The 369th is proud of this achievement. It believes also that it was under fire for a greater number of days than any other American regiment. Its historian will record:

That the regiment never lost a man captured, a trench, or a foot of ground; that it was the only unit in the American Expeditionary Force which bore a State name and carried a State flag;

that it was never in an American brigade or division; that it saw the first and the longest service of any American regiment as part of a foreign army; and that it had less training than any American unit before going into action.

### Letter from Colonel Hayward

A highly significant letter written by Col. Hayward to the author shortly after the 369th reached France and went into training may be quoted:

"DEAR SCOTT:

"Am writing this from away up on the French front where the 'Fighting Fifteenth,' now the 369th U. S., is really fighting in a French Division. We are known to the French as 369 R. I. M. S. and our *Secteur Postal* is No. 54, France.

"I have two battalions in the trenches of the *first* line and the third in relief at rest just behind our trenches. The three rotate. Our boys have had their baptism of fire. They have patrolled No Man's Land. They have gone on raids and one of my lieutenants has been cited for a decoration. Of course, it is still in the experimental stage, but two questions of the gravest importance to our country and to your race have, in my opinion, been answered.

"First: How will American Negro soldiers, including commissioned officers (of whom I still have five), get along in service with French soldiers and officers—as for instance a Negro regiment of infantry serving in a French combat division?

"Second: Will the American Negro stand up under the terrible shell fire of this war as he has always stood under rifle fire and thus prove his superiority, spiritually and intellectually, to all the black men of Africa and Asia, who have failed under these conditions and whose use must be limited to attack or for shock troops?

"We have answered the first question in a most gratifying way. The French soldiers have not the slightest prejudice or feeling. The poilus and my boys are great chums, eat, dance, sing, march and fight together in absolute accord. The French officers have *little,* if any feeling about Negro officers. What little, if any, is not racial but from skepticism that a colored man (judging of course by those they have known) can have the technical education necessary to make an efficient officer. However, as I write these lines, Capt. Napoleon Bonaparte Marshall and Lieut. D. Lincoln Reed are living at the French Officers' Mess at our division *Infanterie* School, honored guests.

"The program I enclose gives you an idea of the way I've cultivated friendship between my boys and the poilus. You should have seen the 500 soldiers, French and mine, all mixed up together, cheering and laughing at the show arranged while the Boche shells (boxcar size) went screaming over our heads.

"Now, on the second question, perhaps I am premature. But both my two battalions which have gone in have been under shell fire, serious and prolonged once, and the boys just laughed and cuddled into their shelter and read old newspapers. French company got shelled and it was getting very warm around the rolling kitchen. The cooks went along about their business in absolute unconcern until the alarmed French soldiers ran to them and told them to beat it. One of the cooks said, 'Oh, that's all right, boss. They ain't hurting us none.' They are positively the most stoical and mysterious men I've ever known. Nothing surprises them. And we now have expert opinion. The French officers say they are entirely different from their own African troops and the Indian troops of the British, who are so excitable under shell fire. Of course, I have explained that my boys are public school boys, wise in their day and generation, no caste prejudice, accustomed to the terrible noises of the subway, elevated and street traffic of New York City (which would drive any desert man or Himalaya mountaineer mad) and are all Christians. Also, that while the more ignorant ones might not like to have a black cat hanging around for fear it would turn into a fish or something, they have no delusions about the Boche shells coming from any Heathen Gods. They know the d—— child-killing Germans are firing at them with pyrocellulose and they know how the breech mechanism works.

"I am very proud of what we've done and are doing. I put the whole regiment through grenade (live grenade) practice. Nasty, dangerous business. They did it beautifully. I found one rank arrant coward, who refused to throw. Said he couldn't. Another threw prematurely after igniting the bomb. We asked him why he did not wait for the command to throw (barrage). He said, 'Kunnel, that old grenade, she begun to swell right in my hand.' The boys keep writing home that the 'war is not so bad if you just go at it right.' Well, a very wise command somewhere, I don't know where, has let us go at it right. You know I've always told these boys I'd never send them anywhere I would not go myself, so I went first to the trenches, prowled around, saw it all and came back to the regiment to take in the battalion which was to go in first. When they saw me covered with mud, but safe and sound they said, 'How is she, Kunnel?' 'She's all right,' I said. They all laughed and then the sick and the lame of that battalion began to get well miraculously and begged to go. Captain Clark called for twelve volunteers for a raid and the company fell in to the last man—all wanted to go, and he had to pick his twelve after all.

"Do you wonder that I love them, every one, good, bad and indifferent?

"Personally I am well, strong, and the happiest man in the world. I've learned more about the military game, at least the fighting of this war, since I have been here with the French than I learned in all the years as drummer boy, private, Sergeant, Captain, Major and Colonel Second Nebraska Infantry, Spanish War, Maneuvers, Officers' School, Gettysburg and Leavenworth problems, etc., etc., and all the time I spent with my present regiment in the New York National Guard.

"And another thing, I believe I know more about Negro soldiers and how to handle them, especially the problem of Negro and white officers, than any other man living today. Of course, the other regiment I commanded for three years was a white regiment, so I had a lot to learn, but I've learned it and I wouldn't trade back now.

"Suppose after I've held my sector up here by blood and iron two or three months, some National Guard Brigadier, who has just arrived in France, will come along and point out all the mistakes I've made and tell me just how to do it. Well, 'C'est la guerre,' as we French say.

"Brother Boche doesn't know who we are yet, as none of my men have been captured so far, and the boys wear a French blue uniform when they go on raids. I've been thinking if they capture one of my Porto Ricans (of whom I have a few) in the uniform of a Normandy French regiment and this black man tells them in Spanish that he is an American soldier in a New York National Guard regiment, it's going to give the German intelligence department a headache trying to figure it out.

"We are proud to think our boys were the first Negro American soldiers in the trenches. Jim Europe was certainly the first Negro officer in. You can imagine how important he feels! In addition to the personal gratification at having done well as a regiment I feel it has been a tremendously important experiment, when one considers the hosts of colored men who must come after us. I wish I had a brigade, yes, a division or a corps of them. We'd make history and plant the hob-nailed boots of the 'Heavy Ethiopian Foot' in the Kaiser's face all right.

"We were so disappointed that the Secretary didn't get up to see us. The town we were holding then had been named by me 'Bakerville' and it is so on our maps.

"Regards and good wishes to you.

"Sincerely,

"WILLIAM HAYWARD."

### Called "Hell Fighters" by the Enemy

The men of the 369th came to be known among the French and the Germans as "Hell Fighters." The regiment participated in the action which followed the German offensive on the 15th of July, 1918, when the Germans were reinforced by released prisoners from Russia, so that they then had their maximum forces. They had broken through the British line and disaster was at hand. This was east of Rheims. The Germans had also torn through the French at Montdidier and had gone through for 30 or 40 kilometers.

During the 191 days that the regiment was in the trenches there were weeks in that immediate sector when there was nothing between the German army and Paris but these black men from America. It was through the action of the men of the 369th in capturing German prisoners on the night of July 14 that the expected German attack was learned. When the French found out that the great German offensive was coming, their forces did not remain a thin blue line. Gen. Gouraud, who commanded the Fourth French Army, took his troops out of the front line trenches over a front of 50 kilometers, and when the attack occurred he had the 369th on one flank of a 50-kilometer line and the old 69th New York, a part of the Rainbow Division, on the other. When the German fire fell on these front line trenches for five hours and twenty minutes, the shells fell on empty trenches except for a few patrols left in reinforced trenches with signal rockets, gas shells, and a few machine guns. When the hour for the German infantry attack came, these patrols let off their gas bombs , and signal rockets and the massed' allied artillery let loose on the massed Germans, who were literally smashed and never got through to the second line of the 369th. On the other end they did get through, crashing into the Rainbow Division and the old 69th New York, which met them hand-to-hand in some of the most terrible fighting of the war.

### Individual Exploits of the 369th

There are many outstanding exploits of the men of the 369th and of Col. Hayward himself. In Belleau Wood on June 6, 1918, the regiment came up to the German front lines where it met a very heavy counter-attack. Some one suggested that they turn back. "Turn back? I should say we won't. We are going through there or we don't come back," was what Colonel Hayward said as he tore off the eagles of his insignia, grabbed a gun from a soldier, and darted out ahead of the rest of Company "K," which went through a barrage of German artillery that was bearing down upon it. A French General ordered the regiment to retire, but Colonel Hayward, who, of course, was under direct command of this French General said: "I do not understand you."

Then the French General raised his arms above his head and cried:

"Retire! Retire!"

And then Colonel Hayward, with his hat knocked off, came running up and cried: "My men never retire. They go forward, or they die!"

A Prussian officer captured by the "Black Watch," as the 369th was called after they had reached the Rhine, is said to have remarked: "We can't hold up against these men. They are devils! They smile while they kill and they won't be taken alive."

The regiment was eleven times cited for bravery in action, and

Colonel Hayward himself received a citation, reading: "Colonel Hayward, though wounded, insisted on leading his regiment in battle."

Following is the citation awarded the 369th for its courage and valor in the great offensive in the Champagne, September and October, 1918, by the French Commanding General:

# CITATION for CROIX de GUERRE

## AWARDED
## 369ᵉ RÉGIMENT d'INFANTERIE U. S.
### (FORMERLY 15ᵗʰ N. Y. INFANTRY)
#### FOR ITS OPERATIONS AS A COMBAT UNIT OF A FRENCH
#### DIVISION IN THE GREAT OFFENSIVE IN
## CHAMPAGNE, SEPT. and OCT. 1918,
### BY THE FRENCH COMMANDING GENERAL

*Sous le Commandement du Colonel HAYWARD qui, bien que blessé, a tenu à conduire son régiment au combat, du Lieutenant Colonel PICKERING, admirable de sang-froid et de courage, du Commandant COBB (tué), du Commandant SPENCER (grièvement blessé), du Commandant LITTLE véritable entraîneur d'hommes, le 369ᵉ R. I. U. S. qui lors des attaques de Septembre 1918, voyait le feu pour la première fois, s'est emparé de puissantes organisations ennemies, énergiquement défendues et a enlevé de haute lutte le village de S. . . . . . . ., a fait des prisonniers, ramené 6 canons et un grand nombre de mitrailleuses.*

### TRANSLATION

*Under command of Colonel HAYWARD, who, though injured, insisted on leading his regiment in the battle, of Lieutenant Colonel PICKERING, admirably cool and brave, of Major COBB, (killed), of Major SPENCER (grievously wounded), of Major LITTLE, a true leader of men, the 369ᵗʰ R. I. U. S. engaging in an offensive for the first time in the drive of September, 1918, stormed powerful enemy positions energetically defended, took, after heavy fighting, the town of S . . . . . . . . . captured prisoners and brought back six cannons and a great number of machine guns.*

A typical story of the dare-devil courage of the men of the 369th is afforded in the exploit of Elmer McCowin of Company

"K," who won the Distinguished Service Cross. He tells his own story as follows: "On September 26 the Captain asked me to carry despatches. The Germans pumped machine-gun bullets at me all the way. But I made the trip and back safely. Then I was sent out again. As I started with the message the Captain yelled to bring him back a can of coffee. He was joking, but I didn't know it at the time.

"Being a foot messenger, I had some time ducking those German bullets. Those bullets seemed very sociable, but I didn't care to meet up with them, so I kept right on traveling on high gear. None touched my skin, though some skinned pretty close.

"On the way back it seemed the whole war was turned on me. One bullet passed through my trousers and it made me hop, step, and jump pretty lively. I saw a shell hole six feet deep. Take it from me, I dented another six feet when I plunged into it hard. In my fist I held the Captain's can of coffee.

"When I climbed out of the shell hole and started running again, a bullet clipped a hole in the can and the coffee started to spill. But I turned around, stopped a second, looked the Kaiser in the face, and held up the can of coffee with my finger plugging up the hole to show the Germans they were fooled. Just then another bullet hit the can and another finger had to act as a stopgap.

"It must have been good luck that saved my life, because bullets were picking at my clothes and so many hit the can that at the end all my fingers were hugging it to keep the coffee in. I jumped into shell holes, wriggled along the ground, and got back safely. And what do you think? When I got back into our own trenches I stumbled and spilled the coffee!"

Not only did Lieut. George Miller, Battalion Adjutant, confirm the story, but he added about Private McCowin: "When that soldier came back with the coffee his clothes were riddled with bullets. Yet half an hour later he went back into No-Man's-Land and brought back a number of wounded until he was badly gassed. Even then he refused to go to the rear and went out again for a. wounded soldier. All this under fire. That's the reason he got the D. S. C."

Corporal Elmer Earl, also of Company "K," living at Middletown, New York, also won the Distinguished Service Cross. He explained: "We had taken a hill September 26 in the Argonne. We came to the edge of a swamp, when enemy machine guns opened fire. It was so bad that of the fifty-eight of us who went into a particular strip, only eight came out without being killed or wounded. I made a number of trips out there and brought back about a dozen wounded men."

### How Sergeant Butler Won the D. S. C.

On authority of General Pershing, Colonel Hayward himself presented the Distinguished Service Crosses to the heroes among his regiment. Then, from the hands of General Collardet, of the French Army, he received the medal of the Legion of Honor. But even among this list of distinguished heroes those who knew of the exploits of Sergeant "Bill" Butler insisted upon calling for him and making him the object of their attentions.

It was on the night of August 12, 1918, while the fighting was raging in the Champagne District, that Sergeant Butler's opportunity came to him. A German raiding party had rushed the American trenches and, after firing a few shots and making murderous use of the short trench knives and clubs carried for such encounters, had captured five privates and a lieutenant. The victorious raiders were making their way back to their own trenches when Butler, occupying a lone position in a forward post, saw that it would be necessary for the party to pass him.

The Negro sergeant waited until the Germans were close to his post, then opened fire upon them with his automatic rifle. He kept the stream of lead upon the raiders until ten of their number had been killed. Then he went forth and took the German lieutenant, who was slightly wounded, a prisoner, released the American lieutenant and five other prisoners, and returned to the American lines with his prisoner and the rescued party.

Under the heading, "Trenton Has Nothing on Salisbury," *The Afro-American* of Baltimore said: "Trenton, New Jersey, may have her Needham Roberts, but it takes Salisbury, Maryland, to produce a William Butler. Roberts had his comrade, Henry Johnson, to help him in repulsing a raiding party of Germans, but Butler took care of a German lieutenant and squad of Boches all by himself. Herbert Corey, a white newspaper correspondent, in telling of the incident said that Butler came 'a-roaring and fogging' through the darkness with his automatic, and 'nobody knows how many Germans he killed.' It was for this that General Pershing awarded him the Distinguished Service Cross recently and the citation read: 'Sergt. William Butler, Company L, 369th Infantry (A. S. No. 104464). For extraordinary heroism in action near Maison de Champagne, France, August 18, 1918. Sergeant Butler broke up a German raiding party which had succeeded in entering our trenches and capturing some of our men. With an automatic rifle he killed four of the raiding party and captured or put to flight the remainder of the invaders. Home address, Mrs. Jennie Butler, Water Street, Salisbury, Maryland.'

"The rest of the State of Maryland and the whole United States now has its hat off to Butler of Salisbury."

And the *New York Tribune*, on April 28, 1919, said: " 'Bill' Butler, a slight, good-natured colored youth, who until two years ago was a jack-of-all-trades in a little Maryland town, yesterday came into his own as a hero among heroes. More than 5,000 men and women arose to their feet in City College stadium and cheered themselves hoarse while representatives of two Governments pinned their highest medals upon the breast of the nervous youth. Sergeant Butler was one of a list of twenty-three members of the famous 15th Regiment upon whom both France and the United States conferred medals of honor because of extraordinary heroism on European battlefields. . But by common consent his name comes first on the list—a list that was made up only after a careful comparison of the deeds of gallantry that finally resulted in the breaking of the Hun lines."

### Won the Cheers of the French

Of the 369th it may be stated that although the Germans never captured a single man, they killed nearly 200 of them and wounded more than 800 others, but on the other side of the score were to be found more than 400 Germans captured by the Third Battalion of the 369th alone, and countless men of the enemy killed and wounded.

It proved itself to be one of the most efficient military units of all the Allied forces. The officers and men were constantly cheered by the gratitude of the French, who never failed to place in evidence their appreciation for the wonderful fighting prowess of the men of the 369th. The French were amazed not only at the proficiency of the men as soldiers but at their proficiency in laying railroad tracks, which was the first duty assigned them near one of the larger French ports. The 369th laid many stretches of track, pushed them into alignment, gave twists to the bolts, and proceeded half a mile farther down to repeat the performance. "Magnifique!" exclaimed a party of French officers who watched them do the work.

The story of the wanderings of "the old 15th," of its hard fighting in France, of its returning to America, and of the triumphant procession through the streets of New York City, down Fifth Avenue, is one of the proudest possessions of the Negro race and of American arms.

Five colored officers went over with the 369th Regiment. These officers were afterwards transferred to the 92nd Division. Considerable criticism followed the transfer of these colored officers from a colored regiment which had won such renown as the 369th. Col. Hayward, however, gave the following as reason for the transfer:

"In August, 1918, the American Expeditionary Force adopted the policy of having either all white or all colored officers with Negro regiments, and so ours were shifted away (though Lieut. Europe later was returned to us as bandmaster, whereas he had been in the machine gun force before). Our colored officers were in the July fighting and did good work, and I felt then and feel now, that if colored officers are available and capable, they, and not white officers, should command colored troops. I hope, if the Fifteenth is reconstructed, as it should be, colored men will have the active work of officering it, from top to bottom.

"There is splendid material there. I sent away forty-two sergeants in France who were commissioned officers in other units. I would have sent others, but they declared they'd rather be sergeants in the Fifteenth than lieutenants or captains in other regiments."

# CHAPTER XV

## "THE EIGHTH ILLINOIS"

*Story of the 370th U. S. Infantry—Another Negro National Guard Regiment That Won Distinction on the Battlefield—Chicago's Colored Fighters—Called "Black Devils" by the Germans and "Partridges" by the French Because of Their Proud Bearing—First American Troops to March into the Fortified City of Laon—Their Stubborn Resistance at the Oise-Aisne Canal.*

The Eighth Illinois National Guard Regiment, which during the great war came to be known as the 370th U. S. Infantry, was the only regiment in the entire United States Army that was called into service with almost a complete complement of colored officers from the highest rank of Colonel to the lowest rank of Corporal. Having been brigaded with French troops and given every opportunity to get into the thickest of the fray and to demonstrate their bravery, ability, and solidarity as fighting men, the brilliant record made by this regiment effectually served to answer the question as to whether colored soldiers would follow colored officers into battle.

Below will be found the record of events of the 370th U. S. Infantry (formerly 8th Illinois Infantry) from July 25, 1917, the date of responding to the call of the President, to March 11, 1919, the date of demobilization of the regiment.

Pursuant to the call of the President, dated July 3, 1917, the regiment reported at the various rendezvous on July 25, 1917, as follows:

At Chicago, Illinois—Headquarters, Headquarters Company, Machine Gun Company, Supply Company, Detachment Medical Department, and Companies A, B, C, D, E, F, G and H.

At Springfield, Illinois—Company I.

At Peoria, Illinois—Company K.

At Danville, Illinois—Company L.

At Metropolis, Illinois—Company M.

On the date of responding to the call, the Field and Staff was as follows:

Colonel Franklin A. Denison, commanding the regiment.

Lt. Col. James H. Johnson, duty with the regiment.

Major Rufus M. Stokes, commanding the 1st Battalion.

Major Charles L. Hunt, commanding the 2nd Battalion.

Major Otis B. Duncan, commanding the 3rd Battalion.

Captain John H. Patton, Regimental Adjutant.

On August 18, 1917, Company G proceeded to Camp Logan, Houston, Texas, for the purpose of preparing camp for the arrival of the remainder of the regiment. This company was present at Camp Logan during the riot in Houston which involved certain colored soldiers of the 24th Infantry, U. S. A., in the latter part of August, 1917, and was commended by the public, the press, and military authorities for its conduct and general bearing.

At the end of October, 1917, on the date of the closing of the Second Liberty Loan campaign, out of a total of 2,166 officers and enlisted men, belonging to the regiment at that time, 1,482 officers and men subscribed $151,400.00 to the Second Liberty Loan. Approximately 96 per cent of the regiment took out $10,000.00 War Risk Insurance.

There was some question in military circles as to whether or not this regiment should be sent overseas, to meet the Huns with its colored Colonel and a full complement of colored officers; but the splendid way in which Colonel Denison had handled his men and maintained discipline at Camp Logan, and at Camp Stuart (Newport News, Virginia), proved to the War Department that he was every inch a man, that he was an intelligent and experienced soldier, and a competent officer who knew how to command and to guard the interests of his regiment. It is especially pertinent to refer to the discussion as to whether this regiment should be sent overseas with a colored commanding officer and its entire colored officers' personnel, because, at that time, Colonel Charles Young, the veteran colored officer, a graduate of West Point, who had given the best years of his life to the United States Regular Army, had been retired from active duty on the strength of a report submitted by a Medical Board of Examiners, before which he was called, and who decided that he was physically disqualified to lead a regiment of colored soldiers on the battlefields of France. Such service was not only Colonel Young's fervent desire, but it was the equally fervent hope of colored Americans that he would be permitted to do so.

The morale of the colored people was, therefore, very much depressed by the retirement of Colonel Charles Young over his earnest protest and the protest of his legion of friends. Negro newspapers, reflecting the sentiment and desire of the Negro people, urged that he be not only retained and actively utilized as an officer of the National Army, but that he be given what they believed to be his rightful reward—namely, promotion in rank to at least that of a Brigadier-General. The futility of these requests and protests, and the failure of repeated efforts to have the findings of the Medical Board which passed upon Colonel Young's case reviewed, and set aside, so that he could be placed in active command of a Negro regimental unit, gave rise to suspicions of unfair play and disturbed the morale of colored Americans generally. For another colored Colonel to be denied active service would have further dampened the morale of the colored people, especially in view of the openly expressed feeling on their part that the highest ranking Negro officer in the United States Regular Army had been unjustly denied active service in the world's greatest war and had been likewise deprived of promotion to the next rank above him—that of Brigadier-General—which he would have automatically received upon being called to active duty.

Colonel Denison, however, proceeded overseas with his regiment, which was the first American regiment to set foot upon the soil of Alsace-Lorraine—territory that had for nearly fifty years been wrongfully held under German domination.

### Equipped with French Arms

After about six weeks' training under French instructors, the regiment was considered sufficiently trained to go into the lines, and on June 12 and 13, 1918, pursuant to *Ordre Particulier* No. 30, Headquarters 10th Division, French Army, dated June 11, 1918, the regiment marched to Morvillars (Haut-Rhin), entrained and proceeded to Ligny-en-Barrois (Meuse), detrained and marched to stations as follows: Headquarters, Headquarters Company, Supply, Company, and the 1st Battalion at Nancois-le-Petit (Meuse); the 2nd Battalion and Company K (Depot Company) at Trouville (Meuse); the 3rd Battalion at Velaines (Meuse).

The French instructors referred to were needed in view of the fact that the men of the 370th Infantry, when they arrived at Grandvillars, were relieved of all of their American equipment, with which they had been trained at home, and were re-equipped with French arms and equipment exclusively, including French rifles, pistols, helmets, machine guns, horses, wagons, and even French rations, which consisted of food sufficient for about two meals per day, while the American ration had provided for three meals per day. But in spite of difficulties arising from difference in languages, the issuing of French arms, ammunition and other equipment, and the French ration, which was considered insufficient, the regiment made rapid progress.

### In the St. Mihiel Sector

On June 21, 1918, the regiment began occupying a sub-sector, Han-Bislee, St. Mihiel sector. This being the first time the regiment had occupied positions in the line, it was deemed advisable by the Division Commander to intermingle the 370th with French troops, in order that officers and men might observe and profit by close association with veteran French troops. Thus, the 1st and 2nd Battalions, commanded by Majors Rufus M. Stokes and Charles L. Hunt respectively, were intermingled with platoons and companies of the French battalions. Except for occasional shelling and rifle and machine gun fire of the enemy, nothing of interest occurred while in the sector, and there were no casualties.

On the night of July 3-4, 1918, the regiment was withdrawn from the St. Mihiel sector, marched to Loxeville, and entrained for the Argonne Forest. Various positions were occupied in the Argonne until August 16, 1918. The particular sector occupied by the 370th Infantry was exceptionally quiet at that time, except on one or two occasions. In this position the regiment suffered its first casualty, namely, Private Robert E. Lee of Chicago, Company E, Machine Gun Company No. 2. It is highly encouraging to note the fact that General Mittlehauser, the French general in command of the entire division, although burdened with important official duties, found time to attend in person the funeral of this brave Negro soldier, who was buried with every military honor.

While in this sector, a portion of the regiment engaged in its first offensive encounter with the enemy. The Stokes mortar platoon, under the command of First Lieutenant Robert A. Ward, took part in a "coup de main" (raid), on August 4, 1918, having as its mission the filling-in of the gaps in the French artillery barrage. For his work during this raid Lieutenant Ward and his platoon were highly commended by General Mittlehauser.

On August 16, 1918, the 370th was relieved from its position in the Argonne Forest and sent for rest behind the lines near Bar-le-Duc. On September 1, the regiment again began to move toward the front lines, and by easy stages, proceeded to positions in the Soissons sector. On September 16 Companies G, H, I, and L were pushed forward to positions in front of Mont des Signes, and from that date to September 21 took part in the various battles and engagements incident to the capture of this exceptionally strong enemy position.

One platoon of Company F, under command of Sergeant Matthew Jenkins, especially distinguished itself by capturing a large section of the enemy works, turning their own guns on them and holding the position for thirty-six hours without food or water, until assistance came and the position was strengthened. For this meritorious work in this engagement Sergeant Jenkins received both the American Distinguished Service Cross and the French Croix de Guerre.

Company F was relieved on September 21, spending the night at Antioche Farm and proceeding to Mont des Tombes (Aisne) the following day and taking position in reserve; Company G was relieved on September 21, 1918, and proceeded to the caves near Les Tueries (Aisne); Companies I and L were relieved on September 22, 1918, and proceeded to Antioche Farm and Tincelle Farm, respectively, and placed in reserve. From September 19 to 21, the organizations not engaged in the front lines were employed in constructing defensive works between Antioche Farm and Vauxaillon.

## Takes Over a Full Sector

Prior to September 21, the regiment had never occupied a full regimental sector, the companies and battalions having been theretofore attached to various French units of the 59th Division. Pursuant to Order 187/S, Headquarters 59th Division, French Army, dated September 21, the regiment for the first time took over a full regimental sector. The 1st Battalion relieved the Battalion Garnier of the 325th Regiment of Infantry, French Army, in the positions outlined by La Folie-l'Ecluse on the Oise-Aisne Canal and the Farm Guilliminet. The 2nd Battalion went into the support position at Mont des Tombes and Les Tueries, and the slopes west of Antioche Farm. The 3rd Battalion went into reserve at Tincelle Farm. The Headquarters Company was stationed at Levilly and the Supply Company at Monte Couve.

On September 25 Company K (Depot Company) changed station from Duvy (Aisne) to Resson le Long (Aisne). On the night of September 26-27 the 2nd Battalion, commanded by Captain John H. Patton, was ordered to relieve with like units one-half of each of the companies of the 1st Battalion in the lines. The relief was completed about 2:00 a. m. An attack along the Oise-Aisne Canal was ordered at dawn on September 27, 1918. By extreme effort the remainder of the 2nd Battalion was brought up to the front, relieved the remainder of the 1st Battalion, commanded by Major Rufus M. Stokes, and the attack began as ordered. The attack continued from the morning of September 27 until October 4. The 2nd Battalion was relieved by the 1st Battalion after having gained possession of the railroad track and woods to the northeast of Guilliminet Farm.

On September 30 the 3rd Battalion, commanded by Lieut. Colonel O. B. Duncan, was ordered to make an attack with the Ferme de la Rivière as the principal objective, and about 3:00 p. m. on that date the attack began. The fighting in front of the Bois de Mortier, which woods the enemy held strongly, continued and it was not until October 4 that it was certain that the enemy had been driven across the canal.

From the 27th of September to the 4th of October the 370th was subjected to severe shelling and to murderous fire of numerous machine guns and rifles. After the 2nd Battalion was relieved by the 1st Battalion on October 17, Company G of the 2nd Battalion supported the 1st Battalion until October 3, 1918. During this time patrols from the 2nd and 3rd Battalions were out between the lines night and day, making effort to locate machine-gun nests in the Bois de Mortier and making other necessary reconnaissances.

On October 4, just before dawn, a reconnaissance in the Bois de Mortier was ordered. As the enemy strongly held the woods, a patrol consisting of volunteers was ordered to make the reconnaissance. Captain Chester Sanders and the necessary 20 men readily volunteered and at 3:30 a. m. crossed the canal and penetrated into the woods about 50 meters east of the Vauxaillon-Bois de Mortier Road, more than a hundred meters within the enemy lines. When reaching this point they were discovered by the enemy and were fired on by numerous machine guns. The mission of the patrol being to discover whether the woods had been abandoned by the enemy, the patrol retired to the French lines under heavy machine gun fire and shelling without the loss of a man.

October 4, 1918, pursuant to Order No. 330/S, Headquarters 59th Division, French Army, the 1st Battalion was ordered to make the following dispositions: Company A sent to the 325th Regiment of Infantry, French Army; Company B sent to the 232nd Regiment of Infantry, French Army. These companies to be used as reinforcements for those regiments. October 6, 1918, General Vincendon, commanding the division, went on leave and General Rondeau assumed command.

October 7, 1918, at 4:30 a. m., after five minutes' violent bombardment by the French artillery, three raiding parties started into the triangle formed by the Oise-Aisne Canal, the railroad, and the Vauxaillon-Bois de Mortier road. The mission of these raiding parties was to capture prisoners. One of these parties under command of 1st Lieutenant Elisha C. Lane entered the triangle, gained the trenches along the south bank of the canal and ejected the enemy after a hand-grenade fight, Lieut. Lane and two enlisted men being wounded. This party was unable to hold this trench on account of its being exposed to enfilade fire from two directions. The other two patrols established themselves along the railroad and sent small patrols into the triangle, but were unable to establish themselves therein. No prisoners were captured.

During the night of October 7-8 Company C of the 1st Battalion relieved Company F of the 2nd Battalion in the lines near l'Ecluse. Company C continued the effort made by Company F to establish themselves in the above mentioned triangle, but were unable to do so for the same reasons that prevented Company F from remaining therein. On October 10 the remainder of the 1st Battalion moved up into the front lines, relieving the rest of the 2nd Battalion, and the units of the 3rd Battalion in the lines along the Oise-Aisne Canal in front of the Bois de Mortier. The 2nd Battalion went into reserve at Antioche Farm and the 3rd Battalion went into division reserve at Mont des Tombes.

### Pushing the Enemy Back

A general advance having been foreseen, Order No. 1978/3 of the Division provided that after the objective, the Laon-La Ferre Railroad, was reached, the Division would be relieved by the 33rd Division, French Army, and sent into the reserve for rest. The alarm for the advance was given at 9:40 a. m., on October 12, and the various units of the regiment proceeded to the Zones of Assembly previously assigned. The 1st Battalion was given the mission of clearing the Bois de Mortier. The 2nd Battalion was placed at the disposition of Lieut.-Colonel Lugand of the 232nd Infantry, French Army. Company F and one section of Company E (Machine Gun Company No. 2), were detached from the 2nd Battalion and sent to join the Battalion Garnier of the 325th Regiment of Infantry, which had as its mission the mopping up of the hills and woods from near Anizy-le-Chateau to a point near Crepy. One company of the 325th Regiment of Infantry, French Army, was attached to the 2nd Battalion to replace Company F. The 3rd Battalion was assigned as reserve of the division, the command of which was assigned to Colonel T. A. Roberts.

Soon after the alert was given, the pursuit began. The 1st Battalion advanced through the Bois de Mortier and successfully reached the first objective, Penancourt, on the same date. The 2nd Battalion began the pursuit on the morning of October 13, having been assigned as the support battalion of the 232nd Infantry, and passed Anizy-le-Chateau, the Farm Fontenille, Tervanne, Cessières, and Butte de Sevresis, and bivouacked at dark with the head of the battalion resting at the north edge of the Bois d'Oiry and the rear on the National Road.

On October 13 the 1st Battalion continued the pursuit via Cessières to a point to the west of Molinchart. The 3rd Battalion rested in the Bois de Mortier the night of October 12, and next day went to Manneux Farm. For the work done in this general advance, the 1st and 2nd Battalions were complimented by the Commanding General—the 1st for its passage of the exceedingly strong position in the Bois de Mortier, and the 2nd for a well-conducted march in pursuit via Anizy-le-Chateau.

The regimental P. C. moved up to Cessières and late in the night of October 13 the division was ordered into rest for twelve days. The first ten days were spent in hard work on the roads, but the last two were given over to the issue of badly needed clothing and equipment. These twelve days found the regiment at the following places: Regimental Headquarters at Susy; 1st and 2nd Battalions in the St. Gobain Forest near Le Cateau; the 3rd Battalion at Manneux Farm. By Order No. 4442, Headquarters 59th Division, French Army, dated October 16, 1918, the General Commanding the division thanked the Colonel of the 370th Infantry for the good work done by the regiment in aiding the Engineers in the repair of roads and the cleaning of villages in the devastated districts.

On October 19, 1918, Major Rufus M. Stokes was relieved from command of the 1st Battalion and Captain John T. Prout assigned to command the battalion, Major Stokes being assigned to the Supply Company as administrative officer.

On October 27 the regiment was again ordered into the lines, and pursuant to *Ordre de Mouvement* No. 30, I. D. 59th Division, French Army, the 2nd Battalion during the night of October 27 proceeded to Farms d'Allemagne and de Cordeau. On the following night, October 28, the 2nd Battalion proceeded to a position in support to the northeast of Grandloup, remaining in various positions near Grandloup until November 5. Except occasional shelling and some machine gun fire on the support positions, nothing of interest occurred to the 2nd Battalion while in position near Grandloup.

On October 29 the 1st Battalion left camp in the St. Gobain

Forest and proceeded to Chambry, rested for the night, and on the following day, October 30, moved up into the support position about one kilometer to the northwest of Grandloup. On November 1 Regimental Headquarters moved up to Chambry.

On November 2 the 1st Battalion was moved to new positions with a view to the defense of Grandloup in case of enemy attack, Companies B and C taking position in the open trenches to the southwest of Grandloup and Company A to the southeast of the village. On November 3, an enemy shell struck in the mess line of Company A, at the Farm Chantrud, killing 35 men and wounding 41, making it necessary to withdraw this company from the lines. On November 4, Company C of the 1st Battalion relieved a company of the 325th Regiment of Infantry in the front lines in the vicinity of Brazicourt Farm. The positions of the 1st and 2nd Battalions received severe intermittent shelling while in these positions.

### Further Pursuit of the Enemy

On November 5, the enemy began again to retreat and the pursuit recommenced and continued until November 11, 1918, the date of the signing of the armistice.

On November 5 the 2nd Battalion, commanded by Capt. John H. Patton, moved out in pursuit of the enemy via Farm Attencourt, Autremontcourt, and bivouacked in the woods north of Ernecourt Farm for the night. The position was shelled intermittently during the entire night. At 6:00 a. m. the following day, in a heavy rain, the pursuit was again taken up, the battalion proceeding to the Farm Bellimont, arriving at about 11:00 p. m., and resting until 6:00 a. m. the following morning, November 7, at which time the battalion moved out and proceeded to Longue Rue de Bas, arriving about 9:30 p. m. At 3:30 a. m. the battalion proceeded to Beaume, arriving at 5:30 a. m., and reporting to Lieutenant-Colonel Lugand, 232nd (French) Regiment of Infantry. An attack was ordered at 6:30 a. m. by the division. The 2nd Battalion occupied a position on the left of the division with the 68th Regiment of Infantry on the left. At 6:30 a. m. the battalion moved out to the attack. The first operation, crossing the River Thon, was successfully accomplished, and the battalion continued the attack eastward towards Aubenton for about one and one-half kilometers, pushing the enemy back as it went. The enemy, fighting a rearguard action, had located numerous machine guns to the south of Leuze and along the heights stretching in the direction of Aubenton. The 68th (French) Regiment of Infantry, on the left, did not advance as anticipated, thus exposing Company H to an enfilade fire from machine guns located to the south of Leuze, and the company suffered severely. About 11:40 a. m. the advance was ordered stopped and preparation made for another attack, which began at 2:00 p. m. and continued until dark, at which time the battalion had reached its objective, the Hirson-Mezières Railroad. Casualties during the day, 4 killed and 2 officers and 33 enlisted men wounded. On the morning of November 9 the advance began again and the battalion continued the pursuit until dark, when it occupied positions from Goncelin, the advance outpost, to the woods northeast of Tarzy. On November 10 the battalion received orders to continue the pursuit with La Verte Place, Belgium, as the objective.

The French military officials, as will be seen by the official communication which follows, always called the battalion by the name of the battalion commander. Thus the 2nd Battalion, just referred to, commanded by Capt. John H. Patton of Chicago, Illinois, was termed "the Battalion Patton."

### 232ND REGIMENT D'INFANTRIE
#### (Translated)

*FROM:* Lieut. Colonel Lugand.

*TO:*　　Captain John H. Patton.　　November 7, 1918.

　1. ORDER OF OPERATIONS FOR THE JOURNEY OF THE 8TH. In the morning of the 8th, the 59th Division will attack as follows:

First Operation: Passage of the River Thon, occupation by the advanced lines of the line Bas-Val-la-Caure to LaHayette.

2. The 6th Battalion of the 232nd Infantry and the Battalion Patton will turn off at Aubenton towards the Northwest. The 325th Infantry will occupy Aubenton. On the left the 68th Infantry will attack Leuze.

3. Axis of the march of the 232nd Infantry Le Four & Chaux, Hill 246, Fligny.

4. Limit of the left of Battalion Patton, Bas-Val-la-Caure. Lisiere, south of Mattin Rieux.

5. *Formation—*

On the right the 6th Battalion of the 232nd Infantry will form an advance guard "in echelon" in rear of the left of the Battalion Patton, having two companies in the first line, one company in the second line. The company on the right of the first line will march on the "axis of the march" of the regiment, so as to be 600 meters from the company on the left of the 6th Battalion. Battalion Patton will attack on the left of the 232nd each time the enemy resists during the forward movement.

6. The movement will commence at 6:30 a. m.

7. Battalion Patton will maintain *"liaison"* (keep in touch) with the 6th Battalion on his right and with the 68th Infantry on his left.

8. The Command Post of the Colonel will be at Beaume.

(Signed)    LUGAND.

On November 6 the 1st Battalion received orders to take up the pursuit in support of the Battalion Michel of the 325th Regiment of Infantry, and proceeded to Hill 150, near St. Pierremont, via Brazicourt, Vesles-et-Caumont, Rapiere. The Battalion P. C. was stationed on the road to Marle and this road was shelled intermittently during the night. On November 7 the battalion continued the pursuit, advancing through St. Pierremont, Taveaux-et-Pontsericourt to Maison De Garde, south of Nampcelles. At Val St. Pierre, Company C of the battalion, commanded by Captain James H. Smith, by a series of flanking operations, drove the enemy from a position they occupied with three field pieces (77's) and two machine guns, causing them to abandon the cannon, which were taken by Company C. The enemy left several dead on the field and evidently had defended the position to the last. For this action, Company C was decorated with the French Croix de Guerre. On November 8, the battalion was ordered to Camp at LaHayette. On November 9 the command advanced to Mont Plaisir. On November 10 the battalion moved south to a position at Farm La-Hayette. On November 11 it proceeded to Fligny, at which place it was found at the signing of the armistice at 11:00 a. m. on November 11, 1918.

On November 5 the 3rd Battalion began the pursuit and rested in the open field at night on the 5th and 6th. On November 7 the battalion moved up and passed Bosmont, Tarveaux, Virginette, Lambercy, Mont Plaisir, and on into the front lines at the Rue Larcher. At the Rue Larcher the battalion passed under command of Colonel Pernin, of the 325th (French) Regiment of Infantry. On November 9, the battalion passed under command of Lieut.-

Colonel Lugand and was ordered to attack Pont d'Any. The objective was reached, the enemy retiring before the advance of the battalion. On November 10 the battalion continued the pursuit to Etignieres, where it was stopped temporarily by heavy shell fire. On November 11 the battalion again took up the pursuit with Reginowez as the principal objective. Later the objective was changed to Gue d'Hossus, Belgium. The battalion reached its objective a few moments before the signing of the armistice.

### After the Armistice

On November 12 the 3rd Battalion, pursuant to Order No. 2082/3, Headquarters 59th Division, French Army, retired from Belgium and took station at Auge (Aisne). On November 15 the regiment changed station as follows: Regimental Headquarters and the 1st Battalion to Dagny (Aisne); the 2nd Battalion to St. Clements (Aisne) and the 3rd Battalion to Morgny (Aisne). On November 16 the regiment changed station as follows: Regimental Headquarters and the 1st Battalion to Barrenton-sur-Serre (Aisne); the 2nd and 3rd Battalions to Froidmont-Cohartille (Aisne). On the following day, November 17, Regimental Headquarters and the 1st Battalion changed station to Verneuil-sur-Serre (Aisne).

From November 17 to December 12, 1918, the regiment was engaged at its various stations in cleaning and repairing roads and villages in the immediate vicinity of its stations. On December 12 the regiment formally passed from under command of the French and on the same date left the various villages in which cantoned and marched to Soissons, arriving in the afternoon of the 13th. On December 15 Capt. John H. Patton was relieved from command of the 2nd Battalion and resumed his duties as Regimental Adjutant and Major R. M. Stokes was relieved from duty with Supply Company and was assigned to command the 2nd Battalion.

The usual cantonment duties were performed at Soissons until December 23, 1918, on which date the regiment entrained for the American Embarkation Center at Le Mans, arriving on December 25, 1918, and going into cantonment. While stationed at Le Mans, the regiment was engaged in the various inspections incident to embarkation for the United States until January 8, 1919, on which date the regiment entrained for Brest, arriving there on January 10 and going into camp at Camp Pontanezen.

Until February 1, 1919, the regiment engaged in the various delousings, inspections, etc., incident to embarkation and on that date began embarking on the SS. La France IV, Colonel T. A. Roberts assuming command of the troops on board and Captain Patton the duties of Transport Adjutant. The embarkation having been completed on February 2, the steamer sailed for the United States, arriving at New York on February 9, and proceeding to Camp Upton, Long Island, for station.

### The Reception in Chicago

February 15, 1919, the regiment entrained at Camp Upton, Long Island, N. Y., en route for Camp Grant, Illinois, via Chicago. On February 17 the regiment arrived at Chicago, detrained, and proceeded to the Coliseum, where the citizens had arranged a reception for the returning regiment. At 2:00 p. m. the regiment paraded through the "Loop" district of Chicago and at about 4:00 p. m. entrained for Camp Grant, Illinois, arriving the same date and going into barracks.

From the date of arrival at Camp Grant, the regiment engaged in the various duties incident to preparation for demobilization until February 24, on which date the discharge of officers and enlisted men began, and continued until March 12, 1919, on which date the regiment formally ceased to exist.

### Cordial Relations Overseas

In commenting upon the friendly and cordial relations which existed between French, English, and Negro officers overseas Capt. John H. Patton, at one time commanding the 2nd Battalion, 370th Infantry (and who, together with Capt. James E. Dunjill and Lieut. Charles S. Parker, 366th Infantry, 92nd Division, were the only three Negroes who served in the capacity of Regimental Adjutants during the war), made the following statement:

"Both French and English officers were very friendly and hospitable in their relations with the colored officers of the 370th Infantry, which unit was brigaded with French troops. They made no discrimination whatsoever in their treatment of Negro officers, with whom they fraternized freely and truly regarded them as brothers in arms.

"Colonel Franklin A. Denison and Lieut.-Colonel Otis B. Duncan were frequently entertained at lunch, not only by officers of their own rank, but occasionally by French generals, for instance, by Gen. Hirshauer, Commander 2nd French Army; Gen. Lebuc, commanding the 73rd Division; Gen. De Boisuide, commanding the 10th Division; Gen. Savatier, commanding the 34th Division; Gen. Pauliner, commanding the 40th Army Corps, and frequently by Gen. Mittlehauser, who was the commanding officer of the 36th (French) Division."

### Awards and Commendations

The first American Distinguished Service Cross won by the 370th Regiment was awarded to Corporal Isaac Valley, Company M, in the following language: "When on July 22, 1918, a hand grenade was dropped among a group of soldiers in the trench and when he might have saved himself by flight he (Corp. Isaac Valley, Company M, 370th Infantry), attempted to cover it with his foot and thereby protect his comrades; in the performance of this brave act he was severely wounded."

While serving under General Mangin, the French commanding officer of the Tenth Army of France, the men of the 370th U. S. Infantry came to be known as the "Black Devils" by the Germans because of their fighting spirit, and were facetiously called "Partridges" by their French comrades because of their proud bearing.

Lieut.-Colonel Otis B. Duncan, commander of the Third Battalion, 370th Infantry, formerly the old Eighth Illinois National Guard Regiment, who was raised from the rank of Major to Lieutenant-Colonel at Camp Stuart, Newport News, Virginia, March, 1918 (being the highest ranking Negro officer in the American Expeditionary Forces), in speaking of the military campaign overseas in which the 370th U. S. Infantry participated, spoke in St. Louis of the difficulties which his men had to face and of the hardships they had to endure. He related some of the deeds of the regiment, but modestly refused to speak of his personal exploits. He wears, however, the French Croix de Guerre, with silver star, conferred by the French Government through General Vincendon, who, in a general order, relates how the Third Battalion (Lieut.-Colonel Duncan's command) took Logny, and *"carried away by their ardor of the previous week could not be stopped short of Gue d'Hossus, on November 11th after the armistice."*

Colonel Duncan continued: "Beginning September 27, 1918, we sailed into them and drove them back to the Ailette Canal, where they made a stand, facing us not 50 yards away. The fighting here was fierce. The Germans had placed barbed-wire entanglements in the canal, but we avoided these with pontoon bridges and continued our drive. We reached what was known as Mont des Signes, or "Monkey Mountain." We took up our position here between "Monkey Mountain" and the German line, near a narrow-gauge railroad. Here we encountered more concrete emplacements, dugouts, and barbed wire, and in getting to the Germans every man of us had to climb up on that railroad embankment, where we were fair marks for any kind of shell the Germans sent over. Naturally we lost many of our men.

"The 370th Infantry," Colonel Duncan said, "was the first regiment of allied troops to enter Petit Chapelle, in Belgium, and the citizens gave them an ovation. In the advance made by Gen. Mangin's army in its 59-day drive, from September 11, 1918, to the date of the Armistice (November 11, 1918), one or another of the units of the regiment was always under shell fire and fighting. In Petit Chapelle the regiment established its lines while German combat troops still were in the town."

Colonel Duncan served for 16 years with the Illinois National Guard, and saw service on the Mexican border, where he held the rank of Major. He was promoted to Lieutenant-Colonel in April, 1917. His home is in Springfield, Illinois, where for twenty years he was connected with the State Department of Education. The order citing him for bravery which was signed by Gen. Vincendon of the French Army, reads:

"The General commanding the Fifty-ninth Division cites to the Order of the Division Military the following names:

"Lieutenant-Colonel Duncan, Otis B., commanding the Third Battalion of the 370th R. I. U. S.

"In command of a battalion during the operations of September, October and November, 1918, up until our victorious armistice, with the very best of tact and highest type of judgment.

"At all times during the pursuit from the 6th of November to November 11th, 1918, he was present in person and was an example of bravery and endurance for his soldiers.

(Signed)　"VINCENDON."

On the Soissons front the 370th Regiment met with the strongest resistance of the enemy. Companies F, G, H, I, and M distinguished themselves in the great drive. They took *"Hill 304"* from the Germans, and the Tenth French Army, with which this unit was fighting renamed it "370th Infantry U. S. Hill" in honor of this Negro regiment.

Death Valley was another exciting place for this unit, for they had advanced into the Hindenburg line and every inch of ground that was won had to be held with science and grit. The "8th Illinois Regiment" gave a splendid account of itself, and proved at the Oise-Aisne Canal to be among the world's greatest troops. Their position was near the center of the 59th Division, in the same spot where France had lost division after division.

### Record of the 370th in France ,

Suffered 20 per cent casualties, lost ninety-five men and one officer killed outright.

Lost only one prisoner to the Germans in all the months they fought.

Captured many German cannon and German machine guns.

Participated in the final drive against the Germans on the French sector, advancing in the final stages of the war as far as thirty-five kilometers in one day.

*Were the first American troops to enter the French fortress of Laon* when it was wrested from the Germans after four years of war.

Won twenty-one American Distinguished Service Crosses, sixty-eight French War Crosses, and one Distinguished Service Medal.

*Fought the last battle of the war,* capturing a German wagon train of fifty wagons and crews a half-hour after the Armistice went into effect.

Refused to fraternize with the Germans even after the Armistice was signed.

# CHAPTER XVI

## THE 371ST INFANTRY IN FRANCE

*How This Colored Regiment of the "Red Hand" Division Helped to Win the War—Service in the Trenches Under General Goybet—In the Great Champagne Offensive—Fierce Fighting and Heavy Losses—The Regiment Decorated by the French—Individual Citations and Awards.*

In addition to the 369th Infantry Regiment (old New York Fifteenth) and the 370th (old Eighth Illinois), the 371st and 372nd Regiments, also composed of colored troops, were brigaded with the French during their active service overseas. It had been first decided by the United States War Department that these four colored regiments should form the nucleus of the 93rd Division (Provisional), but it was finally decided not to organize the 93rd Division, but to brigade these four regiments with French troops.

The 371st Infantry was organized August 31, 1917, at Camp Jackson, South Carolina, in compliance with War Department General Order No. 109, of August 16, 1917, as the First Provisional Infantry Regiment (colored). Col. Perry L. Miles assumed command of the regiment September 1, 1917. All the officers of the 371st regiment were white. On September 5, 1917, fourteen colored men from Pensacola, Florida, were received as the first recruits for the regiment. The time of arrival of recruits for the regiment was delayed by the War Department for about a month, because of the shortage of labor in moving the 1917 cotton crop. It was not until early in October that the first considerable body of recruits was received. By November 20, 1917, however, 3,380 men had been received by the regiment. These men were not all received at once, but in varying sized draft increments at different times. Of this number, 1,680 men were transferred to labor organizations and 500 to a combat organization at Camp Upton.

Under a staff of French officer instructors and interpreters, the 371st Infantry was reorganized on the French plan, soon after its arrival in France (April 23, 1918), with 194 men to the company and three machine gun companies to the regiment instead of one as on the American plan. All the American equipment was turned in, and the men were given the French rifles, bayonets, helmets, packs, and other equipment of the French soldier. Only the American khaki uniform remained. After a few weeks' instruction in this new equipment and in French tactics, the regiment went into the trenches as part of the 157th French Division under General Goybet. It remained in line for over three months, holding first the Avocourt and later the Verrières subsectors (northwest of Verdun). The regiment, with its division, was then taken out of line and thrown into the great September offensive in the Champagne. It took Cote 188, Bussy Ferme, Ardeuil, Montfauxelles, and Trières Ferme near Monthois, and captured a number of prisoners, 47 machine guns, 8 trench engines, 3 field pieces (77s), a munition depot, a number of railroad cars, and enormous quantities of lumber, hay, and other supplies. It shot down three German airplanes by rifle and machine-gun fire during the advance.

During the fighting between September 28 and October 6, 1918, its losses—which were mostly in the first three days—were 1,065 out of 2,384 actually engaged. The regiment was the apex of the attacking salient in this great battle. The percentage of both dead and wounded among the officers was rather greater than among the enlisted men. Realizing their great responsibilities, the wounded officers continued to lead their men until they dropped from exhaustion and lack of blood. The men were devoted to their leaders and as a result stood up against a most gruelling fire, bringing the regiment its well deserved fame.

For its action in the Champagne, the 371st was very highly commended by the French high command and awarded the Army citation. Vice-Admiral Moreau on behalf of the French Government decorated the regimental colors on January 27, 1919, in Brest. In addition to this regimental citation, 146 individual citations were awarded members of the 371st regiment. These were divided as follows:

American Distinguished Service Cross: Officers, 10; enlisted men, 12.

French decorations: Legion of Honor: Officers, 1. Croix de Guerre, in various grades: Officers, 34;. enlisted men, 89.

The 371st went into line for its initial experience in sector work at a time when a big German offensive was expected. From that time until shortly after the Armistice, the regiment remained continuously in line or was on the offensive. It was never in rest.

Returning homeward, the regiment sailed from Brest February 3, 1919, on the U. S. S. Leviathan and arrived at Hoboken, February 11, 1919. From there it went to Camp Upton, where it was broken up into detachments and sent to various camps for demobilization. The largest detachment, nearly 1,400 men with Regimental Headquarters, was sent to Camp Jackson, at Columbia, South Carolina. the place of the regiment's birth. Demobilization was completed and the regiment dissolved February 28, 1919.

### Praise for the Regiment

Col. P. L. Miles, who commanded the 371st, speaks in warm and approving terms of the efficiency of his men. "I never heard of similar performance by any regiment of any nation," Col. Miles writes, commenting on the feat of shooting three Boche airplanes "on the wing." "Our division commander, who had over four years of war over here, said he had heard of a former case where *one* machine had been shot down in a similar manner."

Another officer of the 371st, Capt. J. Leo Collins of East Pittsburgh, Pennsylvania, a member of the Allegheny County bar, who was commissioned an officer at Fort Oglethorpe, Georgia, and assigned to duty at Camp Jackson, South Carolina, where the 371st was organized and trained, says: "The 371st was the first draft regiment to sail from this country, sailing in April, 1918, and the first draft outfit to take the trenches. In the engagements around Verdun the fighting qualities and courage of our boys won the admiration and most profuse praise of the French. Citations were showered upon the valorous boys for their unflinching conduct in the face of withering machine-gun fire, which they overcame and silenced at the point of the bayonet. We broke the Hindenburg line at Monthois, and so rapidly did our boys move that a halt was called to enable the right and left flanks of our line to catch up. An excellent opportunity was furnished by comparisons as to just how good our colored soldiers were. At times we were brigaded with the French Moroccan and with English Canadian troops, with the Germans opposite, and it is quite safe to say that we certainly did not suffer by comparison.''

### Frank Washington's Story

A typical story of the courage and bravery of the men who composed the 371st Regiment is revealed in the record of Frank Washington of Edgefield, South Carolina. He proved his valor under conditions worthy of testing the bravery of the bravest. He was attached to Company B, and received an explosive bullet through the arm at Champagne. His story was as follows:

"It was all bad, but the worst came when the German airplanes flew low and sprayed the wounded with liquid fire. There is no way of putting out that liquid flame, and no one can help you, because the fire spreads so quickly. It is bad enough to be helpless out there, without water or friends, but to have a hellfiend fly over and just squirt torture at you—well, the Indians or the savages of Africa were not much worse. They were not so bad, in fact, for they were savages—while the Germans are supposed to be civilized.

"A Hun plane flew over when I was wounded, but believe me, when I saw that fire coming I sure did some lively hopping around. There wasn't going to be any broiled Washington if I could help it. But some of the mortally wounded were burned to death. Those Huns should be made to pay for that sort of thing. It ain't fighting; it's concentrated hell! But we had to attend to *their* wounded, and one of our officers saw that we did it.

"I went over the top in the fighting on September 29 and 30. We advanced after the usual barrage had been laid down for us. We went up to the Germans, and my platoon found itself under the fire of three machine guns. One of these guns was in front and running like a millrace. The other two kept a-piling into us from the flanks, and the losses were mounting. We got the front one. Its crew surrendered and we stopped. The other guns kept right on going, but we got them, too.

"It was while we were attacking the guns on our flanks that I was wounded. Ordinary bullets are bad enough, but the one that hit me was an explosive bullet. That's me, sir, every time! When things are coming, I am sure to get my share of them. I certainly did get my share.

"While I was knocked down, it was safer to stay down. Those machine guns kept right on pumping, not the ones we captured, but others. The wind they stirred up around your face kept you cool all the time. I finally started back, but found myself in a German barrage. It was shrapnel in front of me and machine guns in back of me. I lay right down and had a heart-to-heart chat with St. Peter. I never expected to get home again.

"They say Edgefield, back home, isn't much to look at, but I would have given two months' pay, including allotments, to get back on my farm about then. But now that I've been there and come back, I feel that I'm square with this country. I did my share, and I'm glad I did it."

### Jim McKinney's Experience

James P. McKinney, of Greeneville, South Carolina, attached to the Headquarters Company of the 371st Infantry, was wounded in the right arm by shrapnel. Gas infection set in and he was invalided out of service.

"The day we went over the top," says McKinney, "we took our positions early in the morning, and waited until our barrage had smashed the German defenses pretty well. About the time our barrage lifted, the Huns sent over a counter-barrage, but we went right through it, and over the slopes commanded by their machine guns. They turned loose everything they had to offer, and the storm of lead and steel got a lot of our men. Still, we followed our officers into the devils' trenches. A few of the Germans tried to fight with their bayonets, but we could all box pretty well, and boxing works with the bayonet. A few feints and then the death-stroke was the rule. Most of the Huns quit as soon as we got at them. Even the ones that had been on the machine guns yelled for us to spare them. I guess in the excitement some of them fared poorly.

"While we were advancing we worked along low and took all

available cover against the machine-gun fire directed against us. As soon as we came within range we opened fire with hand grenades and accounted for the machine-gun nests. I saw some of the gunners chained to their posts. Their barbed wire gave us trouble. Our artillery cut it up pretty badly, but still it was a pretty strong barrier against the advancing infantry. When we got tangled up in the wire, Fritz would play with his rifles. I've seen fellows get into a German trench with their uniforms flying in shreds.

"I was wounded in the arm at the 'big stunt.' We were attacking along the whole front, and the Huns were kept on the hop. While going up I was hit and had to fall behind. My arm was badly mussed up, but I threw a few grenades here and there, and guess I got a few of them.

"The German artillery fire was accurate. They had our ranges down to a science, and while they had good ammunition were hummers. They were good marksmen. Why, I've seen them cut a regular ditch along a row of shell-holes to prevent our troops from using the holes for shelter. There was positively nothing they didn't do that was horrible. I've seen them cut loose at a company runner with three-inch artillery. It was a funny sight for us, but not for the runner. The Huns would drop shells all around him while he fled on wings of terror. I never saw them get a runner with their artillery fire, but I've seen some very close shooting.

"Perhaps the most unusual experience I ever had was one day when we were advancing toward the German positions. They cut loose with their artillery and we were ordered to take open order and hunt cover. For two hours we were violently shelled, but thanks to Providence, none of us was killed. A few were slightly wounded. They mixed high explosives with gas and shrapnel.

"About the hardest luck of the war, though," concluded McKinney, "fell to the lot of a pal of mine. He got a piece of steak somewhere and was cooking it, his first bit of steak in months. While the meat was broiling the Germans began a gas bombardment. The men put on their masks, but the meat was ruined. That's what I call hard luck."

### The Men Never Flinched

Capt. W. R. Richey of Laurens, South Carolina, who commanded a company of the 371st Regiment, in writing of the men of that regiment, said: "On the afternoon of September 26, 1918, we received orders to move forward. We slept that night in a French communicating trench. I say slept, but really there was no sleep, as it was raining, and the noise from the guns would not let one sleep. The French had gone over the top and were pursuing the Huns.

"On Sunday morning my company went over the hill. We arrived at the position the attack was to start from at 7:30, after having a deadly artillery barrage on us over the hill. At 10 o'clock Sunday morning we were ordered to advance up the valley, but in the meantime an enemy plane flew down low, discovered our position, and signalled his artillery, which opened on us, and every minute seemed to be the last one. However, by rifle fire we brought the plane down, killing the pilot and observer.

"Long before we reached the village we could see the cowards running up a steep hill beyond, leaving lots of machine guns to stick out, and, believe me, when we reached our objective and rounded up the machine gunners the men of the 371st made quick work of them.

"In all, during the two days, Sunday and Monday, our battalion advanced about five miles without the aid of a single friendly artillery shot or any other help. We killed lots of Germans, captured lots of them, and also captured any quantity of material and several big guns.

"I am proud of all my officers and all of my men. The whole regiment fought like veterans, and with a fierceness equal to any white regiment. This was the first time any of them had been under aimed shell and machine-gun fire and they stood it like moss-covered old-timers. They never flinched or showed the least sign of fear. All that was necessary was to tell them to go and they went. Lots were killed and wounded, but they will go down in history as brave soldiers."

### "They Were Splendid Fighters"

Lieut. John B. Smith, another Southern officer, residing at Greenville, South Carolina, when asked about the soldierly quality of the colored drafted men who composed the 371st, said: "The men were good soldiers. They were obedient to all commands, and were in every way amenable to discipline. They were drafted men of all sorts, gathered from the farms and cities and towns, from every occupation. To be frank, we were a little dubious about them. We did not know whether they would stand under fire or not. But they did. They would go right into the thickest sort of fight, and they were splendid fighters."

"Would the colored men stand under a losing fight?" Lieut. Smith was asked. "Would they stand the gaff?"

"Yes," was his reply. "We never had that experience but once, for we were usually winning. But in the Argonne Forest we advanced seven kilometers one day, getting ahead of the line. The next day we were subjected to a terrific counter-attack. The enemy used artillery and gas, and airplanes, and rushed us with infantry and machine guns. We held our ground for seven hours, fighting part of the time with our gas masks on. It was as severe a test as any soldier ever had, but our men never faltered once, although our casualties were very heavy that day. No soldiers could have behaved any better under adverse circumstances.

"The colored men were given different treatment by the French people from what they had been accustomed to receive from white people at home," continued Lieut. Smith. "The French people could not grasp the idea of social discrimination on account of color. They said the colored men were soldiers, wearing the American uniform, and fighting in the common cause, and they could not see why they should be discriminated against socially. They received the men in their churches and homes and places of entertainment. The men accepted this, and it did not seem to appear strange to them. They seemed to understand that the customs over there were different from ours in the South, and let it go at that. I don't think anybody need be uneasy or apprehensive. I think these colored men, having made good soldiers, will now be more than anxious to make as good civilians, and that they will do so."

# CHAPTER XVII

## THE RECORD OF THE 372ND

*A Regiment Made Up of National Guard Troops and Drafted Men —Attached to the Famous French "Red Hand" Division—Its Splendid Record in France—At Hill 304—Heroic Exploits of Individuals—The Regiment Decorated With the Croix de Guerre—Citations and Awards.*

The 372nd Regiment of Infantry, United States Army, was a colored regiment composed of the First Separate Battalion of the District of Columbia; the 9th Ohio Separate Battalion; Company L of Massachusetts; the First Separate Company of Connecticut; the First Separate Company of Maryland—all these being National Guard troops, and 250 drafted men from Camp Custer, Michigan, recruited mainly from Michigan and Wisconsin.

It was the fortune of the 372nd Regiment, U. S. Army, to be brigaded, together with the 371st Infantry, throughout its entire period of service overseas, with the 157th Division of the French Army, the famous "Red Hand" Division. Like every other fighting regiment of Negro Americans, whether Regular Army, National Guard, or drafted men who had never handled a rifle or known the meaning of a salute until after the United States entered the war, the men of the 372nd, like those of the 371st, bore themselves throughout with the utmost gallantry and won the highest praise for their military achievements.

No extended narrative of the war could tell as clearly and forcefully, and at the same time concisely just what the 372nd did from the time its members left America until they returned home a little more than ten months later, than the following chronological record:

"Regiment embarked from Newport News, Virginia, March 30, 1918, for overseas duty on board U. S. S. Susquehanna.

"Reached port at St. Nazaire, France, April 13, 1918.

"Landed April 14, 1918, and marched to rest camp.

"Left rest camp Base Section No. 1, France, April 21, 1918, and entrained for Vaubecourt.

"Arrived at Vaubecourt 7:00 P. M., April 23, 1918.

"Left Vaubecourt 8:30 P. M. Sd. (same day), and hiked in a very heavy rain to Conde-en-Barrois, arriving there 2:00 A. M. April 24, 1918.

"Under special instructions with the 13th French Army Corps at Conde-en-Barrois from April 24, 1918, to May 25, 1918.

"Left Conde-en-Barrois 8:05 on the morning of May 28, 1918, in French motor trucks for Les Sennades, arriving at Les Sennades 1:30 P. M. Sd.

"Regiment took sector "Argonne West" May 29, 1918.

"In front line trenches May 31, 1918.

"Regimental Headquarters moved to La Neufour, June 9, 1918.

"Regiment changed sectors June 29-30, 1918, and took over the Vacquois Sector, a sub-sector of the Verdun.

"The 157th Division being a reserve division at this point where the enemy was expected to attack.

"Regimental Headquarters moved to Camp Chillaz June 30, 1918.

"Regiment left Vacquois sector July 13, 1918, *for "Hill 304" of the Verdun sector.*

"Colonel Young relieved from command and Colonel Tupes assumed command at Locheres.

"Regimental Headquarters moved to Bois St. Pierre July 18, 1918, and moved again Sd. to Sivry La Perche.

"Regiment left Sivry La Perche where it had stopped awaiting orders to take over sector July 25, 1918.

"Arrived and took sector about 9:00 P. M. Sd.  Usual trench duty.

"Severe shelling at Regimental P. C. August 3, 1918.

"Heavy shelling at Monzeville August 16, 1918, by a new regiment of Austrians which was opposing us, two American and one Frenchman wounded.  Second Lieut. James E. Sanford, Co. A, 372nd Infantry, captured by German patrol August 20, 1918.

"Left Hill 304 September 8, 1918, being relieved by the 129th U. S. Infantry of the 33rd Illinois Division.

"Hiked in rain and mud to Bois de Brocourt, the trip being a long and disagreeable one.

"Left Bois de Brocourt September 12, 1918, for Souasems La Granges; the trip was a short one and the boys full of fun.

"Arrived at Souasems Sd.

"Left Souasems in motor trucks for Juzanvigny September 13, 1918, an all night trip, arriving at Juzanvigny 12:00 M. September 14, 1918.

"Left for Brienne Le Chateau 8:05 September 17, 1918, to entrain for Jussecourt. (Napoleon attended school at Brienne Le Chateau.)

"Arrived at Vitry La Francois 2:00 P. M. Sd. The city is a beautiful one and overlooks the battlefield "MARNE," the trip being in box cars.

"Left next morning for Jussecourt at 9:00 A. M. on the hardest hike to date and arrived at Jussecourt 8:00 P. M. September 18, 1918.

"Regiment left for Contault September 20, 1918, at 8:00 P. M., arriving there at 12:30 A. M. September 21, 1918.

"Left Contault for Dommartin 9:00 P. M. September 22, 1918. Arrived Sd.

"Left for Camp Des Mangnieux 9:00 P. M. September 23, 1918, arriving at 12:30 P. M. September 24, 1918.

"Left for Hans September 24, 1918, arriving and joining the 9th French Army Corps at Hans Sd.

"Left Hans to take position in attack; the 3rd Battalion leaving September 26, 1918, the 1st September 27, 1918, and the 3rd September 28, 1918.

### "Over the Top" on September Morn

" 'Over the Top' September 28, 1918, the 3rd Battalion started after the Boche. The first blow being delivered by the 2nd Moroccan Division of shock troops. The retreating Boches are still bombarding our position. Machine gun fire is thick and the 88s are falling like hail.

"On the morning of September 29, 1918, we are trying hard to keep up with the retreating enemy, which is retreating fast, unable to stand our assault. This afternoon it is raining which is unfortunate for our wounded, as there are many.

"Today is September 30, 1918, and we find that the 1st Battalion is on our right, and advancing fast in the rain and mud. Machine gun opposition is still stiff. Our casualties are small and we have captured a large number of prisoners.

"October 1, 1918, we are meeting with a stiff resistance from the enemy who has fortified himself in a hill during the past night. Owing to the bad condition of the ground we are not getting any support from the French artillery.

"October 2, 1918, we have driven the enemy out of Fountain-en-Dormois and are now in the village. Still we are giving the enemy no rest, they are retreating across the valley to one of their supply bases which has a railroad running into the same. The enemy is now burning the supplies which cannot be moved.

"October 3, 1918, we have advanced and captured the little village of Ardeuil and a considerable amount of war material. Our losses have been rather heavy during the past 24 hours, but we have inflicted a much heavier loss on the enemy. On our right the 1st Battalion has taken the village of Sechaut after some hard fighting by Company A.

"October 4, 1918, the 2nd Battalion is going in this morning, and we are resting at Vieox, which is about four kilometers from Monthois and is one of the enemy's railroad centers and hospital bases. The enemy is busy destroying supplies and moving wounded. We can see trains moving out of Monthois. Our artillery is bombarding all roads and railroads in the vicinity. The enemies' fire is fierce and we are expecting a counter-attack.

"October 5, 1918, the German artillery has opened up good and strong and we are on the alert. They attacked us and a stiff hand-to-hand combat ensued. Again he has been driven back, suffering an exceedingly heavy loss. We have taken many prisoners from about twelve different regiments. After resting a little, we continued our advance and are now on the outskirts of Monthois.

"October 6, 1918, the enemy is throwing a stiff barrage on our left where the 333rd French Infantry is attacking. The enemy is again being driven back. The liaison work of the 157th Division has been wonderful, not the slightest gap has been left open.

"October 7, 1918, our patrols entered Monthois early in the morning but were driven out by machine gun fire, but returned with a gun and its crew. We have just received word that we are to be relieved by the 76th Regiment, French, sometime during the night; we were relieved at 8:00 P. M. We hiked a very long distance over the ground. We fought so hard to take to Minnecourt where the regiment proceeded to reorganize.

"Regiment reached Somme Bionne Oct. 9, 1918. Regiment left Somme Bionne Oct. 11, 1918 to entrain for Vignemont. Left Valmy 8:00 A. M. Oct. 12, 1918 and arrived at Vignemont Oct. 13, 1918. Hiked 15 kilometers to St. Leonard and arrived Sd. Left St. Leonard for Ban de Laveline in the Dept. of the Bosges Oct. 15, 1918, arrived at Laveline 10:15 P. M. Sd.

"November 7, 1918, 1 officer and 22 enlisted men captured by German patrol. Nov. 10, 1918, a patrol of Co. A, took several prisoners from a German patrol.

### Everybody Happy When the End Came

"November 11, 1918, everybody in the village of Laveline is happy over news of the abdication of the Kaiser and the signing of the armistice. Martial music is plentiful and the colors of the regiment are displayed from the P. C.

"The regiment left the 10th Army Corps Nov. 17th, 1918.

"Left Laveline Nov. 17, 1918 and hiked 45 kilometers to Granges, arrived at Granges the morning of Nov. 18, 1918. Usual close order drill at this station preparing for overseas duty.

"Regiment left 157th Division Dec. 13, 1918, the Commanding General thereof was down to pay his respects to the regiment.

"January 1, 1919, regiment left for Le Mans (forwarding camp). The 92nd Division was assembled here and we met many of our old friends. Left Le Mans January 10, 1919 for Brest (embarkation port). Left Brest February 3, 1919 for Hoboken. Arrived at Hoboken February 11, 1919 on world's greatest ship, The Leviathan, U. S. N. (formerly the Vaterland owned by Germany)."

—

On October 8th the 157th Division with others was transferred from the 9th Army Corps of the French to the 10th Army Corps. General Garnier Duplessis took this occasion to commend the division, particularly mentioning the American regiments in the following general order:

"P. C. October 7th, 1918

"9th Army Corps.
Staff 3rd Bureau
No. 2555

## NOTE

"The 157th, 161st and the 2nd Moroccan Divisions are leaving the Army Corps. The General commanding the 10th Army Corps addressed to them his most sincere thanks and his warmest congratulations for the glorious success achieved by their admirable ardour and their indomitable tenacity. He salutes the brave American Regiments who have rivaled in intrepidity their French Comrades.

"He cannot recount here the feats which have been performed for every one of the days of that victorious journey. They are inscribed on the conquered grounds, materialized by the trophies taken from the enemy and engraved in the heart of the chief who bows before the troops and salutes them profoundly.

GENERAL GARNIER DUPLESSIS,
Commanding the 9th Army Corps."

In transmitting this order to the several regiments comprising the Division, General Goybet reviewed the exploits of the Division in the following order:

"P. C. October 8, 1918.

"157th Division.
"Staff.

### General Order No. 234

"In transmitting to you with legitimate pride the thanks and congratulations of the General Garnier Duplessis, allow me, my dear friends of all ranks, Americans and French, to thank you from the bottom of my heart as a chief and a soldier for the expression of gratitude for the glory which you have lent our good 157th Division. I had full confidence in you but you have surpassed my hopes.

"During these nine days of hard fighting you have progressed nine kilometers through powerful organized defenses, taken nearly 600 prisoners, 15 guns of different calibres, 20 minenwefers, and nearly 150 machine guns, secured an enormous amount of engineering material, an important supply of artillery ammunition, brought down by your fire three enemy aeroplanes.

"THE 'RED HAND' sign of the Division, thanks to you, became a bloody hand which took the Boche by the throat and made him cry for mercy. You have well avenged our glorious dead.

(Signed)  GOYBET,<br>General, Commanding 157th Division."

But even greater distinction was to come. On the following day, October 8th, Colonel Tupes of the 372nd, received notice that his regiment had been recommended for citation in the general orders of the French Army. Following is a translation of the official order conveying this splendid news:

October 8, 1918.

"157th D. I.
No. 5508

"From: Colonel Quillet, Commanding 157th D. I.
   To:     Colonel Tupes, Commanding 372nd Infantry.

"The Colonel Commanding the I. D. has recommended your regiment for citation in the orders of the French Army worded as follows:

" 'Gave proof, during its first engagement, of the finest qualities of bravery and daring which are virtues of assaulting troops.

" 'Under the orders of Colonel Tupes dashed with superb gallantry and admirable scorn of danger to the assault of a position continuously defended by the enemy,—taking it by storm under an exceptionally violent machine gun fire. Continued the progression in spite of enemy artillery fire and very severe losses. They made numerous prisoners, captured cannons, machine guns, and important war material.'

(Signed)  QUILLET."

On October 8 General Goybet of the 157th Division, in a communication addressed to the commanding officers of the 371st and 372nd Infantry Regiments, U. S. A., said:

"Your troops have been admirable in their attack. You must be proud of the courage of your officers and men; and I consider it an honor to have them under my command.

"The bravery and dash of your regiment won the admiration of the 2nd Moroccan Division who are themselves versed in warfare. Thanks to you during those hard days. The Division was at all times in advance of all other divisions of the Army Corps. I am sending you all my thanks and beg you to transmit them to your subordinates.

"I called on your wounded. Their morale is higher than any praise.                                                    GOYBET."

It is to be noted that at the date this communication was received, October 8, 1918, the 372nd had on its roster six colored line officers, who were later transferred to the 92nd Division.

### After the Armistice

On the day of the signing of the Armistice, November 11, 1918, the regiment was at Ban-de-Laveline. How the termination of the war was celebrated is told by Sergeant Wm. J. Huntley of the 372nd Infantry, whose account follows:

"Ban-De-Laveline has today the signs of what one might term a "contented, mirthful, and prosperous village.' It was Ban-De-Laveline before the war. News of the abdication of the Kaiser, a symbol of the total collapse of the German empire, together with the official announcement of the signing of the terms of the armistice, putting an end to the fifty months of anguish, brought out all the legendary light-heartedness of the people of this vicinity.

"One of the most inspiring scenes I ever witnessed was today about 11:05 A. M. The Regimental band played 'Marseillaise', 'The Star Spangled Banner' and 'God Save the King.' As soon as the last note was sounded, hilarious cheers, by both soldiers and civilians, were almost deafening. Old men jumped and threw up their hats, women, whose hearts were heavy from a strain caused by a relentless war, waved their hands and aprons in exultant joy and children romped joyously up and down the streets. The bell and chimes on the church, which had been previously silent, sent their resonant peals far and near. Indeed, they rang out 'glad tidings of joy.' In the meantime, the band struck up a lively march and started up the street followed by 'Old Glory', the regimental colors and soldiers, Americans and French. The scene was a beautiful blending of colors—the khaki and the blue. It seemed as if they wanted to assemble in one great family to celebrate the glorious events, and to see the reflection of their own gladness in the faces of their fellow comrades. The street was filled with a solid, slowly-moving and seething mass of humanity. It appeared to me that the brotherhood of the trenches was heralding the brotherhood of men.

"I should have mentioned one incident in connection with the parade, namely: When the band marched up the street around by the church toward the trenches, which was only about two kilometers, the procession was met by a party bringing to the infirmary a Boche who had been captured and also wounded in the early morning by our boys. This party joined the procession and in regular cadence these stalwart fellows marched in review with their Boche, who later was the occasion of much curiosity. I am quite sure this prisoner rejoiced silently that the horribleness of such hideous work of bestial ferocity, that only the Germans know, was at an end, for according to his own statement he declared his comrades were satisfied with peace negotiations and also stated that the Kaiser must abdicate. Thankful for human hearts, he was not allowed to suffer but was immediately relieved of his humiliation and pain— and such were the scenes, mingled with sadness and gladness, the most inspiring, significant, and most impressive I have ever witnessed.

"Elaborate preparations were made for the grand entertainment which was a part of the day's program. The decorations, prepared by both Americans and French, were as pretentious as though prepared for the metropolis city of France. At nightfall the streets were lighted with electricity (a thing which had not been done since the beginning of the war) with jack o'lanterns, lamps and flares of every description. Long before the hour to begin the program the theatre was filled by civilians from neighboring villages and with soldiers of the cantonment.

"At 7:30 the master of ceremonies announced the beginning of the program and at this time the building's seating capacity was taxed to its utmost and standing room at a premium. The program began with an overture by the band. The significance of the occasion, a most enthusiastic audience that eagerly waited, the contagious gladness which permeated the atmosphere, created an environment in which the band has never appeared to better advantage. At the conclusion of the number, men and women applauded frantically and the American contingent whistled itself breathless.

"The program composed of solos, quartettes, dancing, comic skit by our boys and solos, duets, comic monologues and a pantomime with characters representing Alsace, Lorraine, France, and America, by the French. Some of these were entertaining and some were otherwise. But considering the events of the day, not one left disappointed and felt that the evening was spent without profit. As a closing number, Collins, the Caruso of the Regiment, sang in a pleasing manner "Perfect Day."

"And thus Monday, the eleventh day of the eleventh month, 1918, was passed."

The praise and compliments of the French for the 372nd did not terminate with the cessation of hostilities, for on November 17th, General Vandenberger, commanding the 10th Army Corps, issued the following general order:

November 17, 1918.

"10th Army Corps.
"Staff (French)

## GENERAL ORDER

"It has been an honor for the 10th Army Corps to receive and welcome the 157th Division after its successes in Champagne.

"During the few weeks that the Division belonged to the Army Corps its Regiments of Americans and French have by their conduct and biting activity produced the best impression.

"It had prepared in its sector the ways of penetrating in Alsace and it should have deserved the honor of entering it.

"But military necessities bring today the higher command to consider its use in another part of the front and to give to the Americans a part of the front facing Belgium, Luxemburg and a corner of Lorraine.

"The General commanding the 10th Army Corps sees with pain the gallant Division and her Chief General Goybet move away from him. He cannot defend himself from the painful thought that General Goybet will not have the consolation of treading with his Division that reconquered land that keeps the remains of one of his sons.

"To all he wishes good luck and expresses the hope of meeting again one day.

(Signed) "VANDENBERGER

"General, Commanding the 10th Army Corps."

When the orders were finally issued for the return to America of the 371st and 372nd, Colonel Quillet, commanding the 157th Infantry Division, addressed the following message of farewell to Colonel Miles and Colonel Tupes, commanders respectively of these two Negro regiments::

December 15, 1918.

"157th Division
"Staff of the Infantry.

## ORDER OF THE DIVISIONAL INFANTRY NO. 100

"The 371st and 372nd Infantries are leaving France after having carried on a hard campaign of six months with the I. D. 157.

"After having energetically held a series of difficult sectors, they took a glorious part in the great decisive battle which brought the final Victory.

"In sector, they have shown an endurance, a vigilance, a spirit of devotion and a remarkable discipline.

"In battle they have taken by storm, with a magnificent animation, very strong positions doggedly defended by the enemy.

"In contemplating the departure of these two fine regiments which I commanded with pride, I desire to tell them all how much I think of them and also to thank them for the generous and precious concurrence which they brought to us at the decisive period of the great war.

"I shall keep always in my soldier heart their loyal memories and particularly those of their distinguished commanders who have become my friends: Colonel Miles and Colonel Tupes.

(Signed) QUILLET."

"Commanding the I. D. 157.

On the same day, General Goybet, Commander of the entire 157th Division also took occasion to praise the work of these American fighters.

H. Q., December 15, 1918.

"157th Division
Etat-Major.

### GENERAL ORDERS NO. 245

"On the 12th of December, 1918, the 371st and 372nd R. I. U. S. have been replaced at the disposal of the American Higher Command.

"With a deep feeling of emotion, on behalf of the 157th Division, and in my own personal name, I come to bid farewell to our brave comrades.

"For seven months we have lived as brothers at arms, partaking in the same activities, sharing the same hardships and the same dangers. Side by side we took part in the great Champagne Battle which was to be crowned by a tremendous victory.

"Never will the 157th Division forget the indomitable dash, the heroical rush of the American Regiments up the Observatory Ridge and into the plain of Monthois. The most powerful defenses, the most strongly organized M. G. nests, the heaviest artillery barrages, nothing could stop them. These crack regiments overcame every obstacle with a most complete contempt for danger; through their steady devotion the RED HAND Division, for nine whole days of severe struggle, was constantly leading the way for the victorious advance of the 4th Army.

"Officers, non-commissioned officers, and men, I respectfully salute our glorious comrades who have fallen, and I bow to your colours, side by side with the flag of the 333rd Regiment of Infantry they have shown us the way to VICTORY.

"Dear friends from America, when you will be back again on the other side of the ocean don't forget the Red Hand Division. Our brotherhood has been cemented in the blood of the brave and such bonds will never be destroyed.

"Remember your General who is proud of having commanded you, and be sure of his grateful affection to you all for ever.

"General Goybet, Commanding the 157th Division.

(Signed)　Goybet."

### Washington Men Win Honors

In the 372nd Infantry was the First Battalion of the District of Columbia National Guard, whose heroes were prevented by the Armistice from winning added glory. It would have fallen to its lot to have the honor of being the vanguard of the French Army of Occupation. Of the nearly 600 District of Columbia colored men who were with the 372nd, at least 200 were wounded more or less seriously, and about 33 were killed; probably the first to fall with a fatal wound was Private Kenneth Lewis.

The District of Columbia men proclaimed Sergeant Ira Payne as the hero of heroes among the District of Columbia fighters. He wears the Croix de Guerre and "isn't afraid of the devil himself," according to the men of his company.

Sergeant Payne speaks modestly of his exploits. He says: "During the fighting at Sechault the Germans were picking off the men in my platoon from behind a bush. The Germans had several machine guns behind that bush and kept up a deadly fire in spite of our rifle fire directed at the bush. We did our best to stop those machine guns, but the German aim became so accurate that they were picking off five of my men every minute. We couldn't stand for that, so I decided I would get that little machine gun nest myself and I went after it. I left our company, detoured, and by a piece of luck got behind the bush. I got my rifle into action and 'knocked off' two of those German machine gunners. That ended it. The other Germans couldn't stand so much excitement. The Boches surrendered, and I took them into our trenches as prisoners."

Another hero is Benjamin Butler, a private, awarded the Croix de Guerre. His citation reads: "For displaying gallantry and bravery and distinguishing himself in carrying out orders during the attack on Sechault on September 29, 1918, under heavy bombardment and machine gun fire." Butler said: "I did very little. During this fight with several others, I carried dispatches to the first line trenches from headquarters. They decorated me, I suppose, because I was the only one lucky enough to escape being knocked off."

Private Charles E. Cross was awarded the Croix de Guerre for "his speed and reliability in carrying orders to platoons in the first line under the enemy's bombardment on September 29, 1918." "In some cases," Cross said, "I had to creep across No-Man's-Land, and a greater part of the time I was exposed to enemy fire."

First Sergeant John A. Johnson was termed in his citation and award of the Croix de Guerre "a heroic soldier." "Near Sechault, during the time the District men were making a big effort to capture the town, I was put in the front line not fifty feet away from the enemy," Johnson reports. "A greater part of the time I was exposed to machine-gun fire. I suppose I got my medal just because I stuck with my men. Quite a few District boys were bumped off at this point."

Private William H. Braxton, a member of the Machine Gun Company of the regiment, received the Croix de Guerre for displaying "zealous bravery." "An enemy party," his citation reads, "having filtered through his platoon and attacked same in rear, Private Braxton displayed marked gallantry in opening fire on the enemy and killing one and wounding several others, finally dispersing the entire party." "The men who stuck by me when death stared them in their faces, deserve just as much credit as I," Braxton said. "I was only temporary leader of the men."

The official list of the Washington men of the First Separate Battalion of the District of Columbia who were decorated follows: First Sergeant John A. Johnson, Company B; First Sergeant Ira A. Payne, Company A; Sergeant James A. Marshall, Company B; Sergeant Norman Jones, Company B; Sergeant Homer Crabtree, Company B; Sergeant Norman Winsmore, Company C; Corporal John R. White, Company B; Corporal Benjamin Butler, Company C; Corporal March Graham, Company D; Private Warwick Alexander, Company B; Private George H. Budd, Company B; Private Thomas A. Frederick, Company B; Private John S. Parks, Company B; Private Charles H. Murphy, Company C; Private William N. Mathew, Company D; Private Ernest Payne, Company D; Private Joseph McKamey, Company A; Private William Dickerson, Company A; Sergeant Major Samuel B. Webster.

## Decoration of the Regiment

A special correspondent of the Paris edition of the *New York Herald* transmitted a report to that publication of the distinguished honors shown the 372nd when Vice Admiral Moreau, French Commander of the Port of Brest, decorated the colors of the regiment with the Croix de Guerre and palm for distinguished service in the Champagne offensive, just before the regiment sailed for America. During September and October, 1918, individual honors had been previously conferred as chronicled above. The ceremonies in which Vice Admiral Moreau took part were held at Cours Dajot, overlooking the Port of Commerce and was witnessed by thousands of French civilians and soldiers and sailors of several nations.

The *Herald* report says: "The American fighters, numbering about 3,000, were with the famous French 'Red Hand' division. They became heroes on many fighting-fronts, and were in the Vosges Mountains when the Armistice was signed.

"Vice Admiral Moreau arrived at about 2:30. Major General Helmick, of the American post of Brest, was present as a spectator. The regimental band added much to the program with 'Keep the Home Fires Burning,' patriotic selections, and 'Caesar's Triumphal March.'

"The basis of this citation was included in the Army orders in favor of the 372nd Infantry, which Colonel Quillet, commanding the I. D. of the 157th, submitted to the Commanding General after the Champagne offensive battle.

"The substance of Colonel Quillet's commendation was included in Admiral Moreau's words, to the regiment.

"After the delivery of the Croix de Guerre to the regiment, Admiral Moreau conferred the Croix de Guerre and palm on Adjutant Walsh and read quotations from Colonel Quillet's commendations quoted above, dated and signed December 15, 1918."

## A Monument to the Dead

The regiment did not immediately leave France, however. While waiting for transport, it was decided by the officers and men of the regiment that they would erect a monument with the permission

of the French Government, to mark the ground on which so many
of their comrades had fallen in battle. For the carrying out of
this plan, General Goybet and Colonel Quillet were requested to act
as Trustees for the regimental monument fund, in the following communication from Colonel Tupes:

"HEADQUARTERS 372nd INFANTRY
Forwarding Camp,
A. P. O. 762.

January 9, 1919.

"From: Commanding Officer.
"To General Mariano Goybet and Colonel Augustin Quillet.
"Subject: Trusteeship for Monument.

"1. It is the desire of the officers and enlisted men of this
regiment to erect a monument upon the ground where we have fought
in memory of those who have fallen on the field of battle. In order
to accomplish this, it is necessary that the regiment have representatives residing in France. Due to the high regard we have for our
former French Commanders, it is the request of all ranks of the
regiment that General Mariano Goybet, commanding the 157th D. I.
and Colonel Augustin Quillet, commanding the 157th I. D., act as
trustees of a fund that has been donated by all ranks for the erection
and maintenance of a monument. The fund, consisting of 10,744
francs, has been deposited with the Credit Lyonnais at Le Mans
Sarthe, to the credit of the above mentioned trustees. The trust
fund so deposited is for the purpose of securing a site, purchasing
and erecting a monument upon the site, erecting a suitable fence or
safeguard for the monument and covering all expenses incidental
to the purchasing, erection and maintenance of the monument and
fence or safeguard and for making and forwarding a limited number of photographs of the monument after it is erected.

"2. It is the desire of the members of the regiment that the
monument shall be a plain shaft of granite or other durable stone
with the following inscription in English:

**In Memory of the Members of the
372nd U. S. Infantry, killed in Action September 26,
1918, to October 7, 1918**

"3. It is the desire of the regiment that the monument be erected if practicable, in a conspicuous place near a public roadway and near the most forward point of the advance of the regiment. It is the request of the regiment that the two trustees take all legal measures to put the above in full force with the least possible delay.

"4. It is requested that 24 photographs of the monument, taken after its erection on the site selected, be forwarded to the present Commanding Officer of the 372nd U. S. Infantry.

"HERSCHEL TUPES,<br>
Colonel Infantry."

The trust was accepted by the Gallant French officers, and under their direction there is to be erected in France a massive granite memorial to the heroic American Negroes of the 372nd. May they rest in peace!

# CHAPTER XVIII

## NEGRO HEROES OF THE WAR

*The Exploit of Henry Johnson and Needham Roberts—How one American Soldier in No Man's Land Killed Four Germans and Wounded Twenty-eight Others Single Handed—First American Soldiers to Receive the French Croix de Guerre—Other Instances of Individual Heroism by Negro Soldiers.*

There is no prouder chapter in the history of the Negro race than the records of the American and French Armies that tell of the heroic exploits of colored soldiers, exploits that rank with the most glorious examples of individual courage and devotion to duty in all history. The names of these men who, through their personal bravery and daring, won the coveted Distinguished Service Cross of the American Army or the no less significant *Croix de Guerre* (Cross of War) of the French, will live forever in the annals of the race.

The first American soldiers of any race, white or black, to receive the French *Croix de Guerre*, were Henry Johnson of Albany, N. Y. and Needham Roberts, of Trenton, N. J. Both men were privates in the 369th Infantry, the old Fifteenth New York National Guard regiment. This regiment was brigaded with French troops and early in May, 1918, with other American Negro detachments, was put in charge of a long sector of the front line trenches. The event that gave to Johnson and Roberts the honor of being the first Americans to win the French War Cross is best described in a letter which Colonel William Hayward wrote to Mrs. Edna Johnson, the wife of Private (now Sergeant) Johnson. Colonel Hayward's letter follows:

### Colonel Hayward to Mrs. Johnson

"Your husband, Private Henry Johnson is in my regiment, 369th United States infantry, formerly the Fifteenth New York infantry. He has been at all times a good soldier and a good boy of fine

morale and upright character. To these admirable traits he has
lately added the most convincing numbers of fine courage and fighting ability. I regret to say at the moment that he is in the hospital,
seriously, but not dangerously wounded, the wounds having been
received under such circumstances that every one of us in the regiment would be pleased and proud to trade places with him. It was
as follows:

"He and Private Needham Roberts were on guard together at
a small outpost on the front line trench near the German lines and
during the night a strong raiding party of Germans numbering
from twelve to twenty judging by the weapons, clothing and para-
phernalia they left behind and by their footprints, stole across No
Man's Land and made a surprise attack in the dead of the night on
our two brave soldiers.

### Fighting Against Great Odds

"We had learned some time ago from captured German prisoners that the Germans had heard of the regiment of Black Americans in this sector, and the German officers had told their men
how easy to combat and capture them it would be. So this raiding
party came over, and on the contrary Henry Johnson and Needham
Roberts attended very strictly to their duties. At the beginning
of the attack the Germans fired a volley of bullets and grenades and
both of the boys were wounded, your husband three times and
Roberts twice, then the Germans rushed the post, expecting to make
an easy capture. In spite of their wounds, the two boys waited coolly
and courageously and when the Germans were within striking distance opened fire, your husband with his rifle and Private Roberts
from his helpless position on the ground with hand grenades. But
the German raiding party came on in spite of their wounded and in
a few seconds our boys were at grips with the terrible foe in a
desperate hand-to-hand encounter, in which the enemy outnumbered
them ten to one.

"The boys inflicted great loss on the enemy, but Roberts was
overpowered and about to be carried away when your husband, who
had used up all of the cartridges in the magazine of his rifle and
had knocked one German down with the butt end of it, drew his bolo
from his belt. A bolo is a short heavy weapon carried by the American

soldier, with the edge of a razor, the weight of a cleaver and the point of a butcher knife. He rushed to the rescue of his former comrade, and fighting desperately, opened with his bolo the head of the German who was throttling Roberts, and turned to the boche who had Roberts by the feet, plunging the bolo into the German's bowels. This one was the leader of the German party, and on receiving what must have been this mortal wound, exclaimed in American English, without a trace of accent, "Oh, the son of a —— got me," thus proving that he was undoubtedly one of the so-called German-Americans who came to our country, not to become a good citizen, but to partake of its plenty and bounty and then return to fight for the kaiser and help enslave the world. He was doubtless selected as a leader of the party to speak English and perhaps fool my soldiers, calling to them in English not to fire, that it was a friend.

## Knifing the Hun

"Henry laid about him right and left with his heavy knife, and Roberts, released from the grasp of the scoundrels, began again to throw hand grenades and exploded them in their midst, and the Germans, doubtless thinking it was a host instead of two brave Colored boys fighting like tigers at bay, picked up their dead and wounded and slunk away, leaving many weapons and part of their shot riddled clothing, and leaving a trail of blood, which we followed at dawn near to their lines. We feel certain that one of the enemy was killed by rifle fire, two by your husband's bolo, one by grenades thrown by Private Roberts and several others grievously wounded. So it was in this way the Germans found the Black Americans. Both boys have received a citation of the French general commanding the splendid French division in which my regiment is now serving and will receive the *Croix de Guerre* (Cross of War). The citation translated, is as follows:

"First—Johnson, Henry (13348), private in company C, being on double sentry duty during the night and having been assaulted by a group composed of at least one dozen Germans, shot and disabled one of them and grievously wounded two others with his bolo. In spite of three wounds with pistol bullets and grenades at the beginning of the fight, this man ran to the assistance of his wounded comrade who was about to be carried away prisoner by the enemy, and continued to fight up to the retreat of the Germans. He has given a beautiful example of courage and activity.

"Second—Roberts, Needham (13369), private in Company C, being on double sentry duty during the night was assaulted and grievously wounded in his leg by a group of Germans continuing fighting by throwing grenades, although he was prone on the ground, up to the retreat of the enemy. Good and brave soldier. The general requested that the citation of the division commander to the soldier Johnson be changed to the citation of the orders of the Army.

"Some time ago the great General Gouraud placed in my hands the sum of 100 francs to be sent to the family of the first one of my soldiers wounded in the fight with the enemy under heroic circumstances. Inasmuch as these boys were wounded simultaneously, and both displayed great heroism, I think it but fair to send to each one-half of this sum. Accordingly I am enclosing New York exchange for the equivalent of fifty francs. I am sure that you have made a splendid contribution to the cause of liberty by giving your husband to your country, and it is my hope and prayer to bring him back to you safe and sound, together with as many comrades as it is humanly possible by care and caution to conserve and bring back to America. But it must be borne in mind that we cannot all come back, that none of us can come back until the job is done."

### Whole Regiments Decorated

Four Negro regiments won the signal honor of being awarded the Croix de Guerre as a regiment. These were the 369th, the 370th, the 371st and the 372nd. The 369th (old 15th New York National Guard) was especially honored for its record of 191 days on the firing line, exceeding by five days the term of service at the front of any other American regiment.

Among the honors which France has bestowed upon American soldiers none is more interesting than the "citation" by which the entire 369th Regiment was given the coveted Croix de Guerre. The citation was for gallantry in the September and October offensives in the Champagne sector. By command of General Martin, commanding the 92nd Division, General Orders were issued commending a number of colored officers, non-commissioned officers, and privates of the 369th Infantry for meritorious conduct in action at Bois Frehaut, near Pont-à-Mousson, November 10 and 11, 1918, during the drive on Metz. Those named in this General Order were Captain John H. Allen, First Lieutenants Leon F. Stewart, Frank L. Drye, Walter Lyons, David W. Harris, Benj. F. Ford; Second Lieutenants George L. Gaines and Russell C. Atkins; Sergeants Richard W. White, John Simpson, Robert Townsend, Solomon D. Colston, Ransom Elliott, and Charles Jackson; Corporals Thomas B. Coleman, Albert Taylor, Charles Reed, and James Conley; and Privates Earl Swanson, Jesse Cole, James Hill, Charles White, and George Chaney. In the same General Orders the following were cited for bravery in action: Sergeant Isaac Hill, bravery displayed at Frapelle; First Lieutenant John Q. Lindsey, for bravery at Lesseux, both of the 366th Infantry, and First Lieutenant Edward Bates of the 368th Ambulance Corps, and Sergeant Walter L. Gross of the 266th Infantry, for distinguished service near Hominville.

### Individual Awards for Bravery

Among the first men in the 92nd Division to receive the Distinguished Service Cross for bravery in the fighting in the Argonne was First Lieutenant Robert L. Campbell. He was twice cited for bravery in a single battle. Another instance of his bravery is told, when it became necessary to send a runner with a message to the left flank of an American firing line. The way was across an open field swept by heavy machine-gun fire. Volunteers were called for. Private Edward Saunders of Company "I" responded. Before he had gone far a shell cut him down, when Lieutenant Campbell sprang to his rescue and carried his man back to the American lines. For the valor shown both were cited for the Distinguished Service Cross. Before entering the army Campbell was instructor in mechanical engineering at the Agricultural and Technical College at Greensboro, North Carolina.

Another single detail taken from the record of this same company is the instance of John Baker; having volunteered, he was taking a message through heavy shell fire to another part of the line; a shell struck his hand, tearing away part of it, but he unfalteringly delivered the message.

First Lieutenant T. M. Dent was promoted to a captaincy.

On September 28, 1918, Dent led his platoon in a most heroic charge and captured a German machine gun which covered the bridge crossing the Vallée Moreau, the key to the battle at this point. Captain Dent gained the highest rank of any officer in the 92nd Division under 23 years of age. He was also mentioned by Major-General Ballou as follows: "The Commanding General desires to call the attention of the entire command to the excellent work and meritorious conduct of Captain R. A. Williams and First Lieutenant T. M. Dent, both of the 368th Infantry. During the days of the fight around Vienne-le-Chateau both of these officers displayed courage and leadership and through their conduct should be an example to the other officers of the division."

In another General Order Second Lieutenant Nathan O. Goodloe of the 368th Machine Gun Company was commended for excellent work and meritorious conduct. During the operations in the Argonne Forest Lieutenant Goodloe was attached to the 3rd Battalion; during the course of the action it became necessary to reorganize the battalion and withdraw part of it to a secondary position. He carried out the movement under a continual machine-gun fire from the enemy. General Martin said of him: "Lieutenant Goodloe's calm courage set an example that inspired confidence in his men."

General Martin also cited for meritorious conduct near Vienne-le-Chateau, Tom Brown, a wagoner, who as driver of an ammunition wagon, displayed remarkable courage, coolness, and devotion to duty under fire. Brown hauled his wagon, even after his horse had been hurled into a ditch by shells, and despite his own painful wounds, worked until he had extricated his horse from the ditch, refusing to quit until he had completed his work, even though covered with blood from a painful wound.

Lieutenant Thomas Edward Jones faced a direct machine-gun fire to care for a wounded soldier. A man was killed within a few yards of him. For this deed he was awarded the Croix de Guerre.

When Pershing's infantry swept the Huns from the St. Mihiel salient September 12 and 13, the veteran Pennsylvania machine gunners and automatic riflemen were in the van. Prominent in the attack were Lieutenant John H. Geisel, who was wounded on the first day of action, and Corporal David E. Binkley of Lancaster, who were recommended for a Distinguished Service Cross.

## Awarded the Croix de Guerre

The following officers and privates from different regiments were awarded the Croix de Guerre:

Although severely wounded in action near Lesseau, France, on September 4, 1918, Private Ed Merryfield of Greenville, Illinois, remained at his post and continued to fight a superior enemy force which had attempted to enter our lines, thereby preventing the success of an enemy raid in force.

Sergeant Duncan, formerly an elevator operator in a department store in Philadelphia, took over the command of his platoon when the platoon sergeant was killed and the officer wounded. He was awarded the French War Cross and four hundred francs.

Captain Napoleon B. Marshall, a graduate of the Washington High School and Harvard Law School and an attorney of New York City, served on the firing line, where he was gassed and sent to the hospital. Returning to the battle he was wounded from shell fire on October 21, 1918, in a night raid south of Metz in an effort to capture a machine-gun position.

Sailor Edward Donahue Pierson was wounded when the U. S. S. "Mount Vernon" was torpedoed off the coast of France; he is the son of Professor and Mrs. E. D. Pierson, his father being head of the Science Department of the Colored High School in Houston, Texas.

Lieutenant L. E. Shaw was in one of the most exposed centers of the fighting, being under terrific artillery fire and the fire of two German machine guns. He handled this very difficult situation with cool bravery. The enemy barrage was so close that it was impossible to stand up and Lieutenant Shaw controlled his guns by rolling from one to the other; his two guns fired 5,000 rounds. Lieutenant R. C. Grame was in command of the group which received the brunt of the enemy fire which, besides the barrage, added a heavy fire of large minenwerfers. There was no flinching—the troops always working under perfect control and keeping all combat posts manned, though three men were knocked down by the explosion of shells. Private Howard Gaillard, with a small rapid-fire piece, was unable from position to get a good fire to bear upon the advancing enemy groups, so he coolly and with entire disregard of danger mounted the parapet and while enemy bullets were flying around him, fired his rapid-fire piece from the hip, first at one group and then at the other. Privates Smithfield Jones and George Woods were specially mentioned for their coolness in the face of violent shelling when they dismounted their machine guns and then reassembled them and continued firing until the close of the action. There were other instances of rare bravery and Private Sanders, Corporals Frank Harden and Bean and Sergeant G. A. Morton were also specially mentioned.

Dr. Claudius Ballard, a colored physician of Los Angeles, received the Croix de Guerre for work in the Belgian drive; Henry P. Cheatham, son of former Congressman Henry P. Cheatham of North Carolina, for distinguished service in action under the French General Rondeau, Commandant of l'Infanterie de la 59th Division, with which the 370th Infantry was brigaded, and Captain Samuel R. Gwynne, commanding officer of the Third Machine Gun Company for loyalty and bravery in action, having led his men over the top after having been wounded twice.

For extraordinary heroism under fire 124 soldiers of the 371st and 372nd Infantry have been decorated by the French authorities. Four received the Croix de Guerre. Several exploits stand out prominently. Sergeant Depew Pryor, Corporal Clifton Morrison, Privates Clarence Van Allen and Kenneth Lewis were awarded the Médaille Militaire. All except the last mentioned were Massachusetts boys and belonged to the same company. Lewis is dead, having been killed at his post by hand grenades. He took from the Germans a machine gun while it was in action on Bussy Farm in the Champagne district. Lewis was from Washington, D. C.

Sergeant Robert Terry and Sergeant Charles Hughes were in a big raid and went ahead in spite of a terrible barrage fire from the enemy. Over the top they went and it was due to their coolness under fire that all objectives were gained.

Private George Byrd was in command of a mortar near Verdun. He rendered valuable assistance to a raiding party by cutting wires so that the party could advance into enemy territory. The mortar he was firing had not been securely placed and it began to jump about. In order to secure a steady aim Byrd sat on it while it was piping hot and continued to shoot by feeding the gun from behind. In the same company with Byrd was Corporal Eyre who received the cross for bravery under fire.

Sergeant George H. Jordan received the Croix de Guerre and palm for taking command of an ammunition train at Verdun on October 5, 1918, when the commanding officer had been killed by a shell; he saved and brought through eight of the seventeen wagons of the train.

Private Reuben Burrell, of a machine gun company with the 371st Regiment, was cited for extraordinary heroism in action in the Champagne sector, September 30, 1918, and Private Ellison Moses of Company C went forward and rescued wounded soldiers, working persistently until all of them had been carried to shelter after his company had been forced to withdraw from an advanced position; all the while he was under severe machine-gun and artillery fire. For such services these heroes also were given the Croix de Guerre.

Private James Williams was a member of Company C, of the 369th, and it was in the attack of his regiment on "Snake Hill" in the Champagne sector that he exhibited the valor for which he was awarded the Croix de Guerre.

Private Tom Rivers, of Company G, 366th Infantry, was cited by the commanding general of the American forces in France "for extraordinary heroism in action." Although gassed he volunteered and carried important messages through heavy barrages and refused aid until his company was relieved.

### Heroes of "The Old Eighth" Decorated

The Distinguished Service Cross has been awarded to the following soldiers attached to the old 8th Illinois Regiment. Copies of citations follow:

Private Tom Powell (deceased) for extraordinary heroism in action near Beaume, France, November 8, 1918. He repeatedly carried messages under severe fire to the various units in the vicinity of his company, until he was killed in the performance of his duty.

Private Spirley Irby carried messages to the various units in his vicinity under severe enemy fire. He was badly wounded.

Private Alfred Williamson of the Medical Detachment was assigned to duty at the first-aid station, but volunteered to accompany the attacking lines to more expeditiously attend to the wounded. During the advance he constantly exposed himself to the enemy fire to render first aid.

Acting as ammunition carrier, Private Arthur Johnson received a painful injury in the back from a shell fragment. While engaged in carrying ammunition he found a wounded man in an exposed position, and, regardless of his own wound, carried this man under heavy fire to the first-aid station, a distance of more than a kilometer, returning to his work immediately afterward.

Private Charles T. Monroe, afterward promoted to Sergeant, in the absence of a platoon commander took charge of a platoon of Stokes mortars, directing the work of the men under heavy shell fire. Although the shelling was so intense that guns were at times buried, Sergeant Monroe and his men worked unceasingly in placing them back into action. He himself was buried by the explosion of a shell, but on being dug out continued to direct the work of the men and encouraged them by his fearless example.

During the action at Mont-de-Sanges, September 20 to October 1, 1918, Sergeant Thompson, then a corporal, volunteered and took charge of a detail to secure rations. He succeeded in this mission under very dangerous and trying conditions, and, notwithstanding the fact that his detachment suffered numerous casualties, he remained on this duty, and continued to supply the company with rations until completely exhausted.

A messenger having been wounded by an enemy sniper in the open between the line, Sergeant Lester Fossie immediately went to his rescue and brought him into the company headquarters, over ground swept by machine-gun and sniper's fire.

### Early Instances of Heroism

No one in France was in a better position to report on the heroism of Negro soldiers than Ralph W. Tyler, the Negro war correspondent. Here is Mr. Tyler's report of some of the first instances that came to his attention:

"Somewhere in France.—A successful raid, planned by one of the majors of the old 8th Illinois Regiment, whose home is at Metropolis, Illinois, was made in the Voucharn sector, and with great daring. The motor battery of the regiment first took part in laying down a barrage fire. The barrage fire began at 4 o'clock in the morning—just as the first rays of the sun shone sluggishly, and but dimly, behind the horizon. At the hour named, every gunner was at his post. The Major flashed an electric signal, and within a minute or two thereafter every gun fired simultaneously, as if connected with and controlled by an electric battery. For fifteen minutes the colored gunners kept up their barrage fire, and then a French company was sent out behind the barrage to make the raid. So surprising was the raid, and so quickly made, that but three of the colored soldiers were wounded, and they but slightly, and but eight of the French, with whom they were fighting, while the Germans' casualty toll was eleven killed and three wounded, and the remainder were captured."

### The Negro in the Argonne

"Stories of the fight in the Argonne Forest," said Mr. Tyler in a later report, "and the splendid endurance and valiant fighting of the colored soldiers continue to come in. It is reported that a company of the old Ninth Ohio Battalion, under command of its colored captain from Dayton, Ohio, lay in an open field all night, awaiting orders to go into action, while all the time the Germans were dumping big shells and machine-gun fire into them. But even in the face of such a murderous fire, the colored line stood as firm as if the huge shells and murderous machine-gun fire were but the discharge of toy blowguns. Among their casualties were Anderson Lee and William Chenault, of Dayton, who were killed. The firmness of the line these khaki-garbed black soldiers maintained in the face of a withering fire—a veritable hell—constitutes one more reason why the folks of the race back home should be proud of these, their colored soldiers over here, whose unyielding spirit and bravery is making history for the race.

"I have learned that Hill 304, which the French so valiantly held, and which suffered such a fierce bombardment from the Germans that there is not a single foot of it but what is plowed up by shells, and whose sides, even today, are literally covered with the corpses of French soldiers who still lie where they fell, was later as valiantly held by the colored soldiers from the United States, who fought with all the heroism and endurance the best traditions of the army have chronicled. The colored soldiers, under their own captain from Dayton, Ohio, who so splendidly maintained their line in the Argonne Forest, and those who held that bloody and forever historical Hill 304, had the odds against them, but like Tennyson's immortalized 'Six Hundred,' they fought bravely and well, firmly in the belief it was 'not theirs to reason why, but theirs to do or die,' and, like the patriots they were, they did *DO* and this war's history will so record.''

### How Two Colored Captains Fell

Still another report by Mr. Tyler says: ''Recently, in an engagement already reported, a colored unit was ordered to charge, and take if possible, a very difficult objective held by the Germans. Captains Fairfax and Green, two colored officers, were in command of the detachments. They made the charge, running into several miles of barb-wire entanglements, and hampered by a murderous fire from nests of German machine guns which were camouflaged. Just before charging, one of the colored sergeants, running up to Captain Fairfax, said: 'Do you know there is a nest of German machine guns ahead?' The Captain replied: 'I only know we have been ordered to go forward, and we are going.' Those were the last words he said, before giving the command to charge, 'into the jaws of death.' The colored troops followed their intrepid leader with all the enthusiasm and dash characteristic of patriots and courageous fighters. They went forward, they obeyed the order, and as a result 62 men and two officers were listed in the casualties reported, Captains Fairfax and Green being among those who fell to rise no more. Captain Fairfax's last words: 'I only know we have been ordered to go forward, and we are going,' are words that will forever live in the memory of their race; they are words that match those of Sergeant Carney, the color sergeant of the 54th Massachusetts during the Civil War, who, although badly wounded, held the tattered, shot-pierced Stars and Stripes aloft and exclaimed: 'The old flag never touched the ground.' Men who have served under Captains Fairfax and Green say two braver officers never fought and fell.''

"Since this 92nd Division has been in France there has come to it four promotions for its colored officers, among these being the promotion of Captain Adam E. Patterson and Captain Dean to majorships, the former now serving as Divisional Judge Advocate, while the latter is in command of a munition train. Major Patterson will be remembered as the colored man whom President Wilson, soon after his first inauguration, nominated for the position of Register of the Treasury, but who, on learning certain Southern Senators would prevent his confirmation, wrote the President requesting, in order not to embarrass the President, that he withdraw his name, which was done. The Division Commander speaks in high terms of Major Patterson's ability, his attentiveness to duty, and his fine conduct of the office of Division Judge Advocate. *Both Major Patterson and Major Dean won their promotion, the Division Commander says, on merit alone.*''

### Captain Jones and His Gallant Fighters

"In one engagement in the Argonne woods, where the fighting has been most sanguinary," said Mr. Tyler, "and where the American troops showed their mettle, Captain J. Wormley Jones, of Washington, D. C., is reported to have stood like a stone wall, and rallied his men, when others were wavering in the face of a murderous fire and of great odds. In this particular engagement, Captain Jones displayed such fine leadership, such fearlessness of danger, that his Division Commander, in a personal talk with the writer, praised in highest terms the valor and leadership shown by the Captain. It is such instances as these, and there are many coming to light almost daily, that justify the hope entertained by the race that our colored officers would prove efficient, and that our colored soldiers would fight as well under colored officers as under any others." And in a later dispatch Mr. Tyler continued:

"Realizing that there is nothing more encouraging to the race back in the States than to learn how bravely our colored soldiers over here are enduring and fighting, I made it a point to secure a fuller report of the bravery displayed by Captain J. Wormley Jones, of Washington, D. C., in one of the Argonne engagements.

The place of honor, it appears, fell to Captain Jones's regiment, and to the battalion to which he belongs. Under cover of the night's pitch-black darkness, the Captain led his men into the trenches overlooking No-Man's Land, that grim sepulcher that holds so many thousands of the Allies' and the enemy dead.

"Notwithstanding that Captain Jones and his men had just completed a forced march of some twenty kilometers, the men were in excellent condition and splendid spirits, and eager to demonstrate their fitness to try conclusions with the Huns. Captain Jones was supported by Lieutenants Frank Coleman, C. W. Marshall, D. J. Henderson, and Paul Jones, the last mentioned being a brother of the captain. These men were all of 'the sterner stuff,' and fit for the trying ordeal which awaited them. Space forbids dealing with the blackness of the night, or with the awful bombardment.

"Neither can I individualize respecting the magnificent valor of the men of the company led by Captain Jones in this engagement, which Secretary Baker himself praised. When the awful bombardment died away, just as the gray streaks of early dawn pierced the night's blackness, which was made grayer by a thick heavy fog, the Captain ordered a charge 'over the top' with fixed bayonets; through the treacherous fog and into no-man-knew-what or seemed to care. The first wave, or detachment, went over with a cheer—a triumphant cheer—and the second wave followed their comrades with a dash. It may, perhaps, be best to let these boys and officers tell with their own lips of the terrific, murderous shell, shrapnel, gas, and machine-gun fire which baptized them, only to make them the more hardened and intrepid warriors; of how they contended every inch; fought with marvelous valor, never for an instant faltering. Trench after trench of the enemy was entered and conquered; dugout after dugout was successfully grenaded and made safe for the boys to follow; wires were cut and communicating trenches explored; machine-gun nests were raided and silenced, and still the boys fought their way on. Of course, as a natural sequence to such a daring raid, there were casualties, but the black soldiers, heroes as they were, never flinched at death, and the wounded were too proud of their achievements even to murmur because of the pain they endured. Captain Jones and his men

took over a mile of land and trenches which for four years had
been held by the Germans. The newspapers have given due and
proper credit to the Americans for this daring raid, but the world
has not been informed that it was the colored soldiers of America,
under Captain J. Wormley Jones, a former Washington, D. C.,
policeman, who made the charge that was as daring, and more
successful, than the Tennyson-embalmed charge of 'The Light
Brigade.'"

### A Brave Y. M. C. A. Secretary

To E. T. Banks, of Dayton, Ohio, belongs the honor of being
the first Y. M. C. A. colored secretary to go "over the top," which
he did in one of the Argonne engagements. It was permitted him
to fight for two days and nights in the forests and trenches side
by side with real soldiers. On the last night, while lending first
aid to a wounded black scout soldier, he was fired upon by a German machine gun, but succeeded in bringing his wounded scout
to the American line, though not until they had lain all night in the
forest under a most fearful barrage fire. For his bravery, Banks
was cited and recommended for meritorious service. An officer, in
a personal letter to him commending his splendid service, wrote:
"When the full story of the Argonne is told, the 'Red Triangle'
represented by Mr. Banks will add beauty to the rainbow that is
reflected from the silent tombs of those who sleep the sleep of
death that Democracy may not perish from the earth."

### A Heroic Colored Physician

There was a heroic calmness, according to Ralph W. Tyler,
in the death of Lieutenant Urban F. Bass, of Fredericksburg, Virginia, colored, serving as a physician with one of the colored regiments, and it is deserving of more than a passing notice. He was
directing the affairs of his temporary aid station just behind the
crest of a hill, while the battle was raging, when a shell from the
enemy's gun combed the hill and struck among the group of workers being directed by him, tearing off both legs of the physician.
Lieut. Bass, with remarkable fortitude, as calmly instructed his
hospital corps how to give him first aid as if he was but writing a
prescription for one of his patients back in his Virginia office.

He died a few moments later, from blood hemorrhage. Thus went a most promising colored physician who, although beyond the draft age, volunteered his services; left a splendid practice, wife and children, to serve his country in France, and by so doing help to advance the interests of his race back in America.

Here is another story told by Mr. Tyler: "Yesterday about 10 o'clock, a platoon of colored men, under colored officers, was sent out to reconnoiter, to learn the strength and position of the enemy, and with positive instructions to bring back live prisoners. They went, but discovering that the enemy was strongly entrenched, and realizing that it would be suicidal to attempt to attack almost a regiment with a handful of men, returned and reported. The Major of the battalion thereupon said he would go himself and do the job, and called for eight volunteers to accompany him. There was no lack of volunteers, even from among those of the platoon that had previously returned to make this report. The Major, a white officer, selected eight men from the many who had volunteered to make the perilous trip, and started out to locate the Huns' position and return with a live prisoner. Instead of returning, he, with two of his volunteers, are now prisoners of war in the German camp, for they found, to their Major's regret, that the colored officer had reported correctly the German strength. This is but one more instance showing that the colored soldiers are indifferent to fear; that they quickly, cheerfully, and eagerly volunteer to go even though death or capture is the sure fate awaiting them."

### How Lieutenant Cameron Died

"It was but one of the many small raids nearly every night chronicles here at the front," said Mr. Tyler in another dispatch, "but it demonstrated the daring courage of our colored troops. Some two hundred colored soldiers, under Captain Robert Stephens, of Columbus, Ohio, were ordered to raid the Boche's trenches. They were ordered to do this without a barrage fire being first laid down for them, and without artillery or machine-gun support. They never hesitated, however, but out into the pitch-black darkness of night they moved, encountered the usual barbed-wire entanglements which so fearfully harass advance even in the day, to say nothing of the night. The Germans lay quiet until these black warriors were within forty rods of their trenches, and then they opened up a murderous machine-gun fire, and exploded shells of deadly gas among the black soldiers. But the latter never wavered. They fought manfully against great odds. Among the casualties were Captain Stephens and Lieut. Stewart, badly gassed, and Lieut. Cameron, of Nashville, Tennessee, killed. Bruce McCray, Maxton, North Carolina, just as he was going over the top, was hit by a machine-gun bullet that ripped his stomach, and Cornelius Turner, of Sellars, Louisiana, was stopped from going over the top by a bullet which indented his helmet, cutting a jagged wound in his head. There were a number who were more or less gassed. I visited them in the hospital the following afternoon, and found those injured and gassed getting along as well as could be expected, and had the assurance of the physicians in attendance —careful physicians of their own race—that all would recover. The death of Lieutenant Cameron, however, cast an impenetrable gloom over every one in the regiment, and even in the entire division, for he was loved by officers and men. The draft would not and could not have reached Lieutenant Cameron, but he came —volunteered—to serve his country, and died for it.''

### Badly Wounded, He Fought On

"An incident showing unusual fidelity to duty came to light yesterday. Sergeant Gans, with two other colored comrades, was on guard at a 'strong point' on one of the active fronts. During the night his two comrades were killed by enemy shrapnel, and he himself had ugly wounds in his back and leg, from which the blood flowed freely; still he remained at his post. When it was learned that his two comrades had been killed, and he himself wounded, Captain Harry Atwood sent to have the dead and wounded brought in, but Sergeant Gans refused to leave his post, because a sergeant, as he thought was proper, was not there to relieve him. It became necessary for Captain Atwood to order this badly wounded sergeant to leave his post at the point of a bayonet, to secure medical treatment. All he knew was duty; he was firm in the belief that before he could leave his post for anything, a relief should be there to take his place.''

## A Fighting Colored Chaplain

"The gas mask has saved hundreds from being gassed'," said Mr. Tyler, "but perhaps the first case reported of a gas mask saving a soldier's life by warding off a deadly bit of shrapnel was the case of Chaplain J. T. Simpson, a former Pittsburgh colored minister. The courageous chaplain, as full of fight as of religion, was going over the top with 'his boys,' as he called the troops of his regiment, when a big shell exploded, and a piece of the shrapnel from it hit the mask he was wearing, striking the metal part, otherwise he would now be a dead chaplain instead of confined in the hospital from shell shock. Frequently it takes longer to recover from shell shock than from a shell wound. The chaplain, when I saw him was, however, slowly but surely recovering."

## Mental Effect of a Big Shell

"When one calmly reads of the shelling of a town, he cannot form any adequate knowledge of the feeling which possesses those who experience the shelling. Yesterday afternoon the Boche opened up on the little town at the front, in which I was gathering news," said Ralph W. Tyler in another letter. "The big guns of the Huns sent their awful instruments of death whistling through the air. First a belching sound is heard, and then comes the siren-like whistle of the shell as it races overland to its terminal of destruction, and then a roaring, hellish sound—'Boom!'—shaking hills and vales for miles around. The people are startled. They gather in little knots and look far over the lines, whence came the belching sound, to see if they can get a view of the approaching engine of death. Soldiers hardened to the oft-heard sound, calmly proceed about their duties, when they find the Hun has failed to get the proper range of the town. But the feeling is peculiar. Even when the shell misses, involuntarily there arises, in one's mind, the question: 'Will the next one hit?' There are experiences far more pleasant than seeing a big death-tipped shell—so I thought when two whistled over my head yesterday and struck a few yards to the right and left of me."

# CHAPTER XIX

## THE NEGRO SOLDIER AS A FIGHTER

*Unanimous Praise by Military Observers—Value of Negroes as Shock Troops—Discipline and Morale Under Fire—What the War Correspondents Said About Them—Comments by Foreign Military Observers — Estimates by American and French Officers.*

The Negro has always had the record of being a good soldier. General Pershing has been quoted as to the courage and valor of the colored troops. It may be well to quote here the testimony of four other distinguished Americans as to the faithful service of colored soldiers in other wars. Commodore Perry said after the Battle of Lake Erie: "They seemed to be absolutely insensible to danger." General Jackson asserted on the occasion of the Battle of New Orleans: "You surpassed my hopes. The nation shall applaud your valor." Speaking of the Negro in the Civil War, General Grant said: "The colored troops fought nobly." Colonel Theodore Roosevelt, reporting on the record of the Negro soldiers in the Spanish-American war, said: "No troops could behave better than the colored soldiers."

The reader will have noted that Negro combat units in their fighting overseas lived up to all the traditions of their race. They distinguished themselves by bravery, fortitude, and loyalty, and the records of the regiments of which they were a part compared favorably with any of those who went overseas. Whether in Flanders, in Champagne, in the Argonne Forest, in the Vosges, on the Meuse, or before Metz, it was the old story of indomitable courage, of willingness to go forward always, no matter how murderous the opposing fire. There was the same valor and spirit displayed by them in every action, and they saw some of the most intense and critical fighting of the war.

The Negroes went into the World War with a spirit of the true soldier. They were determined to fight it out at the earliest possible moment. Sixteen Negro soldiers passing through Defiance, Ohio, were asked whether they were going to France.

"No, sir, I am not going to France," replied one of them, "I am going to Berlin and I may stop in France for a short time on the way."

"What we are aiming to do," said a Negro officer, "is to push our way right on into Berlin without stopping, as we promised the folks at home we would do, and we don't intend to be long about it either."

### "Heaven, Hell or Hoboken"

Soldiering for the Negro was a pleasant pastime as long as there were any Germans around. They, therefore, had for their watchword that of the *Black Herald:* "Heaven, Hell, or Hoboken by Christmas." They soon established themselves as being cool and reliable fighters in the front line. Both Americans and French report that if the Germans ever discovered who it was that held part of the line through the Argonne Forest when the Boche failed once to get through, they would have a decidedly high respect for the American Negro infantry.

Their fighting spirit always ran high. They seemed to fear nothing. There is a story of a Negro soldier who was found sitting pensively in a field while shells were roaring overhead like invisible midair express trains.

"What are you thinking about, Buddy? Making your will? Are you wondering why you were nut enough to enlist?"

"No," said the doughboy gloomily, "I was wondering how I was ever nut enough to let a man hold me up in Chicago last spring. He only had a thirty-two."

Upon an occasion of a Negro regiment hammering its way through the German lines the brigade commander summoned the colonel of a Negro regiment before him and demanded to know in terse military fashion, why that colonel had not maintained better control over his troops, and why, above everything else, he had not "stopped" his men and kept them from passing beyond their appointed objectives, and, in fact, hacking their way through ahead of their own protective barrage.

"Stop them?" queried the Colonel. "Stop them? Hell, man, how could you expect me to stop them, when the whole German army couldn't do it?"

Because of these unusual feats in war the Germans soon began to regard the Negroes not with mere curiosity but with unusual fear. Early in the war the German army offered a reward of 400 marks for the capture alive of each Negro as an inducement to German soldiers to overcome the great fear and terror of the Negroes. A discharged German soldier reported that one evening on the front a scouting party consisting of 10 Germans including himself encountered two French Negroes. In a fight which followed, two of the scouting party were killed. One of the Negroes escaped, the other being taken prisoner. In the fight two of the Germans left their comrades and ran to the protection of their own trenches, but these, it was explained, were young soldiers and untrained. The reward of 400 marks subsequently was divided among the remaining six Germans for capturing the Negro.

### German Fear of Colored Troops

How the Germans feared the colored American soldiers is indicated by Mr. Tyler in his report of a conversation with two American aviators, Lieut. V. H. Burgin of Atlanta and Lieut. A. L. Clark of Boston. Both had been forced to descend behind the German lines and had been held as prisoners of war for two months. Writing from Brest, where these airmen were waiting for transport home, Mr. Tyler said:

"The interesting part of these intrepid American airmen's narrative of their fight, capture and imprisonment, to colored people, is that while they were captured at different points, and imprisoned at widely separated prisons, both state that when brought before the German military intelligence department and questioned as to the American force in France, one of the first questions asked of them, and which the Germans seemed most concerned about, was how many colored troops the Americans had over here. Lieut. Burgin, of Atlanta, said he told them there were 13,000,000 American colored troops in France. He stated that this not only surprised the Germans, but appeared to depress them, 'For,' he added, 'the Germans have a holy fear of colored troops and their knives wielded with

skill and dexterity.' He stated that this information made a tremendous impression on the Germans, although he admitted he did
not know, at the time, how many colored troops were in France,
but thought it was best to exaggerate rather than underestimate the
strength of our forces when questioned by the enemy.

"Lieut. Clark, the Boston aviator, also said that the leading question put to him by the German military intelligence officers was:
'How many Negro troops have the Americans got over here?' He
stated that not knowing, he was frank in telling them that he did not
know, but that he believed there were several millions. He, too,
stated that this information regarding the force of colored troops in
France, given to the German officers who questioned him, greatly
depressed them.

"It was a fact patent to every American officer and soldier who
had had contact with German soldiers, that they had a mortal fear
of colored soldiers. This fear had been occasioned by two things.
First, before the American colored soldiers had been put on the
battle front the Germans had encountered the fierce fighting Senegalese and Algerians, fighting with the French, who took no prisoners,
and who were prone to cut off the ears and other parts of a German's
anatomy before dispatching him into eternity. Then again, later,
they had encountered the 372nd, 371st, 370th and 369th colored regiments, the first colored Americans to arrive in France, and who were
brigaded and fought with the French. The Germans had learned
that the American colored soldier, while not brutal like the Senegalese
and Algerians, were even harder, more scientific and more dangerous
fighters. They were men who fought with precision—fought like
trained veterans—were good in trench warfare, in raids, or in attack—any way they were ordered to fight, while the Senegalese and
Algerians were best in attack—being dashing, whirlwind fighters in
attacks, or as shock troops."

### Efficiency of Colored Fighters

Major L'Esperance of the 369th regiment has borne testimony
to the efficiency of his men. Says Major L'Esperance: "The
heaviest fighting was on September 26, 1918, when we went into
action with twenty officers and 700 men in our battalion in the
morning and at the close we had seven officers and 150 men left.

Our boys advanced steadily like seasoned veterans and never lost
a foot of ground they had taken or let a prisoner escape.''

The testimony of Colonel William Hayward of the 369th has
already been quoted to the same general effect.  Colonel T. A.
Roberts, who commanded the 370th referred to in the foregoing
chapters, says: "I have been commended for the fighting qualities
and general bearing of the men who were actually over the Belgian
border when the Armistice was signed, and one of my battalions
was the most advanced unit of the French army with which we were
cooperating at the time."

As the *New York Times* said upon the return of these gallant
soldiers from France: "The American Negro troops in France
never failed to share the glory of battle with the French, or with
their white American comrades.

"In all that makes the soldier, bravery, intelligence, endurance,
and, particularly, good nature under hardship and privation, the
Negro soldier excels.  He is never downhearted, and usually he is
gay and full of humor.  No American army would be complete
without the familiar and historic Negro troops."

In the war of wars in which the Negro has participated it
remained for the American Negro to be represented by a full division, with all the military units thereof.  The band of the 350th
Field Artillery Regiment appeared in Nancy for a concert,
and this was the first information to reach the inhabitants that
the only brigade of Negro artillery ever organized had been
defending Nancy by holding the Marbache sector south of Metz.
This organization came up behind the line about a month before
the end of hostilities.  It was so eager to get into the fray that the
men drew some of the guns into position by hand.  The brigade
participated in the taking of Forêt de Frehaut.  It was the accurate
fire of these colored artillerymen which reduced the resistance and
enabled the infantry to capture the position without great loss.  It
was said by a war correspondent at the front that if Emperor
William in the weeks preceding September, 1918, had been on his
historic observation post at Mount Fauson, where he saw the fighting before Verdun in 1916, he would have seen the American Negro
soldiers holding a portion of the trenches in the Foret de Hesse.
The unanimous opinion of French military observers, with whom

the four regiments of colored troops served, as well as of their commanders who have been quoted (both Northern men and Southern men) was that the colored soldier met every test of service.

Rev. D. Leroy Ferguson, Chaplain in the United States Army, writing from France, is quoted as saying: "The colored soldier here is making a great record in France, and the officers and French people with whom I have talked praise his worth and work. The same bravery and courage and skill that characterized his efforts in other wars in America and Mexico are shown here in an excellent way. They are enduring the hardships and the suffering with smiles; their deportment is good; and whether it is unloading the great cargoes, digging the roads or on the firing line, the black soldier is equal to any. When the history of the war is written our soldiers will have their names written large with honors, and though here in France for victory, they all want to and expect to return to the good old U. S. A. With all her faults we love her still—our wives, our sweethearts, families and our homes. I am proud to be able to contribute something to the war."

## Comparison with European Soldiers

The European war gave colored American soldiers the first opportunity for comparison of their mettle with the best soldiers of Germany, Great Britain and France; and unanimous testimony is more or less to the effect that they were able to hold their own in courage, endurance and aggressiveness without whimper or complaint. Colored Americans are proud of the following two paragraphs which appeared in *The Stars and Stripes,* the organ of the American troops in France:

"The farthest north at 11 o'clock (when the armistice went into effect) on the front of the two armies was held at the extreme American left, up Sedan way, by the troops of the 77th New York Division. The farthest east—the nearest to the Rhine—was held by those New York soldiers who used to make up the 'old 15th New York' and have long been brigaded with the French. They were in Alsace and their line ran through Thann and across the railway that leads to Colmar."

"Probably the hardest fighting by any Americans in the final hour was that which engaged the troops of the 28th, 92d, 81st, and 7th Divisions of the Second American Army. It was no mild thing, that last flare of the battle, and the order to cease firing did not reach the men in the front line until the last moment, when the runners sped with it from foxhole to foxhole."

The gratifying thing is that there should be recorded in the official organ of the American Expeditionary Forces a reference to the fact that colored troops were nearest the Rhine of all American troops, as, indeed, they were later the first of all Allied troops to reach the Rhine, and that the 92d Division—their Division—was engaged "in the hardest fighting of the last hour of the war."

*The Brooklyn Standard Union* epitomizes in an editorial expression the general opinion which obtains as to the fighting quality of the colored American troops sent overseas to fight "for democracy" during the world war:

"Of the American Negro soldiers it has been frequently said since we have been fighting in France, that they are decidedly the most cheerful troops who have spilt blood in this war, and as highly courageous as any who have shouldered guns. This is not an exaggerated tribute, for the testimony of the Allies, and, of course of General Pershing and other white officers bears out this estimate, while the War Department at Washington has abundant proof, in the way of records, showing the bravery of these boys.

"Some of those who recognized the extremely sociable and good natured qualities of the Negro questioned his ability as a fighter. They feared he would not stand up well in a bayonet charge, or in an advance upon singing machine guns, or where shells from the big cannon were bursting and rocking the earth. But that was a superficial view. Under his smile and ready laugh or grin the colored man has the qualities of a fighter—coolness, patience, steadfastness, optimism, pluck and, of course, courage. All these have been brought out in recent months, and honors have fallen upon him in France in a manner that is cause for national pride.

"In every department of the army, from wireless telegraphy to the sanitary squad, the Negro has played his part and played it conscientiously, and it is gratifying to know that this city has contributed a very large number of Negro fighters to the nation's

army, for the percentage of volunteers here has been high. Easy
to mold to the requirements of discipline, happy under any and
all circumstances, he is an exemplary soldier. On the charge he
sees red, as the fighter should, and in rest billets or even in the
trench he seldom loses his cheerful outlook upon life."

### French Wanted Colored Troops

Assigned to the French High Commission in the city of
Washington during the war were two distinguished Frenchmen,
Colonel Edouard Requin and Major L. P. DeMontal. These gentlemen often called at the office of the author to make inquiry as to
when additional combat troops were to be sent to France. They
spoke in terms of gratitude of the services of the S. O. S. men but
their eagerness always manifested was that the War Department
should decide to send over increasingly large numbers of colored
combat troops, for, as they both stated, every report that reached
them from France spoke of the wonderful courage and coolness of
the colored American troops, who made a wonderful impression
upon the French population both civil and military and as will have
been noted from the praise and commendation of high French
officers, they won the respect of those military representatives of
the French army. The courage of these colored American troops
was always in evidence; their cool headedness and bravery under
fire as well as their desire to engage in the aforesaid engagements
went to demonstrate that the colored soldiers were unsurpassed as
fighters. The Germans had little or no respect for the fighting
ability of these soldiers until they encountered them in several
hand-to-hand combats.

The *Bulletin of the Armies* issued by the French government
after the completion of every drive in which the allied armies
participated, gives some of the most amazing records of heroism
in the history of wars. The Algerian and Senegalese soldiers gained
favor continuously as fighters of the first rank. The records of
these soldiers were heralded on the European continent as incomparable achievements of bravery, and upon every occasion when
they paraded the streets preparatory to leaving for the first line
trenches, storms of applause greeted them from every roadside
and tavern, and upon one occasion when these black troops returned

to the city of Paris, after having been engaged in a vigorous drive against the Germans at Verdun, every soldier was bedecked with a shower of flowers tendered him by French women, who wept bitterly as they viewed the wounded Negroes limp through the Paris thoroughfares.

One of the most remarkable feats recorded in the Bulletin was the work performed by a corporal of a French infantry regiment, Louis Hermitte, a Senegalese. After a German attack in December, 1917, he went out of the trench and drove back the enemy by hurling hand grenades. He dug himself into a little corner quite close to the German line and stayed there for several days. He received a military medal.

### Heroism of French Negroes

The black troops of France won many honors and proved themselves unafraid of suffering. One page in the Bulletin was devoted to the mention of five cases of Algerian and Senegalese soldiers, men born in a hot climate and quite unused to frost and snow, who remained at their posts under fire and fought bravely, though all of them were terribly frostbitten—so badly in two cases that both legs had to be amputated. In two other cases the men lost a leg each. One of these men endured the agony of frostbite and of terrific German attacks for nineteen consecutive days and finally fell when his ammunition gave out. Still another, with hands and feet frozen, fought with such fury that he captured several machine guns and single handed brought back sixty German prisoners. These feats of heroism have crowned several of the men with the Croix de Guerre honors, but these honors are not received with a vainglorious boast on the part of the soldiers. It is one of the highest honors that a soldier can receive from the government.

Hard fighting in close quarters calls for a greater measure of athletic ability and superior physical strength and endurance. This the Senegalese seem to possess to a greater degree than any other allied body. In every single close battle with the German they proved themselves masters of the situation and slaughtered their opponents unmercifully. In one instance Corporal Hamilde Annonetti was badly gassed, but continued work until his lungs were overcrowded with the vapor. He was taken to the relief station and begged to go back to the firing line to finish his attack. After being temporarily relieved he escaped from the hospital and dragged himself back two miles over the bullet riddled ground and renewed his attack, killing, it is claimed, five or more Germans who were manning a machine gun. He was picked up by the ambulance corps with both legs shot away.

The high state of discipline and the morale which existed in the 92d (colored) Division was the subject of a great deal of comment from all of the allied officers who had the opportunity to view the troops who composed this command, and is attested by the remarks of General Pershing relative to discipline and morale addressed to the 92d Division at Le Mans, France, just previous to their departure for the United States, when he said:

"The 92d Division has been, without a doubt, a great success, and I desire to commend both the officers and men for the high state of discipline and the excellent morale which has existed in this command during its entire stay in France."

Brig. Gen. W. H. Hay, of the 184th Brigade, 92d Division, said: "I have been with colored troops for 25 years, and I have never seen better soldiers than the drafted men who composed this division." Capt. Willis, of the 365th Infantry, said: "These men are the best disciplined and best saluting soldiers that I have ever seen." An officer en route between Camp Meade and Washington, D. C., on or about February 26, 1919, said, "You just have to give it to these colored troops; they have come back with the stuff; there has been absolutely no slump in their discipline and saluting, but I notice that the white troops have slumped considerably."

# CHAPTER XX

## WITH OUR SOLDIERS IN FRANCE

*Official Reports of the Only Accredited Negro War Correspondent—
Ralph W. Tyler, Representative with the A. E. F. of the U. S.
Committee on Public Information—The Story of the Life and
Fighting of American Negro Soldiers in France as Seen By
This Trained Observer.*

One of the most important results of the conference of Negro
editors held in Washington in June, 1918, was the sending to France
of a trained newspaper writer of the Negro race with instructions
to report on the life and the activities of the Negro soldiers as
he saw things, in order that the Negro press of America might be
furnished with first-hand and accurate information for their readers of the precise conditions under which their people were working and fighting in France. The announcement of Mr. Tyler's
appointment was made by the Committee on Public Information on
September 16, 1918 when the following bulletin was issued to the
press of the country:

"One of the direct requests of the Editors' Conference in June
was that a reliable colored news-writer be sent to France to report
the doings of the colored troops on the western front in France, for
the information of the anxious millions of colored Americans in
this country and to the end that the correct story of the valor and
patriotic devotion of their brethren might be told fully and in a
sympathetic vein by one of their own blood and kindred.

"In compliance with this request, the Committee on Public
Information has designated Ralph W. Tyler, of Columbus, Ohio,
former Auditor of the Navy Department at Washington, as a regu-
larly-commissioned war correspondent, to specialize on the conditions
surrounding the colored troops in France and to make daily reports
of the activities and engagements in which the colored soldiers are
prominent. He will be on the staff of General Pershing, commander-
in-chief of the American Expeditionary Forces overseas. Every

facility has been provided by Mr. George Creel, director of the Committee on Public Information, for the prompt and accurate gathering of all facts that may be of interest to the colored people.

"Mr. Tyler is the first colored man to be named as a regular war correspondent by any Government in the world. He is a native of Ohio. For seventeen years he served in various departments on the Columbus Evening Dispatch and the Ohio State Journal, which gave him experience in the technique of the newspaper craft and afforded him opportunity for association with many influential newspaper men. This intimate contact with such forces will be invaluable to him in his labors as a war correspondent. The fact that he has a wide acquaintance with correspondents now at the front, will make it possible for him to get news concerning colored troops which, perhaps, no other colored correspondent could secure.

"The claims of a number of men were fully considered in connection with this important assignment, but Mr. Tyler was finally selected as the most efficient of those available. Immediately after war was declared by the United States on Germany, Mr. Tyler wrote the President, tendering his services in any capacity. He has three sons, all of whom are at the front in France."

The plan under which Mr. Tyler worked was to send his reports to the Committee on Public Information, which in turn sent them to me for editing and for circulation throughout the country. This news service unquestionably had a tremendously valuable effect in bringing the truth about conditions in France to the colored people of America. As it happened, the war came to an end in less than three months after Mr. Tyler's appointment. In that brief time, however, and in the short time after the armistice was signed during which he remained in France, he wrote and sent to this country the most valuable and interesting first-hand reports about our Negro soldiers that have come from any source. There is no better way in which I can present an adequate picture of the life of our soldiers in France than by reproducing here Mr. Tyler's dispatches, beginning with his graphic account, written after the fighting had ceased, of the last great battle of the war and the glorious part which the Negro soldiers had in it. This is Mr. Tyler's summing up of the work of the 92nd Division:

"Somewhere in France, November 20. They were in it at the

finish, as they were at Verdun, Soissons, Chateau-Thierry, Argonne and Champagne. At the eleventh hour on the eleventh day of the eleventh month in the fifth year of the war, when the signal flashed from Eiffel Tower in Paris stopped hostilities, in conformity with the terms of the armistice just signed by the Germans, the 92nd Division, composed of Colored American Soldiers, occupied the point closest to the German city of Metz, the objective of the last drive of this war. At the stroke of eleven the cannon stopped, the rifles dropped from the shoulders of our Colored soldiers, and their machine guns became silent. Then followed a strange, unbelievable silence as though the world had ceased to exist. It lasted but a moment—lasted for the space of time the breath is held. Then, among these dark-skinned troopers came a sigh of relief—came jubilance, as every colored soldier, in true Parisian vernacular, exclaimed: 'La Guerre est fini'—the war is over, and immediately thoughts turned to dear ones back across the sea, while tears flowed down their war-grimmed black faces for their hundreds of comrades bivouacing forever in sepulchers over here in France. The wish was father to the thought when it was prophesied, back in the states, when the first colored troops sailed for France, that they would be in it at the finish, that their "On to Berlin" slogan would become a reality. The armistice stopped their advance into Berlin, but they did reach the nearest point to the German city of Metz in what was designed as a victorious march to Berlin, and the valor they displayed, their courageous, heroic fighting all along that advance, won for our men in the 92nd Division high praise from superior officers, including the corps and division commander, for they never wavered an instant, not even in that awful hell, the Frehaut Woods, upon which the big guns of Metz constantly played; which the Senegalese were unable to hold, but which our colored soldiers from America did take, and did hold until the signal came announcing the cessation of hostilities." Mr. Tyler also wrote:

### Colored Troops in the Final Drive

"In this last battle of the war to establish world democracy—a thing the colored soldiers and their kinsmen back home crave, the following colored army units effectively took part: 365th, 366th, and 367th Infantry; 349th, 350th, and 351st Field Artillery, and

167th **Machine Gun.** All these were combatants in this final drive, but in this account of the battle the three non-combatant units, the 317th Ammunition Train, under the command of a colored major, Major Milton T. Dean; the 325th Field Signal Battalion; the staff of the 366th Field Hosptial, to which the wounded and gassed were rushed, and the 365th and 366th Ambulance Corps, under the command, respectively, of Captain Sherman Hickman of Memphis, and Captain Charles H. Garvin of Cleveland, must not be over-looked or slighted. The 368th Infantry, while they did not get into this last action, had however been moved up to Guzoncourt, where they were held in reserve.

"If the reader will get out his map of France, and observe it, he will be able to follow the advance of the combatant colored troops in this last drive, which must go down in history as the final battle of the World War. The 367th, or "Buffaloes," as they were familiarly known, had been holding Villers-sous-Preny for many days and up to the time, seven o'clock Sunday morning, November 10, they were ordered to advance to Pagny, which they did, and held. The advance of this regiment was through "Death Valley," exposed to the heavy fire of the German guns stationed on the hill skirting the advance. They made the advance without a single casualty, and that they did so, considering the fire the men were subjected to, appears like a miracle, blind fate, or the will of God. They reached their objective in good form, and it was providential that they did, for it was from this point they were able to open up fire on the German guns, and save the 56th Infantry (white) from annihilation, when it had become pocketed by a murderous German fire which prevented its making Preny, or retreating.

"This saving of the 56th by the 367th was history repeating itself—colored troops saving white troops from destruction in 1918 as the 10th Cavalry saved the Rough Riders during the Spanish-American War in 1898. So splendidly did the 367th colored regiment advance and perform that they wrung from the Corps and Division Commander a letter of praise, in which he paid tribute to the regiment's high qualities. Although the "Buffaloes" had for weeks been holding the front line trenches in a particularly active zone, upon which the Boche rained shells and gas daily and nightly, and although from this regiment, almost daily and nightly, raiding parties of colored soldiers went out and brought in German prisoners, the regiment was the only colored regiment over here, perhaps, that had not been sent into an engagement—something they had longed for. The order to advance, at seven o'clock Sunday morning the 10th of November, gave them the opportunity they had so long waited for impatiently. In spite of the fact that their advance was to be through "Death Valley," a section flanked by big German guns massed on the overlooking hills, the order gave them more enthusiasm and satisfaction than an order to embark for home. When seven o'clock came they were ready to move, these "Buffaloes," and they did move with astonishing rapidity, absolutely indifferent to the bursting shells, which, fortunately, fell a little short of them, or caromed over their heads. "Hail, Hail, the Gang's All Here, What the Hell Do We Care?" greeted many a Boche shell as it fell short, or spent its force a few yards beyond their advancing line. They established and maintained a perfect liaison, and even their Supply Department, under that efficient acting supply officer, Lieut. McKaine, coördinated perfectly with the line advancing "on to Metz."

### Colored Officer Refuses to Retire

"The 366th had been occupying the line at Vaudières, prior to the Metz advance, and the order was to advance into one section of Bois Frehaut and Bois de Voivrotte, which it did in a most effective manner, displaying such bravery, in the face of a deadly shell fire, and its colored line officers displaying such excellent qualities of leadership as to merit unstinted praise from the Division Commander. In the engagement in the Bois Voivrotte, Lieut. Guy W. Canady, of Atlanta, was killed, and Lieut. M. W. Rush, of the same city, fell mortally wounded, dying a few days later in the hospital, after having lain out in the woods, thus terribly wounded, for twenty-four hours. Capt. George A. Holland, of the same regiment, also displayed remarkable courage and leadership. He had been ordered to take a position by his Colonel, and hold it at any cost. With his men he took it, but the fire was so heavy and murderous that his white major, commanding his battalion, sent orders to him to retire. This he positively refused to

*Above*—Some heroes of the famous 15th New York, who went away singing and came back
singing after having earned all the Honors of War.
*Below*—The "Stockholm" with her cargo of "Hell Fighters" under command of Colonel Hayward on deck, just before docking in New York harbor.

Chicago homecoming of the 370th Regiment (Old 8th Illinois) passing in parade at 13th St. and Michigan Ave.

Another Group of Officers of the 370th (Old 8th Illinois) on the deck of the La France before landing. Reading left to right: 2nd Lt. Lawson Price; 2nd Lt. L. W. Stearls; 2nd Lt. Ed. White; 2nd Lt. Ell F. E. Williams; 1st Lt. Oasola Browning; Capt. Louis B. Johnson; 1st Lt. Frank Bates; 1st Lt. Binga Desmond.

The troopship "La France" was still in her war paint as she brought the 370th (Old 8th Illinois National Guard) safely home from the battlefields of France.

Chicago parade of the 370th Regiment (Old 8th Illinois) passing the reviewing stand in Michigan Ave., where the crowds were so dense that troops could not march in regular formation.

Commanders of the 370th Infantry (the old Eighth Illinois): Reading left to right: Col. Frank Denison: Col. Thos. A. Roberts: Lt. Col. Otis B. Duncan.

A group of the "Singing Buffalos" on parade after their return from the battle front in France.

This is the way the people of Buffalo, N. Y., turned out to welcome home the returning heroes of the colored race as they returned from their service in France.

do, sending word back that he had been ordered by his Colonel to hold the position taken, and he and his men would hold it until the last man fell, unless he had orders from his Colonel to retire. Few instances, in the annals of war, are recorded showing equal courage, in the face of heavy odds, to that shown by this colored officer, Captain Holland, and his company of the 366th who obeyed to the letter, the order given to take and to hold a position. As a result of the incomparable courage, endurance, and bravery shown by this company, twenty-five of them were commended, in General Orders, by the Division Commander.

"The First Battalion of the 365th engaged in this final drive of the war, had occupied the front line trenches in the Marbache sector. From almost the moment of occupancy, active patrolling and raiding into the enemy's lines was ordered, to determine the strength of the enemy. Officers and men of this battalion were sent out daily and nightly on such missions, and many instances of conspicuous bravery were displayed. Several of their number, however, were captured, and not a few killed and wounded, but the number of the enemy killed, captured, and wounded greatly outnumbered the casualties suffered by this First Battalion.

### The 365th in the Bois Frehaut

"The 365th, prior to the last drive, had been occupying the front line trenches near Dieulouard, that town being the regimental headquarters. It had orders to advance into, take and hold a position in the Bois Frehaut. It happened that, for one reason or another, all the white officers of this regiment, including the Colonel commanding, and save the Major commanding the 2nd Battalion, had been incapacitated for action, and so the 2nd Battalion went into action with but one white officer, the Major. No unit in the advance had a more difficult position to take and hold than the position assigned to the 2nd Battalion of the 365th. The Bois-Frehaut was a network of barbed-wire entanglements, and the big guns in Metz had nothing to do but sweep the woods with a murderous fire, which they did most effectively. French and Senegalese in turn had failed to hold these woods, for it was worse than a hell—it had become the sepulcher of hundreds. I (Ralph W. Tyler) was over and through these woods; I saw the mass of barbed-wire entanglements; I saw the nests in the trees in which Germans had camouflaged machine guns that rained a fire upon the Allied troops.

"It is impossible to describe this scene of carnage. The order to the colored men of the 365th was to "take and hold," although it was believed, almost to a certainty, that they could not hold it, even if they did take it. But they did take and hold it, and these men of the 2nd Battalion, with Spartan-like courage; with an endurance unbelievable, would be holding the position at this writing had not the Armistice been signed, or had they not received orders to retire. In these woods, at the head of his company, Captain Boutte, and the other line officers, fought tenaciously, heroically— so heroically that the Major commanding stated to me that the world had never produced gamer fighters than the colored men who made up his battalion of the 365th Infantry. The casualty list, because of the savage nature of the resistance the Germans made, because of the heavy, well directed big guns and machine gun fire, was large. But the 365th did take and did hold that which the fighting Senegalese could not hold after they had taken it.

"After sixteen days of activity on this front, the battalion was ordered in support for a week, and on November 5th it was ordered to the front line trenches in the Mousson sector, an intensely active front, that was shelled daily and nightly. On the memorable morning of November 10, 1918, the 1st Battalion was ordered to the "alert," as support for the 2nd Battalion of the same regiment, then engaged in the last drive. On the evening of the 10th it was ordered to attack Champey and LaCote Hill, a very strongly fortified German position. The battalion moved to the attack at five o'clock Sunday evening, entering the position from the rear of the 2nd Battalion's position. A very heavy gas-shell and high explosive barrage laid down by the Germans checked the advance, and the battalion was ordered to remain in its position for the night.

"At five o'clock the next (Monday) morning, the 11th of November, the battalion moved into position for the resumption of the attack. Its line moved into position under cover of our artillery barrage, which began at 4:30 a. m. With two companies in the front line and two in support, the 1st Battalion advanced through the difficult woods, Bois de Frehaut. It advanced with machine-gun support until the northern edge of the woods was reached, overlooking Champey. At this point the advance was met by a most terrific artillery bombardment and machine-gun fire delivered by the Germans stationed on the heights of LaCote Hill. The fighting at this point was bitter. Men and officers, however, remained in action and held their line under extremely adverse conditions. Up to this point the line had advanced, in the face of a terrific fire, about 400 yards, forcing many machine guns of the enemy to retire, and capturing a number of others along with much material. This action continued until 10:45 a. m., at which time the "Cease Fire" was sounded, which ended the hostilities of this titanic war.

"The casualties of the 1st Battalion of the 365th in this engagement were two officers wounded and 61 enlisted men killed, wounded, and gassed. Among the wounded officers was Lieut. Charles H. Fearing, formerly of Washington, D. C., who was slightly cut in the arm by shrapnel. Lieut. Fearing, but a few days before, had escaped death most miraculously.

### Work of the Ammunition Train

"Distributing the many tons of ammunition along the route of the advance, and moving it up to the American combatants in this final drive for the 92nd Division, was a big task, but was successfully done by a colored Ammunition Train, under the command of Major Milton T. Dean, a colored officer. Arranging the telegraphic and signal communications between the various units, was a dangerous—most dangerous—and big achievement, and this was done by the 325th Colored Field Signal Battalion. Caring for and attending to the hundreds of wounded and gassed, as they were rushed back to the field hospital in ambulances driven by colored men and commanded by colored ambulance commanders, was the big task of those sacrificing and sympathetic colored surgeons on the staff of the 366th Field Hospital.

"I was at the front when the drive began—this the last battle of the world war. I was thrilled, and inspired by the enthusiasm of our men, and their eagerness to get into battle. The thundering of the big guns, the terrific explosion of death-carrying shells— hell opening up—served only to inspire our colored soldiers with a grim determination to maintain the race's traditional fighting reputation. As I retraced my steps over the battlefield, the awful field of carnage, and saw the havoc German shells had wrought; saw lifeless, blood-bespattered bodies of colored soldiers lying on the dark and bloody field; saw the maimed and mangled living, the natural feeling of sorrow, of anguish, of pain, was made endurable only by the thought that our men—our colored soldiers— were in it to the end, that they fought like heroes, died like heroes, died like martyrs. And then there was the radiant hope—perhaps they fought and fell, in the last battle of the greatest war ever waged for civilization, *NOT in vain.*

"As the colored troops, in the last battle of the war, the drive on Metz, were the first to reach the nearest point to the city of Metz, so it was colored troops, the old 15th New York, that first reached the point farthest east and nearest to the Rhine in the battle on the Meuse. They were in Alsace, and their line ran through Thann and across the railroad leading to Colmar." Mr. Tyler continues:

### As to Transfers of Officers

"Distance lends enchantment to the view, and likewise, not infrequently, to some degree, distance exaggerates a rule into an exception. The transfer of colored commissioned officers from combatant to non-combatant units is, I know, regarded by a very considerable number of colored people in the States as an 'exception.' I am aware that information has been, or soon will be, received back in the States that a number of colored officers were recently given assignments to casualty camps, and that white officers were assigned to their places in the line. German propaganda is sure to convey these transfers as an 'exception' prompted by racial prejudice. To one who is here on the scene, and who knows of countless number of white officers who are daily being transferred to units and assignments which they would not themselves have selected, and of some having been peremptorily shorn of their rank on the field of battle, the 'rule' carries no evidence of 'exception' due to racial discrimination. *So far as I have been able to ascertain all transfers are made for the good of the service, regardless as to whether the ones transferred are white or colored.*

"The number of colored commissioned officers discharged, or transferred from their units, has been negligible when compared with the number of white officers *honorably* (?) and dishonorably discharged and transferred, even when the proportionate number of each is considered.

"This is *war* over here—*actual,* not theoretical war, and its prosecution to the earliest conclusion is so urgent that commanding generals have no time to consider racial problems, even if they were, ordinarily, so inclined to do. To 'win the war' as speedily as possible, with the best available units and officers, appears to prompt all allied commanders, Americans, French, and British, and if some few colored officers, like hundreds of white officers, fall into the discard, or receive new assignments, the race back in the States must not too quickly assume that race discrimination was the actuating factor. I have learned of instances, over here, where white colonels who had aspired to become brigadier-generals have lost the insignia of colonelcy. I have learned of many white officers whose self-estimate made them available for commanding and directing attacks in battle who have been, much to their chagrin, given desk assignments.

"Just prior to a recent engagement, it is reported, a number of commissioned colored officers were transferred from their units to casualty and other assignments. Had they not been transferred just when they were some of them would have their names now appearing in the list of 'Killed in Battle.' They, doubtless, would have as willingly filled a martyr's grave as they, unwillingly and *uncomplainingly,* accepted other assignments.

"The fact is patent to all who are conversant with the war over here that casualty camp assignments are as necessitous as field assignments; that the stevedore regiments make possible the success of the combatant regiments; that the swivel-office-chair officer performs an important and necessitous function. Secretary of War Baker, although a civilian, performs a duty, the non-performance of which would have made it impossible for General Pershing to achieve glory over here for the United States. I simply want to impress upon my race, back in the States, that in this war 'the hewer of wood and the drawer of water' is as necessary to victory as the man who adjusts the distance for the 75-centimeter gun, and that when the world has been made safe for democracy it will be impossible to deny honor to all who helped to achieve victory, even to those who, having received no assignment in the theater of war, cheerfully stood and waited for an opportunity to serve, even if only in some humble capacity.

"The necessarily quick decisions made on a battlefield, or immediately prior to entering battle, where victory hangs as much on strategy as on man-power and equipment, will ofttimes disillusion even the theorist who employs platitudes, at a safe distance far behind the battle front, rather than bullets and shrapnel with which wars are won. I am now here where life is but a gamble, and the flow of blood is but commonplace, and know whereof I speak, and knowing the necessity of war here at the seat of it, I am willing to stand or fall by the foregoing statement, and in the assurance that our race is actually winning glory over here in France."

### Negroes in the Final Fighting

Following is Mr. Tyler's report of the final fighting, written on the day before the Armistice took effect:

"In the battle raging today in the American advance toward Metz, the 92nd Division played a big role. Not only were its black infantry and machine gun units up at the front, in the thickest of it, but its artillery, the 167th Brigade of Field Artillery, was on the line, behaving like veterans, laying down a barrage for the infantry that was marvelously effective; and they established a reputation which has been made by but few, among French, British or Americans, of laying down a barrage that did not entrap, and fatally so, their own men.

"This has been a glorious day for the black soldiers. The fighting is still on, and I have just received the intimation that the casualty toll may be heavy—depressingly so, for Metz, and the sector around about it, is strongly fortified by the Germans, and resistance determined. Metz is considered by experts to be the strongest fortified city in the world, almost as impregnable as the fortifications of the Dardanelles. But the Americans are hammering away at it, and only the signing of the Armistice terms by the Germans, by eleven o'clock tomorrow, will save Metz from falling. Even as it is, colored soldiers are now on German soil.

"The husky invaders include the colored soldiers of the 92nd Division, embracing the 'Buffaloes' or 367th, the 365th and 366th Regiments of Infantry, and the 167th Brigade of Field Artillery, composed of the 349th, 350th and 351st Regiments and the 317th Trench Mortar Battery, and all are conducting themselves with a fortitude and valor that have won for them high praise from their commanding officers every time they have been put to any test."

And here is Mr. Tyler's report on the very day of the Armistice, November 11, 1918:

"The colored troops who took part in the last battle of this war acquitted themselves splendidly, fought valiantly, and with such precision and order as to earn for them high praise. Reminiscent stories of this engagement will be coming to light for weeks—even months—after this battle has long been a matter of history, for, as in all big battles, the reverberations of the big guns, the rattle of musketry, and the smoke of the battle must have died away before the accounting can be made. There is one remarkable, even astonishing, record made in this last drive, a record that either establishes the fact that God was with the colored regiments engaged, as a protector, or that Fate is not merely a fetish, for the 'Buffaloes' suffered not a single casualty—not one wounded or killed. Just how they could have advanced along the difficult line given them; flanked by heavy German guns—guns from whose rain of hell-made and death-charged shells it seems incredible that any could escape, is beyond the conjecture of man, and yet they made their advance, gained their objective, and held it without the loss of a single man. The 366th, 365th, 351st Machine Gun, and 167th Field Artillery, all colored, engaged in this final battle of the war, suffered a casualty which, in the aggregate, was but slight, and yet they were in the thick of it, and to the finish when the note was sounded that, under the terms of the Armistice signed this morning by the Germans, hostilities cease.

"It will be gratifying to the colored people to know that the colored soldiers and officers have acquitted themselves splendidly, from the first engagement into which the 372nd was rushed soon after landing to the final drive 'on to Metz' in which three colored regiments and colored field artillery took part. And, claim what they will, in every one of these engagements in which colored units took part their colored officers led with commendable bravery and efficiency, and the soldiers in line followed with such a fidelity, loyalty, devotion, and dash as to forever set at rest the claim that colored men are incapable to command as officers, and that colored soldiers best fight under white officers. The drive 'on to Metz' which concluded the four years' titanic war affixes 'finis' to the argument put forth by some as to the loyalty of the race to their own leaders.

"The effect of the signing, and promulgating in the camps of our colored soldiers, of the Armistice today, was like magic in this Marbache sector, where more than 30,000 combatant colored troops are centered. Just out of the trenches, just out of the fierce and bloody battle, they began singing and cheering, and nearly every Frenchman they met, it mattered not the sex, greeted them, these bronzed, khaki-garbed troops, with an embrace and the exhilarating 'La guerre est fini,' meaning 'The war is finished.' This evening, as I am writing this account, colored soldiers are moving up and down, back and forth, over the streets of this little French town at the front, cheering and singing. Their repertoire of songs and hymns, exultingly and plaintively sung, from 'Down on the Suwanee River,' 'Swing Low, Sweet Chariot,' to 'Hail, Hail, the Gang's All Here,' interrupted ever and anon, although strictly forbidden, with the firing of a revolver or gun, tell how happy they are over the conclusion of peace. And many of them—most of them, if not all—are anxiously awaiting the order for embarkation back to America, although they must realize that, of a necessity, many of them will witness the blooming of next June's roses in France, rather than back in the States.

"It is perhaps one of the most glorious epochs in the history of the race, since the issuing of the Emancipation Proclamation, that the race, represented by three regiments—crack fighting regiments—and a field artillery unit, was engaged in the last battle of the war; that the race was among the first of the Allied troops to go over the top and set foot on German soil after more than four years' courageous fighting. Here are some of the expressions with which colored privates gave vent to their happiness at the war being over, in this sector last night:

" 'We done signed another Emancipation Proclamation!'

" 'That "New Freedom" must come—we have won it.'

" 'We came to France and won a man's chance!' "

### How France Received the Negro Soldiers

Let Mr. Tyler's fascinating and gossipy narrative of the life of the American Negro troops in France close with a reproduction of the tribute paid them by the French people themselves. The following is a translation of an article written by a talented French woman and published in the leading newspaper of one of the large French cities:

"A peaceful town, far from the front. A beautiful June day full of perfume of roses; resplendent summer freely bursting into bloom, indifferent to human plaints, frets, and agitations. A boy of ten years, head like the urchin of the year one, runs through the streets crying: 'The Americans are coming to B——; the inhabitants are invited to greet them.'

"The Americans! For months they had been discussed; they had been expected, and there was great curiosity; groups of people go down to the public square of the town, where they see upon our white streets the first ranks of the Allied troops. But what a surprise! They are black soldiers! Black soldiers! There is great astonishment, a little fear. The rural population, not well informed, knows well the Negro of Africa, but those from America's soil, the country of the classical type, characterized by the cold, smooth white face; that from America could come this dark troupe —none could believe his own eyes.

"They dispute among themselves; they are a little irritated; some of the women become afraid; one of them confides to me that she feels the symptoms of an attack of indigestion. Smiling, re-assurably, 'lady with all too emotional stomach, quiet yourself! They do not eat human flesh; two or three days from now you will be perfectly used to them.' I said two or three days, but from

that very evening the ice is broken. Natives and foreigners smile
at each other, and try to understand each other. The next day we
see the little children in the arms of the huge Negroes, confidently
pressing their rosy cheeks to the cheeks of ebony, while their
mothers look on with approbation.

"A deep sympathy is in store for these men, which, yesterday,
was not surmised. Very quickly it is seen they have nothing of the
savage in them, but, on the other hand, one could not find a soldier
more faultless in his bearing, and in his manners more affable, or
more delicate than these children of the sun, whose ancestors
dreamed under the wonderful nights along murmuring streams.
We admire their forms—handsome, vigorous and athletic; their
intelligent and loyal faces with their large gleaming eyes, at times
dreamy, and with a bit of sadness in them.

"Far removed is the time when their inauspicious influence
was felt upon the digestive organs of the affrighted lady. Now one
honors himself to have them at his table. He spends hours in long
talks with them; with a great supply of dictionaries and manuals
of conversation. The white mothers of France weep to see the
photographs of the colored mothers, and display the portraits
of their soldier sons. The fiancées of our own 'Poilus' become
interested in the fiancées across the sea, in their dress, in their
head dress, and in everything which makes woman resemble woman
in every clime. Late at night the workers of the field forget their
fatigue as they hear arise, in the peaceful night, the melancholy
voices which call up to the memory of the exile his distant country,
America. In the lanes along the flowery hedges, more than one
group of colored American soldiers fraternize with our people, while
the setting sun makes blue the neighboring hills, and gently the
song of night is awakened.

"And then these soldiers who had become our friends depart.
One evening sad adieus are exchanged. Adieu! How we wish
they may be only 'Au revoirs.' Promises to correspond, to return
when furloughs are granted. Here and there tears fall, and when,
the next day, the heavy trucks roll off in the chilly morning, carrying away to the front our exotic guests, a veritable sadness
seizes us.

"Soldier friends, our hearts, our wishes, go with you. That destiny may be merciful to you; that the bullets of the enemy may spare you. And if any of you should never see your native home again, may the soil of France give you sweet repose.

"Soldiers, who arrived among us one clear June day, redolent with the scent of roses, you will always live in our hearts."

# CHAPTER XXI

## NEGRO MUSIC THAT STIRRED FRANCE

*Recognition of the Value of Music by the U. S. War Department—
The Patriotic Music of Colored Americans—Lieutenant James
Europe and His Famous "Jazz" Band—Other Leaders and
Aggregations of Musicians—Enthusiasm of the French People
and Officials for American Music as Interpreted by These Colored Artists and Their Bandsmen.*

"You cannot defeat a singing nation," a keen-witted observer
has said, in noting the victory spirit engendered by the martial
music, the patriotic songs and the stirring melodies of hearth
and home that have moved the souls of men to action on all the
battlefields of history.

"Send me more singing regiments," cabled General Pershing,
and Admiral Mayo sent frequent requests that a song leader organize singing on every battleship of the Atlantic Fleet.

Since "the morning stars sang together" in Scriptural narrative, music has exerted a profound influence upon mankind,
be it in peace or in war, in gladness or in sorrow, or in the tender
sentiment that makes for love of country, affection for kindred or
the divine passion for "ye ladye fair." Music knows no land or
clime, no season or circumstance, and no race, creed or clan. It
speaks the language universal, and appeals to all peoples with a
force irresistible, and no training in ethics or science is necessary
to reach the common ground that its philosophy instinctively
creates in the human understanding.

The War Department was conscious of this and gave practical
application to its theory that music makes a soldier "fit to fight"
when it instituted, through the Commission on Training Camp
Activities, a systematic program of musical instruction throughout
the American Army at the home cantonments and followed up the
work overseas. It was the belief that every man became a better

warrior for freedom when his mind could be diverted from the dull routine of camp life by arousing his higher nature by song, and that he fared forth to battle with a stouter heart when his steps were attuned to the march by bands that drove out all fear of bodily danger and robbed "grim-visaged war" of its terrors.        Skilled song leaders were detailed to the various camps and cantonments here and abroad, and bands galore were brought into service for inspiration and cheer.

The emotional nature of the Negro fitted him for this musical program.        The colored American was a "close up" in every picture from the start to the finish and was a conspicuous figure in every scenario, playing with credit and distinction alike in melody or with the musket.

No instrumentality was more potent than music in offsetting the propaganda of the wily German agents, who sought to break down the loyalty of the Negro.        The music he knew was intensely American—in sentiment and rhythm.        It saturated his being—and all the blandishments of the enemy were powerless to sway him from the flag he loved.        His grievances were overshadowed by the realization that the welfare of the nation was menaced and that his help was needed.        American music harmonized with the innate patriotism of the race, and the majestic sweep of "The Star-Spangled Banner" or the sympathetic appeal of "My Country, 'Tis of Thee," were sufficient to counteract the sinister efforts of the missionaries of the Hohenzollerns to move him from his moorings.

No labor is ever so onerous that it can bar music from the soul of black folk.        This race sings at work, at play and in every mood. Visitors to any army camp found the Negro doing musical "stunts" of some kind from reveillé to taps—every hour, every minute of the day.        All the time the trumpeters were not blowing out actual routine bugle calls, they were somewhere practicing them.        Mouth-organs were going, concertinas were being drawn back and forth, and guitars, banjos, mandolins and whatnot were in use—playing all varieties of music, from the classic, like "Lucia," "Poet and Peasant," and "Il Trovatore" to the folk-songs and the rollicking "jazz."        Music is indeed the chiefest outlet of the Negro's emotions, and the state of his soul can best be determined by the type of melody he pours forth.

Some writer has said that a handful of pipers at the head of a Scotch regiment could lead that regiment down the mouth of a cannon. It is not doubted that a Negro regiment could be made to duplicate the "Charge of the Light Brigade" at Balaklava—"into the mouth of hell," as Tennyson puts it, if one of their regimental bands should play—as none but a colored band *can* play, the vivacious strains of "There'll Be a Hot Time in the Old Town Tonight."

The Negro's love of home is an integral part of his nature, and is exemplified in the themes he plaintively crooned in camp on both sides of the ocean. Such melodies as "Carry Me Back to Old Virginia," "My Old Kentucky Home," "In the Evening by de Moonlight," and "Suwanee River" recalled memories of the "old folks at home," and kept his patriotism alive, for he hoped to return to them some day and swell their hearts with pride by reason of the glorious record he made at the front. The Negro is essentially religious, and his deep spiritual temperament is vividly illustrated by the joy he finds in "harmonizing" such ballads of ancient days as "Swing Low, Sweet Chariot," "Steal Away to Jesus," "Standin' in the Need of Prayer," "Every Time I Feel the Spirit," "I Wan' To Be Ready," and 'Roll, Jordan, Roll." The Negro is also an optimist, whether he styles himself by that high-sounding title or not, and the sincerity of his "make the best of it" disposition is noted in the fervor he puts into those uplifting gems, "Pack Up Your Troubles in Your Old Kit Bag and Smile, Smile, Smile," "There's a Long, Long Trail," "Keep the Home Fires Burning," and "Good-bye Broadway, Hello France."

Just as the Negro folk-songs—or songs of war, interpreted with the characteristic Negro flavor—stirred all France and gave *poilu* and populace a taste of the real American music, the marvelous "jazz bands" kept their feet patting and their shoulders "eagle-rocking" to its infectious motion. High officials are said to have been literally "carried away" with the "jazz" music furnished by the colored bands "over there" during the war. General Petain is said to have paid a visit, at the height of the hostilities, to a sector in which there were American troops and had "the time of his life" listening to a colored band playing the entrancing "jazz" music, with some Negro dance stunts in keeping with the spirit of the melodies. He warmly congratulated the colored leader upon the excellence of the work of his organization, and thanked him for the enjoyable entertainment that had been given him. The stolid Briton is scarcely less susceptible to the "jazz" than his volatile French brother, for when another colored band from "The States" went to London to head a parade of American and English soldiers, and halted at Buckingham Palace, it is said that King George V and Queen Mary heard the lively airs with undisguised enthusiasm and were loath to have the players depart for the park where they were scheduled for a concert, with a dance engagement, under British military control, to follow. The colored bands scored heavily with the three great Allied Powers of Europe by rendering with a brilliant touch and matchless finish their national anthems, "God Save the Queen," "La Marseillaise" and the "Marcia Reale."

### "Filling France Full of Jazz"

In an illuminating article, abounding in wit and calling for descriptive powers far out of the ordinary, Mr. Charles Welton, in The World Magazine, New York City, March 30, 1919, using the unique title in the subhead above, tells much of interest concerning the experiences of Lieutenant James Reese Europe and his 369th Regiment Band, which is said to have "jazzed its way through France" and filled up all the vacant spaces in "No Man's Land" with the remnants of notes broken by shells and shrapnel as the one hundred master "jazzers" forced their lines to the very banks of the Rhine, where the world woke up and found them on the day the armistice was signed. Mr. Welton not only gives a clever recital of the way the Europe aggregation "jazzed," but pictures quite realistically the enthusiasm of the French people and the army officials for American music of this new type, as interpreted by these colored artists.

The writer tells engagingly the story of how "Jim" Europe spent his early boyhood on his native heath, Mobile, Alabama, consorting with fiddles and improvised musical instruments until he became acquainted with an upright piano, helped on by a father who was himself something of a sound manipulator on all kinds of "contraptions." Outgrowing his Mobile environs, or "down in 'the

sticks,' " as some facetious Northerners are fond of styling the
South, the youngster migrated to Washington, where he rapidly
advanced in all branches of music and learned to play upon practically every instrument known to an orchestra or brass band and
became a director of musical organizations, vocal and instrumental.

One of Lieut. Europe's particular friends and admirers was
Col. William Hayward, who had fostered the development of the 15th
New York Regiment throughout its long struggle for recognition as
an integral part of the New York National Guard, and at the entrance of the United States into the war, Col. Hayward became the
proud commander of the recruited and accepted "15th," officially
known as the 369th United States Infantry, which later achieved
international fame as "Hell Fighters" and led the Allied van to the
Rhine as the curtain fell upon the greatest tragedy in the annals
of the world.

### How Europe and His "Jazz Outfit" Broke Into the War

Following up the meteoric career of "Jim" Europe, Mr. Welton goes on to say:

"Then the war broke out, and Europe broke in. If he had been
built that way, he could have ducked it and stayed in town with his
bank deposits; but he couldn't figure it. He told Col. Hayward that he
was ready to follow or even go ahead of the flag to the last ounce of
jazz, and there were ninety-nine others like him. So the band was
signed up and sworn in, and Daniel C. Reid and some others made a
pool of enough thousands of dollars to supply instruments that would
stand the wear and tear of war and not go bad if dented up with shrapnel
and such like.

"Among the men who slipped into olive drab with the boss, come
weal, come woe, were Sergeant Noble Sissle, who played the cornet like
anything and knows all the tricks of drum majoring, and sings like a lark,
and writes verses by the yard; Herbert and Steve, whistlers and oh! such
drummers; Raphael Hernandez, baritone saxophoner; Ward Andrews, better known as Trombone Andrews; Elige Rijos, clarinetist, and Frank De
Bronte, who next to Europe himself is called the king of Jazz. The rest
of the band—the marimbaphones, the double B-flat helicons, the bunch of
French horns and all the rest clear down to the cymbals, were manned by
other eminent operators, making what is called a toot ensemble at once
hope-reviving and awe-inspiring.

*Left*—Col. Moss of the "Buffalo's."    *Right*—The Colored Color Bearers of the 15th National Guard, New York.

Group of Negro Officers of the 370th (Old 8th Illinois National Guard) called the Black Devils by the Germans. Reading left to right, Capt. Joe Warner. 1st Lt. Arthur Jones; 2nd Lt. Ed. White. 2nd Lt. Julian D. Rainey. 2nd Lt. M. McGuinn. 2nd Lt. Luther Harris. 2nd Lt. Alvin M. Jordan. 2nd Lt. Edward L. Goodlett. 2nd Lt. J. F. Baker; 2nd Lt. Fred Johnson. 1st Lt. F. Hewitt.

Colored heroes who won the Croix de Guerre. All of these are enlisted men of 369th Infantry who were decorated by the French High Command. In front row from left to right are: Privates Ed. Williams, Herbert Taylor, Leon Fraitor, Leon Fraitor and Ralph Hawkins. In rear row are Private H. D. Prunes. Sgt. D. Stormes. Private Joe Williams. Private Arthur Menly and Corp. Taylor.

*Left*—Presenting the Colors to "The Buffaloes," Governor Charles S. Whitman presenting, on behalf of the New York Union League Club, the National and Regimental Flags to the 367th Infantry, just before they started overseas.
*Right*—American Negro Soldiers in the Spanish-American War. For more than a half century the Negro soldier has played an important part in the Army of the United States. This photograph, taken during the Spanish-American War, shows how our colored troops who fought in 1898 were uniformed and equipped.

Life in the Training Camp. There was a good deal more than drill and work in the training camps as this photograph of a boxing bout at Camp Travis, Texas, under the management of the Y. M. C. A., proves. The man on the stage in the light colored shirt is the Negro Y. M. C. A. Secretary.

*Left.*—Colonel William Hayward, commanding the 369th Infantry, and Major Arthur W. Little of the same regiment. Notice regimental badge, the Coiled Rattlesnake, on Major Little's shoulder.
*Right.*—Major Joseph H. Ward who has the distinction of being one of the only two Negro officers of the Medical Corps to attain the rank of Major.

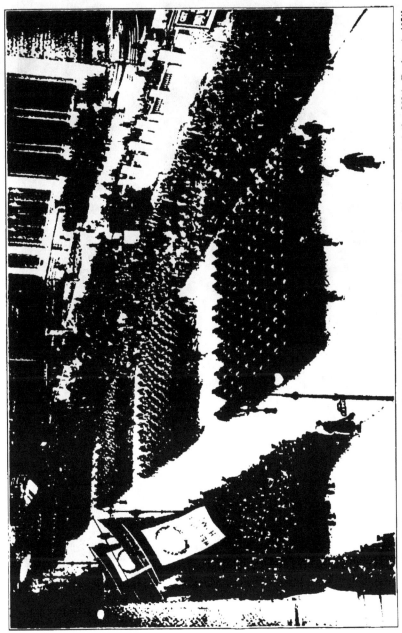

How New York welcomed the famous "Hell Fighters." Triumphal Parade up Fifth Avenue of the 369th Regiment (15th National Guard) on its return from "Over There." Photographed passing the New York Public Library.

GROUP OF OFFICERS OF THE 370TH

Reading from Left to Right—*Top*—1st Lt. Norman Garrett; Capt. John H. Patton, 2nd Batt. 1st Lt. Michael Browning, Machine Gun No. 2.
*Center*—Capt. Spencer C. Dixon. Med Corps; Major Charles H. Hunt. 2nd Battalion; Capt. Libburn Jackson, Machine Gun No. 2.
*Bottom*—1st Lt. Robt. C. Chavis; 1st Lt. Benote H. Lee; 2nd Lt. Frank Corbin. all of the 370th Infantry (formerly old 8th Illinois).

"To understand jazz, it is well to know that it isn't merely a series of uncontrollable spasms or outbursts of enthusiasm scattered through a composition and discharged on the four winds, first by one wing and then by another of the band. Of course if a player feels an attack of something which he believes to be a jazz novelty rumbling in his system it is not the Europe rule to make him choke it back and thus run the risk of cheating the world out of a good thing. Any player can try anything once. If it doesn't come out a fliv on harmony it can remain as a toot to be used whenever there's a place where it won't crowd regular notes over the bars.

"The basic fundamental of jazz, however, is created by means of a variety of cones inserted point down in the bells of the horns. These cones are of two kinds. One is of metal and the other of leather. The leather cones are usually soaked in water before the band goes out for a blow. The metal cones muffle and modify the natural tones of the instruments and make them come across with new sound values.

When a leather cone is wrung out and fitted into the vestibule of a horn, and the man back of the works contributes the best that is in him, it is somewhat difficult to explain what happens, in mere words. You get it with both ears, and almost see it. The cone being wet, the sound might be called liquefied harmony. It runs and ripples, then has a sort of choking sensation;· next it takes on the musical color of Niagara Falls at a distance, and subsides to a trout brook nearby. The brassiness of the horn is changed, and there is sort of a throbbing nasal effect, half moan, half hallelujah. Get me?

"Having set this down, we may now land with the band at Brest, France.

"The first thing that Jim Europe's outfit did when it got ashore wasn't to eat. It wanted France to know that it was present, so it blew some plain ordinary jazz over the town. Twenty minutes before the 369th disembarked, Brest wasn't at all la-la, so to speak; but as soon as Europe had got to work, that part of France could see that hope wasn't entirely dead.

"From Brest the Europe outfit went to St. Nazaire, sowing jazz selections over the agricultural terrain and bunching bits of it in the cantons en route. There was a rest center at St. Nazaire. Europe went to the center of the center, and for two months all he had to do was to help the boys rest by providing a brand of soothing syrup. All the sects in all the sectors round about that had carfare commuted into town and lolled in the rest zone. The city council adopted resolutions and the prefect delivered an eulogium right at Noble Sissle and the backstop of snare drums.

"A call for help from Aix-les-Bains took the band to that resort. It arrived just in time to capture the casino in a night attack. On all fronts at this time soldiers that had been dodging minenwerfers were buoyed by the promise that Jim Europe had enough jazz in stock to last until the war was over, over there. Troops suffering with aches were hurried down to Aix—honest, they were—and the band did the rest.

### Equally Handy With Trombones or Machine Guns.

"Between concerts, so to express it, the 369th band would get from under the coils of horns, unsling its drums, and load up with machine guns and go into the deep and mussy trenches and practice on the unhappy wretches on the other side of no man's land. Europe himself was the first colored officer to rest elbows against a first-line trench in one of the uncomfortable bois countries. He did solo work with a machine gun forty times heavier than a trombone, and actually got it to working in syncopated time. If we ever have another war and it could be fought exclusively by syncopating, Jim Europe would have a Major General's rating."

The people everywhere turned out to hear the 369th Regimental Band, and its magic influence gave proof to the assertion by its devotees that "JAZZ WON THE WAR." The return of "Jim" Europe's band to America, when it led the imposing parade up Fifth Avenue, February 17, 1919, the day the gallant 369th was welcomed home by a grateful nation, was an occasion that will live in history.

Sergeant Noble Sissle, who served as the regimental drum major of the 369th, is one of the musicians whose work has "stood out" in the estimation of the people on the other side of the water. Noble Sissle was reared in Indianapolis, Ind., which boasts of having furnished more real talent to the colored musical and dramatic world than any other spot on earth, and his father, Rev. George A. Sissle, was a one-time pastor of Simpson M. E. Chapel in the Hoosier capital, as well as prominent in ministerial circles at many points in Ohio and Kentucky. Young Sissle has won an enviable reputation as a tenor soloist, composer and pianist, and is regarded as one of Lieutenant Europe's most dependable aids, both in the Clef Club in New York and in the regimental band work overseas.

Sergeant Sissle has made a study of the effect of Yankee ragtime, as interpreted by the colored artists, on French audiences, and advantage may be taken of this opportunity to give a summary of his impressions, as prepared for interested friends "over here." It covers much heretofore unknown matter in connection with the marvelous 369th Infantry Band and the intricacies of ragtime or "jazz" construction in general. Sergeant Sissle wrote, in part, as follows:

"When our country was dance-mad a few years ago, we quite agreed with the popular Broadway song composer who wrote:
'Syncopation rules the nation
You can't get away from it.'

"But if you could see the effect our good old 'jazz' melodies have on the people of every race and creed you would change the word 'nation' quoted above to 'world.'

"Inasmuch as the press seems to have kept the public well informed of our band's effort to make the boys happy in this land where everybody speaks everything but English, I will endeavor to start off with a few notes concerning James Reese Europe, its organizer and conductor. This Lieutenant Europe is the same Europe whose orchestras are considered to have done a goodly share toward making syncopated music popular on Broadway. Having been associated with Lieutenant Europe in civil life during his 'jazz bombardment' on the delicate, classical, musical ears of New York's critics, and having watched 'The Walls of Jericho' come tumbling down, I was naturally curious to see what would be the effect of a 'real American tune,' as Victor Herbert calls our Southern syncopated tunes, as played by a real American band.

"At last the opportunity came, and it was at a town in France where there were no American troops, and our audience, with the exception of an American general and his staff, was all French people. I am sure the greater part of the crowd had never heard a ragtime number. So what happened can be taken as a test of the success of our music in this country, where all is sadness and sorrow.

"The program started with a French march, followed by favorite overtures and vocal selections by our male quartette, all of which were heartily applauded. The second part of the program opened with 'The Stars and Stripes Forever,' the great Sousa march, and before the last note of the martial ending had been finished the house was ringing with applause. Next followed an arrangement of 'Plantation Melodies' and then came the fireworks, 'The Memphis Blues.'

"Lieutenant Europe, before raising his baton, twitched his shoulders, apparently to be sure that his tight-fitting military coat would stand the strain, each musician shifted his feet, the players of brass horns blew the saliva from their instruments, the drummers tightened their drumheads, every one settled back in their seats, half closed their eyes, and when the baton came down with a swoop that brought forth a soul-rousing crash both director and musicians seemed to forget their surroundings; they were lost in scenes and memories. Cornet and clarinet players began to manipulate notes in that typical rhythm (that rhythm which no artist has ever been able to put down on paper); as the drummers struck their stride their shoulders began shaking in time to their syncopated raps.

"Then, it seemed, the whole audience began to sway, dignified French officers began to pat their feet along with the American general, who, temporarily, had lost his style and grace. Lieutenant Europe was no longer the Lieutenant Europe of a moment ago, but once more Jim Europe, who a few months ago rocked New York with his syncopated baton. His body swayed in willowy motions and his head was bobbing as it did in days when tepsichorean festivities reigned supreme. He turned to the trombone players, who sat impatiently waiting for their cue to have a 'Jazz spasm,' and they drew their slides out to the extremity and jerked them back with that characteristic crack.

"The audience could stand it no longer; the 'Jazz germ' hit them, and it seemed to find the vital spot, loosening all muscles and causing what is known in America as an 'Eagle Rocking Fit.' 'There now,' I said to myself. 'Colonel Hayward has brought his band over here and started ragtimitis in France; ain't this an awful thing to visit upon a nation with so many burdens?' But when the band had finished and the people were roaring with laughter, their faces wreathed in smiles, I was forced to say that this is just what France needs at this critical moment.

"All through France the same thing happened. Troop trains carrying Allied soldiers from everywhere passed us en route, and every head came out of the window when we struck up a good old Dixie tune. Even German prisoners forgot they were prisoners, dropped their work to listen and pat their feet to the stirring American tunes.

"But the thing that capped the climax happened up in Northern France. We were playing our Colonel's favorite ragtime, 'The Army Blues,' in a little village where we were the first American troops there, and among the crowd listening to that band was an old lady about sixty years of age. To everyone's surprise, all of a sudden, she started doing a dance that resembled 'Walking the Dog.' Then I was cured, and satisfied that American music would some day be the world's music. While at Aix les Bains other musicians from American bands said their experiences had been the same.

"Who would think that little U. S. A. would ever give to the world a rhythm and melodies that, in the midst of such universal sorrow, would cause all students of music to yearn to learn how to play it? Such is the case, because every musician we meet—and they all seem to be masters of their instruments—are always asking the boys to teach them how to play ragtime. I sometimes think if the Kaiser ever heard a good syncopated melody he would not take himself so seriously.

"If France was well supplied with American bands, playing their lively tunes, I'm sure it would help a good deal in bringing home entertainment to our boys, and at the same time make the heart of sorrow-stricken France beat a deal lighter."

Sissle was made a Lieutenant before he returned with his regiment from overseas.

This resumé of how Negro music thrilled France brings to mind an interesting and pathetic story of an experience in a little war-stricken town of the 369th Infantry Band and its agile drum major—this same Noble Sissle. After the band had finished its output of "Army Blues," etc., the program shifted to plantation melodies, and the auditors were literally overcome by the power of the songs, which were sung as only Negroes can sing them.

Dr. R. R. Moton used to say in his Tuskegee Talks that "the white people can beat the Negro doing a great many things, but there is one thing at which no white man can beat the Negro, and that is in the singing of Negro songs."

The closing piece on this occasion was "Joan of Arc," rendered by Drum Major Sissle, in a beautiful rich baritone. He sang it first in English and then in excellent French. It will be remembered that this Joan of Arc was the "Maid of Orleans" that came as a mysterious child from the womb of destiny to liberate the French at a time when their national existence hung in the balance, and her memory is revered throughout France as a patron saint. As Drum Major Sissle sang, the people wept. One be-whiskered peasant, an elderly man, with tears streaming down his age-hardened cheeks, rushed up to this man of color,—an apostle of liberty, a man with many wrongs, but like the "Man of Galilee," willing to forget—and strenuously attempted to throw his arms around the neck of the singer and kiss him.

### The 350th Field Artillery Band

The 350th Field Artillery Band, led by Lieutenant J. Tim Brymm, of Philadelphia, won fame in France, and received a royal welcome upon its return home in March, after an absence of about a year. The band has about 70 soloists, recruited "from the four corners of the earth," as its organizer, General Fred T. Austin, facetiously puts it. The organization returned to Philadelphia under flattering auspices, and Lieutenant Brymm, who has won distinction as a composer, had two new offerings for the home-coming reception, "The Philadelphia Sunday Blues," a glittering "jazz" conceit, and the "Dieulouard Glide," the latter a fox-trot composed by Lieutenant Brymm as descriptive of an artillery bombardment. It depicts the course of a heavy artillery shell from the beginning of its flight to its explosion, and was composed during one of the regiment's fiercest artillery duels. Lieutenant Brymm has given the country hundreds of popular song hits, the best-known of which is perhaps "Please Go 'Way and Let Me Sleep," which had quite a vogue some years ago.

Among the thousands of appreciative welcomers that packed the Academy of Music was Mme. Ernestine Schumann-Heink, the famous operatic contralto, who has evinced deep interest in a number of aspiring colored composers, and who is styled "the godmother of the 350th band," and its chief sponsor. Some wag has described Tim Brymm's Band as "a military symphony engaged in a battle of jazz." Lieutenant Brymm also did excellent work as leader of the band of the 349th Field Artillery for quite an extended period, and brought it up to a high standard.

### Other Regimental Bands That "Made Good" in France

Other bands that made a record in France, and whose experiences were much the same as those chronicled with reference to the bands of the 369th Infantry and 350th Field Artillery were: The 368th Infantry Band, directed by Lieutenant A. Jack Thomas; the parade at Baltimore before going overseas afforded President and including Edgar Landin, the drum major whose evolutions in Wilson and his party so much solid enjoyment;

The 370th Infantry (the "Old Eighth Illinois" Regiment) Band, directed by Lieutenant George E. Dulf;

The 349th and 351st Field Artillery and the 365th, 366th and 367th Regiments of Infantry all had bands that gave a splendid account of themselves on both sides of the ocean.

Several of these unique organizations toured the country shortly after their return from overseas, visiting many of the principal cities, and were accorded the warmest kind of a reception everywhere arrangements were made for their appearance. Their work was inspirational to the last degree. The band of the 370th Infantry (Eighth Illinois) scored heavily throughout the North and East, with the celebrated coloratura soprano, Mme. Anita Patti Brown, of Chicago, as prima donna and soloist.

Among the bands that have done good work in this country, the 16th Battalion Band of the Minnesota Home Guards, under the leadership of William H. Howard, is warmly praised in the Northwest. Mr. Howard was commissioned as a First Lieutenant. He is a native of Baltimore and for several years conducted one of the leading musical studios in Minneapolis.

### Some of the Song Leaders

The song leaders who trained the soldier lads in mass singing in the home camps contributed largely to the morale of the army and their labors, rendered in many instances at a heavy personal sacrifice, are deserving of the highest commendation. They made camp life happy, when the hearts of the men were sad from homesickness, and every task was made lighter by the song that accompanied it. In Y. M. C. A. huts, in the open field, and as the boys whiled away the time in the highways and byways of the camp area, the song leaders were on deck and had them humming some care-destroying melody which brought a silver lining to the threatening clouds. Of these leaders, J. E. Blanton, Max Weinstein and William C. Elkins, deserve especial mention.

### Service Rendered Colored Soldiers by Mrs. Baker

Among the remembrances of the war period are the visits of Mrs. Newton D. Baker, the wife of the Secretary of War, who sang in the camps and cantonments and the clubs of the War Camp

Community Service, and in various city auditoriums. The appearances of Mrs. Baker at Howard University, at Dunbar High School, at War Camp Community Club No. 3, Camp Meade and other places near Washington, where soldiers and civilians were stationed, were most welcome "breaks" in the daily routine of the soldiers. Her singing always met with an enthusiastic reception, commingling in her selections the military, the folk-song and the ballad of heart-appeal, and the insistent demands for more, despite the extraordinary draft upon her patience and powers, were responded to in a measure that was generous to the last degree. She enjoyed her faculty of giving joy to others, and it cannot be doubted that Mrs. Baker's talents as a singer, and her rare capacity for cheering white and colored Americans "to do their best, whate'er betide," exerted a potent influence toward the winning of the war.

It was arranged with the War Camp Community Service that J. E. Blanton, of the Penn School, should go from camp to camp, leading the men in the singing of the spirituals, teaching them the "Hymn of Freedom," written by Mrs. Burlin, a student of Negro hymn-songs, and exerting his influence in sustaining the morale which has ever characterized the colored troops. The plan was heartily endorsed by Secretary of War Baker, who, in a letter written to Mr. Peabody, said:

"I am quite sure that you are not overestimating the effect of these spirituals. Indeed, there is a certain cadence to these songs which is quite unattainable in any music with which I am acquainted, and I have little doubt that the white soldiers will be singing them as eagerly and effectively as the colored men before we get very far with it."

In an interesting article in *The Outlook* magazine, Miss Grant makes note of the fact that the use of these spirituals was not restricted to colored camps. The "Hymn of Freedom," for instance, she says, has been sung in white churches, schools and service clubs and by choral organizations connected with the war in different parts of the country, thus justifying the hope that the noble old Negro melody would become a bond of sympathy between the races. The statement is made that the writing of the words was in part prompted by Mrs. Burlin's belief that "the artistic utterance of the Negro, which has so important a place in the music of America, might help to build a bridge of understanding between the races, spanning the chasm of prejudice.''

These songs, many of the titles of which have been quoted throughout this chapter on Negro music, along with the hundreds of patriotic war melodies by our skilled composers of the modern school, were carried to France by the colored troops, and toward the close of the conflict they found an additional champion in Dr. Moton, himself an unrivaled interpreter of the "spiritual," who went abroad at the request of President Wilson and Secretary Baker to assist in safeguarding the welfare of the black soldiers on the battle fronts.

Miss Grant is firm in the belief that the work of promoting the folk-song, with its accompanying Americanism, has suggestion for the future in the nation's dealing with the Negro, and the solution of what has come to be known as the "race problem." Her admirable article closes with a quotation from Mrs. Burlin, in the sentiment of which she concurs most heartily:

"Through toil and suffering song has kept the heart of the Negro still unembittered; through prejudice and misunderstanding it has upheld him; through the stress and sacrifice of this white man's war it has cheered him on. And, those who recognize its power are surely not wrong in feeling that in the inspired music of the black man lie a prophecy of the possibilities of the race and an earnest plea for that democracy at home which cannot be won by bomb or bullet, but by sympathy and understanding and a realization of the contribution which each race can make to the civilization of the world."

### Some of the Compositions That Counted

Thousands of creditable compositions, vocal and instrumental, marches, duets, quartets and choruses, have been brought out by gifted colored musicians throughout the land. Of the long list of such compositions, a song "The Colored Soldier Boys of Uncle Sam," by W. J. Nickerson, of New Orleans, Louisiana, dedicated to the colored soldiers of the U. S. A., occupies a conspicuous place. The music is in march time, and has a lively step and a resonant swing that gives it an especial appeal to all who appreciate the combination of classic style with the sprightliness of the melodies that make movement their chief function. The words of this meritorious production are also by Mr. Nickerson, and they carry a sentiment that is at once eloquent and convincing in their patriotism.

> "There'll be no stop, 'till we're over the top,
> We're the colored boys of Uncle Sam!"

Mr. Nickerson's inspiring war song acquired a large measure of popularity through its use by Mme. Anita Patti Brown, prima donna soprano, in the nation-wide concert tour of the 8th Regiment (or 370th) shortly after the signing of the armistice.

The Negro troops of Camp Shelby composed a song of their own and dedicated it to their military cantonment. The men at this camp were all Southern born, and the theme bore strongly upon their attachment to the land in which they first saw the light and their comprehension of the joys of army life. The hymn was entitled "Glory, Glory to Old Shelby," and was sung to the tune of "The Battle Hymn of the Republic."

Miss Nannie G. Board, a young colored woman of Louisville, Kentucky, won first place in a contest for producing the best original war song, securing this laurel in competition with a field of contestants nearly all white. The contest was conducted by the United War Work Campaign Committee of the State of Kentucky. Miss Board graduated from Howard University and became a teacher in the State Agricultural and Industrial Institute, Nashville, Tennessee.

After all is said of the mesmeric influence of Negro music upon France, and of the high-grade morale maintained in camps and communities over here through its magic wand, the world is impressed with the thought that melody is indeed the common tongue of mankind, and that the Negro-American music that filled the hills and dales overseas has forged a link of international friendship that will last for all time, and has built up a spirit of fellowship and *cameraderie* between the races, white and black, that will lay the foundation of an enduring human brotherhood throughout the earth.

# CHAPTER XXII

## THE NEGRO IN THE SERVICE OF SUPPLY

*A Vast Army of Colored Stevedores in France—Their Important and Efficient Work—Essential to the Combatant Army in the Trenches—Their Loyalty and Cheerfulness—Important Lessons Learned in the War — The Labor Battalions — Well-Earned Tributes to These Splendid Colored Workers Overseas.*

War is not all "death and glory." For every soldier who gets even a glimpse of the enemy or risks his life within range of shell-fire, there must, in all modern warfare, be from twenty to thirty men working at such commonplace and routine tasks as loading and unloading ships, building piers, laying railroad tracks, making roads, in a thousand other ways making it possible for the fighting men to get to the front, and for the necessary food, ammunition, and other supplies to reach them. But what man would want to render such service? It was somewhat exciting news for the Negro population of the United States to learn that only about twenty per cent of the colored draftees were to be trained to fight while the remaining Negroes in the military service would constitute non-combatant divisions in the Service of Supply, or other non-fighting organizations. On June 23, 1918, when 237,000 Negroes had been called to the colors, it was estimated that the battalions of the non-combatant to the combatant troops were in the proportion of about four to one.

This vast army of Stevedores in France was composed mostly of men who volunteered when the call was first sounded. The first men who went over early in June, 1917, were with a civilian contract company, experienced as stevedores in America. They served one year and finishing their contract in June, 1918, returned to America. During the early days of July, 1917, other companies of volunteer men arrived, so the army grew until the Stevedore Camps at base ports in France became one great industrial army, numbering about fifty thousand.

The army of Stevedores had all the equipment, regulations, and military rank and uniform that the infantry had. Though industrial in its nature, all the life and workings, and details of procedure, were according to military law and order. This vast army of workers was divided into companies and regiments and had their individual camps regularly officered and numbered. Anything by the way of uniform and ration that other men received, the Stevedore shared equally. They were soldiers and took great pride in the fact that they belonged to Uncle Sam's Army. Including all the display that goes with drills, reviews, and inspections, saluting an officer, flag-raising, and perchance, the grand parades, with companies swinging into line, and the martial music of bands, the Stevedores always stepped proudly and lively enough to suit the keenest military eye for discipline and fine training.

The Stevedores also took great pride in their companies, their camps, and all that belonged to the Army, and because their work and contribution were always emphasized by officers as being essential to the boys in the trenches, the name "Stevedore" finally became a dignified and distinguished term, representing an important part of the great American Army.

To the Negro soldiers of the American Army fell a large part of the work of this "Service of Supply," or, as it was known in Army slang, the "S. O. S." The work of the Negro Stevedore Regiments and Labor Battalions, and their unremitting toil at the French ports—Brest, St. Nazaire, Bordeaux, Havre, Marseilles— won the highest praise from all who have had an opportunity to judge of the efficiency of their work. Every man who served his country in one of these organizations was as truly fighting to save his country as though he had carried a rifle and killed Germans.

The following are the Negro organizations, other than combat troops, that served overseas:

Butchery Companies, Nos. 322 and 363.

Stevedore Regiments, Nos. 301, 302 and 303.

Stevedore Battalions, Nos. 701, 702.

Engineer Service Battalions, Nos. 505 to 550, inclusive.

Labor Battalions, Nos. 304 to 315, inclusive; Nos. 317 to 327, inclusive; Nos. 329 to 348, inclusive, and No. 357.

Labor Companies, Nos. 301 to 324, inclusive.

Pioneer Infantry Battalions, Nos. 801 to 809, inclusive; No. 811 and Nos. 813 to 816, inclusive.

At the same time, there were 207 Labor Battalions in France composed of white soldiers.

As there were not sufficient colored officers to command the colored regiments and no efforts were being made to train colored officers for this purpose, there was much apprehension among the colored people as to how these Negro laborers in the military service would be treated. Some said it meant the re-enslavement of the Negro race. An effort was then made to increase the facilities for military training offered to colored draftees in the various camps to supply this peculiar need of the Service battalions, and some encouragement and some actual deeds to meet this demand followed. It was argued not only that officers to be placed in charge of these noncombatant troops should be well trained themselves, but that the Negro laborers should be given an opportunity to be trained in military tactics. A memorial was, therefore, made to the Secretary of War by the CENTRAL COMMITTEE OF NEGRO COLLEGE MEN, recommending that the noncombatant units excluded from the officer training privileges be allowed through the extension of training privileges to supply their own quota of noncombatant officers, and that for the general good of the service such troops be given at least one month's military training before being assigned to their specific duties.

## Arduous Tasks for the Army

The tasks of these soldiers in the Service of Supply were numerous. On arriving at the ports they were called upon to handle bags of mail and freight sent to supply the Army. The Army had to be furnished with horses and mules, which had to be fed with forage and supplied with saddles and harness. The men needed ice, meat, bacon, flour, and lard, and for comfort shoes, clothes, matches, ipecac, and gasoline. When our Army was in full swing in France we had to hurry up the shipments of millions of rounds of ammunition and large supplies of blankets, rubber-boots, hay, and medicines to carry out the great work of promoting the war.

When brought to the various ports, an unusual number of laborers were required to unload such supplies. When unloaded the task of transporting them to the various points for distribution among the divisions of the Army was a still greater task. As railroads were not always available and railway connections had been broken up by the penetration of the Germans almost into the heart of France, automobile transportation was a necessity. In this same service French cattle cars, the ox-cart, the motorcycle, side-cars, aeroplanes, and human beings as beasts of burden were used.

The task was rendered somewhat easier later when these same men increased sufficiently in numbers to be detached for the special service of building Yankee railroads. This made possible an easier handling of these supplies through storage depots located at various places in France. The storage depot at Gievres, through which millions of American wealth passed in the Army like water over a milldam, covers six square miles. It was started in the fall of 1917 and when the war ended the Army had there about twenty miles of warehouses and shops of modern construction and about 25,000 men handling the enormous masses of stores distributed from that point. From such warehouses were distributed everything except artillery, heavy ammunition and aeroplane products, which had supply depots of their own at Mehun and Romorantin. This depot is diamond-shaped, with 140 miles of interior railroad lines within the reservation for the handling of freight.

How the colored American Stevedores in France worked is told in a report by the Reverend D. Leroy Ferguson, Rector of the Protestant Episcopal Church of Our Merciful Saviour, Louisville, Kentucky. He paid a high tribute to the American Army of Colored Stevedores in a lengthy account which tells of their patriotic deeds.

On the same day that the American Infantry, treading in the wake of the retreating Germans gained the outskirts of Fismes, says he, Colored Stevedores unloading a ship at one of the base ports, unostentatiously won an important victory by discharging 1200 tons of flour in 9½ hours, setting a record for the A. E. F. and a pace which is rarely excelled on the best-equipped docks in the United States. The same group of Stevedores over a period of five days discharged an average of 2000 tons of cargo a day from

one ship, a record more notable still. It was a 24-hour-a-day grind
at the base ports, he says, where thousands of American colored
troops put ashore the million and one articles, big and little, which
are necessary for the maintenance of a modern army. The scarcity
of ocean tonnage made necessary the utilization of every ounce of
ship capacity, and the saving of every possible moment in dispatching supplies to France.

With the same force with which American line units made their
début in a big scale warfare, did the other branches of the service
upon whose efforts depend the potency and effectiveness of the men
in the trenches accomplish their less spectacular but equally important work;—more work was accomplished in the S. O. S. by an
appreciable percentage during July, 1918, than in any previous
month. More dirt was excavated; on the rail lines of communication, more steel was laid; more warehouses were constructed; and
more conspicuous still, at the base ports, more men were landed,
more freight was discharged from incoming ships, and the efficiency
of its handling was materially increased.

Most of the American colored Stevedores had never seen a ship
until they started for France, but they proved their worth as cargo
handlers. Working in the hold of a ship, with the August sun
raising heat waves from the deck, was not the easiest job in the
Army, but they broke records at it, and it did not dampen their
sunny disposition either.

How splendidly the Stevedores measured up to military standards of efficiency while "making good," and with what great
affection their officers regarded them and their work, Dr. Ferguson
had opportunities to witness. And Col. C. E. Goodwyn in a letter
expresses this fact most admirably. His can be taken as a special
standard, because Colonel Goodwyn for over a year was in charge of
the largest camp of Colored Stevedores in France.

"It is with many keen thrusts of sorrow," said he, "that I am
obliged to leave this camp and the men who have made up this
organization. The men for whose uplift you are working have not
only gained but have truly earned a large place in my heart, and
I will always cherish a loving memory of the men of this wonderful organization which I have had the honor and privilege to
command."

That Colonel Goodwyn was also held in high esteem by his
men, may be judged from a conversation which was overheard one
day. After the armistice a group of the boys were discussing what
they had in mind to do first after returning to America. One
ambitious fellow said, "I'm going to marry right away, and get
me a fine little boy stevedore!" Another remarked that "Of course
his name will be Abraham Lincoln." "Oh, no," replied the first
speaker. "There's too many Abe Lincolns in America now; my
first boy's going to be called 'Colonel Goodwyn.'"

### Cheerfulness in the Camps

Very naturally, many amusing stories and jokes, with the war
and France as a background, featured the life of the colored boys
over there. One heard many funny "bon mots" and puns and
clever stories attributed to the Negro soldier, until it seems that
they brought and made most of the humor connected with the grim,
frightful war. Surely, in America, the jokes of their experiences
and life in France, and foreign surroundings, their efforts to imitate
or speak the French language, will, I imagine, serve to increase the
record, which will be all the more laughable, as well as interesting,
because of the new situation and circumstances that enter into the
stories. It is very true that with that native talent and fun-making
nature of his, the Negro soldier found many things in France that
amused him, and made possible for him all sorts of jokes and
clever expressions. Indeed, the Negro soldier was quick to see
whatever was humorous over there; the war, the army, the firing
line, even the serious and dangerous things, that make others sad,
he made the basis of his jokes and ofttimes ridiculed, so that even
his dangers and his tasks seemed to have been less difficult. No
doubt these jokes and comic expressions will be heard over again
and happily enjoyed in America when the boys return home.

As to cheerfulness, the Stevedore Camps had their share of
songs, music, and that gaiety which characterizes a cheerful race.
One thing that most impressed those who were willing to observe,
was that all through those stressful days and anxious, when the
strain of work and the handling of cargoes and ammunition for
the front became really one long grind for the Stevedores, morning,
noon and night, one could see them through all sorts of weather

and hours, swinging by companies into line, marching bravely and merrily to the difficult tasks, singing or whistling some patriotic melody or popular song.

Frequently the base commander and other distinguished officers visited the camps and were seen at the public gatherings and Y. M. C. A. buildings. "I have heard them repeatedly emphasize," writes Dr. Ferguson, "how much the Army at the front depended on the work and loyalty of the Stevedores at the base. They also spoke to them in the highest terms about the way in which they were performing their difficult tasks, without the show, applause, and excitement that inspire the soldier at the front. They were doing the drudgery, the dull routine, the monotonous labor; still they were the foundation and groundwork upon which the whole Army was built. They also were American soldiers and heroes.

"With such patriotic sentiment always encouraging them, I believe the same acted as a spur to keep the morale up to the highest, and the energy with which they worked was all the more vital, because they responded readily to the principles of patriotism that urged them on, believing that through their efforts all the more quickly victory and peace would come. Even after the armistice was signed and their thoughts naturally turned homeward to their families and friends, a new appeal is being made to them, that the Army of Occupation now needs supplies and food, to which they are responding loyally, and the Stevedores are over there still at work, far into the night and even from the rising to the setting of the sun.

"When it is considered to what extent with regard to different States and communities the huge army of Stevedores was organized, and the various types and conditions of men represented, ranging from the young man of school training and city-bred, to those from hamlets and small farms 'way down South, and illiterate, it is remarkable how they were all brought together and welded finally into a fine industrial army that made such a wonderful record of work and efficiency. This credit belongs to the Army discipline and training they received. The traveler was often amazed to see this development of hundreds of young men from crude farmhands, very raw material, indeed, day by day improving under Army discipline, until in these days, after their months of training, they stand forth, erect, alert, earnest, industrious soldiers; and in them is found a type of industrious and useful citizens for the future America.''

### Lessons Learned in the War

They learned remarkable lessons in this experience of war times, aside from the broadening view of life that travel and foreign contact give. These are the lessons of self-control, cleanliness, promptness, obedience, efficiency, and the value of time. Another agency with the camp that greatly influenced the men and urged the development of mind, body, and soul was the Y. M. C. A. In each camp wherever the Stevedores were stationed there were soon established very home-like and commodious ''Y'' buildings, all equipped with the same regular, standardized furnishings and supplies as others, under the able direction of colored secretaries. That the men received additional help and advantage here also is well recognized. The programs were elaborate and interesting, consisting of lectures by eminent men and women, concerts by the leading musicians, singers, and actors that went the rounds of all the camps; moving pictures, athletics, circulating libraries, and educational classes in reading, writing, mathematics; besides regular instruction in French. All these fine influences must have reached the minds and hearts of the Stevedores, and scores of men who came to the Army illiterate were able, after the training received, to write their names and first letters home to wives, sweethearts and friends.

The service rendered by the Negroes of these battalions evoked many expressions of admiration and praise from all persons who saw the Army in action in France. It was observed that the spirit which animated the Americans engaged in the Service of Supply division was the same as that of those in the front-line trenches. The shiploads of products requiring usually four days for unloading were disposed of by these Negroes in half of that time. In fact they did everything on a gigantic scale and did their work quickly. The rapidity then with which the American soldiers were dispatched to France so as to excite surprise at home and abroad was due primarily to the unselfish and patriotic service of the thousands of Negro stevedores who cleared the ports on arrival in France.

Writing of these wonderful feats an observer asserted that when the greatest of American transports first came over, it took 52 days to unload it at Liverpool. Later this period was reduced to 28 days. On the third trip it was decided to send this transport to a French port where Americans could handle the freight in less time. It turned out that on the first arrival 10,000 men and supplies were unloaded and the ship coaled and sent back in four days. On the second arrival the same task was completed in three days; the third arrival in 48 hours, and the fourth arrival in 44 hours. In each case, 5,000 tons of coal had to be put on this large transport and loaded from lighters, as her 41 feet of draft kept her far out in the harbor.

### Work of the Stevedores

Referring to the work done by these stevedores in France, Mr. Ralph W. Tyler, accredited representative of the Committee on Public Information, then in France, said: "Figures just made available show that for the month of September, 1918, there were handled at the American base ports in France 767,648 tons, or a daily average of 25,588 tons, an increase of nearly ten per cent over August. When it is considered that colored stevedores handled by far the largest per cent of this tonnage, some idea can be formed of the very important service colored stevedores are rendering the Government here in France, and how necessary they are to the success of the Allies. The work of colored stevedores may be menial, and is laborious, but it is as essential as the manning of the guns at the front. The fact is, that without these stevedores first unloading and aiding in transporting the guns, munitions, and supplies to the front, there would be no manning of guns at the front. One who sees the stevedores' work notes with what rapidity and cheerfulness they work, and what a very important cog they are in the war machinery. The colored stevedore has greater endurance than the others."

### At a Stevedore Camp

In another letter Mr. Tyler said: "I have just returned from a two days' visit to a point where there are assembled, and at work, some twenty-five thousand service, or stevedore troops. I was particularly impressed with the arrangements, and with the

uniform cheerfulness and splendid morale of the men.  During quite
an extended conference, or audience, with the Colonel in command,
he stated that he would not exchange his men, if it were a matter of
option, for any command in the Army; that he was proud of his
men, and that they not only responded to discipline readily, but most
cheerfully.  He further stated that he would like to lead his men
into action, but that the work they were performing was urgently
necessary to facilitate action at the front, and that his men accepted
their duties, as I learned from the men themselves, knowing that
their work, although non-combatant, was absolutely necessary to the
prosecution of the war.

"The erroneous opinion existing among many of the colored race,
that only colored men are commandeered for the laborious, or manual
work, would quickly be dispelled, among those who hold to such
opinion, were they over here at the front and could observe the many
thousands of white men in the Army performing the same class of
work performed by colored men.  In the assignment of duty over
here, I find that men's racial identity is not considered; that duty is
paramount.  Between the commanding officer, at the point visited,
and the colored stevedores there appears to be a bond of sympathy
akin to that existing between a most considerate employer and satisfied and coöperating employees.  Not only are our men, at this point,
treated with marked consideration, without offending strict military
discipline, but they are wholesomely and abundantly fed, and com-
fortably and sanitarily quartered.  There need not be, back in the
States, any concern whatever felt as to the treatment accorded, or
the provisions made for the maintenance of the colored service battalions in France, so far as I have seen.  Most of the men are faring
as well as they did back in the States, and many of them are faring
infinitely better than they did when at home, and the amusements
and recreations provided for them are excellent.

"The relations existing here between these colored soldiers and
the French people is fine.  Absolutely nothing has transpired here
among these more than 25,000 colored men gathered from every walk
of life, and many of them from the ghettos, to arouse even the suspicion of fear in the most timid of white women.  It was a long,
tedious ride to reach this point, but what I have learned at this camp
abundantly compensates me for the trip.

"Another pleasing thing, to me, about this stevedore camp, was that the guardhouse was, in size, but a small affair, and that its inmates constituted an astonishingly low number, and such as were confined in it were there for trivial offenses—mere infractions of strict military rules rather than crimes.

### The Colored Motorcycle Riders

"There is a glamour about the combatant units of an army in war that very frequently causes the non-combatants who are most essential in war, to be overlooked," continued Mr. Tyler. "Among the non-combatants over here who have been overlooked in all reports are the colored motorcycle riders, who act as couriers and transporters, carrying messages, night and day, from front to front; from headquarters to the front line trenches and battle front, and back, or who rush officers, almost with the velocity of the wind, to distant points. It is really marvelous how these colored motorcyclists ride pell-mell, in the darkest nights, without headlights, along these strange, devious, forking, and merging roads of France, leaving towns, through which they pass, behind in an instant. It is marvelous how these riders so quickly learned these French country roads. They race along, at times, when the darkness is so thick one cannot see his hand before his face, with only their judgment, which never fails them, to tell them the right road to take, or how near a precipice they are riding. They race along these lonely roads at night, whose darkness is only pierced now and then by a bursting German shell just ahead or behind them, or at their side, at the rate of from 65 to 75 miles per hour. Frequently, as they race along, bearing an important message to the front, German shells fall and hit the road so continuously as to be incessant, but these daring colored motorcyclists, never daunted, ride on, indifferent to the shells, as if they were but covering a peaceful road with which they are perfectly familiar back in the states.

"I rode several miles with one last night, from one front to another, at a 65-mile-per-hour clip. He was indifferent to the bursting of American anti-aircraft shells, aimed at the Boche airplane in the sky above us; he was oblivious to the thunder of the German cannon, and their shrieking shells to our right; he merely had his mind, as he kept his eyes to the front, on getting me back to the point which we had left a few hours before, a distance of five miles, in ten minutes. And he made it without slip or hit. When the history of this war is written some space, by right, must be given to telling of the bravery, daring and speed of the colored motorcycle riders, seventy-odd of whom are with the colored division which I am with at present."

In appreciation of the unselfish service rendered by these colored men at one of these ports, General Pershing visited them and paid them a fine compliment. He said: "When this expedition first started, the question was: 'Do you want any colored men over there?' and I said, 'Yes, of course, I want colored men.' I said: 'Aren't they American citizens? Can't they do as much work in the line of fighting and as much work as any other American citizen?'" The General referred to the fact that he was raised in a town where three-fourths of the people were colored, and that he was proud to say that during the Spanish-American War he commanded a colored troop which did splendid work then, just as other Negro troops are doing splendid work now. He said on leaving: "I expect to come back here and organize a few volunteer units and give you guns and let you go to the front and try your hand at it."

One of the largest camps in France, numbering nine thousand Stevedores, frequently had distinguished visitors, who brought greetings from America. How happily the boys heard them, and with what enthusiastic applause they were welcomed! Especially, they will remember Mr. Ralph W. Tyler, war correspondent for the colored press, who brought greetings from the Secretary of War, and their families back home; also, Mr. Julius Rosenwald, who brought to the boys greetings from the Governors of their states, whom the boys all applauded vigorously. Mr. Rosenwald liked so well what he saw that he donated one thousand francs to be spent among the boys. One American representative especially received prolonged applause and a hearty welcome from the stevedores, and that was Ella Wheeler Wilcox. And this because her words were so helpful and friendly. Moreover, this eminent poetess was able to see something of the heroic and splendid in the Stevedores, which inspired her to sing this martial song:

## The Stevedores

We are the Army Stevedores, lusty and virile and strong;
We are given the hardest work of the war, and the hours are long;
We handle the heavy boxes and shovel the dirty coal;
While the soldiers and sailors work in the light,
We burrow below like a mole.

But somebody has to do this work, or the soldiers could not fight;
And whatever work is given a man, is good if he does it right.
We are the Army Stevedores and we are volunteers;
We did not wait for the draft to come, and put aside our fears.
We flung them away to the winds of Fate, at the very first call of our land,
And each of us offered a willing heart, and the strength of a brawny hand.
We are the Army Stevedores, and work as we must and may,
The Cross of Honor will never be ours to proudly wear away.
But the men at the front could not be there
And the battles could not be won,
If the Stevedores stopped in their dull routine,
And left their work undone.
Somebody has to do this work;
Be glad that it isn't you!
We are the Army Stevedores; give us our due!

—Ella Wheeler Wilcox.

# CHAPTER XXIII

## "WITH THOSE WHO WAIT"

*Provision for Technical Training of Draftees—Units That Did Not Get to France—Vocational and Educational Opportunities Opened to Them—The Negro in the Students' Army Training Corps—In the Reserve Officers' Training Corps.*

The progress of the war and the gathering up of miscellaneous men from civil life to serve as defenders of the nation, developed the fact that the education of the youth of the land had been woefully neglected, even in the primary and secondary grades, but particularly in the matter of technical or vocational training. Thousands upon thousands of those inducted into the Army through the operation of the Selective Draft Law, who were ready and eager to battle for the safety of their country's freedom, were sadly deficient in practical knowledge of the simplest things essential to the well-being of a military organization. Their experience had been confined largely to the routine of civil life, and the great majority called to the colors knew nothing of machinery, the handling of tools (as in carpentry, construction and repair), electrical work, woodwork, operation and repair of automobiles, horseshoeing, or the proper care of animals, etc. The number actually illiterate was alarming. It was surprising to those unfamiliar with scholastic conditions among the people of this country, that there should be so many men unable even to sign their names to the Army payrolls.

This deplorable situation led the military officials to cast about for a means of raising the mental tone of the Army, to enhance its efficiency by making provision for technical training, and to carry along with such training a system of scholastic improvement, such as would enable the soldiers to read and understand army orders, to comprehend the meaning and import of signals, to grasp the true spirit of service that had brought them into the great war, and to fit them for the largest measure of usefulness and to be ready for

328

the advancement that would naturally come to those who performed their duty most capably. When it was decided that there should be provision for a double system of education and training for soldiers, the Special Assistant to the Secretary of War looked about to see if *all* soldiers were to be included in this highly important program—that is, if the schedule had in mind the particular needs of *colored soldiers* also. To his regret, he found nothing to indicate that colored soldiers were to be given this training. After several full and free conferences with Dr. C. A. Prosser, Director of the Federal Board for Vocational Training, and his assistant, Dr. W. I. Hamilton, to whom, at first, was confided the responsibility of developing a program of vocational training, a memorandum was drawn up calling attention to the number of colored troops already in the service and the probable number to follow. As a result the whole program was broadened to include also colored soldiers.

### Schools Selected for Training

A Committee on Education and Special Training was afterward designated by the Secretary of War, and entrusted with the execution of this far-reaching program. Certain educational institutions were set apart under Government contract for the training of student-soldiers. Thirteen of the leading colored schools of the land were among the number authorized to undertake the instruction of the colored soldiers. The schools selected and the courses of instruction decided upon, together with the number of soldiers allotted to the various terms were as follows:

HOWARD UNIVERSITY, Washington, D. C.—May 15 and July 15, 1918, 300 men, Capt. Jerome Lavigne, C. O.; bench workers, electricians, wireless operators.

ATLANTA UNIVERSITY, Atlanta, Georgia.—120 men, July 1, 1918; bench workers, general carpenters, army truck drivers, blacksmiths.

FLORIDA AGRICULTURAL AND MECHANICAL COLLEGE, Savannah, Georgia.—125 men; July 1, 1918; blacksmiths, carpenters, electricians, wheelwrights.

GEORGIA STATE INDUSTRIAL COLLEGE, Savannah, Georgia.—200 men, July 1, 1918; army truck drivers, general carpenters, bench workers, blacksmiths.

HAMPTON NORMAL AND AGRICULTURAL INSTITUTE, Hampton, Virginia.—Capt. Robert H. Nealy, C. O.; June 15, 245 men; August 15, 1918, 245 men;

electricians, carpenters, wheelwrights, machinists, chauffeurs, auto repairers, truck drivers, master truck drivers, horseshoers, blacksmiths, pipefitters.

NEGRO AGRICULTURAL AND TECHNICAL COLLEGE, Greensboro, North Carolina.—Capt. C. C. Helmar, C. O.; 260 men, June 15; 280 men, August 15, 1918; chauffeurs, carpenters, tractor operators, truck drivers.

BRANCH NORMAL SCHOOL, Pine Bluff, Arkansas.—120 men, June 15, 1918; carpenters, blacksmiths, auto mechanics.

TUSKEGEE NORMAL AND INDUSTRIAL INSTITUTE, Tuskegee, Alabama.— Capt. Edgar R. Bonsall, C. O.; 380 men, May 15; 380 men, July 15; 380 men, Sept. 15, 1918; auto mechanics, carpenters, blacksmiths, general mechanics.

WESTERN UNIVERSITY, Quindaro, Kansas.—100 men, June 15, 1918; blacksmiths, carpenters, concrete workers, electricians, horseshoers.

PRAIRIE VIEW N. AND I. COLLEGE, Prairie View, Texas.—150 men, June 15, 1918; auto mechanics, chauffeurs, blacksmiths, carpenters.

WILBERFORCE UNIVERSITY, Wilberforce, Ohio.—180 men, July 15; 180 men, August 15, 1918; machine shop, auto gas engines, general mechanics, cobblers, carpenters, blacksmiths.

STATE AGRICULTURAL AND MECHANICAL COLLEGE, Orangeburg, South Carolina.—240 men, July 1, 1918; auto mechanics, truck drivers, tractor operators, concrete workers, blacksmiths, bench woodworking.

WENDELL PHILLIPS HIGH SCHOOL, Chicago, Illinois.—170 men, July 1, 1918; auto mechanics, truck drivers, bench woodworking, electricity.

SUMNER HIGH SCHOOL, St. Louis, Missouri.—275 men.

These military units are listed under the head of "Those Who Wait," although many of them so quickly assimilated the vocational instruction given them that in a few weeks they were ready for overseas service, and actually went over and served in several of the great offensives. The preparedness which was theirs, and the cheerfulness that characterized their every activity were large items in preserving the morale of the Negro people on this side of the ocean.

### Value of the Vocational Detachments

The value of this vocational training cannot be overestimated. The mere fact that the Government should be willing to assume the responsibility for the mental, physical and technical development, pay all the bills, and give these men a brighter outlook for the future, was a revelation to the colored millions of America, and did more to raise the morale of the race than could have been brought about by a thousand speeches or platitudinous proclamations. It was a big, concrete thing, done in a big way, and no single endowment by the Federal authorities in the war period went further to encourage the masses to renewed patriotic endeavors than did the establishment of these vocational detachments in the colored schools of the land. In the first six months more than 3,000 young colored men received the benefits of the training, and plans were laid for an extension of the work to include 20,000 additional men had war continued to the point expected by the military experts.

When the armistice was signed more than 10,000 colored men were on the roster of these Vocational Detachment units and as members of the Students' Army Training Corps, this latter being an outgrowth of the success achieved by the Vocational Detachments.

The War Department recognized that there are many branches of army service in which preliminary technical training is a great asset. This training must be largely secured in intensive, short, practical courses, so that essential industrial production may not be impaired. Much was done at first to meet this need in voluntary classes organized by the Federal Board for Vocational Education, by various divisions of the Army, and by individual schools. Valuable as were the benefits thus secured, however, experience demonstrated that on a civilian basis the desired results could not be obtained; therefore, it was decided to conduct the training under military control.

In order to coördinate the training program with voluntary enlistments and the operations of the selective service regulations, there was established in the War Department, as already noted, the Committee on Education and Special Training reporting to the Chief of Staff. The functions of this committee as stated in the General Order creating it were:

"To study the needs of the various branches of the service for skilled men and technicians; to determine how such needs should be met, whether by selective draft, special training in educational institutions or otherwise; to secure the coöperation of the educational institutions of the country and to represent the War Department in its relations with such institutions; to administer such plan of special training in colleges and schools as may be adopted.''

The War Department undertook to provide this intensive technical training only for soldiers in the service who were under discipline and on pay and subsistence during the period of their training. For the purpose of training them the War Department made use of facilities now in existence, thus offering the different educational centers of the country an opportunity to contribute in a very important way to the preparation of our armies for service in France.

Since the men to be trained were soldiers under military discipline, the War Department was obliged to impose certain general stipulations on communities agreeing to undertake this work. These orders read:

"1. Men will be sent to civilian institutions for technical training in units of from 100 up. Few units will number less than 200 or more than 2,000.

"2. For the maintenance of effective military discipline it is necessary that men be housed and fed in groups of approximately 100-500. Communities and institutions which are willing to receive men for training should note that proper facilities for housing and feeding must be provided. In training centers already established this requirement has been met in various ways; for instance, by utilizing a dormitory or a hotel, by the conversion of a hall or an armory, by the erection of temporary barracks, etc.

"3. Sufficient space suitable for military drill and located at a convenient distance from the quarters must be available.

"4. Institutions providing training and arranging housing and feeding facilities will be compensated at a reasonable per diem rate for each man, which is intended to cover actual costs.

"5. Men will be ordered in some cases to the training centers directly upon their induction into the service; in this case they will bring extra clothing. They will be provided at once with overalls and, as soon as practicable after arrival, with service uniforms and other equipment. In other cases the men will come from the recruit depots, at which they will be equipped.

"6. It is expected that the work involved in the technical training courses will occupy six to seven hours daily, the remaining time available for training being devoted to military drill.

"7. Most of the men thus assigned are inducted under the selective service system. Any one subject to draft, not under call from the Provost

Marshal General, but desiring to volunteer, may be inducted on application to his Local Board, providing such Local Board has been called upon by the Provost Marshal General to supply a share of men and has not already filled the call, and provided he has the qualifications named in such a call. Under special authority given to recruiting officers from time to time this service may be opened also to men not of draft age who can volunteer as enlisted men in the Army."

## Course of Instruction

The training required was such as to give the men some practical skill in the simple underlying operations of carpentry, metalworking, blacksmithing, auto mechanics, and other mechanical activities useful in the Army.

Only fundamental training was possible, and training therefore was thoroughly practical rather than theoretical. Most of the courses of training were two months in length. The work required included the following courses, for which the War Department provided definite directions and outlines:

1. AUTO DRIVING AND REPAIR.—Driving motor vehicles of various types, making all general repairs to motor trucks, cars, motorcycles, tractors.

2. BENCH WOOD WORK.—Splicing frames, joining, pattern making and fine wood work.

3. GENERAL CARPENTRY.—Use of the usual carpenter's tools and materials; practice in rapid rough work with hatchet and saw to qualify the man for building and repairing barracks, erecting concrete forms, rough bridge work.

4. ELECTRICAL COMMUNICATION.—Construction and repair of telephone and telegraph lines; repair, adjustment and operation of telephone and telegraph apparatus; cable splicing.

5. ELECTRICAL WORK.—Installing, operating and repair of electrical machines; inside wiring and power circuits.

6. FORGING OR BLACKSMITHING.—Jobbing blacksmithing; motorcycle, automobile, truck, gas engine and wagon repairing.

7. GAS ENGINE WORK.—Reconstructing and repairing automobile, motorcycle and airplane engines.

8. MACHINE WORK.—General machine shop work on lathe, drill, press, shaper, planer, miller, grinder, etc.

9. SHEET METAL WORK.—Coppersmithing and tinsmithing; soldering, brazing and general repairing.

The widest publicity was given to this program as it affected colored soldiers, through the colored papers, in addition to the use of the official circulars of the War Department, and each of the schools under contract was flooded with applications, sent by mail or brought in person to the institution by the applicant, to be considered by the Commanding Officers of the Training Detachments. Applicants already in the military service or of draft age and yet to be inducted, were required to have a grammar school education, and were assigned to the courses to which the applicant in question seemed best adapted by education, physical condition or experience.

For sympathetic counsel, practical suggestions and constant encouragement in getting the work of these vocational schools before the people and bringing to the Negro the full fruits of this beneficent program, the author was indebted in the largest measure to General Robert I. Rees, of the General Staff Corps, and Chairman of the Committee on Education and Special Training; Major Grenville Clark, of the Adjutant General's Department; Mr. William H. Lough and Dr. Ralph Barton Perry, executive secretaries, and Mr. C. R. Dooley, educational director, of the Committee on Education and Special Training of the War Department. The results of the training received by the thousands of young colored men in the selected schools, under the control of the Government, are reflected not only in the broader opportunities afforded for helpful service and advancement during the war, but in the wider area created for the soldier after the war, in the way of a more lucrative employment and a larger mental and moral endowment.

### The Students' Army Training Corps

The success achieved throughout the country by the Vocational Detachments of the United States Army in the utilization of the young manhood of the Republic, led naturally to a further plan for enlisting the strength of the student forces of the land. The regularly established camps and cantonments were, in many instances, far away from the centers where thousands of youths might be found and who were available for the army of the future, for no one could know at that time how long the war might continue and it was deemed advisable to marshal the entire man-power of the nation to be drawn upon, if the necessity therefor should arise. It occurred to farseeing military authorities that the hundreds of school plants, some of them almost denuded of men by the operation of the draft, might be utilized to train the still younger men and boys who might be needed to defend the flag. The Government perceived the wisdom underlying this plan of providing for future necessities, and out of the mass of suggestions and discussions was born the Students' Army Training Corps, to include qualified young men between the ages of eighteen and twenty-one, not then acceptable under the selective draft law.

The administration of this new instrumentality for the national defense was also placed in the hands of the Committee on Education and Special Training of the War Department at Washington. Through the prompt action of those entrusted with the welfare of the colored people of the land, provision was made for the participation of colored young men in this work, on equal terms with others, and units of the Students' Army Training Corps were established at colored schools which were able to meet the Government's require-, ments.

The primary purpose of the Students' Army Training Corps, as described in the military regulations, was to utilize the executive and teaching personnel and the physical equipment of the educational institutions to supplement the labors of the regular camps and cantonments in the training of the new armies of the nation. Its aim was to train officer-candidates and technical experts of all kinds to meet every need of the service. In the list of colleges, universities, professional, technical and trade schools of the country, totaling about 550, a score or more were conducted for the education of young colored men.

For administrative purposes the Corps was divided into two sections, the Collegiate or "A" Section, and the Vocational or "B" Section. The units of the "B" Section were formerly known as National Army Training Detachments, and their especial function, after being incorporated in the "S. A. T. C." scheme was to continue the program of industrial development and to train soldiers for service as trade specialists in the Army. The colored schools carried into this program included:

Tuskegee Normal and Industrial Institute, Alabama; Hampton Institute, Hampton, Virginia; Howard University, Washington,

D. C.; Atlanta University, Atlanta, Georgia; Georgia State A. and M. College, Savannah, Georgia; North Carolina A. and T. College, Greensboro, N. C.; South Carolina A. and M. College, Orangeburg, S. C.; Prairie View Normal and Industrial College, Prairie View, Texas; Lincoln University, Chester County Pa.; West Virginia Collegiate Institute, Institute, W. Va.; Wilberforce University, Zenia, Ohio; Alabama A. and M. College, Normal, Ala.; Tennessee A. and M. College, Nashville, Tenn.; and Louisiana A. and M. College, Baton Rouge, La.—fourteen in all.

The "A" or Collegiate Section, which was inaugurated October 1, 1918, was open to registrants of authorized colleges, universities or professional schools who were eligible for admission to the S. A. T. C. by voluntary induction into the military service. They thus became members of the Army on active duty, receiving pay and subsistence, subject to military orders, and living in barracks under military discipline in exactly the same manner as any other soldier. The housing, subsistence and instruction of soldiers in both branches of the Students' Army Training Corps were provided by the educational institutions under contract with the Government to furnish the same. Students voluntarily inducted into the service were ordinarily allowed to choose the branch of the service for which they wished to be prepared, but this freedom of choice was not absolute, being subject to a very large extent to the particular qualifications of the individual and upon the needs of the service at any specified time. All students were required to meet the physical standards authorized.

The status of a member of the S. A. T. C. was that of a private; the pay was $30 per month. Students were at the beginning divided into four groups, according to age, and were given the same course of two months' military, industrial or other training, followed by a second two months of higher academic subjects of military value, if the soldier was found capable of greater advancement. Members of the Collegiate or "A" Section, who showed by their rating in academic and military work that they had unusual ability were given opportunities for transfer to a Central Officers' Training School; transfer to a non-commissioned officers' school; or assigned to the institution where they were enrolled for further intensive work in a specified line, as, for instance, in engineering, chemistry or medicine.

Those members of a Collegiate Section whose record was such

as not to justify the Government in continuing their collegiate training were eligible for assignment to a Vocational Training Section for technical training of military value; or transfer to a cantonment for duty with troops as a private.

Men in "B" unit of the S. A. T. C. were given an equal opportunity with those in the college or "A" unit, to demonstrate their fitness for advancement and their qualifications for officers and noncommissioned officers' schools, or for continuance at institutions for more advanced study. The plan adopted provided that student-soldiers would be transferred to the army for active service at stated intervals, and their places would be taken at the school by new contingents, inducted for similar training.

The colored educational institutions embraced in the "A" or Collegiate Section of the Students' Army Training Corps were: Howard University, Washington, D. C.; Lincoln University, Chester county, Pa.; Fisk University, Meharry Medical College, Nashville, Tenn.; Atlanta University and Morehouse College (combined), Atlanta, Ga.; Wiley University and Bishop College (combined), Marshall, Texas; Talladega College, Alabama; Virginia Union University, Richmond, Va.; Wilberforce University, Wilberforce, Ohio.

An instruction camp for colored schools and colleges was held at Howard University, Washington, D. C., August 1 to September 16, 1918. Howard University, Washington, D. C.; Atlanta University, Atlanta, Ga.; Lincoln University, Chester county, Pa.; Raleigh University, Raleigh, N. C.; Shaw University, Raleigh, N. C.; Wilberforce University, Zenia, Ohio; Virginia Union University, Richmond, Va.; Straight University, New Orleans, La.; Morehouse College, Atlanta, Ga.; Talladega College, Talladega, Ala.; Bishop College, Marshall, Texas; Benedict College, Columbia, S. C.; Allen University, Columbia, S. C.; New Orleans University, New Orleans, La.; Florida A. & M. College for Negro Youth, Tallahassee, Fla.; Biddle University, Charlotteville, N. C.; Livingston, College, Salisbury, N. C.; the Tuskegee Normal and Industrial Institute, Alabama; the Hampton Normal and Agricultural Institute, Hampton, Va., and Lincoln Institute, Jefferson City, Mo., were among the schools which were asked to send a student representative for each twenty-five and one faculty member for each one hundred of the male student enrollment. These men were trained forty-seven days on temporary enlistment as privates, during which term they received housing, uniforms, subsistence, equipment, and instruction at the Government's expense with the pay of a private, $30 per month (and reimbursement of transportation to and from camp at 4 cents per mile). The plan of operation and the advantages given these men were identical with those of all other colleges of the country. Wilberforce University, alone of all the schools, however, secured a rating for recognized military training. A group of officers was designated by the War Department to take charge of the instruction, including Lieutenant Russell Smith (afterwards promoted to a captaincy), commanding officer.

### Where the Color Line Was Drawn

As no institution, however well-intentioned, is without its flaws in the administration of its purposes, the S. A. T. C. had its "fly in the ointment." The color question came to the fore, especially as related to those institutions which had not been in the habit of accepting colored students, or in which but few had previously been registered. Trouble on this score was reported by colored students who attempted to secure entrance to the military units at certain colleges in Ohio, Pennsylvania, Nebraska and perhaps other states. A declaration was issued by the War Department officially discountenancing all discriminations based on color. This declaration as officially announced by the War Department was signed by Col. Robert I. Rees, an upstanding American. He always stood for justice and fair play so far as the men of the S. A. T. C. and the R. O. T. C. units were concerned. His declaration read as follows:

"No color line will be drawn in inducting men into the S. A. T. C. Colored men eligible for induction will be inducted at institutions which they attend and will not be required to transfer to other institutions."

Such problems as arose in connection with attendance of colored students at Northern institutions were left by the War Department to be settled by the college authorities, the War Department refusing to be a party to any program which would introduce the color line into those schools where it is not already drawn. At the same time announcement was made that the War Department did not seek through its program to break down the color line in any institution where it was observed. The general effect of this prompt decision on the part of the War Department was gratifying to colored people throughout the country. The controversy and its satisfactory adjustment was described in clear fashion in an interesting news item, making note of the circular letter sent out by the Secretary of the National Association for the Advancement of Colored People. The statement of Mr. John P. Shillady, Secretary of the organization referred to, touching the matter of the rejection of colored student applicants to the Students' Army Training Corps, was:

"Certain college authorities, acting under a misapprehension of War Department regulations, denied the privileges of the Students' Army Training Corps to colored students of Ohio and Nebraska colleges. In one case this action was taken upon instructions of the regional director of a section of the Training and Instruction Branch of the War Department Committee on Education and Special Training, and in another case by direction of the War Department's District Inspector. In the Ohio case inquiries were addressed to the War Department by the students themselves, by the National Office of the National Association for the Advancement of Colored People, and by the Cleveland and Columbus, Ohio, branches. These branches and the students arranged for conferences with the college authorities on the matter. The following telegram on the subject, signed by Emmett J. Scott, Special Assistant to the Secretary of War, under date of September 25, 1918, is self-explanatory:

" 'The War Department has not issued any instructions preventing Negro students from joining Student Army Training Corps at Ohio State University or any other institution. Any student mentally and physically qualified and accepted by the school officials is eligible for admittance into any Student Army organization.

'EMMETT J. SCOTT,
'Special Assistant to Secretary of War.'

"It is apparent from a reading of this telegram and from the statements of Mr. Scott made personally to the Secretary of the National Association for the Advancement of Colored People, while in Washington, on September 28, that the War Department has made no ruling requiring a separation of colored and white students in barracks or dormitory arrangements in the colleges, and that the acceptance of a student by a college under the terms and conditions usual to such colleges qualifies the student for admission to the Students' Army Training Corps provided he is able to qualify.

"The branches and the members of the Association generally are requested to put this matter clearly before the colored students who may desire to enter the Students' Army Training Corps. This will serve as a guide to appropriate action in case any colleges deny admission to colored students under a similar misapprehension to that alluded to above."

## Demobilization of the S. A. T. C.

Although the country was keenly alive to the necessity for some system of general military training for the youth of the land that would serve as a medium for insuring the national safety, when the armistice was signed November 11, 1918, discussion arose at once as to the future of the Students' Army Training Corps. The War Department was at first of the opinion that the organization could be maintained with profit to itself and to the students until the end of the fiscal year at least,.while others high in authority contended that the war emergency being over, the corps should be demobilized at once. Among the forces that desired the continuance of the S. A. T. C. was the Merchants' Association of New York City, which laid before the Department an offer of financial assistance, if necessary, to maintain the organization along the original lines.

Major Ralph Barton Perry, executive secretary of the Committee on Education and Special Training, administering this branch of instruction under the War Plans Division of the General Staff of the Army, replying to the communication of the Merchants' Association urging the continuance of the S. A. T. C., gave as follows the reasons why the War Department did not consider it practical to carry on the military training units in colleges:

"It was not, as had often been assumed, an educational measure, but a plan for creating a reservoir of officer material with which to supply the Officers Training Camps and the other needs of the army for specially trained men. There were certain strong reasons for continuing to June 30, 1919, but these reasons were not military reasons, and did not justify the expenditure of money appropriated for specifically military purposes. While this is the fundamental reason for the demobilization of the Students' Army Training Corps, for various reasons it would have proved difficult, if not impossible, to continue it in any case."

According to Major Perry, about 25 per cent. of the institutions were opposed to maintaining the units, once war ceased. He also said that many of the members of the corps immediately sought discharges in order to pursue civil studies, and these men could not be held in service against their inclinations. "The War Department," said Major Perry, "is fully aware of the force of the arguments in favor of continuing the Students' Army Training Corps. The demobilization will, in some cases, doubtless result in inconvenience to the institution. The Committee on Education and Special Training has, however, been authorized to make equitable financial adjustments. It is also recognized that in many cases the individual students will suffer hardships.

"It should, however, be clearly borne in mind that no man was inducted into the S. A. T. C. on promise of an education at Government expense. He was inducted into the army for the purpose of receiving special additional training in connection with his purely military training, always with a view to the needs of the service."

### To Train Reserve Officers for the Army

On December 21, 1918, Secretary Baker authorized the statement that, with the demobilization of the Students' Army Training Corps, the colleges of the country would turn their attention to another phase of military preparedness—that of establishing the Reserve Officers' Training Corps. This offered another opportunity for the training of youth, colored men along with others, for the national defense, and many of the colored educational institutions which had maintained the S. A. T. C. up to the period of its demobilization, filed application for units of the new R. O. T. C., and also asked that colored officers of experience and capacity be installed as instructors in military science and tactics.

### R. O. T. C. Units and Their Military Instructors

Below is a complete list of the schools selected up to April 1, 1919, together with a roster of the officers designated as military instructors therein. Most of the instruction at the beginning was in infantry movements.

Howard University, Washington, D. C.—Major Milton T. Dean and First Lieutenant Campbell C. Johnson.

Tuskegee Normal and Industrial Institute, Tuskegee, Ala.—

Captain Russell Smith, First Lieutenant James C. Pinkston and Second Lieutenant Harry J. Mack.

Wilberforce University, Wilberforce, Ohio.—First Lieutenant Percival R. Piper.

Negro A. and T. College, Greensboro, N. C.—Second Lieutenant Horace G. Wilder.

South Carolina A. and M. College, Orangeburg, S. C.—First Lieutenant Samuel Hull.

Hampton A. and I. Institute, Hampton, Va.—First Lieutenant Leonard L. McLeod.

Virginia N. and I. Institute, Petersburg, Va.—Second Lieutenant Ernest C. Johnson.

Prairie View N. and I. College, Prairie View, Texas.—First Lieutenant Walter A. Giles.

Tennessee Agricultural and Industrial School, Nashville, Tenn.—First Lieutenant Grant Stuart.

West Virginia Collegiate Institute, Institute, W. Va.—First Lieutenant John H. Purnell.

Branch Normal School, Pine Bluff, Ark.—First Lieutenant Elijah H. Goodwin.

Straight College, New Orleans, La.—Captain Charles C. Cooper.

One important change in the organization was worked out, allowing the units of the R. O. T. C. to specialize in training officer material for Field Artillery, Engineer, Coast Artillery, Ordnance, Medical, and Aeronautics Corps, instead of the uniform training for Infantry, which was the rule before the war. In addition to the collegiate units, plans were formulated for the establishment of junior units in secondary schools. The Committee on Education and Special Training was able to take advantage of the opportunity afforded by the war to make available a large amount of scientific and technical material, which had been developed by the experience of military leaders on both sides of the ocean, and in all units special emphasis is placed on physical training and mass athletics.

The formation of these units of the R. O. T. C. came in response to the national demand for military training for the youth of the land, to provide the preparedness necessary as a safeguard to protect the general welfare. The sentiment was everywhere heard that "Even if we have no wars, universal military training will make better citizens." The discipline and courtesies which grow out of the relations of military men among themselves and the lessons that soldiers learn in keeping themselves "fit to fight" are fine additions to what young men have been able to get in colleges.

The difference between the Students' Army Training Corps and the Reserve Officers' Training Corps is that the S. A. T. C. trained the private; the R. O. T. C. trained officers: the former took a short cut and laid stress on military training; the latter took the long way round and laid stress on the general education of the individual and emphasized the value of administrative or executive ability. One taught the individual to obey without question; the other taught the individual to command judiciously and to get results from the correct application of military science. The Reserve Officers' Training Corps was designed to give a large number of capable young men (colored and white) such training as would qualify them to serve their country as officers in case of another war. All found to be qualified mentally, physically and temperamentally, have been placed on the reserve officers' list subject to call in the event of another war. This branch of the service proved to be of inestimable value to hundreds of live and ambitious young men of the Negro race.

# CHAPTER XXIV

## GERMAN PROPAGANDA AMONG NEGROES

*Insidious Efforts to Create Dissatisfaction Among Colored Americans—Germany's Treacherous Promises—How the Hun Tried to Undermine the Loyalty of Our Negro Citizens—Steps Taken to Combat Enemy Propaganda—Work of the Committee on Public Information.*

Many were the methods resorted to by Germany and her allies in their desperate efforts to win the war. Some of them were among the most despicable, dishonorable, and unscrupulous ever recorded in the annals of military history. By no means did the Imperial German Government confine its war activities to soldiers, to battleships, or to battlefields—those open, legitimate methods which honorable nations use, as a last resort, to settle international differences. On the contrary, Germany sought in many nefarious, secret ways (as was discovered and revealed by the Military Intelligence Bureau and the Department of Justice) to aid her war program right here on American soil, through propaganda work among enemy civilians, and through acts of open outlawry committed either directly by her subjects or by pro-German sympathizers.

Even prior to the breaking out of hostilities, Germany diligently endeavored to promote anti-war sentiment in America, designed to produce an increased number of pacifists who were opposed to the declaration of war as well as to our country's war program. She tried in a number of ingenious ways to appeal to, and to cause dissatisfaction among various racial groups which go to make up America's composite population, and to make them lukewarm in the support of their Government. For instance, in her effort to disaffect the Irish-American group, she paraded before them in certain newspapers, in the form of subsidized articles, by lectures, public speakers, and otherwise, the Irish Home Rule Question so dear to the Irish heart, the alleged mistreatment of Ireland by England, the

344

execution of Sinn Feiners and of Sir Roger Casement; by which sort of propaganda work she hoped to set Americans of Irish descent against the idea of supporting this country as an ally of England.

In order to influence German-Americans, she energetically fostered in this country various kinds of propaganda designed to make this racial group support the "Fatherland" more and America less; she urged German-American workers in munition plants and in other establishments supplying war materials "to be true to the Fatherland" and to withdraw their labor from all such industries, and not only that, but her agents aided and abetted German sympathizers to commit acts of sabotage and violence in order to impair or destroy the power of this country to produce war materials and the implements of war. Her secret service agents and paid hirelings strove to promote strikes and friction among various groups of American workingmen, and even encouraged and engaged in the blowing up of bridges, railroads, munition plants, and other indispensable adjuncts connected with the successful prosecution of war.

In addition to her insidious plans to disaffect those of alien birth or parentage, she also attempted propaganda work among native-born Americans both white and black, and it required all the courage and intelligence of the white press and the Negro press, ably assisted by the Committee on Public Information and its countless number of loyal public speakers, white and black, to counteract the pacifist propaganda, "Made in Germany," which threatened for a time to keep our country from participating in the world's great struggle for freedom and democracy.

Foremost among those who successfully combated this pro-German propaganda was Colonel Theodore Roosevelt, whose forceful opposition to hyphenated Americans and pacifists will ever stand as a monument to his 100-per-cent Americanism. Even before our country's entrance into the arena of war as an ally of Great Britain and France, German propaganda made itself manifest in a determined effort to influence American voters in favor of placing an embargo upon all shipments of arms, ammunition, etc., to belligerent nations; the defeat of Germany's plan in this regard led up, indirectly if not directly, to the Lusitania disaster, which may be said to have brought the United States into the war.

## Propaganda Among Negroes

Active German propaganda of various kinds was attempted, and was officially recognized to exist among the colored people of this country, and it is one of the most remarkable facts of the war that in spite of so many insidious plans to bring about disaffection among them by emphasizing racial discriminations, injustices, and the like, in spite of so many temptations to be disloyal, the entire racial group of colored Americans remained absolutely loyal and actively patriotic. Authentic information that the Germans tried to incite the colored people of the South against the United States was brought out by Mr. A. Bruce Bielaski, Chief of the Bureau of Investigations, Department of Justice, in a Congressional inquiry conducted by the Senate Committee which investigated German propaganda in America. Mr. Bielaski said that "The colored people did not take to these stories, they were too loyal. Money spent among them for propaganda was thrown away." During the course of the same official hearing, Captain George B. Lester, Military Intelligence Officer, told the Senate Propaganda Investigating Committee that German propaganda among Negroes of the South was particularly active in the Spring and Summer of 1918.

## Stirred Race Hatred

In the course of his testimony, Captain Lester said: "When the thirty-one propagandists who reached this country (from Germany) shortly after the outbreak of the war organized the Fuehr publicity bureau in New York, they set aside one 'section' for dealing with American race problems. They kept records of every lynching, every attack by a Negro upon a white person, and every item of alleged oppression of the Negro race by the whites. The directing head of the propaganda was the German ambassador at Mexico City. In this country Reiswitz, former Consul at Chicago, acted as his assistant. The Negroes were told by the propagandists that in Europe there was no color line; that there the blacks were equal to the whites; that if Germany won the war the rights of Negroes throughout the world would equal those of whites. On the military side the propaganda took the form of stories that Negro soldiers were left on the ground to die and that they always were put in the first line trenches in France and used almost exclusively as 'shock troops.' The German agents passed the word among Negro recruits that if Germany won the war, a certain section of the United States would be set aside where the Negroes could rule themselves."

As later developments proved, this was an unsuccessful attempt to weaken the morale of Negro soldiers. In his story of the work of Germans among colored Americans generally, Captain Lester said that *"the propaganda became so annoying that a conference of leading Negroes* (referring to the Negro Editors' Conference which was also attended by a number of other leaders of Negro thought and opinion) *was called in June, 1918, in Washington, D. C., and a movement immediately started through the War Department and the Committee on Public Information to offset it." "As a result,"* he added, *"the activity of the German agents soon ceased."* It was the splendid team work of Negro editors throughout the country that, in large measure, helped to guard colored Americans against such propaganda and to maintain a healthy morale among them.

### Lynchings During the War

While German propaganda failed to affect the colored people to the extent of diverting them from their loyalty to the United States, yet the truth of the matter is that the morale of the colored people was kept more or less disturbed and at a frazzled edge during most of the war by what came to be known as "anti-Negro propaganda." Much of this could not be traced to German sources, but plainly had its origin in age-old prejudices which have existed in America against colored people along certain well defined lines. The number of lynchings of Negroes seemed to be on the increase during the course of the war, and THESE LYNCHINGS, BE IT REMEMBERED, WERE NOT "Made in Germany." According to the records compiled by Monroe N. Work, in charge of records and research of Tuskegee Institute, there were 58 Negroes lynched in 1918 and 38 lynched in 1917, a total of nearly 100 Negroes lynched on American soil while our country was at war and while hundreds of thousands of loyal Negro soldiers and millions of law-abiding colored Americans were supporting the Government with unfaltering patriotism.

This unfortunate condition gave German newspapers abroad much ground for effective criticism, and the following press reports indicate the kind of articles which frequently appeared in the German press, some of which were reprinted in American newspapers. Many of these articles carried the impression to the German people that Germans were being lynched in America.

The Munich *Neueste Nachtrichten* said that at the Berne prisoner-of-war conference the German representatives would have the opportunity of bringing up the question of Praeger, who was lynched, remarking that questions were asked of the foreign office representative at the last session of the Reichstag on this case. It called attention to the cases of Consuls Bopp and Schack of San Francisco, which, it said, should be made the subject of an interpellation in the Reichstag. The paper said that the German delegates should bring up the whole question at the conference and be able to assure better treatment for Germans in America.

The Kolnische *Volkszeitung* published a long article headed "JUDGE LYNCH, MISTER MOB." The article asserted that formerly American writers alleged that the crime of lynching existed only in the black belt, but now, the paper declared, lynch law belongs to the approved rites of "culture" in the United States.

"The most horrible scenes of human bestiality which can be recorded," it goes on, "are quite natural for the Yankee. * * * He no longer gets excited over a lynching, and is only ashamed when foreigners call attention to this 'people culture.' "

It is always asserted, the paper proceeded, that mobs and the scum of the people are responsible for lynchings.

"Every American who uses the word MOB in this sense," it adds, "lies, because he knows that all classes of society, without exception, including men and women, partake."

At Brookhaven, Miss., the paper sets forth, a colored man was lynched by 20,000 persons, and many landowners from Lincoln drove in during the night in order to "enjoy the crime."

That paper also referred to Praeger, and declared that after energetic action by the German government, Washington gave the press the tip to discourage lynching. It scoffed at President Wilson's message regarding crimes committed by the German army, saying "he lives in a glass house and should not throw stones."

Articles of this kind generally appeared prior to and to excuse what the Germans call "reprisals," otherwise Hun brutality.

## A National Danger

No question was fraught with more danger to our national security in time of war, and none will be more deserving of radical treatment in time of peace than the unlawful practice of lynching, regardless of the state or section in which it occurs and regardless of the nationality of the victim.

Some of the lynchings that occurred during the war were cases of colored women (5) accompanied by barbarities that cannot properly be described in print and wholly unworthy of civilized groups of people. There were burnings of human beings at the stake, modeled after medieval horrors, and, in several instances well-known colored citizens of wealth, intelligence, and upright character were tarred and feathered and nameless outrages committed upon their persons and property. Reports of these outrages found their way to the colored people through the Negro press, which stoutly maintained that if America had gone forward to fight battles for freedom and democracy abroad, it should at least give full protection to all of its citizens at home. Foremost among the white friends of the Negro, who vigorously opposed lynching and whose trenchant pen and eloquent voice have always been enlisted on the side of Right and Justice, was Mr. Moorfield Storey, the well known lawyer of Boston, who delivered a most remarkable address on "The Negro Question" before the Wisconsin Bar Association, on June 27, 1918, in the course of which he said:

"Negroes are denied the protection which the law affords the lives and property of other citizens. If only *charged* with crime or even misdemeanor, they are at the mercy of the mob and may be killed and tortured with absolute impunity. In many States they cannot obtain justice in the courts. At hotels, restaurants and theaters they are not admitted or are given poor accommodation. In the public parks and public conveyances, even in the public offices of the nation, they are set apart from their fellow-citizens. The districts which they occupy in cities are neglected by the authorities, and of the money which the community devotes to education, a very small fraction is allotted to them, so that their schoolhouses and their teachers are grossly inadequate.

"It is notorious that in many cities they are wretchedly housed and charged unreasonable rents for their abodes. Labor unions will not receive them as members, and as non-union men they find it hard to get employment. If in spite of every obstacle they gain an education, they find door after door closed to them which would have opened to receive them gladly had their skins been white.

"The deliberate effort is made to stamp them as inferior, to keep them "hewers of wood and drawers of water," to deny them that opportunity which America offers to every other citizen or emigrant no matter how ignorant or how degraded. These are the unquestionable facts, and they are not controverted."

Mr. Storey then proceeded to quote some testimony from the Southern Press, as follows: "Let me give you some testimony from the South. Says *The Atlanta Constitution:* 'We must be fair to the Negro. There is no use in beating about the bush. We have not shown this fairness in the past, nor are we showing it today, either in justice before the laws, in facilities afforded for education, or in other directions.'

"Some years ago," said Mr. Storey, "a Mississippi lawyer, addressing the Bar Association of that State, said: 'A Negro accused of crime during the days of slavery was dealt with more justly than he is today.  *  *  *  It is next to an impossibility to convict, even upon the strongest evidence, any white man of a crime of violence upon the person of a Negro,  *  *  *  and the converse is equally true that it is next to an impossibility to acquit a Negro of any crime or violence where a white man is concerned,' and well did he (the Mississippi lawyer) add: 'We cannot, either as individuals, as a country, as a State, or as a nation continue to mete out one kind of criminal justice to a poor man, a friendless man, or a man of a different race, and another kind of justice to a rich man, an influential man, or a man of our own race without reaping the consequences.'

"From the *Vicksburg Herald* come these words (continued Mr. Storey): 'The Herald *looks with no favor upon drafting Southern Negroes at all,* believing they should be exempt *in toto* because they do not equally 'share in the benefits of government.' To say that they do is to take issue with the palpable truth. 'Taxation without representation,' the war-cry of the Revolutionary wrong against Great Britain, was not half so plain a wrong as requiring military service from a class that is denied suffrage and which lives under such discriminations of inferiority as the 'Jim Crow' law and inferior school equipment and service.' "

It was the attitude and just such sentiments as that voiced by the *Vicksburg Herald* as well as by a number of other Southern white newspapers, and by certain Senators and Congressmen, including Senator Vardaman, of Mississippi, that led the colored people of the United States to feel for a time that it was not desired that they should have any participation in the world-wide struggle for "Freedom and Democracy."

The prevalence of lynching Negroes in America had become so noticeable that not only the German press, but the newspapers and diplomatic representatives of other nations as well, have from time to time commented upon the practice as a sad reflection upon our boasted civilization, our high ideals, and our ability to preserve and enforce law and order. Pregnant with grave danger in time of peace, the lynching evil constituted an even greater menace in time of war, and when the epidemic began to spread and to include white victims as well as black victims, citizens of this country as well as citizens of foreign countries, the President of the United States saw fit to issue from the White House a strong public statement denouncing lynching and mob violence, and later, in New York City, on May 5th and 6th, 1919, a National Conference was held for the purpose of (1) promoting propaganda against lynching in every State of the Union; (2) urging the passage of Federal laws against lynching, and (3) bringing about the formation of white and Negro committees throughout the South to agitate against mob murders and the like.

### Propaganda Among Negroes in New York City

How the Harlem colony of Negroes in New York City was stirred up or, in a measure, influenced by German propaganda, may be gathered from a letter written to Mr. George Creel, Chairman of the Committee on Public Information, by a well-known New York citizen, Mr. Trumbull White, whose wideawake patriotism and deep interest in the welfare of the Negro people are numbered among his many commendable virtues. His letter to Mr. Creel follows:

INVESTORS' PUBLIC SERVICE
(Incorporated)
149 Broadway, New York.

March 15, 1918.

Mr. George Creel,
Chairman of the Committee on Public Information,
Washington, D. C.

Dear George:

This is a matter which seems to me very important and immediate.

The big Negro colony in Harlem is badly infected with a series of rumors arousing great distress and disquiet. I happen to know about it because of very intelligent colored servants at our house who have relatives in the Expeditionary Forces in France.

The rumors are of various kinds. One is that the Negro regiments are being terribly abused by their white officers. Another is that the Negro regiments are being discriminated against in the distribution of troops where the danger and suffering will be the greatest. Another is that the Germans have vowed that they will torture all Negroes who may be captured, in order to prove that this is a white man's war and that no Africans are wanted in Europe. Another is that already more than 200 Negro soldiers with eyes gouged out and arms cut off, after being captured by Germans and then turned loose by them to wander back to the American lines, have been sent home to this country and are now in the Columbia Base Hospital, No. 1, up in The Bronx.

These rumors are spreading like wildfire in the Negro colony through churches, Negro papers, clubs and in general conversation. The colony is seething. I do not know whether German propaganda started the rumors or whether some even less responsible source is the cause. It is clear, however, that serious harm can result and indeed is now resulting.

I have two recommendations. One is that a permit be arranged for one Negro preacher, one Negro doctor, and one Negro woman of intelligence from that colony to be admitted to a complete inspection of the Base Hospital, in order that they may report back to their own people the falsity of the stories.

The other is that some lecturer, preferably Irvin Cobb, if he is in this country, be sent up to that colony to lecture at one of their big churches, specifically on the subject of what he has seen of the Negro troops in France, the work they are doing, and the conditions surrounding them. Cobb has the southern affection for the Negro and could do the thing right. Failing him, can you get a returned Negro minister, Y. M. C. A. worker, or wounded or invalided Negro private of intelligence to tackle that job?

I will help arrange it through the Negro preachers and editors of the colony.

I know that the matter should be expedited. Please do not think this matter a light one.          **As ever yours,**

(Signed) TRUMBULL WHITE.

The following press dispatch further indicates the kind of German propaganda which sought to influence the colored people in New York and elsewhere:

New York, April 11, 1918.—After an alleged threat to kill an aged colored woman in Harlem; Max Freudenheim was arrested yesterday by Agent Davidson of the Department of Justice. He was sent to Newark jail to await internment proceedings.

Charles F. DeWoody, Federal Investigating Chief here, left for Washington last night. *He will lay before Attorney General Gregory today an amazing story of German propaganda among Negroes,* revealed by Freudenheim's arrest.

Mr. DeWoody believes that behind Freudenheim's activities for several months in Harlem lies a Berlin plan like the "Committee for the East," which had for its object the alienation of all the Jews in the world from the allies.

It is known that the trail has led to several States. It was less than a year ago that the same sort of propaganda which had been made rife around One Hundred and Thirty-fifth street and Lenox avenue caused almost a panic among the Negroes of the South. Thousands of them left their homes and fled to Northern States at word of an uprising in favor of Germany which it was said would start in South America and Mexico and sweep through this country.

Freudenheim, who is married and has three children, has been in this country for eighteen years. He says he is an Austrian, but the Federal officials say he was born in Germany.

Posing as an insurance solicitor, the man has been working in Harlem exclusively among Negroes. The Federal authorities say he would meet men and women and when the talk touched on the war, would declare:

"Germany is sure to win this war and it is a good thing for you colored people that she will. Germany is the greatest friend the colored man ever had. All her colonies in East Africa were started to better the conditions of the black man. When she wins the war her intention is to start a colony exclusively for Negroes in one of the Southern States. This will be virtually a Black Republic. The colored men will choose their own rulers.

"In this city the Negroes will get the recognition the United States has denied them so far. They will be made the social equals of white men."

An elderly woman whose mother was a slave freed by Lincoln's Emancipation Proclamation reported Freudenheim's activities to Superintendent DeWoody. Men were sent to shadow the man.

He was followed and his conversations were listened to. He discovered this, and within hearing of a Department of Justice agent he shouted to this woman whom he suspected of betraying him: "I'll see that you are killed long before this war is over. Germany has many friends in New York and they will strike."

As a part of the activities of German propagandists who were seeking to incite the Negro people of the United States to be disloyal to their country and to their flag, they constantly hinted that the Kaiser's love for the Negro was so great that if ever Germany should be triumphant and should win the war, he would dominate affairs in America and would parcel out one or more States of the Union where the Negro would be given real freedom and the full right of self-government. The utter fallacy of such false promises was clearly brought out by Harrison Rhodes (of the Vigilantes), the celebrated newspaper and magazine writer of New York City, who wrote an informing article which was printed in many of the leading newspapers throughout this country.

In order to weaken the morale among colored American soldiers in France, German airships dropped among them all sorts of literature, of which a typical example was given in Chapter XI.

Thus it was, "with fightings within and foes without," *the Negro soldiers and civilians of America stood firm against every temptation to divert them from their primary duty of helping to win the war.* What more remarkable and commendable record could be made, or has ever been made by any class of citizens than was made by Negro Americans who remained steadfastly loyal to the Stars and Stripes notwithstanding the fact that they had been, and were being subjected to unjust and embarrassing conditions and discriminations which even the enemy government noticed, ridiculed, and condemned! It is a record which should, and doubtless will vouchsafe to this racial group not only the eternal respect and gratitude of America but radical reforms and practical rewards befitting their unfaltering patriotism.

# CHAPTER XXV

## HOW COLORED CIVILIANS HELPED TO WIN

*Their Co-operation in All the Liberty Loan Drives—The Negro and the Red Cross—In the United War Work Campaign—How the Negroes Bought War Savings Stamps—Special Contributions and Work of Colored Citizens—The "Committee of One Hundred" and Its Valuable Work.*

Not halting at the cheerful giving of their *man-power* through volunteer enlistment and under the operation of the selective draft, the 12,000,000 American Negroes contributed with equal cheerfulness and promptness and liberality to the call of the Nation for their *money-power*. The total amount of money brought by Negroes to the country's relief through the sale of Liberty Bonds of the first, second, third, fourth and fifth issues, has not been carefully compiled, and may never be definitely known, because of the diffuse method by which the collections were made; but it is safe to say that the figures will run into many millions, representing untold sacrifices and a measure of patriotism unexcelled by any similar number of citizens of the American Republic.

To extend this good work the War Department and the Committee on Public Information, charged with preserving the morale of the great body of American citizens, and especially of groups known to have what they term "special grievances," decided that a vigorous campaign of education was necessary to instruct the Negro on the war aims of the Government, to secure at the hands of the race the full measure of co-operation which it was capable of giving. Early in May, 1918, therefore, a patriotic campaign was determined upon, and upon the recommendation of the author, the Committee on Public Information organized a "Committee of One Hundred," made up of strong, well-poised and thoroughly trained men, representing practically every organization of Negroes in the land, and having undisputed influence with all classes and conditions of the Negro race throughout the land. Bishops and ministers of all denominations, editors of every kind of publication, heads of every known fraternal organization, heads of educational institutions, prominent factors in all of the professions, industries and business agencies formed a part of this unique body of missionaries and messengers.

Zones of activity were worked out and men of varying qualifications were given assignments where they could do the most effective work for the cause at stake and to serve the United States Government in its hour of national emergency and need. These men, without exception, took hold of the work with a will, and their intensive campaign of education, driving home the war aims of the Government in a plain and straightforward fashion, had a powerful influence in inspiring a livelier patriotism throughout the race and encouraging them to engage whole-heartedly in the countless activities designed to help America to win the war. Specially equipped by nature and by experience for dealing with collective humanity, the Committee of One Hundred performed its duty well, and their labors were made more potent for good by the close relationship they were able to establish with the State Councils of Defense in the North, East, South and West, from which they derived much valuable data which enabled them to counteract the particular disadvantage to patriotic endeavor in each of the communities they were called upon to visit and evangelize.

### The Fourth Loan Campaign

At the opening of each specific campaign inaugurated by the Secretary of the Treasury for the flotation of the big loans, running into billions—a denomination which had heretofore held for the Negro, as well as for the white people, a very vague meaning—some well-known member of the race invariably launched the "drive" with a formal address, outlining the necessity for the money asked for and pointing out to the Negro the significance of a victory over the Teutonic allies in its relation to his future, as an integral factor in the American body politic.

The Special Assistant Secretary of War was asked to launch the Fourth Liberty Loan Campaign among the colored citizens of the District of Columbia, and spoke at Howard Theatre, Washington, Saturday evening, October 29, 1918, as follows:

"This is as the President says, the people's war. It is not a white man's war. It is not a black man's war. It is a war of all the people under the Stars and Stripes for the preservation of human liberty throughout the world. Civilization is in peril, and the natural rights of mankind are menaced for all time by the unholy aggressions of the Imperial German Government. The triumph of autocracy means the destruction of the Temple of Freedom which our fathers helped in 1776 to erect, and which their sons have sacrificed blood and treasure ever since to perpetuate. The failure of democracy in this mighty conflict will entail disaster upon humanity throughout generations beyond number.

"The American Negro, is beginning to realize that if the American white man is enslaved by reason of this Republic's inability to rout the Hun in the present struggle, the ultimate result will be his own re-enslavement and the loss of all that he has gained since the Emancipation Proclamation. His fate is indissolubly bound up with the fate of the Republic, and he must join with it, loyally, whole-heartedly and to the finish, in every movement that will add strength to the American arms in the death-grapple with Germany. This common purpose must be contended for by a common brotherhood.

"Already, the Negro has responded promptly and cheerfully to the call for his *man-power*, and three times since the declaration of war against the Imperial German Government he has answered generously, readily and without stint to the call for his *money-power*.

Now comes a fourth call for financial aid and it is not doubted that the 12,000,000 free colored Americans, who wish to remain free, will again respond with the same or greater measure of liberality and enthusiasm that has characterized them when the previous demands were made.

"Appropriately, indeed—in view of the onward march of General Pershing's Invincible Crusaders on France's western front, the Fourth Liberty Loan is styled "The Fighting Loan." Black men are among these Crusaders. We who must remain at home are in duty bound to lend the limit of our aid to those who have gone abroad to bare their breasts to shot and shell in defense of our flag and the sacred ideals for which it stands. We cannot do this in a more effective way than to offer our dollars to sustain the Government—*the only Government we know*—and its fighting men while they are braving death, to insure freedom and justice to all mankind. Even as they are making their bayonet fight in protection of the jewel of liberty, we can make our DOLLARS fight to gird up their loins for stronger efforts in trench and on field.

"We can all rest assured that the response of the colored millions to the fourth call for financial aid will be in keeping with our public-spirited and intensely patriotic rallies of the past. The success of the Fourth Liberty Loan should overtop all of its predecessors in the volume of subscriptions accredited to the Negro race everywhere, and this should be the absorbing mission of colored ministers, editors, teachers, merchants, lawyers, doctors and speakers and workers day by day and night by night until that objective is gained. 'He gives twice who gives quickly.' Let us buy bonds—and then buy *more bonds!*

"Every dollar loaned, every sacrifice made, every useful service performed will give to ourselves the rich consciousness of duty well done and will tend to win for the colored American everywhere the fullest measure of American opportunity."

This address was sent out by Mr. Frank R. Wilson, Director of Publicity for the United States Treasury Department, to all Directors of Publicity, as an appeal to be addressed to the colored people of the United States.

Secretary W. G. McAdoo, of the United States Treasury, made public acknowledgment of the whole-souled coöperation of the colored people throughout the country in connection with the Liberty Loan "drives."

## War Savings Stamps Purchased by Negroes

Although it has not been possible to keep any accurate record of the amount of War Savings Stamps purchased by colored people throughout the country, the scattering reports and personal observations of individuals everywhere indicate that the total is very large. The stamps are purchased through so many and such widely-separated agencies that no accurate compilation by race or creedal groups can be attempted with any hope of success.

A typical instance of the aggressive work done by the War Stamps committees of the colored people is found in the District of Columbia, where during a drive of eight weeks among the children of the public schools, a sale averaging $800 per week was reported—this period covering the months of March and April, 1918. About the same time, the Washington Citizens' Committee on W. S. S., headed by Dr. W. A. Warfield and Dr. D. E. Wiseman, collected $52,000 through their own plan of campaign, in addition to the immense sums subscribed through the government departments and commercial houses where colored people were largely employed. It cannot be doubted that the Washington example was repeated many times over in the many communities all over the land where colored people are found in appreciable numbers.

### Subscribers to the "Victory" Loan

The "Victory" issue of Liberty bonds found colored Americans ready to help the nation finish the job of winning the war, to help furnish funds to bring the boys back home, and to pay the cost connected with the establishment of freedom and democracy for the world.

Throughout the entire country colored organizations and colored leaders set in motion forces which brought from the colored people a response which again served to indicate the willingness of the Negro people to help bring the war to a close with the last of the "drives" for money to complete the financing of the cost of the war.

Mr. John W. Lewis, president of the Industrial Savings Bank, Washington, estimates that the colored people of the District of Columbia purchased $2,200,000 worth of the First, Second, Third and Fourth issues of Liberty bonds. He arrived at this total by checking up as far as was possible the amounts known to have been subscribed by colored men and women through the banks, the Federal departments, and business houses. The Fifth or "Victory Loan" was taken quite largely by Negroes in the Government service, and by persons in private employment as well. For the Fifth Liberty Loan the total subscribed for through his Industrial Savings Bank amounted to something more than $30,000, the investors being exclusively colored.

### Help for the American Red Cross

Notwithstanding certain lack of information at the outset relative to the attitude of the authorities responsible for the management of the American Red Cross Society, the masses of the Negro people early came to realize the vast benefits accruing to them through the universal operations of this great agent of mercy and humanity, and in every community where the colored people constituted any large per cent of the population, they rallied to the standard of the Red Cross. They gave freely of their means, invariably at a large personal sacrifice, and strove earnestly, early and late through existing organizations or to perfect additional organizations for the furtherance of this movement.

In the "drive" of the American Red Cross for a relief fund of $100,000,000 in 1918, the colored citizens of the country contributed their proportionate share. In the churches, schools, theaters, and on the streets, colored speakers eloquently pointed out the duty of the race to give liberally to the fund and women and children daily took up collections in all kinds of public places, and with gratifying results.

### Negroes in Councils of Defense

The State Councils Section of the Council of National Defense early recognized the importance of having the colored people organize under Councils of Defense as was true of other citizens of the republic. It was with this thought in mind that Mr. Arthur H. Fleming, Chief of the State Council Section, addressed the letter following to the Southern State Councils of Defense with reference to this matter, since the great mass of the Negro population is to be found in the Southern section of our country:

COUNCIL OF NATIONAL DEFENSE

WASHINGTON

STATE COUNCIL SECTION　　　　　　　　　　　　February 23, 1918.

*Subject: Organization of the Negroes.*

To the Several Southern State Councils of Defense:

The Negro population can render valuable assistance in the present crisis. Their support of the Government depends largely on their clear understanding of the events which involved the United States in the war, and the purposes and principles which it is upholding. To this end we call to your attention a plan for the organization of Negroes based upon the most successful work for reaching them already accomplished by State Councils of Defense and State Divisions of the Woman's Committee in the South. We ask your opinion of this plan as to its wisdom both in general and in the light of the local conditions in your own State.

We hope that this matter will receive your thoughtful consideration and that you will advise us promptly as to your views.

Yours very truly,

ARTHUR H. FLEMING,

Chief of Section.

The result of the plan referred to was the successful organization of Negroes under the State Councils of Defense.

## The Negro Press

An outstanding force that helped to win the war was the Negro press of the country. Aside from the effective work done by this aggressive element of power through the conference of Editors at Washington, which is referred to elsewhere, the press was an asset of incalculable value in pushing the war work among colored people by the regular publication of the bulletins of information the Special Assistant caused to be sent out from the War Department week after week, beginning shortly after the assumption of his duties. His mailing list embraced more than two hundred Negro journals and magazines, having a large circulation in practically every State in the Union, and reaching every class of the Negro millions, North, East, South and West, besides the Speakers' "Committee of One Hundred" and many newspaper correspondents, special writers, heads of schools and colleges and men of influence and standing in the strategic centers of the nation.

This service proved to be of the greatest possible assistance to those charged with the conduct of the war, as it won and held the confidence of the people, maintaining their morale and stimulating their patriotism at the crucial hour, when the nation needed the loyal and earnest coöperation of every element of its citizenship to assure victory to its cause. Our editors were conservative on all current questions, at no sacrifice of courage and absolute frankness in the upholding of principles. The author has always held to the belief that the only way to gain the united and cordial support of the people is to take them entirely into one's confidence and to throw upon the screen of action the full glare of publicity touching every plan, policy or achievement, withholding nothing that might lead to a suspicion that behind the veil of secrecy there might lurk something that could not stand the light of day.

The superb and generous support given to the war aims of the

Government by the colored press was one of the most gratifying features of the trying conflict, and unstinted praise should be given the colored editors and publishers for their timely services and countless sacrifices, all cheerfully contributed in behalf of the nation's cause.

## Helping to Save Food

The Food Administration, of which Mr. Herbert Hoover was Director, recognizing the importance of having the support of the large colored civilian population, gave attention to organizing them. Some work had been done among the Negroes through one of the divisions of the Educational Department of the Food Administration, and during the carrying out of the preliminary features of this program, A. U. Craig, a teacher of the Paul Laurence Dunbar High School, Washington, D. C., was for awhile in charge of the Negro Press Section of the Educational Division. About September 30, 1918, he gave up his work as director of that section, which was discontinued.

A colored Field Worker, Ernest T. Attwell, who for fifteen years or more had served as Business Agent of the Tuskegee Normal and Industrial Institute, Alabama, was made organizer, first for the State of Alabama, and afterwards for the Southern States. In September, 1918, his activities were enlarged and he was brought to Washington where from September, 1918, to January 1, 1919, he served as director of the activities of the colored people from the headquarters of the Food Administration organization.

## Mr. Hoover's Appeal to the Negro

The campaign of the Food Administration among the colored people was opened by a strong appeal made by Director Herbert Hoover, who circulated an open letter to the 12,000,000 Negroes of the United States, asking for their coöperation as a unit everywhere to help in general food conservation. The appeal indicated a deep appreciation of the potential value of coöperation on the part of this racial group, of which over 2,000,000 were engaged in agricultural pursuits, and, therefore, exerted a tremendous influence in solving the problem of raising food crops. Thousands of the race were also engaged in the domestic occupations, buying and dispensing provisions for the use of many families, serving as cooks, stewards, etc., for hotels, clubs, institutions and restaurants of every conceivable size and grade. This kind of service placed them largely in control of the food consumption in the homes, not only of their own people, but of other races as well. The program of Mr. Hoover contemplated the thorough organization of this important group by, first, naming a national director, in the person of Mr. Attwell, and

## For Freedom

### AN APPEAL TO THE NEGROES OF THE UNITED STATES

OUR Nation is engaged in a war for its very existence. To win this war we must save food, grow great crops of foodstuffs and substitute other foods for those most easily shipped to our associates in this war and our own soldiers in France, thousands of whom are men of your own race. The Food Administration realizes that the Negro people of this Nation can be of the utmost help in food conservation and food production. Every Negro man, woman, and child can render a definite service by responding to the appeal and instructions of the Food Administration and its representatives. The Negroes have shown themselves loyal and responsive in every national crisis. Their greatest opportunity of the present day, to exercise this loyalty, is to help save and grow food. I am confident that they will respond to the suggestions of the Food Administration and thus prove again their patriotism for the winning of this war.

*Herbert Hoover*

then the appointment of Negro State Directors, county deputies, local food committees, and like agencies, taking in every class of helpers, with a view of mobilizing all forces for the purpose of stimulating propaganda work along the line of increased food production and the conservation of the supplies in hand. Mr. Hoover's appeal is reproduced in facsimile above.

One year of food conservation found a colored organization in each of the following named States, with Negro directors as indicated: Alabama, J. H. Phillips; Arkansas, Milton W. Guy; Florida, Nathan B. Young; Georgia, J. P. Davis; Illinois, Alexander L. Jackson; Indiana, F. B. Ransom; Iowa, Herbert R. Wright; Kentucky, Phil H. Brown; Louisiana, J. Madison Vance; Maryland, C. C. Fitzgerald; North Carolina, James B. Dudley; Oklahoma, T. H. Wiseman; South Carolina, R. W. Westberry; Missouri, J. B. Coleman; Tennessee, William J. Hale; Texas, E. J. Howard; West Virginia, C. E. Mitchell; New York, E. P. Roberts.

The publicity system adopted by the Colored Section served to arouse the masses to the necessity for food conservation and production, to supply home needs and to replace the enormous amount of foodstuffs lost at sea on the way to the allied governments. Besides numerous news releases to the colored press a series of striking pamphlets were issued, notable among them being one bearing the admonition, "Don't Cut the Rope!" Illustrated lectures, moving pictures slides in the theaters, public cooking demonstrations, etc., formed a part of the publicity campaign so well carried out by Director Attwell.

The signing of the armistice did not cause the immediate discontinuance of the Food Administration, and the organization of food clubs went on as before. The Director of the Negro Section saw to it that every Negro home was reached with the propaganda of "keeping on in the good work." During "Conservation Week for World Relief," the first week in December, 1918, Mr. Attwell addressed large meetings in Indiana, Ohio and Kentucky, at which he pointed out the necessity for continued conservation of food, in view of the fact that contracts for the current year called for not less than twenty million tons of food products for European countries. In all respects the results flowing out of the activities of the Negro Section of the National Food Administration amply justified its creation and the unstinted praise which Director Hoover and other governmental agents so cheerfully bestowed upon it.

# CHAPTER XXVI

## NEGRO LABOR IN WAR TIME

*Organization for War Work—The Division of Negro Economics—
Pioneer Work of Dr. George E. Haynes—Negro Representation
in Council—Seeking to Improve Race Relations—Good Work
by Negroes in the Shipyards—Attitude of Organized Labor—
The Opportunities of the War.*

Because of unsettled conditions among the Negro people migrating hither and thither during the World War, and still more disturbed conditions obtaining among them after the inter-vention of the United States in the great struggle, it was deemed necessary to make a scientific study of Negro labor and establish an organization for its direction. After considering the available material, the Secretary of Labor decided, in June, 1918, to call as one of his assistants to take charge of this work, Dr. George E. Haynes, founder of the Urban League and Professor of Social Sciences at Fisk University. Dr. Haynes's work was that of a director of the Division of Negro Economics, around which the organization to carry out these purposes would be organized and from which it would receive its direction.

As no special effort had hitherto been made in this field, Dr. Haynes came to his task largely as a pioneer. His first effort was to arouse interest in his cause through personal interviews and conferences with public-spirited citizens of both races, North and South. He, therefore, approached school officials, State Councils of National Defense, Chambers of Commerce, the United States Employment Service, social welfare organizations, and educational societies.

Interest was soon manifested far and wide. The proposed work of the Department of Labor with reference to the Negroes was given careful consideration at a meeting of the Southern

Sociological Congress held at Gulfport, Mississippi, July 12, 1918. Soon there followed a State conference of representative white and Negro citizens at Jacksonville, Florida, called by Governor Sydney J. Catts, who presided at a number of the sessions. On August 5, 1918, a conference was called at Columbus, Ohio, by the Department of Negro Economics with the coöperation of the Federal Director of the United States Employment Service and Governor James M. Cox.

In the meantime conferences of more satisfactory results were being held. The first of these was that called by Governor Bickett of North Carolina, on June 19, 1918. At this meeting the Governor appointed a temporary committee, which drafted a constitution providing for a State Negro Workers' Advisory Committee and for the organization of local, county, and city committees. This plan of organization, with slight modifications and adjustments for other States, served as a model for the development of voluntary field organizations for the Southern States and six Northern States.

An important conference was then held in Kentucky on August 6, 1918. There were both white and colored representatives in attendance. This conference was unique in that the plan of organization adopted was that of a united war work committee, with a special committee of white citizens appointed by the State Council of Defense as coöperating members. This war work committee ' included representatives from the Department of Agriculture, the United States Food Administration, the Red Cross, the Council of Defense, and the Department of Labor. Governor A. O. Stanley of Kentucky attended the morning session and made an enthusiastic address to the delegates. Very soon thereafter the influence of the State conferences so proved their effectiveness and their usefulness as a means of forwarding the State movement and creating good feeling and a favorable sentiment that other conferences followed almost as a matter of course. The most important of these were held in Georgia, Missouri, Illinois, Michigan, Pennsylvania, and New Jersey, and steps were taken for conferences or central organization of the work either in New York or South Carolina.

## Improving Race Relations

The Division of Negro Economics also called upon the Information and Education Service to carry out the departmental plan for publicity and educational campaigns to improve race relations of workers and to increase the morale and efficiency of Negro workers. The Division also assisted the Bureau of Industrial Housing and Transportation in carrying out its purposes. It welcomed also the coöperation of the Public Health Service in its educational campaign among Negro workers, and maintained a similar coöperative relationship with the War Department through the office of the Special Assistant to the Secretary of War.

## Good Work in the Shipyards

It has often been reported that the Division of Negro Economics withheld from rather than conferred upon the Negro the benefits resulting from the scarcity of labor during the World War. For example, Negroes were employed in large numbers in the shipyards, then undertaking to furnish the fleets adequate to the task of transporting American soldiers to France. In the early part of the war the Negroes as illustrated by the unusual record of Charles Knight, at Sparrow's Point, Maryland, exhibited the highest efficiency as riveters in the shipyards. But their increase in efficiency did not lead to an increase in the number employed in the various shipyards. The same condition of affairs, for instance, obtained in the employment of Negroes at Hog Island. After they had manifested the same evidences of efficiency, they suffered from most invidious discriminations while endeavoring to contribute their part to the winning of the war. These untoward conditions tended to continue, and while the number of Negroes employed by the United States Government increased, the Government did little to facilitate their entering the higher pursuits of labor.

It is unfair, however, to charge to the account of Dr. Haynes, the Director of the Division of Negro Economics, the shortcomings of the Department of Labor or of the United States Government. It is decidedly unjust and ludicrous that in the midst of all of these injustices to the Negro laborer there was no effort on the part of the Department to do anything to relieve the situation. A public official is not always in a position every time to divulge exactly what his attitude in a certain situation may be, or whether or not he has taken any steps leading to definite action in matters coming before him for consideration. It may safely be assumed that Dr. Haynes, at all times and in every way possible, did what he could to secure to the Negro laborer the recognition and the remuneration belonging to every man, and in some of these cases he succeeded. That he failed in materially changing the attitude of the Department of Labor or of the country toward the Negro, should not excite surprise. If reformers have had, according to history, to labor for years to effect a change in public opinion it is ludicrous to expect that one colored man could, by holding office two years in a Department of the United States Government solve the economic problems of the race.

### Attitude of Organized Labor

During these same years other forces were at work to assist in the solution of the same problems. Organized labor had become somewhat excited and finally concluded that because of a scarcity of labor it would soon need the support of the Negro. During these, their trying hours, therefore, leading Negroes of the country were approached with a view to obtaining their support toward the end of organizing all Negro wage-earners.

This proposal did not generally appeal to the Negroes throughout the United States. Their attitude was rather, "Beware of the Greeks bearing gifts." Negroes had for so many years been barred by the trades unions and had suffered so much at their hands that they saw in this change of attitude only some advantage which the trades unions hoped to obtain thereby. Why was it that no effort had ever been put forth by white unions in all these years when the Negro was forced to work for starvation wages? Why is it that Negro laborers have been driven away and in some cases, as in East St. Louis, exterminated by the agents of the trades unions—and could now be received with open arms? "Believing that the need of Negro labor was absolute and imperative in unionized territory and that efforts to exclude the Negro from employment would be futile," said these Negroes, "great solicitude was then expressed for the Negro, at the very time that he was so well treated and so well paid and his prospects for even better treatment so much brighter.'' Some Negroes, therefore, advised that nothing could be hoped for but base betrayal, and that it would be a blunder to surrender their independence to accept work when they could get it, and on terms suitable to their own peculiar needs. They openly declared that trades unions were planning, not for the Negroes but for the whites, and Negro leaders were cautioned not to be induced thereby and advised the people not to accept these ''gifts of the Greeks,'' who intended thereby merely to control the Negroes for their own good, having seen that they could no longer keep them down.

These leaders, however, did not oppose the organization of the laborers of their race in separate units primárily concerned with their own welfare, but maintaining their independence of the white unions. They were urged to unite among themselves, but not to connect with any movement which convenienced, encouraged, or incited lawlessness, or that sought to prevent men who desired to work from working because they did not wear the badge of an organization. Complying with such suggestions a number of Negroes' organizations were formed. Chief among these was that of the Associated Colored Employees of America, which aimed to bring about a systematic distribution of laborers.

### The Opportunities of the War

The majority of the Negroes of this country, however, were not of this opinion. They felt that the time had come for the two races to unite and this was its greatest opportunity. As a step in this direction the American Federation of Labor at its meeting in Buffalo in 1917 passed a resolution to this effect. On the 12th of February in 1918, therefore, the Council of the American Federation of Labor met according to appointment a number of representative Negroes who were invited to discuss with that body plans for carrying out these resolutions. Among the persons invited were Dr. R. R. Moton, Principal of Tuskegee; Mr. Emmett J. Scott, Special Assistant to the Secretary of War; Mr. George W. Harris, Editor of the New York News; Mr. A. H. Grimke, President of the Washington Branch, National Association for the Advancement of Colored People; Mr. E. K. Jones, Executive Secretary of the League on Urban Conditions Among Negroes; Mr. John Shillady, Secretary of the National Association for the Advancement of Colored People, and Mr. Fred R. Moore, Editor of the New York Age.

These gentlemen, representing the colored people, set forth as a vital war measure the necessity for the removal of the barriers preventing Negroes from entering the higher pursuits of labor. They asked that the American Federation of Labor organize the Negroes in the various trades to include skilled as well as unskilled workmen, Northern as well as Southern; Government as well as civilian employees; women as well as men workers. They wanted Negro labor directed by the American Federation of Labor in the same way as white labor, when workmen are returning to work after a successful strike, when shops are declared open or closed, and when union workers apply for jobs.

When the American Federation of Labor held its meeting in Atlantic City, New Jersey, in June, 1919, it voted with only one dissenting vote, and that the Railway Postal Clerks' Union, to give full membership rights to Negro wage-earners. The discussion of the question, and there were some seven hundred delegates in the convention, was very general, broad and fair, with few exceptions. For some time past Negroes have enjoyed membership privileges in the Federation, but in a restricted sense only. It now remains for them to make their standing in the American Federation what it should be. Several causes contributed toward this decision. The World War taught the American Federation and all others that Negroes were prepared, by the industrial and technical teaching and instruction they have been subjected to for the past twenty-five years, to do the highly necessary work required by the Government and the essential industry corporations; while the migration movement indicated that there was plenty of labor to be had for the asking.

### The Case of Mrs. Douglass

As soon as the Special Assistant to the Secretary of War entered upon his duties in the War Department he found that there was need of building up a healthy morale among the colored people. Aside from what seemed to be a regular epidemic of racial disturbances culminating in riots, lynching, mob violence, and the like, he found many other conditions that were making for disquiet and

unrest. Although colored men were being drafted and called to fight
for their country on battlefields abroad, many of their relatives and
dependents at home, even those upon the Civil Service register as
eligible for appointment, were being denied employment and discriminated against in nearly every branch of the departmental service
in Washington. One of the first cases brought to his attention was
that of a cultured and refined young colored woman, a relative by
marriage of the late Frederick Douglass, the great Negro leader.
She had met the Civil Service requirements, had been duly certified
to serve the Government as "Index and Catalogue Clerk," but when
she reported for duty and was found to have an admixture of Negro
blood, she was told that a *"MISTAKE HAD BEEN MADE."*
Manifestly the same racial discrimination was practiced in dozens
of similar cases, and led to the author's taking up the matter with a
number of the Government officials who were responsible for such
injustices. While he always recognized the fact that his duties were
primarily to look after the interests of colored soldiers, yet as far
as was practicable, he endeavored to look after the interests of colored civilians as well, and the attached correspondence concerning
the young woman above referred to is typical of his efforts in this
direction, though he frankly admits that such cases of racial discrimination in the Government bureaus at Washington have been far
too numerous for him to give to each of them the personal attention
required:

December 13, 1917.

Memorandum—For Lieut. Ernest J. Wesson,

Officer in Charge, Civilian Personnel Section,

Administration Division, U. S. Signal Corps:

At the instance of Dean F. P. Keppel, Confidential Adviser, Office of the
Secretary of War, I am writing you in the following matter which has been
brought to my attention.

Mrs. Fannie H. Douglass, 910 T Street, N. W., Washington, D. C., has
brought to the Office of the Secretary of War, a telegram received by her,
dated December 7, 1917, which reads as follows:

"Mrs. Fannie H. Douglass, 329 You St., N. W. (which was her former
address), Washington, D. C.:

"Your name certified by Civil Service Commission for appointment
Chief Signal Officer, twelve hundred dollars per annum; if you accept, report

as soon as possible, Room 826, Mills Building Annex, this city, for duty. Wire reply, Government, collect.

(Signed)   SQUIRE, Chief Signal Officer.''

Mrs. Douglass states that she telegraphed her acceptance of the offer, and reported for duty as requested; that she was given certain blank forms to fill out; that she filled out the forms given her, and that a detached portion, headed: ''The appointee will detach this portion of the sheet and retain it for his information and guidance,'' was given her, which detached portion she has brought to the Office of the Secretary of War; and that, after these proceedings, she was informed that ''*there had been a mistake.*''

Inquiry at the office of the Appointment Division elicits the information that Mrs. Fannie H. Douglass was certified to the office of the Chief Signal Officer on December 6, 1917, as Index and Catalogue Clerk, grade of clerkship for which she had been examined, and to which position she has been certified.

Will you kindly let me have, for the Secretary of War, all the facts bearing on this matter?

(Signed)   EMMETT J. SCOTT,
Special Assistant to Secretary of War.

—

War Department, Washington, December 15, 1917.
Memorandum—Mr. Emmett J. Scott,
Special Assistant,
Office of Secretary of War.

In reply to yours of December 13, 1917, you are advised from the investigation in this office it would appear that Mrs. Fannie H. Douglass has been the innocent victim of a series of unfortunate errors. The facts surrounding this case are as follows:

On December 6th the Equipment Division of the Signal Corps applied for certification of a large number of Index and Catalogue Clerks. This application was referred to the Appointment Division by telephone and this office was informed that all certificates covering the eligibles for this position were in the Ordnance Department, that these people probably being engaged in that Department, this office was authorized to make temporary appointments of that grade. The Equipment Division informed the undersigned that they had the names of persons at various points in the United States to fill these positions. Upon receipt of this authority to make temporary appointments they were to telegraph these persons to come to Washington, D. C., and did so. Shortly afterwards fourteen certificates covering eligibles for the position of Index and Catalogue Clerks were received in this office from the Appointment Division, they undoubtedly having received these from the Civil Service Commission subsequent to our telephonic conversation.

In view of the fact that a large number of persons had been directed to proceed to Washington at their own expense from various parts of the United States to accept temporary appointments, the undersigned did not care to take any action on these certificates, knowing that vacancies would shortly occur in the Air Division in which the appointees covered by such certificates could be placed. Nevertheless, through clerical error, all of these persons were notified by telegram. However, Mrs. Douglass was the first person to report, and as no transportation had been involved in her case, and further, that upon questioning the clerk in this office, who handles these matters, it was found that Mrs. Douglass had not given up her position and would not suffer any pecuniary loss, the undersigned instructed this clerk to inform Mrs. Douglass that she had been notified to appear through error, this due to the fact that vacancies existing had been filled by temporary appointments and it seemed hardly just to displace these persons who had come to Washington at their own expense, and that the undersigned had full knowledge that further openings were to occur in the near future when the services of all Index and Catalogue clerks could be utilized.

At a later date, which cannot be recalled, Mrs. Douglass called at this office and was voluntarily informed by the undersigned that vacancies were now existing and she would receive telegram in due time to report to this office for duty.

With reference to Mrs. Douglass filling out the blank forms, you are advised that the first impression in this office was that she had been certified as a Departmental Clerk, certain statements on her papers that she had taken the Departmental examination, being the cause of this error, and it was not until after these forms had been completed, was it determined that she had been erroneously summoned as Index and Catalogue Clerk.

Mrs. Douglass has been notified to appear for duty Monday morning next, as Index and Catalogue Clerk.

By direction of the Chief Signal Officer,

(Signed) E. J. WESSON,

1st Lt., Signal Corps, U. S. R.

It is worth while remarking that this young woman proved so capable and painstaking that she was afterward placed in charge of the group of young women who did the file-indexing in her division.

# CHAPTER XXVII

## NEGRO WOMEN IN WAR WORK

*Enthusiastic Service of Colored Women in the Wartime Emergency
—Overcoming the Problems of Race by Pure Patriotism—
Work for the Red Cross—The Young Women's Christian As-
_sociation—The Colored Hostess Houses and Rest Rooms for
Soldiers—War Problems of Living—The Circle for Negro
War Relief—Colored Women in the Loan Drives—Important
Work in War Industries.*

### By Alice Dunbar-Nelson

When the world war began, even before the United States
had entered the conflict, the women of this country were thrilled
as women have ever been since wars began, with the desire to
serve. As if in anticipation of the days soon to come when their
own men would be sent forth to battle, they began to sew and
knit and plan relief work for the men of other nations. It was
but an earnest of the days to come, when every nerve of the nation
would be strained to care for its own men.

When, after that day in April, 1917, so filled with direful possibilities for the nation, the women realized that they were indeed
to be called upon to give up their all, there was but one desire
in the hearts of all the women of the country—to do their utmost
for the men who were about to go forth to battle for an ideal.
Overnight careless idlers were transformed into busy workers;
social butterflies into earnest grubs; thoughtless girls into poised
women; card clubs into knitting circles; aspirants to social honors
into workers whose sole ambition was to be a definite factor in
helpful service. Where there had been petty bickering, there was
now a realization that this was no time for the small things of
life. The one common sorrow of loss of the men dearest to them,
of seeing their sons, brothers, fathers and husbands in the great
conflict, welded together the women of the nation, and purged the
dross of littleness from their souls by the fire of service.

One thing which served to strengthen and intensify the feeling of responsibility and seriousness of the women of the country was the fact that for the first time in the history of the world, a nation at war recognized its women as a definite asset in the conduct of the war. Hitherto, her place had been that of those in the poem, "For men must work, and women must weep." Hers was the task of sending her men forth to return with their shields or upon them, while she remained at home to weep and perhaps make bandages against the return of her wounded men. As a factor in the war she was nil, save in those isolated and abortive cases in history where she became an Amazon or a Molly Pitcher.

But in April, 1917, all this was changed! The nation called upon its women to do definite and constructive work, far-reaching and real. It called them not only to nurse the wounded, but to conserve the health of those at home; not only to give aid and comfort to the fighting men, but to preserve the health and morals of the women whom they must meet, love, and marry; not only to make bandages for the stricken soldiers, but to provide ambulances and even drive them; not only to give love and tears, but money, which they raised from every legitimate source; not only to cheer the men as they marched to the front, but to keep up the morale of those left at home; and to fan into a flame the sparks of patriotism in the breasts of those whom the country denied the privilege of bearing arms. With one stroke the Government organized every woman of the nation into an inclusive body, and mobilized the formerly overlooked greatest asset of the nation.

Into this maelstrom of war activity the women of the Negro race hurled themselves joyously. They asked no odds, remembered no grudges, solicited no favors, pleaded for no privileges. They came by the thousands, hands opened wide to give of love and service and patriotism. It was enough for them that their country was at war; it was enough for them that there was work to do. Centuries of labor had taught them the love of labor; a heritage of service had taught them the beauty of giving of themselves, and a race record of patriotism and loyalty had imbued them inherently with the flaming desire to do their part in the struggle of their native land.

The problem of the woman of the Negro race was a peculiar one. Was she to do her work independently of the women of the other race, or was she to merge herself into their organizations? There were separate regiments for Negro soldiers; should there be separate organizations for relief work among Negro women? If she joined relief organizations, such as the Red Cross Society, and worked with them, would she be assured that her handiwork would reach black hands on the other side of the world, or should she be great-hearted and give her service, simply for the sake of giving, not caring who was to be benefited? Could she be sure that when she offered her services she would be understood as desiring to be a help, and not wishing to be an associate? As is usually the case when any problem presents itself to the nation at large, the Negro faces a double problem should he essay a solution—the great issue and the lesser problem of racial adjustment to that issue.

However, the women of the race cut the Gordian knot with magnificent simplicity. They offered their services and gave them freely, in whatsoever form was most pleasing to the local organizations of white women. They accepted without a murmur the place assigned them in the ranks. They placed the national need before the local prejudice; they put great-heartedness and pure patriotism above the ancient creed of racial antagonism. For pure, unalloyed unselfishness of the highest order, the conduct of the Negro women of the United States during the world war stands out in splendid relief, a lesson to the entire world of what womanhood of the best type really means.

### Colored Women and the Red Cross

At the very beginning of the war, the first organization to which the women of the country naturally turned was the Red Cross Society. It was to be expected that the colored woman, pre-eminently the best nurse in the world, would necessarily turn to the Red Cross Society as a field in which to exercise her peculiar gifts. Red Cross branches were organized in practically every community in the country. Yet it is extremely difficult to tell just what the contribution of the colored woman has been to this organization. We are told that, "The American Red Cross during the war enlisted workers without regard to creed or color and no separate records were maintained of the work of any particular Auxiliary. We know that some eight million women worked for the Red Cross in one way or another during the war, but we have no figures indicating how many of them were colored.''

In the Northern cities the colored women merged their identity in their Red Cross work with the white women, that is, in some Northern cities. In others, and in the South, they formed independent units, auxiliaries to the local branches presided over by the women of the other race. These auxiliaries sent hundreds of thousands of knitted garments to the front, maintained restaurants, did canteen service where they could; sent men from the local draft boards to the camps with comfort kits; in short, did all that could be done—all that they were allowed to do.

But the story of the colored woman and the Red Cross is not altogether a pleasant one. Unfortunately, her activities in this direction were considerably curtailed in many localities. There were whole sections of the country in which she was denied the privilege of doing canteen service. There were other sections in which canteen service was so managed as to be canteen service in name only. Local conditions, racial antipathies, ancient prejudices militated sadly against her usefulness in this work. To the everlasting and eternal credit of the colored woman be it said that, in spite of what might have been absolute deterrents, she persisted in her service and was not downcast in the face of difficulties.

The best part of the whole situation lies in the fact that in the local organizations of the Red Cross the Negro woman was the beneficiary. The Home Nursing classes and the classes in Dietetics not only served to strengthen the morale of the women engaged therein, but raised the tone of every community in which they were organized. This was shown during the influenza epidemic of 1918, when a panic-stricken nation called upon its volunteer nurses of every race and color, and the women of the Red Cross were ready in response and in training.

Theodore Roosevelt has said, ''All of us who give service and stand ready for sacrifice, are the torch-bearers. We run with the torches until we fall, content if we can then pass them to the hands of other runners.'' If that be the case, the gray chapter of the colored nurses in overseas service is a golden one. Early in 1918 the Government issued a call for nurses. The need was great overseas; it was greater at home. Colored women since the inception of the war had felt keenly their exclusion from overseas service. The need for them was acute; their willingness to go was complete; the only thing that was wanted was authoritative sanction. In June, 1918, it was officially announced that the Secretary of War had authorized the calling of colored nurses in the national service. It was an act that did more complete justice to our people, in enfranchising our women for this noble service than any other of the war. All colored nurses who had been registered by the American Red Cross Society were thus given the right to render service to their own race in the army. Colored nurses were assigned to the base hospitals at Camp Funston, Kansas; Camp Grant, Rockford, Illinois; Camp Dodge, Des Moines, Iowa; Camp Taylor, Louisville, Kentucky; Camp Sherman, Chillicothe, Ohio, and Camp Dix, Wrightstown, New Jersey. At these camps a total of about 38,000 colored troops were located.

### The Service of Colored Nurses

Colored people throughout the country felt deep satisfaction over this authorization of the enrollment of colored nurses at the base hospitals and camps. Hundreds of competent colored nurses had registered their names for many months with the Nursing Division of the American Red Cross, in the hope of finally securing positions where their skill and experience could be utilized to proper advantage. These last were particularly gratified over the happy turn of affairs. At the convention of the National Association of Colored Graduate Nurses held at St. Louis, Missouri, a formal message of appreciation was sent to the War Department, the American Red Cross Society, and other agencies that had been instrumental in pushing their claims.

Mrs. Adah B. Thomas, R. N., president of the National Association of Graduate Nurses, attached to the staff of the Lincoln Hospital and Home in New York City, gave a typical expression of the sentiment of the colored nurses and the colored people generally with reference to the admission of colored women to this branch of service. She was the first to offer herself for overseas service. Indianapolis, Indiana, sent a contingent for active service at once. Elizabeth Miller of Meharry Medical College, Nashville,

Tennessee, answered the Government call and was assigned to duty at a nitrate plant in Alabama.

These were but sporadic instances indicating the instant response to the long-waited call to service. Unfortunately, before any considerable change in existing circumstances surrounding this branch of service could be made, the Armistice was signed and history will never know what the colored woman might have done on the battlefields of France as a Red Cross Nurse. Rumor, more or less authentic, states that over 300 colored nurses were on the battlefields, though their complexion disguised their racial identity.

### Young Women's Christian Association

Of the remedial agencies at work for the relief of humanity, and the shouldering of responsibility for the health, morals, and happiness of those also working for the relief of humanity, the Young Women's Christian Association in its operation among the colored girls, women, and men stands out pre-eminently. The reason for this is not hard to seek—the qualities of personality in the leader of this work among colored women, Miss Eva D. Bowles.

At the time the country faced the possibility of war, the National Board of the Young Women's Christian Association was confronted with the great responsibility of helping to safeguard the moral life of women and girls as affected by war conditions. Request came from the United States War Department Commission on Training Camp Activities and from the Young Men's Christian Association, for women workers to undertake work among girls in communities adjacent to army and navy training camps. Hence the formation of the War Work Council. It was organized in June, 1917, with a membership of 100, its function to help meet the special needs of girls and young women in all countries affected by the war. Allied with this was the Junior War Work Council, and the Patriotic League. The extension of these activities among colored girls and women was simultaneous, and one of the brightest chapters in the story of women in the war is the one which records how this work measured up to the responsibilities laid upon it.

The War Work Council of the Young Women's Christian Association, recognizing the loyalty and the need of the colored women and girls of the country, devoted $400,000 of its 1918 budget to the work among the colored girls. When it was organized there was one colored National Secretary and sixteen associations or communities, with nine paid workers. The great demand for a better morale among the girls of the country soon raised that number to twelve National workers, three field supervisors, and forty-two centers, with sixty-three paid workers.

There were opened up in the various camps fifteen hostess houses with complete staffs of colored women. These houses served a splendid purpose. When the War Department planned the great training camps it may not have remembered the women of the country in the stress of making up the army of men, or it may have thought that if it said that there were to be no women in the camps, there would be none. But every woman knows that as long as there is a path to the camps, that path the women will follow; be it on foot, by boat, in cars, trains, trolleys, motor cars, or on horseback; and if there be no trail, the women will blaze one. They must see if their men are ill, or living, and how they are living. If they are ill, they must get to them; if homesick, they must cheer them; if they are leaving for overseas, they must say good-bye to them. And if there are none of their own, they must be charitable enough to extend their good-will to the lonely and heart-hungry of others.

Hence the birth of the Hostess House idea; a bit of home in the camps, a place of rest and refreshment for the women folks belonging to the soldiers; a sheltering chaperonage for the too-enthusiastic girl; a dainty supplement to the stern face of the camp-life of the soldiers; an information bureau for women and soldiers alike; a clearing-house for the social activities which included the men in camps and their women visitors.

As the colored troops came into the camps in large numbers, there was an urgent appeal to meet the needs of their women. The first house to be opened was at Camp Upton, when the "Buffaloes" (367th) were being made into the crack regiment that it afterward became; Mrs. Hannah C. Smith, the pioneer among the Hostess House leaders, going there to take charge in the early part of November, 1917. Only great enthusiasm and faith in the value of the work to be done could have brought about the results which Mrs. Smith achieved at Camp Upton at this time. The temporary headquarters for the hostess house were in a barracks with few conveniences and almost no possibilities. Mrs. Smith, with her co-worker, Mrs. Norcomb, soon made the place as homelike as possible. This was the beginning of the Hostess House work for colored women.

In no very great while Hostess Houses in seven of the large camps were in operation and others soon followed. In some camps, where there was a definite surety, work was begun in the barracks. From many Southern camps came the request for the immediate erection of houses on an insufficient plan, but these plans were rejected. Finally, in the natural progress that came, the houses were erected, and used the same as other Hostess Houses. The relationship of the staff to the whole staff of the camp developed into an ideal, and all groups working under the general tutelage of the Young Women's Christian Association understood each other and had a better appreciation of mutual problems by working together.

### The Y. W. C. A. and War Industries

As the war progressed, our colored girls were taken into almost every phase of the industrial field. It was then recognized early in the work that the success of the movement depended largely upon the correct interpretation of the colored girl to her employer and her white co-worker, and of a fair, just attitude of the white worker toward the colored girl. The war opened up many avenues of employment and service to the colored girls that had not hitherto been her privilege to accept, principally in the industrial field, and with the opening up of these new lines of work, new problems were developed; consequently there came a demand for women to go into localities where factories were located, to make investigations as to working conditions, housing and recreational facilities; to create a better understanding between the employer and employee, and to assist in the opening up of new opportunities for work. As a result of this, an industrial worker was placed at such vital points as Detroit, St. Louis, Louisville, East St. Louis, Nitro, West Virginia; Penniman, Virginia, and Philadelphia, with one appointed for Baltimore, and an acute situation in Washington cared for.

Not only was there need for the care and protection of the girl in the factory, but equally as much so for those in more social communities. This led to the development of club and recreational centers especially in cities near which camps were located. To-day, these centers reach from New York to Los Angeles, California, and from St. Paul, Minnesota, to San Antonio, Texas. These clubs and recreational centers are also an important feature in industrial communities.

### Splendid Colored Women Workers

Not only in groups, but as individuals, the women felt the call of this great and important work, and responded from every walk of life. There were many offers of volunteer service, and Miss Mary Cromwell, of Washington, D. C., was one of those to offer. She spent the summer at Camp Dix as a volunteer information and emergency hostess, and completed her two months of observation and service, feeling that there was an imperative need for the workers to be able to differentiate between types of people and to deal with each type scientifically as well as sympathetically; to know enough about such things as Home Service, War Risk Insurance, Protective Agencies, and Allotments, to answer any question that might be asked.

Miss Cromwell was well fitted both by training and experience for her work. As an undergraduate at Ann Arbor, she spent her summers in New York doing special investigations for the Charity Organization Society. After graduating, she became a teacher in the Dunbar High School of Washington, and there she became interested in the Washington alleys, and opened a settlement in one of the most congested districts. Later, she received her "master's degree" from the University of Pennsylvania for special research work in psychology.

The arduous task of directing the work of the Industrial Section of the War Work Council was given over to Miss Mary E. Jackson, as Special Industrial Worker among Colored Women for the War Work Council. She was appointed in December, 1917. Prior to that time, Miss Jackson did statistical work in the Labor Department of the State of Rhode Island.

· Associated with Miss Bowles in this War Work Council of colored women as heads of departments in addition to Miss Mary E. Jackson, were Miss Crystal Bird, girls' worker; Mrs. Vivian W. Stokes, who at one time was associated with the National Urban

League and assisted in making a survey of New York City in connection with the Urban League of New York (Mrs. Stokes' work in connection with the Room Registry work has already been mentioned); Mrs. Lucy B. Richmond, special worker for town and country; Miss Mabel S. Brady, recruiting secretary in the Personnel Bureau; Miss Juliette Dericotte, special student worker; Mrs. Cordelia A. Winn, formerly a teacher in the public schools of Columbus, Ohio; Mrs. Ethel J. Kindle, special office worker. Miss Josephine V. Pinyon was appointed a special war worker in August, 1917. She is a graduate of Cornell University, a former teacher, and a student Y. W. C. A. secretary from 1912 to 1916.

The field workers were Mrs. Adele Ruffin, South Atlantic Field, appointed in October, 1917. Mrs. Ruffin was a teacher for some years at Kittrell College, and then secretary of the Y. W. C. A. branch at Richmond, Virginia. Miss May Belcher had charge of the South Central field and Miss Maria L. Wilder of the Southwestern field. Miss Elizabeth Carter was loaned to the Association work by the Board of Education of New Bedford, Massachusetts, where she is the only colored teacher in the city. She is chairman of the Northeastern Federation of Colored Women's Clubs, and former president of the National Association of Colored Women's Clubs. She was placed in charge of the center in Washington, D. C.

Aside from these, there was a small army of club and recreation workers, Hostess House workers, industrial workers, and supervisors. Throughout the trying ordeal of directing the work of these assistants, and meeting the huge problems presented to the council, Miss Bowles remained perhaps the most effective and achieving, and at the same time, noiseless worker among the colored women in this country.

### Women's Division, Council of National Defense

The Council of National Defense made the best organized attempt at mobilizing the colored women of all the war organizations. In most Northern States it was felt that separate organizations were superfluous, yet, on the other hand, in many cases it was agreed that the work could be best served by distinct units. There were many ramifications to the work of the Council of Defense; registration of women, the weighing and measuring of babies, the establishment of milk stations, health and recreations centers, supervision of women in industry, correlation with other war organizations. Different States excelled in different phases of the work. In the establishment of Child Welfare and the conservation of infancy Alabama seems to be the banner state, the best work emanating from Tuskegee, where the examination of infants was under the care of Mrs. J. W. Whitaker. At Birmingham, Alabama, Mrs. H. C. Davenport had charge of the activities of the Council and was particularly successful in the establishment of Community houses at two great industrial centers, Acipco and Bessemer. In the first community, where the managers of the plant had established a model village with community house and all forms of Community life, the entire program of the Council of Defense was carried through, conservation of children, attention to health and recreation, with a very strong emphasis on food conservation. In the latter instance, a Community house established in the heart of the village of Bessemer concentrated on child welfare, food conservation, and war gardens.

### Service in Various States

Two women in Florida stand out as doing yeoman service under the work of the Women's Committee of the Council of Defense. Mrs. Mary McLeod Bethune, who at Daytona, where her splendid school is situated, pushed forward the work of the Emergency Circle, Negro War Relief, and Miss Eartha White, the State Chairman of the Colored Woman's Section of the Council of Defense. Under her direction Florida was organized into excellent working units, with a particular concentration on a Mutual Protection League for Working Girls, who had taken up the unfamiliar work of elevator girls, bell girls in hotels, and chauffeurs. From this it was not far to a Union of Girls in Domestic Service, a by-product of war conditions that might well be continued in every city and hamlet in the country.

In Colorado, the women formed themselves into a Negro Women's Auxiliary War Council, a Negro Women's League for Service, and a Red Cross Auxiliary, all apparently working under the general management of the Council of Defense. In Georgia, the president of the Georgia State Federation of Colored Women's Clubs, Mrs. Alice Dugged Carey of Atlanta, reported organizations in Tallapoosa County, a community canning center in Bremen, Coweta and Cobb counties, with other organizations in every important city. The Illinois women, organized into a Committee on Colored Women, worked in coöperation with the Urban League for training of Negro Women.

Delaware did not have a separate organization of the Council of Defense, but the race was represented on the State Committee, and through them work was carried on. Mrs. Blanche W. Stubbs, president of the City Federation of Christian Workers, represented the women, and through her efforts the usual classes in food conservation were established at the Thomas Garrett Settlement, while a baby-weighing station was established, and a public nurse appointed.

The work in Indiana was carried on by a separate division, largely directed by the State President of Colored Women's Clubs, Mrs. Gertrude B. Hill. Kentucky, with no special woman's division, specialized on the protection of girls. The best work done in Louisiana was in the conservation of children through the weighing and measuring of babies, and in the effective registration of the women and the conservation of food.

Maryland did some splendid and effective work under the direction of Miss Ida Cummings, the State Chairman of the Colored Women's Committee. Practically every phase of the inclusive program mapped out by the Council of Defense was carried through, and a public-speaking class at the Bowie Summer School was most successful. Mississippi was organized by Miss Sallie Green, of Sardis, into eleven sections, corresponding with a similar organization among the white women, with good work done in child conservation at Jackson. Mrs. Victoria Clay Haley saw to it that Missouri did effective work. Colored women in North Carolina merged their war activities into one, and were most successful in training camp activities, the War Camp Community Service maintaining an interesting work at Charlotte. In Portland, Oregon, the Rosebud Study Club, as was the case with so many clubs, turned its attention to knitting and a practical study of food conservation. In Columbia, South Carolina, the Phyllis Wheatley Club opened a community center to be used as a clearing-house for war activities, welcoming all war organizations to work within its walls—Y. W. C. A., Red Cross, War Camp Community Service, and Council of Defense.

In Tennessee, Mrs. Cora Burke, of Knoxville had a successful work; registration of nurses was particularly complete. The colored women of Nashville had a tag day to raise funds for their Branch Council of National Defense. Virginia concentrated on food conservation and the Children's Year, with most successful war gardens. A Colored Woman's Volunteer League was organized at Newark, New Jersey, as a branch of the Mayor's committee, of the Woman's Committee of the Council of National Defense, Mrs. Amorel Cook, president. This league established a canteen and specialized on making soldiers feel at home.

### War Problems of Living

The problems of living, made by the war, which were solved sometimes in whole, sometimes in part by the Woman's Committee of National Defense, were many and various. For instance there was the shifting of the percentage of women in the rural population particularly in the South, the same condition which was met in the North in industrial plants. The employment of women in the cotton fields was as great a problem in its way as the mass of girlhood in the Northern mills. This employment of the women could not but react upon the child, with a consequent lowering of child vitality and raising of infant mortality. It was this condition which the Council of Defense tried to meet, and to forestall the inevitable problems of reconstruction. Hence the establishment of stations where babies were weighed, measured, tested, and placed under weekly supervision with competent nurses in charge. Perhaps the various units did not always accomplish this end, but it was an ideal worth striving for.

### "The Lure of the Khaki"

One of the fundamental problems of the War—no new one but suddenly aggravated by the abnormal atmosphere and excitement accompanying the presence of large numbers of soldiers—was that of the relationship of the young girl and the soldier. What has been called "the lure of the khaki" is but an expression on the part of the girl of her admiration for the spirit of the men who are willing to give their lives, if need be, in the defense of their country. How to win this feeling into the right channels was one of the problems of the women in the war. It was met by two organizations, the Young Women's Christian Association, of which we have spoken, and the War Camp Community Service. It was the duty of the latter organi-

zation to recreate home ties for enlisted men in cities adjacent to
training camps.

It was in providing this home atmosphere that the War Camp
Community Service was most successful. Entertainment was developed for the colored soldiers; concessions let for poolrooms, picture
shows, canteens and cafeterias in connection with the work. But
where the War Camp Community Service was most successful was
in the chaperoned dances, given at the clubrooms. Here "the lure
of the khaki" might find conventional self-expression. The largest
of the Negro Community Service Clubs were in Des Moines, Iowa;
Battle Creek, Michigan; Louisville, Kentucky; Chillicothe, Ohio;
Charlotte, North Carolina; Petersburg and Newport News, Virginia;
Washington, D. C.; Baltimore, Maryland; Atlanta, Georgia; Montgomery, Alabama; and Columbia, South Carolina.

This working together for a common purpose is resulting in
building up a new community consciousness among our own people
and in turning our thoughts to community projects of a permanent
nature. Early in the war, work was started at Des Moines, Iowa.
From that time, with the next two centers at Chattanooga, Tennessee,
there were established in all sixty-six centers, located in Richmond,
Newport News, Lynchburg, Norfolk, Petersburg and Peniman, Vir-
ginia; Nitro, West Virginia; Pittsburgh, Philadelphia, Williamsport,
Germantown, Pennsylvania; San Antonio, Houston and Fort Worth,
Texas; St. Louis and Kansas City, Missouri; Washington, D. C.;
Winston-Salem and Charlotte, North Carolina; Youngstown, Day-
ton, Cincinnati and Columbus, Ohio; St. Paul, Minnesota; Orange,
Jersey City, Burlington and Montclair, New Jersey; Atlanta and
Augusta, Georgia; Brooklyn and New York City; Charleston and
Columbia, South Carolina; Detroit, Michigan; Indianapolis, Indiana;
Little Rock, Arkansas; Louisville, Kentucky; Chicago, Illinois; with
a special industrial worker at Chester, Pennsylvania, in the person
of Mrs. Sarah Fernandis, of Baltimore, an experienced social worker.

## The Circle for Negro War Relief

Time and time again it was borne in upon the inner consciousness of the women of the race that though the various organizations
for war relief were doing all that was humanly possible for the soldiers of both races, they were inadequate for all the needs of the
Negro soldier and his family. There were avenues open for more

extensive relief; there were places as yet untouched by any organization; there were programs of direct War Relief and Constructive Relief work which needed to be carried out and some separate organization for this work was an imperative necessity. So the Circle for Negro War Relief came into existence in November, 1917. The leading spirit in this movement was Mrs. Emily Bigelow Hapgood, the president, and associated around her were the best minds of the country, white and colored. The Circle was incorporated, and dedicated itself to the purpose of promoting the welfare of Negro soldiers and their dependent families as they might be affected by the emergencies of war.

The success of this Circle was immediate and phenomenal. Within a few months, sixty "units" were formed, extending from New York to Utah, to the far South, throughout the East, and middle West. Each unit dedicated itself in its particular locality to the relief of some vital need either in the Community or in some nearby camp. For instance Ambulance Unit of N. Y. gave a two-thousand dollar ambulance to Camp Upton. Unit No. 29 in St. Helena, South Carolina, not only did the usual war knitting and letter writing, but during the influenza epidemic formed itself into a health committee in coöperation with the Red Cross.

It would be difficult to give a complete report of the work of all the units. It forms a voluminous mass of interesting and illuminating statistics. The activities of the Circle ranged from the making of comfort kits to the furnishing of chewing gum to the soldiers; from the supplying of victrolas and records to the introduction of Theodore Roosevelt, Irvin Cobb and Needham Roberts at Carnegie Hall; from the giving of Christmas trees in Harlem to Southern dinners for the home-sick boys in Augusta, Georgia; from contributions of air-cushions from Altoona, Pennsylvania, to the issuing of educational pamphlets on the subject of the Negro soldier.

The Circle of Negro War Relief and the Crispus Attucks Circle organized in Philadelphia in March, 1918, constituted the nearest approach to a Red Cross or other organization of this character through which the colored people coöperated during the war. - The Crispus Attucks Circle did for Philadelphia what the Circle of Negro War Relief did for New York. Its name fitly commemorated the first Negro who gave up his life to help make "the world safe for democracy." The one great project to which it directed all its energies was the attempted establishment in Philadelphia of a base hospital for Negro soldiers, in which Negro physicians and Negro nurses should care for their own.

It may be objected and is frequently a source of controversy that separate hospitals are non-essential. Idle and fallacious reasoning! They are needed in some places as schools, churches and social organizations are needed. A moot question, not to be thrashed out here; merely a remark in passing that the Crispus Attuck Circle saw a need, a vital need, and aimed to fill it. Certainly if every individual in the world saw the vital need in his own particular home circle or community and met that need with joyous service, there would be no more wars. This is what the women of the race have done since April, 1917.

As the Circle of Negro War Relief radiated its influence from New York City and the Crispus Attucks Circle concentrated its efforts in Philadelphia, so all over the United States various independent and private organizations for the relief of the soldier came into being. The Soldiers' Comfort Unit of the War Service Center opened headquarters on Massachusetts Avenue, Boston. It was one of the hundreds of similar organizations made up of women who instinctively got together to work for the great cause, and who, with a small beginning, found themselves a part of a big work with possibilities only limited by the ability to meet them. In February, 1918, Mrs. H. C. Lewis called together a small group of women who in a week's time supplied an urgent need for knitted garments at Newport News. From this beginning, made with a dozen women, the unit grew into an organization of a hundred and seventy-seven women and eventually connected itself with the Circle of Negro War Relief.

In the first days the work was almost exclusively for the comfort of the soldiers, but before many months had passed the scope of the organization had widened to a place of entertainment for the soldiers, visits to hospitals, visits to the nearby camp—Devens, with home-made pies and cakes; liberty sings on Sunday afternoons; lectures on social hygiene and special educational lectures; coöperation with "Company L" auxiliary, and with the Red Cross.

The officers of the Soldiers' Comfort Unit were: President, Miss M. L. Baldwin; first vice-president, Mrs. C. H. Garland; second vice-president, Mrs. Mary E. Rollins; recording secretary, Mrs.

Geo. W. Torbey; financial secretary, Mrs. Wm. L. Reed; treasurer, Mrs. C. Henry Robbins; executive secretary, Mrs. U. A. Ridley.

Executive Committee—Mrs. Lucy Lewis, Chairman; Mrs. Wm. J. Williams, Mrs. Maud Cuney Hare, Mrs. Wm. Cromwell, Mrs. Geo. B. Lewis, Mrs. Amos Mason, Mrs. Alice Casneau, Mrs. Jas Hinton, Mrs. Agnes Adams. Chairman Red Cross, Mrs. A. M. Gilbert; Chairman House Committee, Mrs. Geo. Drummond; Chairman Hospitality Committee, Mrs. Nellie Brown Mitchell.

After a year of work the Soldiers' Comfort Unit found itself facing a still larger field, the returning soldiers coming from scenes of horror and devastation with problems and needs. Like all of the war organizations of the women of the race, they found their work had only just begun.

## Woman's Auxiliary of the 15th Regiment

In the early days of the old Fifteenth New York Regiment, when colored men were volunteering as members of the military organization which was to become the first New York State Guard composed of colored men, it occurred to a thoughtful woman of the race, a New Yorker by birth, that earnest colored women banded together could be a potent factor in the life of the regiment.

The idea was carried out, and the Woman's Auxiliary, Fifteenth Regiment, was organized May 2, 1917, with one hundred members. It received its credentials from Colonel William Hayward, May 9. The first definite work undertaken was the investigation of the cases of men whose dependents claimed exemption for them. This was an important factor in the perfect recruiting of the regiment and won commendation from the commanding officer and his official staff.

It is the exclusive privilege of the colored people to adopt the slogan, "No Color Line." It would seem a strange commentary on the magnanimity of the American people to note that those who are the first to adopt the policy of no discrimination are the ones against whom that discrimination is most often practiced. We have noted how in every instance where organizations of colored women have been formed for War Relief there is a definite policy of "No Color Line." Now and then the fact was proclaimed publicly in sign or in motto, as in Boston and by the Josephine Gray Colored

Lady Knitters of Detroit, Michigan, who "knitted for all American soldiers regardless of race, color, or nationality."

## Colored Women in the Loan Drives

But not only in the definite work of relief, in knitting, sewing, care of dependents of soldiers or in the more spectacular forms of war work were the women engaged. The raising of the sinews of War was a problem which the United States faced. Every man, woman, and child in the country needed to be taxed to the utmost. How to make the giving a pleasing privilege rather than a doleful duty devolved upon the women of the country. Five Liberty Loan drives, six Red Cross drives, the constant Thrift Stamp Drive, and a tremendous United War Camp Drive, wherein uncountable billions were spoken of airily, staggered the average mind both in prospect and retrospect. But Americans learned to think in big figures. Every one got the habit of saving; and the purse-strings of America were permanently opened for the relief of the needs of the nation and to aid needy peoples overseas.

This reaction on the national conscience is of inestimable value. Charity will never again be the perfunctory thing that it was before the Great War. Penury in giving will be frowned down upon as immoral. And this quickening of the national conscience, this loosening of the national purse, is due in no small measure to the fervor and zeal with which the women of the nation threw themselves into the campaigns for filling the war coffers.

As was to be expected, the colored women were foremost in all the financial campaigns. The National Association of Colored Women organized at the very beginning of the war to coöperate in every way with the Woman's Council of Defense. Mrs. Philip North Moore, President of the National Council of Women, says, "No women worked harder than the women of the National Association of Colored Women."

Mrs. Mary B. Talbert, President of the National Association of Colored Women, which has a membership of a hundred thousand, is authority for the statement that in the Third Liberty Loan the colored women of the United States raised about five million dollars. Savannah, Georgia, alone raised a quarter of a million dollars. Poor colored women in a tobacco factory of Norfolk, Virginia, subscribed ninety-one thousand dollars. Macon, Georgia, subscribed about twenty thousand.

The National War Savings Committee appointed colored women to conduct campaigns for the War Savings Committee. One of the most notable of these appointments by the Secretary of the Treasury was that of Mrs. Laura Brown, of Pittsburgh. She maintained an office from which whirlwind campaigns emanated, and set a standard of efficiency of organization not easily equaled.

### War Work Among Negro Children

One of the most effective ways of reaching the people of any community is through the children. Hence the work of the colored teachers in reaching the race through the children under their care, has been in the highest degree effectual. Throughout the South, in the middle Atlantic states in which there is a separate school system, in the Middle West, and in the Southwest; in public schools, in endowed institutions, in colleges—in short wherever colored teachers are employed to teach colored children, there was a constant and beneficial influence being exerted in the entire race through its children. This influence made for loyalty, patriotism unquestioning and devoted; and particularly did this influence raise the quota of the race's contribution to the National war chest. Colored schools taught by colored teachers sent in every community a pro rata to the Thrift Stamp, Red Cross, United War Campaign, and Liberty Loans in considerable excess of the natural percentage. It would have been easy to have failed just here with the children; it was difficult in many communities to overcome the natural obstacles. But they were overcome. The amounts raised in all National drives through the colored women teachers working with their children, are a monumental credit to the women of the race.

### The Negro Exodus of 1917-18

Such a move as this was more important than appears on the face of the bald statement of the fact. In the Northern cities directly affected by the exodus of Southern Negroes in 1917 and 1918, a by-product of the war, there was suffering, intense and widespread, among the Negroes suddenly thrust into a climate and conditions for which their life in the South had given them no preparation. Some cities, notably Detroit, met the situation with a whole-hearted desire on the part of the civic authorities to cope with the condition correctly and humanely. Other cities lamented the influx into their borders, and let the new population shift for itself as best it could, resulting in a pitiful increase of the death rate in pneumonia. The unprecedentedly hard winter of 1917-1918 was trying even to those inured to the rigors of a Northern winter. Some cities drove out the invaders, or made conditions so uncomfortable that they drifted away, or suffered in silence. In other cases, notably Chester, Pennsylvania, the colored women of the city took the matter in their own hands, and saved as best they could the pitiful strugglers in their search for homes and work.

The tide of migration swept northward, and broke in a huge wave, beginning at Chester, Pennsylvania, in the East, St. Louis and East St. Louis in the Middle West, and Los Angeles in the West, the crest of the wave breaking in Philadelphia, Detroit and Chicago. It was a situation which the war had inevitably brought about—the increase in munition plants and shipyards, with their need for more help, and consequent high wages; it was helped by nature—the boll-weevil devastating the little which the Southern laborers owned in cotton-field and home; it was fostered by the growing unrest and bitterness due to lack of economic and educational opportunities and to injustice dealt at home. When the true history of the great Negro Exodus of 1917-1918 shall be written, it will prove as fascinating and as peculiar in its psychological ramifications as the story of the Exodus from Egypt.

Not the least interesting and splendid is the part played by the colored women in those cities where the crest of the wave broke. Hunger and privation, even in the face of the big wages paid by the huge war plants, stared the newcomers in the face, for there was not always work enough, and illness laid off many of those who had made places for themselves in the industrial elysium. The housing conditions, or rather the lack of them, constitute one of the blackest chapters in the history of the movement. Here is where the Christian fortitude and love of the colored women who lived in those cities shine forth resplendently. They gave up their own homes to the newcomers; they endured discomforts and inconveniences to help the women thus pitifully thrust into these adverse conditions; they taught the women from the South the art of coping with the northern climate; they nursed them when the inevitable sickness broke out; they gave them warm clothing and taught them how to spend money to the best advantage in purchasing suitable clothes and proper food; they took women and children into their homes, and helped them in ways that only women understand how to help each other.

## Maintaining the Negro Morale

Rumors, many and various, of the disaffection of the Negro, of his lack of patriotism, of the influence upon him of so-called German propaganda, of the need of stimulating his patriotic fervor, swept through the country in the spring and summer of 1918. Just how much of this so-called propaganda was German, and how much American, and how much of it rumors which had their rise in hysterical fear, it is not given us to know. Why there was a loss of patriotic interest in certain localities was not hard to discover. Here and there studied indifference on the part of certain organizations toward the well-meant efforts of the colored women in attempting to help in war relief; labor conditions; the old, old stories of prejudice and growing bitterness in the labor situation; rumors of increased lynching activities—from all these a lukewarmness towards the conduct of the war had grown up in various cities. And it was here again that the women met a difficult problem and helped to solve it.

Again we look to the army of women teachers, and their subtle and pervasive influence over the youth of the race, and through children over their parents. It would be difficult to measure the service of these women in this particular direction.

Here and there, however, there was a more spectacular appeal made to the patriotic emotions of the race through pageants, demonstrations, or mass meetings. In some cases, the schools through school pageants and plays appealed directly to the patriotic emotions; plays written by Negro authors were staged, commencement exercises became rallying grounds of calls to the warmth of the race in its love for the nation.

## Colored Women in War Industries

War has a way of forcing expedients. From 1914 until November, 1918, the economic balance of the nation was sadly upset, first by the stopping of the tide of immigration from Europe, second by the exodus of the Negro to the North, third by the drastic sweep of the draft law. The first opened the door of opportunity to the Negro laborer, the second depleted the fields of the South, the third plunged the colored woman pell-mell into the industrial world—an entirely new place for her.

"For generations colored women have been working in the fields of the South. They have been the domestic servants of both the South and the North, accepting the positions of personal service open to them. Hard work and unpleasant work has been their lot, but they have been almost entirely excluded from our shops and factories. Tradition and race prejudice have played the largest part in their exclusion. The tardy development of the South and the failure of the colored woman to demand industrial opportunities have added further values. Clearly, also, two hundred years of slavery and fifty years of industrial boycott in both the North and the South, following the Civil War, have done little to encourage or to develop industrial aptitudes. For these reasons, the colored women have not entered the ranks of the industrial army in the past."

But war expediency, for a time at least, partially opened the door of industry to them. It was an experiment and like all experiments, it fell against problems, and those problems were met by the earnest consideration of several agencies. We have already spoken of the splendid work of this department of the Young Women's Christian Association, under the direction of Miss Mary E. Jackson of Providence, Rhode Island. In June, 1918, a joint committee was formed in New York to study the employment of colored women in that city and its environs. Serving on that committee were representatives from practically all the philanthropic organizations in the city, and the result of its labors through two investigators, Mrs. Gertrude McDougald (colored) and Miss Jesse Clarke (white), were given publicity in an interesting pamphlet, from which the above paragraph was quoted. It is a significant fact that the colored woman in industry in a short time had reached the point where she merited trained investigation.

"Come out of the kitchen, Mary," was the slogan of the colored woman in war time. She doffed her cap and apron and donned her overalls. Some States, such as Maryland and Florida, specialized in courses in motor mechanics and automobile driving.

The munition factories took the girls in gladly. Grim statistics prove that their scale of wages was definitely lower than a man's doing the same work, and sad to say a considerable fraction below that of white girls in the same service, although Delaware reports some very high-priced, skilled ammunition testers, averaging seven to twelve dollars a day. The colored girls blossomed out as switchboard operators, stock takers, wrappers, elevator operators, subway porters, ticket choppers, track-walkers, trained signallers, yard-walkers. They went into every possible kind of factory devoted to the production of war materials, from the most dangerous posts in munition plants to the delicate sewing in aeroplane factories. Colored girls and colored women drove motor trucks, unloaded freight cars, dug ditches, handled hardware around shipways and hardware houses, packed boxes. They struggled with the discomforts of ice and fertilizing plants. They learned the delicate intricacies of all kinds of machines, and the colored woman running the elevator or speeding a railroad on its way by signals was a common sight.

Just what the effect of this marvelous influx of colored women into the industrial world would have upon the race was a problem viewed with considerable interest. Pessimists predicted a sociological and psychological upheaval in the ranks of the women of the race. A strange thing about it was that there was no perceptible racial disintegration and the colored women bore their changed status and higher economic independence with much more equanimity than white women on a corresponding scale of living. The reason for this may perhaps be found in the fact that the colored woman had a heritage of 300 years of work back of her. Her children were used to being left to shift for themselves; her home was used to being cared for after sundown. The careful supervision of the War Work Council and the Council of Defense over the health and hours of the woman in industry averted the cataclysm of lowered vitality and eventual unfitness for maternity.

The possible economic effect of this entrance into the unknown fields of industry on the part of the colored woman will be that when pre-war conditions return and she is displaced by men and is forced to make her way back into domestic service, the latter will be placed on a strictly business basis and the vocation of is forced to make her way back into domestic service, the latter will be placed on a strictly business basis and the vocation of housekeeping and home-making will be raised to the dignity of a profession.

We have touched lightly the Negro woman in the world war. Lightly perforce, because of her innate modesty and reticent carelessness in proclaiming her own good deeds. She emerges from the war more serious-minded, more responsible, with a higher opinion of her own economic-importance; with a distinct and definite aim and ambition to devote her life to the furthering of the cause for which her men died on Flanders fields. She has served the Red Cross at home and begged to serve it abroad; she has probed to the depths the real meaning of the word Christianity; she has formed a second line of defense at home; she has learned the real value of community service, and what it means to give of her time, means, and smiles to the weary soldiers passing through her town; she has organized special circles of war relief on her own initiative, and given all that she could afford, from the homely apple and sandwich and cigarette to an ambulance for service overseas.

She has given regally, munificently of her little to help fill the national war chest, and when there was no more in her slender purse she has given her time and persuasiveness to induce others to follow her example. She has endowed and maintained Hostess Houses and helped support the wives and children of the men in service. When disaffection threatened, she fostered patriotism and overcame propaganda with simple splendid loyalty. She gave up ease and clear skies for the dangers and hardships of death-dealing labor. She shut her eyes to past wrongs and present discomforts and future uncertainties. She stood large-hearted, strong-handed, clear-minded, splendidly capable, and did, not her bit, but her best, and the world is better for her work and her worth.

*Alice Dunbar-Nelson*

# CHAPTER XXVIII

## SOCIAL WELFARE AGENCIES

*Important Welfare Work of the Young Men's Christian Association and Other Organized Bodies—Negro Secretaries of the Y. M. C. A.—The Problem of Illiteracy in the Camps—The Social Secretaries—Results of Education—The Y. W. C. A. Hostess Houses—The Knights of Columbus—Caring for Returned Soldiers.*

Prior to the outbreak of the war it was a well-established fact that the Young Men's Christian Association, the Young Women's Christian Association, the Red Cross, and other organized bodies primarily concerned with the welfare of people in general, had figured so largely in the life of the young men prior to their call to arms that something should be done to enable these agencies to throw around them the same influences under which they came when at home. One of the first efforts, therefore, to provide for the social betterment of the men under arms was to connect these movements officially with the Government, that they might function efficiently in caring for the soldiers at the front. It was observed that the social welfare organizations could adapt themselves as successfully to the needs of men in times of war as in times of peace. At the beginning of the war the War Work Council declared that the same thing done for white men would be done for colored men when in the various cantonments, and while it has been difficult to carry out this letter of the law, for many reasons too tedious to be mentioned, Dr. J. E. Moorland, the Senior Secretary of the Young Men's Christian Association in charge of colored men's work, believes that the Negro has come more nearly to receiving a square deal in this instance than in anything else in the history of the country.

When the unusual appeal was made to the American people, adequate funds were raised to finance the work of the welfare organizations. Nearer to the end of hostilities, however, when a more systematic effort for financing all of these social organizations had to be made, the Government provided that all such agencies should be absorbed by the seven recognized groups, and a national drive for $170,000,000 was made by these organizations, resulting in raising the desired amount. They were therefore at an early period in a position to construct successful machinery for the training of social workers to supply these needs throughout the camps in this country and among the soldiers overseas. While it must be admitted that it was impossible to choose upon such short notice persons who met in every way the requirements for this unusual task, the personnel of the Young Men's Christian Association staff so far as the colored workers were concerned were of a high class.

At the head of this staff, to select and equip for this unusual service the numerous secretaries needed in the camps and cantonments, was Dr. J. E. Moorland, Senior Secretary of the Young Men's Christian Association. Associated with him was Mr. Robert B. DeFrantz, visiting secretary of the Des Moines camp, and formerly engaged in the work at Kansas City, Missouri. There were also the placement secretaries, Mr. William J. Faulkner and Mr. Max Yergan, who after his return from Africa, assisted in recruiting men; Professor Charles H. Wesley of Howard University doing similar work. J. Francis Gregory and George L. Johnson, two specialists in religious work, were later added. The former directed his efforts toward the religious life of the men in the camps, while the latter, a noted tenor, rendered valuable service with his singing.

### Negro Secretaries of the Y. M. C. A.

At the beginning of the War Work Council it was decided to send Negro secretaries to care for troops of their own race. There were fifty-five centers or groups in Army camps with Association privileges, served by two hundred and sixty-eight secretaries in the home camps and forty-nine secretaries serving overseas. The grand total of all colored secretaries was three hundred and thirty-one. The buildings in which these secretaries worked were twenty-five "E" type and National Guard buildings. The other centers were housed in barracks, mess halls, and tents.

"This work, too," according to Dr. J. E. Moorland, its moving spirit, "was not a haphazard one. It had a definite purpose, promoted by carefully selected specialists. To be more explicit, it is well to describe a staff organization which is responsible for the work in a building. It is composed of a building secretary, who is the executive; a religious work secretary, who has charge of the religious activities, including personal work among the soldiers, Bible class and religious meetings; an educational secretary, who promotes lectures and educational classes, and uses whatever means he may have at hand to encourage intellectual development; a physical secretary, who has charge of athletics and various activities for the physical welfare of the soldiers, works in the closest relationship with the military officers and is often made responsible for all of the physical activities in the camp; a social secretary, who promotes the social activities, including entertainments, "stunts" and moving pictures; a business secretary, who keeps close tab on the sale of stamps, postcards, and such supplies as may be handled by the Association, and is held responsible for the proper accounting of finances. In every case these secretaries were thoroughly investigated before being appointed and were required to be members of evangelical churches in good standing, and men capable of commanding the respect of the soldiers with whom they work.

### The Problem of Illiteracy

' The large number of illiterates who were brought into the various camps of the country brought with them a tremendous problem. Many of them could not sign the payroll. Some of them did not know the right from the left hand, and not a few were not sure about their names. The Association was able to solve this problem by teaching thousands of men to read and write their names. Some men. after having learned to write their names," says Dr. Moorland, "have actually shouted for joy over the new-found power which at last had released them from the shackles of an oppressive ignorance. Speakers of both races have inspired the men and enlarged their vision. Many men with a better educational equipment have increased their talents by sober thinking along with purposeful programs of reading.

*Above*—Colored Women War Workers of the Young Women's Christian Association at
  Hostess House, Camp Upton, Long Island.
*Below*—Colored American Red Cross Canteen War Workers who canteened all Colored
  soldier troop trains passing through Chicago to and from the front.
*First Row Left to Right*—Mrs. Eva Jenifer, Captain Dr. Mary Fitzbutler Waring, Mrs.
  DeWitt Smith.
*Second Row Left to Right*—Lieut. Hattie Oldham, Mrs. Sadie Anderson, Mrs. Helen Thorne
  Mrs. Juanita Hawkins, Mrs. Mary Wickliffe, Mrs. Lillian Gully, Lieut. Mayme Haddox
Dr. Mary Fitzbutler Waring is also Chairman of the Col. Denison Red Cross Auxiliary, and
  Chairman of Red Cross Work of the Colored Women's Clubs of the U S

*Above*—Negro American Red Cross Workers of the Byhalia Colored Auxiliary of northern Mississippi where Negroes outnumber the whites five to one.
*Below*—Colored boys on troop train passing through New Orleans to training camps being served with chocolates and cigarettes by Colored Auxiliary of American Red Cross.

*Top, Left to Right*—1st Lt. Ewell W. Clarke, Asst. Personnel Adjutant Hdq. Staff, 92nd Div. 1st Lt. Almando Henderson, 367th Inf. 1st Lt. F. S. Upshur, 350th F. A. *Center, Left to Right*—2nd Lt. R. D. Hardeway, 367th Inf. Capt. Aaron Day, Jr., 317th Am. Tr. 2nd Lt. A. M. Watson, 350th Mchn. Gun Bat. *Below, Left to Right*—2nd Lt. Scott A. Moyer, 349th F. A.; 2nd Lt. Wm. F. Grady, 368th Inf., and 2nd Lt. Walter W. Scott, 368th Inf., who was gassed at the Argonne Forest in an attack on Binarville.

*Above*—Colored messengers of Motorcycle Corps, 372nd Headquarters, who kept communication lines alive at all hours during the big drive in Champagne, Argonne and at Verdun.

*Below*—American White and Negro soldiers being served to chocolate and sandwich rolls in canteen established in basement of American Red Cross Bureau of Refugees at Toulouse

*1bove*—Burial place of the 92nd Division near a roadside leading out of Pont-a-Mousson to Metz. Here are laid to rest those who fell in the operations against Metz and those who died of sickness during that period.

*Below*—A wayside church near the front lines in a French sector occupied by American Negro Soldiers

OVERSEAS SECRETARIES OF THE YOUNG MEN'S CHRISTIAN ASSOCIATION.

*Left Top*—E. L. Snyder.  *Left Center*—J. A. Croon.  *Below*—Moses A. Davis.
*Center Top*—Group of "Y" Secretaries ready to sail for France.
*Below*—L. F. Seldon behind the lines in France just emerging from the trip through the
    trenches.
*Right*, at top—Thos. M. Clayton.  *Right Center*—Gary Ward Moore.  *Below*—G. W. Jackson.
All the above overseas Y. M. C. A. Secretaries are well known to the American Negro
    Soldiers who served overseas.

*Above*—"Big Nims" of the 3rd Battalion, 366th Infantry, who found great amusement in contemplating the grotesque appearance of his comrade with a gas mask adjusted over his face and head. Many hours of gloom was dispelled by the good humor of Nims which together with his unquestionable courage at many times served to cheer the flagging spirits of his comrades.

*Below*—Group of Negro Soldiers behind the lines being instructed in approved methods of using gas masks before going forward to the trenches.

**NEGRO OFFICERS OF THE FAMOUS 8th ILLINOIS** (fought in France as the 370th Infantry) decorated by French Government for gallantry in action. *Front Row*, left to right.—Capt. G. M. Allen, Lt. O. A. Browning, Capt. D. J. Warner, Lt. Roy B. Tisdell. *Back*, left to right.—Lt. P. Hurd, Col. Otis B. Duncan, Major J. R. White, Capt. William W. Crawford, Lt. W. J. Warfield, Capt. M. Jackson. Lieutenant Warfield also received Distinguished Service Cross of United States by order of General Pershing (shown in the picture), likewise badge as expert rifleman.

"The religion of the soldiers was not neglected. Hundreds of Bible classes were conducted and religious meetings with purpose were largely attended. The best of both races have been able to give encouragement and helpful messages to the men, many of whom have had their faith strengthened; many others for the first time in their lives accepted the Christian faith. The effort was to give a religious program adapted to the lives of the men and enable them to go overseas and come back fit to look mother, wife, sister, and sweetheart in the face and not be ashamed.

"The emphasis, however, was placed upon life, and speakers were requested to avoid emphasizing death. Although the training in the army camps is physical development to a very marked degree, it was soon learned that there must be a recreational side. The physical director had to meet this need to prevent men from becoming sullen and morose. Baseball teams, football teams, boxing and all sorts of recreational games were staged. These proved to be as essential in the matter of self-defense as lectures and private talks on health and the protection of the body against the ravages of every form of vice."

### Work of the Social Secretaries

The social secretaries rendered no less a service than the other workers. In providing programs for the entertainment of the men, in presenting interesting moving pictures, in utilizing the talent of various communities near the camps for the needs of the men in camps, they accomplished a task which in the past had seemed impossible. The social secretary, moreover, enabled these men to entertain themselves. The Selective Draft brought together men of all grades, from the most illiterate to the highly trained university graduate, messing together side by side daily. Men who had lived in the atmosphere of vice and those who had been trained in the best Christian homes were thrown together in a common cause, wearing the same uniform, obeying the same orders. In this great mass the social secretary discovered remarkable talent, which was able to provide entertainment for the soldiers in the camps and at certain times for the people outside the camps.

According to Dr. Moorland, the letters of appreciation received from many of the soldiers for the service rendered by these faithful secretaries sound like a new edition of the Acts of the Apostles. "Not only in France are our men serving. We also have secretaries in East Africa, working with natives and British troops, and their story is that of pioneers laying foundations as Christian statesmen for the building of future manhood in that great continent; for they are serving men representing tribes from all parts of the continent of Africa, and these men are learning what unselfish service means as well as, in many cases, learning to read and write in the little evening schools provided for them."

There were thirty-nine official directors, giving their entire attention to directing recreational activities and thirty secretaries who served as song leaders. There were six or more secretaries, physical and social directors, however, to do recreational work and direct singing. It has been estimated that two million men attended these various centers for Negro soldiers every month; that there were two hundred lectures with an attendance of eighty a month; ten thousand Scriptures circulated every month; nine thousand personal interviews; seven thousand Christian decisions; eleven thousand war roll singers; one hundred and twenty-five thousand taking part in physical activities; five hundred motion picture exhibitions with an attendance of three hundred thousand; 1,250,000 letters written, and $110,000 worth of money orders sold.

## Important Results of Education

Out of such unusual efforts to educate, in fact to remake, the enlisted man, came important results. The Negro soldier was brought, so to speak, from a sequestered vale into the broad light of modern times, where various agencies which have constituted a leverage in the elevation of men gave him during these few months more opportunity for mental improvement than he had experienced during the other part of his life. Thousands of men were not only taught to read and write, but also formed the habit of reading good books, which in a short time showed results in the appreciation of higher ideals and in giving them a more intelligent attitude toward life. These agencies, too, operating among the whites and the blacks equally deficient in education during their early careers, tended to promote better relationship between the races and as a result to produce a higher class of men.

The record of these secretaries was highly commendable. First among those to attain recognition was Dr. Geo. W. Cabaniss, of Washington, D. C., known for a long time as the dean of the colored secretaries, a man who had much to do with making possible the camp for the training of the colored officers at Fort Des Moines; and who after the camp had been provided went into the service with them to serve these young men as a Y. M. C. A. secretary. Returning home after they were commissioned, Dr. Cabaniss abandoned his lucrative practice in the city of Washington and went to Camp Meade to serve as a secretary at one of the Y. M. C. A. huts. Being a Christian gentleman, Dr. Cabaniss was especially anxious to look after the morals of the young men, and in the end he was glad to report that the habits in general of the men who came under his supervision were of a very high order, and that they exhibited evidences of being men who would make good at the front. Among those who won distinction in reaching men may also be mentioned Matthew W. Bullock, William Stevenson, and J. C. Wright.

### Distinguished Service of Supervisors

Some mention should be made also of those men of color who although Y. M. C. A. workers went to France for supervision, to render a larger service than that of the average social worker. Among them were Mr. Max Yergan, President John Hope of Morehouse College, and Dr. H. H. Proctor of the First Congregational Church, Atlanta, Georgia. Mr. Max Yergan had already rendered distinguished service as an earnest worker among the British troops of color in Africa. His work in France, like that of President Hope, was largely that of a field secretary to consider cases of friction, discipline, and general difficulty and to administer affairs which could not be attended to by the staff on this side of the Atlantic. It was only late in the war that Dr. Proctor answered the call to engage in this same work. These gentlemen, in manifesting a spirit of sacrifice and interest in the welfare of the men at the front, not only exhibited examples worthy of emulation, but rendered the race and the country a distinguished service.

## The Y. W. C. A. Hostess Houses

The work had not gone forward very far when the peculiar need for a plan by which the wives and daughters of the enlisted men might visit them at camp necessitated the bringing in of women as Y. W. C. A. workers. It was accordingly provided that each of these camps, wherever practicable, should have hostess houses, to be placed in charge of a woman of honor. The hostess house was a means of communication between the enlisted men and their relatives. Here the sweetheart came to say goodbye to her loved one, the wife to see her husband for the last time, and the mother to bid her son farewell. The Y. W. C. A. maintained a colored hostess house in every camp where there were colored soldiers, the plan being the same as that for the white soldiers. The official report states that these houses "are not only hospitality centers, but also demonstrations to visitors of the best ways of entertaining and of serving food. Many men and women are here first brought in contact with high yet simple standards of social intercourse. Each house is a training center for new colored social workers."

The heads of these houses are among the best known women of the race, many of whom have been doing social work of a high type among their people for years. The need for such women, of course, was experienced abroad, but there was much objection to the sending of women of color to the front, just as there had been in the case of barring them from the Red Cross units. In the course of time, however, this prejudice was overcome and it was possible to send a number of women of color to serve in the hostess houses in France. The first of these to sail was Mrs. Helen Noble Curtis of New York, the widow of the late James L. Curtis, Minister Resident of the United States to Liberia. For a number of years she had been a member of the committee of management of the colored women's branch of the Y. W. C. A. As she had been in France and had learned to speak the language thoroughly, she was much desired for this work.

The appointment of Mrs. Curtis proved to be such a success that another colored secretary was sent over in the following month. This was Mrs. Addie W. Hunton of Brooklyn, New York, widow of the late William A. Hunton, the first International

Secretary of the Y. M. C. A. for colored men in America. She is an educated woman of excellent standing and had for a number of years been a moving spirit in Y. W. C. A. work. She had also traveled in Europe, studied at the University of Strasburg, and formed certain connections which enabled her to render the race invaluable service abroad. Mrs. Hunton was soon followed by Miss Kathryn M. Johnson, and later by twelve or more women of the same high character.

### Tributes to Y. M. C. A. Workers

"The colored Y. M. C. A. workers here in France," said Ralph W. Tyler, "working under handicaps, and limited, as to numbers, in proportion to the number of white Y. M. C. A. workers, and considering the proportionate number of colored soldiers in France, have been paid a high tribute by Colonel (now General) W. F. Creary. Writing to Wm. Stevenson, colored Y. M. C. A. secretary of Hut No. 2, General Creary said:

" 'I have seen the workings of your huts along the line, from the front line trenches to the base ports, and have been a personal recipient of the comforts afforded by them on many occasions.

" 'I have always been impressed by the zeal with which the secretaries, and others, have prosecuted their work, with untiring energy, and with their valor and bravery, for the work at the front cannot be done except by real red-blooded men.

" 'I have been particularly interested in the activities of your huts, devoted exclusively to the interests of colored soldiers since my assumption of the command of this camp, and I congratulate you on the progress you have made, and are making now.

" 'Besides the splendid athletic, social, and canteen service offered by yourself and your assistants, I have been much impressed by your activities in the educational departments, and have been much pleased to see many of OUR Colored soldiers, who have had but few advantages of early education, availing themselves of the advantages offered by you for the acquirement of knowledge of the elementary branches of education.

" 'Your thrift department is the means of many of OUR men saving their money and purchasing money orders to send back home, thereby placing their money where it should be.'

"In Mr. Stevenson's hut, Mrs. James L. Curtis looks after the canteen, and most laudably aids in the work of comforting the thousands of colored boys who are contributing their might in the interest of world democracy. Mr. Stevenson, to whom General Creary wrote this commendatory letter, is a Cincinnati, Ohio, boy, and he fairly bubbles in his enthusiasm in his work for colored soldiers.

"While visiting this particular point, I came in contact with the work of colored Y. M. C. A. people, who are seconding and coöperating with the work of the Army in a most effective way. Here I met Mrs. James L. Curtis, widow of our late Minister to Liberia, who is idolized by the men in the camp in which is located the particular Y. M. C. A. hut in which she labors. I also came in contact with and investigated the splendid work of Miss Kathryn Johnson, of Chicago, and Mrs. A. W. Hunton, the other two colored women Y. M. C. A. workers over here, and, unfortunately, the only three (with Mrs. Curtis) colored women assigned over here for war work by the Y. M. C. A. The effect of the work these three splendid colored women have done, and will continue to do, will be in evidence long after this war has been fought to a glorious peace. Here I also met the following colored Y. M. C. A. secretaries: Franklin Nichols, of Philadelphia, who has been here for more than a year; Prof. Moses A. Davis, of Evansville, Ind.; Rev. D. Leroy Ferguson, erstwhile rector of the Colored Episcopal church at Louisville, Ky.; Leon James, J. Green, and Wm. Stevenson. When I considered that all these Y. M. C. A. people, and most especially the women, forsook comfortable homes and zones of culture and refinement to come over here and, far from immediate relatives and friends, bury themselves among these colored soldiers in order that the greatest possible amount of sunshine might be shoved into the lives of these men helping to establish world democracy, I could not help but feel that those of the race, back in the states, who are at an absolutely safe distance from German bullets, shrapnel and gas, should consecrate themselves, also, so far as within their power, to the rendering of aid and comfort to these soldiers of ours.

"When I visited the hospital at this point and noted the many colored boys who were bearing their illness with a cheerfulness that was amazing, I could not help but feel much of the criticism one hears back in the states could well be held in abeyance and instead the efforts put forth in criticism expended in sympathy and efforts for 'our own' boys who are here so many thousand miles from home, enduring cheerfully for their country's sake.

"The work being performed by the stevedores, and by these colored Y. M. C. A. workers in the camps I have just visited, and the amicable relations existing between them and superior army officers, I feel certain, would be as disillusioning to the race back home as it has been, in many respects, to me.

"Here one finds these colored men performing nearly every kind of work, skilled and unskilled. Their camp is a model of cleanliness—a cleanliness that would put to shame most of our cities back in the States, and a cleanliness in which the colored boys take a commendable pride. A fine brass band here, composed exclusively of stevedores, frequent moving picture showings, educational work, etc., conspire to make the 'after work' hours of these thousands of colored service men pass quickly and profitably. Recently General Pershing visited this camp and gave the boys an interesting talk, which has since been regarded by them as epochal.

"Thus far, my only regret is that there were not more colored Y. M. C. A. workers over here to enlarge and spread the splendid work being done by Mrs. Curtis, Mrs. Hunton and Miss Johnson. The right sort of women, fine, big-hearted, devoted colored women, have such a refining influence in camps such as this, and the colored Y. M. C. A. secretaries themselves are anxious for them, and feel that colored women, to a number proportionate with the number of white women sent over by the Y. M. C. A., would further tend to make camp life for these soldiers ideal, and render easier the disciplinary work of the army."

Early in April, 1919, some ten or twelve additional well-educated, solid, substantial women were selected and sent to France to work among colored soldiers and to supply the need mentioned by Mr. Tyler.

### The Knights of Columbus

Another organization was of much service in making Negro soldiers comfortable at the front. This was the Knights of Columbus, a Catholic society, which has to its credit that, unlike the other social welfare organizations operating in the war, it never drew the color line. It provided separate huts for Negroes at some of the camps when special requests to this effect were received. These were recreational buildings, provided with home surroundings for the preparation of which no pains were spared. Such arrangements were made at Camp Meade, Camp Dodge, Camp Funston, Fort Riley, and Camp Taylor. As an evidence of the general liberality of the management of the war work conducted by the Knights of Columbus, no better testimony can be given than that by Joseph J. Canavan in a report to the Kansas Plain-Dealer.

"Under the system as it now has been working out," says he, "the Negro soldier needs no other countersign than his khaki uniform to gain for him every advantage offered by the Knights' service. True there are places both in this country and abroad where the Knights of Columbus have erected special huts for the use of the Negro soldiers, but where that has been done it has been at the express request of the Negro soldiers themselves, who in numerous instances have expressed a preference for a building of their own where they may enjoy their own pleasure in their own way and be assured of meeting their own friends when and where and under circumstances they desired. Similarly the other day," says he, "when there were six Negro soldiers in training at Port Jervis, New York, on their way to Goshen, New York, whence they were to start upon their journey to a training camp, it was a group of Knights of Columbus' secretaries who met them and supplied them with cigarettes and tobacco." It happened, however, that the six Negroes did not take a train for Port Jervis. Instead the Knights loaded them into automobiles and drove them across the pretty hilly country to their point of departure for the camps. There were only six men in that draft consignment, but the Knights would have been as hearty and as generous if there had been 600. There have been innumerable instances where a larger number of men have been cared for and had their wants provided for by the Knights, as the men themselves have testified.

### Caring for Returned Soldiers

Upon the signing of the Armistice and the return of soldiers from France, severing their connections with the social welfare organizations which had once cared for them, a serious problem presented itself to the American people. Many cities were stunned by the sudden influx of so many soldiers. In some cases small towns did not have facilities adequate to the task of accommodating the number which came even if it had been expecting them. Vice conditions in the communities became unspeakably bad, soldiers were mingling with lewd women, and when their funds became exhausted, they became dissatisfied and even rebellious. The situation was in every sense an acute one, but no one could be blamed and no one was willing to accept the responsibility for improving the situation.

Realizing the seriousness of this problem the whites and blacks endeavored to find some solution of the peculiar problem. This, however, was no problem peculiar to the Negro soldiers, for the whites were similarly situated. There were, however, a few narrow and prejudiced whites believing that anything was good enough for Negroes. There were also a good many men of color, and especially ministers and the like, who maintained an attitude of apathy towards these men returning from the war. Then there was, worst of all, a strained feeling between the whites and blacks in the various communities—a feeling apparently of long standing and intensified by war conditions. Upon the appearance, therefore, of a few unusual types of soldiers of both races, with the misdemeanors which usually characterize persons lacking self-control, the situation was decidedly aggravated.

### The War Camp Community Service

To find a way out of this difficulty it was planned to extend the War Camp Community Service. To various cities, and especially to Philadelphia, Baltimore, Richmond, Newport News, Norfolk, Portsmouth, Augusta, Chattanooga, Indianapolis, Kansas City, and San Antonio, Texas, were sent directors to enlighten the communities as to the inevitable results of the war, the reason for the appearance of the returned soldiers in the towns, and their responsibility to these veterans. Their first problem was to reach the churches and the schools. They addressed mass meetings, spoke before social groups, and had personal conferences with men of influence, to find their way into the hearts of the people. The next step was to convince the community that such an effort was worth while. A club house, too often some abandoned dilapidated

building, was secured and remodeled to suit the peculiar needs of
the time.  Adequate furniture and equipment for dormitories and
cafeteria service were supplied and a desirable club with a file of
newspapers, branch circulating library, a hall for entertainments,
in fact a social center, was provided for service in the community.
Men generally stood aloof, but it was soon found that while in
some cases the support of the schools and the churches could not
be obtained, some business men and professional men of intelligence, character, and vision came to the support of these War
Camp Community Service workers, and it was not long before the
entertainment and the atmosphere maintained by the center convinced a majority of the people of their importance and value.

It was soon possible thereafter to enlist the support of a larger
number of influential people in the various communities.  One
organization after another engaged in the service and appeared at
various times to entertain the soldiers assembled at these centers.
Out of such beginnings came the support of the churches and other
religious organizations.  It was necessary to add other men and
even women to the staff, so rapid was the progress and so extensive was the work.  Club activities increased; soldiers were visited
in the various camps and hospitals, friendly relations were established and business men were brought together, so as to cause a
contact helpful to them in other ways.  It then became possible to
organize clubs in school buildings and Sunday schools, and women
in clubs worked together in a practical way whenever the opportunity came.  Various ways in which they contributed may be
summarized as follows:  The community became reconciled and
active in the service; it was then an easy matter to welcome the
returning soldiers.  Provision was made for their entertainment
in the theaters; community centers and concerts were arranged for
them; large numbers of citizens attended the recreation rallies
and entertainments, dinners, and dances multiplied throughout
the period of demobilization.

# CHAPTER XXIX

## NEGRO LOYALTY AND MORALE

*Eager Response of Colored Draftees—Notable Tributes to the Patriotism of the Negro Race by the White Press—Also by President Wilson, Secretary Baker, Secretary Daniels, and Others—Negro Loyalty Never Doubted—Patriotic Negro Demonstrations and Other Instances of Loyalty.*

When the United States declared war against Germany and the Teutonic allies, there were internal conditions existing in America that were by no means ideal so far as the Negro was concerned, nor were they altogether conducive to *loyalty* and a healthy *morale* among this particular group of American citizens. Beset by a vicious and persistent propaganda on the one side, and by continued instances of lynching and mob violence of which he was the chief victim on the other, the Negro in America faced a real crisis at the beginning of the war. Temptation after temptation was presented to him to render lukewarm and half-hearted support to the Government in the prosecution of the war, without making himself criminally liable, but Negro leaders in all parts of the country recognized at once that the national crisis demanded, and the plain duty and best interests of the Negro racial group required that, without bargaining, there must be a pledge on the part of the Negro of his undiluted and unfaltering loyalty.

History records no parallel where, under similar conditions, any racial group has been more loyal to the Government or has maintained a higher morale than was true of colored Americans during the trying period of the recent war. The Negro pledged his loyalty and was depended upon in all sections of our country. He entered fully and bravely into the work of defending the "Stars and Stripes." All propaganda efforts to weaken his morale absolutely failed. A black skin during the war was a badge of patriotism.

The Negro was not unmindful of certain wrongs, injustices, and discriminations which were heaped upon his race in many sections of the country, but in the face of it all he remained adamant against all attempts to lower his morale, and realized that his first duty was *loyalty* to his country. America is indeed the Negro's country, for he has been here three hundred years, which is about two hundred years longer than many of the white racial groups; he realized that he was formally declared a citizen of this country by the Constitution of the United States, and that although many of the rights and privileges of citizenship were still denied him, yet the plain course before him was to perform all of the duties of citizenship and at the same time continue to press his demands for all of the rights and privileges which the Constitution has vouchsafed to him. He realized that he would not be in a position to demand his rights unless he fully performed his duties as an American citizen, and in thus lending his loyal allegiance he exemplified his belief in the doctrine expounded by Colonel Theodore Roosevèlt to the effect that "rights and privileges" are contingent upon the faithful discharge of the "duties and responsibilities" of citizenship in any country. And so it was that although the lynching evil and other wrongs against the Negro proceeded with unabated fury, unrestrained even by the President's proclamation, the Negro remained steadfast in his loyalty to the Government. His last ounce of devotion was pledged without question to the principles of *freedom and democracy* for which America stood, and the thought uppermost in the minds of twelve million colored Americans was that the Teutonic allies should be brought to their knees, and that the war would result in the downfall of all kinds of tyranny and oppression.

### Eager Response to the Draft

If there was ever any question as to the Negro's loyalty, it was soon dispelled by the readiness with which he answered the draft call, by his eagerness to volunteer, even though in many instances denied this privilege; by the splendid spirit in which thousands of Negroes, educated and uneducated, accepted tasks assigned to them in non-combatant and Service of Supply regiments; and by the whole-hearted way in which Negro civilians, men, women, and children, representing every section of the country and every walk of life, responded to every call of the Nation. The valiant, varied, and effective services rendered by four hundred thousand Negro soldiers who were called to the colors, both in camps and cantonments at home as well as upon the battlefields of Europe, canceled every possible doubt and furnished proof positive of the Negro's unfaltering loyalty.

Many agencies sought to lower the morale of the Negro. Not only did German propagandists labor diligently i n certain sections of the country, particularly among the unlettered element of the Negro population, in the effort to impress upon their minds the two fallacies that (1) America had no right or cause to engage in a foreign war, and (2) that the Negro was foolish in fighting for a country which did not fully protect him in his rights as a citizen. Propagandists sought to advertise every instance of lynching, mob violence, or other wrong visited upon a member of the Negro race, with a view of turning him against his own country, and found additional fuel for their seditious flames in the anti-Negro attitude manifested by a number of white newspapers, governors of states, mayors of cities, legislators, race-prejudice-breeding moving picture shows, etc., that were allowed to propagate a dangerous hate doctrine and to exert a disquieting influence even in the critical period of war.

Propagandists emphasized racial discriminations of one kind or another and unfortunately were able to refer to the facts that the black American, supposedly a citizen, was in many states denied the ballot; that he was "Jim Crowed" on many of the railroads and public carriers, although charged first-class fare for transportation; that he was denied admission to most public places of amusement, hotels and the like. Using such arguments as a basis, the question was raised as to why the Negro was willing to jeopardize his life, his liberty, and his pursuit of happiness in coming to the rescue of America in her extremity and thus helping to defeat Germany—a country where, it was said, such racial discriminations did not exist.

None of these questions, however, disturbed the thoughtful leaders of the Negro people. They knew the designing motive back of such propaganda. They recognized, without question, that the moment the American Negro failed to perform all of the duties of citizenship, he immediately abdicated the right of claiming the full privileges of citizenship. The Negro leaders knew that the central thought in the German mind and the traditional policy of the Central Powers was *"might,"* and that *"compelling force"* was intended to be used, as a part of a world-wide conquest, to reduce to German domination the weaker and other peace-loving peoples of the earth. They remembered something of the history of Germany's African colonies. They recognized that the great masses of the Negro race in America belong to a submerged group —seeking education, industrial opportunity, wealth—and, more than all, *liberty, freedom,* and the *pursuit of happiness,* and as a means of obtaining possession and permanent enjoyment of those price-less privileges (along with white Americans who were fighting for the same cause), they declared in the public press, in pulpits, upon the public rostrum, in lodge-rooms, in schools and everywhere —that no discouraging or untoward conditions existing among the Negro people must interfere with their whole-hearted support of their country's war program.

### Promoting the Negro Morale

As a part of the Government's program of promoting a healthy morale among colored soldiers and colored Americans generally, the author was delegated by the Secretary of War to visit various camps and cantonments where colored soldiers were stationed, also leading centers of Negro population; first, for the purpose of learning as to conditions existing likely to affect their patriotism; and, second, for the purpose of delivering addresses such as would be calculated to promote the continued loyalty and a healthy morale among the members of this racial group.

Preliminary to his tour of the Middle-West he made a careful investigation of conditions existing in Camps Meade, Dix, Lee, Upton, and others, and had sought to ameliorate conditions existing among colored soldiers stationed at those camps. This middle-western itinerary served to give the colored people full opportunity of hearing directly from a representative of the War Department with respect to its policy concerning Negro troops.

The 92nd Division (colored) was trained at seven different cantonments. Early in May, 1918, it became evident that orders would shortly be issued for the entire division to go overseas, and it was therefore arranged that the author should "swing around the circle," visiting all camps not already visited, where any units of the 92nd Division were stationed, and speaking at such strategic centers en route through the West Where his itinerary would permit. As a part of this program he spoke at various times in all parts of the country, including Boston, Massachusetts; Chicago, Illinois; Kansas City, Missouri; New York City; St. Louis, Missouri; Indianapolis, Indiana; Cincinnati, Cleveland, and Columbus, Ohio; Atlanta, Georgia; Philadelphia, Pennsylvania, and Baltimore, Maryland.

His return to Washington about the middle of May brought the itinerary to a close. Though the gait at which he traveled was a strenuous one, he was immeasurably strengthened for his work by this intimate contact with the people of the country of both races, soldiers and civilians. Wise counsel and friendly encouragement were met with at every turn and he was convinced that the extended tour had not been made in vain. He had spoken thirty-two times, to thousands of his fellow-citizens, all of whom were impelled by a common impulse of patriotism.

A high note of patriotism was sounded by thoughtful leaders of the Negro people in all walks of life. Negro editors, with but few exceptions, rallied to the Nation's call and wrote in a martial spirit; the Negro clergy put on the whole armor of patriotism and awakened the Negro laity to a sense of its duty, opportunity, and responsibility; Negro educators in all sections taught loyalty as a cardinal virtue and representative Negro public speakers sought diligently to maintain a healthy morale among the rank and file of colored Americans.

It was also recognized on the part of the white people of the South and elsewhere that the Negro's loyalty was not to be questioned, and representative white Americans, both North and South, testified in the public press that they regarded the Negro's undivided loyalty as a valuable asset to the Nation. White newspapers all over the country devoted column after column of space to the whole-souled loyalty of colored Americans.

### Notable Newspaper Tribute

"The Negro population of the United States," said the St. Louis Globe Democrat, "is loyal to the core, and of all the fantasies of Germany diplomacy toward the alienation of elements of our composite population, after it was recognized that our declaration of war was coming—none was more fantastic than the well-accredited plot to turn our native colored citizens against the country with which all their fortunes are bound up and identified.

"It has been possible for Prussianism to find among us some weak and credulous people and some even who, coming here as aliens, have prospered greatly under our institutions, to be deluded with the notion that they could reap advantage out of the nation's humiliation and defeat. *The colored citizen of the United States has a shrewd understanding of the fact that we must all stand or fall together,* and he doesn't want to fall.

"Aside from all such practical considerations," continued the editor, "there is a *Negro loyalty which is one of the finest traits of the race.* It has been sung in song and story. The older generations were loyal even to those who were fighting to hold them in slavery, out of ties of love and affection which nothing could break. Men of the South, intelligent and high-charactered men, some of whom had personal and family knowledge of this fine fidelity and devotion, have permitted grosser elements to persecute the race, purely out of political considerations. We trust, and now believe, that that discreditable era is drawing to a close. It has been the one blot on an escutcheon never marred by want of valor or chivalry in fighting for a lost cause.

*"The colored people are justifying all of our faith. Not only are they, at home, responding to every patriotic need, but their men in the field, in France, are proving themselves worthy comrades of those who so signally earned laurels at San Juan, and those who, on the Mexican border, under Pershing, proved themselves at Carrizal to be of the stuff American soldiers are made of."*

In Jackson, Mississippi, in the heart of the South, Rev. George Luther Cady, pastor of the First Congregational Church, preached a special sermon pleading for a deeper consideration of the black man and a fairer judgment of him in view of his demonstrated patriotism and dependability, especially in time of war. He emphasized the fact that the crimes with which the Negro is charged are few in number and in proportion to those of the white population, and that, through the narrow viewpoint of the whites, his

Left—Dr. George Edmund Haynes, Director of Negro Economics, Department of Labor, Washington. D. C.
Center—Dr. Robert R. Moton, Principal, Tuskegee Normal and Industrial Institute, who went to France during the war on
a special mission.
Right—Lester A. Walton. member Military Entertainment Service. War Department Commission on Training Camp Activities.

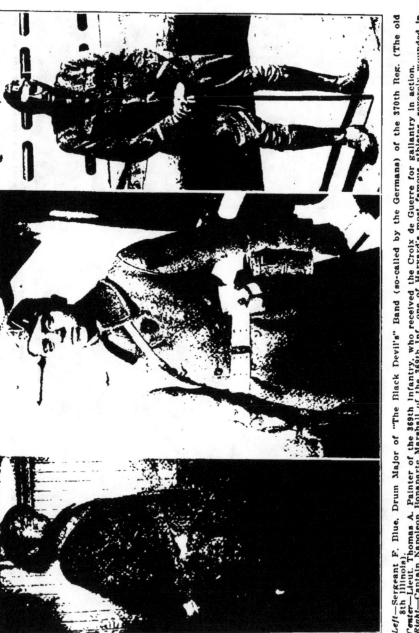

*Left*—Sergeant F. Blue, Drum Major of "The Black Devil's" Band (so-called by the Germans) of the 370th Reg. (The old 8th Illinois).
*Center*—Lieut. Thomas A. Painter of the 369th Infantry, who received the Croix de Guerre for gallantry in action.
*Right*—Captain Napoleon Bonaparte Marshall of the 369th Inf., one of Harvard's most famous athletes, severely wounded in spine, during fighting south of Metz, must wear a steel brace during the remainder of his life.

*Left*—Group of Colored Red Cross Nurses on duty at the base hospital at Camp Grant, Illinois. *Right*—Some of the Negro Officers who were helping to hold the lines with the 366th Infantry, when the Armistice was signed. *Front*, left to right— Captain A. L. Simpson, 1st Lieutenants, Morris, Booker and Ellis. *Back Row*, left to right—2nd Lieutenants Taylor, Wright and McEwen.

American Negro troops returning from their gallant service in France. The above photograph was taken at meal-time aboard a United States Transport just entering New York Harbor. The demonstration would signify that the men were ready for the mess call.

*Above*—Colored American Soldiers being decorated with Distinguished Service Cross by Major-General Eli Helmick of the United States Army in presence of Admiral Moreau of the French Navy. *Below*—Group of Negro Officers, 366th Infantry, U. S. A. *Left to Right*—Capt. L. H. Godman, Lt. and Adj. Chas. S. Parker, Capt. Chas. G. Kelley, Capt. Wm. Hill, Capt. C. W. Owens, Capt. Geo. A. Holland, Capt. W. T. Thompson, 2nd Lt. Wm. D. Nabors

*Above*—The Curtis brothers, three sons of Dr. and Mrs. A. M. Curtis, Washington, D. C., commissioned as Officers in United States Army. *Left to Right*—A. Maurice Curtis, Medical Reserve Corps; Arthur L. Curtis, 368th Medical Corps; Merrill H. Curtis, 349th Field Artillery, all First Lieutenants.

*Below*—The Gould family of fighters. Seated in front is Wm. B. Gould of East Dedham, Mass., a veteran of the Civil War. Standing are his six sons who have also served their country. *Left to Right*—Lawrence W. Gould, 1st Lt. James E. Gould, Major W. B. Gould, Jr., Lt. Herbert R. Gould, 1st Lt. Ernest M Gould, and Frederick C. Gould.

*Top,* Left to Right—2nd Lt. Jas. L. Horace, Intel. Officer, 365th Inf.; 2nd Lt. Stephen E. Moses, Jr., 351st F. A.; 1st Lt. Marion C. Rhoten, Hdqrs. Troop, 92nd Div.; Lt. Frank L. Frances, M. G. Co. 366th Inf.
*Left,* Center—1st Lt. Edward C. Knox, 349th Mchn. Gun Bat. *Right,* Center—Capt. Spahr H. Dickey, 351st Mchn. Gun Bat.
*Bottom,* Left—Capt. Beverley L. Dorsey, 317th Am. Tr. *Bottom,* Right—Capt. Robert B. Chubb, 367th Inf.
*Center Panel*—Sergt. Wm. Butler of Salisbury, Md., who received the Croix de Guerre from the French Government and Distinguished Service Cross and Sharpshooter's Medal from the United States Government. The story of Sergt. Butler and his hand to hand encounters with the Boches is related in full in this volume.

Dr. Emmett J. Scott and his faithful office corps, who co-operated in the performance of his duties as Special Assistant to the Secretary of War, at Washington. *Left to Right*—William H. Davis, Ernestine B. English, Dr. Scott, Madeline P. Childs, Richard W. Thompson, Joseph H. Nelson, J. Bernard Smith, Charles I. Webb.

crimes have been magnified without keeping in mind the short-comings of his white brothers.

Mr. Bolton Smith, a representative white Southern gentleman of Memphis, Tennessee, impressed by Negro loyalty and possessed with a high sense of justice, wrote Governor Tom C. Rye, of Tennessee, as follows: "The Government of the United States is controlled by Southern men. It has called the Negro to the defense of the colors, and the American people will demand that a race thus honored shall be granted the justice of a fair trial when accused of crime. We all know that when guilty there is no doubt of full punishment. As Secretary of the Tennessee Law and Order League, organized to stop lynching, I urge you to issue a proclamation to our people pointing out the treasonable effect of such lynchings."

A white newspaper of Texas published an article that was reprinted in the *Houston Observer* and other Negro journals, headed "*The Black Man Stood Pat and Fought the Good Fight.*" In the course of the article it was stated: "The war did more for the American Negro than had been accomplished in several decades of peace. He demonstrated that he could fight—that his willing-ness and capacity for work were unlimited; that he could easily adapt himself to strange surroundings and that *he understood the purpose of Liberty Bonds, which he almost invariably bought until it actually and positively 'hurt.' One of the most glorious things that happened to the Negro, however, was the revelation of his absolute, unshakable loyalty to the Stars and Stripes.* Evidence adduced before a Senate Committee shows that German propa-gandists failed miserably in their efforts among the blacks. That they operated principally among the plantation Negroes of the South and there made no headway whatever, is significant. *It is a splendid tribute to the Americanism of the Negro.* It might be supposed that among men and women who are not regular readers of the newspapers, who trust to the 'grapevine,' which makes a wireless station of every cabin, for most of their informa-tion, the fairy tales of the paid German agents would find fertile ground. *But the Negro stood pat.* 'You have no country,' was an insidious remark that was dinned into his ears night and day. 'You'll never get your Liberty Bond money back,' was another.

'You'll get forty acres of land if the Germans win,' they were told. And they were assured that victory for the 'humane' Germans meant an end of all hangings and instant leveling of all social lines in the United States. *Many white 'intellectuals' in the North succumbed to sophistries and lies, but those black millions did not. Their hearts proved pure gold and they stood by Uncle Sam. The Secret Service needed no special trains for Negro excursions to internment camps. It is that same inborn spirit of loyalty to the Government that has prevented the I. W. W. from gaining converts among the blacks of the South, no matter how poor they are or how unjust their position economically."*

### Tributes by Wilson, Baker and Daniels

President Woodrow Wilson, in a special memorandum which accompanied his commutation of the sentences of a group of Negro soldiers who were charged with being implicated in the Houston (Texas) riot, paid tribute to the loyalty and fidelity of colored Americans. Similar tributes were frequently paid by Hon. Newton D. Baker, Secretary of War. In a special message of encouragement and confidence which he addressed to the Chicago Branch of the National Security League, which held a patriotic mass meeting at the Coliseum in Chicago, February 12, 1918, the Secretary of War wrote: "As stated to you in the telegraphic reply which Mr. Emmett J. Scott, my Special Assistant, forwarded to you at my instance and request, I sincerely wish it were possible for me to be present on the occasion referred to, for *I would then have a splendid opportunity to tell of the fine spirit with which the great test of the quality of America is being met by the colored people of our country.* * * * I wish, however, in view of my enforced absence, to send, especially to the colored Americans of your community and elsewhere, just a few words of encouragement and confidence. * * * In a most encouraging degree, it is being regarded by colored citizens throughout the country as a privilege and as a duty to give liberally of their substance, of their time, of their talents, of their energy, of their influence, and in every way possible, to contribute toward the comfort and success of our fighting units and those of our allies across the seas. The colored men, who were subject to draft, are to be commended upon their promptness and eagerness in registering their names for service in the National Army, and likewise mention is made of the relatively low percentage of exemption claims filed by them. Those in the service of their country, I am sure, will prove faithful and efficient, and will uphold the traditions of their race."

In addition to the splendid tributes paid to Negro loyalty, time after time, by Colonel Theodore Roosevelt and William H. Taft, both former Presidents of the United States, Hon. Josephus Daniels, Secretary of the Navy, at a banquet given in his honor by the citizens of Albany, N. Y., on Flag Day, June 14, 1918, warmly commended the colored people for their never-failing devotion to the American flag. In introducing Secretary Daniels at the afternoon gathering, following a monster parade, former Governor Martin H. Glynn referred to the fact that Henry Johnson, an Albany colored soldier who was cited by General Pershing for extreme valor on the battlefield, was born in North Carolina, near Secretary Daniel's home. The Secretary, in mentioning Private Johnson in his speech, paid a high tribute to the colored people of the South; he said that while "there has been occasion to question the patriotism of *some* of the people in this country, *the loyalty of the colored citizens had never been in doubt.*"

Upon the floor of the House of Representatives of the United States, a Southern Congressman—Hon. R. W. Austin, of Tennessee, paid glowing tribute to Negro soldiers and warmly commended the loyal part that the Negro citizenship of the country was playing in helping to win the war. He read into the Congressional Record the wonderful tribute which General Pershing, Commanding Officer of the American Expeditionary Forces, paid to the colored soldiers, and stated that not only in the military ranks were Negro patriots to be found, but likewise they were serving in munition plants, in mines, in factories, foundries, and upon the farm, doing their utmost to support their Government in the time of stress and storm. He bore cheerful testimony to the loyalty of this racial group and stated that in his section of the country, the South, the Negro people had not only furnished their full quota for the Army but had liberally subscribed to Liberty Loans, the Red Cross, and the Army Y. M. C. A. funds. He closed his address by saying: "It gives me pleasure to place upon the enduring records of the Government this brief but true and deserved tribute to the loyalty, fidelity, and patriotism of the colored citizens of America.''

## Negro Loyalty Never Doubted

Even though white men who held positions high in the public life of the country were, in some cases, under suspicion as to their loyalty and several members of the United States Congress were charged with entertaining anti-American ideas—one of the latter being convicted in a court of law on the charge of disloyalty, *be it said to the everlasting credit of the American Negro, it was never necessary to question his loyalty.* This racial group placed itself squarely on the side of a wider democracy for all peoples, as expressed by the President in his public utterances, and gave cordial sanction to that sentiment contained in the President's address delivered July 4, 1918, at Washington's Tomb, when he said: ''What we seek is the reign of law based upon the consent of the governed and sustained by the organized opinion of mankind.''

Notable among the patriotic meetings and parades conducted in all sections of the country to sustain the morale of the colored people were those which occurred (1) at Wilmington, Delaware, under the direction of Mrs. Alice Dunbar-Nelson, whose splendid efforts in mobilizing the colored women of the country for war work is referred to elsewhere in this volume; and (2) at St. Louis, Missouri, where a ''Negro Loyalty Day'' was observed, June 13, 1918, featured by a ''Loyalty Day Parade and Patriotic Benefit'' under the auspices of the Colored Women's Unit of the Council of National Defense, with Mrs. Victoria Clay Haley, as Chairman. Colored men and women from every walk of life, including thousands of school children enthusiastically took a part in these patriotic demonstrations; some of the special sections of the St. Louis parade included representatives of the Colored Waiters' Alliance, Wayman A. M. E. Church, Summer High School, Banneker School, Simmons School, Cottage School, Dessalines School, Lincoln School, Delany School, colored employees of the Post Office, St. Louis Medical Forum, Boosters' Club, Young Ladies' Reading Club, colored Patrons from Kinlock and Ferguson, Missouri, First

Baptist Church, Church of God, A. M. E. Church, Olive Street Terrace Realty Company, Negro business and professional men of St. Louis, and others. The two parades mentioned above, and many others, reached the high-water mark of Negro patriotism.

In New Orleans, La., a monster parade was held by colored citizens, each marcher carrying an American flag. Some of the strikingly worded banners were: "Stand by Our President"; "What It Takes To Lick the Kaiser, We've Got It"; "Victory Calls Us"; "The Colored Man Is No Slacker." A squad of stevedores who had served under General Pershing in France and sailors from the Algiers Naval Training Station headed the parade; they were some of the troops who built the great docks in France.

In point of numbers, enthusiasm and fidelity to the cause the parade held in Atlanta, Georgia, was also a tremendously significant demonstration. Negro laborers, factory hands, porters, and workers in stores and office buildings, chauffeurs, gardeners, and other colored employees were granted by their employers a special half-holiday in order that they might participate in the Loyalty Parade; and along with them marched hundreds of other men, women, and children, representing practically every phase of Negro life. Along the route of the parade the marchers were liberally applauded by their white fellow-citizens, who were much impressed with the spirit of the occasion and who gladly contributed to its success.

### Other Instances of Loyalty

The enthusiastic farewells that were given to departing Negro draftees and soldiers by their mothers, wives, and other relatives and friends furnished by no means the least valuable evidence of the self-sacrificing loyalty of this entire racial group. In numerous cities could be witnessed scenes where Negro enlisted men marched through the streets, on their way to camp, accompanied by cheering throngs of colored women, men, and children carrying flags and filling the air with shoutings of patriotism. Nor was their loyalty merely vocal, for it found additional concrete expression in the purchase of Liberty Bonds, War Savings Stamps, and the like. Miss Kate M. Herring, Director of Publicity for the North Carolina War Savings Committee, has published in Northern and South-

ern magazines some interesting facts in regard to the thrift campaigns among Negroes in her State. *In the "Black Belt," where
in fourteen counties the Negroes average 56 per cent of the population,* she wrote, *the average subscription was 80 per cent of the
allotment, 4 per cent more than in the State at large.* In the
county which subscribed 128 per cent of its allotment, the Negroes
constitute 47 per cent of the population. *They furnished 42 to
61 per cent of the thirteen of the nineteen counties which subscribed
100 per cent or over.* Subscriptions ranged from that of *a Negro
who took the limit of one thousand dollars for each member of his
family* to those whose subscriptions were paid for in 25-cent stamps,
including a washerwoman with a blind husband who subscribed for
$50 worth for herself and him.

Another extraordinary case indicating the sublime patriotism
and loyalty of the Negro was that of David H. Haynes, a colored
farmer of Thibodeaux, Louisiana, who subscribed for $100,000
worth of the Fourth issue of Liberty Bonds while fighting was at
its height, making note of his confidence in the Government and
his determination to risk his all in defense of the lofty purpose and
high ideals that caused America's entrance into the arena of war.
This is said to be the largest individual subscription made by any
citizen in the state of Louisiana and was certainly the largest purchase of its kind made in the country by a colored man.

That the Negro was a willing factor in the war has been so
convincingly demonstrated on so many occasions that additional
evidence is scarcely necessary; a striking case in point, however,
may be noted in the journeying at his own expense from Birmingham, Alabama, to Washington, D. C., of Archie Neely, a stalwart
young colored American, to enlist in the Army. It was stated that
he had been refused by the Local Boards at his home, denied the
privilege of voluntary enlistment, but was so determined to battle
for Uncle Sam that he scraped together the necessary funds and
came to Washington to see the officials of the War Department in
person and tender his services; his personality was so inviting and
his plea so effective that he left the War Department with a paper
authorizing him to proceed at once to Camp Meade.

Another striking individual case is that of John Ward, colored,
of Goldsboro, North Carolina, who, according to the sheriff of the

county, had thirteen (13) of his eighteen (18) sons in the United States Army, while his daughters were busy with war work.

Aside from the immensely valuable part performed by the Negro press during the war, representative colored men and women in every section of the country appeared upon the public platform and delivered patriotic addresses before countless audiences composed of members of their racial group with a view of stimulating their patriotism, and to prevent any possibility of their yielding to sinister influences which tended to weaken their morale. All of them seemed to realize the fact that no matter how well equipped a nation may be in a material way, it cannot win any worth-while victory unless it is able to maintain among all groups of citizens that indefinable, spiritual something which is called "MORALE." In its general application it is a "moral condition" or a "mental state" which renders a man capable of endurance and of exhibiting courage in the presence of danger, but in time of war it becomes a spiritual force which keeps men constant in their devotion to their country's flag. Whether the Stars and Stripes was carried into battle by Negro soldiers or held in the hands of patriotic Negro citizens—during the recent war as in all other wars, "the old flag *never touched the ground.*"

## A Negro's Idea of Loyalty

Henry Watterson, editor of the Louisville Courier-Journal, a Democratic newspaper, published an editorial expression regarding the address of a colored man which was quite generally republished throughout the country. The address was also published in the Congressional Record. Mr. Watterson wrote:

With all his genius and culture, Roscoe Conkling Simmons is a Negro. His college degrees and personal refinement cannot change his blood or color or make him one bit less a member of a race regarded as socially, economically and mentally inferior to the white.

That Louisville is proud of him as a citizen; that the Negro people of the country look to him for leadership much as they did to his illustrious uncle, Booker T. Washington; that men of prominence in the nation accord him fellowship and a place in high councils, does not change his status.

For these very reasons, his words, spoken the other day before a gathering of his own race, should spread a blush of shame on the Caucasian skins of some who are conspicuous in the eyes of the nation just now. When men

of superior learning and vaunted super-race connections, intrusted with the
solemn duty of serving and protecting their country's destiny, join with
foreign tyrant cut-throats to heap contumely upon the nation's head and tie
the hands stretched out to protect the lives and rights of Americans; when
sniveling white pacifists join with all the traitor-slacker crew to invite
national disgrace and ruin, well may this member of an "inferior race" boast:

"We have a record to defend, but no treason, thank God, to atone or
explain. While in chains we fought to free white men—from Lexington to
Carrizal—and returned again to our chains. No Negro has ever insulted the
flag. No Negro ever struck down a President of these United States. No
Negro ever sold a military map or secret to a foreign government. No Negro
ever ran under fire or lost an opportunity to serve, to fight, to bleed and to
die in the republic's cause. Accuse us of what you will—justly and wrongly—
no man can point to a single instance of our disloyalty.

"We have but one country and one flag, the flag that set us free. Its
language is our only tongue, and no hyphen bridges or qualifies our loyalty.
Today the nation faces danger from a foreign foe, treason stalks and skulks
up and down our land. In dark councils intrigue is being hatched. I am a
Republican, but a Wilson Republican. Woodrow Wilson is my leader. What
he commands me to do I shall do. Where he commands me to go I shall go.
If he calls me to the colors, I shall not ask whether my colonel is black or
white. I shall be there to pick out no color except the white of the enemy's
eye. Grievances I have against this people, against this Government. Injustice to me there is, bad laws there are upon the statute books, but in this
hour of peril I forget—and you must forget—all thoughts of self or race or
creed or politics or color. *That, boys, is loyalty."*

That this address was a notable piece of diction and oratory means little,
save as a tribute to the talent and erudition of its author and an augury of
what may come from others of his race when given his opportunities. As a
rebuke to the traitors and Americans not worthy of the name it deserves the
widest reading, while such white men as La Follette, Stone, O'Gorman, Vardaman, Works, Bryan and all their ilk, instead, perhaps, of being tarred and
feathered black, should be forced to read these words of a black man.

## Negro Love for the United States

In one of his interesting letters from France, Ralph W. Tyler,
the accredited representative of the Committee on Public Information, wrote as follows:

"For some time, prior to sailing for France, I was cognizant
of a very general belief that many of the colored soldiers here in
France, because of the unrestricted freedom and absolute equality

doled out cheerfully to all people of the Allies, without respect to color, would locate here after the war. I have interviewed hundreds of the boys, and I have not found one who expressed a desire to remain here. This reluctance to remain in France longer than the close of the war is no reflection upon La Belle France, but rather a high testimony to the loyalty of the colored man to his own and native land. I have talked with colored men who came from Dr. Vernon's "Everglades of Florida"; with many who came from the State of Texas, made famous so far as colored men are concerned, by Emmett J. Scott, the achieving Special Assistant to the Secretary of War; with those from Alabama, known principally because of the fact that the late Dr. Booker T. Washington laid the foundation for his fame there. I have talked with many from Mississippi, Georgia, and other Southern States, and, without exception, all, while willing to remain here until German militarism is crushed, want to get back 'home' to the States as soon as peace is declared. The burden of their song is: 'My country! Right or wrong, my country!' 'With all thy faults, I love thee still.'

"To me this eagerness, on the part of colored soldiers, in the face of the absolutely unrestricted freedom offered them by France, and while willing cheerfully to remain here, and die here if necessary, to secure world democracy, is the finest possible testimony to the loyalty to their country—the United States—of the *175,000 colored soldiers who are now in the service of their country on French soil.* To a man they will return to the States as gladly as they embarked for France.

"Those of the race back in the States who complain because of a restricted sugar and flour allowance, etc., but who, nevertheless, enjoy Sundays and holidays for themselves as days bereft of work, perhaps would not complain were they over here at the front where there is neither rest nor Sundays for the boys who must fight and work seven days in the week, rain or shine, hot or cold. But these boys over here accept most cheerfully the inclusion of Sundays and holidays as duty days, and rain and cold as no excuse for relief from work and fight—a necessity, now, to achieve world democracy. The colored men of this Division, commissioned officers and men in the ranks, I find, are anxious to contribute their mite and their *MIGHT* to maintain the best traditions of the American Army."

# CHAPTER XXX

## DID THE NEGRO SOLDIER GET A SQUARE DEAL?

*Reports of Widespread Discrimination and Harsh Treatment in Camp—Many Manifestations of Prejudice by White Officers— The Question of White or Negro Officers for Negro Regiments—Higher Officers of the Army Usually Fair—Disinclination to Utilize Colored Nurses and Colored Medical Men—Secretary Baker's Efforts to Prevent Race Discrimination— Reports of Negro Observers on Conditions Overseas.*

In discussing the question, "Did the Negro soldier get a square deal?" it is pertinent, first, to show the occasion for the inquiry, and, incidentally, such worthy purpose as will be served by the treatment of that question in this volume. It is a question that has been repeatedly suggested by articles and editorials, reports of war correspondents, and the like, which have appeared in the Negro press and other publications of the country, based upon information received from various sources, including letters of criticism written by Negro soldiers and officers, chaplains, Y. M. C. A. secretaries, special investigators, and others, concerning conditions among Negro soldiers in camps at home as well as overseas, and, in some cases, based upon official orders that have been issued with reference to Negro soldiers in the Army of the United States.

It is a question necessarily affecting the morale of colored Americans which must be frankly met and impartially considered. To dodge it would be unworthy of an honest historian whose duty it is to chronicle facts, and might deny to the Negro race and also the Government the opportunity of learning some valuable lessons from the war, of mutual profit not only in the present but possibly in the future. Therefore its discussion in this volume has a three-fold purpose: (1) To enable colored Americans to know the truth about conditions which existed among soldiers of their race during the war; (2) to correct certain false impressions which have been made upon the minds and hearts of colored Americans based, in some in-

426

stances at least, upon certain exaggerated, erroneous, and incomplete statements they may have read or heard with reference to such conditions and which impressions, unless corrected, are capable of working serious harm; (3) to disclose what opportunities were accorded, and what measure of justice was meted out to Negro soldiers, officers, and war workers by the War Department and by others in authority.

*A grave mistake can be made by any one who looks only on one side of a question!* While it has been the consistent policy of the Special Assistant never to condone nor minimize wrong or injustice in any form or wherever found, yet it is no less important that we should never be so completely absorbed and overwhelmed with our grievances that we cannot find time and have vision to "look on the other side of the shield,"—thereby gaining encouragement and strength to fight for improved conditions. Therefore, it is hoped that the frank discussion contained in this chapter will make for a better understanding between the Negro and the Government he has served so well. May it also tend toward the adoption of a better attitude and policy on the part of the Government toward the Negro soldier and citizen and, at the same time, enable colored Americans generally to properly appreciate the difficulties which were confronted, as well as the measure of justice which was attempted and meted out by the Government during the recent war, which involved the handling of millions of men.

## Instances of Unfair Treatment

In view of the fact that the majority of Negro soldiers were commanded largely by white men and the records which they will finally make will most likely defend their own side of the case, it will be difficult to bring a majority of the white people of the country around to the position of thinking that the treatment of Negro soldiers in the Army was other than honorable. With all those who are fair-minded, however, due weight will be given to the complainants in the case, namely the thousands of Negro soldiers who complained and protested. It must also be remembered in this connection that Army rules and regulations rigidly require all complaints to be made. by a soldier through regular military channels,—that is through his immediate commanding officer, and, in the very nature of the case, it becomes at times extremely difficult for a soldier, even though unjustly treated, to publish his grievances or to obtain proper and prompt redress.

In the beginning of the draft, when men were being first called to the colors, there was much apprehension among Negroes as to whether they would be treated as other soldiers in the camps. The manifest discrimination practiced by various Local Draft Boards against Negro men in many sections under the Selective Service Law, together with the almost certain knowledge that they would, in many instances, be placed under the command of white officers, some of whom at least, it was feared, would not entertain a friendly and sympathetic attitude toward them, increased their apprehension. The fact that three Local Draft Boards were peremptorily ordered removed by the Secretary of War because of their flagrant injustice to Negro draftees is in itself a "straw" which shows that the wind was blowing in the *wrong* direction. Instances upon instances can be cited to show that the Negro did not get a "square deal" in the draft; in many sections he contributed many more than his quota; and in defiance of both the spirit and letter of the draft law, Negro married men with large families to support were impressed into military service regardless of their protests and appeals, and their wives, children, and dependents suffered uncalled-for hardships. Local Draft Boards, in almost every instance composed exclusively of white men, were in a position, if so inclined, to show favoritism to men of their own race; the official figures of the draft reveal the fact that in many sections of the country exemptions were granted white men who were single with practically *no dependents,* while Negroes were conscripted into service regardless of their urgent need in Agriculture or the essential industries, and without considering their family relations or obligations.

Would it not have been eminently just and fair, and more in line with the spirit of the American Constitution, *to have granted the Negro his rightful quota of representation on Local Draft Boards and District Boards of Appeal which passed upon matters of such vital consequence to him?* This is a question which should be answered in the affirmative.

*The Negro was willing* to do his full share of the fighting, but the official record shows that he was called upon to do more than his share under the Draft Law, for, although constituting 10.7 per cent of the total population of the United States, he contributed 13.08 per cent of the total colored and white inductions from June 5, 1917, to November 11, 1918. He had practically no representation upon the Draft Boards which passed upon his appeals—an arrangement which was wholly at variance with the theory of American institutions.

To catalogue or specify all of the complaints that have come to the War Department, that have been published in the Negro press, and that have been contained in letters written to the relatives of Negro soldiers with reference to unfair treatment accorded them would be an almost endless task, and would consume far more space than can possibly be allotted in this volume, but a few typical ones are given herein. They include charges of harsh and even brutal treatment by some of their commanding officers and especially by white "non-coms" who were placed over them.

Colored Americans have deeply resented the "table of organization" which denied colored soldiers the privilege of serving as non-commissioned officers over men of their own race. It was further alleged in numerous cases that white officers and white "non-coms" required of them unusually hard tasks under the most trying circumstances and frequently cursed them, beat them, domineered over them as if they were "slaves" instead of fellows in a common cause, and applied to them all manner of epithets and opprobrious terms such as "nigger," "darkey," "coon," and other more objectionable terms. A lack of medical care and proper nursing, inferior food, clothing, and sleeping accommodations were also alleged. In one camp in Virginia it was actually found that no adequate facilities whatsoever had been provided for Negro soldiers who were sick; they were huddled together, fourteen, sixteen and eighteen in one tent, without any wooden floors in the tents, although it was in the midst of the cold winter of 1917, and with practically no hospital accommodations. The official record of conditions then obtaining at Camp Hill, Virginia, conclusively proves that the Negro soldier did not get a square deal at that particular camp, at that particular time, for white soldiers had ample hospital accommodations, suitable barracks or floors in their tents, and were not huddled together as were the Negro soldiers, whose abnormally high death rate, due to pneumonia, was directly traceable to the unfair conditions they were forced to endure.

Similar disparities between accommodations provided for white and colored soldiers occurred at other camps and occasioned considerable complaint. *Perhaps, however, nothing contributed so much to friction in the Army as did the assignment of, and the wrongful attitude manifested by white "non-coms" who served in connection with Negro troops.*

## Comments by the White Press

Not only did the Negro press notice, and protest against various indignities visited upon Negro soldiers, but *many of the white newspapers made comments thereupon.* An editorial in the *New York World* read in part as follows:

"It is our claim that we are fighting this war to make the world safe for DEMOCRACY. Democracy implies equality of privilege and equal obligation of service. *If we fight for this for the world in general we ought to be prepared to practice it among ourselves. At present we mingle democracy with discriminations.* All the elements of our citizenship do not stand on the same level. But there is no way of evading the fact that under a modern military régime—one of universal service—*all elements of our citizenship must stand on the same level. No distinction can be drawn in applying the military code between white soldiers and black soldiers, between white officers and black officers. They are all fighting for the same cause and deserve the same credit for doing so.* Yet, only the other day a Negro officer revisiting his home in Vicksburg, Mississippi, was counseled by friends to put on civilian clothes, for fear that he might be mobbed if he appeared on the streets in the uniform of a United States Army officer. * * * The Government is telling all Americans that they have an equal stake in the war. All are invited to put their energies and resources into a common pool. But if the enterprise is common and the burdens are common, the glory must also be common."

It has been reliably reported that Lieutenant Joseph B. Saunders, the Negro army officer evidently referred to in the article just quoted, was abused, knocked off the sidewalk, and set upon by certain residents or citizens of Vicksburg, Mississippi, where he had gone to visit his parents; and compelled to remove his uniform and escape from that city in disguise to avoid mob violence.

The effort to humiliate Negro officers and to either prevent or limit their utilization in the Army assumed what appeared to be a decidedly organized form. In the first place the West Point officers' group seemed to look with resentment upon all army officers who, after a few months' intensive training in camp were awarded the same commissions for which they had had to sudy four years at the West Point Military Academy, and they seemed especially disinclined to regard favorably colored officers so easily elevated to their rank.

The colored people had cause to feel that there seemed to be a common understanding in many quarters that, wherever possible, the Negro officer should be discredited and that the Negro soldier should be praised only for what he did when led by white officers. To get rid of the Negro officers serving overseas, the plan was usually that set forth in the following document:

*FROM:*      The Commanding Officer, 372nd Infantry.
*TO:*      The Commanding General, American Expeditionary Forces.
*SUBJECT:*   Replacement of colored officers by white officers.

1. Request that colored officers of this regiment be replaced by white officers for the following reasons:

*First:* The racial distinctions which are recognized in civilian life naturally continue to be recognized in the military life and present a formidable barrier to the existence of that feeling of comradeship which is essential to mutual confidence and *esprit de corps.*

*Second:* With a few exceptions there is a characteristic tendency among colored officers to neglect the welfare of their men and to perform their duties in a perfunctory manner. They are lacking in initiative. These defects entail a constant supervision and attention to petty details by battalion commanders and other senior officers which distract their attention from their wider duties; with harmful results.

2. To facilitate the desired readjustment of official personnel it is recommended:

(A) That no colored officers be forwarded to this regiment, replacements or otherwise.

(B) That officers removed upon recommendation of efficiency boards be promptly replaced by white officers of like grade. But, if white officers are not available as replacements, white officers of lower grades be forwarded instead.

(C)   That the opportunity be afforded to transfer the remaining colored combat officer personnel to labor organizations or to replacement units for other colored combat organizations according to their suitability.

3.   Reference letter No. 616-3s written by Commanding General 157th D. I. on the subject August 21, 1918, and forwarded to your office through military channels.

(Signed)   HERSCHEL TUPES,
Colonel, 372nd Infantry.

Received A. G. O.
26th Aug., 1918.
G. H. Q., A. E. F.
*1st Ind. (Endorsement.)*
G. H. Q., A. E. F., France, August 28, 1918.
To Commanding Officer, 372nd Infantry, A. E. F.

1.   Returned.

2.   Paragraph two is approved.

3.   You will submit by special courier requisition for white officers to replace officers relieved upon the recommendation of efficiency board.

4.   You will submit list of names of officers that you recommend to be transferred to labor organization or to replacement units for other colored combat organizations; stating in each case the qualifications of the officers recommended.

By Command of General Pershing:
(Signed)   W. P. BENNETT, *Adjutant General.*
*2nd Ind. (Endorsement.)*
Hq. 372nd Infantry, S. P., 179, France, September 4, 1918.
To Commanding General, A. E. F., France.

1.   Requisition in compliance with par. 3, 1st Ind., is enclosed herewith. Special attention is invited to the filling of two original vacancies by appointment.

In the carrying out of these apparently well-matured plans, various Negro officers were cited to appear before Efficiency Boards, and in practically every case the decision seemed to go against them.  Those pronounced "inefficient" were easily disposed of and when the question arose as to how their positions might be filled there was not in France every time a sufficiency of Negro officers in reserve for this purpose. The military staff then availed themselves of the opportunity to make the claim that inasmuch as additional Negro officers were not available, and white officers would not serve in the same regiment with Negro officers, it was

necessary to turn over the command *entirely to white officers.*
Only in rarely exceptional cases were any of the colored officers
promoted while overseas.

In keeping with the prevailing custom at that time of discrediting Negro officers, desperate efforts were made, it seemed,
to show the unusual efficiency of Negro soldiers when led by white
officers, and their inefficiency when led by officers of their own
race.  Negro officers were often charged with "cowardice" in
spite of demonstrated valor of Negro troops in all the wars of the
Republic.  Such a complaint was brought against four Negro
officers of the 368th Infantry, who uniformly stated that they retreated only when they found themselves surrounded by barbed-
wire entanglements with the enemy using machine guns with deadly
effect, and when they themselves had no wire cutters and other
implements necessary to extricate them from such a dangerous
position.  They were without maps, without hand grenades, and
lacked sufficient ammunition.  Their Major, a white officer supposed
to be leading them, was nowhere to be found during the engagement.  Two of the colored Captains, according to Ralph W. Tyler,
special war correspondent—after they had gone over the top and
had run into a nest of machine guns—turned back and asked for
support and got the Third battalion.  But they could not get in
touch with their Major, who had gone to the rear "somewhere"
immediately after the engagement got hot, thus preventing company commanders from connecting with him to secure orders.  The
Major, however, because of the failure of the engagement, under
such circumstances, charged the colored officers with cowardice
and inefficiency.  Seemingly as a reward for his shifting the blame
so successfully, he was a few days thereafter raised to the rank
of Lieutenant Colonel and given command of a colored regiment.
Too many Negro officers and soldiers won the Croix de Guerre,
Distinguished Service Medals or Crosses, etc., to lend any color to
the charge that Negro officers were inefficient or cowards.

### The Case of the 92nd Division

In connection with the organization of the 92nd Division,
made up entirely of colored units, a certain measure of injustice

was involved in that *the official order creating that Division recognized the color line as such,* and specifically provided that colored men, however capable, were not to be permitted to hold certain positions as officers of said Division. It practically announced to them, so far as their military opportunity was concerned: *"Thus far shalt thou go, and no farther."* The order was as follows:

### WAR DEPARTMENT TELEGRAM.
Washington, October 26, 1917.

Commanding General,
Camp Funston, Kansas:

The Ninety-Second Division (colored), with headquarters at Camp Funston, Kansas, will be organized at that place, and Brigadier-General C. C. Ballou has been directed to proceed with his authorized aides to that place and organize following troops from white officers, who will be directed to report to him and from colored officers and men who will be designated by you to report to him; Division Headquarters, including Headquarters Troops, Three Hundred Forty-Ninth Machine Gun Battalion, four companies, Division Trains to include: Three Hundred Seventeenth Headquarters and Military Police, Ammunition Train, Supply Motor Train, Engineer Train and Sanitary Train. *Following officers of Division will be white:* All officers of general and Field rank, such medical officers and veterinarians as the Surgeon-General may designate, all officers attached to Division Headquarters, except the Lieutenants of the Headquarters Troop, all Regimental Adjutants, Supply Officers, commanding officers of Headquarters Companies and of Engineer Train, Adjutants of Train Headquarters, and Ammunition Trains and Supply Officers of Sanitary Train, all captains of the Field Artillery Brigade and Engineer Regiment and aides to Brigade Commanders. You will transfer to the Ninety-Second Division the necessary colored officers and men to organize the units indicated above.

(Signed)   McCAIN,
(Adjutant-General.)

First Lieutenant T. T. Thompson, of Houston, Texas, went up against this rule in his efforts to be appointed a Captain in the Adjutant General's Department, and to be assigned as Division Personnel Officer of the 92nd Division; although admittedly competent and strongly recommended by Major General C. C. Ballou, Commander of that Division—simply because he was a colored man whose promotion was specifically prohibited by the War Department telegram which prescribed that a "white" man should occupy the

position to which he rightfully aspired, and which position he had
filled as Acting Personnel Officer practically from the time of the
organization of the 92nd Division. The following communications
explain themselves:

(Exhibit "A")
*Headquarters Ninety-Second Division.*
Camp Funston, Kansas.
April 30, 1918.
FROM:　　Commanding General, 92nd Division.
TO:　　The Adjutant General of the Army, Washington, D. C.
SUBJECT:　Appointment of Division Personnel Officer.

1. It is recommended that *First Lieutenant T. T. Thompson, Inf., N. A.,
be appointed a Captain* in the Adjutant General's Department and assigned
to this Division as Assistant-Adjutant *to be in charge of the Personnel Section*
as authorized by the Tables of Organization.

2. *This officer has been in charge of the Personnel work of this Division
practically from the time of its organization and his work has been found to
be thoroughly satisfactory, and his promotion is therefore recommended so
that he may continue on his present duty with adequate rank.*

(Signed)　C. C. BALLOU,
Major-General.

—

(Exhibit "B")
(A competent Negro officer, officially prohibited from promotion in the
Army, becomes discouraged and asks for an Honorable Discharge.)
HEADQUARTERS NINETY-SECOND DIVISION
American Expeditionary Forces
A. P. O. 766

October 21, 1918.

FROM:　　T. T. Thompson, 1st Lt. Inf. U. S. A.
TO:　　Commanding General, 92nd Division, A. E. F.
SUBJECT:　Discharge.

1. *Application is respectfully made herein for discharge from the Military Service of the United States.* Reasons for this application may be summarized by the following notations:

　(a)　By S. O. 82 Hqs. 92d Division, April 25, 1918, I was detailed as
　　　Acting Division Personnel Officer.

　(b)　By announcement of Division Adjutant, the work of the Personnel
　　　Department was merged into and placed under the head of Statisti-
　　　cal Officer on arrival of the Division overseas and I was designated
　　　as an assistant to the Statistical Officer.

(c)  Under this arrangement *other officers were placed in charge of the work which I had begun, SYSTEMATIZED, AND BUILT UP, and I was given a subordinate place. Since that time other officers have been assigned and detailed to the department and each addition lowers me, but has not lessened my work or responsibilities.*

(d)  Paragraph 4, G. O. 100, G. H. Q., A. E. F., June 20, 1918, specifies that Personnel officers will also perform the duties laid down as functions of Statistical Officers.  From which it appears that where a Division brings over its Personnel Officer, he is eligible to become Statistical Officer (not an *assistant* to Statistical Officer).

(e)  G. O. 60. W. D., June 24, 1918, also contemplates that the Personnel Officer under the change of name, becomes the Personnel Adjutant.  When this order was issued, another officer was designated as Personnel Adjutant and I was designated as an assistant.

2.  Without questioning any of the actions above mentioned as to *fairness* or wisdom, *I have felt that each change has advanced others and lowered me and it has discouraged and disheartened me to the extent that I cannot work with the same spirit as an officer who feels that he is getting a square deal.*

3.  *No one has ever charged me with inefficiency.*  As assistant to the first Personnel Officer, *my work was satisfactory in every respect,* and when I afterward relieved him, *my work continued to be satisfactory and was commended by the commanding general of the division.*

   *The only conclusion I have been able to reach is that others are placed in charge of the work because I am a Negro, and under the plan of organization as promulgated in Memo. dated September 11, 1918, Headquarters 92nd Division, ineligible to be attached to division headquarters.*

4.  *Under these circumstances,* and without having had any experience in any other divisional branch of duty, I respectfully ask to be discharged.

(Signed)  T. T. THOMPSON,

1st Lt. Inf. U. S. A., Assistant Personnel Adjutant.

—

(Exhibit ''C'')

(Official Evidence showing how the ''color line'' in the Army decreases the Negro's efficiency.)

**HEADQUARTERS NINETY-SECOND DIVISION**

Camp Funston, Kansas.

Forwarded recommending approval.

(Copy)

This officer (Lieutenant T. T. Thompson) was originally assigned to duty as Acting Personnel Officer, in which capacity *he did good work, and was recommended to be promoted Captain with a view to being assigned to duty as permanent Personnel Officer. This was disapproved by the War Department on the ground that the Personnel Officer should be "white."*

Lieutenant Thompson was *continued as an assistant, there being no other line of work to which he was so well adapted.*

*The ruling of the War Department made his advancement impossible and others passed him as stated in his letter.*

*The result has been the discouragement and lessened efficiency of an officer of considerable promise, who has much justice on his side in alleging race discrimination.*

(Signed)   C. C. BALLOU,
Commanding General.

—

When Lieutenant Thompson brought his case to the attention of the Special Assistant he took up the matter with the War Department, and received the following reply from the Adjutant General's office:

MEMORANDUM for Mr. Emmett J. Scott, Special Assistant to the Secretary of War.

In compliance with your memorandum request of March 10th, I have had the record in the case of Lieutenant Toliver T. Thompson carefully examined and can find no evidence of the fact that he has been discriminated against in any way.

The instructions of the Secretary of War dated October 20, 1917, which referred to the organization of the 92d Division require,

*"That the following officers of the division be WHITE:*

(a)   All officers of General and Field Rank.

(b)   Such Medical officers and Veterinarians as the Surgeon General may decide.

(c)   All officers attached to Division Headquarters except the Lieutenants of the Headquarters Troop.

(d)   All Regimental Adjutants, Supply Officers, Commanding Officers of Headquarters Companies and of Engineer Train, Adjutants of Train Headquarters and Ammunition Train, and Supply Officers of Sanitary Train.

(e)   All Captains of the Field Artillery Brigade and Engineer Regiments.

(f)   Aides to Brigade Commanders."

In view of the above instructions of the Secretary of War dated October 20, 1917, you will see that the recommendation made on April 30, 1918, for the appointment of Lieutenant Thompson as Division Personnel Officer was in direct violation of the above quoted orders. For this reason the recommendation was filed without action.

(Signed)  P. C. HARRIS,<br>
The Adjutant General.

March 12, 1919.

To further the project of eliminating Negro officers from the Army forever, it was reported to the Special Assistant, in a letter sent from France by Ralph W. Tyler, the accredited Negro War Correspondent of the Committee on Public Information, that Colonel Allen J. Greer of the United States Army, 92nd Division, had addressed a letter to this effect to Senator Kenneth D. Mc-Kellar, in violation of a law which would subject him to court-martial. Among other things Colonel Greer was reported as writing:

"Now that a reorganization of the Army is in prospect, and as all officers of the temporary forces have been asked if they desire to remain in the Regular Army, I think *I ought to bring a matter to your attention that is of vital importance not only from a military point of view, but from that which all Southerners have. I refer to the question of Negro officers and Negro troops.* The records of the Division will probably never be given full publicity, but the bare facts are facts about as follows. We came to France in June, were given seven weeks in training area instead of four weeks in training area usually allotted, then went to a quiet sector of the front. From there we went to the Argonne and, in the offensive starting there on September 26 (1918) had one regiment in the line, attached to the 38th French Corps. They failed there in all their missions, lay down and sneaked to the rear, until they were withdrawn. Thirty of the officers of this regiment alone were reported either for cowardice or failure to prevent their men from retreating —and this against very little opposition. The French and our white field officers did all that could possibly have been done; but the troops were impossible. One of our Majors commanding a battalion said: "The men are rank cowards; there is no other word for it. During the entire time we have been operating, there has never been a single operation conducted by a colored officer, where his report did not have to be investigated by some field officer to find out what the real facts were. Accuracy and ability to describe facts is lacking in all, and most of them are just plain liars in addition.''

This manifestly prejudiced statement by Colonel Allen J. Greer has been disproved *in toto* by men who know of the unquestioned valor of Negro troops and the high percentage of efficiency obtaining among Negro officers, many of whom have been awarded the Croix de Guerre and Distinguished Service Medals; it constitutes one of the basest misrepresentations (born of race prejudice, which he openly confesses) that were ever made concerning the efficiency and fearlessness of Negro men in the United States Army, and is in striking contrast to numerous views expressed by other American and by French officers. Colonel Greer entirely overlooked numerous citations to Negro men and officers of the 92nd Division that he had personally signed as Chief of Staff of the 92nd Division.

The Negro press, as a unit, vigorously resented Colonel Greer's insinuation that Negro officers and Negro troops were cowards and incompetents, and, in the interest of national unity and national security, hammered away at injustice and racial discrimination wherever it was shown. Typical of the attitude of the Negro press, is the following editorial comment from the facile pen of that veteran Negro journalist, John Mitchell, editor of *The Richmond* (Va.) *Planet:*

"Complaint is not made of the hardships to which our colored troops were subjected, but on account of discriminations made on account of race and color. They went over there to take a soldier's fare but they did not go over there to feel the pangs of American race prejudice in the midst of a people who made no discrimination on account of race or color."

The following statement of the Negro officers' case comes from Colonel Charles Young, a graduate of West Point, who reached the highest rank ever held by a Negro in the United States Army.

### Colonel Young's Statement

"The black officer feels that there was a prejudgment against him at the outset, and that nearly every move that has been made was for the purpose of bolstering up his prejudgment and discrediting him in the eyes of the world and the men whom he was to lead and will lead in the future.

"Unpatriotic and unwarranted statements do no good and lull the country to sleep, and throw it off its guard while the effects of these statements are causing just rankling in the breasts of the Negro people who have had a new vision.

"The Negro officers know the psychology of their own race and also of the white race; but it is to be feared the latter will never know the mind and motive forces of the Negro if he imagines that this group has not had a new birth in America, whose language it speaks, whose thought it thinks for its own betterment, and whose ideals, both social, political and economic, it emulates."

Under such circumstances, therefore, with the Hun as an enemy in front and certain American army officials utilizing race prejudice as a destructive agency against him in the rear, the Negro officer seriously suffered during the World War, and upon the return from overseas of the regiments formerly commanded by Negroes, it was most disappointing to the colored people in the various cities of this country where parades were held, to see black men led by white officers, their colored officers in many cases having been removed.

### Race Discrimination Overseas

In keeping with this policy, there were many instances of color discrimination in France. On one occasion, after an order had been issued to the effect that certain Negro troops should be carried on the battleship *"Virginia,"* the executive officer requested the Admiral to have these troops *removed on the ground that no colored troops had ever traveled on board a United States battleship.* The Negroes were accordingly removed to a tug and subjected to unusual hardships in being brought back to port. In certain places where it was sometimes necessary for officers of both races belonging to the American Expeditionary Forces to eat together, peculiar provisions were made so as to have Negro officers report to certain quarters, or sections of the same messroom, inasmuch as white officers refused to sit at mess with them. There is ample evidence to show that in most cases the Negro officers had inferior accommodations. On one occasion, in providing for the reception of General John Pershing, the Commanding Officer of the American Expeditionary Forces, at one of the forwarding camps in France, the order was given that *"all troops possible (except colored) should be under arms;"* colored troops, who were not at work, were to be in their quarters or in their tents, according to the command of Brigadier General Longan.

This order, however, was later revoked, after a firm protest by Negro officers and men, and, as a result, colored troops did appear "under arms" in General Pershing's review.

With reference to conditions existing among Negro soldiers overseas and to certain discriminations which were attempted and practiced against them, *Lieutenant Charles S. Parker*, of Spokane, Washington, connected with the 366th Infantry, and who was *the only Negro who served as a Regimental Adjutant in the 92nd Division*, made the following statement:

"At Brest, France, a Memorandum was issued by the Commander of Zone Five, *prescribing mess hours for colored officers* (a) one hour earlier than the usual hour for breakfast; (b) one hour later for the mid-day meal, and (c) one hour later for the supper meal—*thus requiring colored soldiers to get up one hour earlier in the morning for their breakfast and to wait until after the white officers had eaten at the other two meals.* Before publishing the order, I took up the matter with my Colonel, stated the injustice of the proposed arrangement, and he approved of my taking the matter up with the Company Headquarters, at which point I had the order revoked. Thus it was that the order indicating separate hours for Negro officers and white officers to eat, was never published to our command, though a number of the colored officers had positive knowledge of its existence. Likewise, in the case of the Order directing all troops, *except colored troops*, to appear in General Pershing's review 'under arms'— that order, like other attempted discriminations, was only revoked after an earnest protest had been made by colored officers. Also at Brest, France, an order was issued, directing that all Negro orderlies from colored units, who were stationed at Headquarters, should use the open latrines which were unsheltered and which made it very disagreeable during rainy weather, while orderlies from white units, also stationed at Headquarters, were permitted to use the sheltered latrines. When this matter was taken up and properly protested against, the order was revoked as being a 'mistake.'

"The revocation of these orders did much toward keeping down friction between the races in the American army overseas, and I attribute their cancellation not to any particular ability on my part as a Negro Regimental Adjutant, but to the fact that my position put me in close contact with the white officers commanding troops and I was familiar with and could clearly represent to them the feelings and requirements of colored officers and colored men. *This only emphasizes in my mind the wisdom and justice of appointing Negro Regimental Adjutants and Negro officers for all Negro troops, for they and they alone, can properly interpret the sentiments and needs of Negro soldiers and help maintain the highest possible morale among them.*"

The humiliation of the Negro in France, however, was not restricted to army circles. Military staff officers seemed to be firm in the conviction that it was necessary to prejudice the minds of the French people against the Negroes in order that they might be held down to the same status they had in the United States. General Ervin, who succeeded General Ballou in the command of the 92nd Division—complying with the wishes of his co-workers—issued among other regulations, Order No. 40—a proclamation that Negroes should not speak with or to French women. Carrying out this order the Military Police overseas undertook to arrest Negroes found talking to French women while the *white privates and officers were not molested.* This led to a serious misunderstanding between the French and the Americans and to a number of brawls in which the white and black soldiers participated. In addition to orders issued designed to prevent Negro soldiers overseas from coming into social contact with French civilians, French officers were also advised not to present any semblance of mixing socially with Negro officers, especially not to eat with them, and also not to praise the Negro in the presence of white Americans for any military action in which he participated.

For instance,—in order to make such a program as that of General Ervin's more successful, biased Americans succeeded in having issued, on August 7, 1918, from General Pershing's headquarters, through the military mission stationed with the American army, certain *secret information* concerning black American troops. This document began with the observation that *"it is important for French officers in command of black American troops to have an idea as to the position occupied by the race in the United States."* The Negroes were referred to as a "menace of degeneracy which had to be prevented by the gulf established between the two races," and especially so "because of the fact that they were given to the loathsome vice of criminally assaulting women, as evidenced by the record," they said, "they had already made in France." *The French were,* therefore, *called upon "not to treat the Negroes with familiarity and indulgence which are matters of grievous concern to Americans and an affront to their national policy."* *The Americans,* it continued, *are afraid that the blacks might thereby be inspired with undesirable aspirations.* It was carefully explained that although the black man as a citizen of the United States is regarded by the whites as *inferior,* with whom relations of business and service only are possible, that the black is noted for his want of intelligence, lack of discretion, and lack of civic and professional conscience. *The French army then was advised to prevent the rise of any pronounced degree of intimacy between French officers and black officers, not to eat with them, not to shake hands or seek to talk or meet with them outside of the requirements of military service. They were asked also not to commend too highly the black American troops in the presence of white Americans.* Although it is all right to recognize the good qualities and services of black Americans, *it must be done in moderate terms,* strictly in keeping with the truth.

French officers and French civilians, as a rule, could not understand why the black soldiers should not be treated identically as white American soldiers; when French officers were alone with Negro officers, the latter were treated with the utmost friendliness and consideration, and it was only when in the presence of American officers that they reluctantly observed the official order, inspired by race prejudice, which positively forbade them from fraternizing with Negro soldiers and officers. *Thus it was that race prejudice in the Army was carried overseas—to a land where discriminations on account of race or color are neither practiced nor encouraged— to a land where freedom, liberty, and equality are truly exemplified.*

When reports began to come back from France, in divers and sundry ways—alleging unfair treatment of colored soldiers, the Special Assistant immediately assembled these complaints and brought them to the attention of the proper officials in the War Department, including the Military Intelligence Bureau. The Military Intelligence officers ferreted out a number of these complaints, although some of them were contained in anonymous communications. While some of them were found to be justifiable and worthy of corrections, others were found to represent only the exaggerated statement of some individual soldier whose own indiscretion or violation of military law and regulations had brought upon him the punishment or hardships concerning which he complained. Determined to do his utmost to find out the real facts regarding conditions among Negro soldiers in France, and realizing the serious effect that a continuance of such complaints would have upon the morale of colored soldiers and colored Americans generally, the author on August 10, 1918, recommended the special inquiry outlined in the letter to Mr. George Creel, Director of the Committee on Public Information, which will be found on pages 114-116.

### Conditions in the Labor Battalions

In the Labor Battalions sent abroad were impressed many Negroes who went to the front with the hope of bearing arms, but, in conformity with the idea prevailing in some sections of making the Negro a laborer only—thousands of Negro soldiers who had been drilled for service at the front were, for various excuses, reduced and placed in these Labor Battalions. Speaking of the conditions at one camp a Negro officer reported: "The conditions are simply awful; mud everywhere, leaky tents and barracks and lack of sufficient food and proper toilets. The men are worked hard, some at night and others in the day, rain or shine. As a consequence there are quite a number of sick men in our organization." The Fifteenth Regiment of New York, for example, was made to render such service for a time, but was finally placed in a somewhat quiet sector where it was supposed they would not have to engage in hard military fighting. It turned out, however, that the Germans, in their advance, attacked this point, making it necessary for the Old Fifteenth to defend the

# THEY LIE IN FRANCE
# WHERE LILIES BLOOM

They lie in France
Where lilies bloom;
Those flowers pale
That guard each tomb
Are saintly souls
That smiling stand
Close, by them in
That martyred land,
And mutely there the long night shadows creep
From quiet hills to mourn for them who sleep,
While o'er them through the dusk go silently
The grieving clouds that slowly drift to sea,
And lately round them moaned the Winter wind
Whose voice, lamenting, sounds so coldly kind,
Yet in their faith those waiting hearts abide
The time when turns forever that false tide.
In France they lie
Where lilies bloom,
Those flowers fair
For them made room.
Not vainly placed
The crosses stand
Within that brave
And stricken land;
Their honor lives,
Their love endures,
Their noble death
The right assures,
For they shall have their hearts' desire,
They who, unflinching, braved the fire,
Across the fields their eyes at last shall see
Through clouds and mist the hosts of victory.

PERCIVAL ALLEN, in the New York *Times*.

line, *and history shows that these black men designed to play the inconspicuous role of laborers in the war, won for themselves the greatest honor of the war in that they were the first regiment summoned as a whole for citation by the French Government because of the valor they displayed upon the battlefield.* Thus, in military as well as in civil life—out of trials and hardships there often flow counterbalancing benefits and unexpected opportunities for advancement.

After the signing of the Armistice, it was repeatedly stated in the Negro press and in numerous letters from soldiers and others received at Washington, that Reserve Labor Battalions and similar military units composed of colored men were being kept in the Army out of proportion to the number of white troops that were discharged in various camps through the country. Using Newport News as a typical case, and as related by a Director of Colored Work in close touch with the situation, this officer stated: "The causes of unrest as heard from the men themselves are: First: The unfair type of white officers. The commanding officer is very popular with the men, but I have heard no soldier speak a good word for the majority of officers on his staff. Second: They resent being kept in the Army for the purpose of doing all kinds of menial work every day of the week for the good of this section of the country, which they hate with a holy hate. They say that the war is over and why should they be kept at work on something that does not pertain to war; that they enlisted in the Army to defeat Germany and now that Germany is defeated, their job is done and they are anxious to get back to their families and their normal activities. They are the two fundamental causes of unrest. The low morale is something appalling; the men hang around in groups brooding and grumbling. They are beginning to look upon the uniforms as emblems of slavery. You can readily see where this condition of mind is leading to. It strikes me that seeds of anarchy are being planted. * * * There is but one remedy and that is to demobilize them. To keep these men here in their present state of mind means two things—it is preparing the way for serious disturbances at this particular point; and second, it is implanting a bitterness in the souls of these men that will stay with them as long as life lasts. They will leave here with their patriotism destroyed, with a stronger prejudice against the white race, and contempt for the flag itself. For the sake of these men's futures, if for nothing else, they ought to be sent away. The greatest injustice that can be done them is to continue to hold them and later send them back to their homes with an embittered spirit."

### Attitude Toward Colored Medical Officers

Much dissatisfaction arose and was voiced in the Negro press and elsewhere concerning the seeming disinclination on the part of the Surgeon General's office to commission and utilize an adequate number of colored medical officers to minister to the physical needs of the 400,000 Negroes who served in the Army. Still more resentment was felt and expressed by reason of the fact that a large number of Negro physicians, surgeons and dentists were not permitted to serve the Government in their professional capacities, but were drafted into service as privates, while many white physicians, surgeons, and dentists served, in many instances, in connection with Negro troops. This was considered not only a denial of their right to serve as medical officers at least in connection with men of their own race, but was also regarded as an unwarranted reflection upon their professional ability. Colored Medical Societies all over the country protested against the manifest policy of the Government not to commission an adequate number of colored medical officers as well as against the idea of permitting white physicians to serve in connection with colored units, and compelling many Negro physicians to serve as "privates." Repeated efforts were made by the author to bring about the increased utilization of colored medical officers, but the effort was persistently blocked by the Surgeon General's office, and in response to numerous Memoranda sent to that office in behalf of Negro physicians and surgeons, the Special Assistant almost invariably received the following reply: "At the present time there are no vacancies in the Medical Corps to which colored medical officers can be assigned, and until such vacancies occur, or additional divisions of colored troops are organized, it is not the intention of the Department to recommend the appointment of additional colored medical officers." At the same time these replies were received, white medical officers were serving in connection with a number of stevedore regiments, labor battalions and other non-combatant units composed of colored men, while competent colored physicians were serving as privates in the Army—some of them in work battalions. Was this a "square deal" in the matter of colored medical officers? A rightful quota of them was, by no means, commissioned and utilized.

### Attitude Toward Colored Nurses

The situation with regard to *colored nurses* was even more difficult of adjustment and far less satisfactorily handled. In the whole matter of trying to have colored nurses accepted in the Army for the purpose of nursing sick and wounded soldiers—especially those of their own race who uniformly preferred colored nurses—the whole situation (as will be noted in the correspondence which follows) resolved itself into a matter of "passing the buck" from the Surgeon General's office to the American Red Cross, and from the Red Cross Society to the Surgeon General's office. There was a manifest disinclination to utilize colored nurses, and not because they were not competent. Thus racial discrimination triumphed again, and although a few colored nurses were assigned to half a dozen or more camps, practically none of them were sent overseas to nurse and minister to the fighting men of their own race. Was this a "square deal" either for the Negro soldier or for the scores of competent nurses all over the country who tendered their services to the Government? The appended correspondence reveals the "battledore and shuttlecock" policy which was used in shifting the blame for the non-assignment of colored nurses.

February 14, 1918.

Referring to your memorandum of February 12th, *relative to the appointment and training of colored nurses for colored soldiers*, at the present time *colored nurses are not being accepted for service in the Army Nurse Corps*, as there are *no separate quarters available for them*, and *it is not deemed advisable to assign white and colored nurses to the same posts*.

Colored nurses who have applied for admission to the Corps are advised to *apply to the American Red Cross*, as should they be used later in the Army hospital of this country, *they will*, in all probability, *be selected from the Red Cross list*.

(Signed)  W. C. GORGAS,
Surgeon General, U. S. Army.

It will be noted in the above communication that colored nurses were directed to "apply to the American Red Cross," and in the following communication it is stated, by the Director of the Red Cross Department of Nursing, that the utilization or assignment of colored nurses "after all is a matter for the Surgeon General to decide rather than our office."

THE AMERICAN RED CROSS

National Headquarters,

Washington, D. C.

January 9th, 1918.

Mr. John M. Glenn, General Director,

Russell Sage Foundation,

New York City.

My Dear Sir:

The RED CROSS is entirely willing to enroll colored nurses whenever there is an opportunity for their service in military hospitals. We communicated with the superintendents of training schools admitting colored pupils, asking them to submit the names of graduates whom they would recommend for Red Cross nurses.

Several attempts have been made to organize a Base Hospital Unit composed of colored nurses only, and we hope to do this in connection with the Lincoln Hospital in New York and with the Freedmen's Hospital, in Washington. A cantonment for colored troops was originally planned at Des Moines, and we hoped to utilize such a base hospital unit in connection with this cantonment. The colored soldiers were later distributed throughout the cantonments, and there were practical difficulties in the way of assigning the colored nurses to duty with the white nurses.

The Surgeon General's office has been informed that we have such lists available, and that these nurses can be quickly enrolled, whenever there is a possibility of their assignment to duty.

There has never been any question in regard to our willingness to enroll colored nurses and the only *question is how best to assign them to duty, which, after all is a matter for the Surgeon General to decide, rather than our office.*

This matter was fully discussed by the National Committee on Red Cross Nursing Service in the very beginning of the war, and they unanimously agreed that whenever colored nurses could be used, they should be enrolled on exactly the same status as white nurses. It does not seem desirable, however, to enroll them without reference to their color.

I am glad of the opportunity to send you this explanation.

Yours very truly,

(Signed)  JANE A. DELANO,
Director, Department of Nursing.

In view of the conflicting circumstances set forth above with reference to colored nurses in the Army, the Special Assistant made an earnest effort to cure the situation, as the following Memorandum will show:

February 28, 1918.

MEMORANDUM FOR DEAN F. P. KEPPEL,
Office of the Secretary of War.

My Dear Dean Keppel:

I confess my inability to altogether understand the situation *with refer-ence to the utilization of colored nurses during the present war.*

ATTITUDE OF THE RED CROSS ORGANIZATION.

Let me put it before you in this way: *The Red Cross organization has been industriously writing letters to the effect that they are perfectly willing to enroll colored nurses,* as will be noted in the following extract taken from a letter written by the Director of the Department of Nursing under date of January 9, 1918:

"There has never been any question in regard to our willingness to enroll colored nurses and *the only question is how best to assign them to duty, which, after all is a matter for the Surgeon General to decide rather than our office.*

"This matter was fully discussed by the National Committee on Red Cross Nursing Service in the very beginning of the war, and they unanimously agreed that whenever colored nurses could be used, they should be enrolled on exactly the same status as white nurses. It does not seem desirable, however, to enroll them without reference to their color."

This seems to pass the matter, as you will note, to the Surgeon General.

ATTITUDE OF THE SURGEON GENERAL.

*The Surgeon General's attitude* is reflected in his letter of February 14, 1918, and is stated as follows:

"Referring to your memorandum of February 12th relative to the appointment and training of colored nurses for colored soldiers, *at the present time colored nurses are not being accepted for service in the Army Nurse Corps* as there are no separate quarters available for them, and it is not deemed advisable to assign white and colored nurses to the same posts."

"Colored nurses who have applied for admission to the Corps are advised to apply to the American Red Cross for enrollment, as should they be used later in the army hospitals of this country, they will, in all probability, be selected from the Red Cross list."

From the above, it will be seen that the whole matter of utilizing colored nurses is still very much "up in the air."

The upshot of the whole matter is that, while there are thousands of colored men who have been called to the colors as soldiers, no colored nurses have been admitted to the service although quite a number have enrolled with the Red Cross organization as suggested, and they, together with many more well-trained, competent, and registered nurses are ready and willing to look after sick and wounded soldiers who are now and soon will be facing shot and shell upon battlefields abroad.

I would most earnestly recommend that some satisfactory way be found that will offer to colored nurses in the Army Nurse Corps and in the Red Cross organization the same opportunity for serving sick and wounded soldiers as has been so wisely and timely provided for white nurses.

Waiving all discussion as to the matter of assigning white and colored nurses to the same posts or quarters, it is difficult for me to understand why some colored nurses have not been given an opportunity to serve.

This vexing question is being put to me almost daily by colored newspaper editors, colored physicians, surgeons, etc., who are constantly bombarding my sector of the War Department, inquiring what has been done, and urging that something should be done in the direction of utilizing professionally trained and efficient colored nurses.

I recognize the "problems," but can't they be solved?

(Signed) EMMETT J. SCOTT,
WHD                                                      Special Assistant.

## Discriminations in the Government Service

While Negro soldiers were fighting overseas in defense of their country, race prejudice was denying to many members of their families and dependents at home the chance of earning a livelihood in the Government service in Washington and elsewhere. Hundreds of instances can be cited where Negroes, even after qualifying as eligibles by successfully passing civil service examinations for various positions in the Government service, were absolutely "turned down" and denied appointment—in many cases after they had been definitely certified for appointment by the U. S. Civil Service Commission and had journeyed long distances from their home cities to Washington in response to notices by mail or telegrams announcing their appointment. This was not only a source of disappointment and chagrin, as well as financial loss, to the individual Negro applicant, but the widespread prevalence of such an unjust policy constituted a serious menace to the morale of colored Americans generally, who felt and knew that *in this very vital respect,* namely, the opportunity to earn a living after proving one's self fully qualified, THEIR RACE WAS NOT GETTING A "SQUARE DEAL." It placed the Government in the attitude of *"drawing the color line"* in the matter of employment, which was never contemplated by the enactment of the Civil Service law. The following letter received by the author from Mr. Archibald H. Grimke, a member of the Executive Committee of the Washington Branch of the National Association for the Advancement of Colored People, indicates the state of feeling existing among colored Americans in this respect:

### THE NATIONAL ASSOCIATION FOR THE ADVANCEMENT OF COLORED PEOPLE

Washington, D. C., September 17, 1918.

Dr. Emmett J. Scott,
 Special Assistant to the Secretary of War,
  War Department.

My dear Mr. Scott:

I find in almost all Departments of the Government discriminations against colored applicants for clerkships. I will name the following where this discrimination seems to flourish, viz: The Quartermaster's Bureau, the Ordnance Bureau, the Adjutant General's Office, the War Risk Bureau, the U. S. Shipping Board, the Civilian Personnel Division of the War Department, the Food and Animal Industry Bureau, the U. S. Employment Bureau.

I name these merely because I have had more to do with these in behalf of colored applicants for clerkships, but these unfortunate American citizens are up against it hard all along the line of Government where they come into competition with white applicants for the same jobs. I hope that you with others may find some cure for this evil.

Gratefully yours,

(Signed)	ARCHIBALD H. GRIMKE,
President, Local Branch.

In a number of instances the Special Assistant was successful in having the rights of Negro applicants upheld, but in the large majority of cases devious ways were found to sidestep the civil service law. True it was that Negroes in considerable number were employed in various offices and branches of the government service, but even then, in most instances, they were segregated or "Jim Crow-ed" and unnecessary indignities were visited upon them. While full credit is given to the number of Negroes who were appointed to and who rightfully held Government positions during the war, the fact still remains, AND A LESSON WHICH SHOULD BE LEARNED FROM, AND APPLIED AFTER THE WAR, that it is un-American, inconsistent, unjust, and destructive of a healthy morale for the Government, especially, to discriminate against any group of citizens simply and solely on account of their race or color.

### False Impressions and Evidences of Fair Play

It is wrong to assume, because the Negro soldier suffered many hardships during the war,. and was the victim of various forms of racial discrimination, that he was the only one who suffered and it is manifestly unfair to make a wholesale condemnation of Army and Government officials, many of whom sympathized with his position and were actively working for his welfare. White soldiers and white officers suffered many of the hardships of war the same as Negroes did, and many were the complaints and grievances that were registered by them at the War Department. While they were exempted from many of the racial discriminations hereinabove recited, nevertheless the kind of treatment they received was largely dependent upon the character and temperament of the superior officer under whom they served.

It would be wholly unfair to the Secretary of War, to his Assistants, to many members of his Staff, to certain officials of the War Department and to a number of white officers in command of Negro troops, if it were not specifically stated that, on numerous occasions, impelled by a high sense of justice, they actively indicated their earnest desire to give the Negro soldier "a square deal," and it was their consistent policy to rectify, as far as possible, all complaints that were in their power to remedy. It is easy to substantiate the fact that, as a rule, the "men higher up" in Army circles were disposed to be fair and just in their attitude toward the Negro soldier.

The Secretary of War is to be especially commended upon his willingness at all times to listen to the pleas of the Special Assistant on behalf of Negro soldiers and to any other matter calculated to affect the morale of colored Americans generally. Not only did he sympathetically listen, but he actively sought in many ways to remedy the conditions concerning which complaints were made. Unfortunately, however, in a number of instances the Secretary of War could not give his personal attention to every complaint and had to deal with "human instrumentalities" in bringing things to pass, and ofttimes those "human instrumentalities," that were expected to, and relied upon to carry out the letter and spirit of his purposes, did not synchronize with his own high ideals of justice and fair play, and, therefore, in some instances the desired result was not obtained.

No set of men, in my opinion, could have been fairer in their general attitude toward the Negro people than were those connected with the Office of the Secretary of War. Aside from the splendid spirit of fair play shown by Secretary Baker and the Assistant Secretaries of War, his private secretaries, Mr. Ralph A. Hayes, and Mr. Stanley King, aided in many ways in securing prompt consideration and correction of numerous complaints and grievances. The office of Dr. F. P. Keppel, Third Assistant Secretary of War, was especially charged with the duty of looking after many complaints and matters of vital concern to colored soldiers and colored Americans generally, and not only did he manifest a keen interest in their welfare but, in many cases, was successful in translating that interest into remedial action.

In all dealings with the Provost Marshal General's Office, looking after the interests of Negro men who were drafted into the Army, the Special Assistant found in every case a disposition to thoroughly investigate such grievances and to carefully consider such appeals as were presented. The Provost Marshal General's Office carefully investigated and furnished to him, as Special Assistant to the Secretary of War, full and complete reports in each and every complaint or case referred to it for attention, involving discriminations, race prejudice, erroneous classification of draftees, etc., and rectified such complaints wherever it was found, upon investigation, that there was just ground for the same. Especially in the matter of applying and carrying out the Selective Service Regulations, the Provost Marshal General's office kept a watchful eye upon certain local exemption boards which seemed disinclined to treat Negro draftees on the same basis as other Americans subject to the draft law. It is an actual fact that in a number of instances where flagrant violations occurred in the application of the Draft Law to Negro men in certain sections of the country, local exemption boards were removed bodily and new boards were appoint to supplant them. In several instances these new boards so appointed were ordered by the Provost Marshal General to reclassify all colored men who had been unlawfully conscripted into the Army or who had been wrongly classified; as a result of this action, hundreds of colored men had their complaints remedied and were properly classified. Of course, there were a number of such worthy cases that were neither presented to my office, nor to the office of the Provost Marshal General.

Numbers of white Commanding Officers displayed a most friendly and sympathetic attitude toward Negro soldiers and Negro officers and gave them opportunities to demonstrate their efficiency and to earn promotions.

With regard to overseas complaints, as well as complaints emanating from camps at home, it seems not to have been generally known that in the recent war, where millions of men were called to serve in the American Army, it was not possible for the Secretary of War or any other one official to read all of the complaints and grievances even if they had been presented. The fact that no one person could administer all of the affairs of such an immense Army was the reason why all of the camps, both home and abroad, were "decentralized," that is to say, the Camp Commanders at home, and General Pershing abroad were practically supreme in their own military bailiwick, and exercised full charge over the handling and settling of all such complaints. In previous wars, involving only a few hundred thousand men, complaints were usually appealable to, and handled by one central authority, namely the War Department at Washington. It can, therefore, be readily understood that the settlement of complaints made by soldiers, whether black or white, depended almost wholly upon the character of officers under whom they served.

Not only were about 1,200 Negroes commissioned as Army officers, and thousands of Negro soldiers furnished educational opportunities in connection with Vocational Detachments and Students' Army Training Corps located at 18 or 20 of the leading colored institutions of the country, thus showing some regard to their mental qualifications and special adaptabilities, but a number of other signal honors were conferred upon Negro soldiers and Negro officers. For instance, it is not generally known that *Camp Alexander, at Newport News, Virginia, was so named in honor of a Negro officer who has served in the Army of the United States.* Following is a copy of the Official Order conferring that honor:

HEADQUARTERS, PORT OF EMBARKATION
Newport News, Virginia

General Orders No. 294

August 15, 1918.

The Stevedore Cantonment and the Labor Encampments in the vicinity of North Newport News will hereafter be known collectively as CAMP ALEXANDER, Newport News, Virginia.

*The above designation is in honor of the late Lieutenant John H. Alexander, 9th U. S. Cavalry, a colored graduate of the United States military academy, who served from the time of his graduation until his death as an officer of the army. A man of ability, attainments and energy, who was a credit to himself, to his race and to the service.*

By command of Brigadier-General Grote Hutcheson.

(Signed)  DANIEL VAN VOORHIS,

Official:                                        Colonel, General Staff,
C. W. BELL,                                           Chief of Staff.
        Colonel, Adjutant General,
        Adjutant.

The Chief of Staff, General Peyton C. March, the Military Intelligence Bureau, of which General Marlborough Churchill was the directing head, and the morale section of the office of the Chief of Staff, of which General E. L. Munson was in charge,—all deserve much credit for the effective manner in which they handled the numerous complaints of Negro soldiers, Negro officers, and civilians, that were referred to them for attention by my office and which reached them from various other sources. Scores of such complaints were ferreted out by them and, while the methods employed to cure the evils complained of were necessarily secret and confidential, they were vitally helpful in remedying a number of conditions tending to depress the morale of colored soldiers and colored Americans generally. After taking definite steps to improve conditions among Negro soldiers at Camp Alexander, Va., the Office of the Chief of Staff, Military Intelligence Branch, wrote:

February 7, 1919.

Dear Mr. Scott:

Information has come to this office that the situation at Camp Alexander has greatly improved during the past few weeks.

*An improvement both in discipline and morale has been noted. The instituting of military drill seems to have had a good effect in the labor battalions, where the men had previously received no military training.*

*The men seem to feel that they are being treated as soldiers,* and they begin to exhibit soldierly qualities in their deportment and appearance.

Also in a Memorandum, under date of February 18, 1919, addressed to the Special Assistant by E. L. Munson, Chief of the Morale Branch, the following observation was made:

*"One change which proved very helpful to the morale, was the transfer of a large number of unsatisfactory non-commissioned officers who were replaced by colored non-commissioned officers selected in their own organizations."*

Major J. E. Spingarn, Captain J. E. Cutler, and others connected with the Military Intelligence branches of the Government made diligent effort to find out the facts in every case where complaint was made. They, together with many officials of the War Department, *seemed to realize the fact that,* like the white man, *the black man is intensely human; that he thrives when his good works and worth are recognized and appreciated, and droops and wilts when they are disparaged and condemned.*

*Thus it appears that while the Negro was, in many instances, the victim of racial discrimination and injustice in time of war, yet*—by his demonstrated loyalty, valor, and efficiency in practically every branch of military service (to some of which he was reluctantly admitted), *he has proved his right to be granted a fuller measure of justice, respect, opportunity, and fair play in time of peace!*

# CHAPTER XXXI

## WHAT THE NEGRO GOT OUT OF THE WAR

*A Keener Sense of His Rights and Privileges as a Citizen of the United States—The Attitude of the South—Returning Negro Soldiers and Conditions in the North—The Attitude of Organized Labor—Instances of Discrimination—The Black Man and His Claims to Equal Treatment.*

What the Negro should get out of the war ought to be determined largely by what he put into it. Practically all colored leaders of consequence felt that in spite of the wrongs the race had from time immemorial suffered every member of the race should be loyal. To secure coöperation to this end special appeals were made to the colored people of the country for their unstinted support. A specially selected Committee of One Hundred colored speakers to whom reference has been made, acting with local groups everywhere, was appointed and materially assisted in the work of maintaining the morale of the Negro race throughout the war, the demobilization of the army and the reconstruction of the nation on a peace basis.

Briefly stated, the Negroes did their full share in the great struggle to make the world safe for democracy. Four hundred thousand Negro soldiers were drafted or enlisted and 200,000 served in France under white officers and 1,200 officers of color. Negroes served in all branches of the military establishment—the cavalry, infantry, artillery, signal corps, medical corps, aviation corps, hospital corps, ammunition trains, stevedore regiments, labor battalions, depot brigades, engineer regiments, as regimental clerks, surveyors and draftsmen. Negro soldiers acquitted themselves with honor in the battles of the Argonne Forest, at Chateau Thierry, Belleau Wood, at St. Mihiel, in Champagne, in the Vosges, and at Metz, and when the Armistice was signed Negro troops as has been pointed out were nearest the Rhine. Entire regiments of colored troops, including the 369th, 370th, 371st, and 372nd, were cited for exceptional valor and decorated with the French Croix de Guerre. Groups of officers and men of the 92nd Division were likewise decorated. The first battalion of the 367th also received the Croix de Guerre. Many individuals like Harry Johnson, Needham Roberts, and William Butler were awarded the Croix de Guerre and scores of officers by devotion to duty earned, even if they did not receive, promotion in their military units.

What has the American Negro got out of the war? Time alone can bring the full answer to this sweeping question. To some of the manifold implications which the query itself involves, however, some answers can already be made. For one thing, the war has brought to the American Negro a keener and more sharply defined consciousness, not only of his duties as a citizen, but of his rights and privileges as a citizen of the United States. The colored people of America performed to the utmost of their ability the duties which the war imposed upon all citizens, black and white alike.

A summary of what the Negro wants may be stated: He wants justice in the courts substituted for lynching, the privilege of serving on juries, the right to vote, and the right to hold office like other citizens. He wants, moreover, universal suffrage, better educational facilities, the abolition of the "Jim Crow" car, discontinuance of unjust discriminatory regulations and segregation in the various departments of the Government, the same military training for Negro youths as for white, the removal of "dead lines" in the recognition of fitness for promotion in the army and navy, the destruction of the peonage system, an economic wage scale to be applied to whites and blacks alike, better housing conditions for Negro employees in industrial centers, better sanitary conditions in the Negro sections of cities, and reforms in the Southern penal institutions. If, after having fulfilled the obligations of citizenship Negroes do not get these things, then indeed, they feel, will the war have been fought in vain.

## Racial Attitude of the South

Judging from the favorable comments in Southern newspapers as to the desire for more amicable relations between the races and the tendency of Southern whites to labor for a new day of brotherhood, many have thought that this enviable situation would result as a sequel of the World War. In fact there have been a few instances

of distinguished white men who have interfered in behalf of the
Negro soldiers subjected to indignities on their return from the war.
A number of white people on a train refused to permit a conductor
to eject from the passenger car reserved for whites a Negro soldier
who returned from France with his Croix de Guerre and Distinguished Service Medal. A Southern officer on one occasion boldly
upbraided his people for their failure to accord to Negro soldiers
the treatment due those who have offered their lives to defend the
honor of this country.

Most of the professed friendship for the Negro in the South,
however, is largely an economic one, peculiar to the whites who have
materially suffered by the migration of the Negroes and who are
now very much disturbed by social unrest among the thousands of
returned Negro soldiers who find in the South conditions too in-
tolerable to be longer endured. The South as a whole is much disturbed by the question as to whether these soldiers who got a glimpse
of real democracy in France will patiently submit to the treatment
they received in the South before the World War. A larger number
of Southerners have tried to bring about a recrudescence of the
Ku Klux Klan to instill fear into the hearts of these Negroes, that
they may keep the social status assigned them. There are many
signs of opposition and discontent. Segregation and much ostra-
cism still face the Negro and lynching is about as rampant as ever.
So far as the South is concerned, therefore, it is not yet known
whether or not the Negro will benefit by the sacrifices he has made
for democracy.

### Conditions in the North

The North too has not been found a paradise for the returning
Negro soldiers. One hundred thousand of them have on account of
conditions obtaining in the South declared that they will not again
live in that section. In the North they must crowd into cities already
grappling with the problems of an increasing Negro population resulting from the migration during the World War. One finds in the
North, therefore, some of the same conditions obtaining in the South.
In Pittsburg the whites posted threatening signs on the doors of the
colored people declaring that the war is over and Negroes must stay
in their place. Recently Chicago became the scene of a race riot

between Negroes and whites who bore it grievously that their community is being invaded by an increasing number of blacks. The chances for employment, moreover, have not increased. Unusual efforts have been made to find employment for the demobilized white soldiers but the Negro soldiers experience much difficulty in finding a free opportunity to live in this country for which they so nobly fought.

In the North, however, there is a growing healthy sentiment in the interest of fair play. Many of the best citizens contend that the largest task of democracy is that of keeping her own house in order. The mere talking about ideals and theories is not so difficult as to practice them. These gentlemen deplore the fact that race prejudice seems inbred in the spirit of men and that the claims of aristocracy make a difference in one's feelings toward those who seem to be less fortunately situated. Democracy, they contend, must be made a reality. It must be considered an ideal toward which we struggle and we must not grow impatient and discouraged when we fail to realize it. Democracy must not find it difficult to provide a place for the Negro. He must be treated with justice, his interests must be protected, his life must be held precious, his children must be educated, his health must be preserved, and his rights as an American must be defended. These things they claim for the Negro because of his unusual loyalty, because he is not inoculated with any social theories, because he does not contribute to industrial discontent, because, above all, his patriotism is without alloy. Since he has made a good soldier, borne wounds, privations and death in the nation's battles to make the world safe for democracy, he deserves to find a place for himself beneath the flag for which he has fought and within the borders of the country for which he was willing to die.

In view of the fact that the Negro faithfully supported the government he expected to get a much larger portion of the benefits of democracy than was given him. The Negro expected above all that as a fundamental concession in the adjustment of affairs necessary for the reconstruction to herald a new day for the man farthest down, that colored men would at least be given full opportunity to earn a living. Much was expected from the Department of Labor when Dr. George E. Haynes was appointed as a Director of Negro

Economics to mobilize colored labor to help win the war and secure for it a higher position when industrial reconstruction should follow a victorious peace. When, however, the Department of Labor itself drew the color line, refusing to employ Negroes for certain purposes altogether on account of their color and regardless of their efficiency, this proposed good to come to the Negro caused many Negroes to call upon Dr. Haynes to emulate the example of the traditional Arab by folding his tent and quietly stealing away back to the schoolroom to teach the untutored of his race the real meaning of democracy, rather than permit himself to be a party to the camouflage of mobilizing Negro labor of the country.

### Attitude of Organized Labor

The Negroes expected too that the hard and fast rules of labor organizations which have for years barred men of color from the higher pursuits of labor, would be abrogated. It was believed that there would be new avenues for the employment of Negroes and that the so-called friends of Negro labor would be able to effect more than to secure from trade unions mere expressions of interest in behalf of the Negro laborers. It is unfortunate, however, that the Negro still finds himself refused admission to labor unions and then told that he cannot work because he is not a union man. He is denied the chance to care for his family properly and then censured because of his failure to do so. In Northern States where these restrictions have been very rigid it has been difficult to maintain order. Almost any day we hear of reports that some "gang" is hunting Negroes with the intention to do them violence and disturbances and race riots growing out of these conditions are now becoming common.

The Negro, moreover, was disappointed in his expectation to get fair play in the Civil Service of the Government. In the midst of the war, when at an unusually heavy expense to the Government, thousands of agencies had to be quickly established to expedite military preparations as much as possible, the United States Government found itself seriously suffering from a dearth of civil employees in its offices. As the demand was so great that it was necessary to waive the regulations that each should pass the civil service examination, the colored people instead of having a larger opportunity seemed to be less considered than formerly. The Civil Service

Commission has inaugurated the scheme of requiring every applicant in a civil service examination to present his photograph so as
to eliminate, it is quite generally felt, the Negro; and when the examinations were waived altogether their problem of restricting the
service entirely to white people was easily solved.

### Instances of Discrimination

Some of these instances are interesting. Mrs. Sitka D. Thomas
of Washington, D. C., and hundreds of others were certified to
Departments for clerical appointments but were rejected. One Miss
Taylor, a graduate of Howard University, was certified numerous
times to various bureaus in the service, rejected 16 times and finally
on personal appeal from her father was given a clerical position at
$720 per annum when $1,000 appointments were literally going
begging. One Miss Roberts, a graduate of the Boston Latin
School, was certified five times as a clerk to different bureaus and
rejected every time. A Mr. Thompson, now employed in the Department of Justice, was certified to the Ordnance Bureau, where he was
told that colored clerks were not wanted. Miss Aurelia Ferguson,
formerly a teacher in the public schools of New Hampshire, was
certified to the War Department, but rejected on the grounds that
she was already employed in the civil service and could not be appointed to a position paying a higher salary. She was again certified
to the War Trade Board and when she presented her telegram was
told that "some mistake had been made" as her card could not be
found. In April, 1918, she was again notified by telegram that she
had been appointed in the Bureau of War Risk at a salary of $1000
and that her services were urgently needed. Upon reporting, she
was again informed that her card could not be found. She took up
the matter with one of the Senators from New Hampshire, but he
was compelled in the end to report that nothing could be done as it
seemed to be the policy of that Bureau not to appoint colored clerks,
—only a few out of the 14,000, or more, clerks are colored.

The Negro race and especially the Negro soldier expected that
in consideration of what the race as a whole did for the winning of
the war, it would receive more consideration in the army when,
upon a revelation as to the truth about the slander upon Negro

officers the fairminded people of this country would be convinced as to the worth of the Negroes who led their fellow men at the front and would see to it that hereafter Negro troops be commanded by Negro officers. On the contrary, however, coming out here and there in the army wherever the Negro officer has endeavored permanently to attach himself to the service, have been what appear to be definite efforts to eliminate the Negro officer entirely. As a means to this end certain officers in charge of such recommendations have turned down several colored officers who were awarded medals of honor for distinguished service in France. In the case of Thomas M. Dent, who attained distinction in France, the prejudiced officers in charge undertook to brand him as disqualified "because of qualities inherent in the Negro race which make Negroes incapable of being leaders and officers." Upon appeal to the War Department, however, this decision was set aside.

Not only has there been an effort to get rid of the Negro officer but in many cases also the Negro private. When, after demobilization of most of the army, it became necessary to call for 50,000 volunteers for special duty it was specifically stated that these volunteers were to be *white,* not Negroes. Here was an opportunity to show one's patriotism and the Negroes nobly volunteered to manifest theirs, but considering the opportunity a much more desirable one than the ordinary enlistment of soldiers, it was reserved to white men. The Negroes then, it would seem, must be patriotic, must make personal sacrifices for the country, and even give their lives to defend it, but they must not expect to get out of it the same returns which will come to white men.

Upon the return to the United States, the Negro soldiers expected that "Jim Crowism" and segregation would receive a check if not eliminated altogether. The Negro soldier returning from the front bore it grievously that on arriving home he had to ride in "Jim Crow" cars, and be excluded from the use of public places. Their contention is that these places are licensed by the Government, established and often wholly maintained by it and, therefore, should be accessible to all. They contended, moreover, that exclusion from these public places often means no-such facilities for Negroes or, if at all, decidedly inferior accommodations.

### Better Treatment Demanded

The Negro expected, too, a change in the attitude of the white man toward the right of the blacks to exercise the highest functions of citizenship. It has required little argument to convince the Negroes that they are powerless in the hands of the militant whites when the former can neither vote nor hold office. Relying then upon principles long since set forth by the fathers of the Republic that the men who fight for the country ought to share the control of its government, the Negroes have boldly presented their case to the world. This petition has, in most places, fallen upon deaf ears. Instead of a tendency to extend the right of franchise there has been something like a recrudescence, as already stated, of the Ku Klux Klan so as to intimidate the Negroes of the South that they may not seek to reach this end.

Intelligent Negroes, therefore, who got some idea of the real liberty in France although they were not permitted to enjoy it overmuch, are united in demanding better treatment from the American people and to this end have organized a League of Democracy to further their interest. They will not accept excuses, they say; they will not keep silence, they must be heard. They want to enjoy the same rights and privileges vouchsafed to all other citizens regardless of race, creed, or condition. Americans, therefore, they hope, will oppose those enemies to democracy at home that the Junkers were to democracy in Europe. There must come a new day, Negroes feel, for the United States when the country will square itself with its own conscience and with the world in regard to its attitude toward the Negroes in America.

It will be interesting, therefore, to understand exactly what some of the colored leaders are thinking. A very advanced position has been taken by Dr. A. A. Graham, of Phoebus, Virginia, whose words may be quoted here:

"It is necessary now as never before that the black man press his claims as an American citizen. He should demand every right which this government owes to those who maintain its life and defend its honor. He should be willing to make no compromise of any kind, nor be satisfied with anything less than full justice. He has paid the price which all men have had to pay for liberty within the law. He has made the supreme sacrifice which entitled men to every just consideration of the government to which they pay allegiance. His shortcomings as a man and a human being did not excuse him from any of the duties and sacred responsibilities which the government imposed upon those whom it recognized as worthy of its claim upon them. He was called to volunteer when the country was in danger, as other men were called. He was conscripted. He was subjected to all the hard disciplines and exposures to death to which other men of the nation were exposed, and as an unquestioned American citizen, was asked to support all the war program from the purchase of savings stamps to the suffering and death in the trenches and on the battle field.

"No allowance was made for his so-called inferiority, and none was spoken of. The Government laid claim to him, both body and soul, and used him as freely as if he were the equal of any other man behind the guns or who had curly hair and blue eyes. The path he had to walk was just as rough, the load he had to carry was just as heavy, and the life he gave just as sweet, as that of any other man who laid his all upon the altar. He should contend, therefore, for every privilege, every comfort, every right which other men enjoy. He should fight wrong and injustice for himself and his children with the very same valor that he fought the Hun for the nation, and he should fight with the same good judgment and wisdom."

### The Negro as a Citizen

And in the *Southwestern Christian Advocate*, of New Orleans, Louisiana, the Reverend Dr. Robert E. Jones, an outstanding leader of the Negro race, voices the sense of this new recognition of the Negro's position as a citizen. He says:

"The statement of Lincoln, that this country could not exist half slave and half free, has been thoroughly vindicated by subsequent history. Just as that statement was a true interpretation of the life of the American Republic, at the time it was uttered, so is a modern application of that statement equally true. This country cannot exist half democratic and half autocratic. This country cannot exist with a part of its citizenship enjoying the full privileges guaranteed by the Constitution, while a large segment of our citizenship is oppressed, discriminated against and hindered in many ways.

"*The London Guardian* in referring to a statement of the boundary question between Holland and Belgium said that in ordinary times such questions would be the making of serious trouble and then the Guardian pertinently adds, 'The times, however, are not ordinary.' And these are not ordinary times. They are very unusual. The pot of civilization is boiling. Things are to be settled, but they will not be settled unless they are settled right. And the Negro wants his status changed from that of practical peonage to that of free, independent manhood with an upward look and an unhindered pathway. He wants this, first of all, on the basis of his place in the human brotherhood of divine right. He wants this on the basis of the marvelous progress that he has made in freedom.

"It has often been said that no race in all history matches the progress in the same length of time of the Negro race during the past 50 years. He wants it by the revelation of his soul life as shown forth in slavery as well as in freedom. That superb fidelity of the Negro slave to the trusts of those who left him behind should bring a blush of shame to the South when it permits now such frequent lynchings without redress and in many cases without investigation. But the Negro wants also his status fixed on the basis of what he has earned by the force of arms. With our allies we won a mighty victory over Germany. It was a triumph of democracy over autocracy. The Negro had a hand directly in this victory, but did he not also indirectly win for himself by every rule of the game, larger privileges than he had heretofore enjoyed?

"The *New York World* in a recent editorial says: 'War has sinister markings of its own, won in all sufficiency. There is no room for the color line across its horrid front. Such is the thought that suggests itself afresh, for there have been other events calling to mind the gallantry of our colored troops.' And then the *New York World* refers to the fact that the Negro soldiers were decorated by the French authorities, 'For extraordinary heroism under fire.' The *World* continues: 'The words sweep aside every consideration other than that of soldierly merit. The man who dares and does, he is a man for all this and all that.'

"The Negro has WON his decorations in France on 'soldierly merit.' He has WON at the same time by the manifestation of his courage, and his devotion and his loyalty, a more even chance in American life. And the victory should be made sure. And let us not mince words. We do not intend now that we have served the Nation in every war of the Republic and that we have borne our full share, according to our capacity, in every phase of the World War, to further accept the indignities heaped upon us as a race without a solemn protest to every sense of conscience and right in America and without appeal to the sense of conscience of civilization the world over.

"There is one thing this World War has done. It has lifted the Negro problem out of the provincialism of America into the circumspection of the civilized world. We purpose to carry our cause into the open forum of the world. We purpose to let the world know that the soldiers that brought glory to the American flag on the fields of France are denied the common courtesies in too many cases when they return home. And surely our appeal to the world will not fall altogether on deaf ears. There will be an awakening, you may rest assured, a sense of right and of justice that will react upon American life. We make this appeal to the world in no sense of disloyalty to our Nation. We do it because we are loyal. We will be heard. We will not be lynched and robbed and hedged about without a solemn protest. We do not plead for pity or sympathy. We want what we have earned by every rule of the game.

### The Negro's Wonderful Patience

"A white man said the other day, in discussing relations between the races, 'No other race under the sun would endure what the Negro does except the Negro.' White men would not stand for a moment, if they had our status of intelligence and of wealth and of numbers, or submit to the disfranchisement, the uneven opportunities, the oppression and discriminations that we meet on every hand. Someone has said much about race consciousness. Whatever that means, we know this, that much the Negro suffers white men would not endure for twenty-four hours, nor will we in the future without a protest. And we expect to find in the heart of the Nation, North and South, East and West, among those who are supposedly opposed to us, as well as among our friends, men and women who will lend themselves to a readjustment of our life in the Nation, so that we shall have a measure of peace and the pursuit of happiness. We will make our appeal with the certainty that we do not stand alone. If we did, the appeal would be worthless. But there will stand with us a powerful minority, a minority even in the South that is prophetic of a better day. But it must not be thought that this minority, North or South, will champion our cause unless we have a personal appreciation of our own condition and an intense desire for real freedom. He who would be free must strike the first blow. Statutes and proclamations by the score will not help the Negro unless the Negro first is in a position to be helped. Our friends must know our desires. We are making them known in as plain a way as we know how. We do this in love out of a desire for peace and good-will, believing that a more equitable readjustment of the relations of the races in this country will strengthen our National bonds, increase our National wealth, add to our National contentment and hasten the coming of the Kingdom of God on earth as it is in heaven.''

With a broad vision, too, the Negroes of this country have looked forward to a better day for the Negro race throughout the world. From the League of Nations the race has expected an amicable adjustment of relations in Africa so as to secure to the natives the opportunities for social, economic and political development. The author urged in an address delivered in Carnegie Hall, New York, November 2, 1918, that with a view to granting larger liberties for African allies the Peace Conference would establish an International Commission, one member of which would be an American Negro. Because of the revolting crueīties perpetrated upon the natives in the African dependencies, American Negroes have protested against any contemplation of restoring to Germany her African colonies. Is it too much to say that to restore these helpless black men to their former oppressors would be a terrible betrayal? Has not the hour come when men even in darkest

Africa may cry out for the right to elect or ordain their own destinies under an acceptable tutelage, and the guidance of enlightened men rather than under oppressive and cruel masters? If the Senegalese, Algerian and Sudanese troops stayed the Hun and saved civilization to the world, the nations of the world should see to it that these people be removed from the iron heel of malignant oppressors.

With a similar plan in view, Dr. W. E. B. DuBois was enenabled to go to France as a newspaper correspondent during the session of the Peace Conference and there, with a permit from Premier Clemenceau and his co-workers, succeeded in bringing together a sufficiently large number of intelligent Negroes and sympathetic whites to hold what he called a Pan-African Congress of which he was made secretary. There was much discussion as to the rights of the Negroes throughout the world and plans for establishing the same. The Congress was not of one accord in expressing an attitude of censure toward those nations in control of the blacks in various parts of the world, for the reason that all of these nations are not equally culpable. The Congress did make some impression in Paris and passed the following significant resolutions:

"Wherever persons of African descent are civilized and able to meet the tests of surrounding culture, they shall be accorded the same rights as their fellow citizens; they shall not be denied on account of race or color a voice in their own government, justice before the courts and economic and social equality according to ability and desert.

"Whenever it is proven that African natives are not receiving just treatment at the hands of any State or that any State deliberately excludes its civilized citizens from its body politic and cultural, it shall be the duty of the League of Nations to bring the matter to the attention of the civilized world."

# APPENDIX

## (A)

## COMMISSIONED AT FT. DES MOINES

*Colored Officers of the Seventeenth Provisional Training Regiment Who Won Commissions October 15, 1917—Their Home Addresses, and National Army Camps to which They Were Assigned.*

Cleve L. Abbott, First Lieut., O. R. C., Watertown, South Dakota, to Camp Meade.
Joseph L. Abernethy, First Lieut., O. R. C., Prairie View, Texas, to Camp Funston.
Ewart G. Abner, Second Lieutenant, O. R. C., Conroe, Texas, to Camp Funston.
Charles J. Adams, First Lieutenant, National Army, Selma, Alabama, to Camp Dodge.
Aurelious P. Alberga, First Lieutenant, O. R. C., San Francisco, Cal., to Camp Grant.
Ira L. Alridge, Second Lieutenant, O. R. C., New York, to Camp Dodge.
Edward I. Alexander, First Lieut., National Army, Jacksonville, Florida, to Camp Dix.
Fritz W. Alexander, Second Lieut., O. R. C., Donaldsville, Georgia, to Camp Meade.
Lucien V. Alexis, First Lieutenant, O. R. C., Cambridge, Mass., to Camp Upton.
John H. Allen, Captain, O. R. C., U. S. Army, to Camp Grant.
Levi Alexander, Jr., First Lieutenant, National Army, Ocala, Florida, to Camp Dix.
Clarence W. Allen, Second Lieutenant, O. R. C., Mobile, Alabama to Camp Dodge.
Richard S. Allen, Second Lieut., National Army, Atlantic City, N. J., to Camp Dix.
James W. Alston, First Lt., National Army, Raleigh, North Carolina, to Camp Grant.
Benjamin E. Ammons, First Lieut., O. R. C., Kansas City, Mo., to Camp Funston.
Leon M. Anderson, First Lieutenant, O. R. C., Washington, D C., to Camp Meade.
Levi Anderson, First Lieutenant, National Army, Washington, D. C., to Camp Meade.
Robert Anderson, First Lieutenant, National Army, U. S. Army, to Camp Sherman.
David W. Anthony, Jr., First Lieutenant, O. R. C., St. Louis, Mo., to Camp Funston.
James C. Arnold, First Lieutenant, O. R. C., Atlanta, Georgia, to Camp Dodge.
Russell C. Atkins, Second Lieutenant, O. R. C., Winston-Salem, N. C., to Camp Grant.
Henry O. Atwood, Captain, O. R. C., Washington, D. C., to Camp Meade.
Charles H. Austin, Second Lieutenant, National Army, U. S. Army, to Camp Upton.
George J. Austin, First Lieutenant, National Army, New York, N. Y., to Camp Upton.
Herbert Avery, Captain, National Army, U. S. Army, to Camp Meade.
Robert S. Bampfield, Second Lieut., O. R. C., Wilmington, N. C., to Camp Grant.
Julian C. Banks, Second Lieutenant, O. R. C., Kansas City, Mo., to Camp Funston.
Charles H. Barbour, Captain, O. R. C., United States Army, to Camp Funston.
Walter B. Barnes, First Lieut., National Army, United States Army, to Camp Funston.
William I. Barnes, First Lieutenant, O. R. C., Washington, D. C., to Camp Meade.
Stephen B. Barrows, Second Lieut., National Army, U. S. Army, to Camp Sherman.
Thomas J. Batey, First Lieutenant, O. R. C., Oakland, California, to Camp Grant.
Wilfrid Bazil, Second Lieutenant, National Army, Brooklyn, N. Y., to Camp Upton.
James E. Beard, First Lieutenant, O. R. C., U. S. Army to Camp Funston.
Ether Beattie, Second Lieutenant, National Army, U. S. Army, to Camp Meade.
William H. Benson, First Lieutenant, O. R. C., Atlanta, Georgia, to Camp Dodge.
Albert P. Bentley, First Lieutenant, O. R. C., Memphis, Tenn., to Camp Grant.
Benjamin Bettis, Second Lieutenant, National Army, U. S. Army, to Camp Meade.
Harrison W. Black, First Lieutenant, O. R. C., Lexington, Ky., to Camp Grant.
Charles J. Blackwood, First Lieutenant, O. R. C., Trinidad, Colorado, to Camp Grant.

William Blaney, First Lieutenant, National Army, U. S. Army, to Camp Upton.
Isaiah S. Blocker, First Lieutenant, O. R. C., Atlanta, Georgia, to Camp Dodge.
William D. Bly, First Lieutenant, O. R. C., Leavenworth, Kansas, to Camp Funston.
Henry H. Boger, Second Lieutenant, O. R. C., Aurora, Illinois, to Camp Grant.
Elbert L. Booker, First Lieutenant, O. R. C., Wymer, Washington, to Camp Dodge.
James F. Booker, Captain, National Army, U. S. Army, to Camp Upton.
William R. Bowie, Second Lieutenant, O. R. C., Washington, D. C., to Camp Dix.
Virgil M. Boutte, Captain, O. R. C., Nashville, Tenn., to Camp Grant.
Clyde R. Brannon, First Lieutenant, O. R. C., Fremont, Nebraska, to Camp Dodge.
Lewis Broadus, Captain, National Army, U. S. Army, to Camp Funston.
Deton J. Brooks, First Lieut., National Army, Chicago, Illinois, to Camp Grant.
William M. Brooks, Second Lieutenant, O. R. C., Des Moines, Iowa, to Camp Dodge.
Carter N. Brown, First Lieutenant, O. R. C., Atlanta, Georgia, to Camp Dodge.
Emmet Brown, First Lieutenant, O. R. C., St. Louis, Missouri, to Camp Funston.
George E. Brown, Second Lieutenant, O. R. C., New York City, N. W., to Camp Upton.
Oscar C. Brown, First Lieutenant, O. R. C., Edwards, Miss. to Camp Upton.
Rosen T. Brown, First Lieutenant, O. R. C., United States Army, to Camp Dix.
Samuel C. Brown, Second Lieut., National Army, Delaware, Ohio, to Camp Sherman.
William H. Brown, Jr., First Lieutenant, O. R. C., U. S. Army, to Camp Upton.
Arthur A. Browne, First Lieutenant, O. R. C., Xenia, Ohio, to Camp Grant.
Howard R. M. Browne, First Lieut., O. R. C., Kansas City, Kansas, to Camp Funston.
Sylvanus Brown, First Lieut., National Army, San Antonio, Texas, to Camp Funston.
Charles C. Bruen, First Lieutenant, O. R. C., Mayslick, Kentucky, to Camp Grant.
William T. Burns, First Lieutenant, O. R. C., United States Army, to Camp Dodge.
James A. Bryant, First Lieut., N. Army, Indianapolis, Indiana, to Camp Sherman.
William L. Bryson, Captain, O. R. C., United States Army, to Camp Dix.
John E. Buford, Second Lieutenant, O. R. C., Langston, Oklahoma, to Camp Dix.
Thomas J. Bullock, Second Lieut., N. Army, New York City, N. W., to Camp Upton.
John W. Bundrant, Second Lieutenant, O. R. C., Omaha, Nebraska, to Camp Dodge.
John P. Burgess, First Lieutenant, O. R. C., Mullens, S. C., to Camp Grant.
Dace H. Burns, First Lieutenant, O. R. C., Chicago, Ill., to Camp Grant.
William H. Burrel, Second Lieut., National Army, Washington, D. C., to Camp Meade.
John M. Burrell, Second Lieutenant, O. R. C., East Orange, N. J., to Camp Dix.
Herman L. Butler, First Lieutenant, O. R. C., United States Army, to Camp Dodge.
Homer C. Butler, First Lieutenant, O. R. C., New York, N. Y., to Camp Upton.
Felix Buggs, Second Lieutenant, National Army, U. S. Army, to Camp Grant.
Napoleon L. Byrd, First Lieutenant, O. R. C., Madison, Wisconsin, to Camp Grant.
John B. Cade, Second Lieutenant, O. R. C., Ellerton, Georgia, to Camp Dodge.
Walter W. Cagle, First Lieutenant, National Army, U. S. Army, to Camp Grant.
Charles W. Caldwell, Second Lieut., National Army, Orangeburg, S. C., to Camp Meade.
Andrew B. Callahan, Second Lieutenant, O. R. C., Montgomery, Ala., to Camp Dodge.
Alvin H. Cameron, First Lieutenant, National Army, Nashville, Tenn. to Camp Grant.
Alonzo Campbell, Captain, O. R. C., United States Army, to Camp Upton.
Lafayette Campbell, Second Lieutenant, O. R. C., Union, W. Va., to Camp Dix.
Robert L. Campbell, First Lieutenant, O. R. C., Greensboro, N. C., to Camp Grant.
William B. Campbell, First Lieutenant, O. R. C., Austin, Texas, to Camp Funston.
Guy W. Canady, First Lieutenant, O. R. C., Atlanta, Georgia, to Camp Dodge.
Lovelace B. Capehart, Jr., Second Lieutenant, O. R. C., Raleigh, N. C., to Camp Grant.
Adolphus F. Capps, Second Lieutenant, O. R. C., Philadelphia, Pa., to Camp Dix.
Curtis W. Carpenter, Second Lieutenant, O. R. C., Baltimore, Md., to Camp Meade.
Early Carson, Captain, National Army, United States Army, to Camp Grant.
John C. Carter, First Lieutenant, O. R. C., Washington, D. C., to Camp Meade.
Wilson Cary, Second Lieutenant, National Army, U. S. Army, to Camp Funston.
Robert W. Cheers, Second Lieutenant, O. R. C., Baltimore, Md., to Camp Meade.
David K. Cherry, Captain, O. R. C., Greensboro, N. C., to Camp Dix.
Frank R. Chisholm, First Lieut., National Army, Brooklyn, N. W., to Camp Upton.
Robert B. Chubb, Captain, National Army, U. S. Army, to Camp Dix.
Ewell W. Clark, First Lieutenant, O. R. C., Giddings, Texas, to Camp Funston.
Frank C. Clark, Second Lt., O. R. C., N. Guard, Washington, D. C., to Camp Meade.
William H. Clarke, First Lieut., National Army, Birmingham. Ala., to Camp Dodge.
William H. Clarke, First Lieutenant, O. R. C., Helena, Arkansas, to Camp Dodge.
Roscoe Clayton, Captain, O. R. C., United States Army, to Camp Funston.

Lane G. Cleaves, Second Lieutenant, O. R. C., Memphis, Tennessee, to Camp Meade.
Joshua W. Clifford, First Lieutenant, O. R. C., Washington, D. C., to Camp Meade.
Sprigg B. Coates, Captain, National Army, United States Army, to Camp Meade.
Frank Coleman, First Lieutenant, O. R. C., Washington, D. C., to Camp Dix.
William Collier, Second Lieutenant, National Army, U. S. Army, to Camp Dix.
William N. Colson, Second Lieut., O. R. C., Cambridge, Massachusetts, to Camp Upton.
Leonard O. Colston, First Lieutenant, O. R.'C., U. S. Army, to Camp Funston.
Jones A. Coltrane, First Lieutenant, National Army, Spokane, Wash., to Camp Dodge.
John Combs, First Lieutenant, National Army, U. S. Army, to Camp Funston.
Barton W. Conrad, First Lieut., National Army, Cambridge, Mass., to Camp Upton.
Lloyd F. Cook, First Lieutenant, O. R. C., U. S. Army, to Camp Funston.
Charles C. Cooper, Capt., National Army, National Guard, D. C. to Camp Meade.
George P. Cooper, First Lieutenant, National Army, U. S. Army, to Camp Upton.
Joseph H. Cooper, First Lieutenant, O. R. C., Washington, D. C., to Camp Dix.
Chesley E. Corbett, First Lieutenant, O. R. C., Wewoka, Oklahoma, to Camp Grant.
Harry W. Cox, First Lieutenant, O. R. C., Sedalia, Missouri, to Camp Funston.
James W. Cranson, Captain, National Army, U. S. Army, to Camp Grant.
Horace R. Crawford, First Lieutenant, O. R. C., Washington, D. C., to Camp Meade.
Judge Cross, First Lieutenant, O. R. C., 'United States Army, to Camp Meade.
Clarence B. Curley, First Lieutenant, O. R. C., Washington, D. C., to Camp Meade.
Merrill H. Curtis, First Lieutenant, O. R. C., Washington, D. C., to Camp Dix.
Edward L. Dabney, First Lieutenant, O. R. C., Hampton, Va., to Camp Upton.
Joe Dabney, Captain, O. R. C., United States Army, to Camp Meade.
Victor R. Daly, First Lieutenant, O. R. C., Corona, Long Island, N. Y., to Camp Upton.
Eugene A. Dandridge, First Lieut., O. R. C., National Guard, D. C., to Camp Meade.
Eugene L. C. Davidson, First Lieutenant, O. R. C., Cambridge, Mass., to Camp Upton.
Henry G. Davis, First Lieutenant, O. R. C., Atlanta, Georgia, to Camp Grant.
Irby D. Davis, First Lieutenant, O. R. C., Sumter, S. C., to Camp Grant.
William E. Davis, Captain, O. R. C., Washington, D. C., to Camp Upton
Charles C Dawson, First Lieutenant, O. R. C., Chicago, Illinois, to Camp Grant.
William S. Dawson, First Lieutenant, O. R. C., Chicago, Illinois, to Camp Grant.
Aaron Day, Jr., Captain, O. R. C., Prairie View, Texas, to Camp Funston.
Milton T. Dean, Captain, O. R. C., United States Army, to Camp Funston.
Francis M. Dent, First Lieutenant, O. R. C., Washington, D. C., to Camp Meade.
Thomas M. Dent, Jr., First Lieutenant, O. R. C., Washington, D. C., to Camp Meade.
James B. Dickson, Second Lieutenant, O. R. C., Asheville, N. C., to Camp Grant.
Spahr H. Dickey, Captain, O. R. C., San Francisco, Cal., to Camp Funston.
Elder W. Diggs, First Lieut., National Army, Indianapolis, Ind., to Camp Sherman.
William H. Dinkins, First Lieutenant, O. R. C., Selma, Ala., to Camp Dodge.
Beverly L. Dorsey, Captain, O. R. C., United States Army, to Camp Upton.
Edward C. Dorsey, Captain, O. R. C., U. S. Army, to Camp Dodge.
Harris N. Dorsey, First Lieutenant, O. R. C., U. S. Army, to Camp Upton.
Seaborn Douglas, Second Lieutenant, O. R. C., Hartford, Conn., to Camp Upton.
Vest Douglas, First Lieutenant, National Army, U. S. Army, to Camp Upton.
Frank L. Drye, First Lieutenant, O. R. C., Little Rock, Arkansas, to Camp Grant.
Edward Dugger, First Lieutenant, O. R. C., Roxbury, Mass., to Camp Upton.
Henry E. Dunn, Second Lieutenant, National Army, Kinston, N. C., to Camp Grant.
Jackson E. Dunn, First Lieutenant, National Army, U. S. Army, to Camp Upton.
Benjamin F. Dunning, Second Lieutenant, O. R. C., Norfolk, Virginia, to Camp Dix.
Charles J. Echols, Jr., Captain, O. R. C., U. S. Army, to Camp Dodge.
Charles Ecton, Captain, O. R. C., U. S. Army, to Camp Funston.
George E. Edwards, First Lieutenant, O. R. C., U. S. Army, to Camp Funston.
Leonard Edwards, Second Lieutenant, O. R. C., Augusta, Georgia, to Camp Grant.
James L. Elliott, Second Lieutenant, O. R. C., Atlanta, Georgia, to Camp Dodge.
Charles J. Ellis, Second Lieutenant, O. R. C., Springfield, Ill. to Camp Dodge.
Harry C. Ellis, First Lieutenant, O. R. C., Patrick, Louisiana, to Camp Dodge.
Roscoe Ellis, Captain, O. R. C., United States Army, to Camp Dix.
Leslie H. Engram, Second Lieutenant, O. R. C., Montezuma, Ga., to Camp Grant.
Alexander E. Evans, First Lieutenant, O. R. C., Columbia, S. C., to Camp Grant.
Wil H. Evans, Second Lieutenant, O. R. C., Montgomery, Texas, to Camp Funston.
Norwood C. Fairfax, Second Lieut., O. R. C., Eagle Rock, Virginia, to Camp Meade.
John R. Fairley, First Lieut., National Army, Kansas City, Mo., to Camp Funston.

Clifford L. Farrer, First Lieut., O. R. C., El Paso, Texas, to Camp Funston.
Leonard J. Faulkner, First Lieutenant, O. R. C., Columbus, Ohio, to Camp Sherman.
William H. Fearence, First Lieutenant, O. R. C., Texarkana, Texas, to Camp Funston.
Charles H. Fearing, First Lieutenant, National Army, St. Louis, Mo., to Camp Grant.
Robert W. Fearing, Second Lieut., National Army,. Brooklyn, N. Y., to Camp Upton.
Alonzo, G. Ferguson, First Lieutenant, O. R. C., Washington, D. C. to Camp Meade.
Gurnett E. Ferguson, Captain, O. R. C., Dunbar, W. Va. to Camp Grant.
Thomas A. Firmes, Captain, O. R. C., United States Army, to Camp Grant.
Dillard J. Firse, First Lieutenant, O. R. C., Cleveland, Ohio, to Camp Sherman.
Octavius Fisher, First Lieutenant, O. R. C., Detroit, Michigan, to Camp Sherman.
James E. Fladger, Second Lieutenant, O. R. C., Kansas City, Mo., to Camp Upton.
Benjamin F. Ford, First Lieutenant, National Army, U. S. Army, to Camp Grant.
Edward W. Ford, Second Lieutenant, National Army, Philadelphia, Pa., to Camp Dix.
Frank L. Francis, Second Lieutenant, National Army, U. S. Army, to Camp Dodge.
Henry O. Franklin, Second Lt., National Army, San Francisco, Cal., to Camp Funston.
Ernest C. Frazier, Second Lieutenant, O. R. C., Washington, D. C., to Camp Dix.
Arthur Freeman, First Lieutenant, O. R. C., U. S. Army, to Camp Upton.
Sewell C. Freeman, Second Lieutenant, O. R. C., Aragon, Georgia, to Camp Meade.
Edward S. Gaillard, First Lieut., National Army, Indianapolis, Ind., to Camp Grant.
Tacitus E. Gaillard, Second Lieutenant, O. R. C., aKnsas City, Mo., to Camp Funston.
James H. L. Gaines, Second Lieutenant, O. R. C., Little Rock, Ark., to Camp Dodge.
Ellsworth Gamblee, First Lieutenant, O. R. C., Cincinnati, Ohio, to Camp Sherman.
Lucian P. Garrett, Second Lieutenant, O. R. C., Louisville, Ky., to Camp Sherman.
William L. Lee, First Lieutenant, National Army, Gallipolis, Ohio, to Camp Grant.
Clayborne George, First Lieutenant, O. R. C., Washington, D. C., to Camp Meade.
Warmith T. Gibbs, Second Lieutenant, O. R. C., Cambridge, Mass., to Camp Upton.
Howard C. Gilbert, First Lieutenant, National Army, Columbus, Ohio, to Camp Grant.
Walter A. Giles, First Lieutenant, National Army, St. Louis, Mo., to Camp Dix.
Archie H. Gillespie, Captain, National Army, U. S. Army, to Camp Upton.
William Gillum, Captain, O. R. C., U. S. Army, to Camp Grant.
Floyd Gilmer, First Lieutenant, National Army, United States Army, to Camp Grant.
William Glass, Captain, National Army, U. S. Army, to Camp Sherman.
Jesse J. Gleeden, Second Lieutenant O. R. C., Little Rock, Ark., to Camp Grant.
Leroy H. Godman, Captain, O. R. C., Columbus, Ohio, to Camp Sherman.
Edward L. Goodlett, Second Lieutenant, O. R. C., Atlanta, Georgia, to Camp Dodge.
Nathan O. Goodloe, Second Lieutenant, O. R. C., Washington, D. C., to Camp Meade.
Frank M. Goodner, First Lieutenant, O. R. C., U. S. Army, to Camp Dix.
Elijah H. Goodwin, First Lieutenant, National Army, U. S. Army, to Camp Dix.
James A. Gordon, First Lieutenant, O. R. C., St. Joseph, Mo., to Camp Dix.
Herbert R. Gould, First Lieutenant, National Army, Dedham, Mass., to Camp Upton.
James E. Gould, First Lieutenant, National Army, Dedham, Mass., to Camp Upton.
Francis H. Gow, First Lieutenant, O. R. C., Charleston, W. Va., to Camp Grant.
William T. Grady, Second Lieutenant, O. R. C., Dudley, N. C., to Camp Grant.
Jesse M. H. Graham Second Lieut., Nat. Army, Clarksville, Tenn., to Camp Sherman.
William H. Graham, Captain, O. R. C., U. S. Army, to Camp Upton.
Towson S. Grasty, First Lieutenant, National Army, Pittsburgh, Pa., to Camp Dix.
Thornton H. Gray, First Lieut., Nat. Army, Fairmount Heights, Md., to Camp Upton.
Miles M. Green, Captain, O. R. C., U. S. Army, to Camp Upton.
Thomas E. Green, First Lieutenant, National Army, U. S. Army, to Camp Sherman.
Walter Green, Captain, O. R. C., U. S. Army, to Camp Meade.
Jesse J. Green, First Lieutenant, O. R. C., Georgetown, Ky., to Camp Grant.
Thomas M. Gregory, First Lieutenant, O. R. C., Newark, N. J., to Camp Dix.
Jefferson E. Grigsby, Second Lieutenant, O. R. C., Chappelle, S. C., to Camp Dix.
Thomas Grundy, Captain, O. R. C., United States Army, to Camp Dix.
William W. Green, Captain, O. R. C., United States Army, to Camp Grant.
George B. Greenlee, First Lieutenant, O. R. C., Marion, N. C., to Camp Grant.
Nello B. Greenlee, Second Lieutenant, O. R. C., New York, N. Y., to Camp Upton.
Herbert H. Guppy, Second Lieutenant, O. R. C., Boston, Mass., to Camp Upton.
George C. Hall, Captain, O. R. C., United States Army, to Camp Dodge.
Leonidas H. Hall, Jr., Second Lieutenant, O. R. C., Philadelphia, Pa., to Camp Dix.
George W. Hamilton, Jr., First Lieut., O. R. C., Topeka, Kansas, to Camp Funston.
Rodney D. Hardeway, Second Lieutenant, O. R. C., Houston, Texas, to Camp Funston.

Clarence W. Harding, First Lieutenant, O. R. C., U. S. Army, to Camp Dodge.
Clifton S. Hardy, Second Lieutenant, O. R. C., Champaign, Ill., to Camp Dodge.
Clay Harper, First Lieutenant, National Army, U. S. Army, to Camp Funston.
Ted O. Harper, Second Lieut., National Army, Columbus, Ohio, to Camp Sherman.
Tillman H. Harpole, First Lieutenant, O. R. C., Kansas City Mo., to Camp Funston.
Bravid W. Harris, Jr., First Lieutenant, O. R. C., Warrenton, N. C., to Camp Grant.
Edward H. Harris, First Lieutenant, O. R. C., U. S. Army, to Camp Meade.
Eugene Harris, Captain, O. R. C., U. S. Army, to Camp Funston.
William Harris, First Lieutenant, O. R. C., U. S. Army, to Camp Meade.
Byrd McD. Hart, Captain, O. R. C., U. S. Army, to Camp Dodge.
Albert L. Hatchett, First Lieutenant, O. R. C., San Antonio, Texas, to Camp Funston.
Lawrence Hawkins, Second Lieutenant, O. R. C., Bowie, Md., to Camp Meade.
Charles M. Hayes, Second Lieutenant, O. R. C., Hopkinsville, Ky., to Camp Sherman.
Merriam C. Hayson, First Lieutenant, O. R. C., Kenilworth, D. C., to Camp Meade.
Alonzo Heard, Captain, National Army, U. S. Army, to Camp Dodge.
Almando Henderson, First Lieutenant, O. R. C., U. S. Army, to Camp Upton.
Douglas J. Henderson, First Lieutenant, O. R. C., Washington, D. C., to Camp Meade.
Robert M. Hendrick, First Lieutenant, O. R. C., Tallahassee. Fla., to Camp Dix.
Thomas J. Henry, Jr., First Lieutenant, O. R. C., Atlanta, Georgia, to Camp Dodge.
Vodrey Henry, First Lieutenant, National Army, U. S. Army, to Camp Funston.
Jesse S. Heslip, First Lieutenant, O. R. C., Toledo, Ohio, to Camp Grant.
Lee J. Hicks, Captain, O. R. C., Ottawa, Kansas, to Camp Funston.
Victor LaNaire Hicks, Second Lieutenant, O. R. C., Columbia, Mo., to Camp Funston.
Arthur A. Hill, First Lieutenant, National Army, Lawrence Kansas, to Camp Funston.
Daniel G. Hill, Jr., Second Lieutenant, O. R. C., Cantonsville, Md., to Camp Meade.
Walter Hill, First Lieutenant, O. R. C., U. S. Army, to Camp Dodge.
William Hill, Captain, O. R. C., United States Army, to Camp Dodge.
Clarence O. Hilton, First Lieutenant, O. R. C., Farmville, Virginia, to Camp Dix.
Lowell B. Hodges, First Lieutenant, O. R. C., Houston, Texas, to Camp Funston.
Horatio B. Holder, First Lieutenant, O. R. C., Cairo, Ga., to Camp Dodge.
George A. Holland, Captain, O. R. C., U. S. Army, to Camp Dodge.
James G. Hollingsworth, Captain, O. R. C., U. S. Army, to Camp Grant.
George C. Hollomand, Second Lieutenant, O. R. C., Washington, D. C., to Camp Dix.
Wayne L. Hopkins, Second Lieutenant, O. R. C., Columbus, Ohio, to Camp Sherman.
James L. Horace, Second Lieutenant, O. R. C., Little Rock, Arkansas, to Camp Grant.
Reuben Horner, Captain, O. R. C., United States Army, to Camp Dix.
Charles S. Hough, Second Lieutenant, O. R. C., Jamestown, Ohio, to Camp Sherman.
Charles H. Houston, First Lieutenant, O. R. C., Washington, D. C., to Camp Meade.
Henry C. Houston, Captain, O. R. C., United States Army, to Camp Meade.
Cecil A. Howard, First Lieutenant, O. R. C., Washington, D. C., to Camp Dix.
Clarence K. Howard, Second Lieut., O. R. C., Montgomery, Alabama, to Camp Dodge.
Charles P. Howard, First Lieutenant, O. R. C., Des Moines, Iowa, to Camp Dodge.
Arthur Hubbard, First Lieutenant, O. R. C., U. S. Army, to Camp Funston.
Jerome L. Hubert, First Lieutenant, O. R. C., Houston, Texas, to Camp Funston.
William H. Hubert, Second Lieutenant, O. R. C., Mayfield, Georgia, to Camp Meade.
Jefferson E. Hudging, First Lieutenant, O. R. C., U. S. Army, to Camp Grant.
Samuel M. Huffman, First Lieutenant, O. R. C., Columbus, Ohio, to Camp Sherman.
Samuel A. Hull, First Lieutenant, National Army, Jacksonville, Florida, to Camp Dix.
John R. Hunt, First Lieutenant, O. R. C., Washington, D. C., to Camp Meade.
Bush A. Hunter, Second Lieutenant, O. R. C., Lexington, Ky., to Camp Sherman.
Benjamin H. Hunton, First Lieutenant, O. R. C., Newport News, Va., to Camp Upton.
Frederick A. Hurt, First Lieutenant, O. R. C., Washington, D. C., to Camp Dix.
Walter L. Hutcherson, First Lieut., O. R. C., Amherst (post office) Va., to Camp Upton.
Samuel B. Hutchinson, Jr., Second Lieutenant, O. R. C., Boston, Mass., to Camp Upton.
James E. Ivey, Second Lieutenant, O. R. C., Atlanta, Georgia, to Camp Dodge.
Beecher A. Jackson, First Lieutenant, O. R. C., Texarkana, Texas, to Camp Funston.
George W. Jackson, First Lieutenant, O. R. C., Ardmore, Mo., to Camp Grant.
Joseph T. Jackson, First Lieutenant, O. R. C., Charleston, W. Va., to Camp Grant.
Landen Jackson, First Lieutenant, National Army, U. S. Army, to Camp Grant.
Matthew Jackson, Captain, O. R. C., U. S. Army, to Camp Grant.
Maxey A. Jackson, Second Lieutenant, O. R. C., Marian, Ky., to Camp Sherman.
Joyce G. Jacobs, Second Lieutenant, O. R. C., Chicago, Ill., to Camp Grant.

Wesley H. Jamison, Second Lieutenant, O. R. C., Topeka, Kansas, to Camp Funston.
Charles Jefferson, Second Lieutenant, National Army, U. S. Army, to Camp Sherman.
Benjamin R. Johnson, First Lieutenant, O. R. C., New York, N. Y., to Camp Upton.
Campbell C. Johnson, First Lieutenant, O. R. C., Washington, D. C., to Camp Dix.
Ernest C. Johnson, Second Lieutenant, O. R. C., Washington, D. C., to Camp Dix.
Everett W. Johnson, First Lieutenant, O. R. C., Philadelphia, Pa., to Camp Dix.
Hanson Johnson, Captain, National Army, U. S. Army, to Camp Funston.
Hillery W. Johnson, Second Lieutenant, O. R. C., Philadelphia, Pa., to Camp Dix.
Joseph L. Johnson, Second Lieutenant, O. R. C., Philadelphia, Pa., to Camp Dix.
Merle O. Johnson, First Lieutenant, O. R. C., United States Army, to Camp Grant.
Robert E. Johnson, Second Lieutenant, O. R. C., Washington, D. C., to Camp Meade.
Thomas Johnson, Captain, National Army, United States Army, to Camp Dix.
Virginius D. Johnson, First Lieutenant, O. R. C., Richmond, Va., to Camp Upton.
William N. Johnson, Second Lieut., National Army, Omaha, Nebraska, to Camp Dodge.
William T. Johnson, First Lieutenant, O. R. C., U. S. Army, to Camp Dodge.
Willie Johnson, First Lieutenant, O. R. C., U. S. Army, to Camp Dodge.
Charles A. Jones, Second Lieutenant, O. R. C., San Antonio, Texas, to Camp Funston.
Clifford W. Jones, First Lieutenant, O. R. C., U. S. Army, to Camp Dodge.
Dee Jones, Captain, O. R. C., U. S. Army, to Camp Dodge.
Edward D. Jones, Second Lieutenant, O. R. C., Hartford, Conn., to Camp Upton.
James W. Jones, Captain, O. R. C., Washington, D. C., to Camp Meade.
James O. Jones, Second Lieut., National Army, Paulding, Ohio, to Camp Sherman.
Paul W. Jones, First Lieutenant, National Army, Washington, D. C., to Camp Meade.
Percy L. Jones, Second Lieutenant, O. R. C., U. S. Army, to Camp Upton.
Vivian L. Jones, Second Lieutenant, O. R. C., Des Moines, Iowa, to Camp Dodge.
Warren F. Jones, Captain, O. R. C., United States Army, to Camp Funston.
William Jones, First Lieutenant, O. R. C., U. S. Army, to Camp Dodge.
Charles G. Kelly, Captain, National Army, Tuskegee, Alabama, to Camp Dodge.
Elliott H. Kelly, First Lieutenant, O. R. C., Camden, S. C., to Camp Upton.
John B. Kemp, Captain, National Army, U. S. Army, to Camp Grant.
John M. Kenney, Captain, National Army, U. S. Army, to Camp Upton.
Will Kernts, First Lieutenant, National Army, U. S. Army, to Camp Dix.
Otho E. Kerr, First Lieutenant, O. R. C., Hampton, Virginia, to Camp Upton.
Orestus J. Kincaid, First Lieutenant, O. R. C., U. S. Army, to Camp Meade.
Jesse L. Kimbrough, First Lieutenant, O. R. C., Los Angeles, Cal., to Camp Funston.
Moses King, First Lieutenant, O. R. C., United States Army, to Camp Grant.
Lawrence E. Knight, First Lieutenant, O. R. C., U. S. Army, to Camp Sherman.
Edward C. Knox, First Lieutenant, National Army, U. S. Army, to Camp Funston.
John W. Knox, Second Lieutenant, O. R. C., Washington, D. C., to Camp Dix.
Azzie B. Koger, First Lieutenant, O. R. C., Reidsville, N C., to Camp Grant.
Linwood G. Koger, First Lieutenant, O. R. C., Washington, D. C., to Camp Meade.
Charles E. Lane, Jr., First Lieutenant, O. R. C., Washington, D. C., to Camp Meade.
David A. Lane, Jr., First Lieutenant, O. R. C., Washington, D. C. to Camp Dix.
Frank L. Lane, Second Lieutenant, O. R. C., Houston, Texas, to Camp Funston.
Benton R. Latimer, First Lieutenant, O. R. C., Warrenton, Georgia, to Camp Dodge.
Ernest W. Latson, First Lieutenant, O. R. C., Jacksonville, Fla., to Camp Dix.
Paige I. Lancaster, First Lieutenant, O. R. C., Hampton, Va., to Camp Upton.
Oscar G. Lawless, First Lieutenant, O. R. C., New Orleans, La., to Camp Grant.
Samuel Lawson, Second Lieutenant, National Army, Philadelphia, Pa., to Camp Dix.
Wilfred W. Lawson, First Lieutenant, O. R. C., Washington, D. C., to Camp Grant.
George E. Lee, Second Lieutenant, O. R. C., Washington, D. C., to Camp Meade.
George W. Lee, Second Lieutenant, O. R. C., Memphis, Tenn., to Camp Meade.
Lawrence A. Lee, Second Lieutenant, O. R. C., Hampton, Virginia, to Camp Upton.
John E. Leonard, First Lieutenant, National Army, U. S. Army, to Camp Meade.
Garrett M. Lewis, First Lieutenant, O. R. C., San Antonio, Texas, to Camp Funston.
Henry O. Lewis, First Lieutenant, O. R. C., Boston, Mass., to Camp Upton.
Everett B. Liggins, Second Lieutenant, O. R. C., Austin, Texas, to Camp Funston.
Victor C. Lightfoot, Second Lieut., O. R. C., South Pittsburg, Tenn., to Camp Grant.
John Q. Lindsey, First Lieutenant, O. R. C., U. S. Army, to Camp Dodge.
Redden L. Linton, Second Lieutenant, O. R. C., Boston, Georgia, to Camp Grant.
Glenda W. Locust, Second Lieutenant, O. R. C., Sealy, Tenn., to Camp Funston.
Aldon L. Logan, First Lieutenant, O. R. C., Lawrence, Kansas, to Camp Funston.

James B. Lomack, First Lieutenant, O. R. C., National Guard, D. C., to Camp Meade.
Howard H. Long, First Lieutenant, O. R. C., Washington, D. C., to Camp Meade.
James B. Lomack, First Lieutenant, O. R. C., National Guard, D. C., to Camp Meade.
Victor Long, First Lieutenant, O. R. C., United States Army, to Camp Dodge.
Lonnie W. Lott, Second Lieutenant, O. R. C., Austin, Texas, to Camp Funston.
Charles H. Love, Second Lieutenant, O. R. C., Atlanta, Georgia, to Camp Grant.
Edgar A. Love, First Lieutenant, O. R. C., Baltimore, Md., to Camp Meade.
Frank W. Love, Captain, O. R. C., U. S. Army, to Camp Dodge.
George B. Love, First Lieutenant, O. R. C., Greensboro, N. C., to Camp Grant.
John W. Love, First Lieutenant, O. R. C., Baltimore, Md., to Camp Dix.
Joseph Lowe, Captain, O. R. C., U. S. Army, to Camp Sherman.
Walter Lowe, First Lieutenant, O. R. C., St. Louis, Mo., to Camp Dix.
Charles C. Luck, Jr., Second Lieutenant, O. R. C., San Marcus, Texas, to Camp Funston.
Walter Lyons, First Lieutenant, National Army, U. S. Army, to Camp Grant.
Harry J. Mack, Second Lieutenant, O. R. C., Cheney, Pa., to Camp Dix.
Amos B. Madison, First Lieutenant, O. R. C., Omaha, Nebr., to Camp Dodge.
Edgar F. Malone, Second Lieutenant, O. R. C., U. S. Army, to Camp Dix.
Edgar O. Malone, Captain, O. R. C., U. S., Army, to Camp Sherman.
Earl W. Mann, First Lieutenant, O. R. C., Champaign, Ill., to Camp Dodge.
Vance H. Marchbanks, Captain, National Army, U. S. Army, to Camp Meade.
Leon F. Marsh, First Lieutenant, O. R. C., Berkeley, Cal., to Camp Grant.
Alfred E. Marshall, Second Lieutenant, O. R. C., Greenwood, S. C., to Camp Dix.
Cyrus W. Marshall, Second Lieutenant, O. R. C., Baltimore, Md., to Camp Dodge.
Cuby Martin, First Lieutenant, National Army, U. S. Army, to Camp Dodge.
Joseph H. Martin, First Lieutenant, O. R. C., Washington, D. C., to Camp Meade.
Eric P. Mason, First Lieutenant, O. R. C., Giddings, Texas, to Camp Funston.
Denis McG. Matthews, First Lieut., National Army, Los Angeles, Cal., to Camp Grant.
Joseph E. Matthews, Second Lieutenant, O. R. C., Cleburne, Texas, to Camp Funston.
Anderson N. May, Captain, O. R. C., Atlanta, Georgia, to Camp Dodge.
Walter H. Mazyck, First Lieutenant, O. R. C., Washington, D. C., to Camp Meade.
Peter McCall, Captain, O. R. C., U. S. Army, to Camp Dodge.
Milton A. McCrimmon, Captain, O. R. C., U. S. Army, to Camp Meade.
Robert A. McEwen, Second Lieutenant, O. R. C., East St. Louis, Ill., to Camp Dodge.
Osceola E. McKaine, First Lieutenant, O. R. C., U. S. Army, to Camp Upton.
James E. McKey, First Lieutenant, National Army, U. S. Army, to Camp Meade.
Carey McLane, First Lieutenant, National Army, U. S. Army, to Camp Grant.
Archie McLee, First Lieutenant, O. R. C., New York, N. Y., to Camp Upton.
Leonard W. McLeod, First Lieutenant, O. R. C., Hampton, Virginia, to Camp Upton.
Albert McReynolds, First Lieutenant, National Army, U. S. Army, to Camp Meade.
Marshall Meadows, First Lieutenant, O. R. C., U. S. Army, to Camp Dodge.
Louis R. Mehlinger, Captain, O. R. C., Washington, D. C., to Camp Meade.
Louis R. Middleton, First Lieutenant, O. R. C., Washington, D. C., to Camp Upton.
Benjamin H. Mills, First Lieutenant, O. R. C., U. S. Army, to Camp Dix.
Harry W. Mills, Captain, O. R. C., U. S. Army, to Camp Grant.
Warren N. Mins, First Lieutenant, National Army, U. S. Army, to Camp Dix.
J. Wardlaw Mitchell, Second Lieut., O. R. C., Milledgeville, Ga., to Camp Dodge.
Pinkney L. Mitchell, Second Lieutenant, O. R. C., Austin, Texas, to Camp Funston.
John H. Mitcherson, First Lieutenant, O. R. C., U. S. Army, to Camp Dix.
Ralph E. Mizell, Second Lieutenant, O. R. C., Champaign, Illinois, to Camp Grant.
Hubert M. Moman, Second Lieutenant, O. R. C., Tougalo, Miss., to Camp Funston.
John M. Moore, First Lieutenant, O. R. C., Meridan, Miss., to Camp Funston.
Loring B. Moore, Second Lieutenant, O. R. C., Brunswick, Ga., to Camp Meade.
Elias A. Morris, First Lieutenant, O. R. C., Helena, Ark., to Camp Dodge.
Thomas E. Morris, Captain, O. R. C., United States Army, to Camp Upton.
James B. Morris, Second Lieutenant, O. R. C., Des Moines, Iowa, to Camp Dodge.
Cleveland Morrow, First Lieutenant, National Army, U. S. Army, to Camp Dix.
Henry Morrow, First Lieutenant, National Army, U. S. Army, to Camp Dix.
Abraham Morse, First Lieutenant, National Army, U. S. Army, to Camp Upton.
Benjamin H. Mosby, First Lieutenant, O. R. C., St. Louis, Mo., to Camp Funston.
Benedict Mosley, First Lieutenant, O. R. C., United States Army, to Camp Grant.
Scott A. Moyer, Second Lieutenant, National Army, U. S. Army, to Camp Dix.
Albert C. Murdaugh, Second Lieutenant, O. R. C., Columbia, S. C., to Camp Dix.

Alonzo Myers, Captain, O. R. C., Philadelphia, Pa., to Camp Dix.
Thomas J. Narcisse, Second Lieutenant, O. R. C., Jeanerette, Louisiana, to Camp Grant.
Earl H. Nash, Second Lieutenant, O. R. C., Atlanta, Ga., to Camp Dodge.
Homer G. Neely, First Lieutenant, O. R. C., Palestine, Texas, to Camp Funston.
Gurney E. Nelson, Second Lieutenant, O. R. C., Greensboro, N. C., to Camp Grant.
William F. Nelson, First Lieutenant, O. R. C., Atlanta, Ga., to Camp Dodge.
William S. Nelson, First Lieutenant, O. R. C., Washington, D. C., to Camp Meade.
James P. Nobles, First Lieutenant, O. R. C., United States Army, to Camp Upton.
Grafton S. Norman, First Lieut., National Army, Atlanta, Georgia, to Camp Dodge.
Richard M. Norris, First Lieutenant, O. R. C., U. S. Army, to Camp Funston.
Ambrose B. Nutt, Second Lieutenant, O. R. C., Cambridge, Mass., to Camp Upton.
Benjamin L. Ousley, Second Lieutenant, O. R. C., Tougaloo, Miss., to Camp Funston.
Charles W. Owens, Captain, National Army, U. S. Army, to Camp Dodge.
Charles G. Owings, Second Lieutenant, O. R. C., Norfolk, Va., to Camp Upton.
William W. Oxley, First Lieut., National Army, Cambridge, Mass., to Camp Upton.
Wilbur E. Pannell, Second Lieutenant, O. R. C., Stanton, Va., to Camp Upton.
Charles S. Parker, Second Lieut., National Army, Spokane, Wash., to Camp Dodge.
Walter E. Parker, Second Lieutenant, National Army, Little Rock, Ark., to Camp Dix.
Clemmie C. Parks, First Lieutenant, O. R. C., Ft. Scott, Kans., to Camp Funston.
Adam E. Patterson, Captain, National Army, Chicago, Illinois, to Camp Dodge.
Himphrey C. Patton, First Lieutenant, O. R. C., Washington, D. C., to Camp Dix.
Clarence H. Payne, First Lieutenant, O. R. C., Chicago, Ill., to Camp Grant.
William D. Peeks, Captain, O. R. C., United States Army, to Camp Dix.
Robert R. Penn., First Lieutenant, O. R. C., New York, N. Y., to Camp Upton.
Marion R. Perry, Second Lieutenant, O. R. C., Pine Bluff, Ark., to Camp Funston.
Hanson A. Person, Second Lieutenant, O. R. C., Wynne, Ark., to Camp Sherman.
Harry B. Peters, Second Lieutenant, O. R. C., Atlanta, Georgia, to Camp Grant.
James H. Peyton, Second Lieutenant, O. R. C., Montgomery, Alabama, to Camp Dodge.
Joseph Phillips, Captain, O. R. C., Columbus, Ohio, to Camp Sherman.
David A. Pierce, Second Lieutenant, O. R. C., Clarksville, Texas, to Camp Funston.
Harrison J. Pinkett, First Lieutenant, O. R. C., Omaha, Nebr., to Camp Dodge.
James C. Pinkston, First Lieutenant, National Army, U. S. Army, to Camp Funston.
Percival R. Piper, First Lieutenant, O. R. C., Washington, D. C., to Camp Dix.    ·
Anderson F. Pitts, First Lieutenant, O. R. C., Chicago, Ill., to Camp Grant.
Fisher Pride, First Lieutenant, O. R. C., U. S. Army, to Camp Dix.
Herman W. Porter, Second Lieutenant, O. R. C., Cambridge, Mass., to Camp Upton.
James C. Powell, First Lieutenant, O. R. C., Washington, D. C., to Camp Meade.
Wade H. Powell, Second Lieutenant, O. R. C., Atlanta, Georgia, to Camp Dodge.
William J. Powell, First Lieutenant, O. R. C., Chicago, Ill., to Camp Grant.
Gloucester A. Price, Second Lieutenant, O. R. C., Ft. Meyer, Fla., to Camp Upton.
John F. Pritchard, First Lieutenant, O. R. C., U. S. Army, to Camp Grant.
Henry H. Proctor, First Lieutenant, O. R. C., Atlanta, Georgia, to Camp Dodge.
John H. Purnell, First Lieutenant, O. R. C., Trappe, Md., to Camp Dix.
Washington H. Racks, Second Lieut., National Army, U. S. Army, to Camp Grant.
Howard D. Queen, Captain, O. R. C., United States Army, to Camp Funston.
Richard R. Queen, Second Lieutenant, O. R. C., Washington, D. C., to Camp Meade.
Harold L. Quivers, First Lieutenant, O. R. C., Washington, D. C., to Camp Meade.
John E. Raiford, Second Lieutenant, O. R. C., Atlanta, Ga., to Camp Meade.
Hazel L. Raine, First Lieutenant, O. R. C., United States Army, to Camp Sherman.
Fred D. Ramsey, First Lieutenant, O. R. C., Wedgefield, S. C., to Camp Upton.
James O: Redmon, Second Lieutenant, O. R. C., Newton, Iowa, to Camp Grant.
Charles G. Reed, First Lieutenant, O. R. C., Charleston, S. C., to Camp Sherman.
Rufus Reed, Captain, O. R. C., United States Army, to Camp Funston.
Lightfoot H. Reese, Second Lieutenant, O. R. C., Newman, Ga., to Camp Grant.
William L. Reese, Second Lieutenant, O. R. C., Bennetsville, S. C., to Camp Meade.
Robert S. Reid, Second Lieutenant, O. R. C., Newman, Ga., to Camp Grant.
Samuel Reid, Captain, National Army, United States Army, to Camp Funston.
Adolph Reyes, Second Lieutenant, National Army, Philadelphia, Pa., to Camp Dix.
Elijah Reynolds, Captain, National Army, United States Army, to Camp Meade.
John F. Rice, First Lieutenant, O. R. C., Chicago, Illinois, to Camp Dodge.
Douglas C. Richardson, Second Lieut., O. R. C., Washington, D. C., to Camp Meade.
Harry D. Richardson, First Lieut., National Army, Washington, D. C., to Camp Meade.

Leonard H. Richardson, First Lieutenant, O. R. C., Oakland Cal., to Camp Funston.
Maceo A. Richmond, Second Lieutenant, . R. C., Des Moines, Iowa, to Camp Dodge.
Francis E. Rivers, First Lieutenant, O. R. C., New Haven, Conn., to Camp Upton.
Marion C. Rhoten, First Lieut., National Army, U. S. Army, to Camp Meade.
Charles E. Roberts, First Lieutenant, O. R. C., Atlantic City, N. J., to Camp Dix.
Clyde Roberts, Second Lieutenant, O. R. C., United States Army, to Camp Grant.
Edward Robertson, Second Lieutenant, National Army, U. S. Army, to Camp Meade.
Charles W. Robinson, Second Lieutenant, O. R. C., Cleveland, Ohio, to Camp Sherman.
George C. Robinson First Lieutenant, O. R. C., Atlanta, Ga., to Camp Dodge.
Peter L. Robinson, First Lieutenant, O. R. C., Washington, D. C., to Camp Meade.
William W. Robinson, First Lieut., National Army, U. S. Army, to Camp Sherman.
Julian P. Rodgers, First Lieut., National Army, Montgomery, Ala., to Camp Dodge.
John W. Rowe, First Lieutenant, O. R. C., Danville, Ky., to Camp Grant.
Thomas Rucker, Captain, O. R. C., United States Army, to Camp Dix.
Edward P. Rudd, First Lieutenant, O. R. C., New York City, to Camp Upton.
Mallalieu W. Rush, First Lieutenant, O. R. C., Atlanta, Ga., to Camp Dodge.
John Russell, Captain, National Army, United States Army, to Camp Upton.
Louis H. Russell, Second Lieutenant, O. R. C., New York, N. Y., to Camp Upton.
Earl Ryder, Second Lieutenant, O. R. C., Springfield, Ill., to Camp Grant.
Chester Sanders, Captain, O. R. C., United States Army, to Camp Meade.
Joseph B. Sanders, Second Lieutenant, O. R. C., U. S. Army, to Camp Dodge.
Walter R. Sanders, Captain, O. R. C., U. S. Army, to Camp Sherman.
Clifford A. Sandridge, Captain, National Army, United States Army, to Camp Dix.
Lorin O. Sanford, Captain, O. R. C., United States Army, to Camp Upton.
Elliott D. Saunders, Second Lieutenant, National Army, U. S. Army, to Camp Dodge.
Walker L. Savoy, Second Lieutenant, O. R. C., Washington, D. C., to Camp Meade.
Elmer P. Sawyer, Second Lieutenant, O. R. C., Providence, R. I., to Camp Upton.
George S. Schuyler, First Lieutenant, O. R. C., U. S. Army, to Camp Dix.
James E. Scott, Second Lieutenant, O. R. C., Washington, D. C., to Camp Meade.
James E. Scott, First Lieutenant, O. R. C., Hampton, Va., to Camp Upton.
Joseph H. Scott, First Lieutenant, O. R. C., Darlington, S. C., to Camp Dix.
Walter W. Scott, Second Lieutenant, O. R. C., Brooksville, Miss., to Camp Funston.
William F. Scott, Captain, O. R. C., United States Army, to Camp Upton.
Fletcher Sewell, Captain, National Army, United States Army, to Camp Meade.
Shermont R. Sewell, First Lieutenant, O. R. C., Washington, D. C., to Camp Meade.
Charles A. Shaw, First Lieutenant, O. R. C., Atlanta, Ga., to Camp Dodge.
Warren B. Shelton, Second Lieutenant, O. R. C., Hot Springs, Ark., to Camp Sherman.
Robert T. Shobe, First Lieutenant, National Army, U. S. Army, to Camp Funston.
Hal Short, First Lieutenant, O. R. C., Iowa, to Camp Dodge.
Harry W. Short, Second Lieutenant, O. R. C., Iowa City, Iowa, to Camp Dodge.
Ogbon N. Simmons, First Lieutenant, O. R. C., Waldo, Fla., to Camp Dix.
Richard Simmons, Captain, O. R. C., United States Army, to Camp Dix.
William E. Simmons, First Lieutenant, O. R. C., Burlington, Vt., to Camp Upton.
Austin Simms, Second Lieutenant, O. R. C., Dearien, Ga., to Camp Dodge.
John H. Simms, Jr., First Lieutenant, O. R. C., Jacksonville, Fla., to Camp Dix.
Abraham L. Simpson, Captain, O. R. C., Louisville, Ky., to Camp Funston.
Lawrence Simpson, First Lieutenant, O. R. C., Chicago, Ill., to Camp Grant.
William R. Smalls, First Lieutenant, O. R. C., Manassas, Va., to Camp Dix.
Daniel Smith, Captain, O. R. C., United States Army, to Camp Dix.
Enos B. Smith, Second Lieutenant, National Army, U. S. Army, to Camp Meade.
Ernest Smith, Second Lieutenant, National Army, Philadelphia, Pa., to Camp Dix.
Fairel N. Smith, First Lieutenant, O. R. C., Orangeburg, S. C., to Camp Upton.
Joseph W. Smith, Second Lieutenant, O. R. C., Concord, S. C., to Camp Meade.
Oscar H. Smith, First Lieutenant, O. R. C., United States Army, to Camp Meade.
Pitman E. Smith, First Lieutenant, O. R. C., Columbus, Ohio, to Camp Sherman.
Russell Smith, First Lieutenant, O. R. C., United States Army, to Camp Dix.
Walter H. Smith, First Lieutenant, O. R. C., Chattanooga, Tenn., to Camp Grant.
Levi E. Southe, Second Lieutenant, O. R. C., Chicago, Ill., to Camp Grant.
Carlos Sowards, Second Lieutenant, O. R. C., United States Army, to Camp Upton.
Edward W. Spearman, Captain, O. R. C., United States Army, to Camp Upton.
Walter R. St. Clair, Second Lieutenant, O. R. C., Philadelphia, Pa., to Camp Dix.
Lloyd A. Stafford, Captain, O. R. C., United States Army, to Camp Dix.

Moody Staten, Captain, O. R. C., United States Army, to Camp Upton.
Percy H. Steele, First Lieutenant, O. R. C., Washington, D. C., to Camp Meade.
Waddell C. Steele, First Lieutenant, O. R. C., United States Army, to Camp Grant.
Grant Stewart, First Lieutenant, O. R. C., United States Army, to Camp Dix.
Robert K. Stephens, Captain, O. R. C., United States Army, to Camp Sherman.
Leon Stewart, First Lieutenant, O. R. C., United States Army, to Camp Grant.
Thomas R. Stewart, First Lieutenant, O. R. C., Fort Wayne, Ind., to Camp Grant.
William A. Stith, First Lieutenant, O. R. C., United States Army, to Camp Meade.
James M. Stockett, Jr., First Lieutenant, O. R. C., Providence, R. I., to Camp Upton.
Wilbur F. Stonestreet, Second Lieutenant, O. R. C., Topeka, Kansas, to Camp Funston.
Daniel T. Taylor, Second Lieut., National Army, United States Army, to Camp Grant.
Hannibal B. Taylor, Second Lieutenant, O. R. C., Guthrie, Okla., to Camp Funston.
Pearl E. Taylor, First Lieutenant, National Army, St. Louis, Mo., to Camp Dix.
Benjamin F. Thomas, Captain, O. R. C., United States Army, to Camp Grant.
Bob Thomas, Captain, O. R. C., United States Army, to Camp Meade.
Vincent B. Thomas, Second Lieutenant, O. R. C., Washington, D. C., to Camp Meade.
Charles M. Thompson, First Lieutenant, O. R. C., Columbia, S. C., to Camp Dix.
Joseph Thompson, Captain, O. R. C., United States Army, to Camp Grant.
Pierce McN. Thompson, First Lieutenant, O. R. C., Albany, Ga., to Camp Dodge.
Richard C. Thompson, First Lieutenant, O. R. C., Harrisburg, Pa., to Camp Dix.
Roliver T. Thompson, First Lieut., National Army, Houston, Texas, to Camp Funston.
William H. Thompson, First Lieut., National Army, Jacksonville, Fla., to Camp Dix.
William H. Thompson, Captain, O. R. C., United States Army, to Camp Sherman.
James W. Thorton, First Lieutenant, O. R. C., West Raleigh, N. C., to Camp Grant.
Leslie J. Thurman, Captain, O. R. C., United States Army, to Camp Upton.
Samuel J. Tipton, Captain, National Army, United States Army, to Camp Dodge.
Frederick H. Townsend, Second Lieutenant, O. R. C., Newport, R. I., to Camp Upton.
Anderson Trapp, First Lieutenant, O. R. C., United States Army, to Camp Dodge.
Charles A. Tribbett, First Lieutenant, O. R. C., New Haven, Conn., to Camp Upton.
Joseph E. Trigg, Captain, O. R. C., Syracuse, N. Y., to Camp Dix.
Archibald R. Tuck, Second Lieutenant, O. R. C., Oberlin, Ohio, to Camp Sherman.
Victor J. Tulane, First Lieutenant, O. R. C., Montgomery, Ala., to Camp Dodge.
William J. Trunbow, First Lieutenant, O. R. C., United States Army, to Camp Upton.
Allen Turner, First Lieutenant, National Army, United States Army, to Camp Dix.
Edward Turner, First Lieutenant, O. R. C., Omaha, Nebr., to Camp Dodge.
Samuel Turner, Second Lieut., National Army, United States Army, to Camp Upton.
Shadrach W. Upshaw, Second Lieutenant, O. R. C., Austin, Texas, to Camp Funston.
Ferdinand S. Upshur, Second Lieutenant, O. R. C., Philadelphia, Pa., to Camp Dix.
George L. Vaughn, First Lieutenant, National Army, St. Louis, Mo., to Camp Dix.
Austin T. Walden, Captain, O. R. C., Macon, Ga., to Camp Dix.
John P. Walker, First Lieutenant, National Army, U. S. Army, to Camp Dodge.
Lewis W. Wallace, Captain, O. R. C., United States Army, to Camp Funston.
Thomas H. Walters, First Lieutenant, O. R. C., New York, N. Y., to Camp Upton.
Robert L. Ward, First Lieutenant, O. R. C., Detroit, Mich., to Camp Sherman.
James H. N. Waring, Jr., First Lieut., O. R. C., Washington, D. C., to Camp Meade.
Genoa S. Washington, Captain, O. R. C., United States Army, to Camp Upton.
George G. Washington, Second Lieut., National Army, U. S. Army to Camp Funston.
Bolivar E. Watkins, First Lieutenant, O. R. C., St. Louis, Mo., to Camp Funston.
Alstyne M. Watson, Second Lieut., O. R. C., Tallapoosa, Ga., to Camp Grant.
Baxter W. Watson, Second Lt., National Army, United States Army, to Camp Funston.
Louis L. Watson, First Lieutenant, O. R. C., Washington, D. C., to Camp Dix.
William H. Weare, First Lieutenant, O. R. C., United States Army, to Camp Funston.
Walter T. Webb, First Lieutenant, O. R. C., Baltimore, Md., to Camp Meade.
Carter W. Wesley, First Lieutenant, O. R. C., Houston, Tex., to Camp Funston.
Harry Wheeler, First Lieut., National Army, United States Army, to Camp Meade.
Chauncey D. White, First Lieutenant, O. R. C., Mathews, Va., to Camp Upton.
Emmett White, Captain, O. R. C., United States Army, to Camp Grant.
Journee W. White, Second Lieut., National Army, Los Angeles, Cal., to Camp Dix.
Lorenzo C. White, Second Lieutenant, O. R. C., Hampton, Va., to Camp Upton.
Johnson C. Whittaker, First Lieutenant, O. R. C., Lawrence, Kans., to Camp Funston.
Horace G. Wilder Second Lieutenant, National Army, United States, to Camp Dix.
Arthur R. Williams, Second Lieut., O. R. C., Edwards, Miss., to Camp Funston.

Everett B. Williams, First Lieutenant, O. R. C., Syracuse, N. Y., to Camp Dix.
Gus Williams, First Lieutenant, National Army, United States Army, to Camp Upton.
James B. Williams, First Lieut., National Army, Baltimore, Md., to Camp Meade.
John Williams, Second Lieutenant, National Army, U. S. Army, to Camp Grant.
Oscar H. Williams, Second Lieut., National Army, New York, N. Y., to Camp Upton.
Richard A. Williams, Captain, O. R. C., Lawnside, N. J., to Camp Dix.
Robert G. Williams, First Lieutenant, O. R. C., U. S. Army, to Camp Sherman.
Seymour E. Williams, Second Lieutenant, O. R. C., Muskogee, Okla., to Camp Funston.
Major Williams, Second Lieutenant, National Army, U. S. Army, to Camp Dodge.
Walter B. Williams, Captain, National Army, U. S. Army, to Camp Upton.
William H. Williams, Captain, O. R. C., United States Army, to Camp Grant.
Elmore S. Willie, First Lieut., O. R. C., U. S. Army, to Camp Sherman.
Harry E. Wilson, First Lieutenant, O. R. C., Des Moines, Iowa, to Camp Dodge.
John E. Wilson, First Lieut., National Army, Leavenworth, Kans., to Camp Funston.
William H. Wilson, Second Lieut., O. R. C., Greensboro, N. C., to Camp Grant.
Meredith B. Wily, First Lieut., O. R. C., El Paso, Texas, to Camp Funston.
Christopher C. Wimbish, First Lieutenant, O. R. C., Atlanta, Ga. to Camp Dodge.
Hugh H. Wimbish, Second Lieutenant, O. R. C., Atlanta, Ga., to Camp Meade.
Rolland T. Winstead, Second Lieut., O. R. C., Rocky Mount, N. C., to Camp Grant.
George W. Winston, Captain, O. R. C., United States Army, to Camp Dodge.
Ernest M. Wood, Second Lieutenant, O. R. C., Mebane, N. C., to Camp Grant.
Benjamin F. Wright, Second Lieutenant, O. R. C., New York, N. Y., to Camp Upton.
Elbert S. Wright, Second Lieutenant, O. R. C., Baldwin, Kansas, to Camp Funston.
John Wynn, Second Lieutenant, National Army, U. S. Army, to Camp Funston.
Edward York, Captain, O. R. C., United States Army, to Camp Upton.
Charles Young First Lieutenant, National Army, U. S. Army, to Camp Dodge.
William A. Young, Second Lieutenant, O. R. C., Sumter, S. C., to Camp Dix.
Charles G. Young First Lieutenant, O. R. C., Washington, D. C., to Camp Meade.

The above officers do not represent the full number of Colored men who were commissioned in the United States Army, however. In the series of Officers' Training Camps which were conducted after the draftees were called to service, 107 were commissioned in Infantry from various camps, and 33 in Artillery from Camp Zachary Taylor, Louisville, Kentucky.

## (B)

**Colored Chaplains in the United States Army When the Armistice was Signed, November 11, 1918**

| Name. | Denomination. | Assigned tr— |
|---|---|---|
| Louis A. Carter, | Baptist, | 9th U. S. Cavalry. |
| O. J. W. Scott, | Methodist, | 10th U. S. Cavalry. |
| Alexander W. Thomas, | Methodist, | 24th Infantry. |
| George W. Prioleau, | Methodist, | 25th Infantry. |
| William S. Braddon, | Baptist, | (Former Nat'l Guard) 370th Inf., A. E. F. |
| John S. Hawkins, | | (Former Nat'l Guard) 151st Inf., A. E. F. |
| Arrington S. Helm, | Baptist, | (Former Nat'l Guard) Camp Upton, N. Y. |
| Charles R. Winthrop, | Presbyterian, | (Former Nat'l Guard) 372nd Inf., A. E. F. |
| Uriah J. Robinson, | Baptist, | 365 Infantry, A. E. F. |
| Allen O. Newman, | Baptist, | 366th Infantry, A. E. F. |
| George S. Stark, | Presbyterian, | 367th Infantry, A. E. F. |
| Edgar A. Love | Methodist, | 367th Infantry, A. E. F. |
| A. E. Rankin, | Presbyterian, | 349th Field Artillery, A. E. F. |
| Cornelius G. Parks, | Methodist, | 350th Field Artillery. |
| E. O. Woolfolk, | Methodist, | |
| George A. Singleton, | Methodist, | 317th Engineers, A. E. F. |
| Henry M. Collins, | Methodist, | 309th Labor Battalion. |
| Lincoln C. Jenkins, | Baptist, | 310th Labor Battalion. |
| Julian L. Brown, | Baptist, | 302nd Stevedore Regiment. |
| Hugh A. Rogers, | Baptist, | |
| Elbert S. M. Dinsmore, | Methodist, | 314th Labor Battalion. |
| E. M. M. Wright, | Episcopal, | Engineer Service Battalion, A. E. F. |
| Clifford L. Miller, | Congregational, | 506th Service Battalion, Engrs., A. E. F. |
| John T. Clemons, | Congregational, | 370th Infantry, A. E. F. |
| Matthew M. Jefferson, | Methodist, | American Expeditionary Forces. |
| John W. Oveltrea, | Methodist, | American Expeditionary Forces. |
| Benjamin C. Robeson, | Methodist, | American Expeditionary Forces. |
| James T. Simpson, | Methodist, | American Expeditionary Forces. |
| Thomas W. Wallace, | Zion Methodist, | American Expeditionary Forces. |
| Charles T. Isom, | Methodist, | 157th Depot Brigade, Camp Gordon, Ga. |
| Monroe S. Caver, | Baptist, | Camp Taylor, Kentucky. |
| George A. Thomas, | Methodist, | Camp Hill, Newport News, Virginia. |
| Richard A. Greene, | Methodist, | Camp Taylor, Kentucky. |
| William T. Amiger, | Baptist, | Camp Hill, Virginia. |
| Alfred G. Casper, | Methodist, | Camp Stuart, Virginia. |
| John A. Hill, | Methodist, | |
| Blair T. Hunt, | Baptist, | Camp Stuart, Virginia. |
| Noah W. Williams, | Methodist, | Camp Stuart, Virginia. |
| Frank C. Shirley, | Presbyterian, | Camp Meade, Maryland, 11th Division. |
| George A. Rosedom, | Baptist, | Camp Meade, Maryland. |
| Thomas E. Davis, | Methodist, | |
| Matthew W. Clair, Jr., | Methodist, | American Expeditionary Forces. |
| Lewis A. McGee, | Methodist, | |
| John W. E. Bowen, Jr., | Methodist, | |
| Frank W. Brown, | Baptist, | Camp Lee, Virginia. |
| Ellis A. Christian, | Episcopal, | Camp Travis, Texas. |
| Eugene H. Hamilton, | Congregational, | |
| Frederick D. L. McDonald, | Methodist, | |
| A. Huntington Hatwoood, | Methodist, | Camp Taylor, Kentucky. |
| Max Yergan, | Congregational, | Camp Lee, Virginia. |
| Charles Y. Trigg, | Methodist, | Camp Alexander, Virginia. |
| Needham M. Means, | Methodist, | Camp Travis, Texas. |
| James B. Adams, | Baptist, | Camp Lee, Virginia. |
| Robert G. Morris, | Methodist, | Camp Meade, Maryland. |
| Robert W. Jefferson, | Baptist, | Camp Sevier, South Carolina. |
| George C. Parker, | Methodist, | Camp Jackson, South Carolina. |
| Isaac C. Snowden, | Methodist, | 25th Infantry, Nogales, Arizona. |
| Frank R. Arnold, | Methodist, | Camp Sherman, Ohio. |
| William Y. Bell, | Methodist, | Port Newark, New Jersey. |
| Berryman H. Johnson, | Baptist, | Camp Lee, Virginia. |

# THE TREATY OF PEACE

## Official Summary of the Covenant of the League of Nations and Terms Imposed Upon Germany as Decided by the Peace Conference

The official summary of the treaty of peace, given to the public on May 7, 1919, at the time the text of the treaty was handed to the German peace delegates, was as follows:

The preamble names as parties of the one part the United States, the British empire, France, Italy, and Japan, described as the five allied and associated powers, and Belgium, Bolivia, Brazil, China, Cuba, Ecuador, Greece, Guatemala, Haiti, the Hedjaz, Honduras, Liberia, Nicaragua, Panama, Peru, Poland, Portugal, Roumania, Serbia, Siam, Czecho-Slovakia, and Uruguay, who with the five above are described as the allied and associated powers, and on the other part Germany.

It states that: Bearing in mind that on the request of the then imperial German government an armistice was granted on November 11, 1918, by the five allied and associated powers in order that a treaty of peace might be concluded with her, and whereas the allied and associated powers being equally desirous that the war in which they were successfully involved, directly or indirectly, and which originated in the declaration of war by Austria-Hungary on July 28, 1914, against Serbia, the declaration of war by Germany against Russia on August 1, 1914, and against France on August 3, 1914, and in the invasion of Belgium, should be replaced by a firm, just, and durable peace, the plenipotentiaries having communicated their full powers found in good and due form have agreed as follows:

From the coming into force of the present treaty, the state of war will terminate. From the moment and subject to the provisions of this treaty official relations with Germany, and with each of the German states, will be resumed by the allied and associated powers.

### The League of Nations

#### SECTION I

The covenant of the league of nations constitutes section 1 of the peace treaty, which places upon the league many specific duties in addition to its general duties.

It may question Germany at any time for a violation of the neutralized zone east of the Rhine as a threat against the world's peace.

It will appoint three of the five members of the Saar commission, oversee its régime, and carry out the plebiscite.

It will appoint the high commissioner of Danzig, guarantee the independence of the free city, and arrange for treaties betwen Danzig and Germany and Poland.

It will work out the mandatory system to be applied to the former German colonies, and act as a final court in part of the plebiscites of the Belgian-German frontier and in disputes as to the Kiel canal, and decide certain of the economic and financial problems.

An international conference on labor is to be held in October under its direction, and another on the international control of ports, waterways, and railways is foreshadowed.

The members of the league will be the signatories of the covenant and other states invited to accede, who must lodge a declaration of accession without reservation within two months.

A new state, dominion, or colony may be admitted provided its admission is agreed to by two-thirds of the assembly.

A state may withdraw upon giving two years' notice, if it has fulfilled all its international obligations.

# THE TREATY OF PEACE

## SECTION II

A permanent secretariat will be established at the seat of the league, which will be at Geneva.

**Assembly**—The assembly will consist of representatives of the members of the league, and will meet at stated intervals. Voting will be by states. Each member will have one vote and not more than three representatives.

**Council**—The council will consist of representatives of the five great allied powers, together with representatives of four members selected by the assembly from time to time; it may co-operate with additional states and will meet at least once a year. Members not represented will be invited to send a representative when questions affecting their interests are discussed. Voting will be by states. Each state will have one vote and not more than one representative. Decisions taken by the assembly and council must be unanimous, except in regard to procedure and in certain cases specified in the covenant and in the treaty, where decisions will be by a majority.

**Armaments**—The council will formulate plans for a reduction of armaments for consideration and adoption. These plans will be revised every ten years. Once they are adopted, no member must exceed the armaments text without the concurrence of the council. All members will exchange full information as to armaments and programs, and a permanent commission will advise the council on military and naval questions.

**Preventing of war**—Upon any war or threat of war the council will meet to consider what common action shall be taken. Members are pledged to submit matters of dispute to arbitration or inquiry and not to resort to war until three months after the award.

Members agree to carry out an arbitral award and not to go to war with any party to the dispute which complies with it; if a member fails to carry out the award the council will propose the necessary measures.

The council will formulate plans for the establishment of a permanent court of international justice to determine international disputes or to give advisory opinions.

Members who do not submit their cases to arbitration must accept the jurisdiction of the assembly. If the council, less the parties to the dispute, is unanimously agreed upon the rights of it, the members agree that they will not go to war with any party to the dispute which complies with its recommendations. In this case a recommendation by the assembly, concurred in by all its members represented, less the parties to the dispute will have the force of a unanimous recommendation by the council.

In either case if the necessary agreement cannot be secured the members reserve the right to take such action as may be necessary for the maintenance of right and justice.

Members resorting to war in disregard of the covenant will immediately be debarred from all intercourse with other members. The council will in such cases consider what military or naval action can be taken by the league collectively for the protection of the covenants and will afford facilities to members co-operating in this enterprise.

**Validity of Treaties**—All treaties or international engagements concluded after the institution of the league will be registered with the secretariat and published.

The assembly may from time to time advise members to reconsider treaties which have become inapplicable or involve danger of peace.

The covenant abrogates all obligations between members inconsistent with its terms, but nothing in it shall affect the validity of international engagements, such as treaties of arbitration or regional understandings, like the Monroe doctrine, for securing the maintenance of peace.

**The Mandatory System**—The tutelage of nations not yet able to stand by themselves will be intrusted to advanced nations who are best fitted to undertake it.

The covenant recognizes three different stages of development, requiring different kinds of mandatories:

Communities like those belonging to the Turkish empire, which can be provisionally recognized as independent, subject to advice and assistance from a mandatory in whose selection they would be allowed a voice.

# THE TREATY OF PEACE

Communities like those of Central Africa, to be administered by the mandatory, under conditions generally approved by the members of the league, where equal opportunities for trade will be allowed to all members; certain abuses, such as trade in slaves, arms, and liquor, will be prohibited, and the construction of military and naval bases and the introduction of compulsory military training will be disallowed.

Other communities, such as Southwest Africa and the south Pacific islands, but administered under the laws of the mandatory as integral portions of its territory. In every case the mandatory will render an annual report, and the degree of its authority will be defined.

## Conditions of World Labor

Subject to and in accordance with the provisions of international conventions existing, or hereafter to be agreed upon, the members of the league will, in general, endeavor through the international organization established by the labor convention to secure and maintain fair conditions of labor for men, women, and children in their own countries, and other countries, and undertake to secure just treatment of the native inhabitants of territories under their control; they will intrust the league with the general supervision over the execution of agreements for the suppression of traffic in women and children, etc.; and the control of the trade in arms and ammunition with countries in which control is necessary; they will make provision for freedom of communications and transit and equitable treatment for commerce of all members of the league, with special reference to the necessities of regions devastated during the war; and they will endeavor to take steps for international prevention and control of disease.

International bureaus and commissions already established will be placed under the league, as well as those to be established in the future.

Amendments to the covenant will take effect when ratified by the council and by a majority of the assembly.

## New Limits for Germany

**Boundaries of Germany**—Germany cedes to France Alsace-Lorraine, 5,600 square miles, it to be southwest, and to Belgium two small districts between Luxemburg and Holland totaling 382 square miles.

She also cedes to Poland the southeastern tip of Silesia, beyond and including Oppeln, most of Posen, and West Prussia, 27,686 square miles, East Prussia being isolated from the main body by a part of Poland.

She loses sovereignty over the northeasternmost tip of East Prussia, forty square miles north of the river Memel, and the internationalized areas about Danzig, 729 square miles, and the basin of the Saar, 738 square miles, between the western border of the Rhenish Palatinate of Bavaria and the southeast corner of Luxemburg.

The Danzig area consists of the V between the Nogat and Vistula rivers made a W by the addition of a similar V on the west, including the city of Danzig.

The southeastern third of East Prussia and the area between East Prussia and the Vistula north of latitude 53 degrees 3 minutes is to have its nationality determined by popular vote, 5,785 square miles, as is to be the case in part of Schleswig, 2,787 square miles.

## Recovered Lands

### SECTION III

**Belgium**—Germany is to consent to the abrogation of the treaties of 1839, by which Belgium was established as a neutral state, and to agree in advance to any convention with which the allied and associated powers may determine to replace them.

Germany is to recognize the full sovereignty of Belgium over the contested territory of Morenet and over part of Prussian Morenet, and to renounce in favor of Belgium all rights of the circles of Eupen and Malmedy, the inhabitants of which are to be entitled, within six months, to protest against this change of sovereignty, either in whole or in part, the final decision to be reserved to the league of nations.

A commission is to settle the details of the frontier, and various regulations for change of nationality are laid down.

# THE TREATY OF PEACE

**Luxemburg**—Germany renounces her various treaties and conventions with the Grand Duchy of Luxemburg, recognizes that it ceased to be a part of the German Zollverein from January 1, last, renounces all right of exploitation of the railroads, adheres to the abrogation of its neutrality, and accepts in advance any international agreement as to it, reached by the allied and associated powers.

**Left Bank of the Rhine**—As provided in the military (armistice) clauses, Germany will not maintain any fortifications or armed forces less than fifty kilometers to the east of the Rhine, hold any maneuvers, nor maintain any works to facilitate mobilization.

In case of violation, ''she shall be regarded as committing a hostile act against the powers who sign the present treaty and as intending to disturb the peace of the world.''

By virtue of the present treaty, Germany shall be bound to respond to any request for an explanation which the council of the league of nations may think it necessary to address to her.

**Alsace-Lorraine**—After recognition of the moral obligation to repair the wrong done in 1871 by Germany to France and the people of Alsace-Lorraine, the territories ceded to Germany by the treaty of Frankfort are restored to France with their frontiers as before 1871, to date from the signing of the armistice, and to be free of all public debts.

Citizenship is regulated by detailed provisions distinguishing those who are immediately restored to full French citizenship, those who have to make formal applications therefor, and those for whom naturalization is open after three years.

The last named class includes German residents in Alsace-Lorraine, as distinguished from those who acquire the position of Alsace-Lorrainers as defined in the treaty.

All public property and all private property of German ex-sovereigns passes to France without payment or credit, France is substituted for Germany as regards ownership of the railroads and rights over concessions of tramways.

The Rhine bridges pass to France with the obligation for their upkeep.

For five years manufactured products of Alsace-Lorraine will be admitted to Germany free of duty to a total amount not exceeding in any year the average of the three years preceding the war, and textile materials may be imported from Germany to Alsace-Lorraine and re-exported free of duty. Contracts for electric power from the right bank must be continued for ten years.

For seven years, with possible extension to ten, the ports of Kehae and Strasbourg shall be administered as a single unit by a French administrator appointed and supervised by the Central Rhine commission.

Property rights will be safeguarded in both ports and equality of treatment as respects traffic assured the nationals, vessels, and goods of every country.

Contracts between Alsace-Lorrainers and Germans are maintained, except for France's right to annul on grounds of public interest judgments of courts held in certain classes of cases, while in others a judicial exequatur is first required.

Political condemnations during the war are null and void and the obligation to repay war fines is established as in other parts of allied territory.

Various clauses adjust the general provisions of the treaty to the special conditions of Alsace-Lorraine, certain matters of execution being left to conventions to be made between France and Germany.

## The Saar Valley Question

**The Saar**—In compensation for the destruction of coal mines for northern France and as payment on account of reparation, Germany cedes to France full ownership of the coal mines of the Saar basin with their subsidiaries, accessories, and facilities.

Their value will be estimated by the reparation commission and credited against that account. The French rights will be governed by German law in force at the armistice excepting war legislation, France replacing the present owners whom Germany undertakes to indemnify. France will continue to furnish the present proportion of coal for local needs and contribute in just proportion to local taxes.

# THE TREATY OF PEACE

The basin extends from the frontier of Lorraine as reannexed to France north as far as St. Wendel, including on the west the valley of the Saar as far as Saarkolzbach and on the east the town of Homburg.

In order to secure the rights and welfare of the population and to guarantee to France entire freedom in working the mines, the territory will be governed by a commission appointed by the league of nations and consisting of five members, one French, one a native inhabitant of the Saar and three representing three different countries other than France and Germany.

The league will appoint a member of the commission as chairman to act as executive of the commission. The commission will have all powers of government formerly belonging to the German empire.

Prussia and Bavaria will administer the railroads and other public services and have full power to interpret the treaty clauses.

The local courts will continue, but subject to the commission. Existing German legislation will remain the basis of the law, but the commission may make modification after consulting a local representative assembly which it will organize. It will have the taxing power, but for local purposes only. New taxes must be approved by this assembly.

Labor legislation will consider the wishes of the local labor organizations and the labor program of the league. French and other labor may be freely utilized, the former being free to belong to French unions. All rights acquired as to pensions and social insurance will be maintained by Germany and the Saar commission.

There will be no military service, but only a local gendarmerie to preserve order.

The people will preserve their local assemblies, religious liberties, schools, and language, but may vote only for local assemblies. They will keep their present nationality except so far as individuals may change it. Those wishing to leave will have every facility with respect to their property.

The territory will form part of the French customs system, with no export tax on coal and metallurgical products going to Germany nor on German products entering the basin, and for five years no import duties on products of the basin going to Germany or German products coming into the basin for local consumption.

French money may circulate without restriction. After fifteen years a plebiscite will be held by communes to ascertain the desires of the population as to continuance of the existing regime under the league of nations, union with France, or union with Germany. The right to vote will belong to all inhabitants over 20 resident therein at the signature.

Taking into account the opinions thus expressed, the league will decide the ultimate sovereignty. In any portion restored to Germany the German government must buy out the French mines at an appraised valuation.

If the price is not paid within six months thereafter this portion passes finally to France. If Germany buys back the mines, the league will determine how much of the coal shall be annually sold to France.

## New Nations Recognized
### SECTION IV

**German Austria.**—Germany recognizes the total independence of German-Austria in the boundaries traced.

**Czecho-Slovakia.**—Germany recognizes the entire independence of the Czecho-Slovak state, including the autonomous territory of the Ruthenians south of the Carpathians and accepts the frontiers of this state as to be determined, which in the case of the German frontier shall follow the frontier of Bohemia in 1914. The usual stipulations as to acquisition and change of nationality follow.

**Poland.**—Germany cedes to Poland the greater part of upper Silesia, Posen and the province of West Prussia on the left bank of the Vistula. A field boundary commission of seven—five representing the allied and associated powers and one each representing Poland and Germany—shall be constituted within fifteen days of the peace to delimit this boundary. Such special provisions as are necessary to protect racial, linguistic, or religious minority and to protect freedom of transit and equitable treatment of commerce of other nations shall be laid down in a subsequent treaty between the five allied and associated powers and Poland.

**East Prussia.**—The southern and eastern frontier of East Prussia as sueing (word obscure) Poland is to be fixed by plebiscite, the first in the regency of Allenstein between the southern frontier of East Prussia and the northern frontier of Regierungsbezirk Allenstein, from where it meets the boundary between East and West Prussia to its junction with the boundary between the circles of Oletsko and Augersburg, thence the northern boundary of Oletsko to its junction with the present frontier, and the second in the area comprising the circles of Stuhm and Rosenburg and the parts of the circles of Marienburg and Marienwerder east of the Vistula.

In each case German troops and authorities will move out within fifteen days of the peace and the territories be placed under an international commission of five members appointed by the five allied and associated powers, with the particular duty of arranging for a free, fair, and secret vote. The commission will report the results of the plebiscites to the five powers with a recommendation for the boundary, and will terminate its work as soon as the boundary has been laid down and new authorities set up.

The five allied and associated powers will draw up regulations assuring East Prussia full and equitable access to and use of the Vistula. A subsequent convention, of which the terms will be fixed by the five allied and associated powers, will be entered into between Poland, Germany and Danzig, to assure suitable railroad communication across German territory on the right bank of the Vistula between Poland and Danzig while Poland shall grant free passage from East Prussia to Germany.

The northeastern corner of East Prussia, about Memel, is to be ceded by Germany to the associated powers, the former agreeing to accept the settlement made, especially as regards the nationality of the inhabitants.

## Danzig a Free City

**Danzig.**—Danzig and the District immediately about it is to be constituted into the "free city of Danzig," under the guarantee of the league of nations. A high commissioner, appointed by the league and president at Danzig shall draw up a constitution in agreement with the duly appointed representatives of the city, and shall deal in the first instance with all differences arising between the city and Poland.

The actual boundaries of the city shall be delimited by a commission appointed within six months from the peace and to include three representatives chosen by the allied and associated powers and one each by Germany and Poland.

A convention, the terms of which shall be fixed by the five allied and associated powers, shall be concluded between Poland and Danzig, which shall include Danzig within the Polish custom frontiers, though a free area in the port; insure to Poland the free use of all the city's waterways, docks, and other port facilities, the control and administration of the Vistula and the whole through railway systems within the city and postal, telegraphic, and telephonic communication between Poland and Danzig; provide against discrimination against Poles within the city and place its foreign relations and the diplomatic protection of its citizens abroad in charge of Poland.

**Denmark.**—The frontier between Germany and Denmark will be fixed by the self-determination of the population. Ten days from the peace German troops and authorities shall evacuate the region north of the line running from the mouth of the Schlei south of Kappel, Schleswig, and Friedrichstadt, along the Eider to the North sea, south of Tonning; the workmen and soldiers' councils shall be dissolved; and the territory administered by an international commission of five, of whom Norway and Sweden shall be invited to name two.

The commission shall insure a free and secret vote in three zones. That between the German-Danish frontier and line running south of the Island of Alsen, north of Flensburg and south of Tondern to the North sea, north of the Island of Sylt, will vote as a unit within three weeks after the evacuation. Within five weeks after this vote the second zone, whose southern boundary runs from the North sea south of the Island of Fehr to the Baltic, south of Sygum, will vote by communes.

Two weeks after that vote the third zone, running to the limit of evacuation, also will vote by communes. The international commission will then draw a new frontier on the basis of these plebiscites and with due regard for geographical and economic conditions. Germany will renounce all sovereignty over the territories north of this line in favor of the associate governments, who will hand them over to Denmark.

**Helgoland**—The fortifications, military establishments, and harbors of the islands of Helgoland and Dune are to be destroyed under the supervision of the allies by German labor and at Germany's expense. They may not be reconstructed or any similar fortification built in the future.

**Russia**—Germany agrees to respect as permanent and inalienable the independency of all territories which were part of the former Russian empire, to accept the abrogation of the Brest-Litovsk and other treaties entered into with the Maximalist government of Russia, to recognize the full force of all treaties entered into by the allied and associated powers with states which were a part of the former Russian empire, and to recognize the frontiers as determined thereon.

The allied and associated powers formally reserve the right of Russia to obtain restitution and reparation on the principles of the present treaty.

### Colonies and Overseas Possessions

### SECTION V

Outside Europe, Germany renounces all rights, titles, and privileges as to her own or her allies' territories to all the allied and associated powers and undertakes to accept whatever measures are taken by the five allied powers in relation thereto.

**Colonies and overseas possessions**—Germany renounces in favor of the allied and associated powers her overseas possessions, with all rights and titles therein. All movable and immovable property belonging to the German empire or to any German state shall pass to the government exercising authority therein.

These governments may make whatever provisions seem suitable for the repatriation of German nationals and as to the conditions on which German subjects of European origin shall reside, hold property, or carry on business.

Germany undertakes to pay reparation for damage suffered by French nationals in the Cameroons or its frontier zone through the acts of German civil and military authorities and of individual Germans from Jan. 1, 1900, to Aug. 1, 1914.

Germany renounces all rights under the convention of Nov. 4, 1911, and Sept. 29, 1912, and undertakes to pay to France in accordance with an estimate presented and approved by the repatriation commission all deposits, credits, advances, etc., thereby secured.

Germany undertakes to accept and observe any provisions by the allied and associated powers as to the trade in arms and spirits in Africa, as well as to the general act of Berlin of 1885 and the general act of Brussels of 1890. Diplomatic protection to inhabitants of former German colonies is to be given by the governments exercising authority.

**China**—Germany renounces in favor of China all privileges and indemnities resulting from the Boxer protocol of 1901, and all buildings, wharves, barracks, forts, munitions of warships, wireless plants, and other public property except diplomatic or consular establishments in the German concessions of Tientsin and Hankow and in other Chinese territory except Kiau-Chau, and agrees to return to China, at its own expense, all the astronomical instruments seized in 1901.

China will, however, take no measures for disposal of German property in the legation quarter at Peking without the consent of the powers signatory to the Boxer protocol.

# THE TREATY OF PEACE

Germany accepts all abrogation of the concessions at Hankow and Tientsin, China agreeing to open them to international use.

Germany renounces all claims against China or any allied and associated government for the internment or repatriation of her citizens in China and for the seizure or liquidation of German interests there since Aug. 1917.

She renounces in favor of Great Britain her state property in the British concession at Canton and of France and China jointly of the property of the German school in the French concession at Shanghai.

**Siam**—Germany recognizes that all agreements between herself and Siam, including the right of extra-territoriality ceased July 22, 1917. All German public property except consular and diplomatic premises passes without compensation to Siam, German private property to be dealt with in accordance with the economic clauses. Germany waives all claims against Siam for the seizure and condemnation of her ships, liquidation of her property, or internment of her nationals.

**Liberia**—Germany renounces all rights under the international arrangements of 1911 and 1912 regarding Liberia, more particularly the right to nominate a receiver of the customs, and disinterests herself in any further negotiations for the rehabilitation of Liberia.

She regards as abrogated all commercial treaties and agreements between herself and Liberia, and recognizes Liberia's right to determine the status and condition of the re-establishment of Germans in Liberia.

**Morocco**—Germany renounces all her rights, titles and privileges under the act of Algeciras and the Franco-German agreements of 1909 and 1911, and under all treaties and arrangements with the Sherifian empire.

She undertakes not to intervene in any negotiations as to Morocco between France and other powers, accepts all the consequences of the French protectorate and renounces the capitulations. The Sherifian government shall have complete liberty of action in regard to German nationals, and all German protected persons shall be subject to the common law.

All movable and immovable German property, including mining rights may be sold at public auction, the proceeds to be paid to the Sherifian government and deducted from the reparation account. Germany is also required to reliquish her interests in the state bank of Morocco. All Moroccan goods entering Germany shall have the same privilege as French goods.

**Egypt**—Germany recognizes the British protectorate over Egypt declared on Dec. 18, 1914, and renounces as from Aug. 4, 1914, the capitulation and all the treaties, agreements, etc., concluded by her with Egypt. She undertakes not to intervene in any negotiations about Egypt between Great Britain and other powers. There are provisions for jurisdiction over German nationals and property, and for German consent to any changes which may be made in relation to the commission of public debt.

Germany consents to the transfer to Great Britain of the powers given to the late sultan of Turkey for securing the free navigation of the Suez canal.

Arrangements for property belonging to German nationals in Egypt are made similar to those in the case of Morocco and other countries. Anglo-Egyptian goods entering Germany shall enjoy the same treatment as British goods.

**Turkey and Bulgaria**—Germany accepts all arrangements which the allied and associated powers make with Turkey and Bulgaria with reference to any right, privileges, or interests claimed in those countries by Germany or her nationals and not dealt with elsewhere.

**Shantung**—Germany cedes to Japan all rights, titles and privileges, notably as to Kiau-Chau and the railroads, mines and cables acquired by her treaty with China of March 6, 1897, and other agreements as to Shantung.

All German rights to the railroad from Tsingtao to Tsinaufu, including all facilities and mining rights and rights of exploitation, pass equally to Japan and the cables from Tsingtao to Shanghai and Chefoo, the cables free of all charges.

All German state property, movable or immovable, in Kiau-Chau is acquired by Japan free of all charges.

# THE TREATY OF PEACE

In order to render possible the initiation of a general limitation of the armaments of all nations Germany undertakes directly to observe the military, naval, and air clauses which follow:

**Military forces**—The demobilization of the German army must take place within two months of the peace. Its strength may not exceed 100,000, including 4,000 officers, with not over seven divisions of infantry, and three of cavalry, to be devoted exclusively to maintenance of internal order and control of frontiers. Divisions may not be grouped under more than two army corps headquarters staffs.

The great German general staff is abolished. The army administrative service, consisting of civilian personnel not included in the number of effectives, is reduced to one-tenth the total in the 1913 budget.

Employes of the German states such as customs officers, first guards and coast guards may not exceed the number in 1913. Gendarmes and local police may be increased only in accordance with the growth of population. None of these may be assembled for military training.

**Armaments**—All establishments for the manufacturing, preparation, storage, or design of arms and munitions of war, except those specifically excepted, must be closed within three months of the peace and their personnel dismissed.

The exact amount of armament and munitions allowed Germany is laid down in detail tables, all in excess to be surrendered or rendered useless.

The manufacture or importation of asphyxiating, poisonous, or other gases and all analogous liquids is forbidden as well as the importation of arms, munitions, and war materials. Germany may not manufacture such materials for foreign governments.

**Conscription**—Conscription is abolished in Germany. The enlisted personnel must be maintained by voluntary enlistments for terms of twelve consecutive years, the number of discharges before the expiration of that term not in any years to exceed 5 per cent of the total effectives.

Officers remaining in the service must agree to serve to the age of 45 years and newly appointed officers must agree to serve actively for twenty-five years.

No military schools, except those absolutely indispensable for the units allowed, shall exist in Germany two months after the peace. No associations, such as societies of discharged soldiers, shooting or touring clubs, educational establishments or universities, may occupy themselves with military matters. All measures of mobilization are forbidden.

**Fortresses**—All fortified works, fortresses, and field works situated in German territory within a zone fifty kilometers east of the Rhine will be dismantled within three months. The construction of any new fortifications there is forbidden. The fortified works on the southern and eastern frontiers, however, may remain.

**Control**—Interallied commissions of control will see to the execution of the provisions for which a time limit is set, the maximum named being three months. They may establish headquarters at the German seat of government and go to any part of Germany desired.

Germany must give them complete facilities, pay their expenses, and also the expenses of execution of the treaty, including the labor and material necessary in demolition, destruction, or surrender of war equipment.

**Naval**—The German navy must be demobilized within a period of two months after the peace. She will be allowed six small battleships, six light cruisers, twelve destroyers, twelve torpedo boats, and no submarines, either military or commercial, with a personnel of 15,000 men, including officers, and no reserve force of any character.

Conscription is abolished, only voluntary service being permitted, with a minimum period of twenty-five years' service for officers and twelve for men. No member of the German mercantile marine will be permitted any naval training.

# THE TREATY OF PEACE

All German vessels of war in foreign ports and the German high sea fleet interned at Scapa Flow, will be surrendered, the final disposition of these ships to be decided upon by the allied and associated powers. Germany must surrender forty-two modern destroyers, fifty modern torpedo boats and all submarines, with their salvage vessels and all war vessels under construction, including submarines, must be broken up.

War vessels not otherwise provided for are to be placed in reserve or used for commercial purposes. Replacement of ships, except those lost, can take place only at the end of twenty years for battleships and fifteen years for destroyers. The largest armored ship Germany will be permitted will be 10,000 tons.

Germany is required to sweep up the mines in the North sea and the Baltic sea, as decided upon by the allies. All German fortifications in the Baltic defending the passages through the Delts must be demolished. Other coast defenses are permitted, but the number and caliber of the guns must not be increased.

During a period of three months after the peace, German high power wireless stations at Nauen, Hanover, and Berlin will not be permitted to send any messages except for commercial purposes and under supervision of the allied and associated governments, nor may any more be constructed.

Germany will be allowed to repair German submarine cables which have been cut but are not being utilized by the allied powers, and also portions of cables which after having been cut have been removed or at any rate not being utilized by any one of the allied and associated powers. In such cases the cables or portions of cables removed or utilized remain the property of allied and associated powers, and accordingly fourteen cables or parts of cables are specified, which will not be restored to Germany.

**Air**—The armed forces of Germany must not include any military or naval air forces except for not over 100 unarmed seaplanes to be retained till Oct. 1 to search for submarine mines. No dirigible shall be kept.

The entire air personnel is to be demobilized within two months, except for 1,000 officers and men retained till October.

No aviation grounds or dirigible sheds are to be allowed within 150 kilometers of the Rhine or the eastern or southern frontiers, existing installations within these limits to be destroyed.

The manufacture of aircraft and parts of aircraft is forbidden for six months. All military and naval aeronautical material under a most exhaustive definition must be surrendered within three months, except for the 100 seaplanes already specified.

**Prisoners of War**—The repatriation of German prisoners and interned civilians is to be carried out without delay and at Germany's expense by a commission composed of representatives of the allies in Germany. Those under sentence for offenses against discipline are to be repatriated without regard to the completion of their sentence.

Until Germany has surrendered persons guilty of offenses against the laws and customs of war, the allies have the right to retain selected German officers.

The allies may deal at their own discretion with German nationals who do not desire to be repatriated, all repatriation being conditional on the immediate release of any allied subjects still in Germany.

Germany is to accord facilities to commission of inquiry in collecting information in regard to missing prisoners of war and of imposing penalties on German officials who have concealed allied nationals.

Germany is to restore all property belonging to allied prisoners. There is to be a reciprocal exchange of information as to dead prisoners and their graves.

**Graves**—Both parties will respect and maintain the graves of soldiers and sailors buried on their territories, agree to recognize and assist any commission charged by any allied or associate government with identifying, registering, maintaining, or erecting suitable monuments over the graves, and to afford to each other all facilities for the repatriation of the remains of their soldiers.

## Trial of Wilhelm

**Responsibilities**—The allied and associated powers publicly arraign William Second of Hohenzollern, formerly German emporer, not for an offense against criminal law, but for a supreme offense against international morality and the sanctity of treaties.

The ex-emperor's surrender is to be requested of Holland and a special tribunal set up composed of one judge from each of the five great powers. With full guarantees of the right of defense, it is to be guided by the highest of international policy with a view of vindicating the solemn obligations of international undertakings and the validity of international morality, and will fix the punishment it feels should be imposed.

Persons accused of having committed acts in violation of the laws and customs of war are to be tried and punished by military tribunals under military law. If the charges affect nationals of only one state they will be tried before the tribunal of that state; if they affect nationals of several states, they will be tried before joint tribunals of the states concerned.

Germany shall hand over to the associated governments, either jointly or severally, all persons so accused and all documents and information necessary to insure full knowledge of the incriminating acts, the discovery of the offenders, and the just appreciation of the responsibility.

The judge (probably error for accused) will be entitled to name his own counsel.

## Reparations
### SECTION VII

**Reparations**—The allied and associated goverments affirm, and Germany accepts, the responsibility of herself and her allies for causing all the loss and damage to which the allied and associated governments and their nationals have been subjected as a consequence of the war imposed upon them by the aggression of Germany and her allies.

While the allied and associated governments recognize that the resources of Germany are not adequate after taking into account permanent diminutions of such resources which will result from other treaty claims, to make complete reparation for all such loss and damage, they require her to make compensation for all damages caused to civilians under seven main categories:

A—Damages by personal injury to civilians caused by acts of war, directly or indirectly, including bombardments from the air.

B—Damages caused to civilians, including exposure at sea, resulting from acts of cruelty ordered by the enemy and to civilians in the occupied territories.

C—Damages caused by maltreatment of prisoners.

D—Damages to the allied peoples represented by pensions and separation allowances, capitalized at the signature of this treaty.

E—Damages to property other than naval or military materials.

F—Damages to civilians by being forced to labor.

G—Damages in the form of levies or fines imposed by the enemy.

Germany further binds herself to repay all sums borrowed by Belgium from her allies as a result of Germany's violation of the treaty of 1839 up to Nov. 11, 1918, and for this purpose will issue at once and hand over to the reparation commission 5 per cent gold bonds falling due in 1926.

The total obligation of Germany to pay as defined in the category of damages is to be determined and notified to her after a fair hearing and not later than May 1, 1921, by an interallied reparation commission.

At the same time a schedule of payments to discharge the obligation within thirty years shall be presented. These payments are subject to postponement in certain contingencies.

Germany irrevocably recognizes the full authority of this commission, agrees to supply it with all the necessary information and to pass legislation to effectuate its findings. She further agrees to restore to the allies cash and certain articles which can be identified.

# THE TREATY OF PEACE

As an immediate step toward restoration Germany shall pay within two years one thousand million pounds sterling ($5,000,000,000), in either gold, goods, ships, or other specific forms of payment, this sum being included in and not additional to first thousand million bond issue referred to below, with the understanding that certain expenses, such as those of the armies of occupation and payments for food and raw materials, may be deducted at the discretion of the allies.

In periodically estimating Germany's capacity to pay, the reparation commission shall examine the German system of taxation, to the end that the sums for reparation which Germany is required to pay shall become a charge upon all her revenues, prior to that for the service or discharge of any domestic loan, and secondly, so as to satisfy itself that, in general, the German scheme of taxation is fully as heavy proportionately as that of any of the powers represented on the commission.

The measures which the allied and associated powers shall have the right to take, in case of voluntary default by Germany and which Germany agrees not to regard as acts of war, may include economic and financial prohibitions and reprisals and in general such other measures as the respective governments may determine to be necessary in the circumstances.

The commission shall consist of one representative each of the United States, Great Britain, France, Italy and Belgium, a representative of Serbia or Japan taking the place of the Belgian representative when the interests of either country are particularly affected, with all other allied powers entitled when their claims are under consideration to the right of representation without voting power. It shall permit Germany to give evidence regarding her capacity to pay and shall assure a just opportunity to be heard.

It shall make its headquarters at Paris, establish its own procedure and personnel, have general control of the whole reparation problem, and become the exclusive agency of the allies for receiving, holding, selling, and distributing reparation payments.

Majority vote shall prevail except that unanimity is required on questions involving the sovereignty of any of the allies, the cancellation of all or part of Germany's obligations, the time and manner of selling, distributing, and negotiating bonds issued by Germany, any postponement between 1921 and 1926 of annual payments beyond 1930, and any postponment after 1926 for a period of more than three years of the application of a different method of measuring damage than in a similar form or case and the interpretation of provisions.

Withdrawal from representation on the commission is permitted upon twelve months' notice. The commission may require Germany to give from time to time, by way of guarantee, issues of bonds or other obligations to cover such claims as are not otherwise satisfied.

In this connection and on account of the total amount of claims, bond issues are presently to be required of Germany in acknowledgment of its debt as follows:

One thousand million pounds sterling ($5,000,000,000) payable not later than May 1, 1921, without interest; $10,000,000,000, bearing 2½ per cent interest between 1921 and 1926, and thereafter 5 per cent, with a 1 per cent sinking fund payment beginning in 1926, and an undertaking to deliver bonds to an additional amount of $10,000,000,000, bearing interest at 5 per cent.

Under terms to be fixed by the commission, interest on Germany's debt will be 5 per cent, unless otherwise determined by the commission in the future, and payments that are not made in gold may be accepted by the commission in the form of properties, commodities, businesses, rights, concessions, etc.

Certificates of beneficial interest, representing either bonds or goods delivered by Germany may be issued by the commission to the interested powers. As bonds are distributed and pass from the control of the commission an amount of Germany's debt equivalent to their par value is to be considered as liquidated.

**Shipping**—The German government recognizes the right of the allies to the replacement, ton for ton and class for class, of all merchant ships and fishing boats lost or damaged owing to the war, and agrees to cede to the allies all German merchant ships of 1,600 tons gross and upwards, one-half of her ships between 1,000 and 1,600 tons gross, and one-quarter of her steam trawlers and other fishing boats. These ships are to be delivered within two months to the reparation commission, together with documents of title evidencing the transfer of the ships free from incumbrance.

"As an additional part of reparation" the German government further agrees to build merchant ships for the account of the allies to the amount of not exceeding 200,000 tons gross annually during the next five years.

All ships used for inland navigation taken by Germany from the allies are to be restored within two months, the amount of loss not covered by such restitution to be made up by the cession of the German river fleet up to 20 per cent thereof.

## Devastated Areas

### SECTION VIII

**Devastated areas**—Germany undertakes to devote her economic resources directly to the physical restoration of the invaded areas. The reparation commission is authorized to require Germany to replace the destroyed articles by the delivery of animals, machinery, etc., existing in Germany and to manufacture materials required for reconstruction purposes, with due consideration for Germany's essential domestic requirements.

**Coal, etc.**—Germany is to deliver annually for ten years to France coal equivalent to the difference between annual pre-war output of Nord and Pas de Calais mines and annual production during above ten years. Germany, further, gives options over ten years for delivery of 7,000,000 tons coal per year to France, in addition to the above; of 8,000,000 tons to Belgium, and of an amount rising from 4,500,000 tons in 1919 to 1920 to 8,500,000 tons in 1923 to 1924 to Italy at prices to be fixed as prescribed in the treaty. Coke may be taken in place of coal in ratio of three tons to four. Provision is also made for delivery to France over three years of benzol, coal tar, and sulphate of ammonia. The commission has powers to postpone or annul the above deliveries should they interfere unduly with industrial requirements of Germany.

**Dyestuffs**—Germany accords option to the commission on dyestuffs and chemical drugs, including quinine, up to 50 per cent of total stock in Germany at the time the treaty comes in force and similar options during each six months to end of 1924 up to 25 per cent of previous six months' output.

**Cables**—Germany renounces all title to specified cables, value of such as were privately owned being credited to her against reparation indebtedness.

**Special provisions**—As reparation for the destruction of the library of Louvain, Germany is to hand over manuscripts, early printed books, prints, etc., to be equivalent to those destroyed.

In addition to the above, Germany is to hand over to Belgium wings now at Berlin belonging to the altar piece of the "Adoration of the Lamb," by Hubert and Jan Van Eyck, the center of which is now in the church of St. Bavo at Ghent, and the wings now at Berlin and Munich, of the altar piece of "Last Supper," by Dirk Bouts, the center of which belongs to the church of St. Peter at Louvain.

Germany is to restore within six months the koran of the Caliph Ottman, formerly at Medina to the king of the Hedjaz, and the skull of the Sultan Mkwawa, formerly in German East Africa, to His Britannic Majesty's government.

## Pre-War Debts

### SECTION IX

**Finance**—Powers to which German territory is ceded will assume a certain portion of the German pre-war debt, the amount to be fixed by the reparations commission on the basis of the ratio between the revenue of the ceded territory and Germany's total revenues for the three years preceding the war.

In view, however, of the special circumstances under which Alsace-Lorraine was separated from France in 1871, when Germany refused to accept any part of the French public debt, France will not assume any part of Germany's pre-war debt there, nor will Poland share in certain German debts incurred for the oppression of Poland.

If the value of the German public property in ceded territory exceeds the amount of debt assumed, the states to which property is ceded give credit on reparation for the excess, with the exception of Alsace-Lorraine.

Mandatory powers will not assume any German debts or give any credit for German government property.

Germany renounces all right of representation on, or control of, state banks, commissions, or other similar international financial and economic organizations.

## Must Pay For Occupation

Germany is required to pay for the total cost of the armies of occupation from the date of the armistice as long as they are maintained in German territory, this cost to be the first charge on her resources. The cost of reparation is the next charge, after making such provisions for payments for imports as the allies may deem necessary.

Germany is to deliver to the allied and associated powers all sums deposited in Germany by Turkey and Austria-Hungary in connection with the financial support extended by her to them during the war, and to transfer to the allies all claims against Austria-Hungary, Bulgaria or Turkey in connection with agreements made during the war.

Germany confirms the renunciation of the treaties of Bucharest and Brest-Litovsk.

On the request of the reparations commission, Germany will expropriate any right, rights or interests of her nationals in public utilities in ceded territories or those administered by mandatories, and in Turkey, China, Russia, Austria-Hungary, and Bulgaria, and transfer them to the reparations commission, which will credit her with their value.

Germany guarantees to repay to Brazil the fund arising from the sale of Sao Paulo coffee which she refused to allow Brazil to withdraw from Germany.

## Economic Clauses

### SECTION X

Customs—For a period of six months Germany shall impose no tariff duties higher than the lowest in force in 1914, and for certain agricultural products, wines, vegetables, oils, artificial silk, and washed or scoured wool this restriction obtains for two and a half years, or for five years unless further extended by the league of nations.

Germany must give most favored nation treatment to the allied and associated powers. She shall impose no customs tariff for five years on goods originating in Alsace-Lorraine and for three years on goods originating in former German territory ceded to Poland with the right of observation of a similar exception for Luxemburg.

Shipping—Ships of the allied and associated powers shall for five years, and thereafter under condition of reciprocity, unless the league of nations otherwise decides, enjoy the same rights in German ports as German vessels and have most favored nation treatment in fishing, coasting trade, and towage even in territorial waters. Ships of a country having no sea coast may be registered at some one place within its territory.

Unfair competition—Germany undertakes to give the trade of the allied and associated powers adequate safeguards against unfair competition and in particular to suppress the use of false wrappings and markings and on condition of reciprocity to respect the laws and judicial decisions of allied and associated states, in respect of regional appellations of wines and spirits.

Treatment of Nationals—Germany shall impose no exceptional taxes or restriction upon the nationals of the allied and associated states for a period of five years and unless the league of nations acts for an additional five years, German nationality shall not continue to attach to a person who has become a national of an allied or associated state.

**Conventions**—Some forty multilateral conventions are renewed between Germany and the allied and associated powers, but special conditions are attached to Germany's readmission to several.

As to postal and telegraphic conventions Germany must not refuse to make reciprocal agreements with the new states. She must agree as respects the radio-telegraphic convention to provisional rules to be communicated to it and adheres to the new convention when formulated.

In the North sea fisheries and North sea liquor traffic convention, rights of inspection and police over associated fishing boats shall be exercised for at least five years only by vessels of these powers. As to the international railway union Germany shall adhere to the new convention when formulated.

As to the Chinese customs tariff arrangement, the arrangements of 1905 regarding Whangpoo and the Boxer indemnity of 1901; France, Portugal, and Roumania, as to the Hague convention of 1903 relating to civil procedure; and Great Britain and the United States, as to article 3 of the Samoan treaty of 1899, are relieved of all obligation toward Germany.

Each allied and associated state may renew any treaty with Germany insofar as consistent with the peace treaty by giving notice within six months. Treaties entered into by Germany since Aug. 1, 1914, with other enemy states and before or since that date with Roumania, Russia, and governments representing parts of Russia are abrogated and any concession granted under pressure by Russia to German subjects annulled.

The allied and associated states are to enjoy most favored nation treatment under treaties entered into by Germany and other enemy states before Aug. 1, 1914, and under treaties entered into by Germany and neutral states during the war.

**Pre-War Debts**—A system of clearing houses is to be created within three months, one in Germany and one in each allied and associated state which adopts the plan for the payment of pre-war debts, including those arising from contracts suspended by the war, for the adjustment of the proceeds of the liquidation of enemy property and the settlement of other obligations.

Each participating state assumes responsibility for the payment of all debts owing by its nationals to nationals of the enemy states except in cases of pre-war insolvency of the debtor.

The proceeds of the sale of private enemy property in each participating state may be used to pay the debts owed to the nationals of that state, direct payment from debtor to creditor and all communications relating thereto being prohibited.

Disputes may be settled by arbitration by the courts of the debtor country or by the mixed arbitral tribunal. Any ally or associated power may, however, decline to participate in this system by giving Germany six months' notice.

**Enemy Property**—Germany shall restore or pay for all private enemy property seized or damaged by her, the amount of damages to be fixed by the mixed arbitral tribunal. The allied and associated states may liquidate German private property within their territories as compensation for property of their nationals not restored or paid for by Germany, for debts owed to their nationals by German nationals. and for other claims against Germany.

Germany is to compensate its nationals for such losses and to deliver within six months all documents relating to property held by its nationals in allied and associated states.

All war legislation as to enemy property rights and interests is confirmed and all claims by Germany against the allied or associated governments for acts under exceptional war measures abandoned.

**Contracts**—Pre-war contracts between allied and associated nationals, excepting the United States, Japan, and Brazil, and German nationals are cancelled, except for debts for accounts already performed, agreements for the transfer of property where the property had already passed, leases of land and houses, contracts of mortgage. pledge of lien, mining concessions. contracts with governments, and insurance contracts.

Mixed arbitral tribunals shall be established, of three members, one choosen by Germany, one by the associated states, and the third by agreement, or, failing which, by the president of Switzerland. They shall have jurisdiction over all disputes as to contracts concluded before the present peace treaty.

Fire insurance contracts are not considered dissolved by the war, even if premiums have not been paid, but lapse at the date of the first annual premium falling due three months after the peace.

Life insurance contracts may be restored by payments of accumulated premiums with the interest, sums falling due on such contracts during the war to be recoverable with interest. Marine insurance contracts are dissolved by the outbreak of war, except where the risk insured against had already been incurred.

Where the risk had not attached, premiums paid are recoverable; otherwise, premiums due and sums due on losses are recoverable. Reinsurance treaties are abrogated unless invasion had made it impossible for the reinsured to find another reinsurer.

Any allied or associated power, however, may cancel all the contracts running between its nations and a German life insurance company, the latter being obligated to hand over the proportion of its assets attributable to such policies.

**Industrial Property**—Rights as to industrial, literary and artistic property are re-established, the special war measures of the allied and associated powers are ratified and the right reserved to impose conditions on the use of German patents and copyrights when in the public interest. Except as between the United States and Germany, pre-war licenses and rights to sue for infringements committed during the war are cancelled.

**Opium**—The contracting powers agree, whether or not they have signed and ratified the opium convention of Jan. 23, 1912, or signed the special protocol opened at the Hague in accordance with resolutions adopted by the third opium conference in 1914, to bring the said convention into force by enacting within twelve months of the peace the necessary legislation.

**Religious Missions**—The allied and associated powers agree that the properties of religious missions in territories belonging or ceded to them shall continue in their work under the control of the powers, Germany renouncing all claims in their behalf.

### Air Control

### SECTION XI

**Aerial Navigation**—Aircraft of the allied and associated powers shall have full liberty of passage and landing over and in German territory, equal treatment with German planes as to use of German airdromes, and with most favored nation planes as to internal commercial traffic in Germany.

Germany agrees to accept allied certificates of nationality, airworthiness or competency or licenses and to apply the convention relative to aerial navigation concluded between the allied and associated powers to her own aircraft over her own territory. These rules apply until 1923 unless Germany has since been admitted to the league of nations or to the above convention.

**Freedom of transit**—Germany must grant freedom of transit through her territories by rail or water to persons, goods, ships, carriages, and mails from or to any of the allied or associated powers, without customs or transit duties, undue delays, restrictions, or discriminations based on nationality, means of transport, or place of entry or departure.

Goods in transit shall be assured all possible speed of journey, especially perishable goods.

Germany may not divert traffic from its normal course in favor of her own transport routes or maintain "control stations" in connection with trans-migration traffic. She may not establish any tax discrimination against the ports of allied or associated powers; must grant the latter's seaports all factors and reduced tariffs granted her own or other nationals, and afford the allied and associated powers equal rights with those of her own nationals in her ports and waterways, save that she is free to open or close her maritime coasting trade.

**Free zones in ports**—Free zones existing in German ports on Aug. 1, 1914, must be maintained with due facilities as to warehouses and packing, without discrimination and without charges except for expenses of administration and use. Goods leaving the free zones for consumption in Germany and goods brought into the free zones from Germany shall be subject to the ordinary import and export taxes.

## German Rivers Open To All

### SECTION XII

**International Rivers**—The Elbe from the junction of the Vltava, the Vltava from Prague, the Oder from Oppa, the Niemen from Grodno, and the Danube from Ulm are declared international together with their connections. The riparian states must ensure good conditions of navigation within their territories unless a special organization exists therefor. Otherwise appeal may be had to a special tribunal of the league of nations, which also may arrange for a general international waterways convention.

The Elbe and the Oder are to be placed under international commissions to meet within three months, that for the Elbe composed of four representatives of Germany, two from Czecho-Slovakia, and one each from Great Britain, France, Italy, and Belgium, and that for the Oder composed of one each from Poland, Russia, Czecho-Slovakia, Great Britain, France, Denmark and Sweden.

If any riparian state on the Niemen should so request of the league of nations a similar commission shall be established there. These commissions shall, upon request of any riparian state, meet within three months to revise existing international agreement.

**The Danube**—The European Danube commission reassumes its pre-war powers, for the time being, with representatives of only Great Britain, Italy and Roumania. The upper Danube is to be administered by a new international commission until a definitive state be drawn up at a conference of the powers nominated by the allied and associated governments within one year after the peace.

The enemy governments shall make full reparations for all war damages caused to the European commission; shall cede their river facilities in surrendered territory, and give Czecho-Slovakia, Serbia and Roumania any rights necessary on their shores for carrying out improvements in navigation.

**Rhine and Moselle**—The Rhine is placed under the central commission to meet at Strasbourg within six months after the peace and to be composed of four representatives of France, which shall in addition select the president; four of Germany, and two each of Great Britain, Italy, Belgium, Switzerland and the Netherlands.

Germany must give France on the course of the Rhine included between the two extreme points of her frontiers all rights to take water to feed canals, while herself agreeing not to make canals on the right bank opposite France. She must also hand over to France all her drafts and designs for this part of the river.

Belgium is to be permitted to build a deep draft Rhine-Meuse canal if she so desires within twenty-five years, in which case Germany must construct the part within her territory on plans drawn by Belgium; similarly, the interested allied governments may construct a Rhine-Meuse canal, both, if constructed, to come under the competent international commission.

Germany may not object if the central Rhine commission desires to extend its jurisdiction over the lower Moselle, the upper Rhine, or lateral canals.

Germany must cede to the allied and associated governments certain tugs, vessels, and facilities for navigation on all these rivers, the specific details to be established by an arbiter named by the United States. Decision will be based on the legitimate needs of the parties concerned and on the shipping traffic during the five years before the war. The value will be included in the regular reparation account. In the case of the Rhine shares in the German navigation companies and property such as wharves and warehouses held by Germany in Rotterdam at the outbreak of war must be handed over.

**Railways**—Germany, in addition to most favored nation treatment on her railways, agrees to co-operate in the establishment of through ticket services for passengers and baggage; to ensure communication by rail between the allied, associated and other states; to allow the construction or improvement within twenty-five years of such lines as necessary, and to conform her rolling stock to enable its incorporation in trains of the allied or associated powers.

She also agrees to accept the denunciation of the St. Gothard convention if Switzerland and Italy so request, and temporarily to execute instructions as to the transport of troops and supplies and the establishment of postal and telegraphic service, as provided.

**Czecho-Slovakia**—To assure Czecho-Slovakia access to the sea, special rights are given her both north and south. Towards the Adriatic, she is permitted to run her own through trains to Fiume and Trieste. To the north, Germany is to lease her for ninety-nine years spaces in Hamburg and Stettin, the details to be worked out by a commission of three representing Czecho-Slovakia, Germany, and Great Britain.

**The Kiel canal**—The Kiel canal is to remain free and open to war and merchant ships of all nations at peace with Germany. Goods and ships of all states are to be treated on terms of absolute equality, and no taxes to be imposed beyond those necessary for upkeep and improvement for which Germany is responsible.

In case of violation of or disagreement as to these provisions, any state may appeal to the league of nations, and may demand the appointment of an international commission. For preliminary hearing of complaints Germany shall establish a local authority at Kiel.

## Aid for Labor
### SECTION XIII

Members of the league of nations agree to establish a permanent organization to promote international adjustment of labor conditions, to consist of an annual international labor conference and an international labor office.

The former is composed of four representatives of each state, two from the government and one each from the employers and the employed; each of them may vote individually. It will be a deliberative, legislative body, its measures taking the form of draft conventions or recommendations for legislation, which, if passed by two-thirds vote, must be submitted to the law-making authority in every state participating.

Each government may either enact the terms into law; approve the principle, but modify them to local needs; leave the actual legislation, in case of a federal state, to local legislatures, or reject the convention altogether, without further obligation.

The international labor office is established at the seat of the league of nations, as part of its organization. It is to collect and distribute information on labor throughout the world and prepare agenda for the conference. It will publish a periodical in French and English, and possibly other languages.

Each state agrees to make to it, for presentation to the conference, an annual report of measures taken to execute accepted conventions; the governing body is its executive. It consists of twenty-four members, twelve representing the governments, six the employers, and six the employes, to serve for three years.

On complaint that any government has failed to carry out a convention to which it is a party, the governing body may make inquiries directly to that government, and, in case the reply is unsatisfactory, may publish the complaint with comment.

A complaint by one government against another may be referred by the governing body to a commission of inquiry nominated by the secretary general of the league.

If the commission report fails to bring satisfactory action, the matter may be taken to a permanent court of international justice for final decision. The chief reliance for securing enforcement of the law will be publicity, with a possibility of economic action in the background.

# THE TREATY OF PEACE

The first meeting of the conference will take place in October, 1919, at Washington, to discuss the eight hour day, or forty-eight hour week; prevention of unemployment; extension and application of the international conventions adopted at Berne in 1906, prohibiting night work for women and the use of white phosphorus in the manufacture of matches; and employment of women and children at night or in unhealthy work, of women before and after childbirth, including maternity benefit, and of children as regards minimum age.

Nine principles of labor conditions we recognize on the ground that ''the well being, physical and moral, of the industrial wage earners is of supreme international importance.'' With exceptions necessitated by differences of climate, habits, and economic development, they include: The guiding principle that labor should not be regarded merely as a commodity or article of commerce; right of association of employers and employes; a wage adequate to maintain a reasonable standard of life; the eight hour day, or forty-eight hour week; a weekly rest of at least twenty-four hours, which should include Sunday wherever practicable; abolition of child labor and assurance of the continuation of the education and proper physical development of children; equal pay for equal work as between men and women; equitable treatment of all workers lawfully resident therein, including foreigners, and a system of inspection in which women should take part.

## Safeguards and Guarantees
### SECTION XIV

**Guarantee**—Western Europe. As a guarantee for the execution of the treaty, German territory to the west of the Rhine, together with the bridgeheads, will be occupied by allied and associated troops for fifteen years.

If the conditions are faithfully carried out by Germany certain districts, including the bridgehead of Cologne, will be evacuated at the expiration of five years; certain other districts, including the bridgehead of Coblenz, and the territories nearest the Belgian frontier, will be evacuated after ten years, and the remainder, including the bridgehead of Mainz, will be evacuated after fifteen years.

In case the interallied reparation commission finds that Germany has failed to observe the whole or part of her obligation, either during the occupation or after the fifteen years have expired, the whole or part of the areas specified will be reoccupied immediately. If before the expiration of the fifteen years Germany complies with all the treaty undertakings, the occupying forces will be withdrawn immediately.

**Eastern Europe**—All German troops at present in territories to the east of the new frontier shall return as soon as the allied and associated governments deem wise. They are to abstain from all requisitions and are in no way to interfere with measures for national defense taken by the government concerned.

All questions regarding occupation not provided for by the treaty will be regulated by a subsequent convention or convention which will have similar force and effect.

## No Counter-Claims Allowed
### SECTION XV

**Miscellaneous**—Germany agrees to recognize the full validity of the treaties of peace and additional conventions to be concluded by the allied and associated powers with the powers allied with Germany; to agree to the decisions to be taken as to the territories of Austria-Hungary, Bulgaria, and Turkey, and to recognize the new states in the frontiers to be fixed for them.

Germany agrees not to put forward any pecuniary claims against any allied or associated power signing the present treaty based on events previous to the coming into force of the treaty.

Germany accepts all decrees as to German ships and goods made by any allied or associated prize court. The allies reserve the right to examine all decisions of German prize courts. The present treaty, of which the French and British texts are both authentic, shall be ratified and the depositions of ratifications made in Paris as soon as possible. The treaty is to become effective in all respects for each power on the date of deposition of its ratification.

Map of Central Europe, Showing the Territorial Effects of the Peace Treaty.
See Key on Opposite Page.

# CHANGES IN MAP OF EUROPE
## Key to Map on Opposite Page

*The changes made in the map of Central Europe by the terms of the Treaty of Peace handed to the German peace delegates at Versailles on May 7, 1919, are shown on the opposite page. The principal issues, in a territorial or geographic sense, are (See corresponding figures and letters in the map):*

1. Alsace-Lorraine, the territories which were wrenched from France in 1871, are restored to the republic. The French in the lost provinces now regained are repatriated, and the Germans there may become French citizens, if they so desire, by naturalization after three years. The public debt is cancelled.

2. The Saar valley will pass into the hands of the French, together with the output of the mines. After fifteen years the people of the district will vote whether they shall remain under French control, under the guidance of the league of nations, or return to Germany. This voting will be open to all inhabitants over 20 years of age.

3. Germany must renounce all treaties with Luxembourg and must give up the German control of the railways and other facilities in the grand duchy. The duchy is considered to have ceased to have been part of the German Zollverein from Jan. 1, 1919.

4. Germany must recognise the sovereignty of Belgium over the contested territory of Morenet, and must cede all rights to the districts of Malmedy and Eupen. The people in six months may protest, if they wish to, this change. The districts affected comprise 382 square miles.

5. Germany must create a neutral zone thirty miles in depth east of the Rhine. The bridgeheads will be occupied fifteen years.

6. Helgoland, the island fortress, is to be dismantled at German expense and by German labor.

7. The frontier between Germany and Denmark will be decided by a plebiscite. The people of Schleswig-Holstein will decide under the right of self-determination.

8. Danzig and the immediate vicinity will be a free port, giving Poland an outlet to the sea. It will be protected by the league of nations.

9. The territory around Memel must be given up to the allies, who will decide on its destination.

10. The boundaries of southern and eastern Prussia will be decided by a vote of the people. The German troops must move out within fifteen days after peace is signed.

11. Germany must recognize the independence of the new Poland.

12. The portion of West Prussia on the left bank of the Vistula must be ceded to Poland.

13. Posen must be ceded to Poland.

14. The greater part of Upper Silesia is to go to Poland.

15. The present border between Germany and Bohemia is to remain unchanged.

16. Germany must recognise the independence of the new nation of Czecho-Slovakia. Access to the sea must be provided by railroads to the Adriatic at Fiume and Triest, and in the north Germany must lease spaces in Hamburg and Stettin.

17. Germany must recognize the independence of German Austria.

18. The Ruthenians in Hungary are to be recognized as independent.

19. The entire Russian boundary must be restored to the lines of the old Russian empire. The treaties of Brest-Litovsk and other treaties with the Russian soviet government are abrogated.

20. Germany must accept any arrangement the allies make with Bulgaria.

21. The Germans must accept any arrangement the allies make with Turkey.

---

The rivers running through the old Germany and Austria-Hungary are to be internationalized and largely controlled by representatives of the allies:

A. The Rhine will be internationalized on the whole of its navigable course.

B. The Kiel canal, base of the German fleet, is to be opened to the ships of the world.

C. The Elbe river from the juncture of the Vltava to its mouth is to be internationalized.

D. The Vltava as far up as Prague is to be internationalized, giving the city an outlet to the sea.

E. The internationalization of the Oder will be between Oppa and the mouth of the stream.

F. The Niemen river must be opened to the vessels of the world as far up as Grodno.

G. The entire course of the Danube from Ulm to the Black sea is internationalized.

H. The Moselle river is placed under the same international river control commission as the Rhine.

# CHANGES IN THE PEACE TREATY

The changes in the treaty of peace agreed upon by the Allies and promulgated June 16, 1919, when the revised treaty was handed to the Germans, included the following:

1. A plebiscite for Upper Silesia, with guarantees of coal from that territory.

2. Frontier rectifications in West Prussia.

3. Omission of the third zone in the Schleswig plebiscite.

4. Temporary increase of the German army from 100,000 to 200,000 men.

5. Declaration of the intention to submit within a month of signature a list of those accused of violation of the laws and customs of war.

6. Offer to co-operate with a German commission on reparations, and to receive suggestions for discharging the obligation.

7. Certain detailed modifications in the finance, economic, and ports and waterways clauses, including abolition of the proposed Kiel canal commission.

8. Assurance of membership in the League of Nations in the early future, if Germany fulfills her obligations.

After the German national assembly at Weimar had voted in favor of signing the treaty of peace, Sunday, June 22, 1919, and the Scheidemann government had been replaced by a cabinet headed by Herr Bauer, a new set of plenipotentiaries was named to sign on behalf of Germany, and the treaty was finally signed by the representatives of the Allied powers and Germany, at Versailles, Saturday, June 28, 1919.

The Germans delegated by the Bauer government to sign the treaty were: Dr. Herman Mueller, foreign minister; Dr. Bell, minister of colonies; Herr Leinert, and Herr Giesberts. With their signatures came the conclusion of peace—the official end of the great World War.

# CHRONOLOGY OF THE WORLD WAR

*Dates of Important Battles, Naval Engagements, and Principal
Events of the War from 1914 to the Signing of the Peace Treaty
in June, 1919.*

## 1914

**June 28**—Archduke Ferdinand and wife assassinated in Sarajevo, Bosnia.

**July 28**—Austria-Hungary declares war on Serbia.

**August 1**—Germany declares war on Russia and general mobilization is
under way in France and Austria-Hungary. **Aug. 2**—German troops enter
France at Cirey; Russian troops enter Germany at Schwidden; German army
enters Luxemburg over protest, and Germany asks Belgium for free passage of
her troops. **Aug. 3**—British fleet mobilizes; Belgium appeals to Great Britain
for diplomatic aid and German ambassador quits Paris.

**Aug. 4**—France declares war on Germany; Germany declares war on Belgium; Great Britain sends Belgium neutrality ultimatum to Germany; British
army mobilized and state of war between Great Britain and Germany is declared.
President. Wilson issues neutrality proclamation. **Aug. 5**—Germans begin
fighting on Belgium frontier; Germany asks for Italy's help. **Aug. 6**—Austria
declares war on Russia. **Aug. 7**—Germans defeated by French at Altkirch.
**Aug. 9**—Germans capture Liege. Portugal announces it will support Great
Britain; British land troops in France. **Aug. 10**—France declares war on
Austria-Hungary.

**Aug. 12**—Great Britain declares war on Austria-Hungary; Montenegro
declares war on Germany. **Aug. 15**—Japan sends ultimatum to Germany to
withdraw from Japanese and Chinese waters and evacuate Kiao-chow; Russia
offers autonomy to Poland. **Aug. 20**—German army enters Brussels. **Aug. 23**—
Japan declares war on Germany; Russia victorious in battles in East Prussia.
**Aug. 24**—Japanese warships bombard Tsingtao. **Aug. 25**—Japan and Austria
break off diplomatic relations. **Aug. 28**—English win naval battle over German
fleet near Helgoland. **Aug. 29**—Germans defeat Russians at Allenstein; occupy
Amiens; advance to La Fere, sixty-five miles from Paris.

**September 1**—Germans cross Marne; bombs dropped on Paris; Turkish
army mobilized; Zeppelins drop bombs on Antwerp. **Sept. 2**—Government of
France transferred to Bordeaux; Russians capture Lemberg. **Sept. 4**—Germans
cross the Marne. **Sept. 5**—England, France, and Russia sign pact to make no
separate peace. **Sept. 6**—French win battle of Marne; British cruiser Path-
finder sunk in North sea by a German submarine. **Sept. 7**—Germans retreat
from the Marne. **Sept. 14**—Battle of Aisne starts; German retreat halted.
**Sept. 15**—First battle of Soissons fought. **Sept. 20**—Russians capture Jaroslau
and begin siege of Przemysl.

**October 9-10**—Germans capture Antwerp. **Oct. 12**—Germans take Ghent.
**Oct. 20**—Fighting along Yser river begins. **Oct. 29**—Turkey begins war on
Russia.

**November 7**—Tsingtro falls before Japanese troops. **Nov. 9**—German
cruiser Emden destroyed.

**December 11**—German advance on Warsaw checked. **Dec. 14**—Belgrade
recaptured by Serbians. **Dec. 16**—German cruisers bombard Scarborough,
Hartlepool, and Whitby, on English coast, killing fifty or more persons; Austrians said to have lost upwards of 100,000 men in Serbian defeat. **Dec. 25**
—Italy occupies Avlona, Albania.

# CHRONOLOGY OF THE WORLD WAR

## 1915

**January** 1—British battleship Formidable sunk. **Jan.** 8—Roumania mobilizes 750,000 men; violent fighting in the Argonne. **Jan.** 11—Germans cross the Rawka, thirty miles from Warsaw. **Jan.** 24—British win naval battle in North sea. **Jan.** 29—Russian army invades Hungary; German efforts to cross Aisne repulsed.

**February** 1—British repel strong German attack near La Bassee. **Feb.** 2 —Turks are defeated in attack on Suez canal. **Feb.** 4— Russians capture Tarnow in Galicia. **Feb.** 8—Turks along Suez canal in full retreat; Turkish land defenses at the Dardanelles shelled by British torpedo boats. **Feb.** 11— Germans evacuate Lodz. **Feb.** 12—Germans drive Russians from positions in East Prussia, taking 26,000 prisoners. **Feb.** 14—Russians report capture of fortifications at Smolnik. **Feb.** 16—Germans capture Plock and Bielsk in Poland; French capture two miles of German trenches in Champagne district.

**February** 17—Germans report they have taken 50,000 Russian prisoners in Mazurian lake district. **Feb.** 18—German blockade of English and French coasts put into effect. **Feb.** 19-20—British and French fleets bombard Dardanelles forts. **Feb.** 21—American steamer Evelyn sunk by mine in North sea. **Feb.** 22—German war office announces capture of 100,000 Russian prisoners in engagements in Mazurian lake region; American steamer Carib sunk by mine in North sea. **Feb.** 28—Dardanelles entrance forts capitulate to English and French.

**March** 4—Landing of allied troops on both sides of Dardanelles straits reported; German U-4 sunk by French destroyers. **March** 10—Battle of Neuve Chapelle begins. **March** 14—German cruiser Dresden sunk in Pacific by English. **March** 18—British battleships Irresistible and Ocean and French battleship Bouvet sunk in Dardanelles strait. **March** 22—Fort of Przemysl surrenders to Russians. **March** 23—Allies land troops on Gallipoli peninsula. **March** 25— Russians victorious over Austrians in Carpathians.

**April** 8—German auxiliary cruiser, Prinz Eitel Friedrich, interned at Newport News, Va. **April** 16—Italy has 1,200,000 men mobilized under arms; Austrians report complete defeat of Russians in Carpathian campaign. **April** 23—Germans force way across Ypres canal and take 1,600 prisoners. **April** 25 —Allies stop German drive on Ypres line in Belgium. **April** 29—British report regaining of two-thirds of lost ground in Ypres battle.

**May** 7—Liner Lusitania torpedoed and sunk by German submarine off the coast of Ireland with the loss of more than 1,000 lives, 102 Americans. **May** 9—French advance two and one-half miles against German forces north of Arras, taking 2,000 prisoners. **May** 23—Italy declares war on Austria.

**June** 3—Germans recapture Przemysl with Austrian help. **June** 18— British suffer defeat north of La Bassee canal. **June** 28—Italians enter Austrian territory south of Riva on western shore of Lake Garda.

**July** 3—Tolmino falls into Italian hands. **July** 9—British make gains north of Ypres and French retake trenches in the Vosges. **July** 13—Germans defeated in the Argonne. **July** 29—Warsaw evacuated; Lublin captured by Austrians.

**August** 4—Germans occupy Warsaw. **Aug.** 14—Austrians and Germans concentrate 400,000 soldiers on Serbian frontier. **Aug.** 21—Italy declares war on Turkey.

**September** 1—Ambassador Bernstorff announces Germans will sink no more liners without warning. **Sept.** 4—German submarine torpedoes liner Hesperian. **Sept.** 9—Germans make air raid on London, killing twenty persons and wounding 100 others; United States asks Austria to recall Ambassador

Dumba. **Sept.** 20—Germans begin drive on Serbia to open route to Turkey. **Sept.** 22—Russian army retreating from Vilna, escapes German encircling movement. **Sept.** 25-30—Battle of Champagne, resulting in great advance for allied armies and causing Kaiser Wilhelm to rush to the west front; German counter attacks repulsed.

**October** 5—Russia and Bulgaria sever diplomatic relations; Russian, French, British, Italian, and Serbian diplomatic representatives ask for passports in Sofia. **Oct.** 10—Gen. Mackensen's forces take Belgrade. **Oct.** 12—Edith Cavell executed by Germans. **Oct.** 13—Bulgaria declares war on Serbia. **Oct.** 15—Great Britain declares war on Bulgaria. **Oct.** 16—France declares war on Bulgaria. **Oct.** 19—Russia and Italy declare war on Bulgaria. **Oct.** 27—Germans join Bulgarians in northeastern Serbia and open way to Constantinople. **Oct.** 30—Germans defeated at Mitau.

**November** 9—Italian liner Ancona torpedoed.

**December** 1—British retreat from near Bagdad. **Dec.** 4—Ford "peace party" sails for Europe. **Dec.** 8-9—Allies defeated in Macedonia. **Dec.** 15—Sir John Douglas Haig succeeds Sir John French as chief of English armies on west front.

## 1916

**January** 3—British troops at Kut-el-Amara surrounded. **Jan.** 9—British evacuate Gallipoli peninsula. **Jan.** 13—Austrians capture Cetinje, capital of Montenegro. **Jan.** 23—Scutari, capital of Albania, captured by Austrians.

**February** 22—Crown prince's army begins attack on Verdun.

**March** 8—Germany declares war on Portugal. **March** 15—Austria-Hungary declares war on Portugal. **March** 24—Steamer Sussex torpedoed and sunk.

**April** 18—President Wilson sends note to Germany. **April** 19—President Wilson speaks to congress, explaining diplomatic situation. **April** 24—Insurrection in Dublin. **April** 29—British troops at Kut-el-Amara surrender to Turks. **April** 30—Irish revolution suppressed.

**May** 3—Irish leaders of insurrection executed. **May** 4—Germany makes promise to change methods of submarine warfare. **May** 13—Austrians begin great offensive against Italians in Trentino. **May** 31—Great naval battle off Danish coast.

**June** 5—Lord Kitchener lost with cruiser Hampshire. **June** 11—Russians capture Dubno. **June** 29—Sir Roger Casement sentenced to be hanged for treason

**July** 1—British and French begin great offensive on the Somme. **July** 6—David Lloyd George appointed secretary of war. **July** 9—German merchant submarine Deutschland arrives at Baltimore. **July** 23—Gen. Kuropatkin's army wins battle near Riga. **July** 27—English take Delville wood; Serbian forces begin attack on Bulgars in Macedonia.

**August** 2—French take Fleury. **Aug.** 3—Sir Roger Casement executed for treason. **Aug.** 4—French recapture Thiaumont for fourth time; British repulse Turkish attack on Suez canal. **Aug.** 7—Italians on Isonzo front capture Monte Sabotino and Monte San Michele. **Aug.** 8—Turks force Russian evacuation of Bitlis and Mush. **Aug.** 9—Italians cross Isonzo river and occupy Austrian city of Goeritz. **Aug.** 10—Austrians evacuate Stanislau; allies take Doiran, near Saloniki, from Bulgarians.

**August** 19—German submarines sink British light cruisers Nottingham and Falmouth. **Aug.** 24—French occupy Maurepas, north of the Somme; Russians recapture Mush in Armenia. **Aug.** 27—Italy declares war on Germany; Roumania enters war on side of allies. **Aug.** 29—Field Marshal von Hindenburg made chief of staff of German armies, succeeding Gen. von Falkenhayn. August 30—Russian armies seize all five passes in Carpathians into Hungary.

September 3—Allies renew offensive north of Somme; Bulgarian and German troops invade Dobrudja, in Roumania. Sept. 7—Germans and Bulgarians capture Roumanian fortress of Tutrakan; Roumanians take Orsova, Bulgarian city. Sept. 19—German-Bulgarian army captures Roumanian fortress of Silistria. Sept. 14—British for first time use "tanks." Sept. 15—Italians begin new offensive on Carso.

October 2—Roumanian army of invasion in Bulgaria defeated by Germans and Bulgarians under Von Mackensen. Oct. 4—German submarines sink French cruiser Gallia and Cunard liner Franconia. Oct. 8—German submarines sink six merchant steamships off Nantucket, Mass. Oct. 11—Greek seacoast forts dismantled and turned over to allies on demand of England and France. Oct. 23—German-Bulgar armies capture Constanza, Roumania. Oct. 24—French win back Douaumont, Thiaumont field work, Haudromont quarries, and Caillette wood near Verdun, in smash of two miles.

November 1—Italians, in new offensive on the Carso plateau, capture 5,000 Austrians. Nov. 2—Germans evacuate Fort Vaux at Verdun. Nov. 5—Germans and Austrians proclaim new kingdom of Poland, of territory captured from Russia. Nov. 6—Submarine sinks British passenger steamer Arabia. Nov. 7—Cardinal Mercier protests against German deportation of Belgians; submarine sinks American steamer Columbian. Nov. 8—Russian army invades Transylvania, Hungary. Nov. 9—Austro-German armies defeat Russians in Volhyina and take 4,000 prisoners.

November 13—British launch new offensive in Somme region on both sides of Ancre. Nov. 14—British capture fortified village of Beacourt, near the Ancre. Nov. 19—Serbian, French, and Russian troops recapture Monastir; Germans cross Transylvania Alps and enter western Roumania. Nov. 21—British hospital ship Britannic sunk by mine in Aegean sea. Nov. 23—Roumanian army retreats ninety miles from Bucharest. Nov. 24—German-Bulgarian armies take Orsova and Turnu-Severin from Roumanians. Nov. 25—Greek provisional government declares war on Germany and Bulgaria. Nov. 28—Roumanian government abandons Bucharest and moves capital to Jassy.

December 5—Premier Herbert Asquith of England resigns. Dec. 7—David Lloyd George accepts British premiership. Dec. 8—Gen. von Mackensen captures big Roumanian army in Prohova valley. Dec. 12—Chancellor von Bethman-Hollweg announces in reichstag that Germany will propose peace; new cabinet in France under Aristide Briand as premier, and Gen. Robert Georges Nivelle given chief of command of French army. Dec. 15—French at Verdun win two miles of front and capture 11,000.

December 19—Llloyd George declines German peace proposals. Dec. 23—Baron Burian succeeded as minister of foreign affairs in Austria by Count Czernin. Dec. 26—Germany proposes to President Wilson "an immediate meeting of delegates of the belligerents." Dec 27—Russians defeated in five-day battle in eastern Wallachia, Roumania.

## 1917

January 1—Submarine sinks British transport Ivernia. Jan. 9—Russian premier, Trepoff, resigns. Golitzin succeeds him. Jan. 31—Germany announces unrestricted submarine warfare.

February 3—President Wilson reviews submarine controversy before congress; United States severs diplomatic relations with Germany; American steamer Housatonic sunk without warning. Feb. 7—Senate indorses President's act of breaking off diplomatic relations. **Feb. 12**—United States refuses German request to discuss matters of difference unless Germany withdraws unrestricted submarine warfare order.

**February 14**—Von Bernstorff sails for Germany. **Feb. 25**—British under Gen. Maude capture Kut-el-Amara; submarine sinks liner Laconia without warning; many lost including two Americans. **Feb. 26**—President Wilson asks congress for authority to arm American merchantships. **Feb. 28**—Secretary Lansing makes public Zimmerman note to Mexico, proposing Mexican-Japanese-German alliance.

**March 9**—President Wilson calls extra session of congress for April 16. **March 11**—British under Gen. Maude capture Bagdad; revolution starts in Petrograd. **March 15**—Czar Nicholas of Russia abdicates. **March 17**—French and British capture Bapaume. **March 18**—New French ministry formed by Alexander Ribot.

**March 21**—Russian forces cross Persian border into Turkish territory; American oil steamer Healdton torpedoed without warning. **March 22**—United States recognizes new government of Russia. **March 27**—Gen. Murray's British expedition into the Holy Land defeats Turkish army near Gaza.

**April 2**—President Wilson asks congress to declare that acts of Germany constitute a state of war; submarine sinks American steamer Aztec without warning. **April 4**—United States senate passes resolution declaring a state of war exists with Germany. **April 6**—House passes war resolution and President Wilson signs joint resolution of congress. **April 8**—Austria declares severance of diplomatic relations with United States.

**April 9**—British defeat Germans at Vimy Ridge and take 6,000 prisoners; United States seizes fourteen Austrian interned ships. **April 20**—Turkey severs diplomatic relations with the U. S. **April 28**—Congress passes selective service act for raising of army of 500,000; Guatemala severs diplomatic relations with Germany.

**May 7**—War department orders raising of nine volunteer regiments of engineers to go to France. **May 14**—Espionage act becomes law by passing senate. **May 18**—President Wilson signs selective service act. Also directs expeditionary force of regulars under Gen. Pershing to go to France. **May 19**—Congress passes war appropriation bill of $3,000,000,000.

**June 5**—Nearly 10,000,000 men in U. S. register for military service. **June 12**—King Constantine of Greece abdicates. **June 13**—Gen. Pershing and staff arrive in Paris. **June 15**—First Liberty loan closes with large over-subscription. **June 26**—First contingent American troops under Gen. Sibert arrives in France. **June 29**—Greece severs diplomatic relations with Teutonic allies.

**July 9**—President Wilson drafts state militia into federal service. Also places food and fuel under federal control. **July 13**—War department order drafts 678,000 men into military service. **July 14**—Aircraft appropriation bill of $640,000,000 passes house; Chancellor von Bethmann-Hollweg's resignation forced by German political crisis.

**July 18**—United States government orders censorship of telegrams and cablegrams crossing frontiers. **July 19**—New German Chancellor Michaelis declares Germany will not war for conquest; radicals and Catholic party ask peace without forced acquisitions of territory. **July 22**—Siam declares war on Germany. **July 23**—Premier Kerensky given unlimited powers in Russia. **July 28**—United States war industries board created to supervise expenditures.

**August 25**—Italian Second army breaks through Austrian line on Isonzo front. **Aug. 28**—President Wilson rejects Pope Benedict's peace plea.

# CHRONOLOGY OF THE WORLD WAR

**September 10**—Gen. Korniloff demands control of Russian government. **Sept. 11**—Russian deputies vote to support Kerensky. Korniloff's generals ordered arrested. **Sept. 16**—Russia proclaims new republic by order of Premier Kerensky. **Sept. 20**—Gen. Haig advances mile through German lines at Ypres. **Sept. 21**—Gen. Tasker H. Bliss named chief of staff, U. S. army.

**October 16**—Germans occupy islands of Runo and Adro in the Gulf of Riga. **Oct. 25**—French under Gen. Petain advance and take 12,000 prisoners on Aisne front. **Oct. 27**—Formal announcement made that American troops in France had fired their first shots in the war. **Oct. 29**—Italian Isonzo front collapses and Austro-German army reaches outposts of Udine.

**November 1**—Secretary Lansing makes public the Luxburg "spurlos versenkt" note. **Nov. 7**—Austro-German troops capture? **Nov. 9**—Permanent interallied military commission created. **Nov. 24**—Navy department announces capture of first German submarine by American destroyer. **Nov. 28**—Bolsheviki get absolute control of Russian assembly in Russian elections.

**December 6**—Submarine sinks the Jacob Jones, first regular warship of American navy destroyed. **Dec. 7**—Congress declares war on Austria-Hungary. **Dec. 8**—Jerusalem surrenders to Gen. Allenby's forces.

## 1918

**January 5**—President Wilson delivers speech to congress giving "fourteen points" necessary to peace. **Jan. 20**—British monitors win seafight with cruisers Goeben and Breslau, sinking latter. **Jan. 28**—Russia and Roumania sever diplomatic relations.

**February 2**—United States troops take over their first sector, near Toul. **Feb. 6**—United States troopship Tuscania sunk by submarine, 126 lost. **Feb. 11**—President Wilson, in address to congress, gives four additional peace principles, including self-determination of nations; Bolsheviki declare war with Germany over, but refuse to sign peace treaty. **Feb. 13**—Bolo Pasha sentenced to death in France for treason. **Feb. 25**—Germans take Reval, Russian naval base, and Pskov; Chancellor von Hertling agrees "in principle" with President Wilson's peace principles, in address to reichstag.

**March 1**—Americans repulse German attack on Toul sector. **March 2**—Treaty of peace with Germany signed by Bolsheviki at Brest-Litovsk. **March 4**—Germany and Roumania sign armistice on German terms. **March 13**—German troops occupy Odessa. **March 14**—All Russian congress of soviets ratifies peace treaty. **March 21**—German spring offensive starts on fifty mile front. **March 22**—Germans take 16,000 British prisoners and 200 guns.

**March 23**—German drive gains nine miles. "Mystery gun" shells Paris. **March 24**—Germans reach the Somme, gaining fifteen miles. American engineers rushed to aid British. **March 25**—Germans take Bapaume. **March 27**—Germans take Albert. **March 28**—British counter attack and gain; French take three towns; Germans advance toward Amiens. **March 29**—"Mystery gun" kills seventy-five churchgoers in Paris on Good Friday.

**April 4**—Germans start second phase of their spring drive on the Somme. **April 10**—Germans take 10,000 British prisoners in Flanders. **April 16**—Germans capture Messines ridge, near Ypres; Bolo Pasha executed. **April 23**—British and French navies "bottle up" Zeebrugge. **April 26**—Germans capture Mount Kemmel, taking 6,500 prisoners.

**May 5**—Austria starts drive on Italy. **May 10**—British navy bottles up Ostend. **May 24**—British ship Moldavia, carrying American troops, torpedoed; 56 lost. **May 27**—Germans begin third phase of drive on west front; gain five miles. **May 28**—Germans take 15,000 prisoners in drive. **May 29**—Germans take Soissons and menace Reims. American troops capture Cantigny. **May**

30—Germans reach the Marne, fifty-five miles from Paris. May 31—Germans take 45,000 prisoners in drive.

June 1—Germans advance nine miles; are forty-six miles from Paris. June 3—Five German submarines attack U. S. coast and sink eleven ships. June 5—U. S. marines fight on the Marne near Chateau Thierry. June 9—Germans start fourth phase of their drive by advancing toward Noyon. June 10—Germans gain two miles. U. S. marines capture south end of Belleau wood.

June 12—French and Americans start counter attack. June 15—Austrians begin another drive on Italy and take 16,000 prisoners. June 17—Italians check Austrians on Piave river. June 19—Austrians cross the Piave. June 22—Italians defeat Austrians on the Piave. June 23—Austrians begin great retreat across the Piave.

July 18—Gen. Foch launches allied offensive, with French, American, British, Italian and Belgian troops. July 21—Americans and French capture Chateau Thierry. July 30—German crown prince flees from the Marne and withdraws army.

August 2—Soissons recaptured by Foch. Aug. 4—Americans take Fismes. Aug. 5—American troops landed at Archangel. Aug. 7—Americans cross the Vesle. Aug. 16—Bapaume recaptured. Aug. 28—French recross the Somme.

September 1—Foch retakes Peronne. Sept. 12—Americans launch successful attack in St. Mihiel salient. Sept. 28—Allies win on 250 mile line, from North sea to Verdun. Sept. 29—Allies cross Hindenburg line. Sept. 30—Bulgaria surrenders, after successful allied campaign in Balkans. October 1—French take St. Quentin. Oct. 4—Austria asks Holland to mediate with allies for peace. Oct. 5—Germans start abandonment of Lille and burn Douai. Oct. 6—Germany asks President Wilson for armistice. Oct. 7—Americans capture hills around Argonne. Oct. 8—President Wilson refuses armistice. Oct. 9—Allies capture Cambrai. Oct. 10—Allies capture Le Cateau. Oct. 11—American transport Otranto torpedoed and sunk; 500 lost. Oct. 13—Foch's troops take Laon and La Fere.

October 14—British and Belgians take Roulers; President Wilson demands surrender by Germany. Oct. 15—British and Belgians cross Lys river, take 12,000 prisoners and 100 guns. Oct. 16—Allies enter Lille outskirts. Oct. 17—Allies capture Lille, Bruges, Zeebrugge, Ostend, and Douai. Oct. 18—Czecho-Slovaks issue declaration of independence; Czechs rebel and seize Prague, captial of Bohemia; French take Thielt.

October 19—President Wilson refuses Austrian peace plea and says Czecho-Slovak state must be considered. Oct. 21—Allies cross the Oise and threaten Valenciennes. Oct. 22—Haig's forces cross the Scheldt. Oct. 23—President Wilson refuses latest German peace plea. Oct. 27—German government asks President Wilson to state terms. Oct. 28—Austria begs for separate peace.

October 29—Austria opens direct negotiations with Secretary Lansing. Oct. 30—Italians inflict great defeat on Austria; capture 33,000 Austrians evacuating Italian territory. Oct. 31—Turkey surrenders; Austrians utterly routed by Italians; lose 50,000; Austrian envoys, under white flag, enter Italian lines.

November 1—Italians pursue beaten Austrians across Tagliamento river; allied conference at Versailles fixes peace terms for Germany. Nov. 3—Austria signs armistice amounting virtually to unconditional surrender. Nov. 4—Allied terms are sent to Germany. Nov. 7—Germany's envoys enter allied lines by arrangement.

November 9—Kaiser Wilhelm abdicates and crown prince renounces throne. Nov. 10—Former Kaiser Wilhelm and his eldest son, Friedrick Wilhelm, flee to Holland to escape widespread revolution throughout Germany.

# CHRONOLOGY OF THE WORLD WAR

**November 9**—Kaiser Wilhelm abdicates and crown prince renounces throne. British battleship Britannia torpedoed and sunk by German submarines off entrance to Straits of Gibraltar.

**November 10**—Former Kaiser Wilhelm and his eldest son, Frederick Wilhelm, flee to Holland to escape widespread revolution throughout Germany. King of Bavaria abdicates.

**November 11**—Armistice in effect at 11 o'clock a. m., Paris time. Firing ceased on all fronts. An American battery from Providence, Rhode Island, fired last shot at exactly 11 o'clock on the front northwest of Verdun. Germans began evacuation of Belgium and Alsace-Lorraine.

**November 12**—German republic proclaimed at Berlin. Emperor Charles of Austria abdicates. Belgium demands complete independence instead of guaranteed neutrality. To secure status as a belligerent at the peace council, Roumania again declares war on Germany. United States stops draft boards and lifts war restrictions of industries.

**November 13**—American troops cross the German former frontier and enter Alsace-Lorraine.

**November 15**—Distinguished Service Medal conferred on General Pershing at his headquarters in France by General Tasker H. Bliss. United States Postoffice department takes control of all ocean cable lines, consent of other governments having been obtained. Prof. Thomas G. Masaryk proclaimed President of the new Czecho-Slav republic.

**November 16**—Copenhagen reported many German ships due for surrender under armistice conditions. Demobilization of United States troops ordered by the government, beginning with those in army camps at home. United States takes over express service. Belgian troops enter Brussels. German cruiser Wiesbaden torpedoed by German revolutionary sailors, with loss of 330 lives.

**November 17**—Two hundred and fifty thousand American troops advance nine miles in French territory evacuated by Germans. French armies advance across the west boundary of Alsace-Lorraine and occupy many towns. People of Luxemburg demand abdication of Grand Duchess.

**November 29**—The President announced names of commissioners to represent the United States at peace conference. They were Woodrow Wilson, President of the United States; Robert Lansing, Secretary of State; Col. Edward M. House; Henry White, former ambassador to Italy and to France, and Gen. Tasker H. Bliss, American adviser of the supreme war council.

**December 4, 1918**—President Wilson and a numerous staff sailed for Europe from New York aboard the George Washington, escorted by warships under command of Admiral Mayo, to attend the Peace Conference at Paris, France.

**May 7, 1919**—Treaty of peace handed to German peace delegates at Versailles by Premier Clemenceau of France.

**June 28, 1919**—Treaty of peace signed by Allied and German plenipotentiaries at Versailles.

---

*The total number of pages in this book is 608, including 96 pages of illustrations, which are not marked by folio numbers, and 512 pages of numbered text.

CPSIA information can be obtained
at www.ICGtesting.com
Printed in the USA
LVHW010237230723
753131LV00005B/414